Lecture Notes in Computer Science 14109

The series Lecture Notes in Computer Science (LNCS), including its subseries Lecture Notes in Artificial Intelligence (LNAI) and Lecture Notes in Bioinformatics (LNBI), has established itself as a medium for the publication of new developments in computer science and information technology research, teaching, and education.

LNCS enjoys close cooperation with the computer science R & D community, the series counts many renowned academics among its volume editors and paper authors, and collaborates with prestigious societies. Its mission is to serve this international community by providing an invaluable service, mainly focused on the publication of conference and workshop proceedings and postproceedings. LNCS commenced publication in 1973.

Osvaldo Gervasi · Beniamino Murgante ·
Ana Maria A. C. Rocha · Chiara Garau ·
Francesco Scorza · Yeliz Karaca ·
Carmelo M. Torre
Editors

Computational Science and Its Applications – ICCSA 2023 Workshops

Athens, Greece, July 3–6, 2023
Proceedings, Part VI

Editors

Osvaldo Gervasi ⓘD
University of Perugia
Perugia, Italy

Ana Maria A. C. Rocha ⓘD
University of Minho
Braga, Portugal

Francesco Scorza ⓘD
University of Basilicata
Potenza, Italy

Carmelo M. Torre ⓘD
Polytechnic University of Bari
Bari, Italy

Beniamino Murgante ⓘD
University of Basilicata
Potenza, Italy

Chiara Garau ⓘD
University of Cagliari
Cagliari, Italy

Yeliz Karaca ⓘD
University of Massachusetts Medical School
Worcester, MA, USA

ISSN 0302-9743   ISSN 1611-3349 (electronic)
Lecture Notes in Computer Science
ISBN 978-3-031-37119-6   ISBN 978-3-031-37120-2 (eBook)
https://doi.org/10.1007/978-3-031-37120-2

This Springer imprint is published by the registered company Springer Nature Switzerland AG
The registered company address is: Gewerbestrasse 11, 6330 Cham, Switzerland

Preface

These 9 volumes (LNCS volumes 14104–14112) consist of the peer-reviewed papers from the 2023 International Conference on Computational Science and Its Applications (ICCSA 2023) which took place during July 3–6, 2023. The peer-reviewed papers of the main conference tracks were published in a separate set consisting of two volumes (LNCS 13956–13957).

The conference was finally held in person after the difficult period of the Covid-19 pandemic in the wonderful city of Athens, in the cosy facilities of the National Technical University. Our experience during the pandemic period allowed us to enable virtual participation also this year for those who were unable to attend the event, due to logistical, political and economic problems, by adopting a technological infrastructure based on open source software (jitsi + riot), and a commercial cloud infrastructure.

ICCSA 2023 was another successful event in the International Conference on Computational Science and Its Applications (ICCSA) series, previously held as a hybrid event (with one third of registered authors attending in person) in Malaga, Spain (2022), Cagliari, Italy (hybrid with few participants in person in 2021 and completely online in 2020), whilst earlier editions took place in Saint Petersburg, Russia (2019), Melbourne, Australia (2018), Trieste, Italy (2017), Beijing, China (2016), Banff, Canada (2015), Guimaraes, Portugal (2014), Ho Chi Minh City, Vietnam (2013), Salvador, Brazil (2012), Santander, Spain (2011), Fukuoka, Japan (2010), Suwon, South Korea (2009), Perugia, Italy (2008), Kuala Lumpur, Malaysia (2007), Glasgow, UK (2006), Singapore (2005), Assisi, Italy (2004), Montreal, Canada (2003), and (as ICCS) Amsterdam, The Netherlands (2002) and San Francisco, USA (2001).

Computational Science is the main pillar of most of the present research, industrial and commercial applications, and plays a unique role in exploiting ICT innovative technologies, and the ICCSA series have been providing a venue to researchers and industry practitioners to discuss new ideas, to share complex problems and their solutions, and to shape new trends in Computational Science. As the conference mirrors society from a scientific point of view, this year's undoubtedly dominant theme was the machine learning and artificial intelligence and their applications in the most diverse economic and industrial fields.

The ICCSA 2023 conference is structured in 6 general tracks covering the fields of computational science and its applications: Computational Methods, Algorithms and Scientific Applications – High Performance Computing and Networks – Geometric Modeling, Graphics and Visualization – Advanced and Emerging Applications – Information Systems and Technologies – Urban and Regional Planning. In addition, the conference consisted of 61 workshops, focusing on very topical issues of importance to science, technology and society: from new mathematical approaches for solving complex computational systems, to information and knowledge in the Internet of Things, new statistical and optimization methods, several Artificial Intelligence approaches, sustainability issues, smart cities and related technologies.

In the workshop proceedings we accepted 350 full papers, 29 short papers and 2 PHD Showcase papers. In the main conference proceedings we accepted 67 full papers, 13 short papers and 6 PHD Showcase papers from 283 submissions to the General Tracks of the conference (acceptance rate 30%). We would like to express our appreciation to the workshops chairs and co-chairs for their hard work and dedication.

The success of the ICCSA conference series in general, and of ICCSA 2023 in particular, vitally depends on the support of many people: authors, presenters, participants, keynote speakers, workshop chairs, session chairs, organizing committee members, student volunteers, Program Committee members, Advisory Committee members, International Liaison chairs, reviewers and others in various roles. We take this opportunity to wholehartedly thank them all.

We also wish to thank our publisher, Springer, for their acceptance to publish the proceedings, for sponsoring part of the best papers awards and for their kind assistance and cooperation during the editing process.

We cordially invite you to visit the ICCSA website https://iccsa.org where you can find all the relevant information about this interesting and exciting event.

July 2023

Osvaldo Gervasi
Beniamino Murgante
Chiara Garau

Welcome Message from Organizers

After the 2021 ICCSA in Cagliari, Italy and the 2022 ICCSA in Malaga, Spain, ICCSA continued its successful scientific endeavours in 2023, hosted again in the Mediterranean neighbourhood. This time, ICCSA 2023 moved a bit more to the east of the Mediterranean Region and was held in the metropolitan city of Athens, the capital of Greece and a vibrant urban environment endowed with a prominent cultural heritage that dates back to the ancient years. As a matter of fact, Athens is one of the oldest cities in the world, and the cradle of democracy. The city has a history of over 3,000 years and, according to the myth, it took its name from Athena, the Goddess of Wisdom and daughter of Zeus.

ICCSA 2023 took place in a secure environment, relieved from the immense stress of the COVID-19 pandemic. This gave us the chance to have a safe and vivid, in-person participation which, combined with the very active engagement of the ICCSA 2023 scientific community, set the ground for highly motivating discussions and interactions as to the latest developments of computer science and its applications in the real world for improving quality of life.

The National Technical University of Athens (NTUA), one of the most prestigious Greek academic institutions, had the honour of hosting ICCSA 2023. The Local Organizing Committee really feels the burden and responsibility of such a demanding task; and puts in all the necessary energy in order to meet participants' expectations and establish a friendly, creative and inspiring, scientific and social/cultural environment that allows for new ideas and perspectives to flourish.

Since all ICCSA participants, either informatics-oriented or application-driven, realize the tremendous steps and evolution of computer science during the last few decades and the huge potential these offer to cope with the enormous challenges of humanity in a globalized, 'wired' and highly competitive world, the expectations from ICCSA 2023 were set high in order for a successful matching between computer science progress and communities' aspirations to be attained, i.e., a progress that serves real, place- and people-based needs and can pave the way towards a visionary, smart, sustainable, resilient and inclusive future for both the current and the next generation.

On behalf of the Local Organizing Committee, I would like to sincerely thank all of you who have contributed to ICCSA 2023 and I cordially welcome you to my 'home', NTUA.

On behalf of the Local Organizing Committee.

Anastasia Stratigea

Organization

ICCSA 2023 was organized by the National Technical University of Athens (Greece), the University of the Aegean (Greece), the University of Perugia (Italy), the University of Basilicata (Italy), Monash University (Australia), Kyushu Sangyo University (Japan), the University of Minho (Portugal). The conference was supported by two NTUA Schools, namely the School of Rural, Surveying and Geoinformatics Engineering and the School of Electrical and Computer Engineering.

Honorary General Chairs

Norio Shiratori	Chuo University, Japan
Kenneth C. J. Tan	Sardina Systems, UK

General Chairs

Osvaldo Gervasi	University of Perugia, Italy
Anastasia Stratigea	National Technical University of Athens, Greece
Bernady O. Apduhan	Kyushu Sangyo University, Japan

Program Committee Chairs

Beniamino Murgante	University of Basilicata, Italy
Dimitris Kavroudakis	University of the Aegean, Greece
Ana Maria A. C. Rocha	University of Minho, Portugal
David Taniar	Monash University, Australia

International Advisory Committee

Jemal Abawajy	Deakin University, Australia
Dharma P. Agarwal	University of Cincinnati, USA
Rajkumar Buyya	Melbourne University, Australia
Claudia Bauzer Medeiros	University of Campinas, Brazil
Manfred M. Fisher	Vienna University of Economics and Business, Austria
Marina L. Gavrilova	University of Calgary, Canada

Sumi Helal	University of Florida, USA and University of Lancaster, UK
Yee Leung	Chinese University of Hong Kong, China

International Liaison Chairs

Ivan Blečić	University of Cagliari, Italy
Giuseppe Borruso	University of Trieste, Italy
Elise De Donker	Western Michigan University, USA
Maria Irene Falcão	University of Minho, Portugal
Inmaculada Garcia Fernandez	University of Malaga, Spain
Eligius Hendrix	University of Malaga, Spain
Robert C. H. Hsu	Chung Hua University, Taiwan
Tai-Hoon Kim	Beijing Jaotong University, China
Vladimir Korkhov	Saint Petersburg University, Russia
Takashi Naka	Kyushu Sangyo University, Japan
Rafael D. C. Santos	National Institute for Space Research, Brazil
Maribel Yasmina Santos	University of Minho, Portugal
Elena Stankova	Saint Petersburg University, Russia

Workshop and Session Organizing Chairs

Beniamino Murgante	University of Basilicata, Italy
Chiara Garau	University of Cagliari, Italy

Award Chair

Wenny Rahayu	La Trobe University, Australia

Publicity Committee Chairs

Elmer Dadios	De La Salle University, Philippines
Nataliia Kulabukhova	Saint Petersburg University, Russia
Daisuke Takahashi	Tsukuba University, Japan
Shangwang Wang	Beijing University of Posts and Telecommunications, China

Local Organizing Committee Chairs

Anastasia Stratigea	National Technical University of Athens, Greece
Dimitris Kavroudakis	University of the Aegean, Greece
Charalambos Ioannidis	National Technical University of Athens, Greece
Nectarios Koziris	National Technical University of Athens, Greece
Efthymios Bakogiannis	National Technical University of Athens, Greece
Yiota Theodora	National Technical University of Athens, Greece
Dimitris Fotakis	National Technical University of Athens, Greece
Apostolos Lagarias	National Technical University of Athens, Greece
Akrivi Leka	National Technical University of Athens, Greece
Dionisia Koutsi	National Technical University of Athens, Greece
Alkistis Dalkavouki	National Technical University of Athens, Greece
Maria Panagiotopoulou	National Technical University of Athens, Greece
Angeliki Papazoglou	National Technical University of Athens, Greece
Natalia Tsigarda	National Technical University of Athens, Greece
Konstantinos Athanasopoulos	National Technical University of Athens, Greece
Ioannis Xatziioannou	National Technical University of Athens, Greece
Vasiliki Krommyda	National Technical University of Athens, Greece
Panayiotis Patsilinakos	National Technical University of Athens, Greece
Sofia Kassiou	National Technical University of Athens, Greece

Technology Chair

Damiano Perri	University of Florence, Italy

Program Committee

Vera Afreixo	University of Aveiro, Portugal
Filipe Alvelos	University of Minho, Portugal
Hartmut Asche	University of Potsdam, Germany
Ginevra Balletto	University of Cagliari, Italy
Michela Bertolotto	University College Dublin, Ireland
Sandro Bimonte	CEMAGREF, TSCF, France
Rod Blais	University of Calgary, Canada
Ivan Blečić	University of Sassari, Italy
Giuseppe Borruso	University of Trieste, Italy
Ana Cristina Braga	University of Minho, Portugal
Massimo Cafaro	University of Salento, Italy
Yves Caniou	Lyon University, France

Ermanno Cardelli	University of Perugia, Italy
José A. Cardoso e Cunha	Universidade Nova de Lisboa, Portugal
Rui Cardoso	University of Beira Interior, Portugal
Leocadio G. Casado	University of Almeria, Spain
Carlo Cattani	University of Salerno, Italy
Mete Celik	Erciyes University, Turkey
Maria Cerreta	University of Naples "Federico II", Italy
Hyunseung Choo	Sungkyunkwan University, Korea
Rachel Chieng-Sing Lee	Sunway University, Malaysia
Min Young Chung	Sungkyunkwan University, Korea
Florbela Maria da Cruz Domingues Correia	Polytechnic Institute of Viana do Castelo, Portugal
Gilberto Corso Pereira	Federal University of Bahia, Brazil
Alessandro Costantini	INFN, Italy
Carla Dal Sasso Freitas	Universidade Federal do Rio Grande do Sul, Brazil
Pradesh Debba	The Council for Scientific and Industrial Research (CSIR), South Africa
Hendrik Decker	Instituto Tecnológico de Informática, Spain
Robertas Damaševičius	Kausan University of Technology, Lithuania
Frank Devai	London South Bank University, UK
Rodolphe Devillers	Memorial University of Newfoundland, Canada
Joana Matos Dias	University of Coimbra, Portugal
Paolino Di Felice	University of L'Aquila, Italy
Prabu Dorairaj	NetApp, India/USA
Noelia Faginas Lago	University of Perugia, Italy
M. Irene Falcao	University of Minho, Portugal
Cherry Liu Fang	U.S. DOE Ames Laboratory, USA
Florbela P. Fernandes	Polytechnic Institute of Bragança, Portugal
Jose-Jesus Fernandez	National Centre for Biotechnology, CSIS, Spain
Paula Odete Fernandes	Polytechnic Institute of Bragança, Portugal
Adelaide de Fátima Baptista Valente Freitas	University of Aveiro, Portugal
Manuel Carlos Figueiredo	University of Minho, Portugal
Maria Celia Furtado Rocha	PRODEB–PósCultura/UFBA, Brazil
Chiara Garau	University of Cagliari, Italy
Paulino Jose Garcia Nieto	University of Oviedo, Spain
Raffaele Garrisi	Polizia di Stato, Italy
Jerome Gensel	LSR-IMAG, France
Maria Giaoutzi	National Technical University, Athens, Greece
Arminda Manuela Andrade Pereira Gonçalves	University of Minho, Portugal

Louiza de Macedo Mourelle	State University of Rio de Janeiro, Brazil
Nadia Nedjah	State University of Rio de Janeiro, Brazil
Laszlo Neumann	University of Girona, Spain
Kok-Leong Ong	Deakin University, Australia
Belen Palop	Universidad de Valladolid, Spain
Marcin Paprzycki	Polish Academy of Sciences, Poland
Eric Pardede	La Trobe University, Australia
Kwangjin Park	Wonkwang University, Korea
Ana Isabel Pereira	Polytechnic Institute of Bragança, Portugal
Massimiliano Petri	University of Pisa, Italy
Telmo Pinto	University of Coimbra, Portugal
Maurizio Pollino	Italian National Agency for New Technologies, Energy and Sustainable Economic Development, Italy
Alenka Poplin	University of Hamburg, Germany
Vidyasagar Potdar	Curtin University of Technology, Australia
David C. Prosperi	Florida Atlantic University, USA
Wenny Rahayu	La Trobe University, Australia
Jerzy Respondek	Silesian University of Technology Poland
Humberto Rocha	INESC-Coimbra, Portugal
Jon Rokne	University of Calgary, Canada
Octavio Roncero	CSIC, Spain
Maytham Safar	Kuwait University, Kuwait
Chiara Saracino	A.O. Ospedale Niguarda Ca' Granda - Milano, Italy
Marco Paulo Seabra dos Reis	University of Coimbra, Portugal
Jie Shen	University of Michigan, USA
Qi Shi	Liverpool John Moores University, UK
Dale Shires	U.S. Army Research Laboratory, USA
Inês Soares	University of Coimbra, Portugal
Elena Stankova	St. Petersburg University, Russia
Takuo Suganuma	Tohoku University, Japan
Eufemia Tarantino	Polytechnic of Bari, Italy
Sergio Tasso	University of Perugia, Italy
Ana Paula Teixeira	University of Trás-os-Montes and Alto Douro, Portugal
M. Filomena Teodoro	Portuguese Naval Academy and University of Lisbon, Portugal
Parimala Thulasiraman	University of Manitoba, Canada
Carmelo Torre	Polytechnic of Bari, Italy
Javier Martinez Torres	Centro Universitario de la Defensa Zaragoza, Spain

Giuseppe A. Trunfio	University of Sassari, Italy
Pablo Vanegas	University of Cuenca, Equador
Marco Vizzari	University of Perugia, Italy
Varun Vohra	Merck Inc., USA
Koichi Wada	University of Tsukuba, Japan
Krzysztof Walkowiak	Wroclaw University of Technology, Poland
Zequn Wang	Intelligent Automation Inc, USA
Robert Weibel	University of Zurich, Switzerland
Frank Westad	Norwegian University of Science and Technology, Norway
Roland Wismüller	Universität Siegen, Germany
Mudasser Wyne	SOET National University, USA
Chung-Huang Yang	National Kaohsiung Normal University, Taiwan
Xin-She Yang	National Physical Laboratory, UK
Salim Zabir	France Telecom Japan Co., Japan
Haifeng Zhao	University of California, Davis, USA
Fabiana Zollo	University of Venice "Cà Foscari", Italy
Albert Y. Zomaya	University of Sydney, Australia

Workshop Organizers

Advanced Data Science Techniques with Applications in Industry and Environmental Sustainability (ATELIERS 2023)

Dario Torregrossa	Goodyear, Luxemburg
Antonino Marvuglia	Luxembourg Institute of Science and Technology, Luxemburg
Valeria Borodin	École des Mines de Saint-Étienne, Luxemburg
Mohamed Laib	Luxembourg Institute of Science and Technology, Luxemburg

Advances in Artificial Intelligence Learning Technologies: Blended Learning, STEM, Computational Thinking and Coding (AAILT 2023)

Alfredo Milani	University of Perugia, Italy
Valentina Franzoni	University of Perugia, Italy
Sergio Tasso	University of Perugia, Italy

Advanced Processes of Mathematics and Computing Models in Complex Computational Systems (ACMC 2023)

Yeliz Karaca	University of Massachusetts Chan Medical School and Massachusetts Institute of Technology, USA
Dumitru Baleanu	Cankaya University, Turkey
Osvaldo Gervasi	University of Perugia, Italy
Yudong Zhang	University of Leicester, UK
Majaz Moonis	University of Massachusetts Medical School, USA

Artificial Intelligence Supported Medical Data Examination (AIM 2023)

David Taniar	Monash University, Australia
Seifedine Kadry	Noroff University College, Norway
Venkatesan Rajinikanth	Saveetha School of Engineering, India

Advanced and Innovative Web Apps (AIWA 2023)

Damiano Perri	University of Perugia, Italy
Osvaldo Gervasi	University of Perugia, Italy

Assessing Urban Sustainability (ASUS 2023)

Elena Todella	Polytechnic of Turin, Italy
Marika Gaballo	Polytechnic of Turin, Italy
Beatrice Mecca	Polytechnic of Turin, Italy

Advances in Web Based Learning (AWBL 2023)

Birol Ciloglugil	Ege University, Turkey
Mustafa Inceoglu	Ege University, Turkey

Blockchain and Distributed Ledgers: Technologies and Applications (BDLTA 2023)

Vladimir Korkhov   Saint Petersburg State University, Russia
Elena Stankova   Saint Petersburg State University, Russia
Nataliia Kulabukhova   Saint Petersburg State University, Russia

Bio and Neuro Inspired Computing and Applications (BIONCA 2023)

Nadia Nedjah   State University of Rio De Janeiro, Brazil
Luiza De Macedo Mourelle   State University of Rio De Janeiro, Brazil

Choices and Actions for Human Scale Cities: Decision Support Systems (CAHSC–DSS 2023)

Giovanna Acampa   University of Florence and University of Enna
     Kore, Italy
Fabrizio Finucci   Roma Tre University, Italy
Luca S. Dacci   Polytechnic of Turin, Italy

Computational and Applied Mathematics (CAM 2023)

Maria Irene Falcao   University of Minho, Portugal
Fernando Miranda   University of Minho, Portugal

Computational and Applied Statistics (CAS 2023)

Ana Cristina Braga   University of Minho, Portugal

Cyber Intelligence and Applications (CIA 2023)

Gianni Dangelo   University of Salerno, Italy
Francesco Palmieri   University of Salerno, Italy
Massimo Ficco   University of Salerno, Italy

Conversations South-North on Climate Change Adaptation Towards Smarter and More Sustainable Cities (CLAPS 2023)

Chiara Garau	University of Cagliari, Italy
Cristina Trois	University of kwaZulu-Natal, South Africa
Claudia Loggia	University of kwaZulu-Natal, South Africa
John Östh	Faculty of Technology, Art and Design, Norway
Mauro Coni	University of Cagliari, Italy
Alessio Satta	MedSea Foundation, Italy

Computational Mathematics, Statistics and Information Management (CMSIM 2023)

Maria Filomena Teodoro	University of Lisbon and Portuguese Naval Academy, Portugal
Marina A. P. Andrade	University Institute of Lisbon, Portugal

Computational Optimization and Applications (COA 2023)

Ana Maria A. C. Rocha	University of Minho, Portugal
Humberto Rocha	University of Coimbra, Portugal

Computational Astrochemistry (CompAstro 2023)

Marzio Rosi	University of Perugia, Italy
Nadia Balucani	University of Perugia, Italy
Cecilia Ceccarelli	University of Grenoble Alpes and Institute for Planetary Sciences and Astrophysics, France
Stefano Falcinelli	University of Perugia, Italy

Computational Methods for Porous Geomaterials (CompPor 2023)

Vadim Lisitsa	Russian Academy of Science, Russia
Evgeniy Romenski	Russian Academy of Science, Russia

Workshop on Computational Science and HPC (CSHPC 2023)

Elise De Doncker	Western Michigan University, USA
Fukuko Yuasa	High Energy Accelerator Research Organization, Japan
Hideo Matsufuru	High Energy Accelerator Research Organization, Japan

Cities, Technologies and Planning (CTP 2023)

Giuseppe Borruso	University of Trieste, Italy
Beniamino Murgante	University of Basilicata, Italy
Malgorzata Hanzl	Lodz University of Technology, Poland
Anastasia Stratigea	National Technical University of Athens, Greece
Ljiljana Zivkovic	Republic Geodetic Authority, Serbia
Ginevra Balletto	University of Cagliari, Italy

Gender Equity/Equality in Transport and Mobility (DELIA 2023)

Tiziana Campisi	University of Enna Kore, Italy
Ines Charradi	Sousse University, Tunisia
Alexandros Nikitas	University of Huddersfield, UK
Kh Md Nahiduzzaman	University of British Columbia, Canada
Andreas Nikiforiadis	Aristotle University of Thessaloniki, Greece
Socrates Basbas	Aristotle University of Thessaloniki, Greece

International Workshop on Defense Technology and Security (DTS 2023)

Yeonseung Ryu	Myongji University, South Korea

Integrated Methods for the Ecosystem-Services Accounting in Urban Decision Process (Ecourbn 2023)

Maria Rosaria Guarini	Sapienza University of Rome, Italy
Francesco Sica	Sapienza University of Rome, Italy
Francesco Tajani	Sapienza University of Rome, Italy

Carmelo Maria Torre	Polytechnic University of Bari, Italy
Pierluigi Morano	Polytechnic University of Bari, Italy
Rossana Ranieri	Sapienza Università di Roma, Italy

Evaluating Inner Areas Potentials (EIAP 2023)

Diana Rolando	Politechnic of Turin, Italy
Manuela Rebaudengo	Politechnic of Turin, Italy
Alice Barreca	Politechnic of Turin, Italy
Giorgia Malavasi	Politechnic of Turin, Italy
Umberto Mecca	Politechnic of Turin, Italy

Sustainable Mobility Last Mile Logistic (ELLIOT 2023)

Tiziana Campisi	University of Enna Kore, Italy
Socrates Basbas	Aristotle University of Thessaloniki, Greece
Grigorios Fountas	Aristotle University of Thessaloniki, Greece
Paraskevas Nikolaou	University of Cyprus, Cyprus
Drazenko Glavic	University of Belgrade, Serbia
Antonio Russo	University of Enna Kore, Italy

Econometrics and Multidimensional Evaluation of Urban Environment (EMEUE 2023)

Maria Cerreta	University of Naples Federico II, Italy
Carmelo Maria Torre	Politechnic of Bari, Italy
Pierluigi Morano	Polytechnic of Bari, Italy
Debora Anelli	Polytechnic of Bari, Italy
Francesco Tajani	Sapienza University of Rome, Italy
Simona Panaro	University of Sussex, UK

Ecosystem Services in Spatial Planning for Resilient Urban and Rural Areas (ESSP 2023)

Sabrina Lai	University of Cagliari, Italy
Francesco Scorza	University of Basilicata, Italy
Corrado Zoppi	University of Cagliari, Italy

Gerardo Carpentieri   University of Naples Federico II, Italy
Floriana Zucaro   University of Naples Federico II, Italy
Ana Clara Mourão Moura   Federal University of Minas Gerais, Brazil

Ethical AI Applications for a Human-Centered Cyber Society (EthicAI 2023)

Valentina Franzoni   University of Perugia, Italy
Alfredo Milani   University of Perugia, Italy
Jordi Vallverdu   University Autonoma Barcelona, Spain
Roberto Capobianco   Sapienza University of Rome, Italy

13th International Workshop on Future Computing System Technologies and Applications (FiSTA 2023)

Bernady Apduhan   Kyushu Sangyo University, Japan
Rafael Santos   National Institute for Space Research, Brazil

Collaborative Planning and Designing for the Future with Geospatial Applications (GeoCollab 2023)

Alenka Poplin   Iowa State University, USA
Rosanna Rivero   University of Georgia, USA
Michele Campagna   University of Cagliari, Italy
Ana Clara Mourão Moura   Federal University of Minas Gerais, Brazil

Geomatics in Agriculture and Forestry: New Advances and Perspectives (GeoForAgr 2023)

Maurizio Pollino   Italian National Agency for New Technologies,
                               Energy and Sustainable Economic
                               Development, Italy
Giuseppe Modica   University of Reggio Calabria, Italy
Marco Vizzari   University of Perugia, Italy
Salvatore Praticò   University of Reggio Calabria, Italy

Geographical Analysis, Urban Modeling, Spatial Statistics (Geog-An-Mod 2023)

Giuseppe Borruso	University of Trieste, Italy
Beniamino Murgante	University of Basilicata, Italy
Harmut Asche	Hasso-Plattner-Institut für Digital Engineering Ggmbh, Germany

Geomatics for Resource Monitoring and Management (GRMM 2023)

Alessandra Capolupo	Polytechnic of Bari, Italy
Eufemia Tarantino	Polytechnic of Bari, Italy
Enrico Borgogno Mondino	University of Turin, Italy

International Workshop on Information and Knowledge in the Internet of Things (IKIT 2023)

Teresa Guarda	Peninsula State University of Santa Elena, Ecuador
Modestos Stavrakis	University of the Aegean, Greece

International Workshop on Collective, Massive and Evolutionary Systems (IWCES 2023)

Alfredo Milani	University of Perugia, Italy
Rajdeep Niyogi	Indian Institute of Technology, India
Valentina Franzoni	University of Perugia, Italy

Multidimensional Evolutionary Evaluations for Transformative Approaches (MEETA 2023)

Maria Cerreta	University of Naples Federico II, Italy
Giuliano Poli	University of Naples Federico II, Italy
Ludovica Larocca	University of Naples Federico II, Italy
Chiara Mazzarella	University of Naples Federico II, Italy

Stefania Regalbuto   University of Naples Federico II, Italy
Maria Somma   University of Naples Federico II, Italy

Building Multi-dimensional Models for Assessing Complex Environmental Systems (MES 2023)

Marta Dell'Ovo   Politechnic of Milan, Italy
Vanessa Assumma   University of Bologna, Italy
Caterina Caprioli   Politechnic of Turin, Italy
Giulia Datola   Politechnic of Turin, Italy
Federico Dellanna   Politechnic of Turin, Italy
Marco Rossitti   Politechnic of Milan, Italy

Metropolitan City Lab (Metro_City_Lab 2023)

Ginevra Balletto   University of Cagliari, Italy
Luigi Mundula   University for Foreigners of Perugia, Italy
Giuseppe Borruso   University of Trieste, Italy
Jacopo Torriti   University of Reading, UK
Isabella Ligia   Metropolitan City of Cagliari, Italy

Mathematical Methods for Image Processing and Understanding (MMIPU 2023)

Ivan Gerace   University of Perugia, Italy
Gianluca Vinti   University of Perugia, Italy
Arianna Travaglini   University of Florence, Italy

Models and Indicators for Assessing and Measuring the Urban Settlement Development in the View of ZERO Net Land Take by 2050 (MOVEto0 2023)

Lucia Saganeiti   University of L'Aquila, Italy
Lorena Fiorini   University of L'Aquila, Italy
Angela Pilogallo   University of L'Aquila, Italy
Alessandro Marucci   University of L'Aquila, Italy
Francesco Zullo   University of L'Aquila, Italy

Modelling Post-Covid Cities (MPCC 2023)

Giuseppe Borruso   University of Trieste, Italy
Beniamino Murgante   University of Basilicata, Italy
Ginevra Balletto   University of Cagliari, Italy
Lucia Saganeiti   University of L'Aquila, Italy
Marco Dettori   University of Sassari, Italy

3rd Workshop on Privacy in the Cloud/Edge/IoT World (PCEIoT 2023)

Michele Mastroianni   University of Salerno, Italy
Lelio Campanile   University of Campania Luigi Vanvitelli, Italy
Mauro Iacono   University of Campania Luigi Vanvitelli, Italy

Port City Interface: Land Use, Logistic and Rear Port Area Planning (PORTUNO 2023)

Tiziana Campisi   University of Enna Kore, Italy
Socrates Basbas   Aristotle University of Thessaloniki, Greece
Efstathios Bouhouras   Aristotle University of Thessaloniki, Greece
Giovanni Tesoriere   University of Enna Kore, Italy
Elena Cocuzza   University of Catania, Italy
Gianfranco Fancello   University of Cagliari, Italy

Scientific Computing Infrastructure (SCI 2023)

Elena Stankova   St. Petersburg State University, Russia
Vladimir Korkhov   St. Petersburg University, Russia

Supply Chains, IoT, and Smart Technologies (SCIS 2023)

Ha Jin Hwang   Sunway University, South Korea
Hangkon Kim   Daegu Catholic University, South Korea
Jan Seruga   Australian Catholic University, Australia

Spatial Cognition in Urban and Regional Planning Under Risk (SCOPUR23)

Domenico Camarda	Polytechnic of Bari, Italy
Giulia Mastrodonato	Polytechnic of Bari, Italy
Stefania Santoro	Polytechnic of Bari, Italy
Maria Rosaria Stufano Melone	Polytechnic of Bari, Italy
Mauro Patano	Polytechnic of Bari, Italy

Socio-Economic and Environmental Models for Land Use Management (SEMLUM 2023)

Debora Anelli	Polytechnic of Bari, Italy
Pierluigi Morano	Polytechnic of Bari, Italy
Benedetto Manganelli	University of Basilicata, Italy
Francesco Tajani	Sapienza University of Rome, Italy
Marco Locurcio	Polytechnic of Bari, Italy
Felicia Di Liddo	Polytechnic of Bari, Italy

Ports of the Future - Smartness and Sustainability (SmartPorts 2023)

Ginevra Balletto	University of Cagliari, Italy
Gianfranco Fancello	University of Cagliari, Italy
Patrizia Serra	University of Cagliari, Italy
Agostino Bruzzone	University of Genoa, Italy
Alberto Camarero	Politechnic of Madrid, Spain
Thierry Vanelslander	University of Antwerp, Belgium

Smart Transport and Logistics - Smart Supply Chains (SmarTransLog 2023)

Giuseppe Borruso	University of Trieste, Italy
Marco Mazzarino	University of Venice, Italy
Marcello Tadini	University of Eastern Piedmont, Italy
Luigi Mundula	University for Foreigners of Perugia, Italy
Mara Ladu	University of Cagliari, Italy
Maria del Mar Munoz Leonisio	University of Cadiz, Spain

Smart Tourism (SmartTourism 2023)

Giuseppe Borruso	University of Trieste, Italy
Silvia Battino	University of Sassari, Italy
Ainhoa Amaro Garcia	University of Alcala and University of Las Palmas, Spain
Francesca Krasna	University of Trieste, Italy
Ginevra Balletto	University of Cagliari, Italy
Maria del Mar Munoz Leonisio	University of Cadiz, Spain

Sustainability Performance Assessment: Models, Approaches, and Applications Toward Interdisciplinary and Integrated Solutions (SPA 2023)

Sabrina Lai	University of Cagliari, Italy
Francesco Scorza	University of Basilicata, Italy
Jolanta Dvarioniene	Kaunas University of Technology, Lithuania
Valentin Grecu	Lucian Blaga University of Sibiu, Romania
Georgia Pozoukidou	Aristotle University of Thessaloniki, Greece

Spatial Energy Planning, City and Urban Heritage (Spatial_Energy_City 2023)

Ginevra Balletto	University of Cagliari, Italy
Mara Ladu	University of Cagliari, Italy
Emilio Ghiani	University of Cagliari, Italy
Roberto De Lotto	University of Pavia, Italy
Roberto Gerundo	University of Salerno, Italy

Specifics of Smart Cities Development in Europe (SPEED 2023)

Chiara Garau	University of Cagliari, Italy
Katarína Vitálišová	Matej Bel University, Slovakia
Paolo Nesi	University of Florence, Italy
Anna Vaňová	Matej Bel University, Slovakia
Kamila Borsekova	Matej Bel University, Slovakia
Paola Zamperlin	University of Pisa, Italy

Smart, Safe and Health Cities (SSHC 2023)

Chiara Garau	University of Cagliari, Italy
Gerardo Carpentieri	University of Naples Federico II, Italy
Floriana Zucaro	University of Naples Federico II, Italy
Aynaz Lotfata	Chicago State University, USA
Alfonso Annunziata	University of Basilicata, Italy
Diego Altafini	University of Pisa, Italy

Smart and Sustainable Island Communities (SSIC_2023)

Chiara Garau	University of Cagliari, Italy
Anastasia Stratigea	National Technical University of Athens, Greece
Yiota Theodora	National Technical University of Athens, Greece
Giulia Desogus	University of Cagliari, Italy

Theoretical and Computational Chemistry and Its Applications (TCCMA 2023)

Noelia Faginas-Lago	University of Perugia, Italy
Andrea Lombardi	University of Perugia, Italy

Transport Infrastructures for Smart Cities (TISC 2023)

Francesca Maltinti	University of Cagliari, Italy
Mauro Coni	University of Cagliari, Italy
Francesco Pinna	University of Cagliari, Italy
Chiara Garau	University of Cagliari, Italy
Nicoletta Rassu	University of Cagliari, Italy
James Rombi	University of Cagliari, Italy

Urban Regeneration: Innovative Tools and Evaluation Model (URITEM 2023)

Fabrizio Battisti	University of Florence, Italy
Giovanna Acampa	University of Florence and University of Enna Kore, Italy
Orazio Campo	La Sapienza University of Rome, Italy

Urban Space Accessibility and Mobilities (USAM 2023)

Chiara Garau	University of Cagliari, Italy
Matteo Ignaccolo	University of Catania, Italy
Michela Tiboni	University of Brescia, Italy
Francesco Pinna	University of Cagliari, Italy
Silvia Rossetti	University of Parma, Italy
Vincenza Torrisi	University of Catania, Italy
Ilaria Delponte	University of Genoa, Italy

Virtual Reality and Augmented Reality and Applications (VRA 2023)

Osvaldo Gervasi	University of Perugia, Italy
Damiano Perri	University of Florence, Italy
Marco Simonetti	University of Florence, Italy
Sergio Tasso	University of Perugia, Italy

Workshop on Advanced and Computational Methods for Earth Science Applications (WACM4ES 2023)

Luca Piroddi	University of Malta, Malta
Sebastiano Damico	University of Malta, Malta
Marilena Cozzolino	Università del Molise, Italy
Adam Gauci	University of Malta, Italy
Giuseppina Vacca	University of Cagliari, Italy
Chiara Garau	University of Cagliari, Italy

Sponsoring Organizations

ICCSA 2023 would not have been possible without the tremendous support of many organizations and institutions, for which all organizers and participants of ICCSA 2023 express their sincere gratitude:

 Springer Nature Switzerland AG, Switzerland
(https://www.springer.com)

 computers Computers Open Access Journal
(https://www.mdpi.com/journal/computers)

 National Technical University of Athens, Greece
(https://www.ntua.gr/)

 University of the Aegean, Greece
(https://www.aegean.edu/)

 University of Perugia, Italy
(https://www.unipg.it)

 University of Basilicata, Italy
(http://www.unibas.it)

 Monash University, Australia
(https://www.monash.edu/)

 Kyushu Sangyo University, Japan
(https://www.kyusan-u.ac.jp/)

 University of Minho, Portugal
(https://www.uminho.pt/)

Universidade do Minho
Escola de Engenharia

Referees

Francesca Abastante	Turin Polytechnic, Italy
Giovanna Acampa	University of Enna Kore, Italy
Adewole Adewumi	Algonquin College, Canada
Vera Afreixo	University of Aveiro, Portugal
Riad Aggoune	Luxembourg Institute of Science and Technology, Luxembourg
Akshat Agrawal	Amity University Haryana, India
Waseem Ahmad	National Institute of Technology Karnataka, India
Oylum Alatlı	Ege University, Turkey
Abraham Alfa	Federal University of Technology Minna, Nigeria
Diego Altafini	University of Pisa, Italy
Filipe Alvelos	University of Minho, Portugal
Marina Alexandra Pedro Andrade	University Institute of Lisbon, Portugal
Debora Anelli	Polytechnic University of Bari, Italy
Mariarosaria Angrisano	Pegaso University, Italy
Alfonso Annunziata	University of Cagliari, Italy
Magarò Antonio	Sapienza University of Rome, Italy
Bernady Apduhan	Kyushu Sangyo University, Japan
Jonathan Apeh	Covenant University, Nigeria
Daniela Ascenzi	University of Trento, Italy
Vanessa Assumma	University of Bologna, Italy
Maria Fernanda Augusto	Bitrum Research Center, Spain
Marco Baioletti	University of Perugia, Italy

Ginevra Balletto	University of Cagliari, Italy
Carlos Balsa	Polytechnic Institute of Bragança, Portugal
Benedetto Barabino	University of Brescia, Italy
Simona Barbaro	University of Palermo, Italy
Sebastiano Barbieri	Turin Polytechnic, Italy
Kousik Barik	University of Alcala, Spain
Alice Barreca	Turin Polytechnic, Italy
Socrates Basbas	Aristotle University of Thessaloniki, Greece
Rosaria Battarra	National Research Council, Italy
Silvia Battino	University of Sassari, Italy
Fabrizio Battisti	University of Florence, Italy
Yaroslav Bazaikin	Jan Evangelista Purkyne University, Czech Republic
Ranjan Kumar Behera	Indian Institute of Information Technology, India
Simone Belli	Complutense University of Madrid, Spain
Oscar Bellini	Polytechnic University of Milan, Italy
Giulio Biondi	University of Perugia, Italy
Adriano Bisello	Eurac Research, Italy
Semen Bochkov	Ulyanovsk State Technical University, Russia
Alexander Bogdanov	St. Petersburg State University, Russia
Letizia Bollini	Free University of Bozen, Italy
Giuseppe Borruso	University of Trieste, Italy
Marilisa Botte	University of Naples Federico II, Italy
Ana Cristina Braga	University of Minho, Portugal
Frederico Branco	University of Trás-os-Montes and Alto Douro, Portugal
Jorge Buele	Indoamérica Technological University, Ecuador
Datzania Lizeth Burgos	Peninsula State University of Santa Elena, Ecuador
Isabel Cacao	University of Aveiro, Portugal
Francesco Calabrò	Mediterranea University of Reggio Calabria, Italy
Rogerio Calazan	Institute of Sea Studies Almirante Paulo Moreira, Brazil
Lelio Campanile	University of Campania Luigi Vanvitelli, Italy
Tiziana Campisi	University of Enna Kore, Italy
Orazio Campo	University of Rome La Sapienza, Italy
Caterina Caprioli	Turin Polytechnic, Italy
Gerardo Carpentieri	University of Naples Federico II, Italy
Martina Carra	University of Brescia, Italy
Barbara Caselli	University of Parma, Italy
Danny Casprini	Politechnic of Milan, Italy

Omar Fernando Castellanos Balleteros	Peninsula State University of Santa Elena, Ecuador
Arcangelo Castiglione	University of Salerno, Italy
Giulio Cavana	Turin Polytechnic, Italy
Maria Cerreta	University of Naples Federico II, Italy
Sabarathinam Chockalingam	Institute for Energy Technology, Norway
Luis Enrique Chuquimarca Jimenez	Peninsula State University of Santa Elena, Ecuador
Birol Ciloglugil	Ege University, Turkey
Elena Cocuzza	Univesity of Catania, Italy
Emanuele Colica	University of Malta, Malta
Mauro Coni	University of Cagliari, Italy
Simone Corrado	University of Basilicata, Italy
Elisete Correia	University of Trás-os-Montes and Alto Douro, Portugal
Florbela Correia	Polytechnic Institute Viana do Castelo, Portugal
Paulo Cortez	University of Minho, Portugal
Martina Corti	Politechnic of Milan, Italy
Lino Costa	Universidade do Minho, Portugal
Cecília Maria Vasconcelos Costa e Castro	University of Minho, Portugal
Alfredo Cuzzocrea	University of Calabria, Italy
Sebastiano D'amico	University of Malta, Malta
Maria Danese	National Research Council, Italy
Gianni Dangelo	University of Salerno, Italy
Ana Daniel	Aveiro University, Portugal
Giulia Datola	Politechnic of Milan, Italy
Regina De Almeida	University of Trás-os-Montes and Alto Douro, Portugal
Maria Stella De Biase	University of Campania Luigi Vanvitelli, Italy
Elise De Doncker	Western Michigan University, USA
Luiza De Macedo Mourelle	State University of Rio de Janeiro, Brazil
Itamir De Morais Barroca Filho	Federal University of Rio Grande do Norte, Brazil
Pierfrancesco De Paola	University of Naples Federico II, Italy
Francesco De Pascale	University of Turin, Italy
Manuela De Ruggiero	University of Calabria, Italy
Alexander Degtyarev	St. Petersburg State University, Russia
Federico Dellanna	Turin Polytechnic, Italy
Marta Dellovo	Politechnic of Milan, Italy
Bashir Derradji	Sfax University, Tunisia
Giulia Desogus	University of Cagliari, Italy
Frank Devai	London South Bank University, UK

Piero Di Bonito	University of Campania Luigi Vanvitelli, Italy
Chiara Di Dato	University of L'Aquila, Italy
Michele Di Giovanni	University of Campania Luigi Vanvitelli, Italy
Felicia Di Liddo	Polytechnic University of Bari, Italy
Joana Dias	University of Coimbra, Portugal
Luigi Dolores	University of Salerno, Italy
Marco Donatelli	University of Insubria, Italy
Aziz Dursun	Virginia Tech University, USA
Jaroslav Dvořak	Klaipeda University, Lithuania
Wolfgang Erb	University of Padova, Italy
Maurizio Francesco Errigo	University of Enna Kore, Italy
Noelia Faginas-Lago	University of Perugia, Italy
Maria Irene Falcao	University of Minho, Portugal
Stefano Falcinelli	University of Perugia, Italy
Grazia Fattoruso	Italian National Agency for New Technologies, Energy and Sustainable Economic Development, Italy
Sara Favargiotti	University of Trento, Italy
Marcin Feltynowski	University of Lodz, Poland
António Fernandes	Polytechnic Institute of Bragança, Portugal
Florbela P. Fernandes	Polytechnic Institute of Bragança, Portugal
Paula Odete Fernandes	Polytechnic Institute of Bragança, Portugal
Luis Fernandez-Sanz	University of Alcala, Spain
Maria Eugenia Ferrao	University of Beira Interior and University of Lisbon, Portugal
Luís Ferrás	University of Minho, Portugal
Angela Ferreira	Polytechnic Institute of Bragança, Portugal
Maddalena Ferretti	Politechnic of Marche, Italy
Manuel Carlos Figueiredo	University of Minho, Portugal
Fabrizio Finucci	Roma Tre University, Italy
Ugo Fiore	University Pathenope of Naples, Italy
Lorena Fiorini	University of L'Aquila, Italy
Valentina Franzoni	Perugia University, Italy
Adelaide Freitas	University of Aveiro, Portugal
Kirill Gadylshin	Russian Academy of Sciences, Russia
Andrea Gallo	University of Trieste, Italy
Luciano Galone	University of Malta, Malta
Chiara Garau	University of Cagliari, Italy
Ernesto Garcia Para	Universidad del País Vasco, Spain
Rachele Vanessa Gatto	Università della Basilicata, Italy
Marina Gavrilova	University of Calgary, Canada
Georgios Georgiadis	Aristotle University of Thessaloniki, Greece

Ivan Gerace	University of Perugia, Italy
Osvaldo Gervasi	University of Perugia, Italy
Alfonso Giancotti	Sapienza University of Rome, Italy
Andrea Gioia	Politechnic of Bari, Italy
Giacomo Giorgi	University of Perugia, Italy
Salvatore Giuffrida	Università di Catania, Italy
A. Manuela Gonçalves	University of Minho, Portugal
Angela Gorgoglione	University of the Republic, Uruguay
Yusuke Gotoh	Okayama University, Japan
Mariolina Grasso	University of Enna Kore, Italy
Silvana Grillo	University of Cagliari, Italy
Teresa Guarda	Universidad Estatal Peninsula de Santa Elena, Ecuador
Eduardo Guerra	Free University of Bozen-Bolzano, Italy
Carmen Guida	University of Napoli Federico II, Italy
Kemal Güven Gülen	Namık Kemal University, Turkey
Malgorzata Hanzl	Technical University of Lodz, Poland
Peter Hegedus	University of Szeged, Hungary
Syeda Sumbul Hossain	Daffodil International University, Bangladesh
Mustafa Inceoglu	Ege University, Turkey
Federica Isola	University of Cagliari, Italy
Seifedine Kadry	Noroff University College, Norway
Yeliz Karaca	University of Massachusetts Chan Medical School and Massachusetts Institute of Technology, USA
Harun Karsli	Bolu Abant Izzet Baysal University, Turkey
Tayana Khachkova	Russian Academy of Sciences, Russia
Manju Khari	Jawaharlal Nehru University, India
Vladimir Korkhov	Saint Petersburg State University, Russia
Dionisia Koutsi	National Technical University of Athens, Greece
Tomonori Kouya	Shizuoka Institute of Science and Technology, Japan
Nataliia Kulabukhova	Saint Petersburg State University, Russia
Anisha Kumari	National Institute of Technology, India
Ludovica La Rocca	University of Napoli Federico II, Italy
Mara Ladu	University of Cagliari, Italy
Sabrina Lai	University of Cagliari, Italy
Mohamed Laib	Luxembourg Institute of Science and Technology, Luxembourg
Giuseppe Francesco Cesare Lama	University of Napoli Federico II, Italy
Isabella Maria Lami	Turin Polytechnic, Italy
Chien Sing Lee	Sunway University, Malaysia

Marcelo Leon	Ecotec University, Ecuador
Federica Leone	University of Cagliari, Italy
Barbara Lino	University of Palermo, Italy
Vadim Lisitsa	Russian Academy of Sciences, Russia
Carla Lobo	Portucalense University, Portugal
Marco Locurcio	Polytechnic University of Bari, Italy
Claudia Loggia	University of KwaZulu-Natal, South Africa
Andrea Lombardi	University of Perugia, Italy
Isabel Lopes	Polytechnic Institut of Bragança, Portugal
Immacolata Lorè	Mediterranean University of Reggio Calabria, Italy
Vanda Lourenco	Nova University of Lisbon, Portugal
Giorgia Malavasi	Turin Polytechnic, Italy
Francesca Maltinti	University of Cagliari, Italy
Luca Mancini	University of Perugia, Italy
Marcos Mandado	University of Vigo, Spain
Benedetto Manganelli	University of Basilicata, Italy
Krassimir Markov	Institute of Electric Engineering and Informatics, Bulgaria
Enzo Martinelli	University of Salerno, Italy
Fiammetta Marulli	University of Campania Luigi Vanvitelli, Italy
Antonino Marvuglia	Luxembourg Institute of Science and Technology, Luxembourg
Rytis Maskeliunas	Kaunas University of Technology, Lithuania
Michele Mastroianni	University of Salerno, Italy
Hideo Matsufuru	High Energy Accelerator Research Organization, Japan
D'Apuzzo Mauro	University of Cassino and Southern Lazio, Italy
Luis Mazon	Bitrum Research Group, Spain
Chiara Mazzarella	University Federico II, Naples, Italy
Beatrice Mecca	Turin Polytechnic, Italy
Umberto Mecca	Turin Polytechnic, Italy
Paolo Mengoni	Hong Kong Baptist University, China
Gaetano Messina	Mediterranean University of Reggio Calabria, Italy
Alfredo Milani	University of Perugia, Italy
Alessandra Milesi	University of Cagliari, Italy
Richard Millham	Durban University of Technology, South Africa
Fernando Miranda	Universidade do Minho, Portugal
Biswajeeban Mishra	University of Szeged, Hungary
Giuseppe Modica	University of Reggio Calabria, Italy
Pierluigi Morano	Polytechnic University of Bari, Italy

Filipe Mota Pinto	Polytechnic Institute of Leiria, Portugal
Maria Mourao	Polytechnic Institute of Viana do Castelo, Portugal
Eugenio Muccio	University of Naples Federico II, Italy
Beniamino Murgante	University of Basilicata, Italy
Rocco Murro	Sapienza University of Rome, Italy
Giuseppe Musolino	Mediterranean University of Reggio Calabria, Italy
Nadia Nedjah	State University of Rio de Janeiro, Brazil
Juraj Nemec	Masaryk University, Czech Republic
Andreas Nikiforiadis	Aristotle University of Thessaloniki, Greece
Silvio Nocera	IUAV University of Venice, Italy
Roseline Ogundokun	Kaunas University of Technology, Lithuania
Emma Okewu	University of Alcala, Spain
Serena Olcuire	Sapienza University of Rome, Italy
Irene Oliveira	University Trás-os-Montes and Alto Douro, Portugal
Samson Oruma	Ostfold University College, Norway
Antonio Pala	University of Cagliari, Italy
Maria Panagiotopoulou	National Technical University of Athens, Greece
Simona Panaro	University of Sussex Business School, UK
Jay Pancham	Durban University of Technology, South Africa
Eric Pardede	La Trobe University, Australia
Hyun Kyoo Park	Ministry of National Defense, South Korea
Damiano Perri	University of Florence, Italy
Quoc Trung Pham	Ho Chi Minh City University of Technology, Vietnam
Claudio Piferi	University of Florence, Italy
Angela Pilogallo	University of L'Aquila, Italy
Francesco Pinna	University of Cagliari, Italy
Telmo Pinto	University of Coimbra, Portugal
Luca Piroddi	University of Malta, Malta
Francesco Pittau	Politechnic of Milan, Italy
Giuliano Poli	Università Federico II di Napoli, Italy
Maurizio Pollino	Italian National Agency for New Technologies, Energy and Sustainable Economic Development, Italy
Vijay Prakash	University of Malta, Malta
Salvatore Praticò	Mediterranean University of Reggio Calabria, Italy
Carlotta Quagliolo	Turin Polytechnic, Italy
Garrisi Raffaele	Operations Center for Cyber Security, Italy
Mariapia Raimondo	Università della Campania Luigi Vanvitelli, Italy

Bruna Ramos	Universidade Lusíada Norte, Portugal
Nicoletta Rassu	University of Cagliari, Italy
Roberta Ravanelli	University of Roma La Sapienza, Italy
Pier Francesco Recchi	University of Naples Federico II, Italy
Stefania Regalbuto	University of Naples Federico II, Italy
Rommel Regis	Saint Joseph's University, USA
Marco Reis	University of Coimbra, Portugal
Jerzy Respondek	Silesian University of Technology, Poland
Isabel Ribeiro	Polytechnic Institut of Bragança, Portugal
Albert Rimola	Autonomous University of Barcelona, Spain
Corrado Rindone	Mediterranean University of Reggio Calabria, Italy
Maria Rocco	Roma Tre University, Italy
Ana Maria A. C. Rocha	University of Minho, Portugal
Fabio Rocha	Universidade Federal de Sergipe, Brazil
Humberto Rocha	University of Coimbra, Portugal
Maria Clara Rocha	Politechnic Institut of Coimbra, Portual
Carlos Rodrigues	Polytechnic Institut of Bragança, Portugal
Diana Rolando	Turin Polytechnic, Italy
James Rombi	University of Cagliari, Italy
Evgeniy Romenskiy	Russian Academy of Sciences, Russia
Marzio Rosi	University of Perugia, Italy
Silvia Rossetti	University of Parma, Italy
Marco Rossitti	Politechnic of Milan, Italy
Antonio Russo	University of Enna, Italy
Insoo Ryu	MoaSoftware, South Korea
Yeonseung Ryu	Myongji University, South Korea
Lucia Saganeiti	University of L'Aquila, Italy
Valentina Santarsiero	University of Basilicata, Italy
Luigi Santopietro	University of Basilicata, Italy
Rafael Santos	National Institute for Space Research, Brazil
Valentino Santucci	University for Foreigners of Perugia, Italy
Alessandra Saponieri	University of Salento, Italy
Mattia Scalas	Turin Polytechnic, Italy
Francesco Scorza	University of Basilicata, Italy
Ester Scotto Di Perta	University of Napoli Federico II, Italy
Nicoletta Setola	University of Florence, Italy
Ricardo Severino	University of Minho, Portugal
Angela Silva	Polytechnic Institut of Viana do Castelo, Portugal
Carina Silva	Polytechnic of Lisbon, Portugal
Marco Simonetti	University of Florence, Italy
Sergey Solovyev	Russian Academy of Sciences, Russia

Maria Somma	University of Naples Federico II, Italy
Changgeun Son	Ministry of National Defense, South Korea
Alberico Sonnessa	Polytechnic of Bari, Italy
Inês Sousa	University of Minho, Portugal
Lisete Sousa	University of Lisbon, Portugal
Elena Stankova	Saint-Petersburg State University, Russia
Modestos Stavrakis	University of the Aegean, Greece
Flavio Stochino	University of Cagliari, Italy
Anastasia Stratigea	National Technical University of Athens, Greece
Yue Sun	European XFEL GmbH, Germany
Anthony Suppa	Turin Polytechnic, Italy
David Taniar	Monash University, Australia
Rodrigo Tapia McClung	Centre for Research in Geospatial Information Sciences, Mexico
Tarek Teba	University of Portsmouth, UK
Ana Paula Teixeira	University of Trás-os-Montes and Alto Douro, Portugal
Tengku Adil Tengku Izhar	Technological University MARA, Malaysia
Maria Filomena Teodoro	University of Lisbon and Portuguese Naval Academy, Portugal
Yiota Theodora	National Technical University of Athens, Greece
Elena Todella	Turin Polytechnic, Italy
Graça Tomaz	Polytechnic Institut of Guarda, Portugal
Anna Tonazzini	National Research Council, Italy
Dario Torregrossa	Goodyear, Luxembourg
Francesca Torrieri	University of Naples Federico II, Italy
Vincenza Torrisi	University of Catania, Italy
Nikola Tosic	Polytechnic University of Catalonia, Spain
Vincenzo Totaro	Polytechnic University of Bari, Italy
Arianna Travaglini	University of Florence, Italy
António Trigo	Polytechnic of Coimbra, Portugal
Giuseppe A. Trunfio	University of Sassari, Italy
Toshihiro Uchibayashi	Kyushu University, Japan
Piero Ugliengo	University of Torino, Italy
Jordi Vallverdu	University Autonoma Barcelona, Spain
Gianmarco Vanuzzo	University of Perugia, Italy
Dmitry Vasyunin	T-Systems, Russia
Laura Verde	University of Campania Luigi Vanvitelli, Italy
Giulio Vignoli	University of Cagliari, Italy
Gianluca Vinti	University of Perugia, Italy
Katarína Vitálišová	Matej Bel University, Slovak Republic
Daniel Mark Vitiello	University of Cagliari

Marco Vizzari — University of Perugia, Italy
Manuel Yañez — Autonomous University of Madrid, Spain
Fenghui Yao — Tennessee State University, USA
Fukuko Yuasa — High Energy Accelerator Research Organization, Japan
Milliam Maxime Zekeng Ndadji — University of Dschang, Cameroon
Ljiljana Zivkovic — Republic Geodetic Authority, Serbia
Camila Zyngier — IBMEC-BH, Brazil

Plenary Lectures

A Multiscale Planning Concept for Sustainable Metropolitan Development

Pierre Frankhauser

Théma, Université de Franche-Comté, 32, rue Mégevand, 20030 Besançon, France
pierre.frankhauser@univ-fcomte.fr

Keywords: Sustainable metropolitan development · Multiscale approach · Urban modelling

Urban sprawl has often been pointed out as having an important negative impact on environment and climate. Residential zones have grown up in what were initially rural areas, located far from employment areas and often lacking shopping opportunities, public services and public transportation. Hence urban sprawl increased car-traffic flows, generating pollution and increasing energy consumption. New road axes consume considerable space and weaken biodiversity by reducing and cutting natural areas. A return to "compact cities" or "dense cities" has often been contemplated as the most efficient way to limit urban sprawl. However, the real impact of density on car use is less clear-cut (Daneshpour and Shakibamanesh 2011). Let us emphasize that moreover climate change will increase the risk of heat islands on an intra-urban scale. This prompts a more nuanced reflection on how urban fabrics should be structured.

Moreover, urban planning cannot ignore social demand. Lower land prices in rural areas, often put forward by economists, is not the only reason of urban sprawl. The quality of the residential environment comes into play, too, through features like noise, pollution, landscape quality, density etc. Schwanen et al. (2004) observe for the Netherlands that households preferring a quiet residential environment and individual housing with a garden will not accept densification, which might even lead them to move to lower-density rural areas even farther away from jobs and shopping amenities. Many scholars emphasize the importance of green amenities for residential environments and report the importance of easy access to leisure areas (Guo and Bhat 2002). Vegetation in the residential environment has an important impact on health and well-being (Lafortezza et al. 2009).

We present here the Fractalopolis concept which we developed in the frame of several research projects and which aims reconciling environmental and social issues (Bonin et al., 2020; Frankhauser 2021; Frankhauser et al. 2018). This concept introduces a multiscale approach based on multifractal geometry for conceiving spatial development for metropolitan areas. For taking into account social demand we refer to the fundamental work of Max-Neef et al. (1991) based on Maslow's work about basic human needs. He introduces the concept of satisfiers assigned to meet the basic needs of "Subsistence, Protection, Affection, Understanding, Participation, Idleness, Creation, Identity and Freedom". Satisfiers thus become the link between the needs of everyone and society and may depend on the cultural context. We consider their importance, their location and their accessibility and we rank the needs according to their importance for individuals or households. In order to enjoy a good quality of life and to shorten trips and to reduce automobile use, it seems important for satisfiers of daily needs to be easily accessible. Hence, we consider the purchase rate when reflecting on the implementation of shops which is reminiscent of central place theory.

The second important feature is taking care of environment and biodiversity by avoiding fragmentation of green space (Ekren and Arslan 2022) which must benefit, moreover, of a good accessibility, as pointed out. These areas must, too, ply the role of cooling areas ensuring ventilation of urbanized areas (Kuttler et al. 1998).

For integrating these different objectives, we propose a concept for developing spatial configurations of metropolitan areas designed which is based on multifractal geometry. It allows combining different issues across a large range of scales in a coherent way. These issues include:

- providing easy access to a large array of amenities to meet social demand;
- promoting the use of public transportation and soft modes instead of automobile use;
- preserving biodiversity and improving the local climate.

The concept distinguishes development zones localized in the vicinity of a nested and hierarchized system of public transport axes. The highest ranked center offers all types of amenities, whereas lower ranked centers lack the highest ranked amenities. The lowest ranked centers just offer the amenities for daily needs. A coding system allows distinguishing the centers according to their rank.

Each subset of central places is in some sense autonomous, since they are not linked by transportation axes to subcenters of the same order. This allows to preserve a linked system of green corridors penetrating the development zones across scales avoiding the fragmentation of green areas and ensuring a good accessibility to recreational areas.

The spatial model is completed by a population distribution model which globally follows the same hierarchical logic. However, we weakened the strong fractal order what allows to conceive a more or less polycentric spatial system.

We can adapt the theoretical concept easily to real world situation without changing the underlying multiscale logic. A decision support system has been developed allowing to simulate development scenarios and to evaluate them. The evaluation procedure is based on fuzzy evaluation of distance acceptance for accessing to the different types of amenities according to the ranking of needs. We used for evaluation data issued from a great set of French planning documents like Master plans. We show an example how the software package can be used concretely.

References

Bonin, O., et al.: Projet SOFT sobriété énergétique par les formes urbaines et le transport (Research Report No. 1717C0003; p. 214). ADEME (2020)

Daneshpour, A., Shakibamanesh, A.: Compact city; dose it create an obligatory context for urban sustainability? Int. J. Archit. Eng. Urban Plann. 21(2), 110–118 (2011)

Ekren, E., Arslan, M.: Functions of greenways as an ecologically-based planning strategy. In: Çakır, M., Tuğluer, M., Fırat Örs, P.: Architectural Sciences and Ecology, pp. 134–156. Iksad Publications (2022)

Frankhauser, P.: Fractalopolis—a fractal concept for the sustainable development of metropolitan areas. In: Sajous, P., Bertelle, C. (eds.) Complex Systems, Smart Territories and Mobility, pp. 15–50. Springer, Cham (2021). https://doi.org/10.1007/978-3-030-59302-5_2

Frankhauser, P., Tannier, C., Vuidel, G., Houot, H.: An integrated multifractal modelling to urban and regional planning. Comput. Environ. Urban Syst. **67**(1), 132–146 (2018). https://doi.org/10.1016/j.compenvurbsys.2017.09.011

Guo, J., Bhat, C.: Residential location modeling: accommodating sociodemographic, school quality and accessibility effects. University of Texas, Austin (2002)

Kuttler, W., Dütemeyer, D., Barlag, A.-B.: Influence of regional and local winds on urban ventilation in Cologne, Germany. Meteorologische Zeitschrift, 77–87 (1998) https://doi.org/10.1127/metz/7/1998/77

Lafortezza, R., Carrus, G., Sanesi, G., Davies, C.: Benefits and well-being perceived by people visiting green spaces in periods of heat stress. Urban For. Urban Green. **8**(2), 97–108 (2009)

Max-Neef, M. A., Elizalde, A., Hopenhayn, M.: Human scale development: conception, application and further reflections. The Apex Press (1991)

Schwanen, T., Dijst, M., Dieleman, F. M.: Policies for urban form and their impact on travel: The Netherlands experience. Urban Stud. **41**(3), 579–603 (2004)

Graph Drawing and Network Visualization – An Overview – (Keynote Speech)

Giuseppe Liotta

Dipartimento di Ingegneria, Università degli Studi di Perugia, Italy
`giuseppe.liotta@unipg.it`

Abstract. Graph Drawing and Network visualization supports the exploration, analysis, and communication of relational data arising in a variety of application domains: from bioinformatics to software engineering, from social media to cyber-security, from data bases to powergrid systems. Aim of this keynote speech is to introduce this thriving research area, highlighting some of its basic approaches and pointing to some promising research directions.

1 Introduction

Graph Drawing and Network Visualization is at the intersection of different disciplines and it combines topics that traditionally belong to theoretical computer science with methods and approaches that characterize more applied disciplines. Namely, it can be related to Graph Algorithms, Geometric Graph Theory and Geometric computing, Combinatorial Optimization, Experimental Analysis, User Studies, System Design and Development, and Human Computer Interaction. This combination of theory and practice is well reflected in the flagship conference of the area, the *International Symposium on Graph Drawing and Network Visualization*, that has two tracks, one focusing on combinatorial and algorithmic aspects and the other on the design of network visualization systems and interfaces. The conference is now at its 31st edition; a full list of the symposia and their proceedings, published by Springer in the LNCS series can be found at the URL: http://www.graphdrawing.org/.

Aim of this short paper is to outline the content of my Keynote Speech at ICCSA 2023, which will be referred to as the "Talk" in the rest of the paper. The talk will introduce the field of Graph Drawing and Network Visualization to a broad audience, with the goal to not only present some key methodological and technological aspects, but also point to some unexplored or partially explored research directions. The rest of this short paper briefly outlines the content of the talk and provides some references that can be a starting point for researchers interested in working on Graph Drawing and Network Visualization.

2 Why Visualize Networks?

Back in 1973 the famous statistician Francis Anscombe, gave a convincing example of why visualization is fundamental component of data analysis. The example is known as the *Anscombe's quartet* [3] and it consists of four sets of 11 points each that are almost identical in terms of the basic statistic properties of their x– and y– coordinates. Namely the mean values and the variance of x and y are exactly the same in the four sets, while the correlation of x and y and the linear regression are the same up to the second decimal. In spite of this statistical similarity, the data look very different when displayed in the Euclidean plane which leads to the conclusion that they correspond to significantly different phenomena. Figure 1 reports the four sets of Anscombe's quartet. After fifty years, with the arrival of AI-based technologies and the need of explaining and interpreting machine-driven suggestions before making strategic decision, the lesson of Anscombe's quartet has not just kept but even increased its relevance.

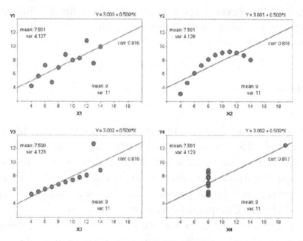

Fig. 1. The four point sets in Anscombe's quartet [3]; the figure also reports statistical values of the x and y variables.

As a matter of fact, nowadays the need of visualization systems goes beyond the verification of the accuracy of some statistical analysis on a set of scattered data. Recent technological advances have generated torrents of data that area relational in nature and typically modeled as networks: the nodes of the networks store the features of the data and the edges of the networks describe the semantic relationships between the data features. Such networked data sets (whose algebraic underlying structure is a called graph in discrete mathematics) arise in a variety of application domains including, for example, Systems Biology, Social Network Analysis, Software Engineering, Networking, Data Bases, Homeland Security, and Business Intelligence. In these (and many other) contexts, systems that support the visual analysis of networks and graphs play a central role in critical decision making processes. These are human-in-the-loop processes where the continuous interaction between humans (decision makers) and data mining or optimization algorithms (AI/ML components) supports the data exploration, the development of verifiable theories about the data, and the extraction of new knowledge that is used to make strategic choices. A seminal book by Keim et al. [33] schematically represents the human-in-the-loop approach to making sense of networked data sets as in Fig. 2. See also [46–49].

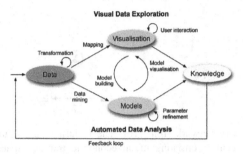

Fig. 2. Sense-making/knowledge generation loop. This conceptual interaction model between human analysts and network visualization system is at the basis of network visual analytics system design [33].

To make a concrete application example of the analysis of a network by interacting with its visualization, consider the problem of contrasting financial crimes such as money laundering or tax evasion. These crimes are based on relevant volumes of financial transactions to conceal the identity, the source, or the destination of illegally gained money. Also, the adopted patterns to pursue the illegal goals continuously change to conceal the crimes. Therefore, contrasting them requires special investigation units which must analyze very large and highly dynamic data sets and discover relationships between different subjects to untangle complex fraudulent plots. The investigative cycle begins with data collection and filtering; it is then followed by modeling the data as a social network (also called *financial activity network* in this context) to which different data mining and data analytic methods are applied, including graph pattern matching, social network analysis, machine learning, and information diffusion. By the network visualization system detectives can interactively explore the data, gain insight and make new hypotheses about possible criminal activities, verify the hypotheses by asking the system to provide more details about specific portions of the network, refine previous outputs, and eventually gain new knowledge. Figure 3 illustrates a small financial activity network where, by means of the interaction between an officer of the Italian Revenue Agency and the MALDIVE system described in [10] a fraudulent pattern has been identified. Precisely, the tax officer has encoded a risky relational scheme among taxpayers into a suspicious graph pattern; in response, the system has made a search in the taxpayer network and it has returned one such pattern. See, e.g., [9, 11, 14, 18, 38] for more papers and references about visual analytic applications to contrasting financial crimes.

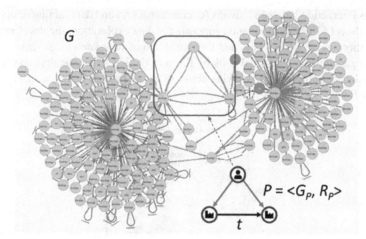

Fig. 3. A financial activity network from [10]. The pattern in the figure represents a SuppliesFromAssociated scheme, consisting of an economic transaction and two shareholding relationships.

3 Facets of Graph Drawing and Network Visualization

The Talk overviews some of the fundamental facets that characterize the research in Graph Drawing and Network Visualization. Namely:

- Graph drawing metaphors: Depending on the application context, different metaphors can be used to represent a relational data set modeled as a graph. The talk will briefly recall the matrix representation, the space filling representation, the contact representation, and the node-link representation which is, by far, the most commonly used (see, e.g., [43]).
- Interaction paradigms: Different interaction paradigms have different impacts on the sense-making process of the user about the visualized network. The Talk will go through the full-view, top-down, bottom-up, incremental, and narrative paradigms. Pros and cons will be highlighted for each approach, also by means of examples and applications. The discussion of the top-down interaction paradigm will also consider the hybrid visualization models (see, e.g., [2, 24, 26, 28, 39]) while the discussion about the incremental paradigm will focus on research about graph storyplans (see, e.g., [4, 6, 7]).
- Graph drawing algorithms: Three main algorithmic approaches will be reviewed, namely the force-directed, the layered), and the planarization-based approach; see, e.g., [5]. We shall also make some remarks about FPT algorithms for graph drawing (see, e.g., [8, 19, 20, 25, 27, 40, 53]) and about how the optimization challenges vary when it is assumed that the input has or does not have a fixed combinatorial embedding (see, e.g., [12, 13, 16, 17, 23]).
- Experimental analysis and user-studies: The Talk will mostly compare two models to define and experimentally validate those optimization goals that define a "readable"

network visualization, i.e. a visualization that in a given application context can easily convey the structure of a relational data set so to guarantee efficiency both in its visual exploration and in the elaboration of new knowledge. Special focus will be given to a set emerging optimization goals related to edge crossings that are currently investigated in the graph drawing and network visualization community unedr the name of "graph drawing beyond planarity" (see, e.g., [1, 15, 29, 35]).

The talk shall also point to some promising research directions, including: (i) Extend the body of papers devoted to user-studies that compare the impact of different graph drawing metaphors on the user perception. (ii) Extend the study of interaction paradigms to extended reality environments (see, e.g., [21, 30, 36, 37]); (iii) Engineer the FPT algorithms for graph drawing and experimentally compare their performances with exact or approximate solutions; and (iv) Develop new algorithmic fameworks in the context of graph drawing beyond planarity.

We conclude this short paper with pointers to publication venues and key references that can be browsed by researchers interested in the fascinating field of Graph Drawing and Network Visualization.

4   Pointers to Publication venues and Key References

A limited list of conferences where Graph Drawing and Network Visualization papers are regularly part of the program includes *IEEE VIS, EuroVis, SoCG, ISAAC, ACM-SIAM SODA, WADS,* and *WG.* Among the many journals where several Graph Drawing and Network Visualization papers have appeared during the last three decades we recall *IEEE Transactions on Visualization and Computer Graphs, SIAM Jounal of Computing, Computer Graphics Forum, Journal of Computer and System Sciences, Algorithmica, Journal of Graph Algorithms and Applications, Theoretical Computer Science, Information Sciences, Discrete and Computational Geometry, Computational Geometry: Theory and Applications, ACM Computing Surveys,* and *Computer Science Review.* A limited list of books, surveys, or papers that contain interesting algorithmic challenges on Graph Drawing and Network Visualization include [5, 15, 22, 29, 31–35, 41–45, 50–52].

References

1. Angelini, P., et al.: Simple k-planar graphs are simple (k+1)-quasiplanar. J. Comb. Theory, Ser. B, **142**, 1–35 (2020)
2. Angori, L., Didimo, W., Montecchiani, F., Pagliuca, D., Tappini, A.: Hybrid graph visualizations with chordlink: Algorithms, experiments, and applications. IEEE Trans. Vis. Comput. Graph. **28**(2), 1288–1300 (2022)
3. Anscombe, F.J.: Graphs in statistical analysis. Am. Stat. **27**(1), 17–21 (1973)
4. Di Battista, G., et al.: Small point-sets supporting graph stories. In: Angelini, P., von Hanxleden, R. (eds.) Graph Drawing and Network Visualization. GD 2022, LNCS, vol. 13764, pp. 289–303. Springer, Cham (2022). https://doi.org/10.1007/978-3-031-22203-0_21

5. Battista, G.D., Eades, P., Tamassia, R., Tollis, I.G.: Graph Drawing: Algorithms for the Visualization of Graphs. Prentice-Hall, Hoboken (1999)
6. Binucci, C., et al.: On the complexity of the storyplan problem. In: Angelini, P., von Hanxleden, R. (eds.) Graph Drawing and Network Visualization. GD 2022. LNCS, vol. 13764, pp. 304–318. Springer, Cham (2023). https://doi.org/10.1007/978-3-031-22203-0_22
7. Borrazzo, M., Lozzo, G.D., Battista, G.D., Frati, F., Patrignani, M.: Graph stories in small area. J. Graph Algorithms Appl. 24(3), 269–292 (2020)
8. Chaplick, S., Giacomo, E.D., Frati, F., Ganian, R., Raftopoulou, C.N., Simonov, K.: Parameterized algorithms for upward planarity. In: Goaoc, X., Kerber, M. (eds.) 38th International Symposium on Computational Geometry, SoCG 2022, June 7–10, 2022, Berlin, Germany, LIPIcs, vol. 224, pp. 26:1–26:16. Schloss Dagstuhl - Leibniz-Zentrum für Informatik (2022)
9. Didimo, W., Giamminonni, L., Liotta, G., Montecchiani, F., Pagliuca, D.: A visual analytics system to support tax evasion discovery. Decis. Support Syst. 110, 71–83 (2018)
10. Didimo, W., Grilli, L., Liotta, G., Menconi, L., Montecchiani, F., Pagliuca, D.: Combining network visualization and data mining for tax risk assessment. IEEE Access 8, 16073–16086 (2020)
11. Didimo, W., Grilli, L., Liotta, G., Montecchiani, F., Pagliuca, D.: Visual querying and analysis of temporal fiscal networks. Inf. Sci. 505, 406–421 (2019)
12. W. Didimo, M. Kaufmann, G. Liotta, and G. Ortali. Didimo, W., Kaufmann, M., Liotta, G., Ortali, G.: Rectilinear planarity testing of plane series-parallel graphs in linear time. In: Auber, D., Valtr, P. (eds.) Graph Drawing and Network Visualization. GD 2020. LNCS, vol. 12590, pp. 436–449. Springer, Cham (2020). https://doi.org/10.1007/978-3-030-68766-3_34
13. Didimo, W., Kaufmann, M., Liotta, G., Ortali, G.: Rectilinear planarity of partial 2-trees. In: Angelini, P., von Hanxleden, R. (eds.) Graph Drawing and Network Visualization. GD 2022. LNCS, vol. 13764, pp. 157–172. Springer, Cham (2023). https://doi.org/10.1007/978-3-031-22203-0_12
14. Didimo, W., Liotta, G., Montecchiani, F.: Network visualization for financial crime detection. J. Vis. Lang. Comput. 25(4), 433–451 (2014)
15. Didimo, W., Liotta, G., Montecchiani, F.: A survey on graph drawing beyond planarity. ACM Comput. Surv. 52(1), 4:1–4:37 (2019)
16. Didimo, W., Liotta, G., Ortali, G., Patrignani, M.: Optimal orthogonal drawings of planar 3-graphs in linear time. In: Chawla, S. (ed.) Proceedings of the 2020 ACM-SIAM Symposium on Discrete Algorithms, SODA 2020, Salt Lake City, UT, USA, January 5–8, 2020, pp. 806–825. SIAM (2020)
17. Didimo, W., Liotta, G., Patrignani, M.: HV-planarity: algorithms and complexity. J. Comput. Syst. Sci. 99, 72–90 (2019)
18. Dilla, W.N., Raschke, R.L.: Data visualization for fraud detection: practice implications and a call for future research. Int. J. Acc. Inf. Syst. 16, 1–22 (2015)
19. Dujmovic, V., et al.: A fixed-parameter approach to 2-layer planarization. Algorithmica 45(2), 159–182 (2006)
20. Dujmovic, V., et al.: On the parameterized complexity of layered graph drawing. Algorithmica 52(2), 267–292 (2008)

21. Dwyer, T., et al.: Immersive analytics: an introduction. In: Marriott, K., et al. (eds.) Immersive Analytics, LNCS, vol. 11190, pp. 1–23. Springer, Cham (2018)
22. Filipov, V., Arleo, A., Miksch, S.: Are we there yet? a roadmap of network visualization from surveys to task taxonomies. Computer Graphics Forum (2023, on print)
23. Garg, A., Tamassia, R.: On the computational complexity of upward and rectilinear planarity testing. SIAM J. Comput. **31**(2), 601–625 (2001)
24. Di Giacomo, E., Didimo, W., Montecchiani, F., Tappini, A.: A user study on hybrid graph visualizations. In: Purchase, H.C., Rutter, I. (eds.) Graph Drawing and Network Visualization. GD 2021. LNCS, vol. 12868, pp. 21–38. Springer, Cham (2021). https://doi.org/10.1007/978-3-030-92931-2_2
25. Giacomo, E.D., Giordano, F., Liotta, G.: Upward topological book embeddings of dags. SIAM J. Discret. Math. **25**(2), 479–489 (2011)
26. Giacomo, E.D., Lenhart, W.J., Liotta, G., Randolph, T.W., Tappini, A.: (k, p)-planarity: a relaxation of hybrid planarity. Theor. Comput. Sci. **896**, 19–30 (2021)
27. Giacomo, E.D., Liotta, G., Montecchiani, F.: Orthogonal planarity testing of bounded treewidth graphs. J. Comput. Syst. Sci. **125**, 129–148 (2022)
28. Giacomo, E.D., Liotta, G., Patrignani, M., Rutter, I., Tappini, A.: Nodetrix planarity testing with small clusters. Algorithmica **81**(9), 3464–3493 (2019)
29. Hong, S., Tokuyama, T. (eds.) Beyond Planar Graphs. Springer, Singapore (2020). https://doi.org/10.1007/978-981-15-6533-5
30. Joos, L., Jaeger-Honz, S., Schreiber, F., Keim, D.A., Klein, K.: Visual comparison of networks in VR. IEEE Trans. Vis. Comput. Graph. **28**(11), 3651–3661 (2022)
31. Jünger, M., Mutzel, P. (eds.) Graph Drawing Software. Springer, Berlin (2004). https://doi.org/10.1007/978-3-642-18638-7
32. Kaufmann, M., Wagner, D. (eds.): Drawing Graphs, Methods and Models (the book grow out of a Dagstuhl Seminar, April 1999), LNCS, vol. 2025. Springer, Berlin (2001). https://doi.org/10.1007/3-540-44969-8
33. Keim, D.A., Kohlhammer, J., Ellis, G.P., Mansmann, F.: Mastering the Information Age - Solving Problems with Visual Analytics. Eurographics Association, Saarbrücken (2010)
34. Keim, D.A., Mansmann, F., Stoffel, A., Ziegler, H.: Visual analytics. In: Liu, L., Özsu, M.T. (eds.) Encyclopedia of Database Systems, 2nd edn. Springer, Berlin (2018)
35. Kobourov, S.G., Liotta, G., Montecchiani, F.: An annotated bibliography on 1-planarity. Comput. Sci. Rev. **25**, 49–67 (2017)
36. Kraus, M., et al.: Immersive analytics with abstract 3D visualizations: a survey. Comput. Graph. Forum **41**(1), 201–229 (2022)
37. Kwon, O., Muelder, C., Lee, K., Ma, K.: A study of layout, rendering, and interaction methods for immersive graph visualization. IEEE Trans. Vis. Comput. Graph. **22**(7), 1802–1815 (2016)
38. Leite, R.A., Gschwandtner, T., Miksch, S., Gstrein, E., Kuntner, J.: NEVA: visual analytics to identify fraudulent networks. Comput. Graph. Forum **39**(6), 344–359 (2020)

39. Liotta, G., Rutter, I., Tappini, A.: Simultaneous FPQ-ordering and hybrid planarity testing. Theor. Comput. Sci. **874**, 59–79 (2021)
40. Liotta, G., Rutter, I., Tappini, A.: Parameterized complexity of graph planarity with restricted cyclic orders. J. Comput. Syst. Sci. **135**, 125–144 (2023)
41. Ma, K.: Pushing visualization research frontiers: essential topics not addressed by machine learning. IEEE Comput. Graphics Appl. **43**(1), 97–102 (2023)
42. McGee, F., et al.: Visual Analysis of Multilayer Networks. Synthesis Lectures on Visualization. Morgan & Claypool Publishers, San Rafael (2021)
43. Munzner, T.: Visualization Analysis and Design. A.K. Peters visualization series. A K Peters (2014)
44. Nishizeki, T., Rahman, M.S.: Planar Graph Drawing, vol. 12. World Scientific, Singapore (2004)
45. Nobre, C., Meyer, M.D., Streit, M., Lex, A.: The state of the art in visualizing multivariate networks. Comput. Graph. Forum **38**(3), 807–832 (2019)
46. Sacha, D.: Knowledge generation in visual analytics: Integrating human and machine intelligence for exploration of big data. In: Apel, S., et al. (eds.) Ausgezeichnete Informatikdissertationen 2018, LNI, vol. D-19, pp. 211–220. GI (2018)
47. Sacha, D., et al.: What you see is what you can change: human-centered machine learning by interactive visualization. Neurocomputing **268**, 164–175 (2017)
48. Sacha, D., Senaratne, H., Kwon, B.C., Ellis, G.P., Keim, D.A.: The role of uncertainty, awareness, and trust in visual analytics. IEEE Trans. Vis. Comput. Graph. **22**(1), 240–249 (2016)
49. Sacha, D., Stoffel, A., Stoffel, F., Kwon, B.C., Ellis, G.P., Keim, D.A.: Knowledge generation model for visual analytics. IEEE Trans. Vis. Comput. Graph. **20**(12), 1604–1613 (2014)
50. Tamassia, R.: Graph drawing. In: Sack, J., Urrutia, J. (eds.) Handbook of Computational Geometry, pp. 937–971. North Holland/Elsevier, Amsterdam (2000)
51. Tamassia, R. (ed.) Handbook on Graph Drawing and Visualization. Chapman and Hall/CRC, Boca Raton (2013)
52. Tamassia, R., Liotta, G.: Graph drawing. In: Goodman, J.E., O'Rourke, J. (eds.) Handbook of Discrete and Computational Geometry, 2nd edn., pp. 1163–1185. Chapman and Hall/CRC, Boca Raton (2004)
53. Zehavi, M.: Parameterized analysis and crossing minimization problems. Comput. Sci. Rev. **45**, 100490 (2022)

Understanding Non-Covalent Interactions in Biological Processes through QM/MM-EDA Dynamic Simulations

Marcos Mandado

Department of Physical Chemistry, University of Vigo, Lagoas-Marcosende s/n, 36310 Vigo, Spain
mandado@uvigo.es

Molecular dynamic simulations in biological environments such as proteins, DNA or lipids involves a large number of atoms, so classical models based on widely parametrized force fields are employed instead of more accurate quantum methods, whose high computational requirements preclude their application. The parametrization of appropriate force fields for classical molecular dynamics relies on the precise knowledge of the non-covalent inter and intramolecular interactions responsible for very important aspects, such as macromolecular arrangements, cell membrane permeation, ion solvation, etc. This implies, among other things, knowledge of the nature of the interaction, which may be governed by electrostatic, repulsion or dispersion forces. In order to know the balance between different forces, quantum calculations are frequently performed on simplified molecular models and the data obtained from these calculations are used to parametrize the force fields employed in classical simulations. These parameters are, among others, atomic charges, permanent electric dipole moments and atomic polarizabilities. However, it sometimes happens that the molecular models used for the quantum calculations are too simple and the results obtained can differ greatly from those of the extended system. As an alternative to classical and quantum methods, hybrid quantum/classical schemes (QM/MM) can be introduced, where the extended system is neither truncated nor simplified, but only the most important region is treated quantum mechanically.

In this presentation, molecular dynamic simulations and calculations with hybrid schemes are first introduced in a simple way for a broad and multidisciplinary audience. Then, a method developed in our group to investigate intermolecular interactions using hybrid quantum/classical schemes (QM/MM-EDA) is presented and some applications to the study of dynamic processes of ion solvation and membrane permeation are discussed [1–3]. Special attention is paid to the implementation details of the method in the EDA-NCI software [4].

References

1. Cárdenas, G., Pérez-Barcia, A., Mandado, M., Nogueira, J.J.: Phys. Chem. Chem. Phys. **23**, 20533 (2021)
2. Pérez-Barcia, A., Cárdenas, G., Nogueira, J.J., Mandado, M.: J. Chem. Inf. Model. **63**, 882 (2023)

3. Alvarado, R., Cárdenas, G., Nogueira, J.J., Ramos-Berdullas, N., Mandado, M.: Membranes **13**, 28 (2023)
4. Mandado, M., Van Alsenoy, C.: EDA-NCI: A program to perform energy decomposition analysis of non-covalent interactions. https://github.com/marcos-mandado/EDA-NCI

Contents – Part VI

Port City Interface: Land Use, Logistic and Rear Port Area Planning (PORTUNO 2023)

Scientific Computing Infrastructure (SCI 2023)

Spatial Cognition in Urban and Regional Planning Under Risk (SCOPUR23)

Socio-Economic and Environmental Models for Land Use Management (SEMLUM 2023)

Specifics of Smart Cities Development in Europe (SPEED 2023)

Models and Indicators for Assessing and Measuring the Urban Settlement Development in the View of ZERO Net Land Take by 2050 (MOVEto0 2023)

Energy Transition and Spatial Transformation: Looking for a Suitable Trade-Off

Angela Pilogallo(✉) and Lucia Saganeiti

Department of Civil, Building-Architecture and Environmental Engineering, University of L'Aquila, Via G. Gronchi, 18, 67100 L'Aquila, Italy
{angela.pilogallo,lucia.saganeiti}@univaq.it

Abstract. The entry of large amounts of funding and the ongoing energy crisis are drivers of large-scale land transformations for which no monitoring plan was framed. Several studies showed that already in the past the uncontrolled development of infrastructure for energy production from renewable sources led to significant environmental impacts, in some cases largely motivated by economic speculation. This paper analyzes the emblematic case study of the Basilicata Region where, since 2006, the number of wind turbines multiplied in the absence of both a monitoring system and a robust planning and programming framework. The paper proposes a spatially explicit methodology to measure the degree of sustainability of land transformations occurred, according to two approaches: ecosystem services, through the analysis of the carbon footprint related to the installation and operation of energy plants; spatial fragmentation, through a density index. The aim is to provide useful indications for addressing investments aimed at repowering existing wind farms in order to improve the overall environmental balance by increasing renewable energy production and minimizing negative environmental effects.

Keywords: Wind energy production · Carbon budget · Territorial fragmentation · holistic environmental impact assessment approach · indicator engineering

1 Introduction

In response to recent global energy crisis, the European Commission unveiled the REPowerEU plan [1] with the twofold aims of accelerating energy transition and increasing Europe's energy autonomy.

This, both in terms of economic-financial incentives and from the permitting simplifications' point of view, is chronologically the latest in a series of acts that, along the hierarchy of actors involved in land governance, has favored the development and spread of technologies for energy production from renewable sources.

Although the growth in the use of renewable energy sources is implicitly linked to an idea of sustainable development even at the local scale [2], several studies now show that the "renewable energy-sustainability" combination has been realized with

O. Gervasi et al. (Eds.): ICCSA 2023 Workshops, LNCS 14109, pp. 3–15, 2023.
https://doi.org/10.1007/978-3-031-37120-2_1

wide variability within the Italian territory [3]. The concept of sustainability is in fact multifaceted, declining within the three dimensions (environmental - economic - social) multiplied by all the spatial scales at which it makes sense to quantify it.

The case of Basilicata Region is particularly representative of the many perspectives from which we should consider territorial transformations induced by the pursuit of renewable energy production models and justified by the sustainability of energy transition. The risk is to incur in an optical illusion (Fig. 1).

According to the R.E.gions2030 Observatory [4], founded to monitor the *fluidity of authorization processes* and to evaluate *the appeal for the development of renewables* in Italian regions, Basilicata is defined as *virtuous*.

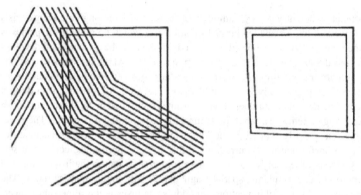

Fig. 1. Optical illusion: a frame between oblique lines appears regular. Removing the lines, it appears distorted [26]

The main reasons are as follows:

1. Basilicata has reached (and exceeded) renewable energy production targets set for 2020;
2. based on the monthly average request for authorizations in the period 2017–2021 (expressed in MW), Basilicata is the second most attractive Italian region;
3. the average time required for authorization procedures in Basilicata is approximately 6 years, an intermediate value between 1.2 years for Abruzzo and 9.2 years for Sardinia.

Several socio-economic studies [5–7], at the same time, suggest alternative readings. The development of renewable energy plants in rural areas with low urbanization, such as the Basilicata Region [8], not only do not effectively contribute to local development, but even risk worsening their marginalization [9, 10]. Furthermore, the ungoverned development of renewable energy production facilities causes significant environmental impacts [11, 12] and changes the landscape and the following territories' identity perception [3, 5].

This paper aims to investigate the cumulative environmental impact of the impressive development of wind energy in the Basilicata Region, proposing analyses and indicators at the territorial scale. The aim is to obtain values with which to compare transformation performance at municipal scale and thus be able to orient future investments towards repowering actions that pursue the dual objective of increasing clean energy production and minimizing impacts deriving from new installations.

The paper presents the case study by describing the increase in number of wind turbines (divided by capacity classes) for different time steps (Sect. 2) and then illustrates the methodology used for calculating the comparison parameters (Sect. 3).

Finally, the results are presented (Sect. 4) and limitations and simplifications adopted in terms of methodology are highlighted (Sect. 5). At the end, the conclusions (Sect. 6) highlight the importance of this work as a contribution to the search for tools to compare performances of territorial transformations.

2 Study Area and Dataset

According to the report of the national (Italian) Energy Services Manager (GSE), in Basilicata region there are 1417 wind farms. The regional wind farm represents in terms of numbers 25% of the national wind farm and in terms of installed power only 12% of the total power of the national wind farm [13].

To understand the magnitude of the phenomenon and the inefficiency of the distribution of wind turbines with respect to the power produced (in the Basilicata region), we point out that on average for the entire national wind farm the installed power is 1.93 MW per turbine (source: GSE) while only for the Basilicata region it is 0.91 MW per turbine. The discussion gets worse if we consider that the GSE surveys do not consider the entire mini wind farm (that with a power output lesser than 1 MW) which in Basilicata region represent a big amount of share.

In this work, reference is made to a larger dataset, obtained through the integration of various databases including the one of the GSE and the one concerning large-scale plants made available on the regional geoportal.

By 2020, there are a total of 2201 turbines with a total installed capacity of approximately 1274 MW.

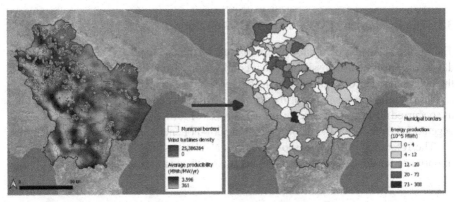

Fig. 2. From the average annual producibility [source: RSE] (MWh/MW/yr) and turbines' capacity (MW) dataset, the overall energy production (MWh) at 2030 was derived.

As can be seen from Fig. 2, the installation of wind turbines has affected a significant part of the regional territory: 72 out of 131 municipalities have at least one installation.

The evolution over time did not happen for everyone in the same way: while in some of them wind farms (capacity $\geq$ 1 MW) prevailed whose authorization process required an Environmental Impact Assessment (EIA), in many others many small size plants (capacity < 1 MW) were installed with no authorization but subjected to a simple notification to the municipal administration.

The result of this uncontrolled transformation process is that in some municipalities there are more than 100 turbines (the regional capital – Potenza - holds the sad record of almost 300 installations) differing in shape, size, height, technology, power.

3   Methodology

The purpose of this paper is to formulate a methodology to support repowering invest-ments and interventions aimed at improving the energy production-environmental impact balance. The first component, related to energy production, is based on a detailed geo-database describing the development of renewable energy sector in the Basilicata Region set out in four different time steps (2008-2013-2017-2020).

Instead, the second was structured to integrate two different approaches to assessing land transformations: ecosystem services and territorial fragmentation.

The methodology consists of several steps. The first one analyzes the carbon balance related to energy production of each wind turbine currently on operation at the regional territory. The result of this phase is the comparison of different plants in terms of their performance as measured by carbon balance. The aim is to obtain a priority scale that identifies which plants reveal ample room for improvement in their carbon balance.

The next step, on the other hand, has the objective of formulating alternative scenar-ios to the existing one and aimed at conserving/improving the share of energy produced by assuming partial restoration interventions and minimizing the value of spatial frag-mentation. A description of the methods and datasets used is given in the following paragraphs for each of the stages just mentioned.

3.1   The Evaluation of Wind Farms' Carbon Budget

The carbon balance is computed by comparing, on the one hand, CO_2 emissions savings due to displacement of fossil fuel sourced electricity from the national supply and, on the other hand, the CO_2 emitted for installation and for turbines' entire life.

The installation-related contributions, in particular, concern both the change in land use occurred during project execution, and the loss of carbon storage due to the removal of vegetation cover during the whole operation period of energy production infrastructures.

The reference year for carbon balance calculations is 2030 as it is of particular importance for the achievement of targets set at European level.

The following paragraphs describe the individual components one by one.

CO_2 Emission Savings

Carbon dioxide emissions from power generation depend on the type of fossil fuel or fuel mix used to produce electricity. Each of these fossil fuels corresponds to an emission factor (E) useful for calculating the tons of CO_2 emitted into the atmosphere for each megawatt-hour of energy produced. Within the scope of this work, ε is equal to $0.337tCO2/MWh$ [14]. By knowing the capacity of each turbine $c_{turb}(MW)$, the average annual production $\varepsilon(MWh)$ was calculated according to the following equations

$$\varepsilon = c_{turb} \cdot \mu_{50} \tag{1}$$

$$\varepsilon = c_{turb} \cdot \mu_{75} \tag{2}$$

where μ_{50} and μ_{75} are the annual average producibility $\left(MWh \cdot MW^{-1} \cdot yr^{-1}\right)$ values at 50 and 75 m above the ground, respectively.

Specifically, in order to consider the different size of existing plants, Eq. (1) was used for turbines of less than $1MW$ capacity, equation number (2) for large generation turbines $(c_{turb} > 1MW)$.

The producibility data are derived from the Wind Atlas made available in a grid format by the Italian Energy System Research (RSE) [15] and based on an anemological database consisting of 30 years of data at hourly and spatial time steps of 1.4 km, using the Weather Research and Forecasting (WRF) meteorological model combined with statistical post-processing based on Analog Ensemble (AnEn).

CO_2 Emission Due to Land Use Change

This component of the carbon budget includes two contributions. The first concerns the emissions of carbon stored in the soil and due to land use changes, that occurred following the construction of the access road, crane hard-standings, works compounds and turbine foundations. The extent of this overall sealed surface varies with plant size and was calculated using an experimental formula already tested for the context of the Basilicata Region in previous works published by the same authors [11, 16]. This surface is in fact approximated to a circular area having a radius proportional to wind turbines' capacity. The land use class considered is the one present at the time of installation of wind turbine.

The second contribution concerns the loss of carbon fixing capacity within different soil layers by the removed vegetated covers. To this end, the lack of carbon absorption relating to the overall operating period of each turbine was calculated. The annual average storage rate for each land use class were derived from literature data collected by the European Environment Agency (EEA) [17]. Also in this case, the working hypothesis is that the land use class would not have undergone variations during the operating time of energy production plants.

CO$_2$ Emission Due to Life Cycle Assessment

The life cycle analysis should consider for each turbine installed specific data relating, for example, to the type of engine, the materials used, the place of production, etc... Since these data were not available, two literature equations [18] were used:

$$L_{life} = 517.62 \times c_{turb} - 0.1788 \tag{3}$$

for turbines of capacity less than $1MW$, and

$$L_{life} = 934.35 \times c_{turb} - 467.55 \tag{4}$$

for turbines with $c_{turb} > 1MW$.

As stated by the authors, these two equations were derived through a linear regression analysis based on 21 case studies collected across Europe.

3.2 Territorial Fragmentation

Fragmentation caused by wind turbines has been the subject of several studies [11, 16, 19] by the same authors in which different indices such as sprinkling index [20] have been tested. The spatial fragmentation caused by the installation of wind turbines was assessed by means of a density of nucleus aggregation (D_{agg}) [20]. In this research, nucleus is understood to be the footprint of the wind turbine useful for considering the area occupied for the construction of the sub-services necessary for the wind turbine's operational use. The core was calculated by means of a buffer whose radius is a function of the power of the blade, the methodology of which was tested in previous research by the same authors [16]. The formulation of this index is given below:

$$D_{agg} = \frac{\Delta n_{agg}}{\Delta \overline{A}} \tag{5}$$

where: Δn_{agg} represents the change in the number of nuclei from a time t1 to a time t0. The range of values can be positive or negative. A positive value represents an increase in the number of nuclei at time t1 compared to time t0. This results in an increase in the fragmentation of the territory. Conversely, a negative value represents a decrease in the number of cores that is significant of a compaction phenomenon. That is, from time t0 to time t1, new wind turbines were built close to the existing ones at such a distance that they formed a single nucleus. $\Delta \overline{A}$ represents the change in average nuclei area from time t1 to time t0. An increase in the average area of the nuclei is reflected in more large nuclei; a decrease, on the other hand, means an increase in small nuclei. The index can take negative or positive values. A value of 0 represents a static situation, while as the absolute value of the index increases, the degree of fragmentation increases. For ease of reading, therefore, the index will be used in absolute value.

4 Results

Carbon Balance

The first result is a representation of the two components of the carbon budget per municipality (Fig. 1), CO_2 emissions from land use change and turbine life cycle, and CO_2 savings calculated by considering the emission equivalent from fossil sources for the same energy production.

The first evidence is the relevant number of municipalities included in the lowest class for both components. Comparison of the two maps shows a good degree of correspondence between the two classifications of municipalities. Thus, an almost linear proportionality between the two components can be assumed, except for some municipalities in central Basilicata.

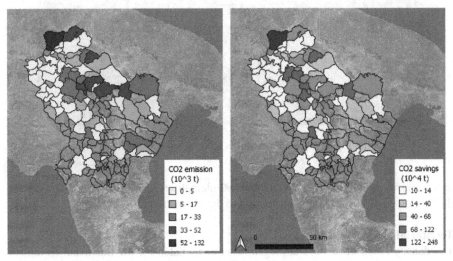

Fig. 3. Comparison between CO_2 emissions (10^3 t) and CO_2 savings (10^4 t) at municipal scale

By subtracting CO_2 savings emissions, Net CO_2 savings were achieved. The map (Fig. 3) then returns a carbon balance picture by 2030 within the municipalities of Basilicata region.

The only municipality in the highest class is Melfi, located in the northern area of the Region. A cluster of municipalities united by a medium-high budget is also located

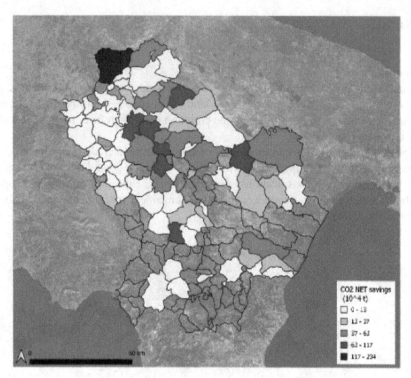

Fig. 4. CO_2 NET savings (10^4 t) at municipal scale

in the central area of the regional territory. Municipalities located in the western part of the Region confirm the small contribution to the contrast to climate change.

Territorial Fragmentation

The density index of nucleus aggregation was calculated for the Basilicata region for each municipality and in the three-time steps: 2013-2008, 2017-2008 and 2020-2008 and are shown in Fig. 5. The maps are representative of the spatial transformations that have occurred as a result of the installation of wind turbines and the degree of fragmentation they have produced on the territory. Municipalities in grey are those in which there are no wind turbines. Fragmentation was assessed by means of the density index of nucleus aggregation, applying it cumulatively in order to make the result comparable with the indices concerning the carbon balance. A value of 0 in the index corresponds to a static situation from one year to the next or very low index variations that cannot be classified as spatial fragmentation.

From 2008 to 2020, the number of municipalities classified as highly fragmented increases from 2 to 9. The municipality of Melfi, which in the previous analysis on CO_2 NET savings (see Fig. 4) falls in the highest class, is also the municipality where wind turbines caused a high degree of fragmentation. Also looking at the CO_2 NET savings, the municipalities located in the western part of the Region show a medium-high degree of fragmentation, while making a small contribution to factors related to climate change.

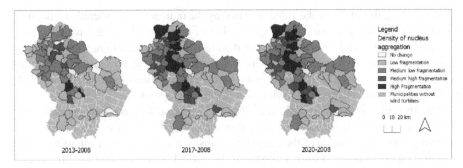

Fig. 5. Density of nucleus aggregation at different years

5 Discussion and Caveats

Environmental sustainability is a complex concept that, for evaluation purposes, needs to be represented from multiple perspectives. Carbon balance and spatial fragmentation are relevant aspects: the former constitutes the foundational motivation behind any transformation dictated by the energy transition; the latter is a direct measure of the transformation-induced change in the environment in which it is embedded, significantly affecting ecological continuity, ecosystem functionality and their ability to deliver ecosystem services.

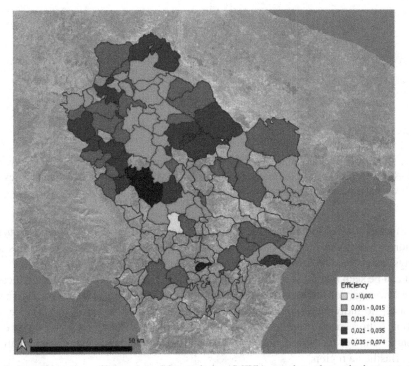

Fig. 6. Transformation efficiency (t CO_2 emissions/MWh) equal to the ratio between total emissions and energy produced at municipal scale

Regardless, therefore, of the value assumed by the indicators considered, a reflection is due first of all with regard to the large number of municipalities that have allowed a profound and irreversible transformation of their territory in the face of negligible energy production. Values such as landscape perception, naturalness, and a sense of belonging to landscapes unchanged in living memory have been sacrificed for a handful of kWh irrelevant to climate change and irrelevant to local development.

The above results provide a static 2030 image of wind turbines impacts measured in terms of carbon balance and territorial fragmentation. An indicator that could better summarize the performance of the ecological transition-induced transformations is the ratio of total emissions and energy produced. We called it "Transformation efficiency" (Fig. 6).

This means that, with equal energy produced by 2030 (see Fig. 2), territorial transformation processes have induced land use changes that result in a variability between performance ranging between three different efficiency classes.

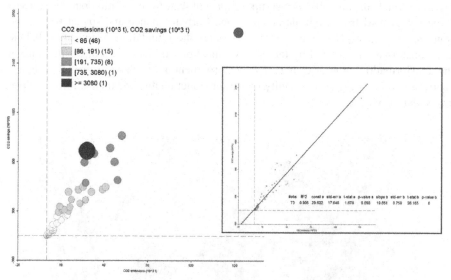

Fig. 7. Bubble chart representing CO_2 emissions (10^3 t) on x axis, CO_2 savings (10^3 t) on y axis. Bubbles' size is proportional to Energy Production (10^4 MWh). In the box, the same regression is showed without considering Energy production.

A further way of looking at this data is the representation in Fig. 7 that depicts the relationship between the two components of the carbon balance (CO_2 emissions and savings) as well as the forecast of energy produced by 2030 (expressed in MWh).

It can be seen that most of the 72 municipalities with wind power plants are located in the lower part of the quadrant, following a linear trend ($R^2 = 0.91$). As the values increase, the individual points deviate from the interpolation line. The distance and position with respect to the interpolation line is not an absolute measure, but it does denote a behavior that can be taken as a benchmark in the panorama of municipalities in the Basilicata region.

6 Conclusions

The paper explores the topic of the integration of energy transition-related dynamics within the wider frame of spatial transformations, also offering a critical reading of tools that spatial planning put in place to manage and monitor these processes. The speed with which these new forms of settlement have spread, in fact, has been much greater than the speed with which plans at different scales have adapted.

The need for rapid decarbonization first, and the recent energy crisis later, have become the main drivers of spatial transformations affecting mainly low-density contexts characterized by fragmented urbanization and scattered settlements of rural nature [21, 22].

The result is a heterogeneous set of landscapes and settlement forms that have greatly altered the quality of scenery, transformed morphological and environmental structures, affected the identity character of local communities, and only in some cases produced energy in non-negligible quantities.

Assessing the sustainability of these transformations becomes even more crucial when thinking about the already wide gap between land take rates and population decline that characterizes these areas [23].

This paper intervenes in this debate by proposing suitable indicators for measuring the sustainability of transformation. Indeed, they concern two key aspects for the purposes of this assessment: transformation efficiency, understood as the ratio between energy production and CO_2 emitted, and spatial fragmentation [24].

The paper applies them to the Basilicata Region case study, showing the contribution they make to an ex-post evaluation and comparison of what happened within different municipalities. The results obtained support several reflections regarding how effectively transformation processes were managed by municipal governments, which are directly responsible for small-scale installations exempt from Environmental Impact Assessment (EIA) [11, 25].

Future research developments will be aimed at exploring the potential of the above indices as components of decision support systems also suitable for comparing alternative transformation scenarios.

References

1. REPowerEU. https://ec.europa.eu/commission/presscorner/detail/en/ip_22_3131. Accessed 03 Apr 2023
2. Johnson, H.G., VanHout, C.A., Wright, J.B.: Esiti controversi delle green energy policy nel Mezzogiorno: il caso della Basilicata. Rivista economica del Mezzogiorno **XXVII**, 671–698 (2013). https://doi.org/10.1432/75851
3. Dechézelles, S., Scotti, I.: Wild wind, social storm: "energy populism" in rural areas? An exploratory analysis of France and Italy*. Rural Sociol. **87**, 784–813 (2022). https://doi.org/10.1111/RUSO.12399
4. R.E.gions 2030 - Rinnovabili, Permitting, Sviluppo. https://regions2030.it/. Accessed 04 Apr 2023
5. Scotti, I.: Controvento: aree marginali e populismo energetico? Indicazioni preliminari su uno studio di caso. Sociol Urbana Rurale (Testo Stamp) 126–143 (2022). https://doi.org/10.3280/SUR2022-128011

6. Magnani, N., Carrosio, G.: Understanding the Energy Transition: Civil Society, Territory and Inequality in Italy. Palgrave Macmillan (2021)
7. Calabrò, F., Massimo, D.E., Musolino, M.: Measures to face population decline of small villages: sustainable and integrated energy strategies for the internal areas. In: Advances in Science, Technology and Innovation, pp. 43–45 (2022). https://doi.org/10.1007/978-3-031-00808-5_11/COVER
8. Saganeiti, L., Favale, A., Pilogallo, A., Scorza, F., Murgante, B.: Assessing urban fragmentation at regional scale using sprinkling indexes. Sustainability 10, 3274 (2018). https://doi.org/10.3390/su10093274
9. Dastoli, P.S., Pontrandolfi, P.: Methods and tools for a participatory local development strategy. In: Calabrò, F., Della Spina, L., Piñeira Mantiñán, M.J. (eds.) NMP 2022. LNNS, vol. 482, pp. 2112–2121 (2022). https://doi.org/10.1007/978-3-031-06825-6_203
10. Kercuku, A.: Forgotten Italy: spaces and identities of a changing geography. Trans. Assoc. Eur. Sch. Plann. 6, 41–54 (2022). https://doi.org/10.24306/TRAESOP.2022.01.004
11. Scorza, F., Pilogallo, A., Saganeiti, L., Murgante, B., Pontrandolfi, P.: Comparing the territorial performances of renewable energy sources' plants with an integrated ecosystem services loss assessment: a case study from the Basilicata region (Italy). Sustain. Cities Soc. 56, 102082 (2020). https://doi.org/10.1016/J.SCS.2020.102082
12. Muzzillo, V., Pilogallo, A., Saganeiti, L., Santarsiero, V., Murgante, B., Bonifazi, A.: Res and habitat quality: ecosystem services evidence based analysis in basilicata area. In: Bevilacqua, C., Calabrò, F., Della Spina, L. (eds.) NMP 2020. SIST, vol. 178, pp. 1714–1721 (2021). https://doi.org/10.1007/978-3-030-48279-4_162
13. Agrillo, A., et al.: Rapporto Statistico 2020 Energia da fonti rinnovabili in Italia (2020)
14. CO2 emission intensity — European Environment Agency. https://www.eea.europa.eu/data-and-maps/daviz/co2-emission-intensity-5#tab-googlechartid_chart_11_filters=%7B%22r owFilters%22%3A%7B%7D%3B%22columnFilters%22%3A%7B%22pre_config_ugeo% 22%3A%5B%22European%20Union%20(current%20composition)%22%3B%22Italy% 22%5D%7D%7D. Accessed 28 Mar 2023
15. Atlante Eolico. https://atlanteeolico.rse-web.it/start.phtml. Accessed 28 Mar 2023
16. Saganeiti, L., Pilogallo, A., Faruolo, G., Scorza, F., Murgante, B.: Territorial fragmentation and renewable energy source plants: which relationship? Sustainability 12, 1828 (2020). https://doi.org/10.3390/su12051828
17. Carbon storage in EU terrestrial and marine ecosystems — European Environment Agency. https://www.eea.europa.eu/data-and-maps/data/carbon-storage-in-global-terrestrial. Accessed 28 Mar 2023
18. Nayak, D.R., Miller, D., Nolan, A.A., Smith, P., Smith, J.U.: Calculating carbon budgets of wind farms on Scottish peatlands. Mires Peat. 4, 9 (2010)
19. Saganeiti, L., Pilogallo, A., Faruolo, G., Scorza, F., Murgante, B.: Energy landscape fragmentation: Basilicata region (Italy) study case. In: Misra, S., et al. (eds.) ICCSA 2019. LNCS, vol. 11621, pp. 692–700. Springer, Cham (2019). https://doi.org/10.1007/978-3-030-24302-9_50
20. Saganeiti, L., Pilogallo, A., Scorza, F., Mussuto, G., Murgante, B.: Spatial indicators to evaluate urban fragmentation in Basilicata region. In: Gervasi, O., et al. (eds.) ICCSA 2018. LNCS, vol. 10964, pp. 100–112. Springer, Cham (2018). https://doi.org/10.1007/978-3-319-95174-4_8
21. Ieluzzi, A., Saganeiti, L., Pilogallo, A., Scorza, F., Murgante, B.: Analyzing the driving factors of urban transformation in the Province of Potenza (Basilicata Region-Italy). In: Gervasi, O., et al. (eds.) ICCSA 2020. LNCS, vol. 12252, pp. 425–434. Springer, Cham (2020). https://doi.org/10.1007/978-3-030-58811-3_31

22. Dotoli, G., Saganeiti, L., Pilogallo, A., Scorza, F., Murgante, B.: Modeling the determinants of urban fragmentation and compaction phenomena in the province of Matera (Basilicata Region - Italy). In: Gervasi, O., et al. (eds.) ICCSA 2020. LNCS, vol. 12252, pp. 566–574 (2020). https://doi.org/10.1007/978-3-030-58811-3_41

23. Scorza, F., Saganeiti, L., Pilogallo, A., Murgante, B.: Ghost planning : the inefficiency of energy sector policies in a low population density region, pp. 34–55 (2020). https://doi.org/10.3280/ASUR2020-127-S1003

24. Saganeiti, L., Pilogallo, A., Scorza, F., Mussuto, G., Murgante, B.: Spatial indicators to evaluate urban fragmentation in Basilicata region. In: Gervasi, O., et al. (eds.) ICCSA. LNCS, vol. 10964, pp. 100–112 (2018). https://doi.org/10.1007/978-3-319-95174-4_8

25. Pilogallo, A., Saganeiti, L., Scorza, F., Murgante, B.: Ecosystem services approach to evaluate renewable energy plants effects. In: Misra, S., et al. (eds.) ICCSA 2019. LNCS, vol. 11624, pp. 281–290. Springer, Cham (2019). https://doi.org/10.1007/978-3-030-24311-1_20

26. Luckiesh, M.: Visual Illusions, their causes, characteristics and applications - Messinissa Libri Shop online. Dover Publications (1965)

Machine Learning Techniques for the Semiautomated Recognition of Urban and Peri-Urban Configurations

Chiara Di Dato$^{(\boxtimes)}$ ⓘ, Federico Falasca ⓘ, and Alessandro Marucci ⓘ

Department of Civil, Building-Architecture and Environmental Engineering, University of
L'Aquila, Via Giovanni Gronchi 18, 67100 L'Aquila, Italy
`chiara.didato@graduate.univaq.it`

Abstract. Smart technologies are becoming increasingly essential in the city of the future. Urban and peri urban dynamics description is a crucial element to manage the changes undergone in the urban settlements. Achieving the sustainability goals set at the global and local levels depends on this. At the same time, the possibility to generalize such approaches to make them universally applicable sees machine learning (ML) techniques as a powerful ally. The enhancement of these models is a topic long since addressed by the scientific community. Nevertheless, such applications focus on a limited in time and space scale.

In the present study a methodology capable of combining semiautomated recognition of urban and peri-urban spatial configurations has been set up. The spatial configurations have been chosen within three different functional urban areas (FUA), considering the broad territorial scale of the Italian central Apennines.

Results represent a first significant step toward the semiautomated urban and peri urban configuration pattern recognition, using supervised machine learning techniques, for an expert based characterization of spatial dynamics.

Keywords: Supervised machine learning · Spatial configurations · Urban planning

1 Introduction

Urban settlements are heterotrophic systems whose sustenance depends on input fluxes from elsewhere [1]. Urban areas are immersed in a territorial framework with which they have direct and indirect interactions. Both these systems are characterized by input and output [2]. The way different urban configurations and forms have different consequences on the environmental, social, and economic aspect of urban and no urban areas has been well deepened in the scientific literature [3].

The transition from urban settlements to natural areas is not even clear because various configurations can occur. The anthropized environment decreases moving away from cores cities and it creates a gradient of different forms of urban structures. The peri-urbanization process has characterized the urban expansion tendence of the 21st

O. Gervasi et al. (Eds.): ICCSA 2023 Workshops, LNCS 14109, pp. 16–29, 2023.
https://doi.org/10.1007/978-3-031-37120-2_2

century and it has increased the spreading of artificial urban surface and fragmentation [4, 5].

Peri-urbanization process refers to the process of rapid creation of new settlements surrounding existent cities and along the main road network. The resulting territory is multifunctional, extensive, with a scattered morphology. It has low-density settlements which requests high mobility and transport dependence longer commuting distances, and it can also imply fragmented communities and degraded landscapes [6, 7]. Generally, the causes are articulate and interconnected such as demographic changes, variation in settlement intensity and economic structures [8].

Studies are extensive because researchers dealt with the topic working on different subjects, scale, methodologies, and purpose [9, 10]. The lack of one singular definition reveals the complexity of associate one singular term to a broad concept. Moreover, as every process which involves land, peri-urbanization is a site-specific issue, and it varies depending on characteristics of geographical context. The uncertainty is given by the genesis of these areas which can be uncontrolled and scattered. Generally, it refers to areas of transition and interaction between urban and rural, which are hybrid landscapes with dispersive urban growth. Peri-urban areas are characterised by an extensive use of the space and low-density settlements [7] which are highly cost-demanding [11].

A univocal systematic approach to classify urban and peri-urban configurations is still missing [10]. Characterization and then classification of different configurations would be indeed desirable. The ability to discriminate such gradient is hence necessary to better define the dynamics occurring between urban and natural territorial systems in terms of pressures, threats, and opportunities.

To accomplish a similar task, machine learning (ML) techniques are nowadays being employed to decline different aspects of territorial dynamics [12].

Among the declinations of these technologies, land use change and urban form hold a lot of importance, together with socio economic considerations, infrastructures, and risk analysis [13, 14].

Mohajeri et al. (2023) used machine learning techniques (Random Forest algorithm) to develop density scenarios for the Oxford–Cambridge Arc region [15]. Similarly, machine learning approaches are used to generate landscape typologies, exploiting remote sensing data [16], as well as to extract, quantify and map urban built-up impervious areas [17].

Machine learning techniques are also used to describe important features of the built environment [18], as well as to model urban forms and their relations with sustainability, socio economic and land use issues [19–21].

The potentialities of ML techniques allow a further deepening of these aspects, also offering predictions and scenarios useful for planning actors and policies.

In the present study a methodology able to discriminate spatial configurations has been set up. Six different supervised machine learning (SML) algorithms have been trained. The semiautomatic recognition task works on an expert-based classification of the urban – peri urban gradient (Fig. 1).

The aim of the present work is to set up as linking point between the unsupervised recognition of the urban and no urban shapes [12] and a deepened description of urban configurations [22].

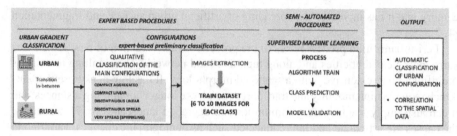

Fig. 1. The main steps of the methodology: the expert based procedure and the semi-automated procedure

2 Materials and Methods

This paragraph aims at comparing three areas around urban centres in central Italy: Perugia, Terni and L'Aquila. The geographical setting is Central Apennines: Perugia and Terni are in Umbria Region and L'Aquila is in Abruzzo Region. Respectively, city's inhabitants are 164880, 110003 and 70019 [23]. Territorial continuity and similarities among the three areas permit to consider them together in this further focus (Fig. 2). They all represent urban poles on the Central Apennines, and they have been involved in recurring seismic events. The geographic area has been subject to seismic events for the last 30 years. Earthquakes of 2009 and 2016 have stroked this geographical area causing differential grades of damage revealing high local level of fragility [24, 25]. Spatial configurations, socio-economic implications and reconstruction processes have influenced actual conditions. Probably, such characteristics will impact also on future development [26]. Phenomena such as seismic events, in fact, emphasise fragilities related to depopulation and abandonment. Such conditions are shared also around such urban centres and then they involve the surrounding minor centres [27].

The analysis is settled inside the perimeters of Functional Urban Areas (FUA) due to reliability of the European standard of Urban Atlas [28] which provides analytical identification of urban poles and their next commuting areas. The Urban Atlas provides pan-European comparable Land Use and Land Cover (LULC) data which describes the spatial distribution analyzed in the present work. Also, the context of FUA is interesting to consider in terms of urban gradient expansion. Such area implicates various processes of land take because its land is the most required for housing, transportation infrastructure, or economic development [5].

2.1 Expert Based Classification of Urban and Peri-Urban Configurations

The first part of the methodology aims at investigating the physical structure of the urban environment. The object is the urban gradient which develops from the main compact urban morphology to the peri-urban areas. Then, the methodology aims at overcoming the vagueness which arises from the multitude of definitions around the urban gradient and peri-urban areas [10]. The methodology introduces the fundamental phase of the expert-based procedure in the process of qualitative evaluation which brings to the further semi-automated procedure.

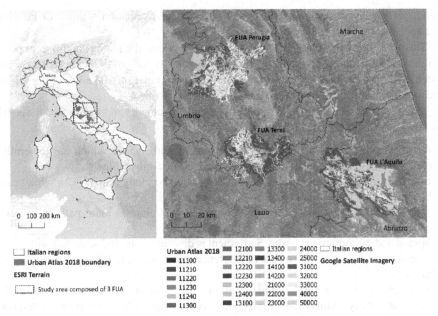

Fig. 2. The FUA of Perugia, Terni and L'Aquila in the context of Central Italy Apennines. Source: Urban Atlas. Authors's elaboration.

LULC data [28] and Google satellite imagery are the main materials of the present analysis. The CORINE Land Cover's layer of artificial surfaces (classes from 1.1 to 1.4) is considered for setting the scale of analysis [29].

Since the medium value of single polygons of artificial surfaces in the CLC is about 100 ha (86,5 ha), the scale of the window of selection is chosen as the double of this data for framing the main geometries of artificial surfaces. In other words, such dimension assures to capture and frame the medium size of the settlements or relevant parts of them. Then, the dimensions of 2 km^2 is taken as reference for capturing the recurrent configurations.

Urban and peri-urban configurations are framed in hexagonal windows of selection. The hexagonal shape is considered suitable for many analyses [12] and it is used for finding recurrent configurations in the case study gradient. The window is arbitrarily stopped where it frames one recurrent configuration.

The process of research of main recurrent configurations is carried out through two steps. Firstly, identification of real settlements approaches the local specificities of the case study. Secondly, the definition of the main classes is guided by the necessity of giving coherence to the specificities in homogeneous classification. The first step of analysis considers qualitative aspects. A punctual, visual, and qualitative analysis is necessary together with process of classification. If classification permits to allocate different examples in different categories due to a process of simplification of the reality, qualitative analysis is fundamental for describing specific characteristics that contribute to allocate examples in classes. Secondly, the classification is organised through the main structures and aggregation features. The shape and structure are taken as primary feature used to classify the settlements. Shapes refers to main conformation of the artificial area as it appears at the chosen scale.

This work implicates the reduction of complex system (the reality) in different possibilities of settlements (the model) which correspond to parts of the real gradient. The match of identification of the urban structure with interpretation of quality of the urban environment is the step that make the classification possible.

Six main models then are classified from the most compact and aggregated tissue to the absence of buildings and urban shapes.

1. Aggregated, compact and dense. Portions of the urban area which are generally comprehensive of historical centre or they are in proximity of that.
2. Linear, compact, and dense. Settlement is aggregated along a main path which can be a provincial or regional road, or a high-speed road.
3. Linear and discontinuous. Settlement is aggregated along a main path and tissue appears discontinuous.
4. Spread and discontinuous tissue. Settlement is discontinuous and scattered with variable density. There is no one path of reference, but some main infrastructures can be present.
5. Very spread tissue in rural context. Settlement is discontinuous and scattered with very low density. In this model rural context is dominant, whereas buildings are spots which follow streets that connect residential areas.
6. Free areas in rural context. The dominant element is a natural area, such as fields, woods, orchards. Buildings are excluded from this pattern.

As the model of the gradient does, such classification comprehends the free areas. Instead, free areas are excluded from the present analysis. It considers the part of the classification which comprehends urban settlements, and the analysis has been conducted on the first 5 classes which are identified with the related acronyms COMP_A, COMP_L, DISC_L, DISC_R, AGR_D (Fig. 3).

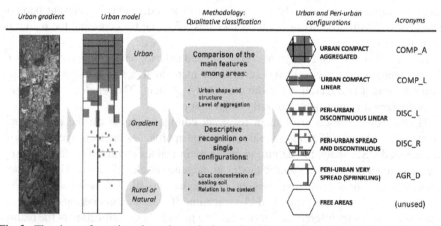

Fig. 3. The six configurations from the analysis on the urban gradient. Source: Google Imagery. Authors' elaboration

2.2 Supervised Machine Learning Algorithms

To perform the analyses open-source software Orange has been used (https://orangedat amining.com/docs/). Despite other software allow a deeper analysis (MATLAB, Rstudio and so on), Orange has been chosen thanks to its user-friendly interface and the possibility to perform machine learning analyses without entering specific procedures that could be less clear for a non-expert user.

To analyse spatial configurations, orange image analysis add-on has been used. This extension allows the user to work with a relatively simple interface, operating some important image analysis operations.

All the following steps have been realized through a train dataset, composed firstly of 30 images, and then expanded to 50 images, equally distributed among 5 classes. Each image has been converted into vector descriptors. To do this, VGG 19 Convolutional Neural Network (CNN) model has been used. This kind of model, pretrained on the ImageNet dataset, has been found to be very useful for image analysis [30].

Based on the information from vector descriptors, the algorithms learn and then formulate a series of rules. Such rules will then help in the association of the categories. In this preliminary step, six different algorithms have been performed (Fig. 4).

For each algorithm cross and stratified validation (k-fold = 5) has been realized. The evaluation of the best algorithm focused on two metrics: Area Under Curve (AUC) and F1-score. AUC is the value of the area under the Receiver Operating Characteristic Curve (ROC curve), which is related to rate of true positive (TP) and rate of false positive (FP). TP are elements assigned to the real class of belonging by the algorithm, whereas FP are assigned to the wrong class compared to the real one. UC values vary from 0 to 1. Values from 0.9 to 1 then provide a highly accurate test [31]. F1-score metrics comes from the harmonic mean of precision and recall. Precision is given by number of TP (elements assigned to the real class of belonging by the algorithm) divided by total number of elements belonging to the class considered (TP and FP) [32]:

$$Precision : \frac{TP}{TP + FP} \tag{1}$$

Recall is the number of TP divided by total number of elements belonging to the class considered (TP and FN). FN represents the number of elements belonging to the class considered but assigned to another class (False Negative):

$$Recall : \frac{TP}{TP + FN} \tag{2}$$

Values of F1-score varies from 0 (worst result) to 1 (best result). Both F1 and AUC metrics are indicative of the model's efficiency based on how it has been trained with the train set.

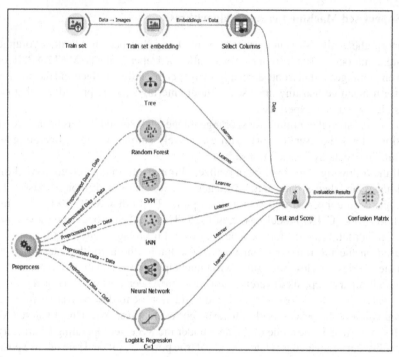

Fig. 4. Learners' performance evaluation. The metrics have been calculated for six main algorithms: Tree; Random Forest; Support Vector Machine (SVM); K-nearest neighbors; Neural Network; Logistic regression. Scheme elaborated by the authors and extracted in Orange. (Colour figure online)

Subsequently, a validation dataset has been realized. It is composed of 25 images and allows validation of the chosen best algorithm, trained with the train set.

The following validation analysis has been conducted firstly associating to each image of the validation set one class, then evaluating the misclassified and the correct ones through a confusion matrix (Fig. 5).

Also for the evaluation of this last step, AUC and F1-score metrics have been used.

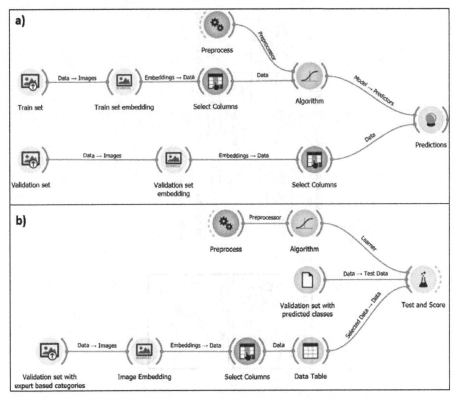

Fig. 5. 1a) First step of class assignment from the chosen best algorithm. After an image embedding, the algorithm learns through the train set and assigns a class to the validation one. 1b) performance evaluation of the validation set, through a comparison with the same images, corresponding to the correct classes (assigned by the operator).

Figure 6 shows a sum up of the followed procedures.

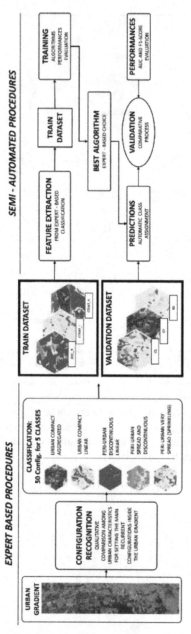

Fig. 6. Explicative workflow of the main passages of the methodological procedures.

3   Results

The first evaluation of algorithms performance returns the highest AUC values for Logistic regression (0.928) and Neural Network (0.898). Instead, highest values of F-1 score corresponds to Logistic regression (0.710), and Random Forest (0.676) algorithms (Table 1). Furthermore, AUC metric slightly decreases for kNN, Tree and SVM algorithms, while remaining quite high for the other ones. F-1 score has instead a fluctuation distributed among all the algorithms, having a clear rise for the logistic regression.

Table 1. Performance metrics algorithms for the training set (30 images). Stratified cross validation (k = 5)

MODEL	AUC	CA	F1	Precision	Recall
Logistic regression C = 1	0.928	0.700	0.710	0.734	0.700
Neural network	0.898	0.600	0.550	0.523	0.600
Random Forest	0.891	0.667	0.676	0.702	0.667
kNN	0.869	0.667	0.670	0.708	0.667
Tree	0.625	0.400	0.405	0.463	0.400
SVM	0.585	0.500	0.508	0.563	0.500

The relative confusion matrix of the train set (composed of 30 images) reports a misclassification of 9 images (about 30%) for logistic regression algorithm. Hence, for the second step of model validation, logistic regression has been used.

The latter algorithm shows performance values for the second step of model validation of 0.796 for the AUC value and 0.556 for the F1-score value, correctly classifying 14 images (56%) out of 25 (Table 2).

Table 2. Confusion matrix validation dataset (train made with 30 images equally distributed among 5 classes, logistic regression algorithm). Acronyms indicate the 5 classes considered out the 6 urban and peri-urban configurations.

		Predicted					
		AGR_D	COMP_A	COMP_L	DISC_L	DISC_R	Σ
Actual	AGR_D	4	0	2	2	2	10
	COMP_A	0	2	0	0	0	2
	COMP_L	1	2	3	0	0	6
	DISC_L	0	0	0	2	0	2
	DISC_R	0	1	0	1	3	5
	Σ	5	5	5	5	5	25

The same computational phases performed with a train set of 50 images, equally distributed into the 5 classes, show the highest performance values for the random forest algorithm (AUC = 0.854, F1 – score = 0.685). The latter correctly classify 34 (68%) out of 50 images (Table 3).

Table 3. Performance metrics algorithms for the training set (50 images). Stratified cross validation (k = 5)

MODEL	AUC	CA	F1	Precision	Recall
Random Forest	0.854	0.680	0.685	0.697	0.680
Neural Network	0.842	0.580	0.582	0.618	0.580
Logistic Regression C = 1	0.828	0.580	0.585	0.597	0.580
kNN	0.799	0.580	0.583	0.597	0.580
SVM	0.613	0.460	0.470	0.557	0.460
Tree	0.613	0.380	0.369	0.380	0.380

These performance values for the validation phase show an AUC value of 0.849 and an F-1 score of 0.692, correctly classifying 17 images (68%) out of 25 (Random Forest algorithm) (Table 4).

Table 4. Confusion matrix validation dataset (train made with 50 images equally distributed among 5 classes, Random Forest algorithm). Acronyms indicate the 5 classes considered out the 6 urban and peri-urban configurations.

		Predicted					
		AGR_D	COMP_A	COMP_L	DISC_L	DISC_R	Σ
Actual	AGR_D	5	0	1	2	0	8
	COMP_A	0	3	0	0	1	4
	COMP_L	0	1	3	0	0	4
	DISC_L	0	0	0	2	0	2
	DISC_R	0	1	1	1	4	7
	Σ	5	5	5	5	5	25

4 Discussion and Conclusion

Though AUC for the logistic regression algorithm has a value of 0.928, it isn't the same for the F1 metric, of 0.710. This means that Logistic regression discriminates quite adequately true positive and true negatives but has some difficulties in correctly classifying false positives and false negatives, having direct consequences when assigning new classes to the validation set.

Using a train set of 30 images, model can correctly classify more than half of the validation set (56%).

When considering the train set implemented with 20 more images, performance values slightly decrease compared to the 30 images dataset train and validation phases.

Despite correctly classifying the 68% of the validation set, performance values of the model trained on 50 images are lower than those of the first 30 train set images analysis (AUC drops from 0.928 to 0.854 and F-1 score drops from 0.710 to 0.685).

This means that the number of images describing each class lowers these values due to the amount of additional information that the model receives. However, the number of images correctly classified increases, potentially meaning that random forest algorithm better describes the classes and their differences. Hence, further studies will be aimed at deepening random forest's performance values, also due to its ability to avoid overfitting and to work with non – linear relationships [33].

Furthermore, being the train set firstly composed of 30 images equally distributed into 5 classes, the capacity of the trained algorithm to assign the correct class is based on the parameters extracted from only 6 figures per class from the train set. Hence, it is likely that the dataset still doesn't reach its full potential, to the point of minimizing its performances. This aspect is supported by the comparison with the same analysis performed using a 50 images train set that, despite being lower than the first train, it returns a higher percentage of correctly classified images.

The passages presented in this article belong to two different approaches, apparently distant from each other. While the classification is based on an expert-based lecture of the spatial configurations, to reach the full potential in its applicability to a wider scale it is necessary to introduce Machine Learning techniques to "teach" to a machine to do this work. Contextually, this kind of technologies can't fulfill the tasks for which they are trained without an operator driven process that connects all the steps to build a reliable, efficient system.

In this sense, integration is the key element able to make it work.

Specifically, the presented work is a systematization aimed at integrating a qualitative-descriptive and a computation approach, for producing integrated land planning tools [34].

Such as other approaches based on machine learning techniques for the automatization of complicated procedures and tasks, also this model is subject to under or overfitting risk [35]. Referring to these aspects, further studies will be aimed not only at extending the areas on which train dataset will be constructed, but also to further deepen the performances of such model, for example in the recognition of other territorial scopes. Regarding this, expert based classification will then need to be finalized to avoid all these potential criticalities, to have not only a model that performs well in the analyzed territorial scope, but is also able to recognize the correct class, regardless of where it belongs.

Although in its embryonal phases, this research encloses a first fundamental step towards the semi-automated recognition of spatial configurations.

The next phase/step will be a finer model tuning and a deeper description of the classes that will then be used to evaluate and map territorial configurations.

References

1. Pickett, S.T.A., et al.: Urban ecological systems: linking terrestrial ecological, physical, and socioeconomic components of metropolitan areas. Annu. Rev. Ecol. Syst. **32**, 127–157 (2001)
2. Pilogallo, A., Saganeiti, L., Fiorini, L., Marucci, A.: Ecosystem services for planning impacts assessment on urban settlement development. In: Gervasi, O., Murgante, B., Misra, S., Rocha, A.M.A.C., Garau, C. (eds.) ICCSA 2022. LNCS, vol. 13380, pp. 241–253 (2022). https://doi.org/10.1007/978-3-031-10542-5_17
3. Marucci, A., Fiorini, L., Dato, C.D., Zullo, F.: Marginality assessment: computational applications on Italian municipalities. Sustainability **12**, 3250 (2020). https://doi.org/10.3390/SU12083250
4. Ravetz, J., Fertner, C., Nielsen, T.S.: The dynamics of peri-urbanization. In: Nilsson, K., Pauleit, S., Bell, S., Aalbers, C., Sick Nielsen, T. (eds.) Peri-Urban Futures: Scenarios and Models for Land use Change in Europe, pp. 13–44. Springer, Heidelberg (2013). https://doi.org/10.1007/978-3-642-30529-0_2
5. European Environment Agency: Land take and land degradation in functional urban areas (2021)
6. ISTAT: Forme, livelli e dinamiche dell'urbanizzazione in Italia (2017)
7. Piorr, A., Ravetz, J., Tosics, I.: Peri-urbanisation in Europe Towards European Policies to Sustain Urban-Rural Futures SyNThESIS REPORT (2011)
8. Cattivelli, V.: Methods for the identification of urban, rural and peri-urban areas in Europe: an overview. J. Urban Regeneration Renewal **14**, 240–246 (2021)
9. Cattivelli, V.: Delimiting rural areas: evidence from the application of different methods elaborated by Italian scholars. Land **11**, 1674 (2022). https://doi.org/10.3390/LAND11101674
10. Sahana, M., Ravetz, J., Patel, P.P., Dadashpoor, H., Follmann, A.: Where is the peri-urban? A systematic review of peri-urban research and approaches for its identification and demarcation worldwide. Remote Sens. **15**, 1316 (2023). https://doi.org/10.3390/RS15051316
11. Manganelli, B., Murgante, B., Saganeiti, L.: The social cost of urban sprinkling. Sustainability **12**, 2236 (2020). https://doi.org/10.3390/SU12062236
12. Fiorini, L., Falasca, F., Marucci, A., Saganeiti, L.: Discretization of the urban and non-urban shape: unsupervised machine learning techniques for territorial planning. Appl. Sci. **12**, 10439 (2022). https://doi.org/10.3390/app122010439
13. Casali, Y., Aydin, N.Y., Comes, T.: Machine learning for spatial analyses in urban areas: a scoping review. Sustain Cities Soc. **85**, 104050 (2022). https://doi.org/10.1016/J.SCS.2022.104050
14. Dobesova, Z.: Experiment in finding look-alike European cities using urban atlas data. ISPRS Int. J. Geoinf. **9**, 406 (2020)
15. Mohajeri, N., et al.: A machine learning methodology to quantify the potential of urban densification in the Oxford-Cambridge Arc, United Kingdom. Sustain Cities Soc. **92**, 104451 (2023). https://doi.org/10.1016/J.SCS.2023.104451

16. van Strien, M.J., Grêt-Regamey, A.: Unsupervised deep learning of landscape typologies from remote sensing images and other continuous spatial data. Environ. Model. Softw. **155**, 105462 (2022). https://doi.org/10.1016/J.ENVSOFT.2022.105462
17. Misra, M., Kumar, D., Shekhar, S.: Assessing machine learning based supervised classifiers for built-up impervious surface area extraction from sentinel-2 images. Urban For. Urban Green. **53**, 126714 (2020). https://doi.org/10.1016/J.UFUG.2020.126714
18. Koc, M., Acar, A.: Investigation of urban climates and built environment relations by using machine learning. Urban Clim. **37**, 100820 (2021). https://doi.org/10.1016/J.UCLIM.2021.100820
19. Koumetio Tekouabou, S.C., Diop, E.B., Azmi, R., Jaligot, R., Chenal, J.: Reviewing the application of machine learning methods to model urban form indicators in planning decision support systems: potential, issues and challenges. J. King Saud Univ. Comput. Inf. Sci. **34**, 5943–5967 (2022). https://doi.org/10.1016/J.JKSUCI.2021.08.007
20. Lin, J., Qiu, S., Tan, X., Zhuang, Y.: Measuring the relationship between morphological spatial pattern of green space and urban heat island using machine learning methods. Build Environ. **228**, 109910 (2023). https://doi.org/10.1016/J.BUILDENV.2022.109910
21. Kafy, A.A., et al.: Predicting the impacts of land use/land cover changes on seasonal urban thermal characteristics using machine learning algorithms. Build. Environ. **217**, 109066 (2022). https://doi.org/10.1016/J.BUILDENV.2022.109066
22. Marucci, A., Di Dato, C.: Urban and peri-urban shapes for sustainable governance. In: Wolski, J., Regulska, E., and Affek, A. (eds.) IALE 2022 European Landscape Ecology Congress Book of Abstracts, p. 341. IGiPZ PAN, Warsaw (2022). https://doi.org/10.7163/Konf.0004
23. ISTAT: Istituto Nazionale di Statistica. https://www.istat.it/. Accessed 14 Apr 2023
24. Forino, G.: Disaster recovery: narrating the resilience process in the reconstruction of L'Aquila (Italy). Geografisk Tidsskrift Danish J. Geogr. **115**, 1–13 (2015). https://doi.org/10.1080/00167223.2014.973056
25. Romano, B., Fiorini, L., Sette, C.: #comeradovera Quale città e quale territorio: L'Aquila a 13 anni dal sisma. EcoWebTown **25**, 28–33 (2022)
26. Compagnucci, F., Morettini, G.: Abandoning the Apennines? The anthropo-systemic value of the Italian inner areas within the 2016-17 seismic crater (2021)
27. Di Dato, C., Marucci, A.: Fragile territories around cities: analysis on small municipalities within functional urban areas. In: Gervasi, O., Murgante, B., Misra, S., Rocha, A.M.A.C., Garau, C. (eds.) ICCSA 2022. LNCS, vol. 13378, pp. 427–438 (2022). https://doi.org/10.1007/978-3-031-10562-3_30
28. Copernicus Land Monitoring Service: Urban Atlas. https://land.copernicus.eu/local/urban-atlas. Accessed 14 Apr 2023
29. Copernicus Land Monitoring Service: CORINE Land Cover. https://land.copernicus.eu/pan-european/corine-land-cover. Accessed 14 Apr 2023
30. Godec, P., et al.: Democratized image analytics by visual programming through integration of deep models and small-scale machine learning. Nat. Commun. **10**(1), 1–7 (2019). https://doi.org/10.1038/s41467-019-12397-x
31. Manning, C.D.: An Introduction to Information Retrieval. Cambridge University Press, Cambridge (2009)
32. Fawcett, T.: An introduction to ROC analysis. Pattern Recognit. Lett. **27**, 861–874 (2006)
33. Lee, H., Wang, J., Leblon, B.: Using linear regression, random forests, and support vector machine with unmanned aerial vehicle multispectral images to predict canopy nitrogen weight in corn. Remote Sens. **12**, 2071 (2020)
34. Koutra, S., Ioakimidis, C.S.: Unveiling the potential of machine learning applications in urban planning challenges. Land **12**, 83 (2023)
35. Jabbar, H., Khan, R.Z.: Methods to avoid over-fitting and under-fitting in supervised machine learning (comparative study). Comput. Sci. Commun. Instrum. Devices **70**, 163–172 (2015)

Modelling Post-Covid Cities (MPCC 2023)

Eco-fashion Luxury Brand: An Empirical Survey on the Attitudes of Millennials and Centennials

Francesca Sinatra(✉)

DEAMS - Department of Economics, Business, Mathematics and Statistics Sciences "Bruno de Finetti", University of Trieste, 34127 Trieste, Italy
francesca.sinatra@phd.units.it

Abstract. Millennials and Centennials represent the largest percentage of consumers in the luxury market, with a great influence on purchase culture and behaviors.

One of the distinguishing features of these generations is their tendency to prefer unique and authentic experiences instead of physical goods. Moreover, Millennials and Centennials are consumers with an increasing attention to issues as sustainability. In fact, they consider fundamental the sustainable values of brands and the environmental impact of fashion companies. As a result, many luxury brands are now investing in sustainable materials and ethical manufacturing in order to meet young consumers' environmental concerns and are trying to develop more personalized and digital purchase experiences.

In this framework, the aim of the paper was to understand what the attitudes and behaviors of Millennials and Centennials are when they faced with the purchase of luxury and sustainable fashion items. In doing that, a survey questionnaire turned out to be the most suitable tool to conduct such investigation. Furthermore, the paper will attempt to understand how the commercial distribution system is undergoing a post-pandemic reorganization.

Keywords: Sustainable Brands · Post-Pandemic · Environmental Issue

1 Introduction

From its beginnings, fashion has been constantly changing and has always played a crucial role in the lives of all individuals. However, today, we are in a social, economic and cultural context in continuous change that determines also transformations within the fashion industry, both at the managerial and communication level, due to the strong influences and changes in customs, costumes and fashion trends. In relation to consumer choices, a detailed profile has been developed with the peculiarities that distinguish consumers in the sector, giving fundamental importance to those who buy luxury products.

Nowadays, consumers' needs have been changed which have led to an increase in brands' diversification and a subdivision of the fashion market in two distinct segments:

O. Gervasi et al. (Eds.): ICCSA 2023 Workshops, LNCS 14109, pp. 33–46, 2023.
https://doi.org/10.1007/978-3-031-37120-2_3

luxury and fast fashion. In particular, the latter has allowed the increase of the production of standardized fashion items at lower costs and with faster production rates. Consequently, the emerge of fast fashion and the increasing attention to sustainability, led businesses and consumers becoming more aware about those issues.

This awareness of both companies and consumers towards ethical issues, within fashion industry, about their impact on environment and society has led over the years to the arose of a new phenomenon, the so-called slow fashion or ethical fashion. This phenomenon has guided the fashion world not only through a slowdown in mass production and consumption of fashion items but also to the use of more sustainable raw materials and the maintenance of certain quality standards.

Within the article, a detailed profile of the consumers most involved in the field of luxury fashion has been developed: the so-called Generation Y and Z also known as Millennials and Centennials. These consumers, in addition to being increasingly proactive and informed, tend to develop a close relationship with brands, through the value co-creation. Then drivers of sustainable fashion consumption were defined, particularly trying to identify the attributes related to the product and the main features that guide consumers' choices.

In this context, Millennials and Centennials seems to constitute a large part of buyers in the luxury fashion market. Furthermore, it appeared necessary try to understand what were the variables that affect consumers' choices in buying eco-sustainable luxury products. From all the topics dealt with in the paper, it did not seem possible to draw certain conclusions, due to the contrasting theories developed in literature. For this reason, it was decided to continue with an empirical survey through a questionnaire with semi-closed questions, in order to better understand consumers' attitudes when they purchase products from luxury brands ad sustainable luxury fashion products.

The paper is organized as it follows: Sect. 2 Eco-Fashion items; Sect. 2.1 Slow Fashion; Sect. 2.2 Drivers of sustainable fashion consumption; Sect. 3 The role of Millennials and Centennials in the luxury market; Sect. 3.1 The Y and Z generations: attitudes for sustainable luxury; Sect. 4 Materials and Methods; Sect. 4.1 Methodology; Sect. 4.2 Data; Sect. 5 Result and Discussion; Sect. 5.1 Socio-demographic area; Sect. 5.2 Consumers behaviors and attitudes towards luxury brands; Sect. 5.3 Perceptions and reasons why consumers are not purchasing luxury items; Sect. 5.4 Eco-Fashion and Sect. 6 Conclusions, limits and future research.

2 Eco-fashion Items

The fashion industry ranks just behind oil as the second most polluting industry worldwide [1]. However, the emergence of sustainable fashion movements indicates that society is starting questioning the dominant consumer-oriented social paradigm, signaling an imminent shift towards more sustainable consumption and a greater commitment to sustainability initiatives [2, 3].

Particularly, an increasing number of fashion companies have launched projects to collect used clothes from customers, in which the obtained items are subsequently resold, donated to second-hand shops or recycled into fibers or fuels, reducing waste and pollution and preserving the environment.

Sustainable fashion is an alternative trend to fast fashion and refers to a series of activities aimed to try to limit damages caused by the fashion industry such as: cruelty to animals, environmental damage and exploitation of workers [4].

So, sustainable fashion, which is also known as "Eco fashion", is part of a philosophy and trend whose goal is to create a system that is sustainable, in terms of human impact on the environment and social responsibility.

Sustainable items provide environmental, social and economic benefits by protecting public health, well-being and the environment throughout their entire business cycle, from raw material extraction to final disposal, taking into account the needs of future generations.

Different ways have been proposed and developed to define and measure the sustainability of a product and one of these consists in make a more sustainable product which must have to respect the following standards:

- during the design phase, particular attention should be placed on raw material selection, the processes used, logistics and packaging optimization;
- ensure the supply chain, responsible work, community and health and safety practices of workers;
- products should have a low carbon footprint and include recycled materials.

Jawahir I. et al. [5] identified the three most common criteria for the development of sustainable products:

- minimization of the material and energy resources needed to combine product function and consumer demand;
- maximizing the use of resources necessary for the items production;
- minimize the negative effects of waste and emissions.

Despite interest in sustainable fashion, consumers also ask for aesthetics and style requirements. Studies have shown that price, quality and style of clothing are features much more relevant than ethics in relation to consumer purchasing decisions. It means that apparel items must not only be sustainable, but also include the aesthetic requirements by consumers. Therefore, the mere fact that a product meets a sustainability criterion does not seem to be a strong enough incentive for the consumer to prefer it over other products [6].

2.1 Slow Fashion

As we have already said, the growing interest in slow fashion is related to a greater awareness of issues as sustainability and the environmental impact of the fashion industry. This concept is associated with fair working conditions, sustainable business models and certifications [7].

The word slow fashion was coined immediately after the huge success of "Slow Food" in food industry. The main feature of the phenomenon of slow fashion is that it acts as a link between raw materials, workforce and environment and his holistic approach takes into account the entire product life cycle.

On the one hand, as for other items, the production process of slow fashion goods begins with the design phase, which however considers sustainability, ecological concerns and raw materials. The second phase, on the other hand, provides for the maintenance of certain quality standards regarding not only production but also the working life of the individuals involved and their salaries. The third and final step encourage recycling and reuse [8].

2.2 Drivers of Sustainable Fashion Consumption

Although most consumers agree that the impact of fashion products on the environment is an important issue when deciding which item to buy, this feature is not considered as important as quality and price (European Commission, 2009). Due to the variety of motivational factors behind buying sustainable fashion products, this concept still represents uncharted territory and consumer's attitude and behaviors gap remains a problem [5, 9].

Literature demonstrates that product attributes play a crucial role in ethical fashion consumption choices. The recurring aspects that tend to influence the consumption of sustainable garments are: price, quality, information, style and availability. Alongside product-related features, literature identifies a number of consumer-related characteristics, which influence ethical fashion consumption choices which are: personal interest, emotions, skepticism, self-expression, social acceptance, effort and behaviors.

3 The Role of Millennials and Centennials in the Luxury Market

In this modern and dynamic business environment, interactions between brands and consumers are growing, especially because customer engagement is now considered as a good tool to generate effective strategies not only for acquiring a greater competitive advantage, but also for sales growth and to increase profitability. Millennials and Centennials represent a fundamental category of individuals within the luxury market, due to their purchasing power and their active interaction on social media. The increasing purchase of luxury brands has led to the need to understand which are the factors behind consumers' attitudes towards these brands [10]. These generations are composed of young, educated, wealthy, increasingly sociable and fashionable individuals [11]. They tend to adopt new fashion trends by researching and gathering information both through traditional channels and social media [12]. In addition, they are groups of younger people who tend to buy goods online and use social media to find more information about items and services offered by brands.

3.1 The Y and Z Generations: Attitudes for Sustainable Luxury

In order to analyze the behaviors and attitudes of the Y and Z generations towards sustainability practices, it is necessary to wonder something interesting: can luxury brands maintain their quality standards and excellence by adding ethical and sustainable practices in their businesses?

Nowadays luxury brands are considering moving towards more ethical and sustainable efforts which should be promoted and brought to the attention of the market. This suggests a positive influence on purchase intentions. Therefore, luxury brands that today incorporate more sustainable efforts, not only keep intact the prestige image of their brand but strengthen it, attracting more consumers pertaining to the Generation Y and generating positive attitudes towards luxury items and brands themselves.

Luxury goods allow consumers to express their individuality. As a result, luxury brands should try to design a reduced supply for consumers, in order to curb the rhythms of fashion through the main features of slow fashion. In this way, the characteristics of luxury as status, power and wealth can be managed providing sustainable material goods.

In conclusion, it can be said that through ethical and sustainable branding efforts and activities, luxury brands can limit their impact on the environment and, at the same time, provide diversified products and reaching new markets by satisfying the sensitivity of these categories of consumers towards sustainability [13].

4 Material and Methods

As we have seen in the previous paragraphs, the economic, cultural, social and technological growth are transforming the luxury apparel industry. However, as noted above, there are often conflicting opinions and assumptions in literature that do not provide a clear insight into consumer attitudes.

The aim of the paper is to investigate analytically different aspects of the purchase of luxury brands, ethical fashion and what the perceptions of consumers are towards these topics. The above macro-themes were explored through a structured survey questionnaire with semi-closed questions.

The selected target for the administration of the questionnaire, in fact, were Millennials and Centennials, also indicated by the expressions Generation Y and Z. As mentioned earlier, the former constitute a group of consumers, between the ages of 24 and 39, who are increasingly proactive, informed and inclined to the technological change. The latter instead include individuals between the ages of 18 and 23. These two groups of consumers were chosen for the reasons listed in the previous paragraphs, as they constitute a set of consumers increasingly involved in the fashion field, and as they are active and prone to the phenomenon of sustainability. Moreover, the choice of this target is also due to the importance they are acquiring within the fashion system.

4.1 Methodology

The first part of the research focuses on luxury brands in order to understand opportunities, frequency and motivations that drive consumers to purchase luxury brand products. In addition, this section investigate the opposite aspect that is understanding if the reasons that push consumers not buying such items are strictly linked to their purchasing power, personal characteristics or a lack of interest in luxury brands [14].

The second section tries to understand if today's consumers are aware of the new ethical and sustainable practices of the fashion world and what are the reasons that encourage the purchase or not of an eco-sustainable item. Today, almost every consumer lives with this phenomenon and for this reason, we tried to study knowledge, propensity, frequency and attitudes towards sustainable fashion products.

In previous paragraphs were extensively discussed different topics including the need to slow down the frenetic production of the fashion industry through the use of the new model of ethical fashion and what are the motivations that push today's consumers to purchase such goods.

As already defined in the previous chapters, the two generations constitute the category of consumers most involved nowadays in the fashion industry and in particular in the luxury market. For this reason, the respondents were selected primarily through the age group to which they belong, to reach a wider number of respondents and to understand the differences between the two generations. Morover, other relevant variables were analyzed as: the income received within the household during the previous year, gender and social status. Those variables were considered for obtaining a heterogeneous sample of consumers, not necessarily identifiable by the designation of luxury consumers.

Furthermore, within the questionnaire, sixteen luxury brands were selected on a personal basis. This choice stems from the fact that luxury brands have a large presence in the fashion market. Moreover, some of them tend to diversify into various sectors of luxury fashion, while others concentrate only on one or a few sectors belonging to the fashion system. These selected and investigated brands were: Luois Vuitton, Gucci, Chanel, Dior, Dolce & Gabbana, Hermès, Rolex, Cartier, Burberry, Yves Saint Laurent, Prada, Lancôme, Faoma, Moët e Chandon, Versace and Tiffany & Co.

4.2 Data

At the end of the design phase of the survey, the next step, data collection, was started to find information about the selected sample and to analyze and measure the results obtained.

The tool that has been used both for the development of the questionnaire and for the collection of data was the web software of Google modules, a platform that allows the dissemination of the questionnaire through associated links.

For the collection of the data which were recorded inside the database in aggregate form in real time, while with reference to the sharing of the questionnaire various online tools have been used as: social media (mainly Instagram and Facebook), emails and private messages.

The link for access to the survey was mainly sent to university students, friends, acquaintances and family members, and consequently spread by them through the word of mouth.

The questionnaire was released on the web on November 6th 2020 and after about a week, the desired result was reached corresponding to 352 respondents. Then, the investigation moved on to the analysis of the results through a descriptive method and the support of graphs to simplify their understanding.

As anticipated, the analysis of the data was carried out based on the most relevant criteria resulting from the survey, in a manner described. During this phase, the aspects were investigate through the help and production of tables and graphs personally made.

5 Result and Discussion

5.1 Socio-Demographic Area

The dissemination of the questionnaire resulted in its elaboration by 352 individuals, including 80 men and 272 women. This result shows a higher percentage of women, equal to 77.3%, probably because the female gender is the most interested and involved in the fashion field.

The respondents were also divided into the two age groups corresponding to the generations studied and from the data result that the sample is distributed almost equally. In addition, 49% of respondents were reached for Millennials, compared to 51% for Generation Z. Within the Millennials category there are mainly graduates and workers; while Generation Z consists of students, recent graduates, workers and unemployed.

Moreover, the sample was then subdivided according to the area of residence. The answers provided by the respondents revealed a majority of individuals living in Southern Italy and the Islands, reaching a percentage equal to 56% of the sample.

The last question in the first section of the questionnaire was about the knowledge and the subdivision of this sample in terms of income received within the household during the year 2019. For this variable there was a strong predominance of the band belonging to 0–18,000.00 euro with a percentage equal to 27% of respondents.

From the analysis of the above data, it can be said that luxury purchases are not only made by those with greater purchasing power, but also by individuals with lower incomes. This is presumably due to the fact that such purchases this type of items bring numerous benefits to buyers, including high brand symbolic values (Fig. 1).

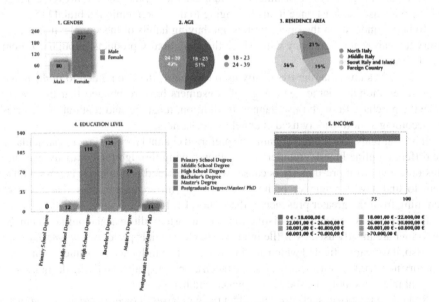

Fig. 1. Socio-demographic area (Author: Sinatra F., 2023)

5.2 Consumers Behaviors and Attitudes Towards Luxury Brands

The second step, in answering the research question, was focused on understanding if the respondents of the sample have bought luxury items during their lives at least once. Out of a total of 352 respondents, it emerged that 194 respondents purchased luxury goods, while 158 respondents never made a luxury purchase.

Regarding the subdivision of the two generations considered within the survey it emerged that among luxury buyers, most are Millennials (110 out of 194), presumably due to their higher purchasing power than the Centennials which mostly consist of non-working students, recent graduates, or unemployed people.

After identifying who were luxury buyers, on a sample of 194 individuals, a question was developed to better understand the frequency with which luxury consumers purchase eight different categories of luxury products. The data obtained have showed a greater propensity to purchase products such as: shoes, glasses, perfumes and food and drinks. Lastly, by carrying out a more in-depth analysis, it emerges that mostly Centennials tend to buy categories such as footwear, glasses and perfumes; in relation to food and drinks categories emerges that Millennials are the category of consumers who mostly buy it.

As anticipated, for the survey, sixteen luxury brands were considered. The results reveal a significant phenomenon: most consumers have never purchased products belonging to the luxury brands taken into account. Another important data comes always from respondents: the frequency with which they purchase one of those brands, named Faoma (which offers luxury furniture products) is extremely low. The hypothesis of such results stems probably from the fact that this brand is not well known by the Z generation or from their lack of interest in this category of products as the youngest category in the study. A small proportion of consumers belonging to the Y generation, however, claimed to have purchased at least once items belonging to the aforementioned brand [15].

To better understand the opportunities and buying habits of the sample, it was necessary to analyze the frequency with which they buy luxury products through different distribution channels.

The Fig. 2 shows that the frequently used channel is the one related to multi-brand stores, even though a large percentage of consumers have responded that they never make the purchase through this channel. In addition, it can be said that outlet factories are becoming a more widely used channel by consumers.

It is clear that e-commerce remains the preferred channel for consumers, particularly the different online brands' retailers rather than buying through the company website. This outcome arose presumably because, within the brand's retailers it is possible for them to find a wider number of items, offered by different brands or the incentive stemming from the greater presence of discounts [12, 16].

From the data came a further distinction in relation to traditional and online channels: the former are mostly used by Millennials while Centennials prefer online purchases.

Also, it were investigated which are the attributes that influence consumers' purchase of luxury items, taking into account features such as: price, quality, made in, design, style, personal interest, emotions, social acceptance and habits.

Regarding the price, such variable affect the purchases choices of luxury consumers [17, 18]. In relation to the other variables analyzed in the analysis emotion emerges because it constitutes a more incisive variable on the purchase choices of the Centennials, presumably due to the fact that they are consumers who seek and desire a high experiential value from the items they purchase.

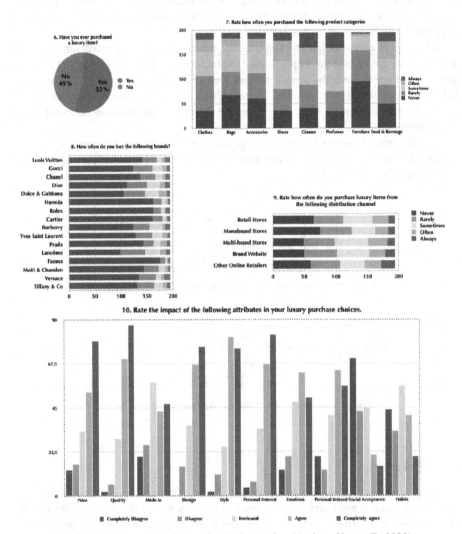

Fig. 2. Consumers behaviors and attitudes section (Author: Sinatra F., 2023)

5.3 Perceptions and Reasons Why Consumers are not Purchasing Luxury Items

Given the strong propensity of consumers to perceive luxury brands as expensive and prestigious, in addition to the analysis of luxury buyers, within the questionnaire was reserved a section dedicated to those who have never made a luxury purchase. The measured variables were multiple to understand which ones really affected purchasing decisions. For this purpose, it was also given the possibility to indicate more than one possible answer, to not to limit respondents having to choose between one or a few options. It appears from the data obtained that the main reason is not the lack of purchasing power as assumed, but the low interest of these individuals in luxury products (91) and the high price of luxury brands (90).

Although in a smaller line, 63 respondents, mostly from the Z generation, indicated as reasons of this choice the impossibility to purchase due to their insufficient income, and 50 of them explain the reason behind their choice as they are not interested in following fashion trends. In addition, 31 individuals indicate that luxury products do not reflect their personal taste while only 4 people the lack of information provided about such products.

Finally, only 2 people belonging to generation Y, indicated the answer "other", stating that they do not perceive the need to buy such items and prefer to use their earnings differently (Fig. 3).

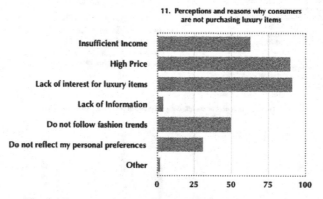

Fig. 3. Consumers' perceptions (Author: Sinatra F., 2023)

5.4 Eco-Fashion

Growing awareness on sustainability and ethical practices among businesses and consumers has made it necessary to slow down the production of the fashion industry and increase the focus on the use of sustainable raw materials in order to reduce the environmental and social impact resulting from the production of fashion items [19]. For this reason, the current situation regarding this phenomenon has been thoroughly analyzed in the previous paragraphs. The aim assigned to the next section of the questionnaire, named eco-fashion, was specifically to better understand the attitudes and propensity of respondents to this phenomenon.

The section opens with a first important question that was whether respondents were aware of the recent arose of the phenomenon of ethical fashion. On the one hand, a relatively high 38% of the sample indicated that it was not aware of this phenomenon. On the other hand, instead, 35% of respondents indicated that they were aware of this phenomenon. As for the remaining 28% of interviewed, they gave a different answer,

("I've heard about it"), presumably because they have less in-depth knowledge of ethical fashion.

The study of eco-sustainable fashion ends with a further question regarding the propensity to purchase eco-sustainable fashion products. From the data collected during the survey, it emerged that only a small percentage of respondents, almost all Millennials, purchased eco-sustainable luxury products at least once, recording a percentage equal to 12% of the sample.

The remaining 88% never made a sustainable luxury purchase, probably because this particular question was addressed to the whole sample, which also includes those who have never purchased luxury products [20, 21] (Fig. 4).

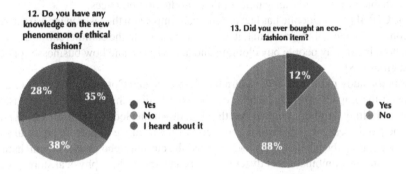

Fig. 4. Eco-Fashion section (Author: Sinatra F., 2023)

6   Conclusions, Limits and Future Research

This article has several limitations. In the first place, it is an elaboration realized through theories often in contrast whose do not to provide an exhaustive answer related to the various topics addressed.

Secondly, having developed a survey limited only to two categories of consumers (Millennials and Generation Z) has not made it possible to compare and examine in depth differences between other consumers' categories.

Third, the use of a limited number of luxury brands led to a circumscription of the sample. This implied an increase in negative responses from consumers, as most of the brands considered belong to the so-called "inaccessible" luxury category. Therefore, it would be interesting in future research to expand not only the sample but also the number of luxury brands investigated. In the future it would be recommended base the research on a more qualitative research model, in order to better understand motivations and attitudes that lead to certain final purchasing choices.

Moreover, in recent years, there have been major changes in the commercial structure of cities in relation to fashion industry. These changes include the rise of online commerce, the concentration of commerce in large shopping centers, the rise of second-hand clothing stores, technological innovation and the evolution of consumer needs.

According to literature [22, 23], e-commerce, social media and crowdfunding are revolutionizing the fashion and retail industry, allowing companies to reach a wider audience and test new products quickly and economically.

As already said, sustainability is another aspect that is becoming increasingly important in the fashion industry. Some authors [24] highlight the need for new supply chain management models [25] to reduce the environmental impact of fashion industry and improve conditions for workers. Also, fashion is becoming increasingly technological [26], with the introduction of smart fabrics, connected clothing and sustainable production technologies.

Furthermore, the influence of digital media [27] on the fashion industry, highlight how companies must adapt to consumers' needs and whose are increasingly interested in sustainable fashion and transparency in the production practices.

The COVID-19 pandemic has had a significant impact on the fashion industry and on the economy in general. In particular, it has led to changes in the commercial structure of cities, both in the way people buy clothing and accessories, and how businesses operate within cities [28].

A major study published in the Journal of Retailing and Consumer Services in 2021 examined the impact of the pandemic on the distribution channel strategy of fashion operators in Italy. Authors pointed out that lockdown has led to a significant increase in online purchases, even for fashion products, with a negative impact on physical store sales. In addition, the pandemic also accelerated the current trend towards omnichannel, which means the combination of different sales channels (online, physical stores, social media, etc.) in order to offer customers a more integrated and personalized shopping experience. This was also highlighted in a study published in the International Journal of Retail & Distribution Management in 2020, which examined the omnichannel strategies adopted by fashion companies in China [29].

The fashion industry is also becoming increasingly aware of the sustainability and environmental impact of its activities, with a growing interest in local production and reducing carbon emissions. This could lead to a greater focus on the production and sale of sustainable clothing and accessories within cities.

Pandemic has increased the focus on the importance of sustainability in the fashion industry. In particular, the industry has started to focus more on the production and sale of sustainable products, with a growing focus on reducing environmental impact. This has led to a greater focus on local production and the reduction of carbon emissions, with possible repercussions on the structure of cities where the fashion industry is present.

In addition, the health emergency has speed up the digitalization of the fashion industry, leading to an increase in online purchases and the growth of e-commerce platforms. This has guided to a restructuring of the commercial structures of the cities, with greater attention to logistics and the organization of home delivery services. Also, pandemic has led an increase in online shopping and has also influenced consumers' choices to purchase in physical stores, leading to a change in the commercial structure of cities.

During the pandemic, the attention of many individuals has moved to issues as inclusiveness and diversity in the fashion industry, with a growing interest in representing people of different ethnicity, gender and involve them in fashion models.

For example, there have been initiatives to promote diversity between fashion models and to ensure that industrial workers are treated fairly and safely.

This could lead to a change in the structure of cities where the fashion industry is present, with a greater focus on promoting diversity and inclusion.

Acknowledgments. This publication was produced while attending the PhD programme in Circula Economy at the University of Trieste, Cycle XXXVIII, with the support of a scholarship financed by the Ministerial Decree no. 351 of 9th April 2022, based on the NRRP - funded by the European Union - NextGenerationEU - Mission 4 "Education and Research", Component 1 "Enhancement of the offer of educational services: from nurseries to universities" - Investment 4.1 "Extension of the number of research doctorates and innovative doctorates for public administration and cultural heritage".

References

1. Muratovski, G.: Paradigm shift: report on the new role of design in business and society. She Ji J. Des. Econ. Innov. **1**(2), 118–139 (2015)
2. Bendell, J., Thomas, L.: The appearance of elegant disruption: theorising sustainable luxury entrepreneurship. J. Corp. Citizsh. **2013**(52), 9–24 (2013)
3. Ozdamar Ertekin, Z., Atik, D.: Sustainable markets: Motivating factors, barriers, and remedies for mobilization of slow fashion. J. Macromark. **35**(1), 53–69 (2015)
4. Lundblad, L., Davies, I.A.: The values and motivations behind sustainable fashion consumption. J. Consum. Behav. **15**(2), 149–162 (2016)
5. Jayal, A.D., Badurdeen, F., Dillon, O.W., Jr., Jawahir, I.S.: Sustainable manufacturing: modeling and optimization challenges at the product, process and system levels. CIRP J. Manuf. Sci. Technol. **2**(3), 144–152 (2010)
6. McNeill, L., Moore, R.: Sustainable fashion consumption and the fast fashion conundrum: fashionable consumers and attitudes to sustainability in clothing choice. Int. J. Consum. Stud. **39**(3), 212–222 (2015)
7. Henninger, C.E., Alevizou, P.J., Oates, C.J.: What is sustainable fashion? J. Fashion Mark. Manag. Int. J. **20**(4), 400–416 (2016)
8. Joy, A., Sherry, J.F., Jr., Venkatesh, A., Wang, J., Chan, R.: Fast fashion, sustainability, and the ethical appeal of luxury brands. Fash. Theory **16**(3), 273–295 (2012)
9. Bucklow, J., Perry, P., Ritch, E.: The influence of eco-labelling on ethical consumption of organic cotton. In: Henninger, C., Alevizou, P., Goworek, H., Ryding, D. (eds.) Sustainability in Fashion: A Cradle to Upcycle Approach, pp. 55–80. Palgrave Macmillan, Cham (2017). https://doi.org/10.1007/978-3-319-51253-2_4
10. Burnasheva, R., GuSuh, Y., Villalobos-Moron, K.: Factors affecting millennials' attitudes toward luxury fashion brands: a cross-cultural study. Int. Bus. Res. **12**(6), 69–81 (2019)
11. Howe, N., Strauss, W.: Millennials Rising: The Next Great Generation. Knopf Doubleday Publishing Group, New York (2009)
12. Geraci, J.C., Nagy, J.: Millennials-the new media generation. Young Consum. **5**(2), 17–24 (2004)
13. Morgan, L.R., Birtwistle, G.: An investigation of young fashion consumers' disposal habits. Int. J. Consum. Stud. **33**(2), 190–198 (2009)
14. Merlo, O., Eisingerich, A.B., Auh, S.: Why customer participation matters. MIT Sloan Manag. Rev. **55**(2), 81 (2014)

15. Gil, L.A., Kwon, K.N., Good, L.K., Johnson, L.W.: Impact of self on attitudes toward luxury brands among teens. J. Bus. Res. **65**(10), 1425–1433 (2012)

16. Aggarwal, P.: The effects of brand relationship norms on consumer attitudes and behavior. J. Consum. Res. **31**(1), 87–101 (2004)

17. Bray, J., Johns, N., Kilburn, D.: An exploratory study into the factors impeding ethical consumption. J. Bus. Ethics **98**, 597–608 (2011)

18. Baek, T.H., Kim, J., Yu, J.H.: The differential roles of brand credibility and brand prestige in consumer brand choice. Psychol. Mark. **27**(7), 662–678 (2010)

19. Goworek, H., Fisher, T., Cooper, T., Woodward, S., Hiller, A.: The sustainable clothing market: an evaluation of potential strategies for UK retailers. Int. J. Retail Distrib. Manag. (2012)

20. Henninger, C. E., Alevizou, P. J., Goworek, H., Ryding, D. (eds.): Sustainability in Fashion: A Cradle to Upcycle Approach. Springer, Cham (2017). https://doi.org/10.1007/978-3-319-51253-2

21. Le Roux, C., Pretorius, M.: Navigating sustainability embeddedness in management decision-making. Sustainability **8**(5), 444 (2016)

22. Roncha, R., Casalegno, A.M.: Fashion and retail: An analysis of e-commerce, social media, and crowdfunding. J. Fash. Mark. Manag. **21**(3), 387–402 (2017)

23. Okonkwo, M.H.: Luxury Fashion Branding: Trends, Tactics, Techniques. Palgrave Macmillan, London (2007)

24. Bianchi, C.: Sustainability and the Fashion Industry: New Models for Supply Chain Management. Springer, Cham (2016)

25. Barnes, L., Lea-Greenwood, G.: Fast fashioning the supply chain: shaping the research agenda. J. Fashion Mark. Manag. Int. J. (2006)

26. Williams, D.R., Martinez, S.S.: Fashion Retailing in the Twenty-First Century. Palgrave Macmillan, London (2016)

27. Koo, A.T., Kim, J.P., Lee, E.K.: A study on the influence of digital media on fast fashion brands. J. Fash. Mark. Manag. **20**(4), 487–499 (2016)

28. Borrello, A., Finotto, V.: Channel strategy and performance during COVID-19 crisis: evidence from Italian fashion retailers. J. Retail. Consum. Serv. **59**, 102348 (2021)

29. Li, Y., Liang, X., Li, X., Huang, Z.: Chinese fashion retailers' omnichannel strategies: an exploratory study. Int. J. Retail Distrib. Manag. **48**(11), 1172–1189 (2020)

Metropolitan City Lab
(Metro_City_Lab 2023)

Minimum Environmental Criteria and Climate Issue in the Metropolitan Urban Ecosystem

Martina Sinatra[1]([✉]) [ID], Ginevra Balletto[1] [ID], and Giuseppe Borruso[2] [ID]

[1] DICAAR – Department of Civil and Environmental Engineering and Architecture, University of Cagliari, Via Marengo 2, Cagliari, Italy
m.sinatra@studenti.unica.it, balletto@unica.it
[2] DEAMS - Department of Economics, Business, Mathematics and Statistics Sciences "Bruno de Finetti", University of Trieste, 34127 Trieste, Italy
giuseppe.borruso@deams.units.it

Abstract. In Italy, the adoption of the Minimum Environmental Criteria (MEC) is associated with Legislative Decree 50/2016, which regulates public tenders. The main objective of the MECs is to promote the purchase of sustainable goods and services thus contributing to the reduction of the environmental impact and the protection of natural resources. Furthermore, the adoption of MEC by public authorities represents a strategic choice to promote the circular economy, reduce waste and greenhouse gas emissions, thus preserving the quality of environmental matrices. MECs, although they are innovative tools, are however lacking in geographic information related to context analysis. In this synthetic framework, the objective of this work is to evaluate a set of contextual environmental indicators to support the MECs. In fact, the knowledge and representation of the context constitutes a fundamental action for recognizing local problems, which are also useful for understanding global issues. Furthermore, how can MECs contribute to adaptation to climate change within the relative territorial context? This question guided the manuscript and the metropolitan city of Cagliari represents the case study.

Keywords: Minimum Environmental Criteria · Climate Issue · Metropolitan City

1 Introduction

The problem of climate change, is the subject of a complex scientific debate and international commitments aimed at reducing climate-altering greenhouse gas emissions [1]. The increase in average temperatures, the frequency of extreme meteorological events such as intense rainfall, heat waves and droughts, constitute the main phenomena of climate change and are closely related to the geographical conditions of the contexts [2].

Climatic variations also have significant impacts on cities as, as a matter of example, increase in temperature, heavy rains and consequent flood risks and other water-related problems, such as the risk of coastal erosion and the risk of drought [3, 4]. Furthermore, in

O. Gervasi et al. (Eds.): ICCSA 2023 Workshops, LNCS 14109, pp. 49–65, 2023.
https://doi.org/10.1007/978-3-031-37120-2_4

cities the combination of the increase in the average annual temperature with the urban heat island effect [5] can amplify climate change, resulting in an increased demand for energy for cooling buildings and infrastructure, whose gas emissions contribute to altering the climate, contributing to the consolidation of the climate-city relationship [6]. Climate adaptation and mitigation strategies in cities are therefore urgently needed, including the reduction of greenhouse gas emissions, the sustainable electricity transition and the promotion of sustainable behavior among citizens, businesses and public administrations [7, 8]. In this sense, the MECs constitute a set of rules and standards that the public administration must respect in order to reduce the environmental impact in the provision of its services. The MECs were introduced to promote the adoption of eco-sustainable behaviors and can concern various aspects, such as the reduction of the environmental impact of production processes, the use of recyclable or biodegradable materials, the reduction of energy consumption, the use of renewable energy sources, the reduction of polluting emissions and water consumption, the management of waste produced during production and distribution and more. The main objective of MEC for public administration is to reduce the environmental impact of services, promoting the adoption of more sustainable technologies and production processes and reducing the overall environmental impact of production and consumption [9]. MECs was born in the 80s, when international governments and then the EU began to recognize the importance of reducing the environmental impact of production and commercial activities. In the following years, MECs have been adopted by many other international organizations, national governments, regional and local authorities, as well as non-governmental organizations [10]. MECs are an important tool to promote environmental sustainability, also contributing to the transition towards a greener and more sustainable economy. However, the MECs have some limitations: they can be interpreted as a minimum and not a maximum requirement, therefore adherence to these criteria may not guarantee maximum environmental sustainability; finally, the application of MECs can be difficult to monitor in the territorial context of reference, also because the context does not constitute a relevant field of investigation.

In this framework, the aim of the paper is to investigate to identify a set of functional environmental indicators to represent the municipal territorial context, within which the urban projects that adhere to the MECs can be monitored in relation to the local sustainable development challenges [11, 12].

The paper is organized as it follows: Sect. 2 Material and Method; Sect. 2.1 Temperatures and human factors; Sect. 2.2 Metropolitan City (MC) and Functional Urban Areas (FUA); Sect. 2.3 Methodology; Sect. 2.4 Data; Sect. 3 Case study; Sect. 4 Results and Discussion and Sect. 5 Conclusions and future development.

2   Material and Method

Luke Howard [13] through the study of the relationships that regulate the relationship between climate and city, managed to systematize about 30 years of observations of this dual relationship. In addition to the influence of large-scale meteorological phenomena, it was the city with its own structure and distribution that significantly influenced the local climate by intervening on the flow of air currents, on the distribution of humidity and on the temperature regime, differentiating the environmental parameters of the cities and nearby areas. However, the scientific debate only became animated in the late 80s and early 90s and since then research, models and methods have been proposed to monitor and/or contrast the change that can also be associated with the progressive phenomenon of metropolisation [14], which requires climatology associated with urban planning and tools to govern the processes of climate-city interaction. In this sense, a set of indicators was selected - sentinel indicators - able to represent the climate_city interaction associated with the territorial dimension of the metropolitan city: land take [15]; green area [16]; sustainable energy [17] and greenhouse gas emission [18] in order to monitor-govern the complex climate-city interaction (Fig. 1).

CRITERIA	INDICATORS	SOURCE
1. Land take	1.1 Airports 1.2 Continuous urban fabric (S.L. : > 80%) 1.3 Discontinuous low density urban fabric (S.L. : 10% - 30%) 1.4 Discontinuous medium density urban fabric (S.L. : 30% - 50%) 1.5 Discontinuous very low density urban fabric (S.L. : < 10%) 1.6 Industrial, commercial, public, military and private units 1.7 Isolated structures 1.8 Land without current use 1.9 Roads, port areas, railways and associated land 1.10 Sports and leisure facilities 1.11 Water	Urban Atlas https://bit.ly/2Kq8Frz
2. Green Areas	2.1 Forests 2.2 Green urban areas	Urban Atlas https://bit.ly/2Kq8Frz
3. Sustainable energy	3.1 Bioenergy 3.2 Eolic 3.3 Photovoltaic 3.2 Hydroelectric	Terna S.p.a. https://bit.ly/3Zo7L7G
4. Greenhouse gas emission	4.1 CO2 emissions	ISTAT https://bit.ly/3K6NQCG

Fig. 1. Set of indicators to represent the climate_city interaction in the territorial dimension of the metropolitan city (Authors: Balletto G. and Sinatra M., 2023)

2.1 Temperatures and Human Factors

New complex challenges between local and global emerge. Identifying strategies to contain environmental impacts, the consumption of resources within a growing and gradually aging international demographic framework represents a shared priority within the scientific debate. Furthermore, the trend of metropolisation [19] of the last decades is bound to go on. It is estimated that the population in 2050 will be approximately 70% urban, which requires urgent sustainable planning strategies. The city, as a spatial organization with a high anthropic concentration: residential, production/services and mobility, as well as being the generator and recipient of numerous and complex environmental impacts, is also subject to significant thermal variations, called heat islands. Forecasts over a period of about forty years show worrying scenarios with an increase in global temperature of 2 to 4 °C, and with greater increases precisely in urban areas [20–22] and heavy consequences on the balance of natural ecosystems. In Italy, inparticular, the average temperature of the period 2009–2018 exceeded that of the years 1961–1970 by more than 2°C. This increase is worrying both in terms of intensity and frequency and for the exposure of communities, in particular for sensitive ones (over 65 - currently growing), as well as for the progressive vulnerability extended to buildings, roads, monuments [23, 24].

2.2 Metropolitan City (MC) and Functional Urban Areas (FUA)

Metropolitan Cities were established in Italy in 2014, with the primary task of promoting socio-economic development and contributing to the competitiveness and growth of the national economy. The metropolitan cities represent the intermediate administrative dimension between the municipal and the regional one, based on the population density, whose trend over time has been increasing towards the peripheral municipalities. In fact, the Italian metropolitan cities have been affected by significant demographic phenomena, first of growth and then of decline, so much so that by 2030 they are expected to be characterized by a significant demographic decline with important socio-economic consequences [25].

The administrative dimension of metropolitan cities derives, however, from a previous definition, that of the FUA -Functional urban area- developed by the OECD in 2004 based on population density to identify urban cores and home-work travel flows to identify the hinterland, or where the labor market is highly dependent on the main urban centres [26]. In particular, by FUA we mean a spatially continuous urban settlement made up of several administrative units. The OCSE methodology makes it possible to compare functional urban areas of similar size, located in various European countries, according to the following classification:

- Small urban areas, with a population >50,000 and <200,000;
- Medium urban areas, with population >200,000 and <500,000;
- Metropolitan areas, with populations >500,000 and <1.5 million;
- Large metropolitan areas, with population >1.5 million.

Europe is made up of a polycentric network of urban areas in which the FUAs defined by the OCSE although the FUAs constitute only a part of its urban structure, nevertheless identify the relationships with the peri-urban areas, in analogy to the "Local systems of the work" defined by ISTAT, on the basis of the "daily commute to work". The metropolitan city therefore represents the administrative dimension for governance, while the FUA represents a compatible dimension for analysis, because it better represents the spatial organization and urban relations such as commuting [27].

2.3 Methodology

The proposed method consists in identifying a set of indicators able to represent the following variations of the phenomena: temperature, soil consumption, green areas, sustainable energy production and greenhouse gas emissions (CO_2) [28, 29]. In particular, the temperature variation was represented by spatial autocorrelation, thus highlighting the positive proximity relationships. All the other indicators, on the other hand, were represented by spatial distribution (Fig. 2).

ID	PHENOMENONS	SPATIAL DIMENSION	LITERATURE
1	Temperature variation	Municipality/ Metropolitan City	Yang et al. (2021)
Representation of the phenomenon		Spatial autocorrelation LISA	Bolletto et al. (2022)
2	2.1 Land take; 2.2 Green areas; 2.3 Sustainable energy; 2.4 Greenhouse gas emission	Municipality/ Metropolitan City/ Regional	Moldan et al. (2007) Verma et al (2018)
Representation of the phenomenon		Spatial distribution	

Fig. 2. Climate_city interaction: Set of indicators and territorial dimension (Authors: Balletto G. and Sinatra M., 2023)

LISA Method

Local Indicators of Spatial Autocorrelation (LISA) were considered useful for examining the phenomenon under observation and, particularly, to analyze the behavior of certain data and variable in the geographical space, taking into consideration the characteristic of geographical feature of autocorrelate in space. Area units in fact can mutually influence each other in geographical terms and in terms of the data referred to such units. In geographic analytical terms, Tobler in his 'First Law of Geography' highlighted [30] as "nearby things are more related than distant things", an intuitive approach [31] recently rediscovered [32], that allows, by means of the appropriate tools for its analysis, to observe the behavior of a variable related to its position in space and with reference to its proximal units. Through two categories of information such as location and related properties it is possible to describe geographic objects. In particular, in analytical terms, spatial autocorrelation can be defined as follows [33]:

$$SAC = \frac{\sum_{i=1}^{N} \sum_{j=1}^{N} c_{ij} w_{ij}}{\sum_{i=1}^{N} \sum_{j=1}^{N} w_{ij}} \tag{1}$$

where:

- i and j are two objects or events in space;
- N is the number of objects or events;
- cij is a degree of similarity of attributes i and j;
- wij is a degree of similarity of location i and j.

From the general formula two indices derive as the Geary C Ratio [34] and the Moran Index I [35]. Defining xi as the value of object i attribute; if $c_{ij} = (x_i - x_j)^2$, Geary C Ratio can be defined as follows:

$$C = \frac{(N - 1)(\sum_i \sum_j w_{ij}(x_i - x_j)^2)}{2(\sum_i \sum_j w_{ij}) \sum_i (x_i - \underline{x})^2} \tag{2}$$

If $c_{ij} = (x_i - x)(x_j - x)$, Moran Index I can be defined as follows:

$$I = \frac{N \sum_i \sum_j w_{ij}(x_i - \underline{x})(x_j - \underline{x})}{\sum_i \sum_j w_{ij}(x_i - \underline{x})^2} \tag{3}$$

Geary and Moran indexes, as recalled and applied in several Italian contexts [36], are similar in their overall meaning and message, differing by the cross-product term in the numerator, calculated using the deviations from the mean in Moran, while directly computed in Geary. The main message coming from the indices is highlighting the presence - or absence - of spatial autocorrelation at a global level in the overall distribution, while the local presence of autocorrelation can be highlighted by the LISA (Local Indicators of Spatial Association) or, as after Anselin [37, 38], a local Moran index, as the sum of all local indices is proportional to the value of the Moran one:

$$\sum_i I_i = \gamma * I \tag{4}$$

The index is calculated as follows:

$$I_i = \frac{(X_i - X)}{S_X^2} \sum_{j=1}^{N} (w_{ij}(X_j - \underline{X})) \tag{5}$$

The index allows assessing for each location assess the similarity of each observation with its neighbors, and five combinations can be obtained from its application:

- hot spots: areas with high values of the phenomenon and a high level of similarity with its surroundings (high-high H-H);
- cold spots, as areas with low values of the phenomenon and a low level of similarity with its surroundings (low-low L-L);
- potentially spatial outliers, with high values of the phenomenon and a low level of similarity with its surroundings (high-low H-L);
- potentially spatial outliers, with low values of the phenomenon and a high level of similarity with its surroundings (low-high L-H);
- lack of significant autocorrelation. The interesting characteristic of LISA is in providing an effective measure of the degree of relative spatial association between each territorial unit and its neighboring elements, thereby highlighting the type of spatial concentration and clustering.

The neighborhood property is based on weights, seen particularly as indicators of contiguity eights, w_{ij}, indicate the presence, or absence, of neighboring spatial units to a given one. A spatial weight matrix is needed, with w_{ij} assuming values of 0 in cases in which i and j are not neighbors, or 1 when i and j are neighbors. Neighborhood is computed in terms of contiguity such as, in the case of areal units, sharing a common border of non-zero length [39].

2.4 Data

The current global warming can be quantified with an increase in average temperatures of over 2 °C in the last 50 years. Among the numerous studies on the climate issue, the Glocal Climate Change (2020) [40] carried out by OBC Transeuropa for the European Data Journalism Network (EDJNet) was selected and focuses on the increase in average temperatures in Europe. The EDJNet reference data were retrieved from the "UERRA regional reanalysis for Europe on single levels from 1961 to 2018", a dataset created by the Copernicus initiative and the European Center for medium-range weather forecasts, containing estimates of the temperature measured at two meters above the ground with reference to a grid composed of cells of 5.5 × 5.5 km.

To evaluate the thermal variation, the value of the annual average temperature was calculated, referring to the two time intervals 1961–1970 and 2009–2018, for each cell. Subsequently, a European municipality was assigned to each of the latter, taking into consideration urban density and the conformation of the coast. Figure 3 shows the temperature values for the Metropolitan City of Cagliari, interval 2006–2018, with the relative absolute variation.

According to the literature review (Sect. 2), a dataset is proposed, as summarised in (Table 1).

Municipality	Assemini	Cagliari	Capoterra	Decimomannu	Elmas	Maracalagonis	Monserrato	Pula	Quartu Sant'Elena	Quartucciu	Sarroch	Selargius	Sestu	Settimo San Pietro	Sinnai	Uta	Villa San Pietro
Temperature 2006 [C°]	17.5	19.3	18.2	17.4	18.0	16.9	18.1	16.6	17.9	17.3	17.4	18.1	17.5	16.6	16.6	17.3	16.6
Temperature 2018 [C°]	17.6	19.2	17.9	17.3	17.7	16.3	17.8	15.9	16.8	16.8	16.8	17.8	17.0	16.0	16.0	17.1	15.9
Temperature variation [C°]	+0.1	−0.1	−0.3	−0.1	−0.3	−0.6	−0.3	−0.7	−0.5	−0.5	−0.6	−0.3	−0.3	−0.6	−0.6	−0.2	−0.7

Fig. 3. Temperatures of the metropolitan city of Cagliari (2006–2018) - EDJNet. Source: https://climatechange.europeandatajournalism.eu/it/

Table 1. Climate city interaction indicators (Authors: Balletto G. and Sinatra M., 2023).

ID	Criteria	Indicators	Source
01	Land take	FUA land-use classes	Urban Atlas (2006–2018)
02	Green Areas		
03	Sustainable energy production	Efficient power for renewable sources	Terna S.p.a. (2006–2018)
04	Greenhouse gas	CO_2	ISTAT (2006–2018)

Sources: Urban Atlas - https://bit.ly/2Kq8Frz; Terna S.p.A. - https://bit.ly/3Zc7L7G; Istat - https://bit.ly/3K6NQCG

3 Case Study

As a study area to test the methodology, the metropolitan city of Cagliari was chosen, because it is also of regional importance. It is an administrative intermediate unit established in Sardinia by the regional law n. 2 of 2016 and became fully operational on 1 January 2017. It consists of 17 municipalities and has a population of 420,000 inhabitants [41]. The city of Cagliari is the capital of the Autonomous Region of Sardinia and of the metropolitan city and is the economic, political and administrative center of Sardinia (Fig. 4).

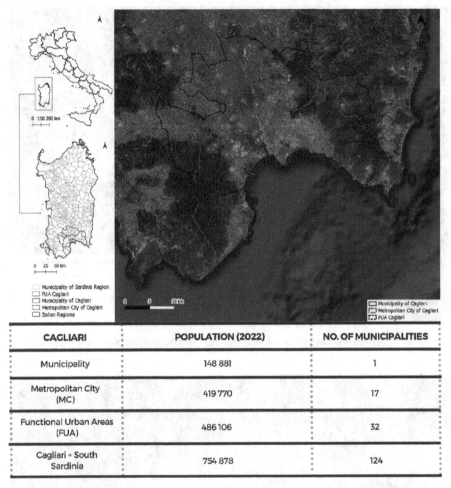

CAGLIARI	POPULATION (2022)	NO. OF MUNICIPALITIES
Municipality	148 881	1
Metropolitan City (MC)	419 770	17
Functional Urban Areas (FUA)	486 106	32
Cagliari + South Sardinia	754 878	124

Fig. 4. Study area and its population (Authors: Balletto G. and Sinatra M., 2023).

4   Result and Discussion

The analysis was carried out considering the average annual temperature recorded over a time interval, from 2006 to 2018, attributed to each municipality of the metropolitan city of Cagliari. These data were then used as input, in particular, for the local Moran's I calculation and the related LISA map. The analysis was conducted on the temperatures of 2006 and 2018.

The results are reported in Fig. 5, Fig. 6 and Fig. 7 (LISA Significance Map and Moran's I Scatterplot).

Fig. 5. Spatial autocorrelation of temperatures (2006) (Authors: Sinatra M., 2023).

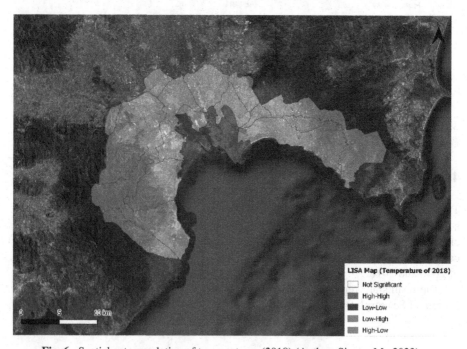

Fig. 6. Spatial autocorrelation of temperatures (2018) (Author: Sinatra M., 2023).

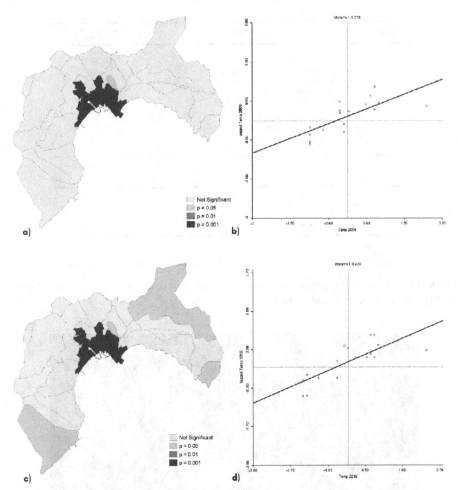

Fig. 7. LISA Significance Map and Moran's I Scatterplot.Significance maps years 2006 (a), 2018 (c), Moran's I scatterplots 2006 (b), 2018 (d).

For the Municipalities of Cagliari and Monserrato with high-high spatial autocorrelation of temperatures, the Climate city interaction assessment was carried out, using the set of indicators, as shown in Fig. 8.

The results of the evaluation of the climate-city interaction (Cagliari and Monserrato) were also spatialized (Fig. 9, Fig. 10, Fig. 11 and Fig. 12) to support MEC monitoring.

CRITERIA	INDICATORS	PERCENTAGE CHANGE (YEARS 2006-2018)
1. Land take	1.1 Airports	+ 0%
	1.2 Continuous urban fabric (S.L. : > 80%)	+ 1%
	1.3 Discontinuous low density urban fabric (S.L. : 10% - 30%)	+ 19%
	1.4 Discontinuous medium density urban fabric (S.L. : 30% - 50%)	+ 6%
	1.5 Discontinuous very low density urban fabric (S.L. : < 10%)	+ 53%
	1.6 Industrial, commercial, public, military and private units	+ 3%
	1.7 Isolated structures	+ 5%
	1.8 Land without current use	+ 30%
	1.9 Roads, port areas, railways and associated land	+ 5%
	1.10 Sports and leisure facilities	+ 4%
	1.11 Water	- 1%
2. Green Areas	2.1 Forests	+ 0%
	2.2 Green urban areas	+ 0%
3. Sustainable energy	3.1 Bioenergy	+ 77%
	3.2 Eolic	- 67%
	3.3 Photovoltaic	+ 99%
	3.2 Hydroelectric	- 98%
4. Greenhouse gas emission	4.1 CO2 emissions	- 33%

Fig. 8. Municipalities of Cagliari and Monserrato: Evaluation of climate-city interaction (2006–2018) (Authors: Sinatra M. and Balletto G., 2023).

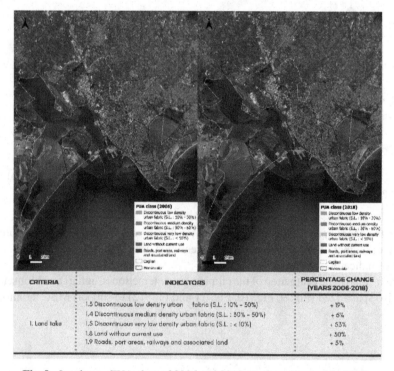

CRITERIA	INDICATORS	PERCENTAGE CHANGE (YEARS 2006-2018)
1. Land take	1.3 Discontinuous low density urban fabric (S.L. : 10% - 50%)	+ 19%
	1.4 Discontinuous medium density urban fabric (S.L. : 30% - 50%)	+ 6%
	1.5 Discontinuous very low density urban fabric (S.L. : < 10%)	+ 53%
	1.8 Land without current use	+ 30%
	1.9 Roads, port areas, railways and associated land	+ 5%

Fig. 9. Land use - FUA class of 2006 and 2018 (Author: Sinatra M., 2023).

The focus was therefore on the two municipalities of Cagliari and Monserrato. Also the following spatial representations, as a consequence, reflect this spatial selection and thematic representation.

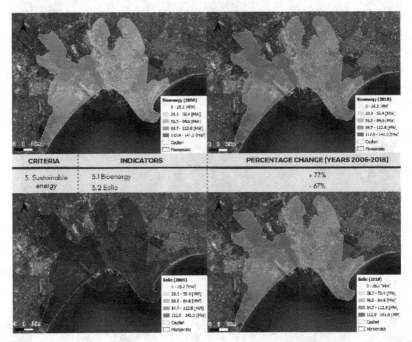

Fig. 10. Sustainable energy production for renewable sources of bioenergy and eolic, years 2006 and 2018 (Author: Sinatra M., 2023).

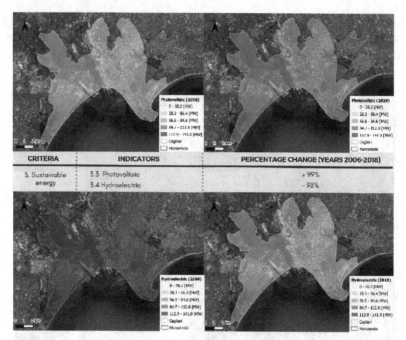

Fig. 11. Sustainable energy production for renewable sources of photovoltaic and hydroelectric, years 2006 and 2018 (Author: Sinatra M., 2023).

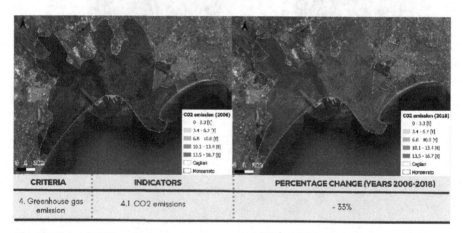

Fig. 12. Tons of CO2 equivalent per person, years 2006 and 2018 (Author: Sinatra M., 2023).

5   Conclusions and Future Development

In Italy, with Legislative Decree 50/2016, it is mandatory to apply the MECs to projects and works for the new construction, renovation and maintenance of buildings and for the management of public administration construction sites. The MECs constitute the environmental requirements useful for identifying the design solution, the product or service that demonstrates the best attention to the life cycle of one or more buildings to be built up to urban regeneration. The latter is to be preferred over the former, because it limits soil consumption to protect environmental sustainability. Urban regeneration also allows the community to reappropriate and relive the regenerated spaces again, with evident improvements in the quality of life and in the social, economic and environmental spheres. In fact, urban regeneration is finding an important space in national and regional legislation. At a central level, the Decree law 18 April 2019, no. 32, "Urgent provisions for the revitalization of the public contracts sector, for the acceleration of infrastructural interventions, urban regeneration and reconstruction following seismic events", set the Government's objective to reduce land take in favor of regeneration of the existing building stock by encouraging rationalisation, promoting and facilitating the redevelopment of degraded urban areas. For this reason the MECs of urban regeneration projects are more powerful than the MECs referred to new construction projects.

However, the urban complexity requires a representation of the territorial context, in order to guarantee the monitoring of the MECs. In fact, the assessment of compliance with the minimum environmental criteria requires to be correlated with the context in order to obtain a real containment of the effects on the environment [7, 42]. In particular, the analysis of the reference context and the basin of influence of urban projects also represents the challenge for regeneration projects [43], so much so that compliance with the minimum environmental criteria must therefore be associated with the context similarly to other tools such as the EIA, evaluation of environmental impact [44]. In this sense, this manuscript intends to provide a first contribution, which will be the subject of subsequent developments and applications to case studies to further test the proposed model.

Acknowledgment. This study was supported by Projects Ecosystem of Innovation for Next Generation Sardinia (e.INS) - approved by MUR, prot. n. 1056 of 23/06/2022; also, this publication was produced while attending the PhD programme in Civil Engineering and Architecture at the University of Cagliari, Cycle XXXVIII, with the support of a scholarship co-financed by the Ministerial Decree no. 352 of 9th April 2022, based on the NRRP - funded by the European Union - NextGenerationEU - Mission 4 "Education and Research", Component 2 "From Research to Business", Investment 3.3, and by the company MLab srl.

Author Contributions. Conceptualization, methodology, formal analysis, materials and resources, software, data curation and validation: all authors. In particular: Balletto wrote Sect. 1, Sect. 2; Sect. 2.2; Borruso and Sinatra wrote Sect. 2.1; Sinatra wrote Sect. 2.2, Sect. 3; Balletto and Sinatra wrote Sect. 4; Balletto and Borruso wrote Sect. 5.

References

1. Santus, K., Corradi, E., Lavagna, M., Valente, I.: Designing forms of regeneration. Spatial implication of strategies to face climate change at neighborhood scale. In: Calabrò, F., Della Spina, L., Piñeira Mantiñán, M.J. (eds.) NMP 2022, pp. 1621–1630. Springer, Cham (2022). https://doi.org/10.1007/978-3-031-06825-6_156
2. Weckroth, M., Ala-Mantila, S.: Socioeconomic geography of climate change views in Europe. Glob. Environ. Chang. **72**, 102453 (2022)

3. Pörtner, H.O., et al.: Climate change 2022: impacts, adaptation and vulnerability, p. 3056. IPCC, Geneva, Switzerland (2022)
4. Fantini, A.: Climate change impact on flood hazard over Italy (2019)
5. Yang, M., Wang, H., Yu, C.W., Cao, S.J.: A global challenge of accurately predicting building energy consumption under urban heat island effect. Indoor Built Environ. **32**(3), 455–459 (2023)
6. Huovila, A., et al.: Carbon-neutral cities: critical review of theory and practice. J. Cleaner Prod. 130912 (2022)
7. Balletto, G., Ladu, M., Camerin, F., Ghiani, E., Torriti, J.: More circular city in the energy and ecological transition: a methodological approach to sustainable urban regeneration. Sustainability **14**(22), 14995 (2022)
8. Grossi, G., Barontini, S., Berteni, F., Balistrocchi, M., Ranzi, R.: Nature-based solutions as climate change adaptation and mitigation measures in Italy. In: Climate Change-Sensitive Water Resources Management, pp. 90–100. CRC Press (2020)
9. Bassi, A., Ottone, C., Dell'Ovo, M.: Minimum environmental criteria in the architectural project. Trade-off between environmental, economic and social sustainability. Valori e Valutazioni (22) (2019)
10. Shang, S.: A multiple criteria decision-making approach to estimate minimum environmental flows based on wetted perimeter. River Res. Appl. **24**(1), 54–67 (2008)
11. Murgante, B., et al.: Health hazard scenarios in Italy after the COVID-19 outbreak: a methodological proposal. Scienze Regionali **20**(3), 327–354 (2021)
12. Balletto, G., Borruso, G., Donato, C.: City dashboards and the Achilles' heel of smart cities: putting governance in action and in space. In: Gervasi, O., et al. (eds.) ICCSA 2018. LNCS, vol. 10962, pp. 654–668. Springer, Cham (2018). https://doi.org/10.1007/978-3-319-95168-3_44
13. Howard, L.: The Climate of London: Deduced from Meteorological Observations, vol. 1. Cambridge University Press, Cambridge (2012)
14. Urso, G.: Metropolisation and the challenge of rural-urban dichotomies. Urban Geogr. **42**(1), 37–57 (2021)
15. Belay, T., Mengistu, D.A.: Impacts of land use/land cover and climate changes on soil erosion in Muga watershed, Upper Blue Nile basin (Abay), Ethiopia. Ecol. Process. **10**(1), 1–23 (2021)
16. Pamukcu-Albers, P., Ugolini, F., La Rosa, D., Grădinaru, S.R., Azevedo, J.C., Wu, J.: Building green infrastructure to enhance urban resilience to climate change and pandemics. Landscape Ecol. **36**(3), 665–673 (2021). https://doi.org/10.1007/s10980-021-01212-y
17. Olabi, A.G., Abdelkareem, M.A.: Renewable energy and climate change. Renew. Sustain. Energy Rev. **158**, 112111 (2022)
18. Manabe, S.: Role of greenhouse gas in climate change. Tellus A: Dyn. Meteorol. Oceanogr. **71**(1), 1620078 (2019)
19. Moya Ortiz, D.: Rethinking the metropolisation process in the global crisis. The Evolving Scholar (2021)
20. Balletto, G., Borruso, G., Donato, C.: City dashboards and the Achilles' heel of smart cities: putting governance in action and in space. In: Gervasi, O., Murgante, B., Misra, S., Stankova, E., Torre, C.M., Rocha, A.M.A.C., Taniar, D., Apduhan, B.O., Tarantino, E., Ryu, Y. (eds.) ICCSA 2018. LNCS, vol. 10962, pp. 654–668. Springer, Cham (2018). https://doi.org/10.1007/978-3-319-95168-3_44
21. Marando, F., et al.: Urban heat island mitigation by green infrastructure in European Functional Urban Areas. Sustain. Cities Soc. **77**, 103564 (2022)
22. Morabito, M., Crisci, A., Guerri, G., Messeri, A., Congedo, L., Munafò, M.: Surface urban heat islands in Italian metropolitan cities: tree cover and impervious surface influences. Sci. Total Environ. **751**, 142334 (2021)

23. Phelps, N.A.: The Urban Planning Imagination: A Critical International Introduction. Wiley, Hoboken (2021)
24. Balletto, G., Sinatra, M., Mura, R., Borruso, G.: Climate variation in metropolitan cities. TeMA-J. Land Use Mobility Environ. **15**(3), 501–516 (2022)
25. Profili delle città metropolitan. https://www.istat.it/it/files//2023/02/Statistica-Focus-Citt%C3%A0-Metropolitane.pdf. Accessed 16 Feb 2023
26. Dijkstra, L., Poelman, H., Veneri, P.: The EU-OECD definition of a functional urban area (2019)
27. Liu, J., Kang, J., Luo, T., Behm, H., Coppack, T.: Spatiotemporal variability of soundscapes in a multiple functional urban area. Landsc. Urban Plan. **115**, 1–9 (2013)
28. Kuik, O.J., Verbruggen, H. (eds.): In Search of Indicators of Sustainable Development, vol. 1. Springer, Dordrecht (2012). https://doi.org/10.1007/978-94-011-3246-6
29. Lowe, M., et al.: City planning policies to support health and sustainability: an international comparison of policy indicators for 25 cities. Lancet Global Health **10**(6), e882–e894 (2022)
30. Tobler, W.R.: A computer movie simulating urban growth in the Detroit Region. Econ. Geogr. **46**, 234–240 (1970)
31. Tobler, W.: On the first law of geography: a reply. Ann. Assoc. Am. Geogr. **94**(2), 304–310 (2004)
32. Sui, D.Z.: Tobler's first law of geography: a big idea for a small world? Ann. Assoc. Am. Geogr. **94**(2), 269–277 (2004)
33. Lee, J., Wong, D.W.S., David, W.S.: GIS and Statistical Analysis with ArcView. Wiley, Hoboken (2000)
34. Geary, R.C.: The contiguity ratio and statistical mapping. Incorporated Stat. **5**(3), 115–146 (1954)
35. Moran, P.A.P.: The interpretation of statistical maps. J. Roy. Stat. Soc. B **10**(2), 243–251 (1948)
36. Murgante, B., Borruso, G.: Analyzing migration phenomena with spatial autocorrelation techniques. In: Murgante, B., et al. (eds.) ICCSA 2012. LNCS, vol. 7334, pp. 670–685. Springer, Heidelberg (2012). https://doi.org/10.1007/978-3-642-31075-1_50
37. Anselin, L.: Spatial Econometrics: Methods and Models. Springer, Dordrecht (1988). https://doi.org/10.1007/978-94-015-7799-1
38. Anselin, L.: Local indicators of spatial association - LISA. Geogr. Anal. **27**(2), 93–115 (1995)
39. O'Sullivan, D., Unwin, D.J.: Geographic Information Analysis, 2nd edn. Wiley, Hoboken (2010)
40. European Data Journalism Network, Glocal Climate Change. https://climatechange.europeandatajournalism.eu/it/. Accessed 20 Mar 2023
41. ISTAT Homepage. http://dati.istat.it/. Accessed 31 Mar 2023
42. Balletto, G., Borruso, G., Mei, G., Milesi, A.: Strategic circular economy in construction: case study in Sardinia, Italy. J. Urban Plann. Dev. **147**(4), 05021034 (2021)
43. Renard, F., Alonso, L., Fitts, Y., Hadjiosif, A., Comby, J.: Evaluation of the effect of urban redevelopment on surface urban heat islands. Remote Sens. **11**(3), 299 (2019)
44. Fonseca, A., de Brito, L.L.A., Gibson, R.B.: Methodological pluralism in environmental impact prediction and significance evaluation: a case for standardization? Environ. Impact Assess. Rev. **80**, 106320 (2020)

A Conceptual Framework to Correlate the Electric Transition and Well-Being and Equity. The Italy Case

Ginevra Balletto[1]([✉]) [iD], Martina Sinatra[1] [iD], Alessandra Milesi[1], Emilio Ghiani[2] [iD], and Giuseppe Borruso[3] [iD]

[1] DICAAR – Department of Civil and Environmental Engineering and Architecture, University of Cagliari, Via Marengo 2, Cagliari, Italy
balletto@unica.it, m.sinatra@studenti.unica.it
[2] DIEE - Department of Electrical and Electronic Engineering, University of Cagliari, Via Marengo 2, Cagliari, Italy
emilio.ghiani@unica.it
[3] DEAMS - Department of Economics, Business, Mathematics and Statistics Sciences "Bruno de Finetti", University of Trieste, 34127 Trieste, Italy
giuseppe.borruso@deams.units.it

Abstract. The macroeconomic indicator of energy efficiency represents the energy performance in spatial terms (nation, region and macro-region) or the amount of energy used to produce a given unit of Gross Domestic Product. However, the electric transition draws attention to the need to pursue combined sustainable objectives, both economic and environmental-well-being.

Through the intermediate spatial dimension-metropolitan city/province, currently the most coherent to represent and support a just energy transition, in this paper it is intended to develop a methodological approach for the com-parative evaluation between electricity energy consumption and the recent equitable and sustainable well-being indicators (BES). In this framework, the objective of the work is the spatial representation of the electricity transition phenomenon in Italy. In particular, the spatial autocorrelation with an intermediate territorial basis in the pre and post-covid period (2017–2021) be-tween electricity consumption and a selected series of BES indicators to recognize spatial equity is investigated.

In order to present the usefulness and effectiveness of the proposed method-ology was applied to the case study covering the Italian territory.

Keywords: Electrical Transition · Metropolitan City Planning · Well-being and equity

1 Introduction

Electrical intensity (EI) was introduced in the economic and environmental literature in the 1970s and 1980s. It is a macroeconomic measure which expresses the quantity of electricity consumed by an economy of a given territory per unit of relative Gross

Domestic Product (GDP) [1, 2]. This measure is used to assess the energy efficiency of an economy, or the amount of energy used to produce a certain amount of goods and services, although some researchers remark that the direct relationship between electricity consumed and economic growth depends on the specific economic structure of Nations and/or Regions [3]. However, EI is an important indicator because it provides information on the energy consumption of a territorial economy. A lower electricity intensity indicates how the economy is becoming more energy efficient and seeks to reduce reliance on non-renewable energy sources. In contrast, an increase in electricity intensity could mean an increase in electricity demand and a greater dependence on non-renewable energy sources [4]. EI is used to track progress in reducing dependence on non-renewable energy sources, particularly in the urban 'smart city' model in line with the 2030 Agenda targets [5]. The complex literature shows how EI can be an indicator of progress in the energy sector, or as a basis for policies and plans to improve energy efficiency, but not for the purpose of reducing negative externalities resulting from increased energy consumption [6, 7] In this sense, the ongoing international electrical transition arises in response to the growing demand of energy. Addressing the complex environmental issue and decarbonization of energy systems requires replacing traditional nonrenewable energy sources (coal, oil, gas) with renewable sources (solar, wind, and hydro) and requires a renewed approach to the assessment of electricity consumption., introducing the BES (Equitable and Sustainable Well-being) indicators to facilitate a transition based on spatial justice [8–11].

The paper is organized as it follows: Sect. 2 Materials and Methods; Sect. 2.1 Equitable and sustainable well-being (BES): beyond the Gross Domestic Product (GDP); Sect. 2.2 Data; Sect. 2.3 Methodology: Local Indicators of Spatial Autocorrelation (LISA); Sect. 3 Case study; Sect. 4 Results and Discussion and Sect. 5 Conclusions and future development.

2 Material and Method

2.1 Equitable and Sustainable Well-Being (BES): Beyond the Gross Domestic Product (GDP)

For more than fifty years, there has been an international debate on the so-called "surpassing GDP" as the only measure of well-being. This is nourished by the consciousness that the parameters on which to evaluate the progress of a society [12] cannot be exclusively economic, but must also address the fundamental social and environmental dimensions of well-being, together with measures of inequality and sustainability [13–15]. In the international scenario, we underline the parameters used by the UN, the EU and the OECD. At national level, through an initiative between CNEL and ISTAT, the BES project has been underway, in order to provide an important contribution along these lines. Figure 1 shows the evolution of growth/development indicators.

The BES arose in 2010 to assess Equitable and Sustainable Well-being, with the purpose to evaluate the progress of society not only from the economic point of view, but also from the social and environmental side [16]. In particular, traditional economic indicators have been implemented by measures concerning people's quality of life and environmental issues. With the approval of the law n. 163/2016 on the National budget

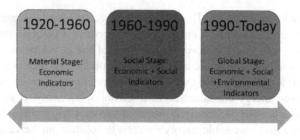

Fig. 1. History of growth/development indicators (Author: E. Ghiani, 2023)

reform, the first regulatory recognition of Equitable and Sustainable Well-being indicators has been achieved. These indicators have been included in the process of the Italian Government's economic planning documents. This innovation seeks to integrate economic measures in order to take account of other dimensions as society's overall well-being and environmental sustainability [17]. Recently, BES indicators have been linked to indicators for monitoring the 2030 Agenda for Sustainable Development targets (Sustainable Development Goals - SDGs - of United Nations), chosen by the global community under an international political agreement to represent their shared values, priorities and goals [18].

2.2 Data

Four indicators were selected (Table 1): two for the electric transition and two BES indicators characterizing the metropolitan urban dimension [19, 20].

The datasets were assembled considering two spatial dimensions, related to two different levels of administrative units in Italy. In particular, some of the data, and therefore the analysis that followed, were referred to Regions that hold an important role in local planning and policies. Other datasets were attributed to Provinces, Metropolitan Cities and Clusters of Municipalities. This latter level represents an intermediate one, between Regions and Municipalities, and allows to observe the territory from a metropolitan, urban and periurban perspective, providing a valid observation point for both the spatial national unbalances and to target ad hoc development policies.

The selected indicators and their sources are listed below.

2.3 Methodology: Local Indicators of Spatial Autocorrelation (LISA)

The energy-well being relation can be examined by means of spatial autocorrelation [21, 22]. Spatial autocorrelation, in particular, can be applied on data or indicators referred to a set of contiguous geographical units, as administrative units, and can be useful for evaluating local effects and clusters in terms of attribute and geographical data. Spatial proximity in fact can influence phenomena under a phenomenon called spatial autocorrelation. Data can be mutually influenced both in terms of the geographical shape and proximity, and in terms of the attribute values attributed to such units. As, Tobler highlighted [23] "nearby things are more related than distant things", apparently intuitive [23], although only recently rediscovered [24]. By analysing spatial autocorrelation it is

Table 1. Set of indicator, spatial dimension and source.

Indicator	Electric energy and BES	Year pre-post Covid	Dimension	Source of database
Electric Transition	Electric energy consumption	2017–2021	Region	Terna S.p.A https://bit.ly/ 3zcPVGR
	Electricity from renewable sources	2017–2021	Province/Metropolitan city	Terna S.p.A https://bit.ly/ 40C1MdA
Equitable and sustainable well-being (BES)	Employment rate (20–64 years old)	2017–2021	Region	ISTAT https://tab soft.co/3K7 wo0X
	Life expectancy at 65 years old	2017–2021	Province/Metropolitan city	BES Province https://bit.ly/ 3nm3Isf

possible to observe how a variable behaves with reference to its location in space and with reference to what happens in its proximity. Geographical elements can be described by two categories of information such as location and related properties. In particular, in analytical terms, spatial autocorrelation can be defined as follows [25]:

$$SAC = \frac{\sum_{i=1}^{N} \sum_{j=1}^{N} c_{ij} w_{ij}}{\sum_{i=1}^{N} \sum_{j=1}^{N} w_{ij}} \quad (1)$$

where:

- i and j are two objects or events in space;
- N is the number of objects or events;
- c_{ij} is a degree of similarity of attributes i and j;
- w_{ij} is a degree of similarity of location i and j;

From the general formula it is possible to derive two indices as the Geary C Ratio [26] and the Moran Index [27]. Defining x_i as the value of object i attribute; if $c_{ij} = (x_i - x_j)^2$, Geary C Ratio can be defined as follows:

$$C = \frac{(N-1)(\sum_i \sum_j w_{ij}(x_i - x_j)^2)}{2(\sum_i \sum_j w_{ij}) \sum_i (x_i - \underline{x})^2} \quad (2)$$

If $c_{ij} = (x_i - x)(x_j - x)$, Moran Index I can be defined as follows:

$$I = \frac{N \sum_i \sum_j w_{ij}(x_i - \underline{x})(x_j - \underline{x})}{\sum_i \sum_j w_{ij}(x_i - \underline{x})^2} \quad (3)$$

As recalled and applied recently in several Italian contexts [28], these indices are quite similar, differing by the cross-product term in the numerator, calculated using the deviations from the mean in Moran, while directly computed in Geary. Both indices lead a common message, as highlighting the presence - or absence - of spatial autocorrelation at a global level in the overall distribution, while the local presence of autocorrelation can be highlighted by the LISA (Local Indicators of Spatial Association), or, as after Anselin [29, 30], a local Moran index. This can be seen as the sum of all local indices and is proportional to the value of the Moran one:

$$\sum_i I_i = \gamma * I \tag{4}$$

The index is calculated as follows:

$$I_i = \frac{(X_i - X)}{S_X^2} \sum_{j=1}^{N} (w_{ij}(X_j - \underline{X})) \tag{5}$$

The index allows assessing for each location assess the similarity of each observation with its neighbors, and five combinations can be obtained from its application:

- hot spots: areas with high values of the phenomenon and a high level of similarity with its surroundings (high-high H-H);
- cold spots, as areas with low values of the phenomenon and a low level of similarity with its surroundings (low-low L-L);
- potentially spatial outliers, with high values of the phenomenon and a low level of similarity with its surroundings (high-low H-L);
- potentially spatial outliers, with low values of the phenomenon and a high level of similarity with its surroundings (low-high L-H);
- lack of significant autocorrelation. The interesting characteristic of LISA is in providing an effective measure of the degree of relative spatial association between each territorial unit and its neighboring elements, thereby highlighting the type of spatial concentration and clustering.

It is important to consider in the above-mentioned equations, the importance of weights, as parameters. The neighborhood property is analyzed by means of the parameter weight, w_{ij}, whose values indicate the presence, or absence, of neighboring spatial units to a given one. A spatial weight matrix is therefore needed, with w_{ij} assuming values of 0 in cases in which i and j are not neighbors, or 1 when i and j are neighbors. Neighborhood is computed in terms of contiguity such as, in the case of areal units, sharing a common border of non-zero length [31]. Rook or Queen contiguity are considered in the realization of the weight matrix.

3   Case Study

The study area chosen to show the effectiveness of the methodology is the Italian territory. Italy is a peninsula located in the southern part of the European continent. The climate is mostly temperate and characterized by dry and warm summers in coastal and southern areas, including islands. Instead, in the major mountain chains, like the Alps and Apennines, there is the prevalence of a cold climate (characterised by no dry season and no cold or hot summers). From west to east borders France, Switzerland, Austria, Slovenia and Croatia.

Italy has a surface area approximately of 302 072.84 km^2 with a population of 59 030 133 (ISTAT, 2022 [32]). From the administrative point of view it is organized in 20 Regions, split into 107 provinces (Fig. 2).

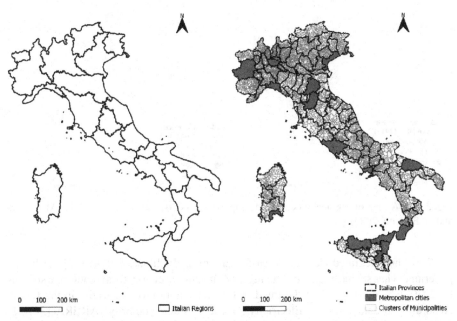

Fig. 2. Italy and its administrative units. Left: Regions; Right: Provinces, Metropolitan Cities, Clusters of Municipalities.

4 Result and Discussion

In this manuscript, the analysis was performed by considering a set of indicators (Table 1) assigned to each Italian Region and Province and their refer to the interval 2017–2021. These data were used as input to calculate LISA and, in particular, for local Moran's I. It is important to highlight that, in order to achieve spatial proximity for the application of the method, some simplifications have been adopted in the spatialization of islands (at regional level). On the one hand, Sicily has been united to Calabria to make it contiguous with Italian territory. On the other hand, Sardinia has been excluded and inserted after the elaborations, due to its distance from other Italian Regions.

The analysis was performed on regional data for the year 2017 and 2021, while on provincial data for 2021 only (the energy consumption indicator is also available for 2017). The application of the method to the set of indicators in the regional and/or provincial dimension yielded the following results (Figs. 5, 6, 7, 8, 9 and 10).

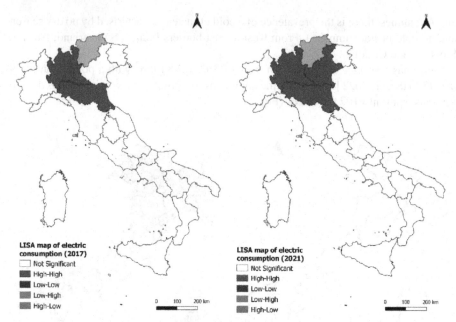

Fig. 3. LISA map of regional electric consumption, years 2017 and 2021 (Authors: M. Sinatra and G. Balletto, 2023).

With the Integrated National Plan for Energy and Climate (2019) [33] the Italian government has set the goal of producing 30% of national energy from renewable sources by 2030, which could affect the trend in the consumption of electricity in the future. According to data from the Electricity, Gas and Water Authority (ARERA [34]), in 2022 electricity consumption in Italy was around 295 TWh, down 3.1% compared to the previous year due to the COVID-19 pandemic and associated restrictions.

Furthermore, electricity consumption in Italy is influenced by various factors, including the physical-geographical conformation with different meteorological conditions, as well as the organization-distribution of economic-productive activities. The LISA elaborations based on the regional and provincial dimension (Fig. 3 and Fig. 4) confirm that Northern Italy is characterized by a high auto-correlation of electricity consumption. In particular, Fig. 3 (2017–2021) shows how the regions with high-high autocorrelation of electricity consumption are located in northern Italy (Lombardy, Emilia-Romagna and Veneto) and are characterized by a climate with more extreme temperatures in winter and summer, but above all they are characterized by a high gross domestic product (Table 2).

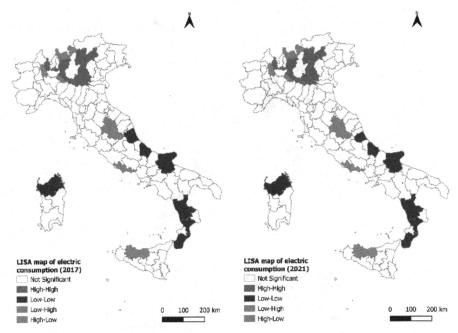

Fig. 4. LISA map of provincial electric consumption, years 2017 and 2021 (Authors: M. Sinatra and G. Balletto, 2023).

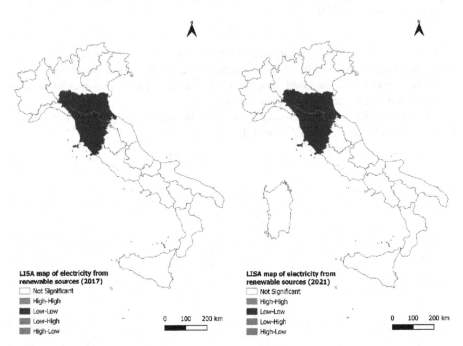

Fig. 5. LISA map of regional electricity from renewable sources, years 2017 and 2021 (Authors: M. Sinatra and G. Balletto, 2023).

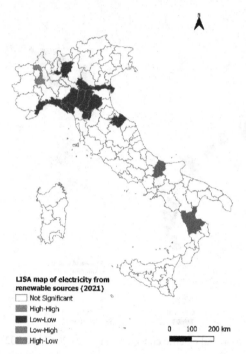

Fig. 6. LISA map of provincial electricity from renewable sources, years 2021 (Authors: M. Sinatra and G. Balletto, 2023).

Figure 4 shows a high-high autocorrelation which respectively affects the Provinces of Bergamo, Cremona, Mantua, Monza, Trento, Varese and Verona, distributed on the border between the regions: Lombardy, Emilia-Romagna and Veneto, also characterized by significant investments also in cohesion policies [35].

The amount of electricity deriving from renewable sources for provinces with high-high auto-correlation is shown below (Table 3).

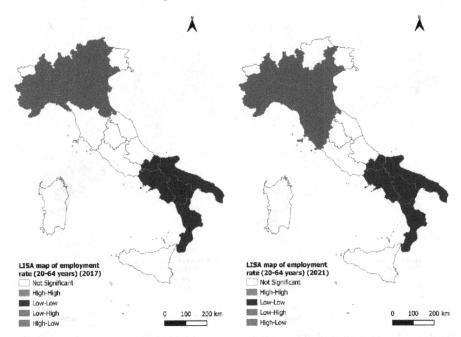

Fig. 7. LISA map of regional employment rate (20–64 years), years 2017 and 2021 (Authors: M. Sinatra and G. Balletto, 2023).

Fig. 8. LISA map of provincial employment rate (20–64 years), year 2021 (Authors: M. Sinatra and G. Balletto, 2023).

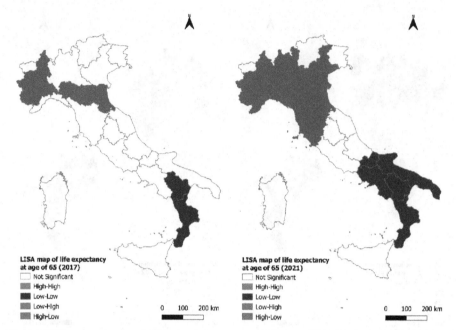

Fig. 9. LISA map of regional life expectancy at age of 65, year 2021 (Authors: M. Sinatra and G. Balletto, 2023).

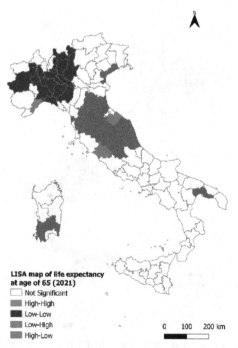

Fig. 10. LISA map of provincial life expectancy at age of 65, year 2021 (Authors: M. Sinatra and G. Balletto, 2023).

Table 2. Regional GDP (2020) and electricity from renewable sources (2021) of Lombardy, Emilia-Romagna e Veneto. (Author: G. Balletto, 2023 from https://ec.europa.eu/eurostat/cache/digpub/regions/#gross-domestic-product and https://bit.ly/40C1MdA)

Region	GDP Gross Domestic Product, 2020 (Purchasing Power Standards per inhabitants)	Share National GDP, 2020 (%)	Electricity from renewable sources, 2021 (%)
Lombardy	37 700	22.5	27.3
Emilia Romagna	34 500	9.1	22.1
Veneto	31 600	9.2	29.3

Table 3. Provincial electricity from renewable sources (2021) of Bergamo, Cremona, Mantova, Monza, Trento, Varese and Verona.

Province	Electricity from renewable sources, 2021 (%)
Bergamo	19.4
Cremona	23.9
Mantova	20.3
Monza	26.9
Trento	109.1
Varese	37.2
Verona	23.6

5 Conclusion and Future Development

The scientific debate focuses on whether anthropogenic emissions of greenhouse gases into the atmosphere are the main cause of complex global climate change, with the average temperature 1.02 degrees higher than in the 1950–1980 period [36]. The main one of these gases is carbon dioxide, which is largely derived from the fossil fuel energy sector. To achieve the so-called Carbon Neutrality by 2050, the main tool is represented by the energy transition, with the transition from an energy mix centered on fossil fuels to one with low or zero carbon emissions, based on renewable sources. A great contribution to decarbonization will come from the electrification of consumption, replacing the electricity produced from fossil sources with that generated from renewable sources, which also makes other sectors cleaner, such as transport, and from the digitalization of networks, which improves energy efficiency.

The energy transition, however, is not limited to the progressive shutting down of coal-fired plants and the development of clean energies: it is a paradigm shift of the entire structure of energy production and utilization, i.e. a transition based on spatial equity [37], with benefits not only for the climate but also for the economy and communities.

Acknowledgment. This study was supported by Projects Ecosystem of Innovation for Next Generation Sardinia (e.INS) - approved by MUR, prot. n. 1056 of 23/06/2022; also, this publication was produced while attending the PhD programme in Civil Engineering and Architecture at the University of Cagliari, Cycle XXXVIII, with the support of a scholarship co-financed by the Ministerial Decree no. 352 of 9th April 2022, based on the NRRP - funded by the European Union - NextGenerationEU - Mission 4 "Education and Research", Component 2 "From Research to Business", Investment 3.3, and by the company MLab srl.

Author Contributions. Conceptualization, methodology, formal analysis, materials and resources, software and data curation: Balletto, Borruso and Sinatra. Validation: all authors. In particular: Balletto wrote Sect. 1, Sect. 2; Balletto, Sinatra and Ghiani wrote Sect. 2.1; Borruso and Sinatra wrote Sect. 2.2 and Sect. 5; Sinatra and Milesi wrote Sect. 3; Balletto and Borruso Sect. 6.

References

1. Fuinhas, J.A., Marques, A.C.: Energy consumption and economic growth nexus in Portugal, Italy, Greece, Spain and Turkey: an ARDL bounds test approach (1965–2009). Energy Econ. **34**, 511–517 (2012)
2. Stamatiou, P.: Modeling electricity consumption for growth in an open economy. Int. J. Energy Econ. Policy (2022)
3. Mohanty, A., Chaturvedi, D.: Relationship between electricity energy consumption and GDP: evidence from India. Int. J. Econ. Financ. **7**(2), 186–202 (2015)
4. Canova, A., Lazzeroni, P., Lorenti, G., Moraglio, F., Porcelli, A., Repetto, M.: Decarbonizing residential energy consumption under the Italian collective self-consumption regulation. Sustain. Cities Soc. **87**, 104196 (2022)
5. Dos Santos, H.T.M., Balestieri, J.A.P.: Spatial analysis of sustainable development goals: a correlation between socioeconomic variables and electricity use. Renew. Sustain. Energy Rev. **97**, 367–376 (2018)
6. Energy Efficiency and Economic Growth" di Richard G. Newell e Daniel L. Kammen (2002), "Energy Efficiency and the Environment" di Thomas F. Rutherford e Richard G. Newell (2010), "Energy Intensity and Economic Development: A Reassessment" di David G. Tawil e David I. Stern (1994), "Energy Efficiency and Climate Change" di Michael P. Toman (2007), "Energy Efficiency and Renewable Energy" di James E. Hansen (2011), "Energy Efficiency Policies" di John A. Riggs e Karen Palmer (2012), "Energy Efficiency and Energy Security" di Richard G. Newell e Daniel L. Kammen (2009)
7. Ozturk, I., Acaravci, A.: The causal relationship between energy consumption and GDP in Albania, Bulgaria, Hungary and Romania: evidence from ARDL bound testing approach. Appl. Energy **87**(19), 38–43 (2010)
8. Ghisellini, P., Passaro, R., Ulgiati, S.: Environmental assessment of multiple "cleaner electricity mix" scenarios within just energy and circular economy transitions, in Italy and Europe. J. Cleaner Prod. 135891 (2023)
9. Wahlund, M., Palm, J.: The role of energy democracy and energy citizenship for participatory energy transitions: a comprehensive review. Energy Res. Soc. Sci. **87**, 102482 (2022)

10. Balletto, G., Ladu, M., Camerin, F., Ghiani, E., Torriti, J.: More circular city in the energy and ecological transition: a methodological approach to sustainable urban regeneration. Sustainability **14**(22), 14995 (2022)

11. Balletto, G., Borruso, G., Murgante, B., Milesi, A., Ladu, M.: Resistance and resilience. A methodological approach for cities and territories in Italy. In: Gervasi, O., et al. (eds.) ICCSA 2021. LNCS, vol. 12952, pp. 218–229. Springer, Cham (2021). https://doi.org/10.1007/978-3-030-86973-1_15

12. Balletto, G., et al.: Sport-city planning. a proposal for an index to support decision-making practice: principles and strategies. In: Gervasi, O., et al. (eds.) ICCSA 2021. LNCS, vol. 12952, pp. 255–269. Springer, Cham (2021). https://doi.org/10.1007/978-3-030-86973-1_18

13. Giannetti, B.F., Agostinho, F., Almeida, C.M.V.B., Huisingh, D.: A review of limitations of GDP and alternative indices to monitor human wellbeing and to manage eco-system functionality. J. Clean. Prod. **87**, 11–25 (2015)

14. Hall, C.A.: The 50th anniversary of the limits to growth: does it have relevance for today's energy issues? Energies **15**(14), 4953 (2022)

15. Murgante, B., et al.: Health hazard scenarios in Italy after the COVID-19 outbreak: a methodological proposal. Scienze Regionali **20**(3), 327–354 (2021)

16. La Torre, M., Salazar Zapata, J.D., Semplici, L.: Un modello di impact finance per i Comuni: il piano strategico di mandato BES-oriented, pp. 143–170 (2020)

17. INAPP Homepage. https://oa.inapp.org/handle/20.500.12916/3558. Accessed 15 Mar 2023

18. Tebala, D., Marino, D.: A synthetic indicator BES-SDGs to describe Italian well-being. In: Bevilacqua, C., Calabrò, F., Della Spina, L. (eds.) NMP 2020. SIST, vol. 178, pp. 1862–1871. Springer, Cham (2021). https://doi.org/10.1007/978-3-030-48279-4_176

19. Leogrande, A.: Healthy Life Expectancy at Birth in the Italian Regions (2022)

20. Qualità della vita. https://lab24.ilsole24ore.com/qualita-della-vita/tabelle/2021/speranza-di-vita-alla-nascita. Accessed 08 Mar 2023

21. Ceci, M., Corizzo, R., Malerba, D., Rashkovska, A.: Spatial autocorrelation and entropy for renewable energy forecasting. Data Min. Knowl. Disc. **33**(3), 698–729 (2019). https://doi.org/10.1007/s10618-018-0605-7

22. Wang, S., Luo, K.: Life expectancy impacts due to heating energy utilization in China: distribution, relations, and policy implications. Sci. Total Environ. **610**, 1047–1056 (2018)

23. Tobler, W.R.: A Computer Movie Simulating Urban Growth in the Detroit Region. Econ. Geogr. **46**, 234 (1970)

24. Sui, D.Z.: Tobler's first law of geography: a big idea for a small world? Geographers **94**(2), 269–277 (2004)

25. Lee, J., Wong, D.W.S., David, W.S.: IS and Statistical Analysis with ArcView. Wiley, Hoboken (2000)

26. Geary, R.C.: The contiguity ratio and statistical mapping. Incorporated Stat. **5**(3), 115–146 (1954)

27. Moran, P.A.P.: The interpretation of statistical maps. J. Roy. Stat. Soc. B **10**(2), 243–251 (1948)

28. Murgante, B., Borruso, G.: Analyzing migration phenomena with spatial autocorrelation techniques. In: Murgante, B., et al. (eds.) ICCSA 2012. LNCS, vol. 7334, pp. 670–685. Springer, Heidelberg (2012). https://doi.org/10.1007/978-3-642-31075-1_50

29. Anselin, L.: Spatial Econometrics: Methods and Models. Springer, Dordrecht (1988). https://doi.org/10.1007/978-94-015-7799-1

30. Anselin, L.: Local indicators of spatial association – LISA. Geogr. Anal. **27**(2), 93–115 (1995)

31. O'Sullivan, D., Unwin, D.J.: Geographic Information Analysis, 2nd edn. Wiley, Hoboken (2010)

32. ISTAT Homepahe. http://dati.istat.it/. Accessed 31 Mar 2023

33. Piano nazionale integrato per l'energia e il clima, https://www.mise.gov.it/images/stories/doc umenti/PNIEC_finale_17012020.pdf. Accessed 22 Mar 2023
34. ARERA Homepage. https://www.arera.it/it/index.htm. Accessed 15 Apr 2023
35. Balletto, G., Mundula, L., Milesi, A., Ladu, M.: Cohesion policies in Italian metropolitan cities. Evaluation and challenges. In: Gervasi, O., et al. (eds.) ICCSA 2020. LNCS, vol. 12255, pp. 441–455. Springer, Cham (2020). https://doi.org/10.1007/978-3-030-58820-5_33
36. Glocal climate change Homepage. https://climatechange.europeandatajournalism.eu/it/map. Accessed 02 Mar 2023
37. Yenneti, K., Day, R., Golubchikov, O.: Spatial justice and the land politics of renewables: dispossessing vulnerable communities through solar energy mega-projects. Geoforum **76**, 90–99 (2016)

3rd Workshop on Privacy in the Cloud/Edge/IoT World (PCEIoT 2023)

FPGA-Enabled Efficient Framework for High-Performance Intrusion Prevention Systems

Cuong Pham-Quoc[1,2]([⊠]) [iD] and Tran Ngoc Thinh[1,2]

[1] Ho Chi Minh City University of Technology (HCMUT),
268 Ly Thuong Kiet Street, District 10, Ho Chi Minh City, Viet Nam
cuongpham@hcmut.edu.vn
[2] Vietnam National University - Ho Chi Minh City (VNU-HCM),
Thu Duc, Ho Chi Minh City, Vietnam

Abstract. With the rapid increase of network-based services during and after the COVID-19 pandemic, preventing network attacks is an essential demand. This paper proposes an efficient FPGA-based framework for developing high-performance intrusion prevention systems. The framework allows both signature/pattern-based and anomaly/AI-based prevention techniques to be deployed. We implement the framework with two efficient FPGA-based network processing platforms, NetFPGA-10G and NetFPGA-SUME, for evaluating the proposed framework. Three signature-based approaches, SYN flood defender, hop count filtering, and port ingress/egress filtering, are applied to the framework with the NetFPGA board. Meanwhile, five different neural network models are deployed with both platforms. Three well-known datasets, NSL-KDD, UNSW-NB15, and CIC-IDS2017, are used for training and testing these models. Experimental results show that we achieve a throughput of up to 39.48 Gbps with the signature-based techniques. Our framework can obtain a throughput of up to 34.74 Gbps for the neural network models. Our network intrusion prevention systems can offer up to 99.48% accuracy with only a 0.05% false positive rate and a 0.99% false negative rate in the best case.

Keywords: FPGA · Network intrusion prevention · Anomaly-based detection · signature-based detection

1 Introduction

The development of internet devices has been exponential in recent years, with a range of smart gadgets and wearable technologies flooding the market. According to a report by Statista [30], the number of internet-connected devices is expected to reach 75 billion by 2025, most of which are smartphones, tablets, and other portable devices. The proliferation of such devices has increased demand for high-speed internet connectivity, resulting in the rapid deployment of 5G networks worldwide.

O. Gervasi et al. (Eds.): ICCSA 2023 Workshops, LNCS 14109, pp. 83–98, 2023.
https://doi.org/10.1007/978-3-031-37120-2_6

As technology and network architectures continue to develop rapidly, cyber-security has become a crucial concern for organizations such as businesses, banks, and military networks. For example, a report by Microsoft reveals that, on average, 1,435 attacks per day are taken into account at the organization in 2022 [32]. Furthermore, the security today report shows that in 2022, compared to 2021, in total 150% DDoS attacks are increased [28]. These intrusion threats can have severe consequences, including financial losses, reputational damage, and legal liabilities. Therefore, developing an efficient framework for creating high-performance network intrusion prevention systems (NIPS) to countermeasure these attacks is essential.

In modern NIPS, two primary approaches have been mainly utilized: pattern-based (signature-based) [20] and anomaly-based [11]. The former method compares network packets with predefined patterns/signatures to detect harmful packets. The latter technique uses AI models to classify packet behaviors and recognize illegitimate flows. While pattern-based NIPS methods are known for their high accuracy rates and throughput, they suffer from inflexibility, the overhead for processing rules, and the need for data storage to store attacking rules [3]. This issue becomes even more problematic when the number of stored patterns is significant and frequently updated. Meanwhile, deep learning has made impressive strides in recent years, and the anomaly-based approach, which relies on deep neural networks (DNN), offers several advantages over the signature-based method. For example, it can efficiently prevent unknown attack types and does not require extensive storage resources [12].

In this work, by taking advantages of the Field Programmable Gate Array (FPGA) technology [8] such as reconfigurability and high parallelism, by a massive amount of resources into account, we design an FPGA-based efficient framework to deploy different IPS techniques from both the above approaches to build high-performance network intrusion prevention systems. The framework allows network administrators to configure the NIPS with hardware computing cores with signature-based or neural network models. The number of cores and types (signature-based or neural networks) depends on the hardware resources available and the system's sensitivity. We implement our prototype system with a NetFPGA 10G board (equipped with a Virtex 5 FPGA device) and a NetF-PGA SUME board (equipped with a Virtex 7 FPGA device). Various techniques, including signature-based hardware cores and AI-based models, have been deployed into the prototype system to evaluate the throughput and accuracy.

The main contributions of our paper can be summarized in three folds.

1. We propose an efficient FPGA-based framework for deploying high performance intrusion prevention systems with signature- and anomaly-based approaches.
2. We present our FPGA-based system implementation for developing different intrusion prevention techniques.
3. We show our experiments with various prevention approaches using the system. Our experimental results can be used for future studies as a reference.

The rest of the paper is organized as follows. Section 2 presents the background of intrusion prevention systems and related work in the literature. We introduce our proposed FPGA-enabled framework in Sect. 3. Section 4 shows the FPGA-based system implementation so that various intrusion prevention techniques can be deployed. Experiments with some approaches, both signature-based and anomaly-based, are discussed in Sect. 5. Finally, Sect. 6 concludes our paper.

2   Background and Related Work

This section presents the background of network intrusion detection/prevention systems (NIDS/NIPS). We also summarize related work of FPGA-based NIDS/NIPS in the literature.

2.1   Background

In this section, we present at first an overview of network intrusion detection/prevention systems, followed by the datasets most used for training and testing these systems.

Network Intrusion Detection/prevention Systems (NIDS/NIPS): are used to detect/react to potential threats on a network by analyzing network traffic and packet behaviors [15]. These systems can respond to threats by either alerting administrators (detection) or blocking network access (prevention). There are two main types of detection/prevention: signature-based and anomaly-based. Signature-based NIDS uses previous knowledge or abnormal behaviors to detect/prevent threats (so-called knowledge-based approaches). In contrast, anomaly-based NIDS uses normal activities as a reference point for identifying/reacting to abnormal behaviors. Recently, many studies have applied machine learning/deep learning for anomaly detection. This can help NIDS adapt quickly to changing environments and identify anomalous intrusions by training machine learning models on normal network activities. However, anomaly-based detection may result in more false positives, generating many alarms in the monitoring system. Nevertheless, this issue is not a concern for protected systems as these alerts do not indicate actual attacks. In contrast, although signature-based techniques suffer from overhead for data storing and low ability to adapt to new attacking types, they offer high throughput and accuracy compared to the anomaly-based approach.

Dataset: Both the approaches for NIDS/NIPS require datasets for building or training and testing to validate the scanning cores. As reported in [2], three most frequently used datasets in the literature are KDD Cup99 & NSL-KDD (60%), UNSW-NB15 (18%), CIC-IDS2017 (12%)in which:

- KDD Cup99 [10] is one of the most well-known and widely used datasets for NIDS/NIPS. The dataset contains about 5M+ and 2M+ records for training and testing purposes, respectively. Each record consists of 41 features labeled as usual or attack. Four attacking types, DoS (Denial of Services), Probe, R2L (Remote to Local), and U2R (User to Root), can be detected with this dataset. Consequently, NSL-KDD [31] is an enhanced version of the KDD Cup99 dataset to overcome the integral issues.
- UNSW-NB15 [22] contains 2M+ records with 49 features per record. The dataset covers nine attacking types: Worms, Shellcode, Reconnaissance, Port Scans, Generic, Backdoor, DoS, Exploits, and Fuzzers.
- CIC-IDS2017 [1] includes normal flows and attacks collected from the real world with common attacking types such as DDoS, Botnet, Brute Force Attack, etc.

In this work, we use three latter datasets for testing our prototype because NSL-KDD already covers KDD Cup99. Along with these two popular datasets, we also use our in-house building dataset collected from our organization network to test the signature-based scanning cores.

2.2 Related Work

In recent years, many studies have focused on building NIDS/NIPS on FPGAs to exploit the parallelism and reconfigurability of this technology. However, they all propose implementing a standalone, signature-based, or anomaly-based approach. Compared to these proposals in the literature, our framework supports both signature- and anomaly-based strategies to be implemented on the FPGA devices. Furthermore, thanks to the reconfigurability, our NIPS system can be switched among different techniques/models based on the two primary approaches. The following summary review FPGA-based NIDS/NIPS published in the literature during the past five years.

FPGA-Based Signature-Based: The work in [35] proposed IDS/IPS Pigasus in which FPGA performs most execution of NIDS to protect a network of 100 Gbps. An FPGA and rule-based NIDS was introduced in [19] with 256 entries. The packet processing latency of this work is only $0.032\,\mu s$. The RegEx matching and NFA (Non-deterministic Finite Automata) were used for building a NIDS [7] and its updated version [6] to offer a Snort rule FPGA-based NIDS with 100 Gbps and 400 Gbps, respectively. Research in [33] used UltraRAMs and rolling hash functions for implementing an FPGA-based intrusion detection with a significant performance improvement. FPGA/Bloom filter-empowered IDS was introduced in [27] with many of Bloom filter's disadvantages removed. The Cuckoo filters and FPGA were used for developing an IDS with improved performance was discussed in [16].

FPGA-Based Anomaly-Based: The k_modes, a modified version of k_mean, was proposed in [21] using the NSL-KDD. Research in [14] used KNN (K-Nearest Neighbours) with a custom dataset to design an FPGA-based NIDS that offers 95% accuracy with 3.913 ms latency. Accepting the low accuracy with BNN (Binary Neural Network), researchers in [23] presented a NIDS system of 90.74% accuracy with only 19.6 ns latency. The same authors continued improving their BNN-based NIDS and reported in [24] with 38.1% higher accuracy than their previous work. Study in [18] implemented an FPGA-based NIDS with runtime updating coefficients. The implementation with Zynq FPGA offered an accuracy of 80.52% with 9.02 ms latency.

3   The FPGA-Enabled Framework

Figure 1 presents our proposed efficient framework for building high-performance network intrusion prevention systems on FPGA. As shown in the figure, the proposed framework consists of three different layers, *Application & Administrator, Communication layer*, and *FPGA-based NIPS*, hosted by both software (CPU or GPU) and hardware (FPGA). The software part mainly manages the entire system by generating anomaly-based models or building signature-based hardware cores to configure the FPGA-based NIPS on-the-fly. Meanwhile, the hardware part performs the main functionalities of the NIPS by executing the neuron network models and hardware computing cores for anomaly-based and signature-based prevention, respectively.

3.1   Application and Administrator Layer

As mentioned above, the primary purpose of this layer, deployed at the software level (CPU or GPU), is to manage the entire system. The layer contains two main components, the visualization report and the FPGA-based computing cores for both neuron networks and signature-based cores. Through the visualization reports, system administrators can recognize attack types and sizes that the system has been preventing currently and in the past. Based on statistical data, administrators can determine which types of prevention (for example, DDoS or virus/malware) should be deployed.

Along with these reports, the layer takes certified datasets into account the generate FPGA-based computing cores for prevention attacks. Furthermore, the layer can generate trained AI neuron network models with different toolchains (such as Tensorflow or Kaffe) for anomaly-based prevention. The trained neuron networks will then be manually implemented by hardware description languages (such as Verilog, VHDL, or SystemVerilog) or high-level synthesis tools (such as Vitis from Xilinx or Stratus HLS from Cadence). Finally, the computing cores are synthesized for programming the FPGA board with the support of the design tools provided by target FPGA device vendors. The output of this layer will be used to configure the system through the communication layer.

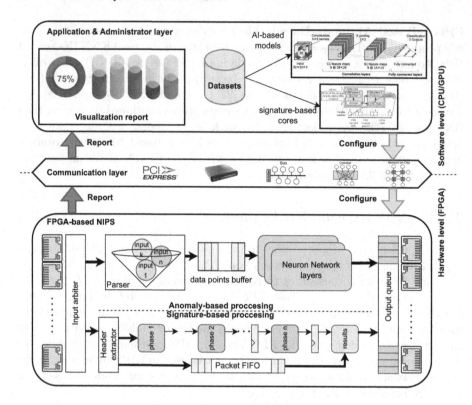

Fig. 1. The FPGA-enabled framework for high-performance NIPS

3.2   Communication Layer

The communication layer is the interface between software and hardware. This layer transfers configuration data (parameters of AI neuron network models and programming files for reconfiguring the FPGA boards). Based on the deployment platforms, the communication layer can be PCI-express, giga-speed switch, high-performance bus, crossbar, or network-on-chip. This layer is mainly responsible for communication overhead that affects the system's downtime (handling for reconfiguration). Therefore, high bandwidth communication infrastructure should be used for the system.

3.3   FPGA-Based NIPS

The FPGA-based NIPS layer is the central part and one of the main contributions of our work. FPGA-enabled NIPS hosts various FPGA-based processing cores to implement the anomaly-based or signature-based prevention approaches[1]. Our NIPS includes high-speed input/output network ports for

---

[1] We call them scanning cores when we do not distinguish them.

incoming network packets receiving and legitimated packets sending. Input packets from ports are pre-processed by the *Input arbiter*. Depending on predefined behaviors, the Input arbiter selects packets coming from a particular port to send to processing cores (by anomaly/signature-based processing) or forward directly to outputs without scanning. This behavior can be reconfigured by administrators because there may exist some ports connected to truth sources.

In contrast to the input, the output queue stores packets waiting for decisions of the scanning cores. Based on classifications from deployed scanning cores, packets in this queue will be forwarded to a desired output port if they are legitimated or removed from the queue to protect the internal systems if they are classified as attacks. The heart of the system is the scanning cores which can be deployed with the anomaly-based approach or a particular technique using the signature-based method to classify packets.

Anomaly-Based: As introduced above, the anomaly-based approach uses neural network models to classify packets as normal or abnormal. Network packets, at first, are analyzed to extract feature vectors for neural networks by the *Parser* module. Next, these input features for AI models are stored in the *data points buffer* to support high-speed incoming network flows. Finally, layers of neurons collect data from the buffer to classify network packets as normal or abnormal. The datasets and models determine the number of layers and neurons per layer.

Signature-Based: Different from the anomaly-based, the signature-based approach implements particular prevention techniques to investigate network packets, such as Hop-count filtering or SYN Flood Defender. Therefore, the architecture of the signature-based scanning cores relies on the selected methods. In general, we need a *Header extractor* to collect features from the header field of packets and send them to computing blocks of the cores. The blocks are usually designed and implemented in the pipeline to improve performance.

To cope with high-speed network packet arriving, signature-based scanning cores are equipped with *packet FIFOs* waiting for decisions. First, a legitimate packet is transferred to the *Output queue* to forward to target ports. Otherwise, it will be removed from the FIFO to protect the local network resources.

4   The FPGA System Implementation

In this section, we present our prototype implementation with two target platforms, NetFPGA-10G and NetFPGA-SUME.

4.1   Signature-Based Techniques

For our implementation to test the proposed framework, we use three prevention techniques, including SYN defender [13], hop-count filtering [34], and port ingress/egress filtering [29]. Figure 2 depicts the implementation architectures for the three signature-based prevention techniques.

As shown in the figure, a table of known data is embedded into each architecture. Then, based on analysis information of incoming packets, the *results* block checks the table to determine whether the packet should be dropped due to its harmfulness or forwarded to destinations. We implement these architectures by Verilog-HDL for building on the two above-mentioned FPGA target platforms.

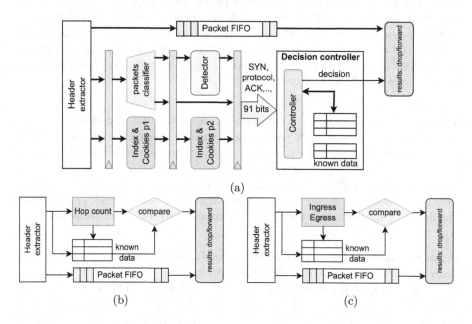

Fig. 2. The implementation architectures for three signature-based prevention techniques: (a) SYN flood, (b) hop-count, (c) port ingress/egress filter.

4.2   Neural Networks

Figure 3 presents our implementation architecture to build an FPGA-based neural network layer. A chain of multiplication and addition blocks are used for calculating a neuron's operations ($y = \sum_{i=1}^{n}(x_i \times w_i) + b$), where x, w, and b are feature vector, weight vector, and bias, respectively. In this work, we apply Nordstroem and Svensson's activation function [26] (depicted in Eq. 1) due to its hardware efficiency.

$$f(x) = \frac{x + |x| + 1}{2(|x| + 1)} \qquad (1)$$

Like the signature-based techniques above, we use Verilog-HDL to describe an FPGA-based IP core for neural network layers. Using the *parameter* directive, we can effectively change the number of elements in input vectors and neurons per layer before synthesizing and programming the platforms. Depending on deployment models, neural network layer cores are connected in cascade form.

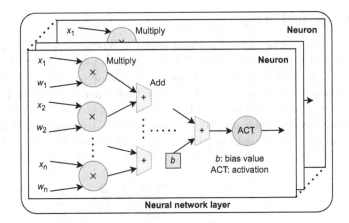

Fig. 3. The implementation architecture a for neural network layer

4.3   Target Platforms

In this work, we use two FPGA platforms dedicated to network processing for building our prototype implementation. The first is the NetFPGA-10G [25] which includes an xc5vtx240t Xilinx FPGA device (149,760 LUTs, 96 DSP48s, 11,664 Kbit block RAM, and 27 MBytes external SDRAM) and 4 SFP+ connections supporting 10 Gbps per port. For our prototype version, we build the three above-mentioned signature-based prevention techniques (SYN flood, hop-count filtering, and port ingress/egress filtering) and three neural network models $(10 \times 1, 10 \times 2 \times 1,$ and $10 \times 4 \times 1)$. The three neural network models are trained and tested with the NSL-KDD dataset.

The second platform for testing the proposed framework is NetFPGA-SUME [9], an updated version of NetFPGA-10G [36]. The platform is equipped with the Xilinx Virtex-7 xc7vx690T-2FFG1761C (433,200 LUTs, 3600 DSPs, 52,920 Kbit block RAM, and three x36 72Mbits QDR II SRAM) and 4 SFP+ interface supporting 10 Gbps per port like the NetFPGA-10G. Due to the massive available resources compared to the NetFPGA-10G platform, we build a neural network model of $40 \times 31 \times 1$ trained and tested by both UNSW-NB15 and CIC-IDS2017 datasets. In addition, we also apply the Autoencoder model with neural networks of $122 \times 64 \times 122$ trained and tested with the NSL-KDD dataset for this platform.

5   Experiments

In this section, we present our experiments to validate and estimate the acceleration ability of the above system. At first, the experimental setup is introduced.

Then, we summarize the results with our experiments to illustrate the goals of our work.

5.1 Experimental Setup

To verify the two platforms implemented with our NIPS, we build the following testing models: (i) we use two NetFPGA boards, for our system and the OSNT (Open Source Network Tester) generator [5] tool as depicted in Fig. 4a to estimate throughput. The board with the OSTN tool generates and sends packets at the maximum bandwidth to our NIPS. (ii) we use two NetFPGA boards and a traditional computer with a gigabit network card to test our neural networks' accuracy and signature-based techniques. Figure 4b shows this testing model.

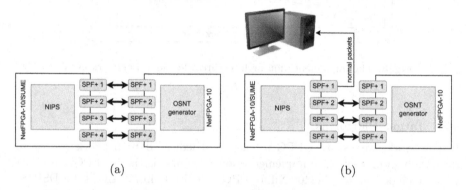

(a)   (b)

Fig. 4. Testbed used for our NIPS: (a) throughput and latency evaluation; (b) accuracy evaluation

5.2 Synthesis Results

Our proposed framework with the aforementioned prevention approaches for the two target FPGA platforms is synthesized with Xilinx Vivado 2022.1 [4]. Table 1 shows the hardware resources usage for our framework with the two target platforms.

The table shows that the system implemented on the NetFPGA-10G platforms with the three signature-based approaches, SYN defender, hop-count, and port ingress/egress filtering, requires almost all on-chip memory (blockRAM) for storing known patterns. Due to the substantial amount of resources used, the working frequency of the system with the three prevention techniques is only 89.254 MHz, the worst compared to other experiments. When neural networks are used on the NetFPGA-board, the system uses less BlockRAM than before. As shown in the table, the number of LUTs, FFs, and DSP48 increases according to the neural network size.

Table 1. Synthesis results for our prototype implementation with both target platforms

Resources	NetFPGA-10G				NetFPGA-SUME	
	Signature	$10 \times 0 \times 1$	$10 \times 2 \times 1$	$10 \times 4 \times 1$	Autoencoder	$40 \times 32 \times 1$
FF	107,275	77,869	95,261	122,085	131,341	131,592
	71.63%	52.00%	63.61%	81.52%	15.61%	15.19%
LUT	96,767	65,621	78,883	99,890	90,869	92,661
	64.61%	43.82%	52.67%	66.70%	20.97%	21.39%
DSP48	0	11	25	49	245	132
	0.00%	11.46%	26.04%	51.04%	6.81%	3.67%
BlockRAM	323	139	139	140	285.5	214.5
	99.69%	42.90%	42.90%	43.21%	19.43%	14.59%
Freq. (MHz)	89.254	102.218	100.644	100.532	206.7	204.2
Power (W)	11.977	10.143	10.364	10.996	11.27	10.32

Regarding the framework implemented on the NetFPGA-SUME, the table shows that our neural networks use a few resources. Due to the many DSP48 embedded, many DSP48 elements are exploited for building neurons. Regarding working frequency, the system can work with more than 200 MHz for both neural network models. The table also shows that the system with neural network models on NetFPGA-SUME requires similar power consumption to the NetFPGA-10G.

5.3   Throughput Results

The signature-based prevention techniques scan both header and payload of packets for detecting attacking packets. Therefore the size of packets will affect the throughput of the system. Hence, for evaluating the throughput of the framework with these approaches, we classify testing packets into six groups based on their sizes, including 64-byte, 128-byte, 256-byte, 512-byte, 1024-byte, and 1500-byte packets. Figure 5 depicts the processing throughput in terms of Gbps of the three signature-based prevention techniques.

Figure 5 shows that with large packet sizes, the system with these prevention techniques offers higher throughput due to the payload. When packets' sizes are 64 B, the throughput is decreased because many packets' headers need to be verified. For all packets' sizes, throughput values with the hop count and port ingress/egress filtering are the same because they share the same structure.

The neural networks, as mentioned above, convert packets to feature vectors to process neurons. Therefore, we do not need to classify packets according to their sizes as the signature-based approaches. We use two platforms, NetFPGA-10G and NetFPGA-SUME, for deploying different neural network models. Due to more resources, the NetFPGA-SUME can host larger models, as mentioned in the previous sections. To estimate the system throughput, we

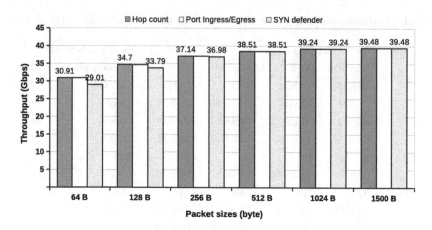

Fig. 5. Processing throughput of signature-based techniques: hop count, port ingress/egress, and SYN defender

leverage the three most frequently used datasets NSL-KDD, UNSW-NB15, and CIC-IDS2017. Figure 6 depicts the throughput of neural network models on the two platforms with different datasets. In this figure, for each model, the above chart bar shows the processing throughput while the below one depicts the maximum packet sending speed that the OSNT tool can send to the testing platform.

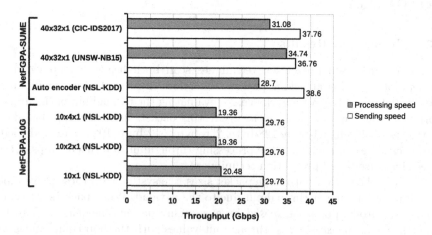

Fig. 6. Processing throughput neural networks with different models and datasets

Figure 6 shows that the neural network models for anomaly-based network intrusion prevention with NetFPGA-10G offer lower throughput than NetFPGA-SUME due to the low working frequency (~100 MHz compared to ~200 MHz). Regarding the NetFPGA-10G platform, three models provide almost similar throughput values with a slightly higher of the simplest model (10 × 1 - no hidden layer).

Consider the NetFPGA-SUME platform, two neural network models, Autoencoder and 40 × 32 × 1, are built. We test the first model with NSL-KDD and the second with CIC-IDS2017 and UNSW-NB15 datasets. Figure 6 shows that the 40 × 32 × 1 model outperforms the Autoencoder model because it is more straightforward than Autoencoder.

5.4 Accuracy Results

To compare the accuracy of neuron network models, we use the evaluation metrics as shown in Eq. 2, including *Accuracy*, *False Negative Rate*, and *False Positive Rate*, in which TP (true positive), TN (true negative), FP (false positive), and FN (false negative) are defined in [17].

$$\text{Accuracy} = \frac{\text{True positive} + \text{True negative}}{\text{Total testing packets}}$$
$$\text{False positive rate (FPR)} = \frac{\text{False positive}}{\text{Total negative in dataset}} \qquad (2)$$
$$\text{False negative rate (FNR)} = \frac{\text{False negative}}{\text{Total positive in dataset}}$$

Figure 7 illustrates the three metrics for evaluating the deployed models with three datasets. The figure shows that we achieve the 10 × 4 × 1 with NSL-KDD and 40 × 32 × 1 with CIC-IDS2017 achieve better accuracy, FNR, and FPR values than the others. Although the same neural network model is used, the 40 × 32 × 1 model with UNSW-NB15 provides low accuracy and high FPR because the dataset includes 68 features after refined, while the model accepts only feature vectors with 40 elements.

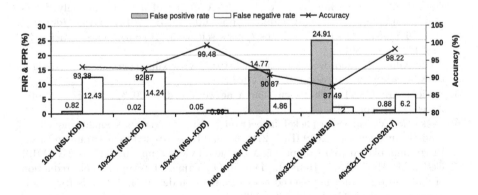

Fig. 7. Accuracy, False Positive Rate (FPR), and False Negative Rate (FNR) of the neural network models

6   Conclusion

As network-based services have rapidly increased during and after the COVID-19 pandemic, preventing network attacks has become essential. This study proposes a high-performance intrusion prevention system framework that utilizes FPGA technology. The framework allows for deploying signature/pattern-based and anomaly/AI-based prevention techniques. Two efficient FPGA-based network processing platforms, NetFPGA-10G and NetFPGA-SUME, are implemented to evaluate the proposed framework. The framework is tested using three well-known datasets, NSL-KDD, UNSW-NB15, and CIC-IDS2017, with three signature-based approaches and five different neural network models. The results show that with signature-based techniques, the framework achieves a throughput of up to 39.48 Gbps, while with neural network models, the throughput can reach up to 34.74 Gbps. Furthermore, the network intrusion prevention system developed using this framework can achieve up to 99.48% accuracy with only a 0.05% false positive rate and a 0.99% false negative rate in the best case.

Acknowledgement. We acknowledge Ho Chi Minh City University of Technology (HCMUT), VNU-HCM for supporting this study.

References

1. Abdulhammed, R., Musafer, H., Alessa, A., Faezipour, M., Abuzneid, A.: Features dimensionality reduction approaches for machine learning based network intrusion detection. Electronics **8**(3), 322 (2019)
2. Ahmad, Z., Shahid Khan, A., Wai Shiang, C., Abdullah, J., Ahmad, F.: Network intrusion detection system: a systematic study of machine learning and deep learning approaches. Trans. Emerg. Telecommun. Technol. (ETT) **32**(1), e4150 (2021). https://doi.org/10.1002/ett.4150. https://onlinelibrary.wiley.com/doi/abs/10.1002/ett.4150
3. Ahmed, M., Naser Mahmood, A., Hu, J.: A survey of network anomaly detection techniques. J. Netw. Comput. Appl. **60**, 19–31 (2016). https://doi.org/10.1016/j.jnca.2015.11.016. https://www.sciencedirect.com/science/article/pii/S1084804515002891
4. AMD Xilinx: Vivado overview (2023). https://www.xilinx.com/products/design-tools/vivado.html. Accessed 01 Apr 2023
5. Antichi, G.: OSNT - the open source network tester (2023). https://osnt.org. Accessed 01 Apr 2023
6. Ceška, M., et al.: Deep packet inspection in FPGAs via approximate nondeterministic automata. In: 2019 IEEE 27th Annual International Symposium on Field-Programmable Custom Computing Machines (FCCM), pp. 109–117. IEEE (2019)
7. Ceška, M., Havlena, V., Holík, L., Lengál, O., Vojnar, T.: Approximate reduction of finite automata for high-speed network intrusion detection. Int. J. Softw. Tools Technol. Transfer **22**(5), 523–539 (2020)
8. Cong, J., et al.: FPGA HLS today: successes, challenges, and opportunities. ACM Trans. Reconfigurable Technol. Syst. **15**(4) (2022). https://doi.org/10.1145/3530775

9. Digilent an NI companay: NetFPGA-SUME virtex-7 FPGA development board (2023). https://digilent.com/shop/netfpga-sume-virtex-7-fpga-development-board/. Accessed 01 Apr 2023

10. Dua, D., Graff, C.: UCI machine learning repository (2017). http://archive.ics.uci.edu/ml. Accessed 01 Apr 2023

11. Garcia-Teodoro, P., Diaz-Verdejo, J., Maciá-Fernández, G., Vázquez, E.: Anomaly-based network intrusion detection: techniques, systems and challenges. Comput. Secur. **28**(1–2), 18–28 (2009)

12. García-Teodoro, P., Díaz-Verdejo, J., Maciá-Fernández, G., Vázquez, E.: Anomaly-based network intrusion detection: techniques, systems and challenges. Comput. Secur. **28**(1), 18–28 (2009). https://doi.org/10.1016/j.cose.2008.08.003. https://www.sciencedirect.com/science/article/pii/S0167404808000692

13. Ghanti, S., Naik, G.M.: Defense techniques of SYN flood attack characterization and comparisons. Int. J. Netw. Secur. **20**, 721–729 (2018)

14. Gordon, H., Park, C., Tushir, B., Liu, Y., Dezfouli, B.: An efficient SDN architecture for smart home security accelerated by FPGA. In: 2021 IEEE International Symposium on Local and Metropolitan Area Networks (LANMAN), pp. 1–3. IEEE (2021)

15. Hindy, H., et al.: A taxonomy of network threats and the effect of current datasets on intrusion detection systems. IEEE Access **8**, 104650–104675 (2020). https://doi.org/10.1109/access.2020.3000179

16. Ho, T., Cho, S.J., Oh, S.R.: Parallel multiple pattern matching schemes based on cuckoo filter for deep packet inspection on graphics processing units. IET Inf. Secur. **12**(4), 381–388 (2018)

17. Hossin, M., Sulaiman, M.N.: A review on evaluation metrics for data classification evaluations. Int. J. Data Mining Knowl. Manag. Process **5**(2), 1 (2015)

18. Ioannou, L., Fahmy, S.A.: Network intrusion detection using neural networks on FPGA SOCS. In: 2019 29th International Conference on Field Programmable Logic and Applications (FPL), pp. 232–238. IEEE (2019)

19. Kang, J., Kim, T., Park, J.: FPGA-based real-time abnormal packet detector for critical industrial network. In: 2019 IEEE Symposium on Computers and Communications (ISCC), pp. 1199–1203. IEEE (2019)

20. Liao, H.J., Lin, C.H.R., Lin, Y.C., Tung, K.Y.: Intrusion detection system: a comprehensive review. J. Netw. Comput. Appl. **36**(1), 16–24 (2013)

21. Maciel, L.A., Souza, M.A., de Freitas, H.C.: Reconfigurable FPGA-based k-means/k-modes architecture for network intrusion detection. IEEE Trans. Circuits Syst. II Express Briefs **67**(8), 1459–1463 (2019)

22. Moustafa, N., Slay, J.: The evaluation of network anomaly detection systems: statistical analysis of the UNSW-NB15 data set and the comparison with the KDD99 data set. Inf. Secur. J. Glob. Perspect. **25**(1–3), 18–31 (2016). https://doi.org/10.1080/19393555.2015.1125974

23. Murovic, T., Trost, A.: Massively parallel combinational binary neural networks for edge processing. Elektrotehniski Vestnik **86**(1/2), 47–53 (2019)

24. Murovič, T., Trost, A.: Resource-optimized combinational binary neural network circuits. Microelectron. J. **97**, 104724 (2020)

25. NetFPGA: NetFPGA 10G information (2023). https://netfpga.org/NetFPGA-10G.html

26. Nordström, T., Svensson, B.: Using and designing massively parallel computers for artificial neural networks. J. Parallel Distrib. Comput. **14**(3), 260–285 (1992). https://doi.org/10.1016/0743-7315(92)90068-X. https://www.sciencedirect.com/science/article/pii/074373159290068X

27. Sateesan, A., Vliegen, J., Daemen, J., Mentens, N.: Novel bloom filter algorithms and architectures for ultra-high-speed network security applications. In: 2020 23rd Euromicro Conference on Digital System Design (DSD), pp. 262–269. IEEE (2020)
28. Security today: Malicious DDoS attacks rise 150% in 2022 according to new report (2023). https://securitytoday.com/articles/2023/02/17/malicious-ddos-attacks-rise-150-in-2022-according-to-new-report.aspx
29. Senie, D., Ferguson, P.: Network Ingress Filtering: Defeating Denial of Service Attacks which employ IP Source Address Spoofing. RFC 2827 (2000). https://doi.org/10.17487/RFC2827. https://www.rfc-editor.org/info/rfc2827
30. Statista Research Department: Internet of things - number of connected devices worldwide 2015–2025 (2016). https://www.statista.com/statistics/471264/iot-number-of-connected-devices-worldwide/. Accessed 01 Apr 2023
31. Tavallaee, M., Bagheri, E., Lu, W., Ghorbani, A.A.: A detailed analysis of the KDD cup 99 data set. In: 2009 IEEE Symposium on Computational Intelligence for Security and Defense Applications, pp. 1–6 (2009). https://doi.org/10.1109/CISDA.2009.5356528
32. Team, A.N.S.: 2022 in review: DDoS attack trends and insights (2023). https://www.microsoft.com/en-us/security/blog/2023/02/21/2022-in-review-ddos-attack-trends-and-insights/. Accessed 01 Apr 2023
33. Wada, T., Matsumura, N., Nakano, K., Ito, Y.: Efficient byte stream pattern test using bloom filter with rolling hash functions on the FPGA. In: 2018 Sixth International Symposium on Computing and Networking (CANDAR), pp. 66–75. IEEE (2018)
34. Wang, H., Jin, C., Shin, K.G.: Defense against spoofed IP traffic using hop-count filtering. IEEE/ACM Trans. Networking **15**(1), 40–53 (2007). https://doi.org/10.1109/TNET.2006.890133
35. Zhao, Z., Sadok, H., Atre, N., Hoe, J.C., Sekar, V., Sherry, J.: Achieving 100Gbps intrusion prevention on a single server. In: Proceedings of the 14th USENIX Conference on Operating Systems Design and Implementation, pp. 1083–1100 (2020)
36. Zilberman, N., Audzevich, Y., Covington, G.A., Moore, A.W.: NetFPGA SUME: Toward 100 Gbps as research commodity. IEEE Micro **34**(5), 32–41 (2014). https://doi.org/10.1109/MM.2014.61

Improving Drone Security in Smart Cities via Lightweight Cryptography

Raffaele Pizzolante$^{(\boxtimes)}$, Arcangelo Castiglione, Francesco Palmieri,
Angelo Passaro, Rocco Zaccagnino, and Samanta La Vecchia

Department of Computer Science, University of Salerno,
Via Giovanni Paolo II, 132, 84084 Fisciano, Italy
rpizzolante@unisa.it

Abstract. In recent years, *Unmanned Aerial Vehicles (UAVs)* have
become increasingly popular. It is estimated that the UAV market will
continue to grow to reach $27.4 billion by 2030. The ability of UAVs to
travel long distances and acquire and process information has made these
devices suitable in many areas. On the other hand, their widespread use
has made UAVs an attractive target for cyberattacks. More precisely,
most of such attacks are targeted to the *MAVLink*, which is the main
communication protocol used by UAVs.

In this paper, we first focus on the main MAVLink security protocol,
namely, the *MAVSec* protocol. MAVSec uses cryptography to encrypt
messages exchanged between the UAV and *ground control station (GCS)*.
However, several security weaknesses still affect the MAVSec protocol, mainly resulting from the lack of authentication and key exchange
between UAV and GCS. To overcome the limitations of this protocol, we
introduce a novel and modular security architecture based on lightweight
cryptography [10,16]. Finally, the effectiveness and efficiency of the proposed solution have been assessed through a proof of concept implemented using the *software in the loop (SITL)* simulator.

Keywords: Drone Security · Lightweight Cryptography · Unmanned
Aerial Vehicles (UAVs) · MAVSec · MAVLink · Unmanned Aircraft
Systems (UAS) · software in the loop

1 Introduction

In recent years, drones, also known as Unmanned Aerial Vehicles (UAVs), have
been spread in many governmental and civilian applications, varying from disaster management to agricultural controlling and from data collection (e.g., image
sensing, environment sensing, and so on) to traffic monitoring [8]. However, it is
essential to point out that originally drones were used for several specific military
aspects.

The spread of commercial drones is expected to continue its growth and,
according to a report of Tractica [1], it is estimated that, in 2025, this market

O. Gervasi et al. (Eds.): ICCSA 2023 Workshops, LNCS 14109, pp. 99–115, 2023.
https://doi.org/10.1007/978-3-031-37120-2_7

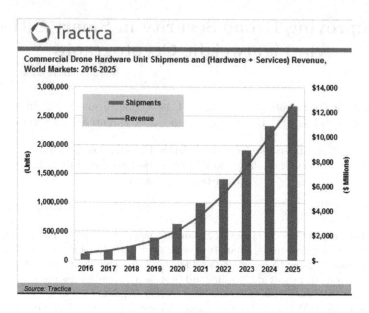

Fig. 1. Commercial Drone Hardware Unit Shipments and Revenue [1].

segment will reach a global income of $12.6 billion by 2025, as it can be observed from Fig. 1.

However, a drone, also known as *Unmanned Aerial Vehicle* (UAV), is a part of a more complex system denoted as *Unmanned Aerial System* (UAS). In detail, as shown in Fig. 2, a UAS is composed of the following key elements:

- One or more drones (UAVs);
- One or more radio controllers for piloting the drones;
- The *Ground Control Station* (GCS) or *Operation Control Unit* (OCU), which can be viewed as a control center that provides all the human facilities for the management of the UAVs;
- The communication links.

As discussed in [8], one of the most valuable and advanced fields of application for drones is related to smart cities. We can informally define a smart city as an urban region with advanced infrastructure and communications facilities [14]. Smart cities can offer many advantages for citizens, businesses, the government, and the environment. In this scenario, drones can be used in several fields of a smart city, such as traffic monitoring, controlling civilian security, and situation awareness. Drones could be more efficient than human-crewed planes. The abovementioned aspect is paramount since it can lead to relevant cost savings. Drones are also more flexible in many scenarios, such as hazard cases for people. In such cases, drones can provide effective and indispensable aid. Again, due to some of their physical characteristics (i.e., small size), drones can accurately perform specific actions close to a destination object or a small location.

By relying on these considerations, it emerges that drones provide tangible benefits in several scenarios in the context of smart cities. On the other hand,

Unmanned Aerial Vehicle (UAV)

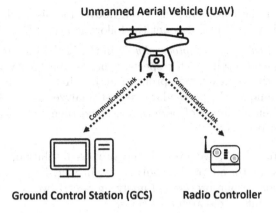

Ground Control Station (GCS)   **Radio Controller**

Fig. 2. The Elements of a UAS.

the drones and all the elements of a UAS system can be affected by several issues related to security and privacy [6,9,12,15], such as attacks on the flight controller and ground control station, attacks on the data link, etc. [6].

Motivation and Contribution. Most of such attacks are targeted to the *MAVLink*, i.e., the main communication protocol used by UAVs. The MAVLink protocol is a *lightweight* messaging protocol for communication with drones and among the components of onboard drones. This protocol ensures efficient, reliable, and extensible communication. Since the MAVLink protocol is widely used, it is affected by several security issues and attacks. [11,13]. MAVLink protocol implements a solution to solve authentication problems, including signatures in the MAVLink messages. However, this solution only solves a small portion of the issues affecting the MAVLink since, in general, the GCSs do not implement signature mechanisms. Other solutions have been proposed to improve the security of MAVLink, and most of them rely on symmetric cryptography. However, due to the hardware constraints and the limited computational capabilities, such solutions could not be suitable for all devices. Allouch et al. [5] proposed MAVSec, a solution based on cryptography that can solve security problems related to confidentiality and privacy. However, even the MAVSec is affected by some safety and scalability issues that do not make it entirely suitable for all modern scenarios where drones are used.

This paper addresses MAVSec issues by improving the communication link security between GCS and UAVs in smart city ecosystems.

First, we focus on the encryption algorithms used by MAVSec, which are insecure or unsuitable for devices with limited hardware capabilities. Furthermore, we observe that the problem of *key exchange* between the UAV and the GCS is not addressed in MAVSec, and this causes a lack of portability. Finally, found out that are no mechanisms that guarantee the *authentication* between the involved entities (i.e., GCS and UAV).

Starting from the considerations given above, in this work, we envision a novel solution that takes into account the following aspects:

- We integrate *lightweight cryptography* [7] in the MAVLink protocol and compare the obtained results with respect to the standard MAVSec protocol;
- We focus on the key exchange problem and address it with *lightweight key exchange* techniques. In particular, we first analyze such techniques to find the best of them in terms of performance, and then we integrate them into the MAVLink protocol.

Organization. In Sect. 3, we present the proposed solution, highlighting its underlying ideas and the adopted design choices; in Sect. 4, we focus on the experimental evaluation of our proposal; Finally, in Sect. 5 we conclude the paper, besides providing future research directions.

2 Background

This section highlights the key points and basic concepts to provide all the necessary background to understand better and contextualize our proposal. In particular, we outline the basic concepts and ideas underlying the MAVLink V2 protocol. More precisely, we focus first on the main aspects of the MAVLink V2, showing its motivations, logical functioning, and exchanged messages. Finally, we focus on the MAVLink V2 security requirements, highlighting the most common attacks proposed against this protocol.

2.1 MAVLink

A UAV can be viewed as an autonomous platform that can be easily programmed to perform missions with or without the intervention of a pilot. Using wireless technologies, a UAV typically communicates with a Ground Control Station (GCS). A GCS can monitor the status and control the actions of one or more UAVs. Furthermore, the communications between the GCS and the UAV occur through ad-hoc hardware and/or software called *autopilot*. More precisely, the autopilot is embedded into the UAV and allows the control of the UAV movements.

Some software has been proposed in the market to perform autopilot functions. Some of these software are:

- *ArduPilot* by *3DR*;
- *Paparazzi UAV* developed by *Ecole Nationale de l'Aviation Civil (ENAC)*;
- *Hangar autopilot*.

One of the most used autopilot software is *ArduPilot*, an open-source project. ArduPilot represents the basis of different types of autonomous systems, and its core is the *Micro Air Vehicle communication Link (MAVLink)* protocol [2,11].

The MAVLink protocol, released in 2009 by Lorenz Meier under the lesser general public license (LGPL), is a *lightweight* messaging protocol for communication with drones and among the components of onboard drones. Until now, two versions of MAVLink have been developed, MAVLink V1 and MAVLink V2.

2.2   MAVLink Insecurity

In this section, we report some possible attacks that can be performed.

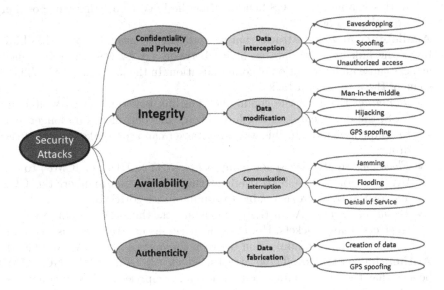

Fig. 3. The MAVLink Security Attacks.

As we showed in Fig. 3, the attacks can be classified according to the following categories:

- **Confidentiality and privacy attacks**: An attacker gains unauthorized access to confidential and sensitive information by intercepting data, commands, or messages exchanged between one or more UAVs and a GCS. In the following, we report some of the most important attacks in this category:
  - *Eavesdropping*: If encryption techniques are not put in place, an attacker can easily intercept communication between a UAV and a GCS, obtaining information of different types through traffic analysis;
  - *Spoofing*: MAVLink uses System IDs to identify elements of a network. However, due to the lack of encryption, such IDs are transmitted in cleartext. Therefore, an attacker could easily use such IDs for malicious purposes;
  - *Unauthorized access*: This attack occurs when an attacker gains access to the UAV and/or GCS.
- **Integrity attacks**: The integrity of MAVLink can be compromised by modifying the sent data. The following attacks are some examples of integrity attacks:
  - *Man-in-the-middle (MITM)*: An attacker can listen to the communication and reconstruct the exchanged commands. Again, the attacker can modify the control and telemetry data, then send this altered data to the GCS or UAV;

- *Hijacking*: Whenever a MITM attack is successful, an attacker can send arbitrary commands to the UAV, making it believe the GCS sent them;
- *GPS spoofing*: An attacker can send false GPS coordinates to the GCS. In this manner, the GCS believes that the UAV is in a different position from the real one.
- **Availability attacks**: Attacks that compromise the availability of MAVLink break the link used for data exchange between a UAV and the GCS. Such attacks cause an interruption of communication. In the following, we highlight some of these types of attacks:
  - *Jamming*: Breaking the communication link between the UAV and the GCS, the drone enters a *lost-link*. Then, the controller is no longer able to send commands. In this way, an attacker can try to take control of the drone;
  - *Flooding*: An attacker sends many packets (SYN, UDP, or ICMP) to the UAV and/or the GCS to overload them/it. In this manner, the GCS and/or the UAV are/is unable to communicate correctly;
  - *Denial of Service*: As in the previous attack, the UAV and/or the GCS receive(s) many packets. However, in this case, an attacker aims to obtain a break in the communication between the parties (i.e., UAV and GCS).
- **Authenticity attacks**: These attacks, which try to make the GCS/UAV believe that the forged data is authentic, can comprise the following actions
  - *Creation of data*: An attacker can analyze the exchanged information between the UAV and the GCS, trying to create forged messages to be sent to one of the two parties;
  - *GPS spoofing*: The UAV connects to the GCS via wireless links to exchange data and commands. However, an attacker could successfully spoof one or more MAVLink command(s) since the wireless environment is open.

3   The Proposed Solution

Although the MAVSec V2 protocol represents an attractive solution, it is still affected by some limitations, which make its use not fully compliant with the security requirements defined in the previous section. In particular, from a critical analysis of the MAVSec protocol, it emerged that it is affected by the following limitation.

First, we focus on the encryption algorithms used by MAVSec, i.e., *RC4* and *AES*. Actually, RC4 cannot guarantee a good level of security. On the other hand, as discussed in the previous section, AES is unsuitable for devices with limited hardware capabilities.

Furthermore, we observe that the problem of *key exchange* between the UAV and the GCS is not addressed in MAVSec. More precisely, the keys are hard-coded in the source code, and this causes a lack of portability. Finally, no mechanisms guarantee the *authentication* between the involved entities (i.e., GCS and UAV).

Starting from the considerations given above, in this work, we envision a novel solution that takes into account the following aspects:

- We integrate *lightweight cryptography* [7] in the MAVLink protocol and compare the obtained results with respect to the standard MAVSec protocol;
- We focus on the key exchange problem and address it with *lightweight key exchange* techniques. In particular, we first analyze such techniques to find the best of them in terms of performance, and then we integrate them into the MAVLink protocol.

This section presents the proposed solution, highlighting its underlying ideas and the adopted design choices. We remark that the proposed solution is modular and can be adapted according to the different operational scenarios. In particular, our solution, based on lightweight cryptography, can be modeled by the following four phases:

1. **Certificate Generation**: In this phase, the certificates for the GCS and the UAV are generated by the GCS;
2. **Certificate Broadcasting**: In this phase, the UAV broadcasts its certificate;
3. **Certificate Management**: The GCS receives a certificate and checks its validity. Then, the following two cases may occur:
   - If the received certificate is not valid, it is ignored;
   - Otherwise, the GCS generates the shared key and sends its certificate to the UAV (if the certificate is valid). The UAV then checks the certificate's validity and generates the shared key. The certificate exchange process is shown in Fig. 4
4. **Secure Data Exchange**: Once both the UAV and the GCS have generated the shared key, the exchange of encrypted messages begins.

3.1   Used Technologies

To realize the proposed solution, we use the following technologies:

- *MAVLink v2*;
- *QGroundControl (QGC)* [3]: QGC is an open-source and well-known cross-platform GCS. QGC is entirely developed in C++ and fully supports MAVLink.
- *SITL (Software in the Loop) Simulator* [4]: SITL Simulator permits to simulate Plane, Copter, or Rover without any specific hardware. More precisely, SITL is a build of the autopilot code that allows testing the behavior of a UAV without using any ad-hoc hardware.

3.2   Certificate Generation

In our solution, the GCS plays the role of the *Certificate Authority (CA)*. The certificates for the GCS and UAVs are created by an ad-hoc *generator* that we will describe below.

In detail, we include two structures in the proposed generator:

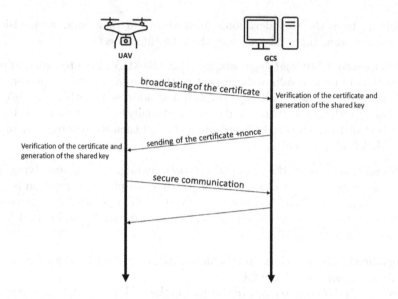

Fig. 4. Exchange of certificates.

- The first one, denoted as *info_s*, contains the information needed to identify the drone. In the following, we report some of the most relevant information contained in such a structure:
  - Serial number of the certificate;
  - Name and identification (ID) of the device;
  - Entity that has signed the certificate and validity of this certificate;
- The second one, denoted as *mavlink_device_certificate*, contains the certificate and other information, such as the *private* and *public key* of the issuer and the *sign* of the certificate. Notice that MAVLink uses these two pieces of information, which are not transmitted when the certificate is sent.

First of all, the certificate for the GCS is generated. In particular, the generator obtains the necessary information to create the certificate (i.e., the issuer, the subject, the device name, and the validity period). Then it generates the pair of keys, which will be used to generate the *shared key*. Subsequently, once the certificate for the GCS is signed, the certificate for the UAV can be generated.

3.3 Certificate Broadcasting

To broadcast the certificates on the network, we define and include two new messages in the MAVLink protocol: one message is intended for the UAV, and the other for the GCS. We remark that to include such new messages in the MAVLink protocol, we need to define their structures in an XML file (i.e., *common.xml*) within the *message_definitions* element. We also define and implement the features needed to interact with certificates and integrate them into the MAVLink protocol. Again, regarding the MAVLink implementation, the features mentioned above have been included in the *mavlink_helpers.h* file. At the same time, the auxiliary structures have been included in *mavlink_types.h*.

In detail, we extended the MAVLink with several new functions. In the following, we outline the most important of them:

- *mavlink_read_certificate*: This function enables reading a certificate from a given file and storing its information;
- *mavlink_check_remote_certificate*: This function checks a remote certificate. First of all, this function checks the validity of the date and then the sign of the certificate;
- *mavlink_get_remote_key*: This function enables access to the keys agreed with remote devices;
- *mavlink_set_remote_key*: This function generates the *shared_key* between two devices, and stores it into the *remote_keys* by also updating the status;
- *mavlink_compute_iv*: This function generates a pseudo-random IV for a specific remote key;
- *mavlink_set_iv*: This function receives an IV and saves it for the specific remote key.

Once we have modified the implementation of the MAVLink protocol, we also modified ArduPilot and QGC according to such new features for the management of the certificates.

3.4 Certificate Management

Besides introducing the new certificate management functions, we modified the ArduPilot and the QGC to allow the certificate exchange. We briefly outline the basic ideas behind the introduced modifications in the following. For what concerns the ArduPilot software, we highlight that it is equipped with a scheduler. Such a scheduler works in the following manner: each time it finds a message, it tries to send it by calling the corresponding function. For example, when the *HEARTBEAT* message is found in the scheduler, the scheduler invokes the *send_heartbeat* message and tries to send this message.

Starting from the considerations given above, we provide the scheduler with a new message, denoted as *CERTIFICATE*. In addition, we include the *send_certificate* function in the scheduler. These modifications allow the scheduler of the ArduPilot software to adequately manage the sending of a certificate when the *CERTIFICATE* message is received.

Furthermore, we modified the QGC software component for receiving incoming messages. The basic idea behind this modification is that when a GCS receives a *certificate* message, it verifies if a key has already been set for the device that has sent such a message. At this point, if the key is not set, the GCS *deserializes* the received message and checks if the certificate is valid. If the certificate is valid, the GCS sets the shared key and the IV. Finally, the GCS reads its certificate, which is serialized so that it can be sent to the UAV. In this manner, the exchange of certificates can be completed.

3.5   Secure Data Exchange

To exchange data securely between the GCS and UAV, we modified three functions in the MAVLink implementation. In detail, we redefine the following functions included in the *mavlink_helpers.h* file:

1. *mavlink_finalize_message_buffer*: This function is used by the GCS to compute the checksum of the payload;
2. *_mav_finalize_message_chan_send*: This function is similar to the *mavlink_finalize_message_buffer*, but it is used by the UAV;
3. *mavlink_frame_char_buffer*: This function parses the received message.

In detail, we modify the functions *1.* and *2.*, enabling them to encrypt the payload before the checksum computation. More precisely, the ID is checked before the encryption of the payload. Then, if the ID denotes a *heartbeat* message or matches one of the two certificates, the payload is not encrypted. We remark that a heartbeat message is a message the UAV sends to the GCS to inform that it is alive and contains some information. When the ID check has been carried out, the function obtains the remote key and performs the encryption.

Finally, we modify function *3.* to enable the decryption of the received message. However, we remark that this encryption can occur only after the checksum's correct verification.

4   Experimental Test Results

In this section, we focus on the experimental evaluation of our proposal. In particular, we highlight and discuss the performance of the proposed solution, comparing it with some other proposals defined in state-of-the-art.

4.1   Testing Environment and Benchmark

The used testing environment is composed of a laptop with the following hardware characteristics:

– *CPU*: Intel i5-8250U, with 4 cores and 8 threads;
– *RAM Capacity*: 8 GB.

The SITL and QGC were run on the laptop described above during the testing phase. In particular, the SITL simulator has been run on a virtual machine (VM) with the following assigned resources: 2 CPU threads and 3192 MB of RAM. On the other hand, the GCS software has been run on the host.

Moreover, to carry out the testing activities, we define a *mission* composed of three waypoints. This mission is used as a test for all the considered algorithms, as shown in Sect. 4.1.

In Fig. 5, we report the three waypoints, denoted as *T*, *2*, and *3*, characterizing the mission used for the testing activity. The UAV starts from *T* and proceeds towards *2* and *3*. Finally, the UAV returns to the point *T*.

The mission characterized above has been used in two phases:

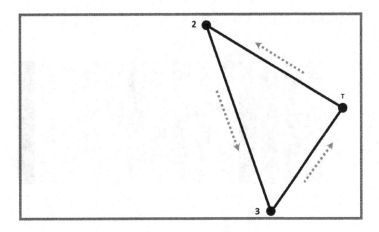

Fig. 5. The three waypoints characterizing the evaluated mission.

1. To determine the best encryption algorithm for memory and energy consumption. In this case, the shared key has been hard-coded within the code. We discuss the details and the motivations behind this phase in Sect. 4.1;
2. To evaluate the overall performance of the proposed solution, taking into account both the encryption and key exchange phases. The details are outlined in Sect. 4.1.

Encryption. This section focuses on the first phase of the testing activity. In particular, we focus on analyzing the encryption algorithms that use a shared key hard-coded in the source code. For each evaluated encryption algorithm integrated into the MAVLink protocol, we completed the mission 10 times. Then, using the *pidstat* utility provided by the SITL simulator, for each second, we collect the CPU consumption and memory usage for the process related to our test. Furthermore, we estimate the energy consumption from the GCS for each flight session. Again, we evaluate the collected results and show them through several graphs. Then, we also provide some comparisons based on the achieved results.

Notice that even though the CBC mode is also supported for *Simon* and *Speck* ciphers, it has not been possible to test it due to some limitations related to modifying the payload size.

From Fig. 6 and Fig. 7, we can observe that there are no relevant differences concerning memory and energy consumption among all the considered algorithms. Again, as we can observe from Fig. 8, the *Trivium* algorithm offers the worst performance in terms of CPU usage. Conversely, all the other evaluated encryption algorithms perform significantly better than *ChaCha20*. In particular, *Speck128/192* in CTR mode offers the best performance. Therefore, our solution uses *Speck128/192* as an encryption algorithm.

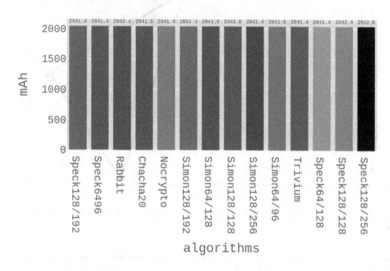

Fig. 6. Encryption algorithms energy consumption.

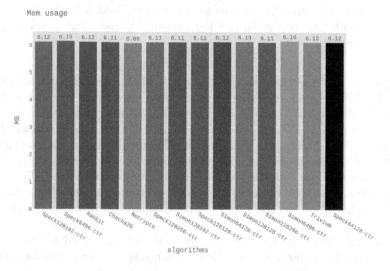

Fig. 7. Encryption algorithms memory consumption.

Key Exchange and Encryption. Once we have determined the best encryption algorithm regarding CPU consumption, i.e., the *Speck128/192*, we performed an evaluation similar to the one outlined in Sect. 4.1. In particular, to analyze the overall performance of our proposal, we repeated 10 times the mission, using the *Speck128/192* algorithm preceded by a key exchange phase.

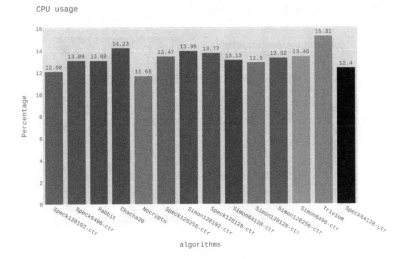

Fig. 8. Encryption algorithms CPU consumption.

The key exchange phase adds only a slight initial overhead with respect to using only the encryption, as it can be observed from Figs. 9 and 10. Therefore, the overall performance of our proposal is not negatively affected by such a phase.

4.2 Correctness

Finally, after choosing the encryption algorithm and applying the key exchange, we intercept and analyze the traffic between UAV and GCS to verify the correct functioning of the proposed solution.

Starting from traffic analysis, we can draw the following considerations:

- *Traffic generated without the proposed solution*: Analyzing the *HOME_ POSITION* message shown in Fig. 11 (a), it is possible to locate the waypoint from which the drone has taken off. This information is leaked due to the lack of encryption.
- *Traffic generated using the proposed solution*: Analyzing the *HOME_ POSITION* message shown in Fig. 11 (b), it is not possible to obtain information on the waypoint thanks to our solution.

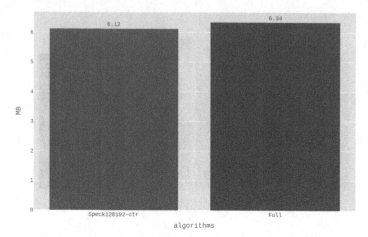

Fig. 9. Memory consumption of the proposed solution.

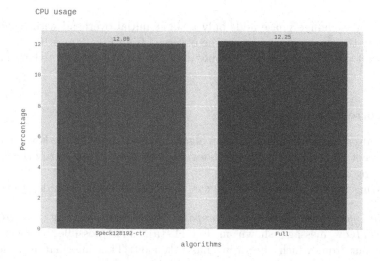

Fig. 10. CPU consumption of the proposed solution.

Payload: HOME_POSITION (242)
  latitude (int32): -353632622
  longitude (int32): 1491652376
  altitude (int32): 584010
  x (float): 0
  y (float): 0
  z (float): 0
  q[0] (float): 1
  q[1] (float): 0
  q[2] (float): 0
  q[3] (float): 0
  approach_x (float): 0
  approach_y (float): 0
  approach_z (float): 0
  time_usec (uint64): 71110711

Payload: HOME_POSITION (242)
  latitude (int32): 863416022
  longitude (int32): 120575720
  altitude (int32): 1374130098
  x (float): -1,34555e-13
  y (float): -1,35936e+18
  z (float): -1,95701e-19
  q[0] (float): 7,94778e-38
  q[1] (float): 3,56239e+12
  q[2] (float): 4,19627e-26
  q[3] (float): -4,32514e+16
  approach_x (float): 7,69489e+25
  approach_y (float): 3,88574e-25
  approach_z (float): 2,17008e+20
  time_usec (uint64): 220134204

(a) An example of an individual figure sub-caption.   (b) A slightly shorter sub-caption.

Fig. 11. The HOME_POSITION Message: Before and After Encryption.

5   Conclusions and Future Directions

In recent years, drones, also known as Unmanned Aerial Vehicles (UAVs), have found fields of application in many environments. As discussed in [8], one of the most valuable and advanced fields of application for drones is related to smart cities [17]. However, a drone, also known as *Unmanned Aerial Vehicle* (UAV), is a part of a more complex system denoted as *Unmanned Aerial System* (UAS). On the other hand, drones and all the elements of a UAS system can be affected by several issues related to security and privacy, such as attacks on the flight controller and ground control station, attacks on the data link, etc. Most of such attacks are targeted to the *MAVLink*, which is the main communication protocol used by UAVs. The MAVLink protocol is a *lightweight* messaging protocol for communication with drones and among the components of onboard drones. Since the MAVLink protocol is widely used, it is affected by several security issues and attacks. MAVLink protocol implements a solution to solve authentication problems, including signatures in the MAVLink messages. However, this solution only solves a small portion of problems affecting the MAVLink since the GCSs do not provide implementations of signature mechanisms. Other solutions have been proposed to improve the security of MAVLink, and most of them rely on symmetric cryptography. However, due to the hardware constraints and the limited computational capabilities, such solutions could not be suitable for all devices. Allouch et al. [5] proposed MAVSec, a solution based on cryptography that can solve security problems related to confidentiality and privacy. However, even the MAVSec is affected by some safety and scalability issues that do not make it fully suitable for all modern scenarios where drones are used.

This paper addresses MAVSec issues by improving the communication link security between GCS and UAVs in smart city ecosystems.

As a future research development, we would like to define an intelligent model that allows establishing, dynamically and adaptively, the best possible combination of security algorithms that guarantees the best compromise between communication security and drone lifetime. Furthermore, we would like to test the feasibility of using safety routines implemented directly onboard the drone.

Acknowledgement. This work was partially supported by project *"SEcurity and RIghts in the CyberSpace (SERICS)"* (PE00000014) under the NRRP MUR program funded by the EU - NGEU.

References

1. Artificial intelligence - omdia - informa. https://omdia.tech.informa.com/topic-pages/artificial-intelligence
2. Mavlink developer guide. https://mavlink.io
3. QGC - qgroundcontrol - drone control. https://qgroundcontrol.com/
4. SITL simulator (software in the loop) - dev documentation. https://ardupilot.org/dev/docs/sitl-simulator-software-in-the-loop.html
5. Allouch, A., Cheikhrouhou, O., Koubâa, A., Khalgui, M., Abbes, T.: Mavsec: securing the mavlink protocol for ardupilot/px4 unmanned aerial systems. In: 2019 15th International Wireless Communications & Mobile Computing Conference (IWCMC), pp. 621–628. IEEE (2019)
6. Altawy, R., Youssef, A.M.: Security, privacy, and safety aspects of civilian drones: a survey. ACM Trans. Cyber-Phys. Syst. **1**(2), 1–25 (2016)
7. Biryukov, A., Perrin, L.P.: State of the art in lightweight symmetric cryptography (2017)
8. Dai Nguyen, H.P., Nguyen, D.D.: Drone application in smart cities: the general overview of security vulnerabilities and countermeasures for data communication. Dev. Future Internet Drones (IoD): Insights Trends Road Ahead **332**, 185 (2021)
9. Dey, V., Pudi, V., Chattopadhyay, A., Elovici, Y.: Security vulnerabilities of unmanned aerial vehicles and countermeasures: an experimental study. In: 2018 31st International Conference on VLSI Design and 2018 17th International Conference on Embedded Systems (VLSID), pp. 398–403 (2018)
10. Duguma, D.G., Kim, J., Lee, S., Jho, N.S., Sharma, V., You, I.: A lightweight D2D security protocol with request-forecasting for next-generation mobile networks. Connect. Sci. 1–25 (2021)
11. Koubâa, A., Allouch, A., Alajlan, M., Javed, Y., Belghith, A., Khalgui, M.: Micro air vehicle link (MAVLink) in a nutshell: a survey. IEEE Access **7**, 87658–87680 (2019)
12. Krishna, C.G.L., Murphy, R.R.: A review on cybersecurity vulnerabilities for unmanned aerial vehicles. In: 2017 IEEE International Symposium on Safety, Security and Rescue Robotics (SSRR), pp. 194–199 (2017). https://doi.org/10.1109/SSRR.2017.8088163
13. Kwon, Y.M., Yu, J., Cho, B.M., Eun, Y., Park, K.J.: Empirical analysis of mavlink protocol vulnerability for attacking unmanned aerial vehicles. IEEE Access **6**, 43203–43212 (2018)

14. Madakam, S., Ramaswamy, R.: 100 new smart cities (India's smart vision). In: 2015 5th National Symposium on Information Technology: Towards New Smart World (NSITNSW), pp. 1–6. IEEE (2015)
15. Rodday, N.M., Schmidt, R.D.O., Pras, A.: Exploring security vulnerabilities of unmanned aerial vehicles. In: NOMS 2016–2016 IEEE/IFIP Network Operations and Management Symposium, pp. 993–994 (2016)
16. Xiao, L., Xie, S., Han, D., Liang, W., Guo, J., Chou, W.K.: A lightweight authentication scheme for telecare medical information system. Connect. Sci. 1–17 (2021)
17. Zheng, Z., Zhou, Y., Sun, Y., Wang, Z., Liu, B., Li, K.: Applications of federated learning in smart cities: recent advances, taxonomy, and open challenges. Connect. Sci. 1–28 (2021)

"SHeMeD": An Application on Secure Computation of Medical Cloud Data Based on Homomorphic Encryption

Hara Salaga[1]([⊠]) [iD], Nikos Karanikolas[1], and Christos Kaklamanis[1,2]

[1] Department of Computer Engineering and Informatics, University of Patras, 26504 Rion, Greece
{salaga,nkaranik,kakl}@ceid.upatras.gr
[2] Computer Technology Institute and Press "Diophantus", 26504 Rion, Greece

Abstract. In today's Internet-centric world, two main challenges have arisen regarding data exploration: a) the privacy of sensitive data and b) the need for users to have an efficient way to manage their data. Cloud computing offers a cost-effective way towards direct data storage and access, which can function as a catalyst to modernize and update legacy systems. Although cloud computing provides efficient dynamic storage space, data security remains a concern. To this end, we propose a novel design and implementation of an application that enables secure storage of personal data in the cloud through a complete homomorphic encryption system. The application is named "SHeMed", which stands for Secure Homomorphic encryption on Medical cloud data. We have concentrated on the secure storage of medical data for breast cancer patients to ensure patients' data privacy and prevent unauthorized access. With the introduction of homomorphic encryption in the core of this application, we achieve four significant milestones regarding the secure "sealing" of data privacy: a) the user does not share the private key with the cloud provider, b) the user can proceed with implementing mathematical operations on encrypted data, c) cloud can be easily scaled and provide a convenient way to store data, d) after the implementation of mathematical operations, the new processed data may be shared with other users, mainly doctors, without providing the original ones. Our design implies that our users will need to retrieve their patient's data just once. In this paper, we present a case study of our application that utilizes homomorphic encryption to eliminate the burden of preserving data confidentiality in the cloud and enable a convenient analysis of medical data through computations on encrypted data.

Keywords: Homomorphic encryption · Cloud computing · Medical data · Data privacy · Data storage · Malicious acts · Confidentiality · Computations · Breast cancer

1 Introduction

Nowadays, the expansion of the Internet has made a tremendous impact on the amount of data exchanged and on the way those data are retrieved, interpreted, and stored. There are two key issues regarding data analysis, i.e., the privacy of sensitive data and

O. Gervasi et al. (Eds.): ICCSA 2023 Workshops, LNCS 14109, pp. 116–133, 2023.
https://doi.org/10.1007/978-3-031-37120-2_8

the data management in the new era of cloud computing. We focus, but not restrict, our attention on medical data analysis for the following reasons. First, medical data privacy and confidentiality are critical and any violation, meaning that integrity may be compromised from adversaries or could be stolen, may even lead to legal sanctions. Second there is a worldwide attempt and ongoing process of medical data digitization and storage. The goal is that health information and patients' records can be created and managed by authorized providers in a digital format having the ability of being shared with other providers across more than one health care organization. For example, healthcare industry proceeds with medical data digitization, referred to as Electronic Health Records (EHR), which is a digital record of a patient's medical history maintained by hospitals or healthcare providers for better handling of medical examinations.

This is likely to improve the quality and efficiency of healthcare as there is ease of access to records, where frequent examinations are required, for example for patients with breast cancer. Given the potential for adversaries to steal or tamper with sensitive data, ensuring its safety is crucial to prevent the dissemination of misleading information. The necessity for full protection of medical digital data is essential, the consequence of which is the rapid development of cryptographic systems as a countermeasure to security threats of third parties.

Homomorphic encryption was first proposed in 1978 [1] as a solution to eliminate the need for multiple decryptions that can potentially compromise the integrity of the information received by the end-user. In other words, homomorphic encryption is a cryptographical method designed to allow mathematical operations to be performed on the already encrypted information while hiding the appearance of plaintext in any third party. Homomorphic encryption enables processing of ciphertext such that the resulting encrypted output data matches the output produced during the first decryption, while preserving the confidentiality of the processed and encrypted data. The practical implementation of homomorphic encryption was introduced by Gentry in 2009 [1]. Homomorphic encryption techniques can be categorized into three groups based on the number and complexity of mathematical operations applied to the encrypted message, resulting in diverse types of homomorphic encryption.

- Partially Homomorphic Encryption (PHE) [13]: Only one mathematical operation is allowed to be performed on the encrypted message, either addition or multiplication, with no limit on the number of repetitions.
- Somewhat Homomorphic Encryption (SWHE) [14]: It becomes possible to use addition and multiplication with a limited number of iterations.
- Fully Homomorphic Encryption (FHE) [15]: It becomes possible to use the mathematical operations, multiplication, and addition, on the encrypted information without limitation in the number of iterations.

Currently, there are several implemented homomorphic encryption libraries. In our implementation, the SHeMed application, SEAL library [3] and specifically EVA compiler [5] have been deployed. SEAL (Simple Encrypted Arithmetic Library), proposed by Microsoft, is an open-source library that implements Fully Homomorphic Encryption (FHE) technology. It provides a set of encryption libraries that allow computation to be performed directly on encrypted data. This enables the creation of encrypted data storage and computation services, where the client never needs to share its key with the service (e.g., cloud). In addition, this library supports two different homomorphic schemes with different properties: the Brakerski-Fan-Vercauteren (BFV) [17], which allows arithmetic operations on encrypted integers and Cheon-Kim-Kim-Song (CKKS) [8] scheme, which allows approximate computations applied on encrypted real or complex data. The latter method yields approximate results, due to Learning With Errors (LWE) [16] noise, which is the foundation of CKKS homomorphic encryption scheme. CKKS aims at applications of medical nature or the application of machine learning models to encrypted data, etc. Encrypted Vector Arithmetic (EVA) is a compiler for fully homomorphic encryption, implementing the functionality of the SEAL library. EVA has a Python frontend system, called PyEVA, which allows calculations to be expressed using basic arithmetic operations in Python.

Furthermore, healthcare industries require to store multiple EHRs for their patients and the conventional hardware storages are not considered flexible while their cost is significant. Thus, modern organizations adopt Cloud computing, which is defined by NIST [12] as a model for enabling ubiquitous, convenient, on-demand network access to a shared pool of configurable computing resources (e.g., networks, servers, storage, applications, and services) that can be rapidly provisioned and released with minimal management effort or service provider interaction. One of the most reliable and widely known cloud providers is Google Cloud Provider (GCP).

It is worth emphasizing the presence of ad hoc algorithms in the medical domain, which have been demonstrated by several recent studies, including those referenced as [6] and [7]. These algorithms are developed on an as-needed basis and are designed to address specific problems, making them highly tailored and efficient. Through these studies, it is shown that machine learning and data mining methods can effectively tackle specific medical issues, including but not limited to tracking COVID-19 cases and analyzing genomic data. The application of these techniques can provide valuable insights and aid medical professionals in making more informed decisions, ultimately improving patient outcomes.

In the same manner, the motivation behind our research is driven by the objective to offer medical professionals valuable insights and support, empowering them to make well-informed decisions and improve patient outcomes. To this end, our proposed application seal the data securely using homomorphic encryption without providing the encryption secret key in the cloud provider. The data in our case study are related to patients with breast cancer and we have demonstrated the way that we managed these big data set. In the following sections, we will analyze the design as well as the implementation of an application that allows the secure storage of medical data using a fully homomorphic encryption scheme in cloud storage. Moreover, we will present relevant screenshots of SHeMed application.

1.1 Related Work

The proposed application "SHeMed", which stands for SEAL Homomorphic encryption on medical data, has a major role in applying arithmetic operations in encrypted data using the homomorphic theory while exploits the capabilities of cloud computing. By implementing homomorphic encryption operations in the cloud provider, we exploit the capabilities of cloud computation while we take advantage of the storage.

However, there has been significant research towards securing cloud data with the aim of homomorphic encryption. The research of Poteya M. M., Dhoteb C. A. and Deepak H. S. in 2016 [11] presents an application in which they demonstrate the functionality of a FHE scheme on the cloud. They use the AWS as a provider and add a simple logic to present the accuracy of data from IDE environment as well as show the storage of the encrypted data in DynamoDB of the AWS cloud provider. Another paper that expanded our knowledge towards homomorphic encryption, was introduced by Chen B., Zhao N. [4], where they analyze two fully homomorphic encryption FHE systems, DHCV and CAFED, along with their capabilities and vulnerabilities towards the cloud. In both systems, they propose alternative improved ways for algorithms having as objective to send the key to the cloud server to retrieve ciphertext. Another research worth to be mentioned by Chauhan K. K., Sanger K. S. A. and Verma A. [10], examines the processing state, which is considered as a critical stage for data security especially in cloud computing. They proceeded with the analyzation of three partial homomorphic encryption HE methods and their applications in cloud computing, expanding traditional encryption techniques which are not efficient for processing state of data. Although, homomorphic encryption methods successfully manage the problem of data security in cloud computing, currently, both fully as well as partial homomorphic methods are not so easy to implement for cloud computing. In addition, similar research has been conducted by Vankudoth, Biksham & Vasumathi [18], where they present an overview of homomorphic encryption in cloud computing area urged from the need of security at infrastructure: network level, host level, application level and data. Kocabaş, Övünç and Soyata, Tolga [9] have contributed to the value of fully homomorphic encryption systems by introducing a health monitoring system that detects patient health issues by continuously monitoring the ECG data. This system consists of ECG acquisition devices, a cloud-based medical application, and back-end devices that display the monitoring results. Thus, in order to override security risks associated with personal health information in cloud providers, such as Amazon, a fully homomorphic encryption scheme has been formulated. With the aim of this encryption schema, the operation on encrypted data can be applied without collisions in the cloud and with no concern about personal health data privacy. The prominent work of Ahmad, I., and Khandekar, A. [2], which enhances the knowledge around homomorphic encryption, suggests RSA and Paillier algorithm for homomorphic encryption by using proxy re-encryption algorithm that prevents cipher data from Chosen Cipher text Attack (CCA).

Overall, the abovementioned papers state that homomorphic encryption schemes introduce a new era for security of cloud computing, since calculations on encrypted data without knowing the plain data can be provided while respecting their confidentiality.

1.2 Our Work

The related work as presented above provides a valuable foundation for the research on homomorphic encryption and its adaptation for cloud computing security, which primarily focuses on theoretical aspects. Unlike other studies in the field, our paper adopts a practical approach and expands on the theoretical concept by introducing a user-friendly graphical user interface (GUI) on a cloud-based implementation. Hence, in comparison with the existing literature our work differs as we bring an applicative dimension to the concept of cloud computing security on medical data. To this end, we introduce a practical implementation of a fully homomorphic encryption scheme to securely store medical records for patients with breast cancer in cloud storage, by introducing the "SHeMed" application. The application offers a convenient way to remove any barriers in terms of confidentiality, availability, integrity of personal medical data in the cloud and enhance doctors to freely use the capabilities of the cloud. For this reason, Google Cloud Provider (GCP) is considered as an appropriate cloud provider in which data can be stored in a single cloud bucket, separated by folders which are used by different users to store their patients' health records, which use the application. Since medical records are decimal results, the implementation of a FHE system, named CKKS, which indicates the capabilities of SEAL library is the most appropriate to be used. To manage quite conveniently the complexity of SEAL library, it has been introduced in the core of SHeMed application the usage of EVA compiler of SEAL library. The user experience has been implemented using the Auth0 page for a flexible and convenient way to identify the application's users. The SHeMed scheme results in improving the communication gap between the cloud provider and the possible users, in our case doctors, having as impact the development of patient's confidence and medical staff in the use and exploitation of personal data in cloud storage.

Our goal is that medical results after the SHeMed usage can be shared freely with other users from around the world for better patients' treatments and for exchanging knowledge without barriers. In short terms, the innovation that homomorphic encryption provides is a "swiss knife" against the struggles that someone may face using cloud providers. We expect our application to trigger the usage of homomorphic encryption in other applications, too. In short, we propose an innovative and convenient solution, where the users can easily navigate through application's UI and the creation of the cryptographic keys can be done through a dedicated terminal locally. The implementation of SEAL library through EVA compiler as we have adjusted it in our application, provides a novel procedure which enables the practical use of homomorphic encryption in medical data towards the aim of breast cancer treatment, expanding most of the research held in this area, which focus on the theoretical issues of homomorphic encryption.

2 Problem Description

The advantages of cloud computing are considered as paramount regarding the usefulness and the easy scalability. Overall cloud computing provides a convenient, easy-to-use way to store personal data with the aim of cloud storage (depending on the provider, buckets etc.). On the contrary, the cloud lacks security which leaves an open gap in healthcare industries and individual doctors, according to their security. The security of medical related data is considered as critical, especially when it comes to patient's data privacy. The health records are required to be confidential because of the protection law between patients and doctors and can be only accessible from them. A patient with breast cancer is required to perform a lot of medical examinations, as well as a doctor needs an efficient way to store her data whiles extracts an output about the progress of medical treatment.

In data's life cycle, as shown in Fig. 1, in every state data need to be accessible by retaining confidentiality for authorized users, integrity for data correctness and availability in any time. One state, which raises concerns about data integrity is the storage.

Despite the storage capabilities of the cloud, which are instantly upgradable based on users demands, the data can be compromised, since to keep the personal data encrypted for safety reasons, public and private keys need to be given in most of cloud providers. The role of homomorphic encryption is a catalyst for this case, since the data stored in the cloud can be changed while are encrypted, using mathematical operations. For enhancing data security, in our application we use Google Cloud Provider (GCP), where private key does not have to be provided. Thus, the state of storage can be locked in the context of security. Hence, in this case of the homomorphic encryption problem studied in this paper, our input is data which contains the frequent results, in a decimal form, of medical examinations of several patients with breast cancer (which are monitored by a doctor) and the goal is to manage and store the patients' data in an encrypted form securely in the cloud while we implement homomorphic operations, which result to a different encrypted form.

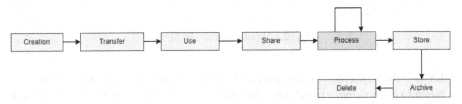

Fig. 1. Data life cycle

3   The Design of the Cloud-Based Application "SHeMeD"

To tackle the problem mentioned above, we propose a cloud-based application SHeMed which is based on storing securely medical examinations for patients with breast cancer on cloud storage using fully homomorphic encryption. The outcome of this application is that users can use the advantages of cloud storage for their patients' medical data, without keeping them in their local systems, something that could compromise the data integrity. The proposed architecture can be shown in Fig. 2 and its components will be analyzed further below.

"Python CLI" Subsystem. The CLI is an external program, part of "SHeMed scheme, that users need to install locally on their computer, so they can use the " SHeMed" application. The possible functions of CLI, use PyEVA, are the following and perform the following actions. First, function "KeyGenerator" is responsible for generating public and private cryptographic keys. Second, "Encryptor", is able to encrypt the initial exam and last, "Decryptor" decrypts the data on its private computer.

"Client" Subsystem. The role of the client subsystem is to provide to the user client, all the necessary services for encryption and decryption of her medical data. To be more precise, through the user's local machine, the following occur:

The user has access to her patient's original medical results for a specific day in excel format, which will be encrypted using the Python CLI. The SEAL library will be implemented for the encryption, key generation, and decryption processes via its compiler,

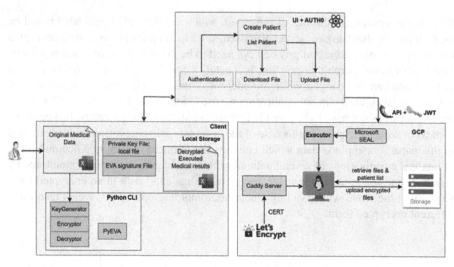

Fig. 2. Architecture of SHeMed

PyEVA. If the required keys are generated via "KeyGenerator", then the "Encryptor" is called to encrypt the original data entered by the user. Finally, the "Decryptor" will decrypt the processed data, which will be received from the cloud provider. Thus, to avoid any compromise of the sensitive information that the data possesses, the private key file is stored locally and the use of the signature of the EVA compiler is also required for the final decryption of the files in their original excel format.

"UI + AUTH0" Subsystem. The function of the "UI + AUTH0" Subsystem is to provide the end user, i.e., the client, all the components needed to interact with the "SHeMed" application. There is an appropriate interface from which the following tasks are performed. In order to ensure authentication, the user should be registered or logged in, otherwise she cannot use it. Then, she can create new patients "Create Patients" to add in bucket, have her total list of patients "List Patients", upload files to the cloud "Upload files" and receive them locally from the cloud "Download files".

"GCP" Subsystem. The "GCP" Subsystem is the server side of the "SHeMed" application and performs the following tasks. First, the interface communicates with the Google Cloud Provider (GCP) using the Flask framework to build REST APIs and establish authentication via JWT generation. Then, Caddy server is responsible for using the SSL protocol through "Let's Encrypt", which provides the appropriate certificate. Next, the virtual machine on which our application code resides is responsible for communicating with the storage in the cloud. Last, the "Executor" call is responsible for performing on the virtual machine the operations on the encrypted data which occur with the aim of SEAL.

4   Implementation of "SHeMeD"

Implementation of Python CLI. The patients' medical examinations need to be encrypted before they are sent to the cloud provider GCP. Hence, an encryption procedure needs to be followed from a user's CLI terminal. Primarily, an input polynomial program is created using PyEVA. Due to some limitations in the CKKS model, the parameters of the vector entered by the user must be of power of two and in this case 16 test results were selected. The aforementioned polynomial program needs to be compiled based on CKKS scheme requirements, which requires two more coefficients: the fixed-point scale for the inputs, i.e., set_input_scales, and the maximum coefficient ranges on the outputs, i.e., set_output_ranges, corresponding to several bits. After the compilation of the program into a fully functional EVA program that can be run on encrypted data, the compile() method returns: the compiled program, the encryption parameters for Microsoft SEAL, and a signature object which specifies how the inputs/outputs should be encoded and decoded, respectively.

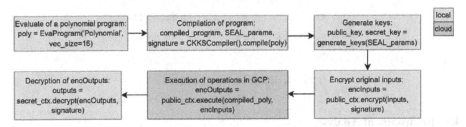

Fig. 3. Process of homomorphic encryption and decryption

Also, EVA through generate_keys() uses SEAL parameters, as an input, to generate a pair of keys: one private and one public, where the public key will be used to encrypt the original input data and the private key will be used to decrypt them after applying homomorphic encryption operations in Google Cloud Provider (GCP). Figure 3 illustrates the prior described process.

Implementation of Backend GCP. The application of the polynomial operation requires the loading of the program (poly), the public key and the encrypted data, entered by the user, from the subfolder (located in medicaleva) of each patient. The call to the EVA compiler's built-in function execute() is responsible for implementing the homomorphic operation, where eventually the result of this function results in an encOutputs vector. Then, again using the save() function, the results end up in a suitably customized file, where it will end up again in the patient's folder.

The application as a backend system is located and "running" on a virtual machine of Ubuntu 22.04 LTS operating system. Therefore, the user from the graphical user interface (UI), selects certain network addresses (endpoints), which through the REST API respond with the corresponding response to the user's request. Below, in Fig. 4, there is a complete scheme of the application's endpoints, that the users can access once they are identified.

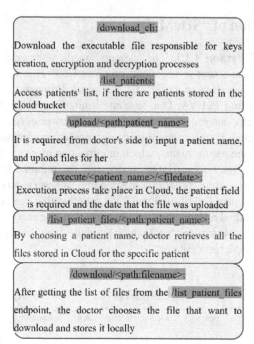

Fig. 4. Endpoints of application

4.1 Environment Analysis

For the implementation of the system, the usability provided by Docker is more convenient as with the implementation of three (3) different Dockerfiles, it is possible to specify all the requirements of the system, without any dependencies installed on a local machine. We have developed a specialized Docker environment that satisfies the functional requirements of the SEAL library and EVA compiler. The second one has been created to cover the appropriate requirements for our backend system, that the application will run on. The last Dockerfile, is responsible for creating appropriate executable files, one for backend application, which can be uploaded in the cloud's virtual machine, and a second one to create an executable SEAL CLI, which end users will store and use in their local machines. The abovementioned Dockerfiles that make up the requirements of the final system, are combined in a bash file to create the final images.

4.2 Theoretical Approach

Our case-study includes a demonstration of program operation and the practical implementation of the CKKS fully homomorphic encryption scheme. This case study uses statistical data for women with breast cancer obtained from [20].

- Initial medical data: The data include measurements from categories of tests for women with benign or malignant disease. A total of 16 categories were sampled from the total. Data obtained from [20]. For these medical records, it is assumed that each test category shares and follows a normal (Gaussian) distribution, $N(\mu, \sigma^2)$. The values for the mean, μ, and standard deviation, σ, are obtained from Eq. (1–2):

$$\mu = \sqrt{\frac{\sum_{i=1}^{N} x_i}{N}} \qquad (1)$$

$$\sigma = \sqrt{\frac{\sum_{i=1}^{N} (x_i - \mu)^2}{N}} \qquad (2)$$

and after examining medical datasets, x_i, from a wide sample of patients, N, the final values are as following: $\mu = 0.1137$ and $\sigma = 0.05689$ (Fig. 5).

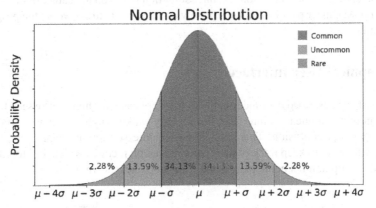

Fig. 5. Normal Distribution indicating three statistical categories [19]

As mentioned, the input data are showcased as part of a normal distribution. A polynomial is, then, calculated as a means of approximating – to some extent – the probability function of the normal distribution. This was achieved by implementing Taylor series of second order, centered around the mean value μ, and based on the maximum range ([0, 1]) of a Probability Density Function (PDF). Hence, the following polynomial is obtained:

$$f(x_i) = \frac{1}{2} - \frac{1}{\sqrt{\pi}} * \left(\frac{\mu - x_i}{\sigma\sqrt{2}}\right) + \frac{1}{5\sqrt{\pi}} * \left(\frac{\mu - x_i}{\sigma\sqrt{2}}\right)^3, x_i : inputdata \qquad (3)$$

In the proposed function, after the replacement of μ and σ the function that results is the following one:

$$f(x_i) = -216.67x_i^3 + 73.91x_i^2 - 1.4x_i + 0.021 \qquad (4)$$

The x_i variable describes the input data of each patient.

- Data output f(x): The values of f(x) belong to the range from 0 to 1. The conceptual meaning of the output indicates a result, ranging from 0 to 1, corresponding to a percentage (%), which categorizes the result of an examination into three different statistical categories (see Fig. 4), based on the rarity of each medical recording. The categorization of the medical records according to the range of the function values is the following.

– functionvaluesof[0.4, 0.6] are considered common,
– functionvaluesof{[0.3, 0.4) ∪ (0.6, 0.7]} are considered uncommon,
– functionvaluesof{(0, 0.3) ∪ (0.7, 1)} are considered rare.

This categorization along with the benignity or malignancy of cancer, could prompt the doctor to conduct the necessary treatment.

It should be mentioned that the aforementioned mathematical polynomial function is not a scientific medical criterion, but an assumption based on the nature of the medical data on breast cancer patients and acts merely as an example to showcase the program's capabilities.

5 Graphical User Interface

So far, we have described the functionality of this application, which can be seen through the layout of the application interface. It is an easy walkthrough for any user to be able to use it without confusion. This application is addressed to particular users, mainly doctors, who want to keep track of their patients' health records, which are stored in the cloud. The application's home page is the following one, shown in Fig. 6.

Fig. 6. Home page

Registered users select the "Log In" button, where the following page appears (Fig. 7):

Fig. 7. Sign In

After logging in, the user may navigate in tabs of SHeMed application. In the next Fig. 8, the user is required to download the executable file to her computer via "Download Seal-CLI" to be able to generate the required keys and encrypt the original data before sending it to the GCP.

The user needs to use the terminal of her operating system to access the executable file and 'run' the command "./seal_cli", which is mentioned in the instructions. The relevant commands are:

- ./seal_cli --action encrypt --mode create --path < PATH > --file < PLAIN_FILE >.xls: user creates the required keys (public, private), the crypto-program, and the medical data entered are encrypted.
- ./seal_cli --action encrypt --mode add_file --path < PATH > --key < PUBLIC_KEY > --file < PLAIN_FILE >.xls: user already has necessary keys at her disposal and simply encrypts new medical data of her patients with the keys to store them in the cloud.
- ./seal_cli --action decrypt --mode decrypt_file --key < PRIVATE_FILE > --path < PATH > --file < ENC_OUTPUTS >: the encrypted data retrieved by the user from
- the cloud is decrypted with the private key, which is located exclusively on the local computer of the treating physician. This data is saved in excel file format and ends up in a new folder "medical_results", which is created when the command is executed.

Then, the user can upload file to corresponding endings (.eva,.sealvals,.sealpublickey) in GCP storage by entering the name of a new patient or by choosing an existing one. Select one or multiple files to upload to the cloud, for which it is ensured through the system that they correspond to an allowed file type. Finally, user

Fig. 8. SEAL CLI

selects the "Submit" button, where she uploads the encrypted medical files to the cloud for the selected patient. The user is presented with a new window with the option to proceed to run the polynomial at the cloud server level (Fig. 9).

Fig. 9. Upload and execution in the cloud

The user is finally able to download the encrypted files for a chosen patient from the corresponding folder in the unified cloud bucket (Fig. 10).

Fig. 10. Download files from the cloud

6 Results and Inferences on Real Data Examples

In this section, we provide our case-study, which was specifically designed for demonstrating the usefulness of our homomorphic scheme. To accomplish this, for the needs of our application, we have used medical breast cancer data from online platform [20], related to smoothness, compactness, concavity, concave points, symmetry, etc. in a decimal form. Mathematical operations combined in a polynomial, which form is encrypted, are implemented in the encrypted form of the original medical data, likewise. After performing mathematical operations, the results were stored in the cloud storage bucket. The EVA compiler of SEAL library was used to perform the mathematical operations inside a cloud VM.

The user can proceed with downloading locally the encrypted modified results from the cloud, by first selecting the patient, and retrieve the relevant ".sealvals" file. The user is now able to decrypt the retrieved cloud data locally. The aforementioned data indicate that the accuracy we achieved is pretty significant. The MSE (Mean Squared Error) is quite low compared to the case where the original data would have been modified after the polynomial was applied: the error approximates the value $1.9878780595116836e - 18$.

In Table 1, there is a demonstration regarding a sample of the medical examinations for a specific day, which indicates for each category the condition of a patient regarding the results. Specifically, a category corresponds to some initial test values from which the results are derived, after the application of the mathematical polynomial. The results indicate the condition of the patient according to the fields of values corresponding to them, as shown in Sect. 4.2.

Table 1. Sample of results for patient's health records

Examination category	Original data	Results	Condition
Smoothness	0.08983	0.334590	Uncommon
Compactness	0.03766	0.061527	Rare
Concavity	0.1063	0.447085	Common
Concave points	0.1322	0.627030	Uncommon
Symmetry	0.1467	0.722176	Rare

7   The Novelty of SHeMed: Features and Outcomes

In this paper, we presented a user-friendly application based on a homomorphic scheme, along with a suitable user interface to store medical data in organized folders on the cloud using the same bucket while applying homomorphic operations on encrypted data with the aim of SEAL library. In a more detailed analysis, the application offers the following outcomes:

- Enables an oncology physician to use the cloud as a method of storing medical examinations of breast cancer patients.
- At the same time, it applies mathematical operations, in particular the application of a probability function to the encrypted results of breast cancer's examinations regarding symmetry, coherence, regularity, etc. This possibility presents three important advantages:

    - Our application utilizes the computational power of cloud computing to securely perform complex mathematical operations on encrypted data, without requiring a powerful computing system on the user's end. This allows users to perform computationally intensive tasks within the application that would otherwise be impractical or impossible.
    - The doctor can draw conclusions about the health history of the patient in question. Based on our approach, the doctor may revisit thoroughly application's results about patient's condition for medical categories, where the states uncommon or rare are present. Thus, the doctor can proceed with changing the patient's current treatment or run additional tests to crossover results.
    - In order to protect patient privacy and maintain data security, oncologists can share modified results, i.e., data output $f(x)$ of medical data with other medical professionals, rather than the original patient data. This approach, known as de-identification, allows doctors to collaborate and share knowledge without compromising the integrity of the medical data or the privacy of their patients. By doing so, medical research and patient care can be improved while still maintaining high standards of data security and privacy.

- The separation of the patients' medical data is delegated through the "SHeMed" application to the cloud provider, GCP in our case, by creating the corresponding folders in the unified bucket. For instance, a user, i.e., a doctor, is advised to categorize her patients with a unique ID or nickname and can upload medical examinations for *"patient_2305"* and a corresponding folder is being created in the bucket.

Therefore, the main conclusion derived from the introduction of this application is the complete security in data lifecycle in the cloud, since:

- A separate CLI is created with the ability for the user to generate the necessary keys and provide the original medical data encrypted, without sharing anything on the web.
- Within the application, appropriate authentication is established using Auth0, where the communication with the provider is done during the respective user sessions.
- The type of files that can be stored on the internet is controlled through the application. The application prevents users from uploading file types *".sealprivatekey"*, which holds the private key that is generated from CLI.
- Only the public key and the encrypted operation defined for the imported data are available to the provider, without the risk of decrypting the medical results, since the private key is in the possession of the user.
- From a list of patients and based on a date, selected by the attending physician, the attending physician selects and retrieves the encrypted tests, which will eventually be decrypted via the CLI with the usage of the private key, which is reserved locally.

In this paper, the usability of SHeMed, as an implementation of a FHE scheme, has been demonstrated through the field of medical data. However, SHeMed application can be easily extended and adapted to a broad range of applicability, including various data and scenarios.

8   Conclusion and Future Work

In this paper, we have proposed an efficient, easy-to-use application for implementing fully homomorphic encryption by using SEAL library for data stored in a cloud provider. The usage of this application indicates that important confidential data can be stored in the cloud securely. Consequently, it can provide the possible elimination of any countermeasure and risk of interception or destruction of personal medical data. Although homomorphic encryption is still an emerging field, research has indicated that it has the potential to protect against attacks from malicious actors, even in the presence of quantum computing. Also, the computational power and complexity that quantum computing offers can provide the resources so that operations take place in less computation time. Thus, this application will provide a practical foundation for working with big data sets of medical data and developing standards for homomorphic encryption in healthcare organizations and other industries. The current implementation has a limited set that can be managed efficiently. However, the problem is expected to be solved with the introduction of quantum theory. Overall, instead of classic encryption techniques, homomorphic encryption will be a milestone in the elimination of the unencrypted security gap, which will provide innovative options for cyber security. The unlimited medical data storage on cloud will introduce a worldwide access for users to gather information without collisions or the fear of compromising the patients' privacy. From homomorphic encryption's perspective, another future research direction would be the enhancement of existing homomorphic encryption techniques, like Fully Homomorphic Encryption (FHE) schemes, which are currently time consuming and cannot support management of unlimited data. Also, another potential avenue for future enhancements is to adapt the secure multi-party computation (MPC) technique to facilitate multiple parties computing a function on their private inputs without compromising their inputs to each other. This advancement holds great promise for the healthcare sector, as it would enable doctors from around the world to collaborate and achieve superior medical outcomes. Further research can concentrate on developing more efficient homomorphic encryption methods that are optimized for secure MPC, improving the privacy, security, and efficiency of healthcare data analytics.

References

1. Acar, A., Aksu, H., Uluagac, S., Conti, M.: A survey on homomorphic encryption schemes: theory and implementation. ACM Comput. Surv. **51**, 1–35 (2017)
2. Ahmad, I., Khandekar, A.: Homomorphic Encryption Method Applied to Cloud Computing. (2014)
3. Chen, H., Laine, K., Player, R.: Simple encrypted arithmetic library - SEAL v2.1. In: Brenner, M., et al. (eds.) Financial Cryptography and Data Security. LNCS, vol. 10323, pp. 3–18. Springer, Cham (2017). https://doi.org/10.1007/978-3-319-70278-0_1
4. Chen, B., Zhao, N.: Fully homomorphic encryption application in cloud computing. In: Proceedings of the 11th International Computer Conference on Wavelet Actiev Media Technology and Information Processing (ICCWAMTIP) (2014)
5. Chowdhary, S., Dai, W., Laine, K., Saarikivi, O.: EVA improved: compiler and extension library for CKKS. In: Proceedings of the 9th on Workshop on Encrypted Computing & Applied Homomorphic Cryptography, pp 43–55 (2021)
6. D'Angelo, G., Palmieri, F.: Discovering genomic patterns in SARS-CoV-2 variants. Int. J. Intell. Syst. **35**(11), 1680–1698 (2020). https://doi.org/10.1002/int.22268
7. D'Angelo, G., Palmieri, F.: Enhancing COVID-19 tracking apps with human activity recognition using a deep convolutional neural network and HAR-images. Neural Comput. Appl. **35**(19), 13861–13877 (2021). https://doi.org/10.1007/s00521-021-05913-y
8. Huynh, D.: CKKS explained, Part 3: Encryption and Decryption. https://blog.openmined.org/ckks-explained-part-3-encryption-and-decryption/ (2020)
9. Kocabas, Ö., Soyata, T.: Medical data analytics in the cloud using homomorphic encryption. In: Raj, P., Deka, G.C. (eds.) Handbook of Research on Cloud Infrastructures for Big Data Analytics, pp. 471–488. IGI Global (2014). https://doi.org/10.4018/978-1-4666-5864-6.ch019
10. Chauhan, K.K., Sanger, A.K., Verma, A.: Homomorphic encryption for data security in cloud computing. In: 2015 International Conference on Information Technology (ICIT), pp. 206–209 (2015)
11. Manish, M.P., Dhote, C.A., Sharma, D.H.: Homomorphic encryption for security of cloud data. Proc. Comput. Sci. **79**, 175–181 (2016)
12. Mell, P., Grance, T.: The NIST Definition of Cloud Computing. Special Publication (NIST SP), National Institute of Standards and Technology, Gaithersburg (2011)
13. Liu, J., Mesnager, S., Chen, L.: Partially homomorphic encryption schemes over finite fields. In: Carlet, C., Hasan, M.A., Saraswat, V. (eds.) Security, Privacy, and Applied Cryptography

Engineering. LNCS, vol. 10076, pp. 109–123. Springer, Cham (2016). https://doi.org/10.1007/978-3-319-49445-6_6

14. Fan, J., Vercauteren, F.: Somewhat practical fully homomorphic encryption. IACR Cryptology ePrint Archive , 144 (2012)
15. Gentry C.: A Fully Homomorphic Encryption scheme. Stanford University. (2009)
16. Regev, O.: On lattices, learning with errors, random linear codes, and cryptography. J. ACM (JACM). **56**, 84–93 (2009)
17. Wibawa, F., Catak, F.O., Sarp, S., Kuzlu, M.: BFV-based homomorphic encryption for privacy preserving CNN models. Cryptography. **6**(3), 34 (2022)
18. Vankudoth, B., Vasumathi, D.: Homomorphic encryption techniques for securing data in cloud computing: a survey. Int. J. Comput. Appl. **160**, 1–5 (2017)
19. Normal distribution. https://money.stackexchange.com/questions/144051/calculate-stock-price-range-using-standard-deviation
20. Kaggle datasets homepage. https://www.kaggle.com/datasets

Evaluating the Effectiveness of Privacy and Security Promotion Strategies

M. Iacono[1] and M. Mastroianni[2(✉)]

[1] Dipartimento di Matematica e Fisica, Università degli Studi della Campania,
"L. Vanvitelli", viale Lincoln, 5,81100 Caserta, Italy
[2] Dipartimento di Informatica, Università degli Studi di Salerno,
Via Giovanni Paolo II, 132, 84084 Fisciano, Italy
mmastroianni@unisa.it

Abstract. Privacy and security concerns are one of the relevant action fields of regulators. The rise of privacy concerns is, due to the capabilities of computing systems to aggregate information to generate profiles or other aggregates that impact the personal life of people. This has led to regulations like the UE General Data Protection Regulation (GDPR) and to the spread of initiatives aiming to raise awareness in people. Data show that privacy problems are known to people; however, practice of privacy and security aware behavior seems to be oddly not part of the habits of the same population. In this paper we propose a model of privacy and security effectiveness promotion strategies and a related evaluation method. The strategies we are interested in aim at aligning actual behavior to awareness levels. We derive an example of strategy starting from literature data and propose an analysis method that is based on Pythia, a tool for the analysis of graph-based probabilistic cause-and-effect models.

Keywords: Privacy · Security · Privacy awareness · Security awareness · Privacy paradox · Risk analysis · GDPR

1 Introduction

Problems created by privacy, and, more in general, security violations may be highly severe and may seriously impact daily life of people. As a consequence, far before the introduction of the GDPR[1] privacy concerns had been raised by the scientific and social studies communities, by industry and by governments. For example, in Italy private and public initiatives and information campaigns were launched, targeting workers, students and citizens, after in 2005 the Codice dell'Amministrazione Digitale[2] law introduced and regulated Information and

---

[1] Regulation (EU) 2016/679 of the European Parliament and of the Council, April 27, 2016, concerning the protection of individuals with regard to the processing of personal data, as well as the free movement of such data and repealing Directive 95/46/EC (General Data Protection Regulation) OJ L 119, 4 May 2016.

[2] D.lg. 7 marzo 2005, n. 82, Codice dell'amministrazione digitale (G.U. n. 112 del 16 maggio 2005, Suppl. ord. n. 93).

© The Author(s), under exclusive license to Springer Nature Switzerland AG 2023
O. Gervasi et al. (Eds.): ICCSA 2023 Workshops, LNCS 14109, pp. 134–148, 2023.
https://doi.org/10.1007/978-3-031-37120-2_9

Communication Technologies (ICT) as the main mean for the reorganization of public administrations, their processes and their interaction with private citizens and other subjects. Analogous initiative were enacted in many Countries.

This notwithstanding, an Eurobarometer[3] survey published in 2018 reveals a surprising discrepancy between data resulting from the answers to the questions on potential privacy problems and those resulting from the answers to the questions about behaviors: apparently, people exhibited high awareness about potential problems but did not enact virtuous and attentive behaviors, as should have been expected as a consequence.

Possibly, the Covid-19 crisis led to an even worse situation, as many citizens that were not familiar with online operations were forced to unfamiliar procedures without any kind of training or support, and this is also confirmed an Interpol report written in August 2020 about Covid-19 impact on cybercrime[4].

In [1] we identified possible levers that might help stimulating people to align their behavior to their knowledge about privacy and security procedures, including better software engineering approaches that conform to GDPR privacy-by-design and privacy-by-default requirements [2,3]. In this paper we propose a methodology and a modeling approach to evaluate the potential effectiveness of such levers by means of a quantitative approach based on an Influence Nets analysis tool [4,5]. At the best of our knowledge, this is a novel approach to the problem and contributes to bridge efforts by software industry, academia and regulator under the umbrella of a tool suitable to analyze complex scenarios subject to complex probabilistic influences.

This paper is organized as follows: Sect. 2 presents related work, Sect. 3 states the problem, Sect. 4 describes the modeling approach, Sect. 5 introduces a case study, Sect. 6 discusses the results of the analysis on the example strategy, and conclusions close the paper.

2   Related Work

The *Privacy Paradox* is a seemingly strange users' behavior that may be defined as *a concept in which online users state that they are concerned about privacy, but disclose personal data nonetheless* [6]. Many researchers deal with this topic, and an interesting starting point to deep into this topic is a systematic literature review [7] that explains the privacy paradox and identified a series of theoretical explanation attempts for the privacy paradox, including decision biases, lack of experience and illusion of control.

The privacy paradox concept is also controversial. Solove [8] argues that it is a myth created by faulty logic, since the people's behavior in their everyday life is not an accurate metric of preferences because behavior is distorted by biases and heuristics, manipulation and skewing, and other factors. Author claims that giving individuals more tasks for managing users' privacy will not

---

[3] https://europa.eu/eurobarometer/.

[4] https://www.interpol.int/content/download/15526/file/COVID-19%20Cybercrime %20Analysis%20Report-%20August%202020.pdf.

provide effective privacy protection, and instead argue that a regulation focused on regulating the way information is used, maintained, and transferred could have more impact on this issue.

Acquisti et al. [9] in their review also highlighted biases and illusory control as an attempt to explain the matter, and include in the explanations the *adaptation* of users. In this research some possible countermeasures are also proposed to be taken to mitigate the issue: i) soft paternalistic interventions, called *nudges*, by authors given from stakeholders such as government, companies etc.; ii) positive impact from privacy regulations; iii) use of privacy-enhancing technologies; iv) market-based data *propertization*[5] schemes that could induce positive response.

An empirical study conducted during Covid-19 pandemic [11] suggests that the users' behavior could vary depending on age and medical condition. In [12] has been studied the case of AIoT-enabled smart surveillance, and stated that transparency in mode and purpose of the information collected could efficiently moderate the privacy paradox effect.

3   Problem Statement

The name Eurobarometer refers to a series of public opinion polls conducted regularly on behalf of the European Commission and other EU institutions since 1974. These polls address a wide variety of topical issues relating to the European Union across the its member states.

The objective of the surveys referred in this analysis is to understand the awareness, experiences and perceptions of EU citizens on cybersecurity issues. Respondents were asked to talk about many specific cybersecurity issues, such as how important they think cybersecurity is to EU internal security, how much they worry about being victims of cybercrime and how they would react in a variety of situations if they were victims of these particular forms of cybercrime. Although the number of questionnaires in the survey is relatively low (around 27,000), this analysis can be a good starting point for understanding how EU citizens deal with Cybersecurity issues. Used data relate to the Europeans' attitudes towards Internet security survey, ref. 2207/480. The survey is based on data collected in October/November 2018, which, at the time the analysis was conducted, was the most recent survey available on the topic.

Eurobarometer surveys have first highlighted a worrying trend in user behavior. The number of EU citizens concerned about cybercrime is on the rise, as is the number of EU citizens who think they are well informed about cybercrime, but are less likely to protect themselves from cyber risks. The following Fig. 1 shows how the view of the respondents regarding concerns and information on cybercrime changed from 2013 to 2018, comparing it with the most basic rule of safe behavior: changing the password in Internet services. In 2018, 40% of users did not change their password (email, social networks, e-banking services...) in the last 12 months, while in 2017 this percentage was 37%. It should be noted

---

[5] The process of coming to treat something as if it were property under the law [10].

that, in the same period, the perception of the interviewees regarding the increase in risks is growing, as is the perception of being well informed about these risks.

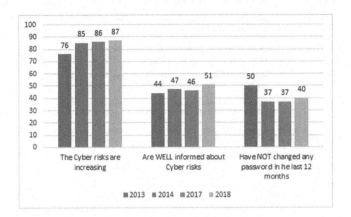

Fig. 1. Cybersecurity risks and users' behavior (Source: Eurobarometer).

Other relevant considerations can be made by analyzing user reaction to an attack. In the Eurobarometer survey there are two sets of questions relating to reactions. In the first group of questions, users were asked what in their opinion the correct behavior should be (respondent's perception); in the second group, users were asked what their real behavior was after they suffered an attack (real behavior). The results are quite surprising and are shown in Fig. 2. The reactions in the figures are grouped into three categories: Law Enforcement (the answer to the Eurobarometer questionnaire was "Call the police"), "Do nothing", same question in the EB questionnaire) and Others, which is the sum of all the other answers in Eurobarometer Questionnaire such as "Contact your Internet provider", "Contact your bank", "Contact a consumer association" and so on.

The first observation that emerges from these figures is the high number of "Do nothing" reactions in real behavior. If it is intuitive to explain this behavior in the case of fraudulent e-mails (e.g., phishing), which can be perceived more as a annoyance rather than a real threat, it is alarming that the reaction of over 30% of users who encounter abuses is to "Do nothing". The "Do nothing" reaction of many users who suffer online fraud or identity theft also deserves further study. Another thing to note is the distance between users' perception and their actual behavior when comparing the pair of rows drawn in Fig. 2. In many cases, users know that it is necessary to report the problem to law enforcement agencies and, in particular, to more serious cases, such as identity theft, bank fraud, ransom demand, but in real cases they choose to call another actor (the Internet provider or the bank, for example), or even do nothing.

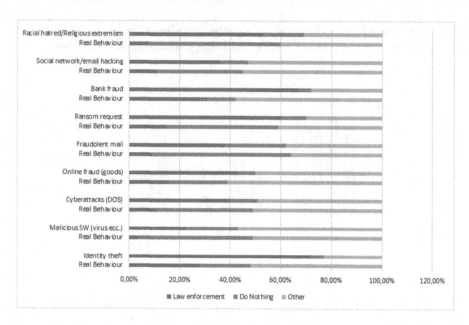

Fig. 2. Reaction to attacks, users' perception vs. real behavior (Source: Eurobarometer).

4 Modeling Approach

The verification of the effectiveness of the proposed actions requires an extended experimental campaign that would impact in vivo on the population, with significant and expensive large-scale interventions by governmental authorities. Enacting a strategy would involve the need for new laws, reorganization of governance processes at all levels and a control system over processes. Consequently, each proposal should be evaluated and compared with alternatives by means of a sound modeling approach capable of supporting a decomposition of the influencing factors and levers into intermediate steps and possible global influences in a quantifiable impact between single related factors and their mutual interference, in terms of a probabilistic framework.

A suitable methodology may consist of the following steps (see Fig. 3):

1. framing the problem;
2. identification of primary and secondary objectives;
3. identification of intermediate influencing objectives;
4. identification of actionable levers;
5. identification of the influence links;
6. definition of the probability with which each of the factors may independently verify or evolve;
7. weights assignment;
8. evaluation of the effects of levers application;

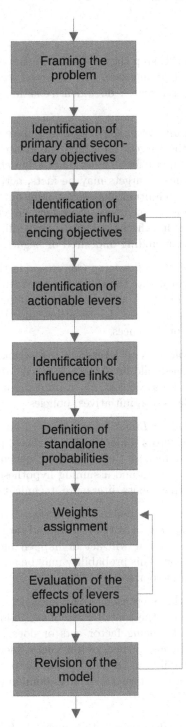

Fig. 3. The steps of the proposed methodology.

9. revision of the model.

Framing the Problem: in this step the relevant elements of the existing scenario are collected, investigated or measured, in order to state the situation as-is. Sources may be official or research document, existing data, experts, panels, reports.

Identification of Primary and Secondary Objectives: once the scenario is defined, primary goals, that is, the targets on which the strategy is meant to act in order to modify them or their effects, must be clearly defined, in order to allow the analysis of the influences. Targets may be facts, actions, effects of actions, measures. As the scenario definition phase may point out that other effects may derive by the application of the strategy, secondary targets may be defined and observed, as additional results, checks to be used for verification, expected effects to be monitored et cetera, including undesired or negative effects.

Identification of Intermediate Influencing Objectives: in this step the intermediate actions or facts that constitute the chain of consequences between levers and targets are discovered. This step, as well as the next ones, requires the intervention of domain experts, both for the definition and the quantification of the elements of the chain of consequences.

Identification of Actionable Levers: levers are the actions that can be used to enact the strategy. Actions should be in the actual availability of the entity that will enact the strategy, and may consist, for example, in investments, regulation, activation of resources, decisions, initiatives, policies.

Identification of the Influence Links: in this step the nature of the influences between the intermediate factors is identified, in terms of potential contributions to the verification of the influenced factor if the influencing factor verifies. This is done by analyzing the domain and assuming hypotheses derived by previous knowledge, documents, experiments, literature, technical reports.

Definition of the Probability with Which Each of the Factors may Independently Verify or Evolve: in this step each of the factors and targets is assigned a probability about the chances that it will act or happen independently from any influence, that is, in isolation. This probability may be already known or in need to be estimated by domain experts.

Weights Assignment: in this step each of the influences is assigned a positive or negative strength, defining the contribution of the influencing factor over the influenced factor if the influencing factor acts or does not act. This strength transmits or mitigates the consequences of influencing factors over an influenced factor modifying the probability of the destination factor as a conditioned probability[6]. The estimation of the strength requires domain experts.

---

[6] In the case study used to demonstrate this approach, CAST logic is applied to combine the influences.

Evaluation of the Effects of Levers Application: a what-if analysis may be performed to investigate the effects of the levers. This may lead to reconsider the weight of the influences of the model, also acting as a first debug step, and to cycle back to the *Weights assignment* step.

Revision of the model: the results of a sensitivity analysis may suggest missing influences in the model. This may lead to reconsider the structure or the influences of the model, also acting as a second debug step, and to cycle back to the *Identification of intermediate influencing objectives* step. The results of the previous steps might also inspire considerations on relations between the modeled entities and suggest the definition of new influences to be established between related levers or actions, contributing to define new or alternative policies; this may lead to fork new, alternate versions of the model, to be compared, on which it is necessary to cycle back to the *Identification of intermediate influencing objectives* step.

5 Case Study

In order to evaluate the impact of the proposed levers that can be used to improve the situation, we analyzed the influences between the goals and the levers. The analysis has been performed by organizing a panel of experts, including the authors. The panel supported the authors in the application of the methodology to the case proposed by the authors in [1] with an evaluation of the probabilities and the strength of influences and by assessing the proposed model. Moreover, the panel discussed the outcomes of the evaluation performed by the authors. The scenario has been modeled as an Influence Net and has been evaluated by means of Pythia [5].

The model is depicted in Fig. 4.

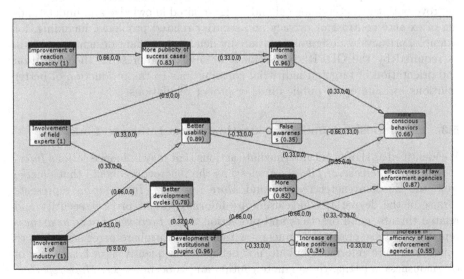

Fig. 4. The Influence Net for the proposed scenario

5.1 Targets Definition

The primary target effect of the model, coherently to what proposed in ?, is action *More conscious behavior*; secondary target effects are actions *Increase in effectiveness of law enforcement agencies* and *Increase in efficiency of law enforcement agencies*, as they are global measures of the potential effects of the strategy on the global level of the overall system defined by the regulations to react to privacy and security threats and to contrast their effects. *More conscious behavior* represents a change in users' behavior in terms of a greater coherence with security and privacy oriented policies, and with their knowledge about them. *Increase in effectiveness of law enforcement agencies* represents an increase of the overall degree of effectiveness of the complex of authorities, forces and institutions that apply a posteriori actions in contrast of privacy or security violations (e.g. courts, police, policy makers et cetera). *Increase in efficiency of law enforcement agencies* represents an increase of the overall efficiency of the said complex in terms of resources (people, funds, equipment) needed to investigate and, in case, sanction violations.

5.2 Levers

Used levers are a synthesis of the ones proposed in [1]. *Improvement of reaction capacity* represents the implementation of better procedures for immediate reaction to violations, both on the technical and the administrative point of view, but in the model the focus is on the administrative procedures, including publicity of success cases and avoided threats as a deterrent. For example, focusing on the Italian case, the national CERT, Agenzia per l'Italia Digitale, and the Autorità per la cybersicurezza nazionale might be involved in such a process. *Involvement of field experts* represents the contribution of academia and reference experts to improve both the methodological and design-related knowledge and understanding of ex-ante contrast of privacy and security related problems, including, for example, privacy-by-design and privacy-by-default compliant design techniques, as required by the GDPR. *Involvement of industry* represents the activation and orientation of targeted industrial contributions to the production of better solutions, stimulated by public funds or proper regulations.

5.3 Decomposition and Identification of the Influence Links

We identified as significant intermediate actions that may influence actions *Information* and *Increase of false awareness*, as the macrocomponents that emerge from the Eurobarometer results, and *More reporting*. *Information* represents a raise of the degree at which users are informed about privacy, security and related threats, good practices and protection tools. *Increase of false awareness* represents a raise of the phenomenon witnessed by Eurobarometer according to which users are informed, but do not behave consequently as a false sense of consciousness is letting them ignore caution and good practices. *More reporting* represents a raise in the amount of potential violations or threats reported by users while using services or accessing the web.

In turn, *More publicity of success cases* has been identified as a factor that may influence *Information*, and may be a consequence of *Improvement of reaction capacity*. This action represents the contribution of media to the diffusion of positive results obtained by reaction among the population, that produces a spread of information reaching also generic citizens.

Better usability has been identified as a factor that may influence *Increase of false awareness*, as, paradoxically, better usability of software promotes routine behaviors, and routine behaviors produce mechanical actions, leading to ignore anomalies or to underestimate the consequences of own actions, as they become a habit. *Better usability* is influenced by both *Involvement of field experts* and *Involvement of industry*, respectively because of the theoretical/methodological and the implementation contributions to this factor. *Better usability* also impacts on *Increase in effectiveness of law enforcement agencies*, as better user interfaces may guide users to avoid bad habits or mistakes that produce exposure to threats and reduce the number of low impact violations, with a lower ordinary workload for contrast authorities.

Another joint effect of *Involvement of field experts* and *Involvement of industry* might be the development of proper methodological software engineering solutions and practices, such as the targeted privacy-by-design and privacy-by-default advocated by the GDPR, represented by *Better development cycles*. This might include the *Development of institutional plugins* to detect threats or produce automatic reports for the law enforcement agencies, which have as a consequence *More reporting* and *Increase in effectiveness of law enforcement agencies*, but may also produce *Increase of false positives* because of malicious or inexpert users, with a negative impact on *Increase in efficiency of law enforcement agencies*. *Development of institutional plugins* might also directly be a consequence of *Involvement of industry* under the push of regulation or as a byproduct of a will for less exposure to legal actions and liability that might involve authorities.

5.4   Probability and Weights

The panel did examine and review the proposed structure for the model and discussed both the probabilities and the weights of the influences, on the basis of an evaluation of the scenario based on the experience, reaching a consensus. In some cases there has been no consensus, so a mediation has been reached as a conservative compromise.

For the sake of space, the results of the analysis about actions probability is summarized in Table 1. In the case of action *False awareness* the baseline probability is set to 0.5 because no consensus has been reached by the panel. Similarly, the results of the analysis about strengths is summarized in Table 2. The reported strengths are relative to the case in which the influencing action is enabled, while in the case in which the influencing action is not enabled the strength of the influence is 0.0, with the only exception of one case, in which respectively the strength is indicated if the influencing action is enabled or not enabled.

Table 1. Baseline probability of actions

Action	Baseline probability
More publicity of success cases	0.20
Information	0.50
More conscious behavior	0.20
Better usability	0.10
False awareness	0.50
Better development cycles	0.20
More reporting	0.10
Increase in effectiveness of law enforcement agencies	0.50
Development of institutional plugins	0
Increase of false positives	0
Increase in efficiency of law enforcement agencies	0.50

Table 2. Influences between actions expressed as strengths of an Influence Net

Influence	Action	Strength
Improvement of reaction capacity	More publicity of success cases	0.66
More publicity of success cases	Information	0.33
Involvement of field experts	Information	0.90
Involvement of field experts	Better usability	0.33
Involvement of field experts	Better development cycles	0.33
Information	More conscious behaviors	0.33
Better usability	False awareness	-0.33
Better usability	Increase in effectiveness of law enforcement agencies	0.33
False awareness	More conscious behaviors	-0.66
Better development cycles	Development of institutional plugins	0.33
Involvement of industry	Development of institutional plugins	0.90
Involvement of industry	Better usability	0.66
Involvement of industry	Better development cycles	0.33
Development of institutional plugins	More reporting	0.33
More reporting	More conscious behaviors	0.33
More reporting	Increase in efficiency of law enforcement agencies	±0.33
Development of institutional plugins	Increase in effectiveness of law enforcement agencies	0.66
Development of institutional plugins	Increase of false positives	0.33
Increase of false positives	Increase in efficiency of law enforcement agencies	-0.33

6   Analysis and Results

The as-is situation of the influence net, considering the effects of the three levers, is in Fig. 4. The primary target has an overall probability of 0.66, 3.3 times the baseline probability: the hypothesized interventions may consequently be beneficial. Secondary targets are also impacted: the probability of increasing the effectiveness is 0.87, with respect to a 0.50 baseline, while the probability of increasing the efficiency is 0.55 with respect to a 0.50. In the first case, the model suggests that the proposed interventions do not have a negative impact on effectiveness and efficiency of contrast initiatives (helping instead it a bit to be more effective).

On these premises, a sensitivity analysis has been performed to understand what is the actual role of the three levers according to their intensity (or absence). The model suggests a very low sensitivity of the primary target with respect to an improvement of the reaction capacity, that is, an investment on first intervention procedures and infrastructures, as the overall oscillation of the final probability is 0.001: consequently, the contribution of this lever is not relevant. This may be motivated by the fact that people is not sensitive to technical procedures and emergency management with respect to the overall information that is available to the public, the baseline probability of spontaneous increase of which has been estimated by the panel to a value of 0.50 considering that workers receive training and that regulation is gaining popularity among the population because of the visible consequences of GDPR requirements in terms of consent forms both online and offline; the structure of the model excludes influences on the secondary targets. The oscillation due to the involvement of experts (including education, research and technical/professional initiatives) and of industry is one magnitude order wider, respectively 0.035 and 0.029.

The impact of an increase of the effectiveness of the law enforcement agencies depends on the involvement of field experts with an oscillation of 0.004, exhibiting a low sensitivity, while the oscillation of the contribution of industry is very relevant and quantifiable in 0.104. This may justify public funding targeted to stimulate industry towards an active collaboration with policy makers in the directions represented by the model.

The efficiency of the law enforcement agencies is a concern, due to the fact that the model exhibits a direct negative influence with a common root with an action that in turn has a positive impact on the previous target. Even if there is a chain of influences between the field experts contribution lever and this target, the only lever to which this target is sensitive, with an oscillation of 0.045, is industry intervention: this may be motivated by the fact that there is a common intermediate action that mediates their influences, with a complex influence subnetwork on which the industry lever has a direct and indirect influence.

If no lever is actually present, the model provides overall probabilities of 0.58, 0.74 and 0.21.

We decided to investigate the effect of a different estimation for the baseline probability of the efficiency target, in order to understand its inertia with respect to influences. With its baseline probability set to 0.20, the resulting overall probability of the target is 0.33; if set to 0.10, 0.25. Consequently, the proposed levers produce anyway a positive overall impact.

6.1 A Proposal to Improve the Effectiveness of the Law Enforcement Agencies

The analysis of the model points out the low impact of an investment on improving the reaction capacity. This insight stimulated further work that led to a proposal of modification of the model, hypothesizing an influence of this lever on the effectiveness secondary target: this corresponds to a direct collaboration between first reaction and contrast authorities, that is between technicians and jurists, that we hypothesize with a moderate strength quantified in 0.33 and consisting in direct and organized communication and regular data and statistics exchange. A suitable model is provided by the introduction of Autorità per la cybersicurezza nazionale in Italy.

In this case, the overall probability of obtaining an increase of effectiveness is 0.91, and the best case is obtained when all levers are enacted, while the worst case is 0.83, when only the first lever is applied (clearly as an obvious consequence of the introduction of the new mechanism). The highest influence is anyway due to the introduction of institutional plugins; consequently, this new influence mitigates the dependency of effectiveness from private initiatives.

7 Conclusions

When the socio-technical perspective has to be considered, evaluating the effects of actions cannot be based the analysis of architectural or functional specifications. The effects of system-wide decisions on technical issues need a different quantification and proper modeling approaches. In this paper we adopted a tool suitable for evaluation of chains of consequences in socio-political systems and a support methodology to evaluate the suitability of a promotion strategy for privacy and security in the perspective of socio-technical systems. We explored how a proper analysis of the results provided by the tool and of sensitivity to levers may inspire and support insight-based improvements, besides informed decisions.

Future work includes the implementation of a more detailed model to obtain further insight and a better analysis of possible oscillation causes, that we expect wider if including a finer decomposition of objectives and levers, a time-based analysis of the same model, with alternative strategies, including proper cost hypotheses, and further quantitative investigation about the possible causes of the privacy paradox, to improve the model structure and define and evaluate more detailed strategies, with special references to the levers that software engineering may provide.

Acknowledgments. This paper is part of the research activity realized within the project PON "Ricerca e Innovazione" 2014–2020, action IV.6 "Contratti di ricerca su tematiche Green", issued by Italian Ministry of University and Research. Part of this work has been finalized in Sala della Regina at Camera dei Deputati, Italy, where Mauro Iacono was attending a meeting; it has been revised after the precious comments formulated while sitting together close to the tower of Pisa by professor emeritus Alexander H. Levis, to which Mauro Iacono wishes to express his gratitude, also for being a continuous inspiration and reference. The Pythia simulator used in this paper has been developed with the support by the Air Force Office for Scientific Research under contract no. F49620-01-1-0008, by the Air Force Research Laboratory, Information Directorate, under contract no. F30602-01-C-0065, and by the Office of Naval Research under contract no. N00014-06-1-0081.

References

1. Iacono, M., Mastroianni, M.: Il curioso caso della divergenza tra consapevolezza e comportamenti in materia di sicurezza informatica dopo la crisi pandemica: quando non bastano norme ed esperienza, Edizioni Scientifiche Italiane, pp. 107–118 (2022)
2. Campanile, L., Iacono, M., Marulli, F., Mastroianni, M.: Designing a GDPR compliant blockchain-based IOV distributed information tracking system. Inf. Process. Manage. **58**(3), 102511 (2021). https://doi.org/10.1016/j.ipm.2021.102511, https://www.sciencedirect.com/science/article/pii/S0306457321000194
3. Campanile, L., Iacono, M., Mastroianni, M.: Towards privacy-aware software design in small and medium enterprises. In: 2022 IEEE International Conference on Dependable, Autonomic and Secure Computing, International Conference on Pervasive Intelligence and Computing, International Conference on Cloud and Big Data Computing, International Conference on Cyber Science and Technology Congress (DASC/PiCom/CBDCom/CyberSciTech), pp. 1–8 (2022). https://doi.org/10.1109/DASC/PiCom/CBDCom/Cy55231.2022.9927958, https://doi.org/10.1109/DASC/PiCom/CBDCom/Cy55231.2022.9927958
4. Zaidi, A., Mansoor, F., Papantoni-Kazakos, T.: Theory of influence networks, J. Intell. Robot Syst. **60**, 457–491 (2010). http://dx.doi.org/https://doi.org/10.1007/s10846-010-9425-8, https://doi.org/10.1007/s10846-010-9425-8
5. Mansoor, F., Zaidi, A.K., Wagenhals, L., Levis, A.H.: Meta-modeling the cultural behavior using timed influence nets. In: Computing, S., Modeling, B. (eds.) Springer, pp. 1–9. MA, US, Boston (2009). https://doi.org/10.1007/978-1-4419-0056-2_19
6. Øverby, H.: The Privacy Paradox, pp. 1–2. Springer, Heidelberg (2019). https://doi.org/10.1007/978-3-642-27739-9_1619-1
7. Gerber, N., Gerber, P., Volkamer, M.: Explaining the privacy paradox: a systematic review of literature investigating privacy attitude and behavior. Comput. Secur. **77**, 226–261 (2018). https://doi.org/10.1016/j.cose.2018.04.002, https://www.sciencedirect.com/science/article/pii/S0167404818303031
8. Solove, D.J.: The myth of the privacy paradox. Geo. Wash. L. Rev. **89**, 1 (2021)
9. Acquisti, A., Brandimarte, L., Loewenstein, G.: Secrets and likes: the drive for privacy and the difficulty of achieving it in the digital age. J. Consum. Psychol. **30**(4), 736–758 (2020)
10. Paul, E.F., Miller Jr, F.D., Paul, J.: Freedom of Speech: Volume 21, Part 2, vol. 21, Cambridge University Press, Cambridge (2004)

11. Fernandes, T., Costa, M.: Privacy concerns with COVID-19 tracking apps: a privacy calculus approach. J. Consum. Mark. **40**(2), 181–192 (2023)
12. Zhang, F., Pan, Z., Lu, Y.: Smart surveillance for personal data digitalization: contextual personalization-privacy paradox in smart home. Inf. Manage. **60**(2), 103736 (2023). https://doi.org/10.1016/j.im.2022.103736, https://www.sciencedirect.com/science/article/pii/S0378720622001446

A Decentralized Smart City Using Solid and Self-Sovereign Identity

Biagio Boi[✉][iD], Marco De Santis[iD], and Christian Esposito[iD]

University of Salerno, Fisciano, Italy
{bboi,esposito}@unisa.it, m.desantis29@studenti.unisa.it

Abstract. In the Internet of Things (IoT) context, a considerable quantity of data flows from sensors to centralized servers, holding sensitive information related to users. Unfortunately, how servers store these data instances is usually poorly documented and does not offer any transparency to the users but may pave the way to possible privacy violations. Web decentralization is a prominent solution to cope with these issues and legal obligations regarding data protection so that multiple domains are progressively adopting it as the principal technological enabler. The IoT is not among them yet, as a centralized approach is still the most common one; however, moving data location away from servers to prefer gateways or directly to devices closer to users and under their direct control can realize a more decentralized approach and alleviate the issues related to performance, throughput as well as data protection. This paper aims to exploit existing data decentralization solutions, like Social Linked Data (Solid), to define a more distributed data management for IoT and propose a proof-of-concept implementation of a Smart City platform where users can store and directly manage data produced by public or private IoT devices. Despite providing decentralized data handling, Solid is still affected by a centralized identity management and authentication implementation represented by OpenID Connect. Therefore, to fulfill our vision of a decentralized IoT, we also investigate how decentralizing authentication within Solid and a new user-centric approach based on Self-Sovereign Identity (SSI) represents a promising solution.

Keywords: Web Decentralization · Solid · Smart City

1 Introduction

Integrating intelligent sensors within the context of cities and their underlying social processes is a practice that positively impacts costs and efficiency [2]. For example, by analyzing real-time data from sensors and cameras placed in specific crucial locations, it's possible to optimize traffic flow, reduce congestion, and improve public transportation services. In addition, smart cities can also be one enabler for citizen empowerment and enhance the interaction of public administrations with their inhabitants by providing personalized services. Due to the characteristics of such sensors, and their massive horizontal and vertical

O. Gervasi et al. (Eds.): ICCSA 2023 Workshops, LNCS 14109, pp. 149–161, 2023.
https://doi.org/10.1007/978-3-031-37120-2_10

scale, it is unfeasible for them to process such data directly on board. Still, it is more reasonable to have them connected among each other by leveraging cellular or mobile networks and/or outsourcing computation and data to external services hosted in the cloud or different virtualized environments. Therefore, it is a practice for IoT devices to continuously send data to external servers, with consequent networking issues that have led to radical transformations, such as 5G to cite the most prominent one.

Problems in such an approach are not only bonded to QoS and technological aspects, but also legal and ethical when collected data are strictly related to the users, so they become instances of personal data. Moreover, collected data are usually stored in centralized databases, subject to possible attacks perpetrated by criminal externals to providers and dishonest employees aimed at stealing sensible information. Furthermore, such collected data can be used to profile a person by tracing down his/her habits for commercial purposes or not only. What is more dangerous is the position taken by some manufacturers which create sensors able to collect undeclared information, without specifying to the final user in which country or who will receive collected data. General Data Protection Regulation (GDPR) plays a vital role in this context by trying to give users control over their data. It defines how applications can collect the data, which limits exists in the data collection, and where a manufacturer can or cannot store user data. Despite this regulation, its application to the concrete case of IoT and smart cities is still fuzzy [10], motivating the EU to issue additional legal tools to discipline better the legal and ethical obligations in these novel ICT contexts.

Over the last few years, the concept of decentralization is taking place, which is the transfer of authority and responsibility from centric servers to decentralized nodes. This shift is motivated by the need to reduce data flows and deal with legal and ethical obligations by restraining outsourcing for personal data. Blockchain is the key technological enabler for decentralization. It can realize a consistent replica of data and state synchronization so that central nodes are removed, and all computations safely and securely occur at local nodes. As a result, we have witnessed a flourishing explosion of academic papers investigating how blockchain-based solutions can be used within the context of IoT and smart cities, where decentralization is made of smart contracts running on blockchain [19]. Using blockchains simplifies handling good performance, reduced network stress, and improved security, but it is not so evident that privacy and legal obligations are also resolved. As proof, frictions between GDPR and blockchain [8] are yet to be completely resolved. Therefore, rather than focusing on GDPR-compliant blockchain-empowered solutions, we turned attention to other existing solutions for decentralization.

Based on the decentralization concept, the major inventor of the Internet - Tim-Bernard Lee, has recently proposed the Solid project, *a decentralized platform for social Web applications*, aimed at changing how users store their data [14]. The architecture defines the concept of *personal online datastore* (pod), an online storage accessible only by the owners without restriction about the provider. Users can only authorize third-party applications to interact (write or read) with their pod. According to Linked Data Platform (LDP) recommendation [11], data within Solid platforms are exposed by using a RESTful way: POST/PUT commands to create data instances in the pod, PUT/PATCH commands to update existing data, and GET commands to retrieve data from the pod. Solid has a natural application to traditional citizen empowerment services and/or social networks, but it is our belief that it can also be successfully used in the context of IoT; as the huge quantity of sensing data can be stored in the related user pod, rather than outsourced in the cloud or other computing environment. Despite being such an application a natural one for Solid, the current academic literature and industrial practice encompass only a few works trying to extend the Solid platform to IoT devices. As widely known, problems in applying this solution are the limitation imposed by IoT nodes, which cannot directly follow the schema defined by LDP due to their communication protocols, such as Bluetooth, usually oriented to connection-less ones [3].

This paper proposes an architecture that includes IoT devices as active nodes in the Solid ecosystem, paving the way for a user-centric and decentralized Iot for smart city. The motivation behind this research starts from the necessity for an always more interconnected world, populated by myriads of smart devices, to guarantee user privacy, which is currently under the control of centralized servers. The proposed architecture will make possible the inclusion of all kinds of smart devices and is not limited to the context of a smart city but can be adapted for each kind of application of IoT such as ehealth, industry 4.0 and so on. The starting point of our work has been the analysis of the Solid project and its related standards and technologies, to better understand the context and the limitations in terms of requested resources for using such an architecture within the IoT context. In particular, as will be explained in the next section, Solid does not use any decentralized authentication protocol for preserving user privacy or any mapping with a digital version of citizens' identities. Considering that multiple studies have been conducted on digital twins within the context of smart cities [17], our work will propose a completely user-centric existing authentication mechanism. Such a mechanism is based on Self-Sovereign Identity (SSI), which completely matches the digital twin concept by giving citizens a digital representation of their identity. The integration of SSI as an authentication mechanism for the Solid ecosystem can be a revolution in this context, guaranteeing users' complete control over their data. The document is structured as follows:

- In the second section, an overview of the Solid architecture is presented jointly with open challenges, which will be considered during the presentation of the architecture;
- The third section discusses state of art of authentication within the context of smart cities, in conjunction with progress done in IoT decentralization;
- In the fourth section, a proof-of-concept architecture that uses Solid for handling data storage decentralization is proposed within the context of IoT, including a prominent solution for decentralized authentication;

– In the last section, conclusions and future developments are discussed, with
 pros in the adoption of such architecture and open challenges.

2   Solid Overview

Solid was born as a solution for privacy concerns within the context of centralized
social web applications and platforms, where a massive number of problems
exist. This technology aims to provide data independence and a simple data
management system by letting the users store data everywhere they want. As
discussed in the introduction, Solid does not leverage blockchain for handling
data decentralization, in favor of a mechanism that let the user the choice of
where to store their data. In what follows, the principal components of such an
ecosystem are presented, with a focus on techniques used for data storage, user
identification, authorization, and authentication. Finally, open challenges and
possible resolutions to cope with decentralization are discussed.

2.1   Architecture

Solid gives users complete control over their data; one can locate their data in
a self-hosted server and some others can locate their data in a server ruined
by big companies. This concept is possible thanks to the abstraction of pod,
which, as said in the introduction, can be seen as the deposit of data created
by the web applications. Data stored in such spaces are well structured and
easily reusable and interactable by applications. Solid uses Resource Descriptor
Framework (RDF) and Semantic Web technologies to store high-quality data;
but agrees also with unstructured data (discourage this approach due to difficulty
in reusing such data).

It's possible to uniquely identify an identity using WebID; it is a decentralized identifier that is used by agents to create their own identities by linking
such identifiers to a profile document. A profile document is a document containing user information formatted according to RDF serialization, including the
location of their pod. As possible to see in Fig. 1 a WebID is similar to a URI,
and different types of WebID currently exist, depending on the provider which
is hosting the pod. Users are able to give applications authorization at different granularity to their pods using the Access Control List (ACL). In according
with Web Access Control (WAC), four access modes are defined: read, write,

https://namesurn.solidcommunity.example/profile/card#

https://id.provider.example/namesurn

Fig. 1. Two types of WebID, where the username is included as subdomain or as path.

append, and full control. In such a way the user can establish who is authorized to write or who is only able to read. The authentication instead, depends on the implementation server.

2.2 Decentralization Challenges

Data produced from applications, according to Solid recommendation [14], are stored directly on the user's pod, guaranteeing users complete control over the data produced, without any possibility for services to store or track user data. The major privacy threats of such a model come from the architecture behind such pods and the authentication mechanisms offered. In Solid users are free to use their own server, or servers that they trust, for hosting their pods, located within a centralized server which can be subject to multiple attacks or to data lock-in. Furthermore, the OIDC protocol does not prevent servers from tracking users' activity, compromising their privacy, while TLS-based authentication is poorly supported and difficult to use on mobile devices. For this reason, two big challenges are still open: the decentralization of **data storage** and the decentralization of **authentication**. An interesting study has been conducted by Parrillo et al. [12], which proposes the Interplanetary File System (IPFS) as a solution for managing data storage using a distributed file system, guaranteeing decouple between pod servers and storage location. Cai et al. [1], instead, try to give a complete view of both challenges by proposing a decentralized schema for both data storage and authentication based on blockchain. In particular, they adopt an off-chain storage repository to help store and encrypt the actual data values while guaranteeing decentralized authentication to such storage using certificateless cryptography. Despite such a solution might be really interesting for the problem of data storage; multiple problems can happen regarding the authentication schema. A strong schema must put in place some mechanism for handling with revocation or updating of user data; if a user lost the private key should be able to recover it or should be able to communicate to the system that he needs a new key pair for the access. Considering the purpose of the paper, which is more interested in user authentication, the proposed architecture will take into consideration this last open challenge by proposing a new schema based on SSI also able to cope with revocation.

3 State of Art on Authentication

The advent of password-less authentication mechanisms has radically changed the way in which users access services while guaranteeing them more control over their credentials. Limited studies have been conducted in trying to adopt these in smart cities, usually characterized by weak authentication mechanisms.

B.-C. Chifor et al. [4] presented a proof-of-concept software solution that uses the FIDO protocol for users to authenticate to their devices. Such a protocol preserves user anonymity without giving the possibility to manufacturers to create a link between different user accounts because the only user-related information is the FIDO public key and a pseudonym. Also if FIDO can be seen as a good authentication mechanism in the case of private devices, it cannot be a suitable solution for the context of smart cities, since it obligates all citizens to buy FIDO-based hardware to comply with the standard. Other implementations of SSI can be deployed, an alternative approach SSI follows a different concept, which is based on Verifiable Credentials (VCs) enabling password-less authentication at reduced cost without the need for proprietary hardware. Sovrin Network [18] is one of the major providers of SSI, giving a solution based on public permissioned blockchain, where nodes validate transactions for issuing and verification. The adoption of such a solution within the context of smart cities can enable the vision for a digital twin of each citizen, who can use SSI to access public services. Rotunua et al. [13] provide an implementation of SSI for digital identity, which is a starting point for initiatives for using the blockchain as a platform for communications and transactions in the public sector.

Despite the decentralization of user identity management can solve privacy problems while enabling digital identity, multiple threats exist in handling data produced by applications within the IoT context, Tahirkheli et al. [15] highlight threats in smart cities that use Cloud Computing that aim at disrupting IAS-octave. Decentralization of user data can be seen as a resolution of multiple privacy issues currently existing within the application [5], their authentication mechanisms are characterized by centralized authentication or by complex mechanisms making citizens difficult to come to terms with. Considering such problems, a solution that is able to include IoT devices as they are, leveraging on gateways as mediators for decentralized solutions and IoT communication protocols must be taken into consideration. An implementation of such mediation has been developed by Troung et al. [16], which uses FIWARE and Hyperledger Fabric for proposing a secure and decentralized data-sharing framework over blockchains. However, in the FIWARE case, we also see the same issue affecting Solid, where authentication is centralised and can be decentralized with permission blockchain as in [6], to deal with identity management and verification. Despite multiple works exist in the literature, the usage of permissioned blockchain can be critical in terms of scalability; making difficult the adoption of such solutions in dense contexts, such as the smart city one.

As a result of these works it's possible to highlight the advantages of adopting SSI for handling user identity while the necessity for a decentralized schema for managing application data considering the limitations of IoT context. Solid can play the role of a data management system without the need for blockchain. This characteristic paves the way for a more secure and interconnected world. In the next section an overview of this ecosystem is given, fixing the challenges that must be taken into consideration for a fully decentralized system.

4   Methodology

A big challenge in IoT scenarios is related to poor battery equipment and power consumption: manufacturers usually deploy devices with a proprietary communication protocol or with protocols that aim to reduce complexity in favor of consumption. As a result, devices in the IoT context usually implement a connection-less protocol making them unable to rely on the advantages introduced by RESTful protocols, required by Solid for the operation of data writing.

The proposed architecture will take into consideration such limitations by moving the data writing requests to the pod at the gateway level, leveraging on the possibility offered by the Gateways to produce well-structured data and connection-oriented protocols like HTTP(s).

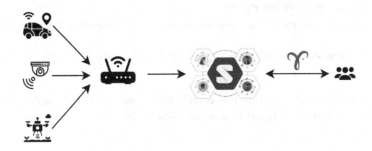

Fig. 2. Proposed Architecture.

Figure 2 depicts the overall architecture, which involves smart devices that use both non-IP and IP protocols creating a secure communication with the gateway, which handles all these communications using mechanisms that support both protocol types, such as FIWARE. As we will explain, the gateway is responsible for producing data in a well-structured form and sending such data directly to the user pod using RESTful mechanisms. To complete our decentralization proposal, an SSI schema based on Hyperledger Aries is taken into consideration for handling user identity, preventing in this way any kind of tracking of user activities.

4.1 Architecture

Before being able to receive data within their pod, citizens must register on the platform. In particular, they have to give the system access to their pod. This is possible using ACL defined within the Solid Server. In Fig. 3 is shown the URL *https://unisa.it* authorized to write into the user pod.

This first step let all the requests coming from the defined domain be accepted for writing in the user pod. At this point, the application is authorized to write to the user pod and must initialize a dataset, or more properly a SolidDataset which stores the data. Data within a dataset are organized in Thing, where each Thing has its own identifier; an example could be https://namesurn.solidcommunity. net/SmartCity#TrafficControl where the SolidDataset SmartCity contains the Thing TrafficControl. Once defined the structure in which data are saved, it's necessary to define a WebID/Things information association. This depends on the nature of the system, if we are interested in traffic control, the information

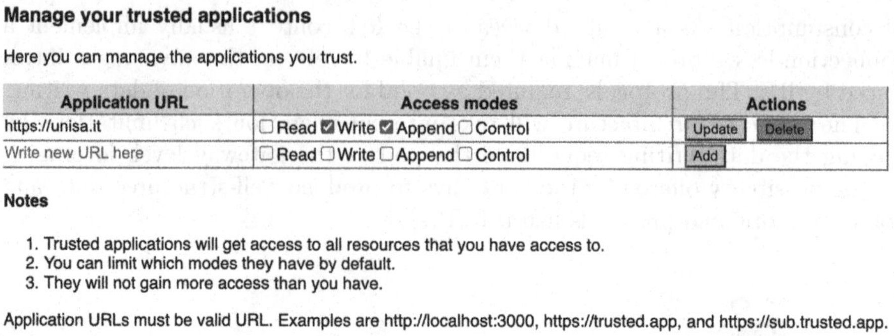

Manage your trusted applications

Here you can manage the applications you trust.

Application URL	Access modes	Actions
https://unisa.it	☐ Read ☑ Write ☑ Append ☐ Control	Update Delete
Write new URL here	☐ Read ☐ Write ☐ Append ☐ Control	Add

Notes

1. Trusted applications will get access to all resources that you have access to.
2. You can limit which modes they have by default.
3. They will not gain more access than you have.

Application URLs must be valid URL. Examples are http://localhost:3000, https://trusted.app, and https://sub.trusted.app.

Fig. 3. Applications authorized to interact with user pod.

needed by the system could be the vehicle identifier. Table 1 shows an example of a table that must be stored in a secure place within the system server.

Table 1. WebID - VehID association.

WebID	VehID
https://namesurn.solidcommunity.net/profile/card#	AA123AA
https://id.provider.example/namesurn	AA123AB

The content of such a table can be extended to include all the information read by sensors used by the system. Such a table will be queried by the gateway to check which is the endpoint of red information. In the next subsection, the data collection step is described.

Data Collection and Writing. IoT nodes will not store any kind of data, but just collect them and transmit them to the nearest gateway. These prerequisites are fundamental for the concept of decentralization that we're implementing since the sensors mustn't know which is the owner of produced data, avoiding possible attacks aimed at stealing such association.

As previously introduced, the association table is securely stored at the gateway or server level, which can put in place security mechanisms aimed at preventing attacks. Data produced by IoT devices are sent to the gateway using secure protocols; for example, BLE can be secured using lightweight cryptography based on a symmetrical key. The structure of received data depends on the application, the gateway is responsible for the production of well-structured data according to RDF. Moreover, the gateway can apply some pre-processing techniques before sending data to the user pod.

```
{                                    @prefix foaf: <http://xmlns.com/foaf/0.1/> .
    "VehID":"AA123AA",               @prefix loc: <http://example.org/location> .
    "average_speed":"70",            @prefix veh: <http://example.org/vehicles> .
    "start":{                        @prefix xsd: <http://www.w3.org/2001/XMLSchema#> .
        "time":"08:10:37",
        "lat":40.777204,             veh:AA123AA a foaf:Agent ;
        "lon":14.785706              veh:end loc:end ;
    },                               veh:speed "70"^^xsd:numeric ;
    "end":{                          veh:start loc:start .
        "time":"08:12:40",
        "lat":40.774389,             loc:end loc:lat "40.774389" ;
        "lon":14.792069              locc:lon "14.792069" ;
    }                                loc:time "08:12:40" .
}
                                     loc:start loc:lat "40.77204" ;
                                     loc:lon "14.785706" ;
                                     loc:time "08:10:37" .
```

Fig. 4. Transformation from JSON to RDF and serialization according to ttl format.

Figure 4 depicts the transformation from JSON to RDF and the consequent serialization in Turtle (ttl) format of data coming from some smart webcam placed in the city. In such a way application can query users' pod using SPARQL language. To perform data writing, Table 1 is queried with the information received. For example, the gateway receiving data related to VehID will query the table with the related identifier receiving as a response the WebID of the user pod. Once the gateway obtains the WebID related to the VehID an authentication is needed to validate the identity of the application. An existing implementation based on token is offered by Enterprise Solid Server (ESS) which agrees users to register a new application by releasing a new token. Such a token is used by applications for writing or reading requests. This approach makes the authentication of applications dependent on a centralized identity provider without any kind of decentralization mechanisms. An SSI-based approach could solve this issue, by deleting the token-based one.

4.2 Solid-SSI Integration

The decentralized application is now able to write to user pod, but to fulfill our vision of a decentralized IoT it's necessary to do something more on authentication of both users and devices. As described in the previous section, Solid authentication is based on centralized methods, which means that every time a user makes a request, a track of user data can be recorded on the authentication server for advertising or tracking purposes. In our proposal users' authentication leverage SSI methods for guaranteeing users' privacy without interacting with the issuer for the verification of attributes related to the identity but relying on a self-verification system. The concept of Verifiable Credentials (VCs) completely matches such a schema, providing self-verifiable attributes using the cryptographic property. The schema to be followed is depicted in Fig. 5, where three authors (Issuer, Holder, and Verifier) interact with a Verifiable Data Registry for the operation related to the identity. By considering the Solid ecosystem, it's possible to assume that Issuer and Verifier are the same actor, namely, the Solid server, responsible for the issuing of VCs and subsequentially for their verification. A really interesting implementation of SSI based on VCs, able to handle revocation problems and data updates is characterized by Hyperledger Aries,

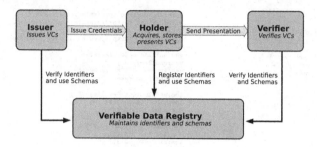

Fig. 5. VC Ecosystem defined by W3C, source: https://www.w3.org/TR/vc-data-model/

which is a project based on Hyperledger Indy for generating and managing Verifiable Credentials (VCs). It's possible to integrate SSI within an authentication mechanism by storing the relevant information in a verifiable way. What's relevant in the Solid ecosystem is the WebID of users, which is released by a Solid server during the registration process and is used by the owner for the identification when needs to authenticate. Hyperledger Aries offers a mechanism based on HTTP API for interacting with Indy wallet, which contains VCs.

WebID Issuing. To include SSI as an authentication means for Solid ecosystem it's necessary to issue the WebID at the registration phase. When a user wants to get a pod from a Solid server must enter his email and choose a username that is used for composing the WebID; for including SSI, it's necessary that the user saves the VC in his wallet to make identity verification possible. Once the Solid server authorizes the registration of a new user, shows a QR Code on the page that must be scanned by the Holder for creating a secure connection with the server. After a secure connection has been established, the Server sends a Credential Offer to the Holder containing the WebID, if the Holder accepts then the data public-facing claims are stored in the Verifiable Data Registry in order to make aware all Solid servers of this new WebID. Such issuing phase can be extended for the authentication of devices by issuing a verifiable token usable for writing and reading requests.

WebID Verification. Differently from password-based authentication mechanisms, which request the user a password, the authentication using a Verifiable WebID can be done by transmitting the proof related to the credential. Hyperledger Aries offers HTTP API for handling such credentials exchange making possible the interaction with a mobile app. Figure 6 depicts the authentication panel including a QR Code which initializes the connection between Holder and Verfier, similarly to what happens during the WebID Issuing phase.

Fig. 6. Authentication form of Solid-SSI compliant server.

Once the connection has been established, the Verifier sends a request containing the requested field and the non-revocation in a given time field. In such a way, the Verifier will be able to check the user's WebID while guaranteeing that no one revoked this VC, which can be useful in case of an identity thief. Once the Holder receives the request can accept it by sharing a cryptographically verifiable proof of possession in conjunction with the requested attribute. When the Verifier receives the proof, using the Hyperledger Aries checks, by consulting the Verifiable Data Registry, if the produced proof is valid.

4.3 Discussion

The adoption of a decentralized approach for handling data produced by sensors can pave the way for a world where each citizen is the owner of data produced by himself. The application that can be built on top of Solid are multiple, for example, a machine learning model that uses data coming from sensors for giving citizens advice on which is the best road considering their habits. Such an approach can facilitate the role of stakeholders interested in users' data by simplifying the request for permission to access to a part of users' data following the WAC and ACL defined by users. More structured data can give access to different granularities, on the basis of user choice.

The other key advantage is that it enables citizens to have a single, unified identity across different services and applications. The adoption of SSI is not limited to Solid but can be adopted also for all the other public services simply by defining the attributes needed for the identification, guaranteeing in this way a more interoperable ecosystem based on SSI. This not only reduces the burden of managing multiple identities but also helps to prevent identity theft and fraud. Furthermore, our approach ensures that residents have full control over their personal data, and can choose what information to share and with whom.

However, there are also challenges associated with building a decentralized smart city using Solid and SSI technologies. For example, there may be technical challenges associated with integrating different systems and applications, and ensuring that they can communicate with each other securely and efficiently.

Data produced by the gateways must be serialized in an RDF-compliant format and require the usage of vocabularies but only a few of them are available at the time of writing. Some future development of them must include the smart city scenario, including vocabularies for sensing temperature, smart agriculture, and so on.

5   Conclusion

A proof-of-concept of a decentralized smart city based on Social Linked Data platform has been proposed and analyzed considering the recommendation of LDP regarding the RESTful way of handling data requests, while decentralized user authentication has been proven to be directly applicable to the Solid platform. We have planned to assess the security of this architecture, performing simulations of malicious attacks on the proposed system and possibly assessing the formal security of the protocol adopted for credentials exchange. Further improvement, instead, can be made on the direct support for leveraging on Web of Things [9] by non-IP protocols [7], making the devices directly responsible for writing on users' pod without the necessity for a mediator. An open challenge in Solid regards centralized data storage, which limits also the usage of SSI. Despite a Verifiable Data Registry is available from all the Solid servers, user data are stored within a pod, which is strictly connected to just one server.

Acknowledgement. This work was partially supported by project SERICS (PE00000014) under the NRRP MUR program funded by the EU - NGEU.

References

1. Cai, T., Chen, W., Yu, Y.: BCSolid: a blockchain-based decentralized data storage and authentication scheme for solid. In: Zheng, Z., Dai, H.-N., Tang, M., Chen, X. (eds.) BlockSys 2019. CCIS, vol. 1156, pp. 676–689. Springer, Singapore (2020). https://doi.org/10.1007/978-981-15-2777-7_55
2. Camero, A., Alba, E.: Smart city and information technology: a review. Cities **93**, 84–94 (2019)
3. Chituc, C.M.: Towards seamless communication in the web of things: are standards sufficient to ensure interoperability? In: 2020 13th International Conference on Communications (COMM), pp. 427–431 (2020). https://doi.org/10.1109/COMM48946.2020.9141996
4. Dissanayake, D., Abineshh, U., Zihara, M., Kuruppu, S., De Silva, D., Vidhanaarachchi, S.: Enhancement to smart cities in Sri Lanka using cutting edge technologies. Int. J. Eng. Manage. Res. **12**(5), 488–493 (2022)
5. Dwivedi, A.D., Srivastava, G., Dhar, S., Singh, R.: A decentralized privacy-preserving healthcare blockchain for IoT. Sensors **19**(2), 326 (2019)
6. Esposito, C., Ficco, M., Gupta, B.B.: Blockchain-based authentication and authorization for smart city applications. Inf. Process. Manage. **58**(2), 102468 (2021)
7. Freund, M., Dorsch, R., Harth, A.: Applying the web of things abstraction to bluetooth low energy communication. arXiv preprint arXiv:2211.12934 (2022)

8. Humbeeck, A.V., et al.: The blockchain-GDPR paradox. J. Data Protect. Priv. **2**(3), 208–212 (2019)
9. Kovatsch, M., Matsukura, R., Lagally, M., Kawaguchi, T., Toumura, K., Kajimoto, K.: Web of things (wot) architecture (2020). https://www.w3.org/TR/2020/REC-wot-architecture-20200409
10. Lučić, D., Boban, M., Mileta, D.: An impact of general data protection regulation on a smart city concept. In: 2018 41st International Convention on Information and Communication Technology, Electronics and Microelectronics (MIPRO), pp. 0390–0394. IEEE (2018)
11. Malhotra, A., Arwe, J., Speicher, S.: Linked data platform specification (2015). https://www.w3.org/TR/ldp/
12. Parrillo, F., Tschudin, C.: Solid over the interplanetary file system. In: 2021 IFIP Networking Conference (IFIP Networking). pp. 1–6 (2021). https://doi.org/10.23919/IFIPNetworking52078.2021.9472772
13. Rotună, C., GHEORGHIĂ, A., Zamfiroiu, A., Smada Anagrama, D.: Smart city ecosystem using blockchain technology. Informatica Economica. **23**(4) (2019)
14. Sambra, A.V., et al.: Solid: a platform for decentralized social applications based on linked data. MIT CSAIL & Qatar Computing Research Institute, Technical report (2016)
15. Tahirkheli, A.I., et al.: A survey on modern cloud computing security over smart city networks: threats, vulnerabilities, consequences, countermeasures, and challenges. Electronics **10**(15), 1811 (2021)
16. Truong, H.T.T., Almeida, M., Karame, G., Soriente, C.: Towards secure and decentralized sharing of iot data. In: 2019 IEEE International Conference on Blockchain (Blockchain), pp. 176–183 (2019). https://doi.org/10.1109/Blockchain.2019.00031
17. White, G., Zink, A., Codecá, L., Clarke, S.: A digital twin smart city for citizen feedback. Cities **110**, 103064 (2021)
18. Windley, P.: How sovrin works. Sovrin Foundation, pp. 1–10 (2016)
19. Xie, J., et al.: A survey of blockchain technology applied to smart cities: research issues and challenges. IEEE Commun. Surv. Tutor. **21**(3), 2794–2830 (2019)

Prevention of Cyber-Attacks and Privacy Breaches in Healthcare Sector

Antonio Scarfò[1]([✉]) [ID], Carmine Piccolo[2], Francesco Palmieri[1] [ID],
and Michele Mastroianni[1] [ID]

[1] Department of Information of Computer Science, University of Salerno, Salerno University of Salerno, 84084 Salerno, Italy
ascarfo@unisa.it
[2] Center for Computer Services, University of Naples Federico II, 80138 Napoli, Italy
carmine.piccolo@unina.it

Abstract. Periodically, analysts in the cybersecurity sector, collect and share relevant data about recent cybercrime trends. These insights cover many aspects of the current cyber-threat scenario, including actors involved, motivations of the attacks, attack vectors, consequences, targets, and so on. Many organizations leverage such data to prepare their risk management plans and cyber defense strategies. This paper illustrates a case study involving two sample structures, a university and its hospital that want to compare the data available in last cyber security reports with the one collected from their actual operating environment, with the aim of being aware of how the mentioned reports could be helpful in reducing cybersecurity risks.

Keywords: Cybersecurity · healthcare · risk · vulnerability · CVE · EPSS

1 Introduction

Nowadays, cybersecurity and risk management scenarios are getting more and more complex and hard to manage. Indeed, attackers can leverage both an always wider attack surface and increasingly powerful attack tools. According to the last IBM report [1] about cyber security trends, from 2020 to 2022 the average cost of data breaches has grown from 3.86 M\$ to 4.35 M\$. The report also says that the healthcare sector resulted in the highest cost per stolen record in data breaches.

Another key insight from IBM is that the average time needed to identify a data breach is 207 days, and the average time necessary to contain an attack is 77 days from its detection. Reducing these times means significantly decreasing the cost of data breaches.

[1] shows the key factors that affect the costs of data breaches. It appears that there are several prevention actions that can reduce considerably its overall cost. The adoption of Artificial Intelligence-driven platforms for the automation of defense tasks, and the arrangement of a more reactive cybersecurity governance model, may be significantly helpful in containing the cost of successful attacks.

© The Author(s), under exclusive license to Springer Nature Switzerland AG 2023
O. Gervasi et al. (Eds.): ICCSA 2023 Workshops, LNCS 14109, pp. 162–178, 2023.
https://doi.org/10.1007/978-3-031-37120-2_11

On the other side, the complexity, and lack of compliance with common security recommendations exacerbate the cost of a data breach. Finally, to better highlight the relevance of the problem, we consider that the healthcare services industry will be one of the most important drivers for the growth of IoT technologies, fostering the Internet of Medical Things (IoMT) ecosystem, which is already one of best potential targets for data breaches. Due to the aforementioned evolution dynamics, the attack surface will expand dramatically in the years coming. Fortune Business Insight forecasts a CAGR of 29.8% for the period 2021–2028, ending in 187 billion dollars.

In EU countries, due to the adoption since 2016 of the General Data Protection Regulation (GDPR), companies and public agencies are forced to comply with such regulation, implementing both technical and organizational security measures [17].

Moreover, the recent COVID-19 pandemic caused a sharp increase in the use of ICT technologies in all fields of real life, mainly within the healthcare sector. Unluckily, the pervasive use of such technologies led to an exponential growth of cybercriminal activities, and the new threats are directed primarily to smartphone apps and healthcare related IoT devices, often affected by severe vulnerabilities [18]. Also, energy-related attacks could play a key role, causing power failures and untimely battery faults on IoT devices [19].

Therefore, the need for network monitoring and breach prevention is increasingly critical to ensure an adequate perimeter defense. In order to help network and security managers to focus on the most frequent and threatening attacks, a number of reports have been periodically redacted by various stakeholders and organizations. This paper aims to investigate about some of the most popular report in the field of cyber-attacks. The reports have also been compared with each other, and then compared with a real-world analysis with two different datasets generated by perimetral firewall of two big organizations: a University and his University hospital in order to verify the coherence of the reports with attacks detected by the university firewalls.

2 The Methodology

The methodology used is structured in three steps, the first one aims to identify the most relevant and common threats, by seeking them in the literature and in recently published reports. The second step is focused on collecting real operational data from the field that are comparable with the one selected in the previous step. The last step consists in comparing the data of step one and step two, with the aim of evaluating the usefulness of the data published against the threats collected from the field. To better introduce the topic, this chapter will present the key concepts and organizations that are useful for our specific purposes.

To compare the data coming from the reports and from the field, a process of standardization is required. The basic element that helps to compare the data collected is the CVE concept.

2.1 CVE Program

The CVE stands for Common Vulnerabilities and Exposures. The CVE has the purpose of "Identify, define, and catalog publicly disclosed cybersecurity vulnerabilities" [7]. The vulnerabilities discovered and verified, are assigned and published by organizations from around the world that have partnered with the CVE Program. These organizations publish CVE Records to communicate consistent descriptions of vulnerabilities. Information technology and cybersecurity professionals use CVE Records to ensure uniqueness in managing the same issues and to coordinate efforts for prioritizing and addressing the vulnerabilities. The Program counts 275 partners, covering several different roles.

The original concept was introduced by the MITRE [5] Corporation's David E. Mann and Steven M. Christey in 1999. Later, the CVE program was recommended by the National Institute of Standards and Technology (NIST) in "NIST Special Publication (SP) 800–51" [6]. In June 2004, the U.S. Defense Information Systems Agency (DISA) issued a task order for information assurance applications that requires the use of products that use CVE IDs.

CVE has also been used as the basis for totally new services. The NIST's U.S. National Vulnerability Database (NVD), a "comprehensive cybersecurity vulnerability database that integrates all publicly available U.S. Government vulnerability resources and provides references to industry resources" is synchronized with, and based upon, the CVE. A CVE must be numbered and clearly described, as well as maintained, according to the form and the rules that govern the Program. A classification of the risk related to the vulnerability is provided by the National Vulnerability Database (NVD) which provides the CVSS (Common Vulnerability Scoring System), which is a method used to provide a qualitative measure of severity and score for almost all known vulnerabilities. CVSS is owned and managed by FIRST.Org, Inc. (FIRST), a US-based non-profit organization, whose mission is to help computer security incident response teams across the world. It should be clear that CVSS is not a measure of risk. CVSS consists of three metric groups: Base, Temporal, and Environmental, and the NVD provides just CVSS 'base scores', which represent the innate characteristics of each vulnerability. The metric group Temporal and Environmental can be used to customize the risk analysis providing a score of a CVE for a specific environment where the product operates. The Base Score metric is both quantitative and qualitative, like Fig. 3 shows. The base score of CVSS, is composed of a set of metrics. These metrics are chosen to take into account both the exploitability of the vulnerability and its impact when it is exploited. These metrics and their granularity have evolved through the different versions of CVSS. Figure 1 shows the qualitative and the quantitative score for CVEs through the releases,

CVSS v2.0 Ratings		CVSS v3.0 Ratings	
Severity	Base Score Range	Severity	Base Score Range
		None	0.0
Low	0.0-3.9	Low	0.1-3.9
Medium	4.0-6.9	Medium	4.0-6.9
High	7.0-10.0	High	7.0-8.9
		Critical	9.0-10.0

Fig. 1. Score and severity model of CVSS.

2.2   EPSS Program

The FIRST organization "aspires to bring together incident response and security teams from every country across the world to ensure a safe internet for all" [8]. So, FIRST wants to create a global language about cybersecurity, make available tools and means for incident responders, and work together with key stakeholders according to clear policy and governance rules.

With the aim of improving, in some ways, the CVSS systems, the organization called FIRST has created the Exploit Prediction Scoring System (EPSS) model, which is an open, data-driven effort for estimating the likelihood that a software vulnerability will be exploited in the wild. The purpose is to help the network defenders to optimize and prioritize the remediation of the vulnerability. The difference with the CVSS standards is clear, since it has been useful for capturing innate characteristics of a vulnerability and providing measures of severity, but it is limited in its ability to assess threats. EPSS was born to fill that gap because it composes current threat information from CVEs and real-world exploit data. The EPSS model produces a probability score between 0 and 1 (0 and 100%). The higher the score, the greater the probability that a vulnerability will be exploited.

3   Analysis of the Reports

In this chapter, we analyze the reports selected to extrapolate and compare data. There are four different reports.

3.1   ENISA Threat Landscape Report 2022

ENISA is the European Union's agency dedicated to achieving a high common level of cybersecurity across Europe. Established in 2004 and strengthened by the EU Cybersecurity Act. As an observatory about cyber security dynamics, ENISA issues an annual report on the status of the cybersecurity threats landscape. The report identifies the prime threats, the major trends observed with respect to threats, the threat actors, and the attack techniques, and describes the relevant mitigation measures. Looking at the ENISA's report of 2022 [2], which provide a wide view about cyber threats from June 2021 to June 2022, it is possible extrapolate the following main threats, limiting the scope to healthcare and education fields.

- Ransomware, the period records an increasing activity of the attackers The most active groups, that produce more than half of the attacks are Lockbit, Conti, and ALPHV, followed by Black Basta and Hive. RDP (Remote Desktop Protocol) and Phishing are the most used vectors of attack. Brute force without multi-factor Authentication is the most common method used.
- Malware, after the Covid crisis, malware is on the rise again, likely because the alert to IT department is re-started since people are back in offices and the increasing precision of the attackers. The increase of malware is related mainly to crypto-jacking and IoT malware. Botnets, crypto miners, and info stealers have been the most common threats. IoT malware are doubled in 2022, and the main actors have been Mirai

and Mozi botnets. Relevant malicious activities are focused on supply-chain attacks, especially related to open-source packages (typo squatting). Also, from the blocking of macros from internet files by Microsoft, the attack is shifted away from VBA and has gone towards container files (ISO, ZIP, RAR, LNK)

• Attacks against availability, DDoSes remain one of the most critical threats. The Pandemic and Ukraine-Russian war influenced the shape of DDoSes like never in the past. An increasing fuel for DDoSes comes from mobile and sensor devices. These devices, whose number is on rapid rise, can be attacked both for exhausting their energy resources and also used as individual bots within a botnet to attack external targets. Multi-vector attacks are preferred as well as applications/protocols-based attacks. A relevant dynamic is that IoT devices are easy to attack since patching and updating are often done too late. A new kind of attack is a combination of DDoS and Ransomware, referred as RDoS attack.

The threat listed by ENISA and mentioned above, are linkable to some kye CVEs, which are summarized below, Table 1.

Table 1. ENISA Top Threats and CVEs

Threats	CVE
Lokbit [9]	CVE-2021-34523, CVE-2021-31207, CVE-2021-34473, CVE-2021-22986, CVE-2018-13379, CVE-2021-36942, CVE-2021-20028, CVE-2020-0787, CVE-2022-36537
BlackCat (ALPHV) [10]	CVE-2016-0099, CVE-2019-7481, CVE-2021-31207, CVE-2021-34473, CVE-2021-34523
Conti [11]	CVE-2018-13379, CVE-2018-13374, CVE-2020-0796, CVE-2020-0609, CVE-2020-0688, CVE-2021-21972, CVE-2021-21985, CVE-2021-22005, CVE-2021-26855, CVE-2015-2546, CVE-2016-3309, CVE-2017-0101, CVE-2018-8120, CVE-2019-0543, CVE-2019-0841, CVE-2019-1064, CVE-2019-1069, CVE-2019-1129, CVE-2019-1130, CVE-2019-1215, CVE-2019-1253, CVE-2019-1315, CVE-2019-1322, CVE-2019-1385, CVE-2019-1388, CVE-2019-1405, CVE-2019-1458, CVE-2020-0638, CVE-2020-0787, CVE-2020-1472, CVE-2021-1675, CVE-2021-1732, CVE-2021-34527
MIRAI [12]	CVE-2012-4869, CVE-2014-9727, CVE-2017-5173, CVE-2019-15107, CVE-2020-8515, CVE-2020-15415, CVE-2022-36267, CVE-2022-26134, CVE-2022-4257
MOZI [16]	CVE-2016-6277, CVE-2014-8361, CVE-2015- 2051, CVE-2008-4873, CVE-2017-17215, CVE-2018-10561, CVE-2018-10562

From the perspective of CVEs, ENISA leverages two reports, [13, 14], by IBM and RedCanary. These reports mention ProxyLogon, ProxyShell, PrintNightmare, whose CVE are included in the following reports and in Conti Botnet. Also mentioned are:

- Kaseya VSA, CVE-2021-30116
- ManageEngine CVE-2021-40539, CVE2021-44077, CVE-2021-44515
- Accellion FTA vulnerability susceptible to SQL injection, CVE-2021-27101
- Liferay Portal deserialization of untrusted data allows for remote code execution via JSON web services, CVE-2020-7961
- MobileIron vulnerability allowing for remote code execution, CVE-2020-15505
- ForgeRock AM server Java deserialization vulnerability allows for remote code execution, CVE-2021-35464
- Citrix Server path traversal flaw, CVE-2019-19781

3.2 CISA Reports 2021

The Cybersecurity and Infrastructure Security Agency (CISA) is an agency of the United States Department of Homeland Security (DHS), which that is responsible for strengthening cybersecurity and infrastructure protection across all levels of government, coordinating cybersecurity programs with U.S. states, and improving the government's cybersecurity protections against private and nation-state hackers (February 19, 2019). The agency covers two key roles: "CISA acts as the quarterback for the federal cybersecurity team, protecting and defending the home front—our federal civilian government networks", also CISA "coordinates the execution of our national cyber defense, leading asset response for significant cyber incidents and ensures that timely and actionable information is shared across federal and non-federal and private sector partners". The mission of the agency requires an intensive collection and analysis of insights from the field, working across the private and public sectors. Periodically, the agency issues reports that light on the threats on the field. One of the most interesting is "2021 Top Routinely Exploited Vulnerabilities" [3], which reports the vulnerabilities most used by attackers, observed by U.S., Australian, Canadian, New Zealand, and UK cybersecurity authorities during the 2021. These CVEs are:

- CVE-2021-44228 (Log4Shell). This vulnerability affects Apache's Open Source Log4j library. It is exploitable to submit a specially crafted request to a vulnerable system, which is open to the execution of an arbitrary code. Log4j is incorporated into thousands of products worldwide. This CVE is critical and scores 10.0.
- CVE-2021-26855, CVE-2021-26858, CVE-2021-26857, CVE-2021-27065 (ProxyLogon). These vulnerabilities, affect Microsoft Exchange email servers. Exploiting them in combination, is possible that an unauthenticated actor executes arbitrary code, allowing to gain persistent access to files and mailboxes on the servers, as well as to credentials stored on the servers.
- CVE-2021-34523, CVE-2021-34473, CVE-2021-31207 (ProxyShell), affect Microsoft Exchange email servers. Like in the previous case, the exploitation of the vulnerabilities in combination allows a remote actor to execute arbitrary code. These vulnerabilities reside within the Microsoft Client Access Service (CAS), CAS is commonly exposed to the internet to enable users to access their email via mobile devices and web browsers.

- CVE-2021-26084. This vulnerability affects Atlassian Confluence Server and Data Center, it allows an unauthenticated attacker to execute arbitrary code on vulnerable systems. This vulnerability quickly became one of the most exploited, mass exploitation attempts of this vulnerability was observed in September 2021, after its disclosure.
- CVE-2021-40539 is a high-rated (9.8) and highly exploited vulnerability, that allows to bypass authentication with remote execution code.
- CVE-2021-21972 is the vulnerability of VMware vCenter plugin that contains remote code execution, also critical with 9.8 score by NIST.
- CVE-2020-0688 is another critical vulnerability for Microsoft Exchange that allows remote code execution. Score 8.8.
- CVE-2019-11510 is a 10.0-scored vulnerability in Pulse Secure Pulse Connect Secure (PCS), which allows an unauthenticated remote attacker to perform an arbitrary file reading vulnerability.
- CVE-2018-13379 is a 9.8-scored vulnerability in Fortinet FortiOS and FortiProxy under SSL VPN web portal that allows an unauthenticated attacker to download system files via specially crafted HTTP resource requests.

2021 Top Malware Strains is another report by CISA, it discloses the top Malware in 2021. These malwares are Agent Tesla (RAT), AZORult (Trojan), Formbook (Trojan), Ursnif (Trojan), LokiBot, (Trojan) MOUSEISLAND (Macro downloader), NanoCore (RAT), Qakbot (Trojan), Remcos (RAT), TrickBot (RAT) and GootLoader (Loader). An interesting insight is that Cyber-criminals have used these malwares in the last five and, in some cases, ten years. The awareness of the methods of attacks may really help to defend infrastructures and data.

3.3 FORTINET'S Report 2022

Fortinet is an American multinational corporation headquartered in Sunnyvale, California. The company develops and sells cybersecurity solutions, such as physical firewalls, antivirus software, intrusion prevention systems, and endpoint security components. The business is the most important at the worldwide level in terms of appliances delivered, it records 37% of the market by IDC.

Based on its threat intelligence activity, Fortinet publishes a biannual report about threats and vulnerabilities observed. The report is called "Global Threat Landscape Report" by Fortiguard labs in the first half of 2022 [4], the company has observed 10.666 ransomware variants. The alarming trend of Wipers malware is increasing at a worldwide level. Finally, OT devices as a target are increasing dramatically, due to the high number of vulnerabilities exposed. From these first three macro-finding appear the main threat of zero-day, which are in significant rising compared to the past, 72 discovered.

Figure 2 shows the top 20 detections by IPS, Intrusion Detection System, which helps to discover exploitation attempts and can log the CVE that is tried to be exploited.

Following the top attacks together with their CVEs:

- Log4j2: CVE-2021-44228, CVE-2021-45046, CVE-2021-45105), that is the Remote Code Execution. The CVE-2021-44228 is already mentioned and scored 10.0, and

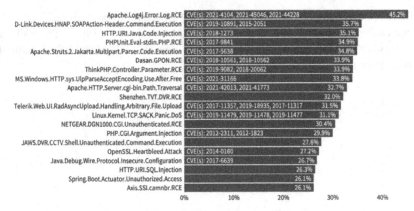

Fig. 2. Top IPS detection H12022

also, the report mentions CVE-2021-45046, a vulnerability that affects the patch of the CVE-2021-44228 and is critical due to its score of 9.0. Also, the 2021-45105 is another but medium base score CVE for Log4j2. The report links the Fortiguard services pages, where some insights are shown.

- D-Link.Devices, CVE-2019-10891, CVE-2015-2051. These are CVEs affecting D-Link Routers. The first allows RCE on the router and score 9.8, the second CVE in under review currently.
- HTTP.URI.Java.Code.Injection CVE 2018-1273, is another RCE by a remote malicious user that affects Java. The CVE scores 9.8 and is critical.
- PHPUnit.Eval-stdin.PHP.RCE, CVE 2017-9841, this is critical, scoring 9.8, vulnerability that allows a RCE in PHPUnit, and the remote attacker can gain control of vulnerable systems.
- Apache.Struts.2.Jakarta.Multipart.Parser.Code.Execution, CVE 2017-5638, this is a critical 10.0 scoring vulnerability, that can exploit a remote Code Execution vulnerability in Apache Struts.
- Dasan.GPON.RCE, CVE(s) 2018-10561, 2018-10562. It is another RCE where a remote attacker can take the control of the device. Both CVEs score 9.8.
- MS.Windows.HTTP.sys.UlpParseAcceptEncoding.Use.After.Free, CVE-2021-31166 scores 9.8. This indicates an attack attempt to exploit a Use After Free Vulnerability in Microsoft Windows HTTP.sys. A remote, authenticated attacker can exploit this vulnerability by sending a crafted HTTP request to the target server.
- ThinkPHP.Controller.Parameter.Remote.Code.Exec utionhis, CVEs 2019-9082, 2018-20062. This is an attack attempt to exploit a Remote Code Execution Vulnerability in ThinkPHP.

3.4 Data from EPSS

As mentioned in paragraph II.B, EPSS is a program that has the mission to predict the most dangerous CVEs in the days coming. Looking at these data is another interesting analysis that can tell us if the ESSP's predictions are observed in the field. With this purpose, hereafter is presented some insights from EPSS data.

There are two main pieces of information that are useful to be analyzed. The first is the relationships between ESPP data and CVE, which is shown in Fig. 3. The CVEs are scored by CVSS v3.0 included in NVD. It comes clear that CVSS and ESPP are totally different approaches, but both useful.

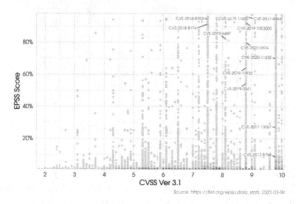

Fig. 3. EPSS compared to CVSS 3.0 (NVD)

The EPSS score is calculated by a Machine Learning system, that collects data from several sources. ML collects data continuously, and, unlike CVSS, also from the field. These data include information coming also from Fortinet Fortiguard labs. Collecting data from the field, EPSS, by its nature, is more dynamic than CVSS,

Both EPSS and CVSS cannot estimate the risks related to the environment where the affected devices are installed. In some way, EPSS is more specific than CVSS, it, analyzing data from the field can include temporal elements.

So, it is interesting to compare the EPSS predictive score with data from the field. With that aim, in the following are reported the most critical CVE, scored by EPSS.

Table 2 shows the riskiest CVEs based on the evaluation of EPSS, all above 96% of score. The list is related to the EPSS report of 15 February 2023, and reports the CVEs that most likely will be exploited in the following 90 days.

3.5 Data from the Field

In this chapter is disclosed the data collected from the field. The architecture of analysis consists in a double pair of Firewalls that act as perimeter protection in a university network infrastructure and its hospital. A couple of Firewall Fortigate 3400E work as perimetral defense internal- internet segmentation, whereas the second couple of firewalls, Fortigate 1800F, act as a perimetral defense for the datacenter of the hospital. These couples of firewalls are equipped with a Fortiguard UTM license of software, which include features like Intrusion Protection System (IPS) and Antivirus. The IPS are system of protection that can detect the attempts to exploit a CVE. The Fig. 4 shows the architecture of the analysis, it highlights the firewall form which are taken the dataset. These firewalls manage two typologies of traffic, the traffic to and from Internet, which

Table 2. Most risky CVE by ESPP march compared to CVSS 3.0 (NVD)

CVE	EPSS Likelihood	CVE	EPSS Likelihood
CVE-2021-26084	97,72%	CVE-2014-6271	96,24%
CVE-2021-40438	97,22%	CVE-2019-0708	96,11%
CVE-2017-12635	97,11%	CVE-2018-0296	96,09%
CVE-2021-44228	97,10%	CVE-2019-17558	96,09%
CVE-2022-47966	96,96%	CVE-2017-0144	96,09%
CVE-2020-5902	96,82%	CVE-2019-3396	96,09%
CVE-2019-16759	96,82%	CVE-2017-0037	96,08%
CVE-2021-26855	96,74%	CVE-2021-21972	96,08%
CVE-2020-1938	96,55%	CVE-2014-0160	96,06%
CVE-2019-11510	96,51%	CVE-2021-26295	96,05%
CVE-2017-8464	96,39%	CVE-2018-7600	96,02%
CVE-2022-28219	96,35%	CVE-2021-44077	96,02%
CVE-2019-2725	96,29%	CVE-2019-11043	96,00%
CVE-2016-10033	96,29%	CVE-2018-15961	96,00%
		CVE-2021-26084	97,72%
		Model Version v2022.01.01 – Score_Date:2023-03-04T00:00:00+0000	

is prefiltered by the second cluster of firewalls 3400E, and the traffic to and from the internal network.

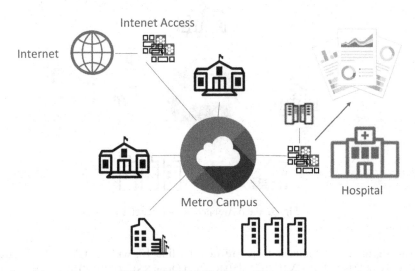

Fig. 4. Field Architecture – Dataset 1

The Dataset 1 is taken for the cluster of Fortigate 1800F in the period from 19 Feb 2023 and 24 Feb 2023, which defend the perimeter of the hospital and its datacenter. The most important intrusions detected by IPS are the of DDoS, mostly, and Malware. Mostly, attacks are related to an old botnet called Andromeda. This botnet was born in 2011 and is quite disappeared since years. The second attack detected is DoublePulsar Backdoor, it allows the connection of remote hosts, thought SMB and RDP (port 3389), for malicious actions. Then, as high-scored threats, there is Robot.PKCS.RSA.Information..Disclosure, this attack exploits some vulnerabilities in TLS protocol cryptographic, vulnerability in TLS protocol in RSA key exchange, to recover private keys. The attack is linked to some CVE. Also, there are Adobe.Acrobat.CVE-2018-16042.Security.Bypass, MS.IE.CTreePos.Objects.Memory.Corruption, Mirai and DCRat.botnet.

Given the not so numerous attempts of threats detected from the IPS protecting the hospital datacenter, another dataset (dataset 2) was carried out from the IPS of the Firewall exposed to the internet, Fig. 5.

Figure 6 shows these intrusions detected and some of the main important: 1.7M critical severity threats, 1.1M high severity threats, 2.4M medium severity threats. The threats detected by the first dataset are related to internal networks, whereas the threats detected by the second dataset from the field are related to the internet. The internet perimetral firewall acts efficiently as a first filter towards the hospital datacenter, analyzing all traffic but the internal one. Looking at the dataset 2, the list of threats detected it is possible identify some relevant attacks already mentioned in the previous analysis.

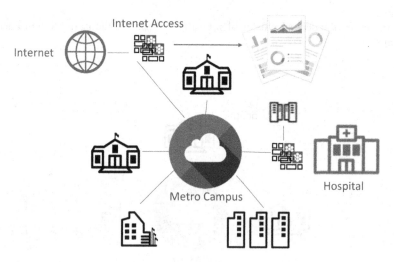

Fig. 5. Field Architecture – Dataset 2

Among the critical attacks there are Log4j2, line 10, with its CVEs (CVE-2021-4104, CVE-2021-44228, CVE-2021-45046), and Open SSL (CVE-2014-0160), line 14. Among the high severity attacks we can identity two critical Botnet: Mirai, line 4, and Mozi, line 9.

Criticity	ID	Attack Name	CVE-ID	Counts
###Critical Severity Intrusions###	1	Realtek.SDK.UDPServer.Command.Execution	CVE-2021-35394	1.501.221,00
	2	MikroTik.RouterOS.Arbitrary.File.Read	CVE-2018-14847	87.799,00
	3	PHPUnit.Eval-stdin.PHP.Remote.Code.Execution	CVE-2017-9841	50.133,00
	4	H-worm.Botnet		47.642,00
	5	D-Link.Devices.HNAP.SOAPAction-Header.Command.Execution	CVE-2015-2051,CVE-2019-10891	18.635,00
	6	Hikvision.Product.SDK.WebLanguage.Tag.Command.Injection	CVE-2021-36260	14.364,00
	7	NETGEAR.DGN1000.CGI.Unauthenticated.Remote.Code.Execution		12.663,00
	8	Dasan.GPON.Remote.Code.Execution	CVE-2018-10561,CVE-2018-10562	12.224,00
	9	ThinkPHP.Controller.Parameter.Remote.Code.Execution	CVE-2019-9082,CVE-2018-20062	5.127,00
	10	Apache.Log4j.Error.Log.Remote.Code.Execution	CVE-2021-4104,CVE-2021-44228,CVE-2021-45046	3.756,00
	11	Telerik.Web.UI.RadAsyncUpload.Handling.Arbitrary.File.Upload	CVE-2017-11317,CVE-2017-11357,CVE-2019-18935	2.753,00
	12	WordPress.HTTP.Path.Traversal	CVE-2019-9618,CVE-2018-16283,CVE-2018-16299,CVE-2020-11738	2.589,00
	13	Bladabindi.Botnet		2.439,00
	14	OpenSSL.Heartbleed.Attack	CVE-2014-0160	242,00
	15	Er.D1000.Modem.CWMP.Command.Injection	CVE-2016-10372	2.341,00
	16	GitLab.Community.and.Enterprise.Edition.Command.Injection	CVE-2021-22205	1.794,00
	17	Gh0st.Rat.Botnet		1.356,00
	18	Zeroshell.Kerbynet.Type.Parameter.Remote.Command.Execution	CVE-2009-0545,CVE-2019-12725	1.333,00
	19	Java.Debug.Wire.Protocol.Insecure.Configuration	CVE-2017-6639	1.263,00
	20	Apache.Struts.2.Jakarta.Multipart.Parser.Code.Execution	CVE-2017-5638	1.106,00
###High Severity Intrusions###	1	Linux.Kernel.TCP.SACK.Panic.DoS	CVE-2019-11477,CVE-2019-11478,CVE-2019-11479	550.495,00
	2	malicious-url		236.099,00
	3	HTTP.URI.SQL.Injection		107.502,00
	4	Mirai.Botnet		103.816,00
	5	Multiple.Routers.GPON.formLogin.Remote.Command.Injection		50.453,00
	6	AndroxGh0st.Malware		40.248,00
	7	RedLine.Stealer.Botnet		24.765,00
	8	Web.Server.Password.File.Access		11.936,00
	9	Mozi.Botnet		10.788,00
	10	Rota.Jakiro.botnet		10.739,00
	11	HTTP.Unix.Shell.IFS.Remote.Code.Execution		4.198,00
	12	MS.Office.EQNEDT32.EXE.Equation.Parsing.Memory.Corruption	CVE-2018-0798,CVE-2018-0802,CVE-2017-11882	376,00
	13	Joomla!.CMS.Webservice.API.index.php.Unauthorized.Access	CVE-2023-23752	1.822,00
	14	JAWS.DVR.CCTV.Shell.Unauthenticated.Command.Execution	CVE-2016-20016	1.525,00
	15	NetSupport.Rat.Botnet		1.277,00
	16	Alcatel-Lucent.OmniPCX.Office.MasterCGI.User.Command.Execution	CVE-2007-3010	1.003,00
	17	PHP.URI.Code.Injection		949,00
	18	MS.IIS.Command.Shell.SQL.Injection	CVE-2005-4149	842,00
	19	VACRON.CCTV.Board.CGI.cmd.Parameter.Command.Execution		806,00
	20	PHP.CGI.Argument.Injection	CVE-2012-1823,CVE-2012-2311,CVE-2012-2688	688,00
###Medium Severity Intrusions###	1	SSLv3.POODLE.Information.Disclosure	CVE-2014-3566	2.298.422,00
	2	HTTP.Referer.Header.SQL.Injection	CVE-2007-1061	99.372,00
	3	WordPress.xmlrpc.php.system.multicall.Amplification.Attack		16.639,00
	4	WordPress.xmlrpc.Pingback.DoS		12.571,00
	5	Android.ADB.Debug.Port.Remote.Access		9.123,00
	6	TCP.Split.Handshake		8.377,00
	7	WordPress.REST.API.Username.Enumeration.Information.Disclosure	CVE-2017-5487	5.972,00
	8	NTP.Monlist.Command.DoS	CVE-2013-5211	3.564,00
	9	PHP.Diescan		1.031,00
	10	MS.IIS.DLL.Request.DoS	CVE-2005-4360	756,00
	11	HTTP.URI.Script.XSS	CVE-2002-1315,CVE-2017-0068	325,00
	12	Sophos.Anti-Virus.Reserved.Device.Name.Handling.SMTP	CVE-2004-0552	192,00
	13	NetworkActiv.Web.Server.XSS		158,00
	14	Atlassian.Server.S.Endpoint.Information.Disclosure	CVE-2021-26085,CVE-2021-26086	140,00
	15	Novell.NetBasic.Scripting.Server.Directory.Traversal	CVE-2002-1417	132,00
	16	Apache.Axis2.Default.Password.Access	CVE-2010-0219	127,00
	17	HTTP.Malformed.Request.Directory.Traversal	CVE-2005-2020,CVE-2008-2938	110,00
	18	PHP.mosConfig_absolute_path.Remote.File.Inclusion	CVE-2004-1693,CVE-2006-3396,CVE-2006-3736,CVE-2006-3773,CVE-2006-377	103,00
	19	VBulletin.Vote.PHP.Nodeid.Parameter.SQL.Injection	CVE-2013-3522	100,00
	20	FCKeditor.CurrentFolder.Arbitrary.File.Upload	CVE-2009-2265	93,00

Fig. 6. Dataset 2, data from the internet perimeter

4   Comparison Between the Reports and the Datasets

In this chapter, the CVEs extrapolated from the four reports taken into consideration are compared. The methodology followed consists of the calculation of the intersections among the four sets of CVEs. The first evaluation is between the set of CVEs form ENISA, CISA and Fortiguard with the CVEs of EPSS. This step is useful to highlight which CVE, part of these reports, are forecasted by EPSS to be exploited. FortiGuard shares with EPSS just the CVE-2021-44228 (10%) related to Log4j2 and, specifically Log4Shell, vulnerability. The set of CVEs by ENISA shares with EPSS two vulnerabilities (3%): CVE-2021-21972, CVE-2021-26855; both related to Conti Botnet. CISA shares with EPSS 5 CVEs: CVE-2021-44228, CVE-2021-26855, CVE-2021-26084, CVE-2021-21972, CVE-2019-11510 (30%). These CVEs are related to Log4j2, ProxyLogon, Atlassian Confluence, VMware vCenter, Pulse Secure Pulse Connect Secure. The CVE reported by CISA will be mostly likely exploited in the next future.

Looking at the correlation between the set of CVEs of the report, there are the following outcomes:

- CISA and ENISA share 8 CVEs. These CVEs are related to the attack techniques of Lokbit, Conti and Mozi. Among these CVEs, EPSS forecasts CVE-2021-21972, CVE-2021-26855 as most likely to be exploited, and both related to Conti.
- ENISA and Fortiguard share 2, that are related to MOZI Botnet for remote control execution. None of these are forecasted to be exploited in the next future by EPSS.
- ForiGuard and CISA shares one CVE, which is related to Log4j2,

If we look at CVEs included in all of three reports by ENIA, CISA and Fortiguard, there are not any CVEs included in all these three reports. Finally, CISA is the report that has in common the majority of CVE with EPSS, and CISA (53%) and ENISA (11%) share the most CVEs among the three reports.

The Venn's Diagram in the Fig. 7 shown the intersection among the set of CVEs of the report analyzed. Then, looking at four reports, ENISA, CISA, FortiGuard and EPSS, the critical CVEs are being extrapolated and correlated. These reports have in common some CVEs, mostly related to recent and widespread threats like Conti, Mozi and Log4j2. The first analysis has been comparing the reports from ENISA, CISA and ForiGuard against EPSS in order to highlights the CVEs belonging to these three reports that will be, most likely, exploited in the next future. CISA lists the most CVEs that EPSS predicted to be exploited, 5 out 15; ENISA share with EPSS 2 CVEs out of 72, and, finally, FortiGuard just 1 CVE out of 20. The CVEs shared by CISA and EPSS are the riskiest because there include all CVEs shared by ENISA and FortiGuard with EPSS.

Then, looking at the intersection among the reports by ENISA, CISA and Forti-Guards, we have seen the all the three reports together do not share any CVEs. ENISA and CISA share 8 CVEs out of the 72 selected from ENISA, 2 are the CVEs shared by ENISA and FortiGuard, only 1 CVE is shared between CISA and FortiGuard.

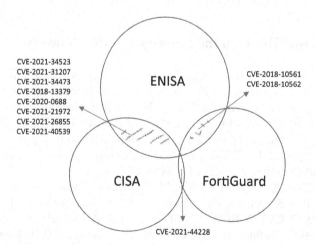

Fig. 7. CVEs shared by ENISA, CISA, FortiGuard, Venn Diagram

CISA is the report that is more aligned with ENISA and EPSS, whereas FortiGuards is the less aligned with the others reports.

Trying to extrapolate the riskiest CVE, the CVEs belonging at least to two reports are 11, and are related to Conti, Mozi, Lokbit and Log4j2. Out these 11, the CVEs also listed by EPPS are 3, that are related to Conti and Log4j2.

Table 3. Riskiest CVEs

CVEs Sets	CVE
$(ENISA \cap CISA) \cup (ENISA \cap Foriguard) \cup (CISA \cap Foriguard)$	CVE-2021-34523
	CVE-2021-31207
	CVE-2021-34473
	CVE-2018-13379
	CVE-2020-0688
	CVE-2021-21972
	CVE-2021-26855
	CVE-2021-40539
	CVE-2018-10561
	CVE-2018-10562
	CVE-2021-44228
$[(ENISA \cap CISA) \cup (ENISA \cap Foriguard) \cup (CISA \cap Foriguard)] \cap ESPP$	CVE-2021-44228
	CVE-2021-21972
	CVE-2021-26855

Looking at the data collected from the field, specifically from the report 1, surprisingly, there are not threats and CVE shared with any of the reports analyzed. Except for CVE-2018-1388, that is a high scored CVE related to GSKit V7 of Tivoli IBM platform. The intrusion detected by the IPS and AV system in place, in the report 1, are related to old CVE and even the attacks that are not listed by no one of the report analyzed in the most critical CVEs.

In we extend the analysis to the report, report 2, from the internet perimeter IPS the scenario completely changes. First, the intersection between the sets of CVEs coming from the report 1 and the report 2 consists in just a CVE: CVE-2005-4360, RCE for Microsoft Internet Information Services (IIS) 5.1. Then, we record the following situation about the internet perimeter IPS:

- the intersection with ENISA's consist in two CVEs, which are about Mozi. ENISA predicts the 2.7% of all the detected exploitations and 10% among the critical attempts of exploitation.
- the intersection with CISA's is one CVE, which is relate to Apache Log4j 2. CISA predicts the 1.35% of all the detected exploitations and 5% among the critical attempts of exploitation.
- the intersection with Fortiguard are ten CVEs. As to be expectable, the CVE shared are the most numerous. The threats are related to Mozi, Log4j2, and ThinkPHP. FortiGuard predicts 13.9% of all the detected exploitations and 50% among the critical CVEs.

- the intersection with EPSS are two CVEs. These are related to Log4j2 and Heartbleed in OpenSSL. EPSS predicts 2.7% of all the detected exploitations and 10% among the critical CVEs. This is a bad data because of EPSS should works as predictive engines for the defenders.

The scenario is summarized in the Table 4, the data form the filed says that FortiGuard report is the most helpful report to arrange an action of defense. Even if it helps to predict just the 50% of the critical threats. Out of the 11 riskiest CVEs of the Table 3 the report 2 lists only 3: Log4j2 CVE-2021-44228 is shared by all reports but the ENISA one, CVE-2018-10561, and CVE-2018-10562. We can deem it as the threat most dangerous and, fortunately, filtered by the perimetral cluster in our scenario.

Table 4. Intersection among CVEs of Report 2 and CVEs of Report 2

CVEs Sets	CVE	Impact
ENISA ∩ Report2	CVE-2018-10561, CVE-2018-10562	2.7% Total CVEs 10% Critical CVEs
CISA ∩ Report2	CVE-2021-44228	1.35% Total CVEs 5% Critical CVEs
Fortiguard ∩ Report2	CVE-2017-9841 CVE-2015-2051 CVE-2019-10891 CVE-2018-10561 CVE-2018-10562 CVE-2019-9082 CVE-2018-20062 CVE-2021-44228 CVE-2021-45046 CVE-2017-5638	13.9% Total CVEs 50% Critical CVEs
EPSS ∩ Report2	CVE-2012-4869 CVE-2014-9727 CVE-2017-5173 CVE-2014-0160 CVE-2021-44228	2.7% Total CVEs 10% Critical CVEs

5 Conclusions and Future Works

The paper has the aim of evaluating the usefulness of data coming from some of the most relevant reports in the cyberspace sector for the operative defense against cyber-attacks. As a matter of fact, models like MITRE allow to prepare infrastructures, organizations, and people against well know attacks, and in [15] is shown how it is possible linking MITRE ATT&CK TTP (Tactics, Techniques and Procedures of attacks) and CVEs, this allows to predict the behaviors of the attackers and, consequently, helps to prepare the defense.

In conclusion, the reports analyzed are not particularly useful with the purpose to prepare the defense, even EPSS does not find confirmation by the data from the field, at least, in this specific case. Even if all reports identify some critical threats observed on the field. And, even putting together ENISA, CISA and EPSS is possible predict just the 5.5% of the attacks overall, and 20% of critical attacks detected from the field. The exception is the FortiGuard Threats Landscape report, which usefulness of the is certainly more interesting. Indeed, following the insights of that report, it is possible to be prepared for the 50% of the critical attacks. Somehow it is something we could imaging.

The works presents a limitation, the miss of the SSL inspection configuration on the firewalls. In this way, the firewall must detect a CVE exploitation through the analysis of encrypted traffic. In that case, the firewall can access just clear text information, limiting its ability to detect CVE exploitation activities. In that constrain, the IPS limiting the analysis just to some features, like IP addresses, time of packets inter-arrival, packets length, number of ACK packets, number of retransmissions, and all statistics linkable with this information. So, the IPS could, mainly, carries out some behavioral analysis that is not its purpose, since it works on signature base.

Future works can be developed on the analysis improvement. Extending, for example, the IPS configuration the mean of SSL inspection, or implementing IPS at host level, with the purpose to detect a most wide set of attempts of CVE exploitations.

References

1. Ponemon Institute LLC, September 16, 2022: Cost of a Data Breach Report 2022. https://www.ibm.com/downloads/cas/3R8N1DZJ. Accessed 25 Mar 2023
2. Ifigeneia Lella, Eleni Tsekmezoglou, Rossen Svetozarov Naydenov, Cosmin Ciobanu, Apostolos Malatras, Marianthi Theocharidou – European Union Agency for Cybersecurit, October 2022, ENISA Threat Landscape 2022. https://www.enisa.europa.eu/publications/enisa-threat-landscape-2022. Accessed 25 Mar 2023
3. Cybersecurity Advisory (CSA), Infrastructure Security Agency (CISA), National Security Agency (NSA), Federal Bureau of Investigation (FBI), Australian Cyber Security Centre (ACSC), Canadian Centre for Cyber Security, (CCCS), New Zealand National Cyber Security Centre (NZ NCSC), United Kingdom's National, Cyber Security Centre (NCSC-UK), 27 April 2022, 2021 Top Routinely Exploited Vulnerabilities. https://www.cisa.gov/sites/default/files/publications/AA22-117A_Joint_CSA_2021_Top_Routinely_Exploited_Vulnerabilities_Final.pdf. Accessed 25 Mar 2023
4. Foriguard Labs, 16 Agust 2022, "Global Threat Landscape Report, 1H 2022. https://www.fortinet.com/content/dam/fortinet/assets/threat-reports/threat-report-1h-2022.pdf. Accessed 25 Mar 2023
5. Ahmed, M., Panda, S., Xenakis, C., Panaousis, E.: MITRE ATT&CK-driven Cyber Risk Assessment. In: Proceedings of the 17th International Conference on Availability, Reliability and Security, ARES 2022. Association for Computing Machinery, New York, NY, USA, Article 107, pp. 1–10 (2022). https://doi.org/10.1145/3538969.3544420
6. Waltermire (NIST), D., Scarfone (G2), K.: Guide to Using Vulnerability Naming Schemes, February 2011. https://csrc.nist.gov/publications/detail/sp/800-51/rev-1/final
7. U.S. Department of Homeland Security (DHS), Cybersecurity and Infrastructure Security Agency (CISA), The MITRE Corporation, About the CVE Program. https://www.cve.org/. Accessed 25 Mar 2023

8. Forum of Incident Response and Security Teams, FIRST Vision and Mission Statement. www. first.org/about/mission. Accessed 25 Mar 2023

9. Aluri, S.: Posted on Sep 28, 2022 and Updated on September 29, 2022, All about LockBit Ransomware. https://cybersecurityworks.com/blog/ransomware/all-about-lockbit-ransomware.html. Accessed 25 Mar 2023

10. By Ravindran, P.: posted on Jul 14, 2022 and Updated on 06 Sep 2022, All about Black-Cat (ALPHV). https://cybersecurityworks.com/blog/ransomware/all-about-blackcat-alphav. html. Accessed 25 Mar 2023

11. Narang, S.: ContiLeaks: Chats Reveal Over 30 Vulnerabilities Used by Conti Ransomware, 24 March 2022. https://www.tenable.com/blog/contileaks-chats-reveal-over-30-vulnerabilit ies-used-by-conti-ransomware-affiliates. Accessed 25 Mar 2023

12. Lei, C., Zhang, Z., Hu, C., Das, A.: Mirai Variant V3G4 Targets IoT Devices, 15 February 2023. https://unit42.paloaltonetworks.com/mirai-variant-v3g4/. Accessed 25 Mar 2023

13. Astle, J., et al.: 2022 Threat Detection Report, Mar 25 2023. https://resource.redcanary.com/ rs/003-YRU-314/images/2022_ThreatDetectionReport_RedCanary.pdf

14. Singleton, C., et al.: X-Force Threat Intelligence Index 2022, February 2022. https://www. ibm.com/downloads/cas/ADLMYLAZ. Accessed 25 Mar 2023

15. Kuppa, A., Aouad, L., Le-Khac, N.-A.: Linking CVE's to MITRE ATT&CK Techniques. In: Proceedings of the 16th International Conference on Availability, Reliability and Security (ARES 21). Association for Computing Machinery, New York, NY, USA, Article 21, pp. 1–12 (2021). https://doi.org/10.1145/3465481.3465758

16. Tu, T.-F., Qin, J.-W., Zhang, H., Chen, M., Xu, T., Huang, Y.: A comprehensive study of Mozi botnet. Int. J. Intell. Syst. **37**, 6877–6908 (2022). https://doi.org/10.1002/int.22866

17. Di Martino, B., Mastroianni, M., Campaiola, M., Morelli, G., Sparaco, E.: Semantic techniques for validation of GDPR compliance of business processes. In: Barolli, L., Hussain, F.K., Ikeda, M. (eds.) Complex, Intelligent, and Software Intensive Systems. AISC, vol. 993, pp. 847–855. Springer, Cham (2020). https://doi.org/10.1007/978-3-030-22354-0_78

18. Bobbio, A., Campanile, L., Gribaudo, M., Iacono M., Marulli F., Mastroianni M.: A cyber warfare perspective on risks related to health IoT devices and contact tracing Neural Comput. Appl. 1–15 (2021).https://doi.org/10.1007/s00521-021-06720-1

19. Palmieri, F., Ricciardi, S., Fiore, U., Ficco, M., Castiglione, A.: Energy-oriented denial of service attacks: an emerging menace for large cloud infrastructures. J. Supercomput. **71**(5), 1620–1641 (2014). https://doi.org/10.1007/s11227-014-1242-6

TokenFuse: A Versatile NFT Marketplace

Ch Sree Kumar[1,2], Akshya Kumar Lenka[2], Surukati Asutosh Dora[2], Ashish Sharma[3],
Ugo Fiore[4(✉)], and Diptendu Sinha Roy[1]

[1] National Institute of Technology Meghalaya, Shillong, Meghalaya, India
diptendu.sr@nitm.ac.in
[2] NIST Institute of Science and Technology (Autonomous), Berhampur, Berhampur, Odisha,
India
{akshyalenka.ele.2019,surukatidora.ece.2019}@nist.edu
[3] Institute of Engineering and Technology, GLA University, Mathura, U.P., India
ashishsharma@gla.ac.in
[4] Department of Computer Science, University of Salerno, Fisciano, Italy
ufiore@unisa.it

Abstract. An NFT (non-fungible token) marketplace is a platform where people can buy and sell one-of-a-kind digital items such as art work, music, and videos. These items are represented by NFTs, which are not exchangeable for other tokens or assets and are stored on a blockchain. The growing use of blockchain technology and the desire for individuals to own and trade rare digital items have fueled the growth of NFT marketplaces. The purpose of this paper is to demonstrate the creation and working of an NFT marketplace named "TokenFuse" and discuss its features as well as the background technologies that keep it running. Our NFT marketplace uses the power of Inter Planetary File System (IPFS) Technology to provide artists with a unique and secure way to sell their original works as NFTs. In contrast to traditional marketplaces that rely on centralized servers and databases, our platform stores and distributes NFTs in a decentralized and peer-to-peer network, ensuring security and redundancy. It also provides a unique and cost-effective way for authors to monetize their works by taking advantage of blockchain technology. Our platform has extremely low fees, making it one of the most affordable options on the market.

Keywords: NFT · Ethereum · IPFS · Solidity · Blockchain

1 Introduction

NFTs (non-fungible tokens) are a mechanism to manage and control digital scarcity so that businesses based on creative work can be created and sustained. Beyond digital art, which NFTs are known for, they can support ownership of anything that is unique. This encompasses a variety of things, from event tickets to real estate and intellectual property rights. NFTs create records of ownership that are stored on a blockchain. Compared to traditional records of ownership, NFTs offer several important characteristics. Authenticity, for example, can be ensured by cryptographic techniques. Transfers of ownership are simple and direct because transactions are recorded on the blockchain. A

O. Gervasi et al. (Eds.): ICCSA 2023 Workshops, LNCS 14109, pp. 179–192, 2023.
https://doi.org/10.1007/978-3-031-37120-2_12

consequence is that the legitimacy of ownership can also be verified by looking at the history of the NFT on the blockchain. Smart contracts allow selective, controlled, and reliable transfers of ownership.

In an NFT marketplace, margins are considerably affected by transaction costs. In particular, since NFTs can be conceived as having a very small value, transaction costs could eat up a significant proportion of revenues, up to the point at which trading becomes uneconomical.

Building a decentralized and price-competitive marketplace requires the careful selection and integration of multiple tools organized in a coherent architecture. This paper describes the lessons learned in designing and building TokenFuse, a blockchain-based NFT marketplace that provides creators and collectors with a safe and dependable platform for trading and managing digital assets. TokenFuse is a marketplace for NFTs that aims to make it easy for creators to mint, list, and sell their digital assets and for collectors to discover, buy, and own them. TokenFuse is built on the Ethereum blockchain [1], which provides a decentralized platform for the creation and transfer of NFTs. This allows for a transparent and secure marketplace where transactions are recorded on an immutable ledger accessible to anyone. TokenFuse also utilizes smart contract [2, 3, 4] technology, which enables automatic and self-executing transactions without the need for intermediaries.

Section 2, Background, explains NFTs trading using them and their relationship to blockchain technology with use cases. Section 3 deals with building a versatile marketplace and covers TokenFuse's architecture, workings, tools used and monetization strategies. Section 4 is about the implementation, which includes screenshots and code snippets to create TokenFuse. Finally, the conclusion section summarizes the main points and emphasizes TokenFuse's potential impact on the NFT market.

2 Background

This Section provides an overview of NFT and how it connects to real blockchain applications.

2.1 NFT for Trading Using Blockchain Use Cases

Blockchain technology is used to create non-fungible tokens (NFTs), allowing for their safe and open purchase, sale, and trading [5]. NFTs are generally considered tokens that are saved on a blockchain, so it is very difficult to change the ownership record or tamper with it. Each NFT is unique and stored on the blockchain, making it simple to confirm that someone is the rightful owner of a particular object [6]. This is crucial for expensive objects that have a high potential for fraud or counterfeiting, such as art and collectibles. Blockchain technology not only offers security and verification but also makes it simple to buy, sell, and trade non-fungible tokens on online exchanges. This enables the development of a liquid market for rare items, making it simple for buyers and sellers to find and conduct business with one another. An art business can thus grow and scale, increasing the revenue generated from creative work [7].

The next section elaborates on the process of building a versatile marketplace for trading NFTs.

2.2 NFT and Trading Using Them

The process of creating and using NFTs involves several steps [8]:

1) Creation: Using blockchain, a creator or artist develops a digital asset, such as a work of art or a collectible, and gives it a special digital signature. The asset has this signature as confirmation of ownership and authenticity.
2) Minting: By uploading the digital asset to a blockchain platform like Ethereum and constructing an NFT utilizing smart contract technology, the creator or artist "mints" the digital asset. This generates a special token that identifies the owner of the digital asset and is stored on the blockchain.
3) Purchasing and selling: The NFT can be purchased and sold in a marketplace that focuses on NFTs, such as TokenFuse. An NFT is not the actual digital asset that is purchased; rather, it is the special token that signifies ownership of the asset. The asset may reside on the blockchain or elsewhere.
4) Storage: The NFT metadata is kept on the blockchain, and the purchaser can view and use the digital asset by utilising the special token.
5) Trading: The NFT can be exchanged for other NFTs on the open market; the value of each NFT depends on demand and rarity.

The next section will discuss the architectural and technological choices in the implementation of TokenFuse.

3 Building TokenFuse

TokenFuse is a blockchain platform that enables minting, browsing, and listing NFTs, as well as profile management for users. It offers a comprehensive set of features to create and tokenize unique digital assets, purchase them using cryptocurrency, and monetize them. Overall, TokenFuse is a versatile and convenient platform for the NFT community.

3.1 Architecture of TokenFuse

An NFT marketplace's architecture can change depending on the particular platform and its characteristics [9]. However, there are a few elements that are frequently found in an NFT market (Fig. 1):

1) Frontend: The user interface on the front end of an NFT marketplace is what customers use to browse and buy NFTs. ReactJs has been chosen for building the front end of TokenFuse.
2) Backend: The server-side technology that drives an NFT marketplace is referred to as the backend. It might have a database for keeping track of NFTs. IPFS is the selected backend for TokenFuse.
3) Blockchain: The technology that drives NFTs and enables safe and open transactions is the blockchain. TokenFuse runs on the Ethereum blockchain network. For writing smart contracts, TokenFuse uses the Solidity language.
4) Smart contracts: These are self-executing pieces of code that run over a blockchain. In TokenFuse, smart contracts are used for minting, buying, and selling NFTs.

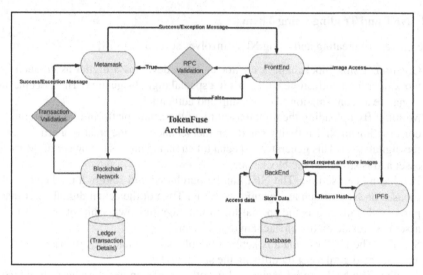

Fig. 1. Architecture of TokenFuse

3.2 Working of TokenFuse

In this section, the main operations within TokenFuse are described.

Connecting a Wallet to TokenFuse: To purchase an NFT, a user must connect their wallet to the NFT marketplace. Web3js and metamask [10] are used to connect the user's wallet to the marketplace platform.

Minting an NFT: Minting an NFT simply means creating NFT for the digital asset. It involves storing the digital asset over IPFs and then updating its metadata to the Blockchain Network. Figure 2 reports the mint function in TokenFuse.

```
function mint(address _to, uint256 _tokenId) public {
        require(!tokenExists[_tokenId]);
        tokenExists[_tokenId] = true;
        tokenOwner[_tokenId] = _to;
        emit Mint(_to, _tokenId);
    }
```

Fig. 2. Solidity code to mint NFT

Sell Function: Minting an NFT automatically triggers the sell functionality i.e., once an NFT is minted it is ready to be sold. Below is the sell function used in the marketplace (Fig. 3).

```
function sell(uint256 _tokenId, uint256 _price) public {
        require(tokenExists[_tokenId]);
        require(tokenOwner[_tokenId] == msg.sender);
        require(_price > 0);

        tokenPrice[_tokenId] = _price;

        emit Sell(msg.sender, _tokenId, _price);
    }
```

Fig. 3. Solidity code to Sell NFT

Buy Function: For buying an NFT from TokenFuse, a user needs to have sufficient eth in his/her account. He/She then chooses a particular NFT from the homepage and, after clicking the buy button, a Metamask prompt will appear to confirm the transaction. The buy function below is used in TokenFuse (Fig. 4).

```
function buy(uint256 _tokenId) public payable {
        require(tokenExists[_tokenId]);
        require(tokenOwner[_tokenId] != address(0));
        require(msg.value >= tokenPrice[_tokenId]);

        address _seller = tokenOwner[_tokenId];
        uint256 _price = tokenPrice[_tokenId];

        tokenOwner[_tokenId] = msg.sender;
        _seller.transfer(_price);

        emit Buy(msg.sender, _tokenId, _price);
    }
```

Fig. 4. Solidity code to Buy NFT

3.3 Tools Used in TokenFuse

Alchemy, IPFS, Hardhat, and OpenZeppelin are just a few of the tools and technologies that were used to build TokenFuse. Alchemy supplies the platform's infrastructure, ensuring dependable connectivity to the Ethereum network. NFT metadata is stored in a decentralized way via IPFS, simplifying retrieval and sharing. The NFT contracts on the platform can be created using Hardhat, a development environment that enables developers to build, test, and deploy smart contracts. To reduce development time and guarantee security, OpenZeppelin offers a library of reusable smart contracts that have been audited and secured. Together, these resources make up the foundation of the TokenFuse NFT market, offering a dependable and secure platform for the production, marketing, and administration of NFTs.

IPFS

IPFS (InterPlanetary File System) is a distributed file system that allows for content-addressable, peer-to-peer storage and retrieval of files using a unique cryptographic hash of their contents, with a built-in mechanism for caching, replication, and resiliency [11].

The process of storing data in IPFS is as follows:

1) Smaller pieces of data are created by subdivision. Each block is a standalone data unit.
2) Each block is used to produce a distinct cryptographic hash.
3) The hashes are then used to locate and identify the blocks, which are then stored on the IPFS network.
4) A client asks for the root block's hash when it wants to retrieve a file.
5) The root block and any other blocks that it is made up of are located by the IPFS network via a distributed hash table (DHT).
6) Blocks are then put back together and provided to the customer.
7) To increase resilience and fault tolerance, IPFS incorporates a concept known as "Content addressability," which states that data is stored and retrieved based on its content rather than its location.
8) Data replication and caching are also incorporated into IPFS, so when a block is requested numerous times, it is cached on adjacent nodes for quicker retrieval.

Hardhat

Hardhat is an open-source Ethereum development environment that is used for testing and debugging smart contracts before deploying to a live blockchain network [12]. It makes it simple for developers to test and debug their contracts on a local machine during the development process.

Developers can compile, test and deploy their contracts locally on Hardhat's built-in "development network", a small blockchain that resembles the Ethereum network. It also comes with a set of testing and debugging tools, including a JavaScript console, commands for contract deployment and maintenance, and support for other development frameworks like Truffle.

Its major objective is to increase smart contract development's efficiency and reduce error-proneness. It is especially helpful for teams creating complex decentralized applications (dApps) that require a stable development setting in order to test and debug their contracts before releasing them onto a live network.

Alchemy

Alchemy is a platform that offers a number of tools that help in creating and monitoring decentralized applications (dApps) by offering a collection of APIs, SDKs, and developer tools that can be used to interface with the blockchain and manage NFTs without having to construct everything from scratch [13]. It also offers a few extra tools to help make your dApp more effective and user-friendly, and it can reduce development time while offering a secure and reliable environment.

The Alchemy platform's user-friendly interface makes it simple to mint, manage, and trade NFTs. Developers may mint NFTs, set their metadata, and post them for sale on the marketplace thanks to the platform's set of APIs and SDKs. The Alchemy platform also has an interaction with MetaMask, which enables users to quickly link their wallet to the market and conduct transactions. Additionally, the platform offers analytics and monitoring capabilities to assist developers in understanding user behaviour, identifying usage trends, and identifying any problems with their NFT marketplace.

OpenZeppelin

On the Ethereum blockchain, OpenZeppelin [14] is an open-source platform for creating smart contracts. It offers a set of reusable, safe, and proven smart contract components for developers to use in their applications. These components include libraries for common contract types like multi-sig wallets and access control, as well as libraries for token standards like ERC20 and ERC721.

OpenZeppelin assists programmers in creating smart contracts that are more secure, as the libraries and contract patterns have been strictly reviewed by security professionals. Developers can reduce the chance of adding security flaws to their contracts by utilizing these pre-built components.

Additionally, OpenZeppelin offers a user-friendly API that enables programmers to create typical contract features like token transfers and contract updates without having to write challenging low-level code platform.

Once the marketplace has been built, it is time to focus on how to monetize it.

3.4   Monetizing Opportunities for TokenFuse

There are several ways to monetize an NFT marketplace, including the following:

1) Commission on sales [15]: One of the most popular ways to monetize the NFT marketplace is by taking a commission on each sale.
2) Listing fees: One more approach to make money is to charge creators a listing fee to list NFTs that are open for sale.
3) Advertising: Selling ad space on TokenFuse is another option to make money off the system.

4   Implementation

This Section will showcase code snippets and screenshots of the TokenFuse application to provide a visual representation of its functionalities.

1. Creating the Smart Contract using Solidity
    i. Importing Libraries from OpenZeppelin
    ii. Defining the buy, sell and mint Functions.
    iii. Enabling a counter to keep track of NFT ID.
2. Using Alchemy as a Node
    i. Creating an Alchemy account
    ii. Creating an app and importing the API key
3. Configuring IPFS for storing the NFTs
    i. Using Pinata to upload data to IPFS
    ii. Coping the Pinata key and using it in the.env file
4. Integrating a wallet for Transaction purpose
    i. Connecting Metamask to Goerli Test Network.
    ii. Obtaining some TestEth using the faucet

iii. Pasting the Private Key of the Wallet in.env file

5. Building the Front-end

    i. Creating the Homepage and User Profile Page

    ii. Creating the Mint and Buy page.

    iii. Integrating Front-end with Back-end using EthersJS.

The above points can be elaborated by the following-

1. Creating smart contracts using Solidity involves importing useful libraries from Open-Zeppelin to make the development faster and secure. We define functions like buy(), sell() and mint() to facilitate transactions. A counter is required to assign unique IDs to each NFT.
2. Alchemy is a popular node used to deploy the smart contracts on different networks like Goerli testnet. We created an Alchemy account, added an app and imported the API key to connect with Alchemy.
3. IPFS is used to store the NFT data permanently. Pinata makes it easy to upload files to IPFS. We just need to get the Pinata key and add it to the.env file.
4. A wallet is mandatory to conduct transactions on the blockchain. Connecting Metamask wallet to Goerli testnet, obtaining some test ETH using the faucet and adding the private key to.env file will enable transactions.
5. The front-end consists of homepage, user profile page, mint page and buy page. Integrating the front-end and back-end using EthersJS will provide a seamless experience to users.
6. In summary, creating NFTs on blockchain involves smart contract development, choosing a suitable node for deployment, storing NFT data on IPFS and enabling transactions through wallets. The front-end and back-end integration completes the project (Figs. 5, 6, 7, 8, 9, 10, 11, 12, 13, 14, 15, 16 and 17).

Fig. 5. Connecting Metamask wallet to TokenFuse

```
const connectwalletHandler = () => {
    if (window.ethereum) {
        provider.send("eth_requestAccounts", [])
            .then(async () => {
                await accountChangedHandler(provider.getSigner());
            })
    } else {
        setErrorMessage("Please Install MetaMask!!!");
    }
}
```

Fig. 6. Code to connect wallet to Marketplace

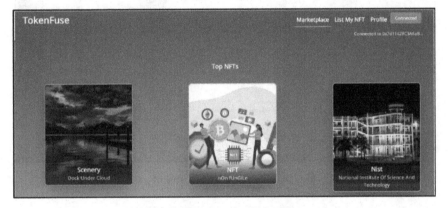

Fig. 7. Home page of TokenFuse

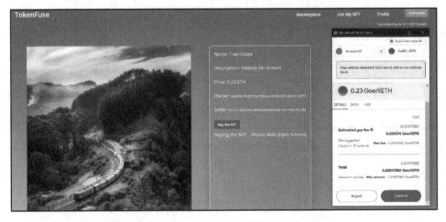

Fig. 8. Minting/ Selling an NFT in TokenFuse

```
function mintAndSellNFT(string memory tokenURI, uint256 price) public {
    _tokenIds.increment();
    uint256 newTokenId = _tokenIds.current();
    _mint(msg.sender, newTokenId);
    _setTokenURI(newTokenId, tokenURI);
    tokenIdToPrice[newTokenId] = price;
}
```

Fig. 9. Solidity Function to Mint and Sell NFT

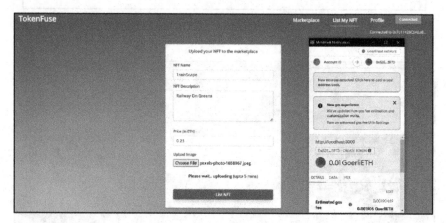

Fig. 10. Buying an NFT in TokenFuse

```
function buyNFT(uint256 tokenId) public payable {
    require(tokenIdToPrice[tokenId] > 0, "NFT is not for sale");
    require(msg.value >= tokenIdToPrice[tokenId], "Not enough ETH sent");

    address owner = ownerOf(tokenId);
    safeTransferFrom(owner, msg.sender, tokenId);

    uint256 amountToPay = tokenIdToPrice[tokenId];
    tokenIdToPrice[tokenId] = 0;
    owner.transfer(amountToPay);
}
```

Fig. 11. Solidity Function to Buy NFT

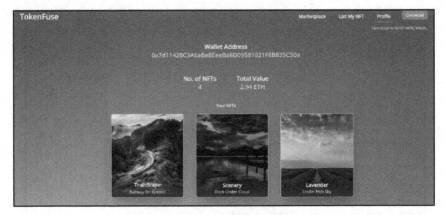

Fig. 12. Profile section of TokenFuse

```
import Navbar from "./Navbar";
import NFTTile from "./NFTTile";
import MarketplaceJSON from "../Marketplace.json";
import axios from "axios";
import { useState } from "react";

export default function Marketplace() {
const sampleData = [
    {
        "name": "NFT#1",
        "description": "Alchemy's First NFT",
        "website":"http://axieinfinity.io",
        "image":"https://gateway.pinata.cloud/ipfs/QmTsRJX7r5gyubjkdmzFrKQhHv74p5wT9LdeF1
        "price":"0.03ETH",
        "currentlySelling":"True",
        "address":"0xe81Bf5A757CB4f7F82a2F23b1e59bE45c33c5b13",
    },
```

Fig. 13. Home page code snippet of TokenFuse

```
import logo from '../logo_3.png';
import fullLogo from '../full_logo.png';
import {
  BrowserRouter as Router,
  Switch,
  Route,
  Link,
  useRouteMatch,
  useParams
} from "react-router-dom";
import { useEffect, useState } from 'react';
import { useLocation } from 'react-router';

function Navbar() {

const [connected, toggleConnect] = useState(false);
const location = useLocation();
const [currAddress, updateAddress] = useState('0x');
```

Fig. 14. Navbar code snippet of TokenFuse

```
import Navbar from "./Navbar";
import axie from "../tile.jpeg";
import { useLocation, useParams } from 'react-router-dom';
import MarketplaceJSON from "../Marketplace.json";
import axios from "axios";
import { useState } from "react";

export default function NFTPage (props) {

const [data, updateData] = useState({});
const [dataFetched, updateDataFetched] = useState(false);
const [message, updateMessage] = useState("");
const [currAddress, updateCurrAddress] = useState("0x");

async function getNFTData(tokenId) {
    const ethers = require("ethers");
```

Fig. 15. Individual NFT page code snippet of TokenFuse

```
import Navbar from "./Navbar";
import { useLocation, useParams } from 'react-router-dom';
import MarketplaceJSON from "../Marketplace.json";
import axios from "axios";
import { useState } from "react";
import NFTTile from "./NFTTile";

export default function Profile () {
    const [data, updateData] = useState([]);
    const [dataFetched, updateFetched] = useState(false);
    const [address, updateAddress] = useState("0x");
    const [totalPrice, updateTotalPrice] = useState("0");

    async function getNFTData(tokenId) {
        const ethers = require("ethers");
        let sumPrice = 0;
```

Fig. 16. Profile page code snippet of TokenFuse

```
import Navbar from "./Navbar";
import { useState } from "react";
import { uploadFileToIPFS, uploadJSONToIPFS } from "../pinata";
import Marketplace from '../Marketplace.json';
import { useLocation } from "react-router";

export default function SellNFT () {
    const [formParams, updateFormParams] = useState({ name: '', description: '', price:
    const [fileURL, setFileURL] = useState(null);
    const ethers = require("ethers");
    const [message, updateMessage] = useState('');
    const location = useLocation();

    //This function uploads the NFT image to IPFS
    async function OnChangeFile(e) {
        var file = e.target.files[0];
```

Fig. 17. Sell NFT page code snippet of TokenFuse

5 Conclusion

The development and commercialization of an NFT marketplace could prove to be a viable and profitable business venture. As the use cases and interest in NFTs expand, there is a growing demand for platforms that enable the buying, selling, and trading of these digital assets. A marketplace such as TokenFuse can attract and retain customers by creating a user-friendly and secure environment, offering a diverse range of NFTs, and implementing efficient monetization mechanisms, such as charging transaction fees or taking a percentage of sales, which will ultimately result in financial success. However, it is also important to remember that it is a topic with a lot of innovation and competition, so investing in it may be both high-risk and high-reward. Furthermore, one must always be aware of and follow rules and regulations strictly.

Future work includes implementing auction functionality, a facility to place bids in an existing auction, support for music, GIFs & video NFTs, implementation of transactionsusing multiple cryptocurrencies, andcustomer support.

References

1. Taş, R., Tanrıöver, Ö.Ö.: Building a decentralized application on the ethereum blockchain. In: 2019 3rd International Symposium on Multidisciplinary Studies and Innovative Technologies (ISMSIT). IEEE (2019)
2. Szabo, N.: Smart contracts: building blocks for digital markets. EXTROPY J. Transhum. Thought (16) **18**(2), 28 (1996)
3. Pradhan, N.R., et al.: A novel blockchain-based healthcare system design and performance benchmarking on a multi-hosted testbed. Sensors **22**(9), 3449 (2022)
4. Pradhan, N.R., Singh, A.P.: Smart contracts for automated control system in blockchain based smart cities. J. Ambient Intell. Smart Environ. **13**(3), 253–267 (2021)
5. Chohan, U.W.: Non-fungible tokens: Blockchains, scarcity, and value. Critical Blockchain Research Initiative (CBRI) Working Papers (2021)
6. Ante, L.: The non-fungible token (NFT) market and its relationship with Bitcoin and Ethereum. FinTech **1**(3), 216–224 (2022)
7. Singh, A.P., et al.: A novel patient-centric architectural framework for blockchain-enabled healthcare applications. IEEE Trans. Industr. Inf. **17**(8), 5779–5789 (2020)
8. Wang, Q., et al.: Non-fungible token (NFT): Overview, evaluation, opportunities and challenges. arXiv preprint arXiv:2105.07447 (2021)
9. Reverse engineering open seas to build an NFT marketplace(2021) Accubits Dev Blog. https://dev.accubits.com/reverse-engineering-openseas-to-build-an-nft-market-place/
10. Lee, W.-M., Lee, W.-M.:Using the meta mask chrome extension. Beginning Ethereum Smart Contracts Programming: With Examples in Python, Solidity, and JavaScript, pp. 93–126 (2019)
11. Zheng, Q., et al.: An innovative IPFS-based storage model for blockchain. In: 2018 IEEE/WIC/ACM International Conference on Web Intelligence (WI). IEEE (2018)
12. Sarmah, M., Saxena, S., Mukherjee, S.: A decentralized crowdfunding solution on top of the ethereum blockchain. In: 2022 IEEE Silchar Subsection Conference (SILCON), Silchar, India, pp. 1–6 (2022). https://doi.org/10.1109/SILCON55242.2022.10028843
13. Chowdhury, T.R., et al.: Crypto Pay: Design of Public Blockchain Platform.AJEC (2023)
14. Pierro, G.A., Tonelli, R.: Analysis of source code duplication in ethreum smart contracts. In: 2021 IEEE International Conference on Software Analysis, Evolution and Reengineering (SANER). IEEE (2021)
15. NonFungible: Market overview (2021). https://nonfungible.com/

Port City Interface: Land Use, Logistic and Rear Port Area Planning (PORTUNO 2023)

Sustainable Maritime Passenger Transport: A Network Analysis Approach on a National Basis

Antonio Russo[1] , Tiziana Campisi[1] (✉) , Efstathios Bouhouras[2] ,
Socrates Basbas[2] , and Giovanni Tesoriere[1]

[1] Faculty of Engineering and Architecture, University of Enna Kore, 94100 Enna, Italy
tiziana.campisi@unikore.it

[2] School of Rural and Surveying Engineering, Aristotle University of Thessaloniki, 54124
Thessaloniki, Greece

Abstract. The goals of United Nations Agenda 2030 for Sustainable Development push the need for a modal shift from the road towards more sustainable modes. The mitigation of the environmental impacts and guarantee of effective connections between distant areas are objectives to be pursued in the logic of greater environmental, economic, and social sustainability. Geographical areas characterized by a big percentage of coastal lines must rethink the potential of their port system. The geographical position of Italy, in the center of the Mediterranean Sea, with the highest length of coast line respect to the national surface, have made it necessary to have a vast port system. The presence of two major islands, Sicily and Sardinia, and many smaller ones has made necessary the creation of a network of passenger transport services. In 2017, 16 Port System Authorities were identified on the Italian territory, including the ports considered to be of national strategic interest. The objective of this research is concentrated on the analysis of maritime passenger transport focusing on the services that connect the ports belonging to the abovementioned network, evaluating their centrality within the national services network. The results highlight an imbalance of the network towards the Tyrrhenian Sea, with the Adriatic mainly delegated to connection services with the Balkans and the East, while the single most central port authorities are the Sicilian and Sardinian ones. This article represents a first step for a better understanding the interconnection between ports around a closed basin in terms of passenger traffic.

Keywords: Maritime transport · Ports Systems · Sea network · Agenda 2030

1 Introduction

For several years, the document entitled 'Transforming our world: the 2030 Agenda for Sustainable Development' has been a guide to the UN's 2030 Sustainable Development Goals (SDGs) [1]. The 17 goals and their subsequent specification in targets, international indicators and national indicators are aiming at the pursuit of economic, social and

O. Gervasi et al. (Eds.): ICCSA 2023 Workshops, LNCS 14109, pp. 195–207, 2023.
https://doi.org/10.1007/978-3-031-37120-2_13

environmental sustainability. The transport sector, by its nature, is largely involved in this process. The problem of passenger transport on a national scale is particularly relevant due to the high number of pax-km.

These concepts are closely connected with some of the goals of Agenda 2030. The first is SDG 13 'Take urgent action to combat climate change and its impacts'. Combating climate change and the need to reduce the carbon footprint is, in the context of the study to be presented, the main goal. Considering how different modes of transport are characterised by different carbon footprints [2] and how it is therefore necessary to pursue a reduction of the same; among the available instruments, it is important to recall the modal shift towards less emissive modes of transport, an objective also pursued by the 2011 White Paper in the European context [3].

SDG 9, 'Build resilient infrastructure, promote inclusive and sustainable industrialisation and foster innovation' is also closely connected to the development of sustainable infrastructure. In this sense, Target 9.1 "Develop quality, reliable, sustainable and resilient infrastructure, including regional and transborder infrastructure, to support economic development and human well-being, with a focus on affordable and equitable access for all" should be specified; of this target, it is interesting to note the specification on cross-border and regional infrastructure.

SDG 11 'Make cities and human settlements inclusive, safe, resilient and sustainable' expresses the necessity to pursue the sustainability of urban settlements. These three SDGs, which describe concepts related to the reduction of pollution, the spread of better infrastructure and the sustainability of cities, represent the reference goals for this work. Among the measures promoted by the Transport White Paper, the aforementioned modal shift must push a share of demand from road to the rail and maritime-port systems.

In all countries, geographical areas characterised by a high ratio of total km of coastline to surface area must naturally pay special attention to the maritime traffic system. Italy is a valid case study because it is geographically positioned at the centre of a Mediterranean port network and has significant maritime traffic with neighbouring countries [4]. The railway relationship with other countries is different, considering that Italy only borders other European countries along the Alps [5]; moreover, its geography includes two major islands and a large number of smaller ones.

To complete the picture, there is a substantial asymmetry in land transport between the southern part of the peninsula and the northern part; as a result, those who need to travel from the southern regions to the northern regions, albeit characterised by land continuity, are forced to turn to air transport.

The 2016 reform [6] identified 15 port system authorities, which were later increased to 16 following the spin-off of the ports of the Strait Area from the Port System Authority of the Southern Tyrrhenian and Ionian Seas [7]. Of the 16 areas, five are on the Adriatic Sea, two entirely on the Ionian Sea, one between the Tyrrhenian and Ionian Seas and the remaining eight on the Tyrrhenian Sea.

There is the need of identifying the degree of centrality in passenger services, freight services and Ro-pax services. Specifically, for passenger services it is necessary to consider both those that take place under ordinary conditions and those that take place with a tourist demand [8]. For freight and Ro-Pax services it is important to know what happens in large national and international basins such as the inland Mediterranean [9,

10]. The present study represents a first step in evaluating the relationships, in terms of passenger and Ro-pax traffic, between these port authorities. In this work, Ro-pax services are studied having systematicity and repetitiveness characteristics during the year and which therefore constitute the lower bound on the relationships to be considered. This is conducted by considering, as data, the passenger traffic services present between ports belonging to different port authorities. The objective is to reconstruct the centrality, in terms of passenger and Ro-pax services, of the various port authorities, in order to identify which are most affected by passenger traffic services, using the centrality tools provided by Network Analysis [11]. Knowledge of the importance of the various nodes makes it possible to enhance them in order to change further demand shares and to adequately support less important ones.

The most important aspects concerning the evolution of ports are recalled in Sect. 2 and contextualised on the basis of the existing literature; in Sect. 3 the methodology adopted for the study is presented in detail by recalling the theoretical cornerstones, in Sect. 4 the dataset and the results obtained are presented. Conclusions and future developments are reported in Sect. 5.

2 State of the Art of Port Evolution

The definition of ports is important to correctly specify the scope of the article. Note that following the UNCTAD approach the notion of generation does not imply a concept of improvement, i.e. ports of generation k are not better than ports of generation $k - 1$. The United Nations Conference on Trade and Development (UNCTAD) approach associates each generation with certain main functions as recalled above. Four generations of ports are identified in the literature [12–16]:

- First-generation ports are the ports directly connected to cities. Often, for first-generation ports, the birth of the port precedes that of the city itself. It is the presence of the port that determines the birth of the urban agglomeration; the port represents the main channel of communication and supply to the urban area. It is the first model to be born in chronological order. Some examples of ports emerging as the first-generation ports in Italy are Trieste, Genoa, Naples, Cagliari, Catania [17–19];
- Second generation ports developed after the Second World War. They are large industrial ports that, as such, must have adequate infrastructure and technology, and are often positioned to serve large industrial agglomerations. In Italy, Taranto and Augusta are examples of second-generation ports, serving their respective industrial systems [20];
- Third-generation ports have emerged since the 1980s. They are ports specialising in container traffic, and must contain all the equipment needed for container handling. The ships serving these ports must also be hyper-specialised [12, 21]. In general, these ports serve the longer Short Sea Shipping and Round the World routes. In Italy, an example of a fourth-generation port is the port of Gioia Tauro;

- Finally, the definition of fourth generation ports is closely connected to the creation of port areas located in different areas but with the management and presence of common operators [13]. Such an example is the joint administration of the ports of Malmoe (Sweden) and Copenhagen (Denmark).

Studying the Italian case is interesting and of reference on a European scale because with the reform of the Port System Authorities, the fourth-generation ports model was tried for different areas. As a result, ports with different characteristics are subject to the same administration. For example, there are different case study such as the Western Sicily Sea Authority, which sees in the same administration the ports of Palermo (mainly passenger port), Trapani and Porto Empedocle (tourist ports serving the system of Sicilian Minor Islands and fishermen) and Termini Imerese (commercial port); the same administration can exploit synergies and differences between the ports subject to it to increase competitiveness [22]. In addition to competitiveness and thus internal efficiency, the Agenda 2030 goals mentioned above must be achieved: reduction of environmental impact, resilient infrastructure, sustainable cities and communities. Central importance is given to first-generation ports, i.e. urban ports where better planning can be directly perceived by communities. Furthermore, the focus is on passenger traffic, and thus the main focus on first-generation ports derives from the better accessibility values that generally characterise these ports, which are not far from historical centres [23–25].

3 Methodology

The methodological tools used are derived from network analysis. Network analysis has a wide range of applications in the literature. Applications of network analysis tools have been proposed in the literature in terms of social sciences [26, 27], in urban planning in the analysis of open spaces [28], in economics in the study of economic exchanges [29, 30] and in transport for the analysis of transport networks [31–36].

Considering the punctual nature of the port, which is identified by a node within the transport network, in order to make an assessment of ports, it is interesting to identify centrality indices.

This preliminary research reconstructs the essential network of national passenger transport services by ship. For the construction of the network, port system authorities were considered as nodes and passenger ferry connections as arcs.

The characteristic of centrality measures is to provide an indicator to classify nodes according to a criterion in terms of weight within the network. The differences in the formulations between the different indicators make it necessary to identify several of them in order to be able to compare the results obtained.

According to Cascetta, 2013 [37], it is possible to represent a transport network with a graph $G = (N, E)$, where N is the number of nodes and E the number of arcs. The generic pair ij represents the arc with nodes i and j as ends. In the case of an undirected graph, it is possible to define the adjacency matrix as A_{ij} as $A_{ij} = [a_{ij}]$ where $a_{ij} = 1$ if i is connected to h, 0 otherwise. One can also define w_{ij} as the weight ascribed to arc ij. Each link ij is referred to direct connection. In the present paper, $a_{ij} = 1$ means the existence of a direct connection between node i and node j.

From these definitions, it is possible to specify the measures adopted in this work to assess the centrality of nodes:

- Degree centrality represents the centrality of the i-th node expressed as

$$c_i = \frac{\sum_j^N a_{ij}}{N - 1} \tag{1}$$

It represents the number of links the i-th node has with other nodes, relative to the total number of nodes. The maximum value of the number of links a node can have is $N - 1$. A value of $c_i = 1$ identifies that the i-th node is directly connected with each of the nodes in the network, while it is worth $1/(N - 1)$ if it is connected with only one other node in the network. This measure is relevant if the links in the network all have the same weight, and it is not essential to distinguish the arcs from each other.

- Strength centrality represents the centrality of the i-th node expressed as

$$s_i = \sum_j^N a_{ij} w_{ij} \tag{2}$$

It represents the sum of the weights of the arcs affecting the generic i-th node, having indicated with w_{ij} the weight of the generic link between node i considered and the generic directly connected node j. This measure is important to define when it is necessary to define the weight of a single arc on the network; the sum of the services from i to j and j to i is considered

- Eigenvector centrality, is a measure that is important because it not only con-siders the number of links and the weight of the direct links of the i-th node, but also the values associated with the generic j-th nodes with which the i-th node is connected. One can define the value of v that satisfies

$$Av = rv \tag{3}$$

where A is the adjacency matrix defined above, and v is the eigenvector associated with the eigenvalue r. Each value of v_i component of the eigenvector v associated with r expresses the eigenvector centrality of the i-th node. According to Perron [38], the matrix A has the following properties: a real square matrix with positive elements has a single largest real eigenvalue; the corresponding eigenvector has a strictly positive real eigenvector.

4 Results

For the identification of the network under examination, only ports belonging to one of the 16 Port System Authorities in Italy were considered as nodes.

Some ports were not considered because they are not equipped with passenger and Ro-pax services. For the evaluation of the arcs, the existence of direct passenger ferry services between two ports represented by previously identified nodes was taken into consideration.

The arcs are only considered between ports belonging to different Port System Authorities. In addition, seasonal connections and connections with only seasonal characteristics were not considered. In this work, $a_{ij} = 1$ indicates the existence of a Ro-Pax transport service of direct, systematic, collective connection between nodes i and j.

The data were obtained by analysing the websites of the Port System Authorities and the main shipping companies.

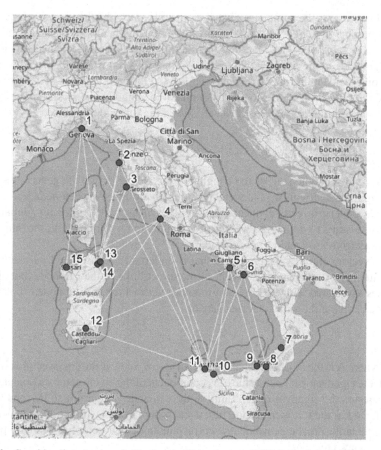

Fig. 1. Considered port network (Authors' elaboration on QGIS https://gisgeography.com/)

The network considered is presented in Fig. 1. The legend is shown in Table 1.

The study takes the first step by aggregating the services of the different ports of each Port System Authority.

This allows the linking strategies between different port authorities to emerge, as well as further emphasising the scale of the link concerned by this article.

The focus of the research is within Short Sea connections and not, for example, related to territorial continuity with smaller islands or tourist navigation.

The final evaluation is carried out on the graph presented in Fig. 2.

Table 1. Port list

ID	Port
1	Genoa
2	Livorno
3	Piombino
4	Civitavecchia
5	Naple
6	Salerno
7	Vibo Valentia
8	Messina
9	Milazzo
10	Termini Imerese
11	Palermo
12	Cagliari
13	Golfo Aranci
14	Olbia
15	Porto Torres

Table 2 presents, in addition to the legend, the reference Core Ports for each Port Authority considered, with reference to the European TEN-T network.

Table 3 presents the main results considering the 3 different indicators introduced in the previous section. For the evaluation of c_i, s_i and v_i, Eqs. (1), (2) and (3), respectively, are considered:

The nodes characterised by greater centrality are the two island nodes and the North Tyrrhenian Sea node. In particular, the West Sicilian Sea sees the highest values of c_i and v_i, having the greatest number of links: the Ports of Palermo and Termini Imerese, in fact, count a total of six direct links with other ports, out of the seven in total. This guarantees the highest values of centrality c_i; moreover, the only port with which they are not connected (South Tyrrhenian Sea and Ionian Sea) is also the one with the lowest number of links. This explains Palermo's centrality in the network.

The Sardinian Sea, although characterised by slightly lower values of c_i and v_i (only 5 out of 7 possible connections), sees a greater number of services (the 221 per week against the approximately 104 on average of the Western Sicilian Sea). This is because in the case of Sardinia, services to the Peninsula are counted as node-to-node connections. The case of Sicily is different, where a large part of the services connecting with the Peninsula pass through the Strait and are therefore intra-nodal connections, which are not reported in this work.

The Strait area is characterised by a lower c_i value (3 out of 7 connections), which is the same value as the Central Tyrrhenian area (Naples). However, the Naples area has a greater number of services, and therefore a higher c_i value; similarly, the Naples links

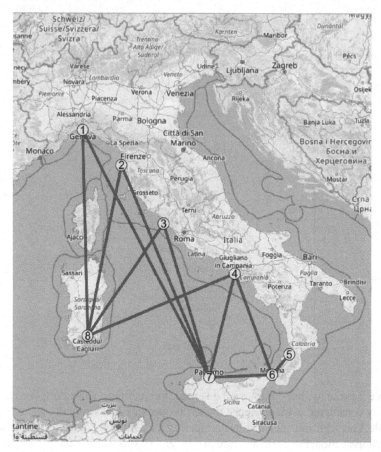

Fig. 2. Port System Authorities network studied (Authors' elaboration on QGis)

Table 2. Port System Authorities list

ID	Port System Authority	Core Port
1	Mar Ligure Occidentale	Genoa
2	Mar Tirreno Settentrionale	Livorno
3	Mar Tirreno Centro-Settentrionale	Civitavecchia
4	Mar Tirreno Centrale	Napoli
5	Mar Tirreno Meridionale e Ionio	Gioia Tauro
6	Stretto	[-]
7	Mar di Sicilia Occidentale	Palermo
8	Mare di Sardegna	Cagliari

Table 3. Values of centrality indicators for each Port System Authority

i	Port System Authority	c_i	s_i	v_i
1	Mar Ligure Occidentale	0,29	60	0,44
2	Mar Tirreno Settentrionale	0,29	107	0,44
3	Mar Tirreno Centro-Settentrionale	0,29	78	0,44
4	Mar Tirreno Centrale	0,43	82	0,56
5	Mar Tirreno Meridionale e Ionio	0,14	4	0,12
6	Stretto	0,43	38	0,42
7	Mar di Sicilia Occidentale	0,86	104	0,85
8	Mare di Sardegna	0,71	221	0,75

are more central than the Strait area links. The two authorities share a link with Western Sicily, they have a link in common, but while Naples is connected with Sardinia (as seen, one of the main nodes of the network) the Strait is connected with the South Tyrrhenian Sea node and Ionio.

The Southern Tyrrhenian and Ionian node is the least central on all three indicators: the only connection considered is the Vibo Valentia - Milazzo link that tours the Aeolian Islands. The geographical continuity on the Italian peninsula of this area makes continuous connections throughout the year by ship unnecessary. This is also essentially due to the nature of this Port Authority, which serves the port of Gioia Tauro, Italy's leading container port and least affected by passenger traffic.

The three nodes in the centre-north show the same values of c_i and v_i, while the Northern Tyrrhenian Sea has a higher value than the others of s_i, the highest after the s_i associated with the Sardinian Sea, precisely because of the high number of weekly connections between Tuscan and Sardinian ports.

Finally, it is useful to highlight a general result that emerged in the work: the role of the closed basin in the activation of maritime services. The Tyrrhenian Sea represents to all intents and purposes a closed basin which is bounded to the east and north by the Italian peninsula, to the south by Sicily and to the west by Sardinia. The Adriatic, considering Italian services, is an open basin. It turns out that in the open basin, services are practically nil because evidently all travel is by land or air. This result, although intuitable, is largely confirmed quantitatively.

5 Conclusions and Future Developments

Three measures of centrality, widely adopted in the literature for undirected graphs, were proposed. Each of the three measures proposed for the proposed Ro-pax port network has its own characteristics and expresses a different dimension of centrality.

A first conclusion concerns the geography of the country, which is reflected in the geography of services. The substantial absence of services on a national scale on the Adriatic and the non-significance of services on the Ionian make these two basins negligible for the evaluation of passenger ship traffic on a national scale. The network, as presented, essentially concerns the Tyrrhenian Sea and some areas immediately adjacent to it (part of the Ligurian Sea and the Sardinian Sea).

On the basis of this conclusion, and of the general result identified in Sect. 4, subsequent developments should include the possibility of extending this research to the Adriatic basin as a whole, considering all the countries bordering the basin, and not limiting it to the Italian ports. In this sense, it should be considered how the Tyrrhenian Sea is, with the exception of Corsica, an Italian basin, while the two eastern seas, the Adriatic and the Ionian, lap up Slovenia, Croatia, Bosnia and Herzegovina, Montenegro, Albania and Greece. The study of the network of passenger services connecting Italian Adriatic and Ionian ports with Balkan ports is the next step in this research to validate the general results obtained in the international case. Similarly, it is particularly important to study other closed basins in Europe, such as the one between the Balearic Islands and Spain and that of the Aegean Sea. In order to better understand the relationship between the different countries and basins, the study of the relations within the entire Mediterranean basin should be considered. An analysis on a Mediterranean scale would make it possible to evaluate the centrality at the port level and consequently the weight of each port in the Southern Range system. This is essential since maritime relations on the Mediterranean, being covered by Short Sea Shipping type services, often represent a valid alternative to land services where available, both in passenger transport and in freight transport. It is highly important that Mediterranean Ports should always aim to increase their capacities in respect to sustainable urban mobility planning [39].

With regard to national traffic, which can be reduced to the single Tyrrhenian basin, it was seen that the highest centrality values are linked to the two largest islands, Sicily and Sardinia. Where Sardinia has a higher value of s_i, Western Sicily has a higher value of overall connections (c_i and v_i). In this regard, the importance of Palermo in national passenger traffic is evident; in a complementary way, the 'ship' mode of transport is also central to Palermo's connections with Italy. Considering how the East Sea of Sicily, on the same island but in the eastern zone, is not considered in the graph: passenger traffic from Catania to Italy is shifted to the aeroplane, in the absence of a stable rail link with the continent. Palermo, which also has an airport, has a position of geographical centrality in the Tyrrhenian and a natural 'push' towards the sea that is reflected in an analytical centrality in the network. This second consideration must lead to the development of studies to verify the modification of the service network, and the centrality of the various ports, in the presence of new modal forms in Sicily. In particular, it is necessary to evaluate whether the centrality of the port of Palermo and the airport of Catania would change in the face of a reduction in rail times.

A further line of development of the research is linked to the possibility of studying the nautical tourism sector, considering the high tourist and seasonal flow of some of the nodes that were found to be more central in the study, like Sardinian Sea port Authority and Western Sicily Port Authority. The study would present different characteristics according to the type of traffic. Specifically, particular attention should be paid to the connections between the ports of the mainland and the smaller islands, like Lampedusa for Sicily and Isola d' Elba for Tuscany. To develop this line of research it is important to move from the aggregate node relating to the port authority to a graph in which the individual ports are represented. This approach would make it possible to study both the national and international scale basins and the regional and local scale basins, often characterized by a strong seasonality of services. The concrete growth capacity of our economy depends on the maritime-port system, considering that 85% of our country's non-EU goods are managed by it. It turns out to be a key sector that in these tragically particular years (due to the pandemic, wars and other events) has demonstrated all its resilience by managing to resist the factors of crisis better than others. This is thanks to a context of clear rules which favours the necessary balance between business competitiveness and job protection. Also guaranteed by the public nature of the Port System Authorities. This research can serve at different levels: public administrators, executives of shipping companies and port companies.

In particular, as regards the administrators, the assessment of the centrality of the ports is fundamental for the planning and design of strategies and actions aimed at improving the port-city connections and at creating sustainable and more accessible solutions both from the point of view of passenger transport and goods.

In addition, shipping and management companies can draw inspiration from the evaluation for an improvement in investments and interconnections between the ports themselves.

References

1. https://sdgs.un.org/2030agenda
2. http://docplayer.it/amp/15743061-Ecocalcolatore-ffs-relazione-di-base-versione-1-0-settembre-2010.html
3. https://eur-lex.europa.eu/LexUriServ/LexUriServ.do?uri=COM:2011:0144:FIN:IT:PDF
4. Comi, A., Polimeni, A.: Assessing the potential of short sea shipping and the benefits in terms of external costs: application to the Mediterranean Basin. Sustainability **12**(13), 5383 (2020)
5. Di Gangi, M., Russo, F.: Potentiality of rail networks: integrated services on conventional and high-speed lines. In: Computers in Railways XVIII: Railway Engineering Design and Operation, vol. 213, p. 101 (2020)
6. Decreto Legislativo 4 agosto 2016 n.169. https://www.mit.gov.it/sites/default/files/media/notizia/2016-09/Testo%20Decreto%20riorganizzazione%20porti%2031_8_16.pdf
7. Decreto legge del 23/10/2018 n.119. https://def.finanze.it/DocTribFrontend/getAttoNormativoDetail.do?ACTION=getSommario&id=%7B1391ECFD-6973-46F7-9DF2-BFD94652EB45%7D
8. Russo, F., Rindone, C.: Aggregate models for planning nautical tourism: basic, trend and seasonal demand. Case Stud. Transp. Policy **10**(4), 1980–1987 (2022)
9. Russo, F., Musolino, G., Assumma, V.: Ro-ro and lo-lo alternatives between Mediterranean countries: factors affecting the service choice. Case Stud. Transp. Policy **11**, 100960 (2023)
10. Serra, P., Fancello, G.: Performance assessment of alternative SSS networks by combining KPIs and factor-cluster analysis. Eur. Transp. Res. Rev. **12**, 57 (2020). https://doi.org/10.1186/s12544-020-00449-z
11. Hossmann, T., Spyropoulos, T., Legendre, F.: A complex network analysis of human mobility. In: 2011 IEEE Conference on Computer Communications Workshops (INFOCOM WKSHPS), pp. 876–881. IEEE, April 2011
12. UNCTAD, Port Marketing and the Challenge of the Third Generation Port. Trade and Development Board Committee on Shipping ad Hoc Inter-Government Group of Port Experts, Geneva, Switzerland (1994)

13. UNCTAD, Fourth-Generation Port: Technical Note. Ports Newsletter N. 19, Prepared by UNCTAD D Secretariat, Geneva, Switzerland (1999)

14. Russo, F., Musolino, G.: Quantitative characteristics for port generations: the Italian case study. Int. J. Transp. Dev. Integr. 4(2), 103–112 (2020)

15. Russo, F., Musolino, G.: Port-city interactions: models and case studies. Transp. Res. Procedia 69, 695–702 (2023)

16. Russo, F., Musolino, G.: Industrial and oil ports: case studies and theoretical approaches. Transp. Res. Procedia 69, 703–710 (2023)

17. Balletto, G., Borruso, G., Campisi, T.: Not only waterfront. The Port-City relations between peripheries and inner harbors. In: Gervasi, O., Murgante, B., Misra, S., Ana, M.A., Rocha, C., Garau, C. (eds.) Computational Science and Its Applications – ICCSA 2022 Workshops: Malaga, Spain, July 4–7, 2022, Proceedings, Part V, pp. 196–208. Springer, Cham (2022). https://doi.org/10.1007/978-3-031-10548-7_15

18. Caballini, C., Gattorna, E.: The expansion of the port of Genoa: the Rivalta Scrivia dry port. Development of dry ports, p. 73 (2009)

19. Castigliano, M., De Martino, P., Russo, M.: Napoli: relazioni irrisolte tra porto e città. Urbanistica Informazioni 45(278–279), 43–45 (2018)

20. Paixão, A.C., Bernard Marlow, P.: Fourth generation ports–a question of agility? Int. J. Phys. Distrib. Logist. Manag. 33(4), 355–376 (2003)

21. Russo, F., Panuccio, P., Rindone, C.: Structural factors for a third-generation port: between hinterland regeneration and smart town in Gioia Tauro, Italy. In: Urban Maritime Transport XXVII, vol. 204, pp. 79–90 (2021)

22. Meersman, H., Van de Voorde, E., Vanelslander, T.: Port competition revisited. J. Pediatr. Matern. Fam. Health-Chiropractic 55(2), 210 (2010)

23. Davis, H.C.: Regional port impact studies: a critique and suggested methodology. Transp. J. 23(2), 61–71 (1983)

24. DeSalvo, J.S.: Measuring the direct impacts of a port. Transp. J. 33(4), 33–42 (1994)

25. Ignaccolo, M., Inturri, G., Le Pira, M.: Framing stakeholder involvement in sustainable port planning. Trans. Marit. Sci. 7(02), 136–142 (2018)

26. Borgatti, S.P., Mehra, A., Brass, D.J., Labianca, G.: Network analysis in the social sciences. Science 323(5916), 892–895 (2009)

27. Das, K., Samanta, S., Pal, M.: Study on centrality measures in social networks: a survey. Soc. Netw. Anal. Min. 8(1), 1–11 (2018). https://doi.org/10.1007/s13278-018-0493-2

28. Porta, S., Crucitti, P., Latora, V.: Multiple centrality assessment in Parma: a network analysis of paths and open spaces. Urban Des. Int. 13, 41–50 (2008). https://doi.org/10.1057/udi.2008.1

29. Bhattacharya, K., Mukherjee, G., Saramäki, J., Kaski, K., Manna, S.S.: The international trade network: weighted network analysis and modelling. J. Stat. Mech Theory Exp. 2008(02), P02002 (2008)

30. De Benedictis, L., Tajoli, L.: The world trade network. The World Econ. 34(8), 1417–1454 (2011)

31. Guimera, R., Mossa, S., Turtschi, A., Amaral, L.N.: The worldwide air transportation network: anomalous centrality, community structure, and cities' global roles. Proc. Natl. Acad. Sci. 102(22), 7794–7799 (2005)

32. Scheurer, J., Porta, S.: Centrality and connectivity in public transport networks and their significance for transport sustainability in cities. In: World Planning Schools Congress, Global Planning Association Education Network (2006)

33. Ducruet, C., Lee, S.W., Ng, A.K.: Centrality and vulnerability in liner shipping networks: revisiting the Northeast Asian port hierarchy. Marit. Policy Manag. 37(1), 17–36 (2010)

34. Wu, J., Zhang, D., Wan, C., Zhang, J., Zhang, M.: Novel approach for comprehensive centrality assessment of ports along the maritime silk road. Transp. Res. Rec. 2673(9), 461–470 (2019)

35. Wang, Y., Cullinane, K.: Determinants of port centrality in maritime container transportation. Transp. Res. Part E Logist. Transp. Rev. **95**, 326–340 (2016)
36. Wan, C., Zhao, Y., Zhang, D., Yip, T.L.: Identifying important ports in maritime container shipping networks along the Maritime Silk Road. Ocean Coast. Manag. **211**, 105738 (2021)
37. Cascetta, E.: Transportation Systems Engineering: Theory and Methods, vol. 49. Springer, New York (2001). https://doi.org/10.1007/978-1-4757-6873-2
38. Perron, O.: Neue Kriterien für die Irreduzibilität algebraischer Gleichungen (1907)
39. Miltiadou, M., Mintsis, G., Basbas, S., Taxiltaris, C., Tsoukala, A.: Sustainable urban mobility plans in Mediterranean Port-Cities: the SUMPORT project. In: Nathanail, E.G., Karakikes, I.D. (eds.) CSUM 2018. AISC, vol. 879, pp. 410–417. Springer, Cham (2019). https://doi.org/10.1007/978-3-030-02305-8_50

Inland Port Areas for Optimal Networks Management in Genoa: From Planning Issues to Artificial Intelligence

Ilaria Delponte[(✉)] [iD]

University of Genoa, 16145 Genoa, Italy
ilaria.delponte@unige.it

Abstract. The application of digitalization and artificial intelligence to the field of infrastructural networks shows broad advantages: the improvement of the data collection quality, the works carried out in more precise environments with a relative lower incidence of discrepancies, reduction of the times of execution. All this, considering the need to make the management of regional and multi-regional transport more efficient, in accordance with the territories and their requests, in a cooperative perspective as much as possible. This is the approach recently promoted by the National Recovery and Resilience Plan PNRR and in particular in the funded Raise Ecosystem "Robotics and Artificial Intelligence for Socio-economic Empowerment", based in Genoa (IT). Within the Ecosystem, in Spoke 4 "Intelligent and sustainable ports", the aforementioned themes find ample space and new life for tackling the needs already claimed for a long time by the port clusters in the Liguria Region and, in general, in Italy. The RAISE approach proposed shows how to decline together social and technological issues, as its complexity requires. Specifically, in this paper, the strategic topic of ancillary inland port areas for the management of port operations (night parking areas, pre-gate areas, buffer areas and Special Logistics Zones) is explored as a fundamental tessera of a Western Liguria port planning system, integrated in its physical aspects related to urban planning and dematerialized data flows.

Keywords: inland port areas · artificial intelligence · strategic planning

1 Introduction

In recent years, the advancements of Information Communication Technology were undeniable. Big Data, Machine Learning and the Internet of Things are the most popular topics in both industry and research [1], and considerably waited by territorial bodies for their potential applications in planning and transport.

In particular, as far as port and infrastructures sectors are concerned, great expectations are addressed towards digital and robotics implementations. These for two fundamental reasons: the increase of safety for workers at risk exposition and the improvement in sustainability (economic, social and environmental) for operations and worksites [2, 3].

O. Gervasi et al. (Eds.): ICCSA 2023 Workshops, LNCS 14109, pp. 208–220, 2023.
https://doi.org/10.1007/978-3-031-37120-2_14

Nevertheless, as shown in Fig. 1 (the green box is referred to Airports and Ports), real experimenntations are poor and at a partial level of maturity [4].

On the contrary, from the territorial institutions point of views, the added value constituted by digitalisations and artificial intelligence for engineering and constructions is well known and considered as promising. Speaking about Italy, one of the most popular feature of the Country -as a whole- is the National priority given to ports' performances, which were -for ages- drivers of innovations and competitiveness within their regions.

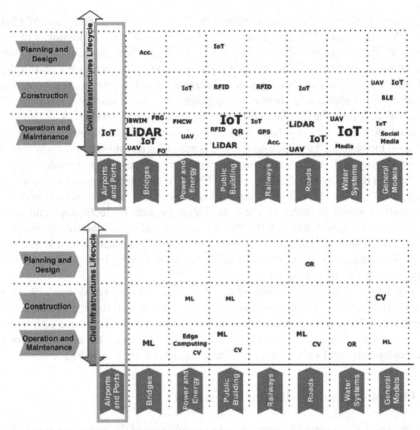

Fig. 1. Map of data acquisition technologies and data processing technologies across infrastructure domains and lifecycle (the content of the green box is referred to "Airports and Ports") (Elaborated from [4])

As a very dinamic context, ports' communities look at tecnologies potentials with a dual mentality: from one hand, dematerialization can cause possible enumployment rates in certain sectors, but, from the other one, the improvements due to acceleration, rationalisation and optimisation of flows, mansions and times are indisputable and strictly connected to global competition rankings (in wich nobody would like to be left behind) [5–7].

Regarding Italian ports positioning in the global scene, Genoa is the most important one, not only because it is the first in terms of tons of goods, but also because plays as the reference point of the productive North-West of Italy and has a long-lasting culture in fact of maritime studies [8].

For the purpose of the paper, Genoa port is an interesting case, because its Port System Authority (Western Ligurian Sea, from now on AdSP) drew up an innovative Strategic Planning Document in which "physical" land and transport planning actions were accompanied by an evident interest towards "digital" models applied for intermodality [9].

Starting from the EU Communication 395 "Ports: an engine for the growth" (2013) [10], which emphasizes how the ports "will be encouraged to act as promoters of intermodality", AdSP underlined the exigence to make traffic flows as uniform as possible from/to the hinterland, by remodulating the volume peaks impacting the port in times and spaces. Interoperability is expected to increase up to the experimentation of a real "synchronized logistic date" between ship/goods and port operators. Considering the lack of spaces due to the morphological asset of the site, AdSP foresees as a competitive potential the availability of inland areas (fully described in the following section), far way from the benches, but which operativity is grounded on info-telematic relations and interoperability of digital systems that also works outside strictly-port borders.

National Recovery and Resilience Plan (PNRR) confirm this perspective through the conceptualization (and funding) of Innovation Ecosystems. In the case of Genoa, local University, National Research Council and Italian Institute of Technology and several local companies were funded by the Plan for the constitution of the RAISE (Robotics and AI for Socio-economic Empowerment) Innovation Ecosystem; its aim is to achieve the goal of digital transition in those sectors acknowledged as territorial vocations, in particular port and infrastructures.

The paper investigates the added value of the Genoese RAISE Ecosystem with respect to territorial priorities and in which way it can support the realization of inland areas needed by AdSP. More specifically, in the following section the Genoa port and the complex design of inland areas are described; then, in the third, the paper deepens the relationship between Ecosystem and inland areas, with some concluding remarks.

2   Port of Genoa and Its Logistic Areas

The trend of port activeness is certainly a meaningful sign of the general economic trend of a city. In the case of Genoa, strictly dependent by nature from maritime traffic and crucial for food and raw materials supply, this indicator is particularly representative of the overall dynamics not only in the city, but in the entire region. In fact, we can say with Hoyle et al. (1997) [11], that a port is structured by the interrelation between an oceanic dependence and a continental one (Fig. 2).

Furthermore, we must not forget that the Ligurian ports always represented a door, an open passage in the Apennines which constitutes the natural outlet of the Po Valley towards the sea.

The XII and XIII centuries had seen the three Republics marinare, Genoa, Pisa and Venice, positioning themselves among the economies that dominated the sea and just

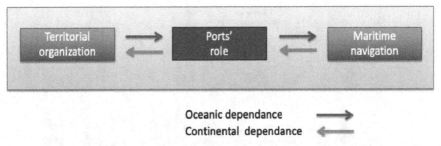

Fig. 2. Relationships between port's role and its territory and sea, according to Hoyle et al. (1997, cit.)

the latter, not being forced like the other two to fight hard to gain a privileged position, it had erected a great protagonist of European trade and beyond. The Ligurian city, after a period in which, despite no longer having a leading role, remains among the richest cities in Europe, rises to prominence again, around the middle of the sixteenth century, thanks to the a certain balance between armament, trade, manufacturing and finance; in fact, that period, thanks to the strategical ability of its merchants and captains, will be defined as the "Century of the Genoeses" [12]. It is possible to consult and access copious documentation about the trend of traffics in the ancient centuries and - with the exception of periods of particular crisis or war - goods have always been increasing up to the present day, although they varied in type and mode of treatment and handling. From the infrastructural viewpoint, in 1874 the city was completely connected by railway lines to France and the rest of Italy: Genoa-Turin, Genoa-Ventimiglia, Genoa-Pisa. Moreover, in the 19th century, Genoa consolidated its role as a major seaport and as important steel and shipbuilding centre, too.

Regarding last century, after a long period of crisis following the economic stagnation of the Seventies and Eighties (due the crisis of heavy industrial plants, especially chemicals), the global increase of maritime traffic (goods and passengers) and the occurrence of urban renewal interventions promoted Genoa, in the the very recent years, as an absolute protagonist of the maritime scene. In 1992 Genoa celebrated the "Colombiadi" or "Genoa Expo '92", the celebration of the 500th anniversary of the discovery of the American Continent by Christopher Columbus. The area of the ancient port of Genoa is restructured and expanded also with the works of the famous architect Renzo Piano. In 2004, the European Union designated Genoa as the European Capital of Culture for that year, because of its historical centre, one of the largest and most-densely populated in Europe: part of it was also inscribed on the World Heritage List (UNESCO) in 2006. The geopolitical positioning of Genoa has increasingly consolidated up to the traffic indicated below (in terms of passengers and goods, Fig. 3). It can be said that, even in a different way compared to the last century in which Genoa was part of the so-called "industrial triangle" with Milan and Turin, it still stands out today as a point of reference for the trade of North-West Italy, of course, but also for in the blue econmy sphere [13].

Starting from the aim to strenghten the Genoa Ports' role, AdSP drew up a Strategic Plan in 2021, in which mjor strategies are contained (Table 1).

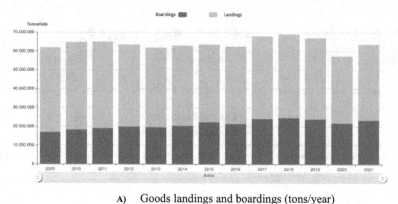

A)   Goods landings and boardings (tons/year)

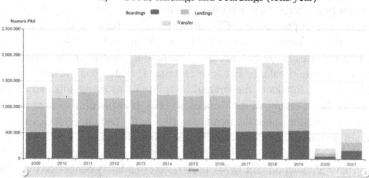

B)   Cruises passengers landings, transfer and boardings (pax/year)

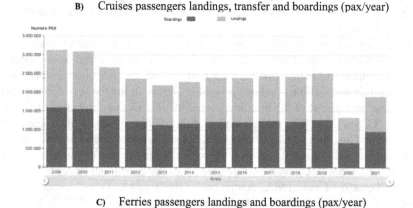

C)   Ferries passengers landings and boardings (pax/year)

Fig. 3. Ports of Genoa traffics, along the years. Source: https://www.portsofgenoa.com/it/chi-siamo/porto-numeri.html

Considering Obj. 2 and the strategic action related to the enhancement of intermodality and actual valorisation of territorial contexts aroung the ports' sites, AdSP proposed a comprehensive project of the whole logistic system, grounded on a shared target: to semplify logistic bureaucratic operations and limitate congestion.

In fact, the second Objective of the Plan focuses on organizing processes and cluster relationships, through the identification of a set of interventions of procedural, technological and organizational innovation. In particular, the development of "infostructures" will allow to rationalize the document exchange while ensuring fluidization of traffic; this will optimize the use of the port spaces and will allow to manage a greater amount of traffic with a relative increase of ground areas. We can also noticed that, specifically, the European Commission puts a special emphasis on promoting unique interoperable interfaces, with the aim of reducing practices administration and the facilitation of traffic. Specific directives on these themes are being implemented such as 2010/65 [14], relating to the formalities of declaration of ships arriving or departing from ports of the Member States and the establishment of the "Single Windows national maritime time".

Table 1. Strategic Plans Objectives and Lines (Source: AdSP)

Objectives	Title	Intervention Lines
1	*Increase in the competitiveness of the port system*	- multi-business vocation of the port system - centrality in the logistics system of the reference hinterland - extension of the reference market beyond national borders
2	*Sustainability of port areas*	- growth of the port system with sensitivity to the environment - reduction of the environmental impacts - enhancement of intermodality
3	*Increase in value for the area*	- strengthening of economic and occupational activities - enhancement of the coexistence between urban and port activities

Particularly, the evolution of the transport and logistics reserch took into account peaks of volumes that occur in conjunction with the ship's dock. The landing of the ship stimulate the infrastructural network systems at a level that has grown considerably in the last few years. This phenomenon is not only linked exclusively to the container sector, but it concerns a large part of the traffic handled within the port system, just think of the case of the passenger sector (ferries and cruises), in which Genoa flourishes. Furthermore, the hinterland production and distribution flows impose rather rigid time windows for loading/unloading operations at the plant/warehouse, helping to make flows from/to the port a variable that is not controllable by the port and its operators. This reflects in traffic peaks, occurring in certain times during the day and during the weekend, which also reverberates in terms of peaks in certain port areas and infrastructures. Additional seasonal peaks contribute to raise the level of operational stress on the facilities of the port.

The Plan identifies therefore, among the prior interventions for the logistics system, the need to soften, as far as possible, traffic peaks, through better distribution of flows both over time (over the day and of the week) both in space (areas, networks).

Better upfront planning and management of the arrival and departure of vehicles (road and rail) to/from and to the hinterland would allow for a more uniform distribution of vehicles throughout the day and along the network, limiting the phenomena of congestion.

In details, promoted actions pertain to:

- "Intermodal appointment": better sharing of information e the introduction of more punctual synchronization elements, new approach in the use of infrastructure and facilities of the port (temporal planning);
- Buffer areas and Simplified Logistics Zones: availability of operational areas outside the port (as in art. 6 National Law 130/2018 [15], Simplified Logistics Zone pursuant to art. 7 of the same Law), which allow the performance of operational activities in these areas, permitting a better distribution, in time and space, of flows from/to the port. In these areas, services for cargo and hauliers will be also included, as functional to both ordinary and in contingency/emergency situations. Furthermore, the flows of vehicles from/to these areas will be organized in order to take advantage of the hours/days off the peak of port operations, relieving congestion port facilities and in general the organization of the port;
- Rest areas and Pre-gates: optimization and flow fluidification also passes through regularization of their trend during the day/week and the organization of a system of passages/gates and related parking areas (internal or immediately outside the port). In particular, regarding rest areas can be identified at least three levels of response that combine with needs different, though often complementary, operations: 1) parking areas/car park 2) areas of pre-gate 3) technical parking areas inside the port. These areas will be digitally equipped to manage remote dialogue and exchange of information.

The network of areas should contribute to raise the level of the service provided, to improve the planning of trips for heavy vehicles and the working conditions of road hauliers, as well as to reduce the level of congestion and externalities of transport. Nevertheless, what has just been reported is sufficient to understand the prominence that innovation and technologies assume at the level of Community policies and how they constitute a new element cornerstone of port planning.

From the research point of view, author prevously focused on the last two types of areas, i.e. rest areas and pre-gates. In fact, following the approach of the AdSP Plan, the features of buffer areas and semplified logistics zones were already determined with a certain level of details (see in Fig. 4: Rivalta Scrivia, Arquata Scrivia, Novi Ligure, Alessandria, Piacenza, Castellazzo, Ovada, Dinazzano, Mi-Smistamento, Melzo, Vado Ligure). While, in the case of the second type, a preliminary areas localisation was already provided but without any indication about how it would be equipped in terms of services.

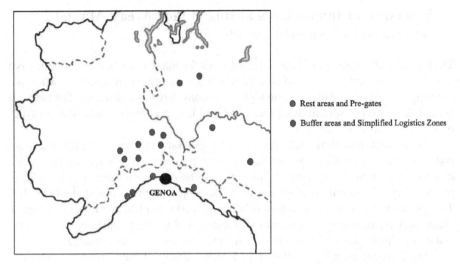

Fig. 4. Inland port areas systems (Elaborated from https://worldmapblank.com/it)

As widely expressed in Delponte et al. (2022) [16], areas devoted to truck drivers services as potential pre-gates of the Genoa port system are:

- two areas are located approximately 30 km from Western part of Genoa Port area along motorway network-Savona, West direction and AdS Stura, North direction;
- two areas are located approximately 30 km from Central part of Genoa Port area along motorway network-Chiavari, East direction and Serravalle Scrivia, North direction;
- one closer area -Ex-Fondega- located between Western and Central Genoa Port Area (distances are approximately 5 km).

The abovementioned paper illustrated the first part of the research (related to the location and provision of services, considering the necessary tools and infrastructures, technical, technological, orographic constraints, etc., and the engagement of the stakeholders and partners) and it can be consulted for further details.

At the end of its preliminary investigation, based on verification of land-use and transport connectivity contraints and key-stakeholders interviews, only two areas resulted properly usable for for pre-gate destination (Fondega and Chiavari) and other two for restoration and services for hauliers' night stop (Savona and Stura).

Nevertheless, despite many project results were already obtained, a wider glance towards such categories of areas in a systematic approach is still lacking. An all-encompassing way to distribute functions and to apply connection and interoperability operations have still to be defined.

At this point of the pursuing of the Strategic Objectives, the RAISE Ecosystem comes to aid for this purpose.

3 Ecosystem of Innovation and Inland Port Areas: Mutual Outcomes and Expected Results

The potential of automation has been talked about for many years now and robotics as a lever to improve performance - of efficiency, efficacy, safety, environmental impact, etc. - in freight transport and distribution logistics is considered as indeniable. The theme is at the intersection of several disciplinary areas of transport and a multiplicity of types of actors are involved.

This is the approach recently promoted by the National Plan of PNRR Recovery and Resilience, but which has very distant roots in time (and in scientific literature): it is the concept of "Ecosystem of innovation". The relationship between knowledge and territory in which it develops has been the subject of numerous studies [17, 18]. The systems premises are constantly evolving (networks, implementation of new supply chains/sectors, local re-composition of businesses e linking them into long value chains) and new technologies are grafted into such an intense and pervasive change.

Therefore, the challenge will be based on the ability of the territories to produce cognitive capital, for which contextual policies will be needed as stimulators of fertile environments for the transposition of new business models. In fact, Ecosystems intervene on areas of technological specialization, consistent with industrial and research vocations of the local territory (regional or supra-regional), promoting and strengthening collaboration between the research system, firms and institutions.

In parallel with the actual challenges promoted by the Strategic Plan of AdSP, Spoke 4 "Smart and Sustainable Ports" has the objective of creating an ecosystem of innovation in support to the several port areas foreseen for the Liguria region. New levels of automation, innovative technologies for collecting data, smarter and optimized processes will be introduced and applied to the big maritime ports (Genova, La Spezia and Savona-Vado) and to the medium/small ones (in the two Rivieras of the region), aiming at reducing the environmental impacts of port activities, improving safety and security, creating a less stressful work environment, defining a new way of experiencing the port within the city. Projects of spoke 4 will be carried out by University of Genova, with affiliates co-founders CNR and IIT, public/research affiliates ENEA and INFN, and industrial affiliates Aitek, algoWatt, Circle, EII, Fincantieri, and Leonardo. These are the main players of this "innovative port ecosystem" and they are currently working together to carry out research and industrial activities, develop technologies, set living labs and demonstration areas, disseminate results to the scientific community, industrial associations, and citizens.

- Spoke 4 "Smart and Sustainable Ports" was built on four strategic lines of research and development (RL) and nineteen research areas (RA). The four strategic lines are:
- RL1. Uncrewed and automated systems for port automation
- RL2. Machine Learning and real-time data for port safety, security, and sustainability
- RL3. Port management in an integrated framework of transport infrastructures
- RL4. AI-powered services for medium and small ports

Considering, in particular, the two lines 2 and 3 -in which the author is involved- RL 3 has the objective of optimizing the performance of the port from many points of view (management, environmental, energy), also exploiting the data collected and analyzed in the second work-package, and even making use of virtual models and digital twins. In this connection, ports are considered -in a systemic approach- as nodes of a regional network of transport infrastructures. This strategic line includes both approaches devised for ports as "nodes" of the integrated network (as the integration of new and smart solutions inside TOSs, advanced AI and IoT schemes for improving processes, solutions for energy and resource efficiency), and methods and tools for transport networks as "lines" (like advanced monitoring, forecasting and optimization of flows of goods, approaches for reacting to disruptions). In parallel, in RL 2, several data and signals will be collected from various heterogeneous sources (also exploiting the resources introduced in the first work-package) and they will be analyzed for the purpose of traffic monitoring, marine and weather forecast, sustainability evaluation, risk assessment, port protection against hazards and infrastructure maintenance. Robotics and AI technologies developed in this strategic line includes IoT- based solutions to localize, track, and recognize in- and out-bound flows of vehicles and persons; data- driven models for nowcast and forecast of marine conditions including weather, fauna, and pollution; tools to evaluate energy consumptions and emissions, as well as for monitoring acoustic signals for workers' health; intelligent sensor networks for port protection; teams of aerial and ground robots for monitoring and inspection of shipbuilding activities, port areas and goods.

The safety of port workers is a sensible item of paramount importance. Using state-of-the-art AI-inspired technologies the project aims to define a modern framework that will reduce and manage risks in port operations. Starting from a deep assessment of the working conditions and stakeholders' needs, the best strategy minimize risks and define a work plan for continuous monitoring of the port environment will be deployed. A combination of hardware (e.g. remotely operated vehicles, robots, and a network of monitor systems) and software technologies (e.g. platforms for big-data collection and elaboration) will be developed and optimized by public and private partners of the project to increase the current safety operations in the port environment and provide a long-range plan to ensure continuous monitoring and risk minimization in future. To this extent, the goal of strengthening port automation processes through a novel combination of data collection and aggregation from IoT devices, AI/ML and optimization algorithms for (predictive) analytics and automation can be implied, in this case, to improve flows in ports.

From the concrete application point of view, many are the disciplines involved; but, the two research lines have a point in common that is Genoa as the test bed.

The paradigm of the innovation ecosystem, according to its own nature, carries out an idea of the future (innovation) on some selected elements/categories/fields, but it is also a project declined locally, as a sort of evolution of its vocations. In this participatory perspective, the "disruptive" technologies that could be progressively introduced thanks to the research progress, should be appropriately introduced to Stakeholders. This can happen by means of models of acceptance (TAM - Technology Acceptance Models), which verify consensus by the actors and often provide suggestions for the consequent rebalancing of the work activities.

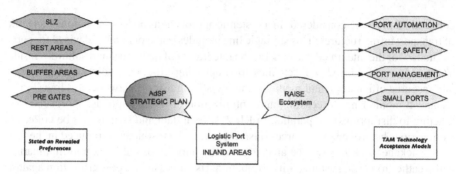

Fig. 5. Inland port areas systems in the Strategic Plan and the RAISE Research Lines.

4 Conclusions

Finally, it seems meaningful to underline that, even if AI and ML are considered "technological" activities, RAISE takes into account the societal empowerment phase equally important, in an all-encompassing way to think about "innovation" in a holistic manner [19]. In fact, one possible objection to the research project could be the will -in some way- to organize the port cluster according to a top-down activity.

However, the shared objective between RAISE and the AdSP Strategic Plan (Fig. 5) is to build a platform -with tested characteristics- able to perform the best in rationalization and optimization of flows, and to precisely define the requirements from a technological point of view. The governance of the process is totally devolved to a sharing process with economic operators; in a possible future, actors will join into a Framework Agreement with detailed procedures and forms. For this reason, likewise important is an active participation of all the parties: port and urban institutions, hauliers, brokers, shippers, carriers, road and motorway managers, etc. Most work will be led not only in the field of AI and ML, but also in other topics/applications such as TAM-Technology Acceptance Models and targeted interviews with stakeholders, which will define the propensities to change and the willingness to pay related to each of the different scenarios. The latter will be accomplished by the Stated Preferences and Revealed Preferences methods (and a connection of the two).

Regarding TAM, we consider it as an information systems theory that models how users come to accept and use a technology; in this, behavioral intention is a key-factor that leads people to use the provided technology [20, 21]. However, when we spoke about Stated and Revealed Preferences as a way to investigate propensity by interviewees, we refer to "stated preferences" (sometimes referred to as contingent valuation) as a survey-based technique for establishing valuations, that is the crucial aim in societal acceptance: in other words, the actor is asked how much they value something. The answer might be based on several elements and it may be very different from the actual behavior. Revealed preferences investigate the actual decisions people make and these may be very different – if not completely opposite from – their stated preferences. Starting from the relationships between the two and the users' profile which comes from them, dissemination and engagement actions can be organize for a better understanding of the project in its complexity.

Considering that the main points of the study concern

- the characterisation of the areas;
- the study of their urban constraints;
- the definition of services in each area
- the feasibility criteria (economic, social and environmental) of intervention in the areas,

it is clear that the acceptance part of the new technologies introduced is an integral and not ancillary part of the proposal considered by the Port Authority and Ecosystem RAISE.

All these components are strategic for an Ecosystem that want to consolidate the local port vocation but also give an added value to its territory, by means of the engagement of its social community.

References

1. Zhu, H., Cao, Y., Wei, X., Wang, W., Jiang, T., Jin, S.: Caching transient data for internet of things: a deep reinforcement learning approach. IEEE Internet Things J. **6**(2), 2074–2083 (2018)
2. Makkawan, K., Muangpan, T.: A conceptual model of smart port performance and smart port indicators in Thailand. J. Int. Logistics Trade **19**(3), 133–146 (2021)
3. Melo, P., Arrais, R., Veiga, G.: Development and deployment of complex robotic applications using containerized infrastructures. In: 2021 IEEE 19th International Conference on Industrial Informatics (INDIN), pp. 1–8. IEEE (2021)
4. Naderi, H., Shojaei, A.: Digital twinning of civil infrastructures: current state of model architectures, interoperability solutions, and future prospects. Autom. Constr. **149**, 104785 (2023). https://doi.org/10.1016/j.autcon.2023.104785
5. Parola, A.F., Risitano, M., Ferretti, M., Panetti, E., Risitano, M., Ferretti, M.: The drivers of port competitiveness: a critical review. Port Econ. **37**, 1–23 (2016)
6. Yu, H., Gong, Y., Liu, J.: A systematic literature review on port competitiveness. International Journal of Logistics Research and Applications, pp. 1–25 (2023)
7. Luo, M., Chen, F., Zhang, J.: Relationships among port competition, cooperation and competitiveness: a literature review. Transp. Policy **118**, 1–9 (2022). https://doi.org/10.1016/j.tranpol.2022.01.014
8. Musso, E., Ghiara, H.: Ancorare i Porti al Territorio. Dai Traffici Alla Marittimizzazione. McGraw Hill Education (2007)
9. Autorità di Sistema Portuale del Mar Ligure Occidentale. Documento di Pianificazione Strategica di Sistema, Genova (2021)
10. EU Communication from the Commission 395: Ports: an engine for the growth (2013). https://eur-lex.europa.eu/LexUriServ/LexUriServ.do?uri=COM%3A2013%3A0295%3AFIN%3AEN%3APDF
11. Hoyle, B., Pinder, D.A., Husain, M.S.: Aree Portuali e Tarsformazioni Urbane: le Dimensioni Internazionali Della Strutturazione Del Waterfront, Mursi (1997)
12. Braudel, F.: Civiltà materiale, II, I giochi dello scambio, Torino, **185** (1981)
13. Carver, R.: Lessons for blue degrowth from Namibia's emerging blue economy. Sustain. Sci. **15**(1), 131–143 (2019). https://doi.org/10.1007/s11625-019-00754-0
14. EU Directive 2010/65: Ing formalities for ships arriving in and/or departing from ports of the Member States (2010)

15. National Law 16 novembre 2018, n. 130: Conversione in legge, con modificazioni, del decreto-legge 28 settembre 2018, n. 109, recante disposizioni urgenti per la citta' di Genova, la sicurezza della rete nazionale delle infrastrutture e dei trasporti, gli eventi sismici del 2016 e 2017, il lavoro e le altre emergenze

16. Delponte, I., Costa, V., Cascetta, E., Cartenì, A., Scisciot, F.: Buffer areas for sustainable logistics. assessing their added value towards port community. TEMA, **3**, 487–500, ISSN: 1970–9889 (2022)

17. Camagni, R., Borri, D., Ferlaino, F.: Per un concetto di capitale territoriale. *Crescita e sviluppo regionale: strumenti, sistemi, azioni*, pp. 66–90 (2009)

18. Di Venosa, M.: L'interfaccia città. Geografie e governance in transizione. urbanistica, **287**, 55 (2019)

19. Moulaert, F., Mehmood, A.: Towards social holism: social innovation, holistic research methodology and pragmatic collective action in spatial planning. In: The Routledge Handbook of Planning Research Methods, pp. 97–106. Routledge (2014)

20. Venkatesh, V., Davis, F.D.: A theoretical extension of the technology acceptance model: four longitudinal field studies. Manage. Sci. **46**(2), 186–204 (2000)

21. Taherdoost, H.: A review of technology acceptance and adoption models and theories. Procedia Manufact. **22**, 960–967 (2018)

Ports in the Port: The Case of Messina

Clara Stella Vicari Aversa[✉] [iD]

dArTe Architecture and Territory Department, Mediterranean University of Reggio Calabria,
89124 Reggio Calabria, Italy
clarastella.vicariaversa@unirc.it

Abstract. In seaside towns, the port has always constituted an essential element of their collective memory. From being the main cultural and identity element, this close port-city relationship has increasingly become a rich ecosystem that only lives with the cooperation of all its parts; ecosystems now more than ever called upon to face future challenges to ensure their sustainability, by creating green ports, from an environmental, economic and social point of view, using appropriate integrated approaches. The case of Messina will be analyzed. The area presents profiles of complexity that can make it a paradigm: the historic port is located in the city center and in it interacts commuter transport for the Calabrian side of the Strait serving workers in the areas, traffic on the Tyrrhenian -Ionian Seas axis and vice versa of pure transit, which in turn intersects with train, vehicle and passenger traffic on the Sicily-Calabria axis of non-commuting traffic. Finally, the port is affected by cruise tourism, the top 10 nationwide. Examining the interactions between these different traffic flows and 'destinations' with the immanent city that is totally integrated with it, may indicate a strategic model that can be adequately developed in larger port areas. And the imminent redevelopment projects of the former market areas with the I-Hub of the Straits and the Customs House for a new cruise terminal in one with the recovery of the *Real Cittadella* in the rear port will also imply a study of the bureaucratic interactions between different bodies.

Keywords: Port-city Interaction · Waterfront Redevelopment · Messina harbour

1 Introduction: Port Cities

In seaside towns, the port has always constituted an essential element of their ancestral and collective memory, becoming in almost all cases the main reference of urban identity itself.

A fundamental value not only at the time of their foundation, but also and above all, over time, for their spatial and productive organisation. The presence of the port is closely related to the historical and cultural memory of a place, to the point of marking it profoundly; it even becomes something with which the inhabitants who live in and pass through it, come to identify themselves, acquiring it and restoring a sense of it even through its very architecture.

O. Gervasi et al. (Eds.): ICCSA 2023 Workshops, LNCS 14109, pp. 221–239, 2023.
https://doi.org/10.1007/978-3-031-37120-2_15

The architectural configuration of the main port cities has always stemmed from the profound relationship with the port itself, a fundamental element of exchange between the land and the sea, between the stable space and the constantly changing one. And this has historically been the case since the ancient Greek or Roman settlements, to the ancient mediaeval walls, to the Renaissance openings, to the most modern architectural and spatial solutions of the waterfront.

The permanent dialectic between land and sea is certainly the main feature in port cities.

Port cities never imagine themselves to be stationary, but always historically hospitable and on the move, always ready for continuous arrivals and departures, for good-byes and new welcomes. It is no coincidence that their growth has always been related to that of the port, just as their crisis, historically, has also coincided with the crisis of the port itself, with the weakening of trade or exchange and/or with changes in flows. Cities and their ports are linked by important, but often conflicting relationships, which have inevitably conditioned their mutual evolutions [2, 9].

In fact, when in many of these seaside cities, the port as a pole of economic development disappeared, and this happened especially in the last decades of the 20th century, with the crisis of maritime transport and heavy industry, the port cities that were unable to cope with the changes coming from the sea entered more into crisis; they did not reinvent themselves on the sea and port front and, closing in on themselves, they almost completely turned their backs on the sea. A strategic error when one considers that this is, after all, their primary source of wealth. But in this way the overwhelming opportunity and wealth of the cities themselves ended up becoming a deep barrier rather than an opportunity. And this has happened because they have lost contact with their raison d'être, their sea, and thus interrupted a centuries-old relationship, which, after all as in all relationships that work, is changeable and must be nurtured and regained.

The focus on port areas, often suddenly freed in central and desirable locations, has forced us to contemplate the different potentials of these areas, which have once again been discovered and thus reinvented and converted to urban uses and functions. Cities such as Marseille, Barcelona, Rotterdam, Hamburg, Malaga, Boston, Yokoama, but also Bilbao, on its *Ria*, have resurrected precisely by recovering their historical port spaces with a profound intervention of recovery of their respective waterfronts and the reconversion and redevelopment of their sea or river ports [5–8] (Fig. 1).

Port cities must consider the richness of the stretch of water in front of them as a determining factor when making important architectural, planning and urban regeneration choices; and they must take it into primary consideration when the need to reinvent themselves and decide on the new face of the city cyclically arrives.

A new face, that of the port waterfront, which involves subjects from different sectors and among them urban planners and designers, politicians and, often, countless other decision-makers or stakeholders.

Fig. 1. Examples of waterfront projects in some city-ports in Europe: Bilbao, Hamburg, Tokyo, Barcelona. Photos by Clara Stella Vicari Aversa.

Indeed, port waterfront areas are often privileged spaces that lend themselves to hosting various functions and no longer those purely related to industry alone, as was the case in the past. Their location makes these areas truly attractive areas close to urban or historical centres; historic city ports, in particular, are ideal places to host activities related to transport, trade, entertainment and, of course, tourism. They can be ideal places to build new housing developments, hotels, recreational areas, sports facilities, and thus become important sources of employment.

These waterfronts along the harbour, which then spread along the waterfront of the cities in which they are located, not only provide breathing space for residents, but also ample space for monuments, housing, recreation and mixed-use developments.

This is certainly an interdisciplinary issue that is becoming an increasingly popular and shared topic in the fields of urban planning, city architecture and should increasingly be integrated as a priority within any development policy process [3, 4, 19].

From being the main cultural and identity element, this close port-city relationship has become an increasingly complex sphere, a rich ecosystem that only lives with the cooperation of all its parts; ecosystems now more than ever called upon to face the present and future challenges regarding the actions necessary to ensure their sustainability [15]. Even the necessary and increasingly urgent focus on issues such as sustainability, urban regeneration, and the need for ever greener spaces and ports, ineluctably tends towards a global social and economic model that works the more it tends to involve all players in the process. It is a matter of getting architects, engineers, town planners, and landscape architects to work together with the political authorities and administrative bodies involved from time to time, all united, it is hoped, by the need to find answers to a new, closer and more contemporary relationship between port and city. Moreover, if we consider that 90% of ports in Europe are located in urban areas, it is clear that their development must necessarily be governed by environmental protection logics and policies. In fact, ports are actually responsible for a substantial share of greenhouse gas emissions, which are certainly harmful both for those who live near these places and for the ecosystem.

Port cities, in these processes of evolution, are also called upon to regenerate by making their ports increasingly green ports. A formula that must be understood from an environmental, economic and social point of view, using appropriate integrated approaches and electrification and decarbonisation interventions, involving the port itself but also the post-port areas intimately connected to it.

The port of Messina, if the ongoing transformation processes are completed, will be able to contribute to the reshaping of port cities; its port and its old new architecture have in fact and in power a dual energy: economic for the territory's gross domestic product, regenerative as a lever for the urban re-modelling of the entire city area.

Administrative and political authorities interacting in the governance of the territory, planners, but also entrepreneurs in port areas could draw indications and references in the performance of their roles or in the protection of their interests.

A necessarily basic technical and historical framing of the Messina port city, of its hybrid character, will be followed by an examination of current or possible projects and processes, all aimed at putting the pieces of the puzzle that make up the identity of a city back in the right place.

2   The Port City of Messina, Its Sickle

Of all the port cities that have begun to undertake these necessary transformations, the case of the city of Messina, historically the 'Gateway to Sicily' from the Italian peninsula, located on the Strait of the same name between Sicily and Calabria, is analysed. The city's original name, 'Zancle', coincides precisely with the conformation of its port. A name given to it by the Siculians, who called it 'Zanklon', due to the configuration of the harbour with the appearance of a sickle, a harbour that still identifies the image of the centre of the city itself. Even the most historically representative and characteristic architectural invention of the city, the *Palazzata*, is none other than the redesign with architecture of the harbour front. The *Palazzata* that exists today, designed by Giuseppe Samonà in the 1930s, still seems to embrace the harbour; a comparison of non-maritime architecture could be the typical Spanish Plaza Mayor (Fig. 2).

The city of Messina, lying longitudinally on a narrow plain between the Peloritani Mountains and the junction of the Tyrrhenian and Ionian Seas, seen from the sea with its *Palazzata* in the foreground, presents several elements of variety and complexity, which derive above all from its particular geographical position and configuration. Messina, in fact, in its characteristic position of 'control' of the Strait of the same name, seems far from representing the 'classic and normal' maritime city, where land and sea, located opposite each other, meet and control each other along a 'simple' edge. The city, on the contrary, is an incredible and almost inextricable crossroads of land and sea but also of exchange between one land and another land that is, in turn, a continent.

"On a map of the world, the Mediterranean is nothing more than a fissure in the earth's crust... These mountains reach out to the sea, sometimes choking to the point of reducing it to a mere corridor of salt water: think... of the Strait of Messina with the swirling eddies of Scylla and Charybdis... It is no longer sea: they are rivers, or even

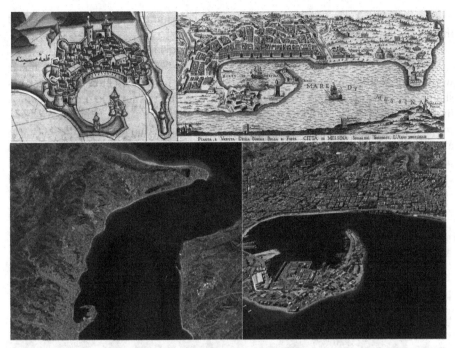

Fig. 2. Messina in a map attributed to the Turkish admiral Piri Reis, circa 1554. Messina in an engraving from 1783 [20]. The Strait and the Port of Messina. Source Geoportale Messina, www. comune.messina.sitr.it - AdSP, https://cpwaterfrontmessina.it.

mere sea gates" writes Fernand Braudel. And the same French historian adds that this liquid space is almost no longer sea, but river, because of the way Sicily and Calabria seem to restrict it.

Messina, as written above, gateway to Sicily, has also been called the 'key to Sicily', due to its strategic geographic location but also due to its natural military and commercial port, a point of union between the Italian peninsula and the East and traditionally one of the most welcoming in the Mediterranean. It is no coincidence that it is a frequent feature in many ancient engravings, especially those of Grand Tour travellers, and a magnificent backdrop in some famous paintings such as Antonello da Messina's Sibiu Crucifixion; but, even before that, a place recounted in Homeric mythology. The city has grown longitudinally around its port since antiquity; it has been a transit route of great importance, attracting enterprising spirits of various nationalities because of the extraordinary beauty of its landscape and the charm of its waters, full of deceptive whirlpools, myths and legends, of monsters with magical powers such as Scylla and Charybdis, 'so distant in nature' -they are separated by three kilometres- 'and which poetry, nevertheless, has located so close', said Goethe; and, finally, never ceasing to produce suggestions even in more recent times, inspiring a wonderful marine poem, Stefano D'Arrigo's Horcinus Orca.

Messina's entire history is linked to its port, living and developing both in a natural symbiosis, passing from the splendour of the 17th century, to the crisis of the 18th century, to the revival years of the 19th century, to the painful post-earthquake years and the gradual decline.

A port and a city profoundly changed between the 19th and 20th centuries.

In the 19th century, the first steamers stopped next to the sailing ships, the quays were full of goods with stretches of barrels ready to be loaded and huge ox-drawn carts shuttled from the factories to the port, especially for citrus products. In the 20th century, the expanse of goods on the quays was replaced by a multitude of men and women leaving for the Americas. At the same time, after the disastrous earthquake of 1908, there was also the slow and more modern reconstruction of the port facilities, with the large cranes on a par with the increasingly large ships, now all made of steel. Throughout the various epochs, the port has never ceased to be the lung and heart of Messina's economic and social reality, while remaining at the centre of the city's life (Fig. 3).

Fig. 3. Current view of Messina from its harbour. Photo by Clara Stella Vicari Aversa.

3   An Inextricable Intertwining of Routes

The special feature of the 'urban' port of Messina is a continuous and inextricable intertwining of routes. There are fast and slow routes, traffic of light vehicles, such as cars, and heavy vehicles, such as trucks; flows of people and goods between one bank and the other and parallel to the city, across the Strait from north to south and vice versa. Small vessels, container ships, ships with trains in them and cruise ships travelling between Sicily and Calabria or transiting the Strait enter or leave the port. There is an unusual overlapping and multiplication of routes, of straight lines, of roads and railway lines interrupted at sea but then resumed on the two shores.

Not only is the Strait traversed seamlessly, 24 h a day, every day of the year, by ships laden with passengers, cars, trucks and even trains connecting the two shores; but oceanic routes also cross on these, with container ships that may come from China, cross Suez and head, if they are lucky, for Gioia Tauro, but sometimes continue on to Rotterdam and into the North Seas [18]. And there is no shortage, of course, and indeed they are constantly increasing, of the gigantic mobile palaces of the sea, the cruise ships.

The port itself of the city of Messina, the historic sickle of the harbour, a decisive junction and strategic crossroads, has evolved for these reasons.

The traditional port of Messina, born and bred as a so-called 'port emporium', with reference to the classification of ports into generations according to their characteristics, is a first-generation port [22]. However, processes are underway to overcome the functioning of the port as an 'independent realm' in which the operators within it often act like atoms. And this also emerges from what is described in this paper.

Today, it is no longer a single port; there are many ports in a port, many ports and berths even intertwined with each other. And in its most intimate and sheltered part, bordering on the remains of the *Real Cittadella* created by Charles V, activities serving the sea such as shipbuilding and those of the Navy.

The historic sickle of the port of Messina, in fact, despite its fairly contained dimensions, actually seems to house a world.

Fig. 4. Cruise ship in the port of Messina in front of the *Palazzata*. Source Port System Authority of the Strait [1]

Right in front of the historical buildings of the *Palazzata*, which redesign the edge of the harbour, cruise ships are arranged every week; they almost seem to be playing doubles and competing in height, and eventually winning, with the *Palazzata* itself (Fig. 4).

Almost at the end of the *Palazzata*, in the area comprised between the old Customs House and the Maritime Station, dock the so-called fast ships, replacing the hydrofoils invented in the 'Rodriquez' shipyards years ago in Messina itself, reserved for passengers, in communication with Reggio Calabria (with connections to the city centre or to the Straits Airport), Villa San Giovanni and the Aeolian islands.

In front of the Maritime Station dock the ships of the State Railways, connecting with both Reggio Calabria and Villa San Giovanni, including special ships equipped with tracks to carry all trains to and from the 'continent'; ships carrying cars, trucks and passengers.

Ships carrying cars, trucks and passengers to and from Salerno also dock daily at the port.

And, as mentioned above, cruise ships, to the great satisfaction of the Port System Authority of the Strait, whose President Mega recently declared: "A great cruise season is on the horizon for the Port of Messina with the arrival of the most beautiful and modern ships that ply the seas all over the world"; the same President underlined that the city port, in April 2023, is confirmed to be of great attractiveness for ship-owners from all over the world, with well-established approval rates; 25 companies will be present, from MSC with 39 stopovers to Norwegian Cruise Line with 24, from Royal Caribbean with 38 ships of the RCCL/Celebrity brand to Viking with 21 calls and many more, also expecting welcome returns such as Carnival and Costa Crociere.

Fig. 5. Port Master Plan. Port System Authority of the Strait. Areas and sub-areas [1]

The area included in the historic port is not the only one with berths, there are others further north and further south that fall under the jurisdiction of the Port System Authority of the Strait. This is an entity established in 2016, with legal personality under public law and endowed with budgetary and financial autonomy, whose main tasks are those of direction, planning, control, coordination, and promotion of port operations and other commercial and industrial activities carried out in the ports of Messina, Tremestieri, Milazzo, Villa San Giovanni, Reggio Calabria, and Saline in an administrative-managerial unicum, thus unifying the development strategies of the port infrastructures of the entire Strait of Messina area [1] (Fig. 5).

Just outside the harbour crescent, a little further north, in front of the Prefecture and the *Passeggiata a Mare* and just before the entrance to the former trade fair citadel, there is a small marina; a short distance away, after passing the trade fair enclosure, in the roadstead of San Francesco di Paola, there has been a berth for private Caronte-Tourist ships since the 1970s. Ships that, like a modern two-faced Janus, load cars and passengers and, whenever the port of Tremestieri is silted up due to storm surges, even trucks, relentlessly linking the Sicilian shore with the Calabrian shore at Villa San Giovanni.

In the southernmost area, about 8 km from the city centre, is the port of Tremestieri, which has recently become an area of strong commercial development. From here, with the entry into operation of the maritime port, a high percentage of the heavy ferry traffic to and from Calabria is handled, shifting here much of the traffic that used to be carried out at the FS embarkation points of the Maritime Station and the San Francesco di Paola roadstead (Fig. 6).

Fig. 6. Some of the ships that cross in the Strait of Messina: FS train-carrying ship, cruise ship near the Maritime Station, Caronte & Tourist car carrier, container ship. First photo by Roberto Di Maria, others photos by Clara Stella Vicari Aversa.

The area of the Strait of Messina therefore presents profiles of complexity that can make it a paradigm: the historic port is located in the historic and current centre of the city; commuter transport for the Calabrian side of the Strait interacts in it, serving workers in the two areas, traffic on the Tyrrhenian-Mar Ionian axis and vice versa of pure transit, which in turn intersects with rail, vehicle and passenger traffic on the Sicily-Calabria axis of non-commuter traffic. Finally, the port is affected by cruise tourism, which places the city among the top 10 nationwide.

It is no coincidence that, on the basis of the *Ispra - Istituto Superiore per la Protezione e la Ricerca Ambientale* surveys, the city of Messina is in the top position for the indicator measuring the size of ports according to the number of passengers transported each year. *Ispra* measures the relevance of European ports by means of two indicators, cargo transit capacity, as a volume of containers, and passenger traffic on arrival and departure [10].

Moreover, according to these findings of the said body, by number of passengers transported each year, the two cities on the Strait, Messina and Reggio Calabria, in just three years, from 2016 to 2019, have even doubled the number of people transported, with a remarkable growth of 90% and 95% respectively.

Messina ranks first, and its neighbour Reggio Calabria fourth, as the main European ports for passenger transport, with 11.7 and 10.9 million passengers transported each year, respectively. An achievement that while on the one hand is a richness and a surprise considering the size of the cities and their inhabitants, on the other hand also opens up an issue and a sore point to be addressed, that of the environment.

It is clear that it is becoming fundamental that the normal process of logistical and economic development of the city, and the inevitable use of the sea as a means of communication and transport, is increasingly accompanied by the need not only to protect the environment of the port areas and those connected to them, but also to minimise the environmental impact of the port infrastructures themselves on the surrounding territory (Fig. 7).

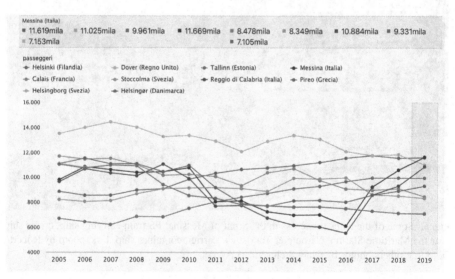

Fig. 7. The main ports in Europe by number of passengers transported each year (2005–2019). Source *Openpolis* processing of *Ispra* data (updated 2 March 2022) [17]

Italy, moreover, is first in Europe for emissions at berth, according to Transport Environment data. [21] (Fig. 8).

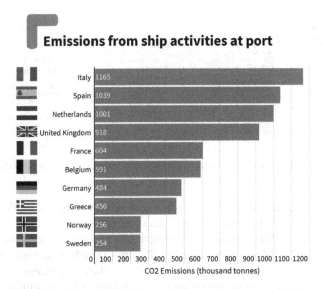

Emissions from ship activities at port

Country	CO2 Emissions (thousand tonnes)
Italy	1165
Spain	1039
Netherlands	1001
United Kingdom	918
France	604
Belgium	591
Germany	484
Greece	456
Norway	256
Sweden	254

0 100 200 300 400 500 600 700 800 900 1000 1100 1200
CO2 Emissions (thousand tonnes)

Note: Ship emissions at port, referred to as 'at-berth' emissions, are those that come from port activities like loading, unloading and refuelling. An alternative to running the ship engine using traditional fuels would be to plug in to shore-side electrification infrastructure at port. Data from 2018.

Fig. 8. Emissions from ship activities at port by Member State. Source *TransportEnvironment.*

4   Green Transition and More

The Messina port, considered, due to its natural strategic position, one of the safest natural harbours in the Mediterranean, if not subject to intervention, risks also becoming one of the most polluted.

One can therefore understand how important it is to intervene urgently and carefully on the area surrounding the port area, but also the strategic role that urban, architectural and technological planning and regeneration of these areas can play. The potential benefits and possible interrelations and uses for the community are enormous. Without forgetting that here, as in other seaside cities, a wide variety of entities and interests are involved and only with dialogue, understanding between all stakeholders and joint planning is it possible to think of contributing to the success of a waterfront redevelopment project. The public entities involved in the management of the areas are, among others, the aforementioned Port Authority, the Municipality of Messina, the Superintendence for Cultural and Environmental Heritage, the Civil Engineers, the Port Authority; and, again, the State Property Agency and the Navy. Interacting with decisions on the area are the companies of the *Ferrovie dello Stato* group, the local Chamber of Commerce (Fig. 9).

GOVERNMENT

National Government			
Regional Government			
Local Government	PUBLIC		
Port Authorities			
Park Authorities	Existing Residents	PRIVATE	
Planners	New Residents		
Development Review	Conservationists	Shop Owners	SERVICES &
Panels	General Public	Investors	OPERATIONS
	Recreational Associations	Land Owners	
	Nature Associations	Developers	Waterway Operators
	Yachting Associations	Surrounding Land	Marina Operators
	Educational Institutions	Owners	Waterfront Planners
		Farmers	Waterfront Designers
		Heavy Industry	Waterfront Engineers
			Architects
			Landscape Architects
			Suppliers
			Construction

Fig. 9. Stakeholders in waterfront development. Source *Waterfronts NL* [23]

In this complex framework of relations between different subjects, the Port Authority of the Strait has a number of interventions underway, as also shown in the AdSP Straits Sustainability Report. With regard to pollution, thanks to an intervention financed under the National Plan Complementary to the PNRR, it has launched the tender for the final and executive design and implementation of works for the electrification of port quays. The interventions aim at a new green transformation foresee the electrification of all the quays of the historical port, from which cruise ships will also be powered, with a total power of about 22 MVA; they already foresee the possibility of a further increase. The characteristics of the port of Messina located within the city and the particular type of traffic present also make the implementation of an On-Shore Power Supply system to electrically power the docked ships highly advisable. This will allow the engines to be switched off and the consequent significant reduction of emissions and air pollutants, including particulates and nitrogen oxides, in the port areas [1].

While electrification is important, it can certainly contribute, but on its own it is not enough to address the port climate problem. Indeed, the enormous energy requirements of individual vessels make electrification of ships for movement at sea unlikely, and so there is a clear need to track down the possible clean liquid fuels of the future.

The only fuels to be proposed as sustainable and scalable for the maritime sector do not seem to be fossil liquid natural gas (LNG) and biofuels, even though they are erroneously proposed as sustainable options, but rather those produced from renewable energy and, where appropriate, direct air capture. This refers to so-called hydrogen-based 'e-fuels', such as e-ammonia, e-methanol or hydrogen itself. Unfortunately, however, the current proposals require the former and not the latter. At the moment, therefore, ports do not invest in clean fuel infrastructure until they are sure that ship owners will demand it, and ship owners refrain from investing in zero-emission ships until there is a clear supply infrastructure for clean fuels.

The climate package with proposals for '*Fit for 55*' transport, adopted by the European Commission on 14 July 2022, which contains legislative proposals to achieve the *Green Deal* targets by 2030, is undoubtedly the most important legislative package in history for shipping. The goal is to reduce greenhouse gas emissions by 55 per cent compared to 1990 levels and with the prospect of achieving 'carbon neutrality' by 2050, the package represents an important opportunity to equip European shipping with an environmentally friendly refuelling and charging infrastructure that will finally address its climate impact [12].

Port authorities and representatives of the European Parliament and the EU Council must support ambitious targets for clean port infrastructure to ensure the green transition of maritime transport.

The Green Transition can also be achieved in other ways and, above all, by reducing the causes to limit the consequences and, in the case of Messina, a big step forward can also be taken by intervening in infrastructure, logistics, and alternative connections, such as the Strait of Messina Bridge, which would greatly reduce polluting emissions due to the routes of ships laden with vehicles between the two shores (Fig. 10).

Fig. 10. Bridge over the Strait of Messina. Project. Source *Webuild S.p.A. – Webuild Group* [24]

The bridge project, moreover, plans to compensate, with large green spaces and parks, the areas on which it rises and those closest to them. And the city of Messina is in great need of green spaces. In fact, according to a study published by *Openpolis*, while Trieste is the metropolitan city capital with the greatest availability of urban green space (62.4 square metres per inhabitant), followed by Venice (43.6 square metres/inhabitant) and Reggio di Calabria (37 square metres/inhabitant), unfortunately Messina is in last place, together with Bari, with extensions of less than 10 square metres/inhabitant [16].

What if the Bridge over the Strait of Messina finally exists and comes true? According to a study conducted by engineers Giovanni Mollica and Nino Musca, of the 'Civic Network for Infrastructure in Southern Italy', the reduction in pollution levels would be drastic: carbon dioxide or carbon dioxide emissions would fall by 94%, carbon monoxide emissions by 73%, nitrogen oxides and sulphur oxides would be cut by almost 100%) and particulate matter would fall by over 80%, in addition to the predictable reduction of THC, total hydrocarbons, by almost 80% [11].

Green transition is also achieved by intervening, with appropriate redesign and careful architectural reconfiguration, in the public spaces and buildings along the maritime edge of the port in a greener and more conscious manner. It means intervening to give back a face, but also a character to the finally regenerated edge, recovering its characteristics, with a targeted and responsible project.

There are some ways, from a design point of view, to encourage this transition and the sustainability of places, starting above all by giving them meaning:

– spaces and architecture in the harbour should be places to accommodate as many useful activities for all as possible;
– there is a need to give awareness and trust to physical places also in the sense of sustainability;
– a search for a balanced relationship between each piece of architecture and the surrounding landscape is necessary;
– there is also a need to rediscover a poetic dimension of design, something that appears as that added value capable of making architecture truly more sustainable.

It is no coincidence that, over time, the major architects and town planners who have worked on the Strait area have not resisted including the port as a founding project of urban redevelopment. Suffice it to think of the new vision of the cities of the Strait with the sea and the port of Messina at the centre, drawn up for the International Ideas Competition for a stable road-rail link between Sicily and the continent, by Giuseppe and Alberto Samonà with the *Gruppo urbanisti architetti siciliani* in 1969, which can probably be considered the paradigm of urban plans for the Strait Area.

The project even envisages a doubling of the historic port with the *Biporto*, a strategic element that coincides with the new land and sea route welded by the road and rail bridge. As Prof. Franco Cardullo well emphasises, these are "visions or ideas such as those of the 'Biport', or the 'City-region' or the 'Future Metropolis of the Strait', all developed in continuity and homogeneity, which relate economic planning, with urban, territorial and landscape design, but always with an architectural capacity, to think physically about forms that reinterpret and enhance the physical environment, projecting it into a future: a future that has been denied" [6] (Fig. 11).

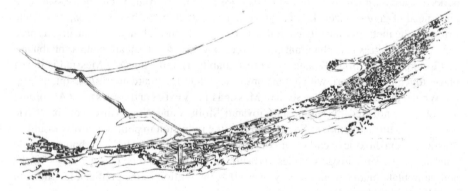

Fig. 11. Competition for the PRG of Messina, motto 'Biporto', 1960, with the *Gruppo urbanisti architetti siciliani*: Antonio Buonafede, Roberto Calandra, Napoleone Cutrufelli, Giuseppe De Cola and Alberto Samonà [7]

5 The Historic Port, the Back Harbour, the *Real Cittadella*, the Areas of the Disused Markets and the Reuse of Existing Architecture

The recovery and regeneration of the historic port and its surrounding areas therefore becomes an urgent measure for a city of the sea such as Messina; and the above-mentioned multifaceted character of the port itself, 'the ports in the port' allows us to state that the model of recovery of Messina's historic port can represent a model for other historic ports in the city centre. With the necessary adaptations deriving from the diversity of geographical dimensions and the presence of all or, more likely, some of the destinations of the port of Messina, other cities and other ports may find indications for development.

The imminent redevelopment projects of the former market areas near the port with the creation of an innovation hub, the *I-Hub dello Stretto*, the reuse of the Customs House areas, once the Royal Palace, for a new cruise terminal together with the recovery of the *Real Cittadella* in the hinterland are some of the pieces of a mosaic to be put together in terms of architectural design and to be added to the green transition of the more specifically port infrastructure. The challenge is not the feasibility of the works but the capacity for dialogue and cooperation between the aforementioned interested bodies that have decision-making power over the future of the areas [14]. The study of the bureaucratic interactions between the various public, local, national and European bodies in order to reduce decision-making deadlocks to zero has the same importance as the complexity of choosing the 'scale' of architecture to be built or demolished or reused and the sources of funding to be found.

Three are, symbolically, the concentric circles on the historic port: the green transition of the port infrastructure, the reuse of architectures of historical importance and new construction of disused areas in the city centre close to and bordering the historic port, the rediscovery and reclamation to make it a living part of the city of the *Real Cittadella* located on the Sickle itself. The first two circles are already 'designed' and underway, the third is still at the planning stage and, perhaps, as will soon be said, it is precisely from the historic port that the favourable wave to restore lustre to the 1600s jewel can start.

The area of the Technological Innovation Pole will be comprised of the buildings between the two Stations, the Central and Maritime, and the Customs House area already occupied by the Royal Palace. It is planned to demolish the buildings that housed the *Magazzini Generali*, the old *Silos Granai* and the Fish Market building to allow, using the same site and footprint but with a different volume, the construction of the Innovation Hub of the Strait.

The Technology and Innovation Hub is expected to attract investment from international companies and, at the same time, will serve to redevelop the real estate of one of the most valuable portions of the city's territory.

The bet is that the SEZ area - *Special Economic Zone* - where the I-Hub will be located will be able to attract multinationals in the high value-added technology sector that will be able to set up in their factories with the constraint of hiring human resources and incubating the most promising start-ups. And the integration and interaction with the port and its role as a connector should enhance the results.

In this context of architectural and urban renaissance, on the side of the redesigning of this part of the city port, between the sea and the city centre, there remains the unknown aspect of the project for a modern cruise terminal on one of the cruise ship docks, between the *Palazzata* and the sea. The contract has been halted and, to date, it is unclear what will happen in the future. A reflection on sea-land, *Palazzata*-Port, full-empty interactions should, in the writer's opinion, lead to the project being abandoned. Messina and its port do not need to add but to subtract cement or, at the very least, to conserve and enhance what exists.

Fig. 12. Outline drawn up on behalf of the Order of Architects of Messina for the Waterfront Boccetta public debate requested by the Port Authority of the Strait of Messina [13]

And in this perspective, the new starting point should be represented by the functional recovery of Angelo Mazzoni's Maritime Station, seen as a hinge capable of connecting the Messina of the *Real Cittadella* and the Sickle, to the Messina of the new *Palazzata*, the Exhibition Citadel, the *MuMe* Museum and the beach leading to Capo Peloro. A hub to be placed, in addition and not as an alternative to the above-mentioned spaces of the Customs House, which can also be used by cruise tourism. A point of convergence of immediately usable attractions and new activities to be launched in the medium-short term, also in view of the redevelopment, already underway, at last even if still only partially, of the southern area's seafront. A new cruise terminal in the Maritime Station, to which other activities are also aggregated, could become, in this way, a central and driving element, due to its position but also to its being a reconversion, a harmonious use, of a pre-existing building. The piers of the maritime station themselves, arranged almost like an open hand towards the sea, seem to constitute an interesting invitation to enter the island, even if not the only possibility of docking and arriving from the sea in a city with a sea front of some 20 kms (Fig. 12).

The symbolic value of such an intervention is evident. In terms of location and conformation, the spaces and areas of the refunctioned Maritime Station in the heart of the port would allow those arriving from the sea to immediately see and get to know the city itself: the remains of the historic city, right behind, in the Spanish Royal Citadel, up to embrace its splendid seafront, the historical and vital core of Messina's *Palazzata* turning their gaze. One would welcome cruise passengers to the city by making them pass through significant architecture. It would act in line with a building policy that tends to prevent an increase in cubic capacity on the territory and favours the reuse of the existing.

With a ripple effect, it was written, the new function of the Maritime Station could accelerate the rebirth of the *Real Cittadella*, located inside the sickle between the two portions of sea separated by it. This is a fortress, the ruins of which remain, built as an imposing military construction with a star-shaped plan and five bastions, between the late 17th and early 18th century by the Spanish, with the dual task of defending and controlling the Strait and the hills above it, and which could also become a defensive stronghold. It is a fine example of military architecture now owned by the Sicilian Region, as a property bound by the Superintendence and falling under the Maritime State Property managed by the Straits Port Authority, which deserves the redevelopment and restoration work that has fortunately just begun.

The interaction between historic port - city centre - disused industrial areas (such is what the sickle has become over time) is clearly underway. The pieces of the mosaic if they find their place with the completion of the work will give Messina, its ports in the harbour in step with the environmental challenges, in dialogue with the economic activities of the city that has among its main streets the road parallel to the docks and capable of stimulating the historical and architectural recovery of the sickle. The port returns to being the vital centre of the city capable of reuniting and revitalising, through the sea, the land on which Messina stands by integrating the sickle into the *Palazzata* (Fig. 13).

Messina is splendid but, too often resigned, lacks courage and ambition. Will it be good enough this time to savour the new changes that come with its being a city by the sea, Bridge over the Strait of Messina included? Will it be able to bet on its new image revolutionised starting from the very heart of the city, making peace with its port and reaffirming its sea front?

Italo Calvino wrote in 'The Invisible Cities' about one of his cities, Zenobia, which is all cities, "*It is useless to establish whether... it should be classified among the happy cities or among the unhappy ones. It is not into these two species that it makes sense to divide the city, but into two others: those that continue through the years and mutations to give their shape to desires and those in which desires succeed in erasing cities or are erased from them*".

Fig. 13. Outline drawn up on behalf of the Order of Architects of Messina for the Waterfront Boccetta public debate requested by the Port Authority of the Strait of Messina [13]

References

1. AUTORITÀ DI SISTEMA PORTUALE DELLO STRETTO. https://adspstretto.it. Accessed 21 Apr 2023
2. Balletto, G., Borruso, G., Campisi, T.: Not only waterfront. the Port-City relations between peripheries and inner harbors. In: Computational Science and Its Applications–ICCSA 2022 Workshops: Malaga, Spain, July 4–7, 2022, Proceedings, Part V, pp. 196–208. Springer International Publishing, Cham, July (2022)
3. Bruni, F., D'Agostino, A., Santangelo, M.R., La,: Trasformazione delle aree portuali, 9° Seminario Internazionale di Progettazione, 1997–98. Edizioni Scientifiche Italiane, Napoli (2002)
4. Bruttomesso, R.: Waterfront, una nuova frontiera urbana. Trenta progetti di riorganizzazione e riuso di aree urbane sul fronte d'acqua, Centro Internazionale città d'acqua, Venezia (1993)
5. Caldeira dos Santos, M.C., Pereira, F.H.: Development and application of a dynamic model for road port access and its impacts on port-city relationship indicators. In: Journal of Transport Geography, n. 96, 103189, October (2021)
6. Cardullo, F.: Architettura e Città. Scritti su Messina. Officina Edizioni, Roma (2010)
7. Cardullo, F.: Giuseppe e Alberto Samonà e la Metropoli dello Stretto di Messina. Officina Edizioni, Roma (2006)
8. Errigo, M.F., Arcuri, F.: Underwater: the relationship city-water in Zuid Holland. sea and the city. In: TRIA, Territorio della Ricerca su Insediamenti e Ambiente, n. 11, pp. 185–199, February (2013)
9. Gasparrini, C.: Porto, spazio pubblico e città metropolitana. In: PORTUS: The on-line magazine of RETE, n, 28, Year XIV October 2014, RETE Publisher, Venice (2014). https://portusonline.org/porto-spazio-pubblico-e-citta-metropolitana-2/
10. ISPRA_Istituto Superiore per la Protezione e la Ricerca Ambientale. https://www.isprambiente.gov.it/it. Accessed 10 Apr 2023
11. Mollica, G., Musca, A.: Stretto di Messina e rispetto della transizione ecologica. Lussografica, Caltanissetta (2021)

12. Morgia, E.: Fit for 55: quali rotte di transizione per lo shipping?. In: Rivista Energia, 7 marzo (2022). https://www.rivistaenergia.it/2022/03/fit-for-55-quali-rotte-di-transizione-per-lo-shipping/
13. Nota sul fronte a mare dell'Ordine degli Architetti P.P. e C. di Messina. Quaderno degli Attori. In: Confronto pubblico Waterfront Boccetta –Annunziata, 24 febbraio (2022). https://www.cpwaterfrontmessina.it/wp-content/uploads/33-ordine-architetti.pdf
14. Nota sul fronte a mare di Rete Civica per le Infrastrutture nel Mezzogiorno. Quaderno degli Attori. In: Confronto pubblico Waterfront Boccetta –Annunziata (2022). https://www.cpwaterfrontmessina.it/wp-content/uploads/47-Rete-Civica-per-le-Infrastrutture-nel-Mezzogiorno.pdf
15. Notteboom, T., Rodrigue, J.P., Pallis, A.: Port-city relationships. In: PORT ECONOMICS, Management and Policy. A comprehensive analysis of the port industry (2023). https://porteconomicsmanagement.org/pemp/contents/part7/port-city-relationships/
16. OPENPOLIS, La disponibilità di verde pubblico nelle città italiane. In: Ecologia e Innovazione, venerdì 21 aprile (2023). https://www.openpolis.it/la-disponibilita-di-verde-pubblico-nelle-citta-italiane/. Accessed 21 Apr 2023
17. OPENPOLIS, La sfida della sostenibilità dei porti. In: Ecologia e Innovazione, venerdì 4 marzo (2022). https://www.openpolis.it/la-sfida-della-sostenibilita-dei-porti/. Accessed 21 Apr 2023
18. Panzarella, M.: Movin' to the future, Globalizzazione e infrastrutture. Visioni da sud, Collana Progetto & Società, Edizioni Arianna, Geraci Siculo, Palermo (2022)
19. Pavia, R., Di Venosa, M.: Waterfront. Dal conflitto all'integrazione. From conflict to integration. In: LISt Lab Laboratorio Internazionale Editoriale, Trento (2012)
20. Riccobono, F.: Il Porto di Messina. Dagli argonauti ai crocieristi, quattromila anni di storia. Skriba, Messina (2006)
21. TRANSPORTENVIRONMENT, "EU Ports' Climate Performance. An analysis of maritime supply chain and at berth emissions" (2022). https://www.transportenvironment.org/wp-content/uploads/2022/02/2202_Port_Rankings_briefing-1.pdf
22. UNCTAD, United Nations Conference on Trade and Development: Port Marketing and the challenge of the Third Generation Port. Trade and Development Board, Committee on Shipping ad hoc Inter-government Group of Port Experts. Geneva, Switzerland (1994)
23. WATERFRONTSNL. https://www.waterfrontsnl.com/about-waterfronts-nl/what-is-waterfront-development. Accessed 21 Apr 2023
24. WEBUILD GROUP. https://www.webuildgroup.com. Accessed 21 Apr 2023

The Stable Strait Crossing System. What Developments and Opportunities?

Celestina Fazia[✉] ⓘ, Tiziana Campisi[✉] ⓘ, and Federica Sortino ⓘ

Faculty of Engineering and Architecture, University of Enna Kore, 94100 Cittadella
Universitaria, Enna, Italy
{celestina.fazia,tiziana.campisi}@unikore.it,
federica.sortino@unikorestudent.it

Abstract. The Strait of Messina area is affected by one of the greatest works of the third millennium: the bridge and related infrastructure that will connect the two sides, Sicilian and Calabrian. Territories will have to be reorganized with respect to the artificial welding, the stable crossing. Territorial continuity will unite two metropolitan cities that will no longer be physically separated. But how will activities be organized along the coast, settlements, ports, relations, and what initiatives will be undertaken to enhance and publicize the cultural and environmental heritage, to revitalize the two territories? Coastal facades will have to be an active part of urban regeneration and development processes, also looking at defense against hydrogeological risk and the long-term effects of climate change.

This is an opportunity to be seized. The essay proposes an interpretation of the environmental, economic and social challenges that the "Bridge on the Strait" project will raise; the Integrated Plan for the Strait Area drafted in 2019 will be illustrated with a far-sighted vision, with and without a stable crossing several.

Keywords: Accessibility · Infrastructure · Strait of Messina

1 Introduction

The bridge over the Strait of Messina is a project for the construction of a road infrastructure between the cities of Messina and Villa San Giovanni, connecting the region of Sicily to Calabria and the European continent, in response to the need for the realization of a stable road and railway connection of the Strait of Messina.

Its realization and all the problems associated with it have been talked about for some time now, but if we tried to reverse the point of view, we would also realize how the current needs are not solely related to the lack of a physical college, but rather to the actual readiness of the host cities.

Real connection would become the outline and consequence of a reorganization of a refocusing of sites of interest.

O. Gervasi et al. (Eds.): ICCSA 2023 Workshops, LNCS 14109, pp. 240–258, 2023.
https://doi.org/10.1007/978-3-031-37120-2_16

It is necessary to start from a reinterpretation of the territory in order to equip it principally with the necessary responses to today's needs and initiate a profound redevelopment of the areas concerned. This process could trigger a medium- and long-range change that could lead to great goals for the island and the peninsula.

A new perspective must be sought, looking at the coastal strip from the sea and laying the groundwork for the change we are heading for. The essay aims to illustrate the necessities of the place, investigate the proposed strategies of the Master Plan drafted for the Straits area, and help the re-launch of the area by placing it at the center of a new social and economic dimension [1] (Fig. 1).

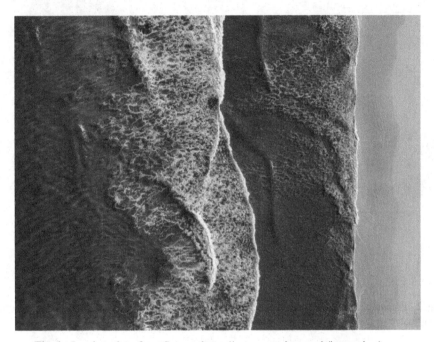

Fig. 1. Land-sea interface. Source: https://www.gettyimages.it/immagine/mare

2 The Master Plan for the Straits Area

The Strait of Messina has always been considered an evocative place rich in history and folklore, just think of the dense web of myths and history that has been woven for years about that portion of the sea that laps two lands not quite distant, but not quite close either.

Their history for years has been bound together by common issues such as the interminable diatribe over the construction of the Straits Bridge, but even more so they are bound together by their incontrovertible nature. They are places of exchange, of connection, strips of land born and developed around their facing the sea, a characteristic that makes them unique and indispensable for the island as for the peninsula [2] (Fig. 2).

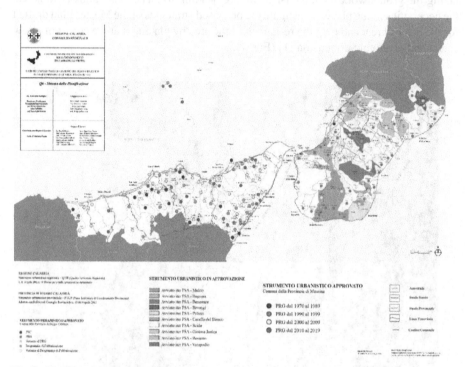

Fig. 2. Planning System Source: Masterplan and graphics drawn up by the group of 13 experts coordinated by Celestina Fazia.

In Greek evocations already their importance and power can be perceived. Scylla, an incredibly beautiful nymph, is transformed by the sorceress Circe into a sea monster, and together with Charybdis, a frightening creature born of ZES, they guard the strait, making that strip of sea difficult to navigate.

Their strategic location has always made these waters and these two cities not only attractive, but above all crucial for cultural, economic and political exchanges.

When talking about the straits, one cannot limit oneself to talking about the settled and settled territory, but a much broader look is necessary. One must talk about their needs as a land-sea interface, a definition inherent in their nature as port and maritime cities. It is this duality that makes the planning process very delicate and complicated.

The Straits area cannot be enclosed only to the mere commercial sphere, but it is also true that it represents a main axis of interchange, a great opportunity to re-evaluate the main and secondary strategic nodes. One of the tools to achieve this ultimate goal is certainly the recently drafted Strategic Plan for the Promotion of the Straits Area, which is preparatory to the Master Plan [1].

The latter by setting as its primary objective the re-functionalization of the areas concerned aims at the better usability of the area, taking into consideration all the actors involved and highlighting the potential of some projects already started, giving space and emphasis to the development of other projects of common interest, creating the right scenarios for the redevelopment of the Strait [2] (Fig. 3).

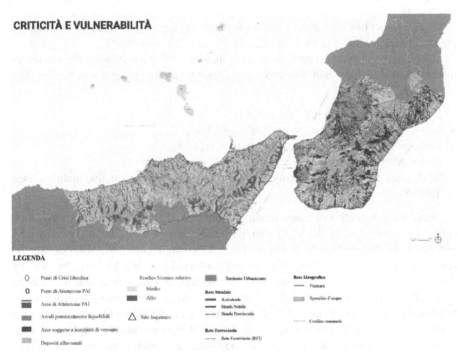

Fig. 3. Strait area criticality and vulenrability. Source: Masterplan and graphics drawn up by the group of 13 experts coordinated by Celestina Fazia.

The Preliminary document for the drafting of the Strategic Plan consists of a reconnaissance analysis document and is accompanied by a variety of graphic works, including a final synthesis document suitable for the definition and overall vision of the project scenarios, gathering and systematizing the outcomes of the analysis work.

In the strategic definition, spatial realities were identified through a macro-zoning that aims to connect the local and wide area systems. Starting from the study of the land-sea interface as locations of flows, interactions, exchanges and opportunities.

The document aims to highlight the hitherto unexpressed possibility of activating territorial coalitions through participation and involvement finally giving the possibility of achieving a metropolitan macro-region gravitating around the identified focal points.

This objective appears to be achievable only by insisting on the right method of planning by placing at the center of the study some salient points such as the accessibility and usability of the Strait area with a multi-level interpretation that interests not only the infrastructural aspect, but also the accessibility of areas with a high tourist vocation, the enhancement of the historical and environmental heritage, of which the area is steeped, and the enhancement of the landscape itself. All this is, of course, aimed at a new promotion of the sites concerned, which will eventually be able to lead to the real interest of economic and innovative development by commanding such important factors as employment growth, the relationship between public administration and business, and much more [3].

The goals set have the ambitious role of triggering the real process of upgrading the physical, infrastructural, environmental, functional and social straits.

Through the analysis process, the five key themes on which to develop the redevelopment process were identified, which compose in summary the strategic actions identified in the plan:

- Infrastructure and mobility (see Table 1).
- Services and metropolitan endowments (see Table 2).
- Environment energy and sustainability (see Table 3).
- Cultural heritage, protected areas and Landscape (see Table 4).
- Settlement systems, socio-demographic dynamics and productive realities (see Table 5).

From the perspective of a new reading of the area, the aspect of port infrastructure cannot be overlooked. In the Strait area, port nodes have very different characteristics and flows. The Strait Port Authority includes Messina, Tremestieri, Milazzo, Reggio Calabria and Villa S. Giovanni. An area daily affected not only by trade, but also by flows of citizens, which also count many commuters. It seems clear that it would be necessary to reinvest in these infrastructures by making the territory's physical and technological connections more efficient. Prepare the infrastructure to accommodate the real flow from which they are interesting and divide it in a more unified way by investing, for example, in other connections such as the Gioia Tauro port.

It seems clear how we need to reinvest in an area with all the qualities needed to live up to today's expectations. Focusing on a medium- and long-range strategy aiming at strengthening the territorial identity, taking advantage of the realization of high-quality works capable of focusing attention on this area of intervention [4].

The strait that has always oscillated between myth and culture, landscape and environmental quality, a place of union and social exchange, can be revitalized in the global scenario and cope with the changes that are affecting the region. A stable physical crossing would certainly underscore the need for a new adjustment to a flow that had hitherto remained only by sea, but the absence of a road infrastructure cannot slow down a reinterpretation of the territory that has already been triggered and is clamoring for its blossoming [5].

Scylla and Charybdis, protective and silent monsters, no longer frighten, but rather must now be the new cradle of the strategic change of which the Strait area is not only deserving, but a necessary spokesman (Fig. 4).

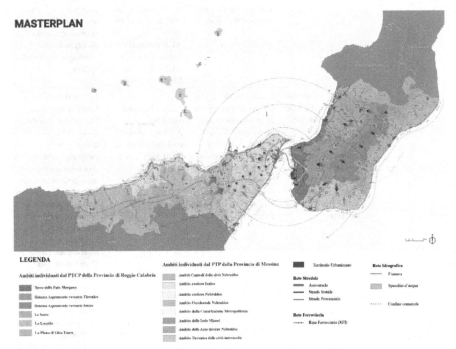

Fig. 4. Master Plan for the Straits area. Source: Masterplan and graphics drawn up by the group of 13 experts coordinated by Celestina Fazia.

Table 1. Summary of the strategies underlying the preliminary document for the Strategic Plan (sector A = Infrastructure and mobility). Source: Masterplan and graphics drawn up by the group of 13 experts coordinated by Celestina Fazia.

Affected sector	General objectives	Specific goals	Strategies	
A Infrastructure and mobility			*N. Identifier*	*Title Action*
	Inner-city cohesion	Improve connections between inland areas and smaller towns, both by upgrading current facilities and reorganizing the public transportation system	A1 A1.1 = aspromonte system/ Ionian slope A1.2 = aspromonte system narrow slope A1.3 = aspromonte system Tyrrhenian slope A1.4 = Nebrodi Milazzo system A1.5 = Nebrodi Messina system	Smart road system_ Improving accessibility by encouraging the use of energy-saving means energy to produce energy from renewable sources (self-producing stations and docks energy/solar) by creating a smart road system
	Countering the spatial and social segregation of urban centers and the territory of the 2 metropolitan cities Facilitate the process of conurbation between the cities of Reggio Calabria and Messina and territorial continuity	Countering the spatial and social segregation of urban centers and the territory of the 2 metropolitan cities Facilitate the process of conurbation between the cities of Reggio Calabria and Messina and territorial continuity	A2 A2.1 = Messina Strait area A2.2 = territorial continuity Messina Strait Area	Intermodality and Crossing the Strait. Intermodality in the Strait and local public transport in the integrated metropolitan area must support the metropolitan strategic plan of the 2 cities in a broader relational and infrastructural logic that integrates urban functions and regeneration processes. Conurbation and Territorial Continuity_ Implementation of the Project Agreement between Reggio Calabria and Messina for Territorial Continuity in the Strait Area, dated 29.5. 2017
	Recovery of disused Infrastructure	Promote sustainable and inclusive mobility, enhancing multi-modality (parking lots intermodal, bicycle lanes, etc.)	A3 A3.1 = disused railway road infrastructure with roadside houses and stations	Slow-road net Recovery of disused infrastructure (rail and road) and creation of a walking and cycling city: New urban connectivity imposing new modes of travel, crossing and emotional enjoyment

(*continued*)

Table 1. (*continued*)

Affected sector	General objectives	Specific goals	Strategies	
			A3.2 = depowered infrastructure, in areas at risk, old disused routes	Life-risk lines_ The system of infrastructures that can perform lifeline functions in the ME and RC metropolitan areas. Management of the infrastructure assets under emergency conditions will take place through the development of new technologies for risk mitigation
		16 Port Authority Organization The creation of the Single System Authority is an answer to the problem of mobility in the Straits Area	A4 A4.1 = Governance and operation 16th Port Authority	16 Port Authority Organization and operation for flow management and crossing in the Straits area

Table 2. Summary of the strategies underlying the preliminary document for the Strategic Plan (sector B = Metropolitan services and endowments). Source: Masterplan and graphics drawn up by the group of 13 experts coordinated by Celestina Fazia.

Affected sector	General objectives	Specific goals	Strategies	
B Metropolitan services and endowments			*N. Identifier*	*Title Action*
	Improve the accessibility conditions of cities and logistics	Reorganize the provision of integrated city and metropolitan level services	B1 Pass and integrated infrastructure	Passenger Modal integration with integrated mobility solutions mainly through the LPT rail and road sector: - Integrated pass, - Integrated logistics, - Integrated infrastructure: effectiveness in programming, planning and management;

(*continued*)

Table 2. (*continued*)

Affected sector	General objectives	Specific goals	Strategies	
	Countering weak urban structure, depopulation of inland areas, abandonment and degradation of historic villages and social isolation	Modernization of urban and intangible services for residents and city users	B2 The new geography of flows B2.1 The new geography of material flows B2.2 The new geography of intangible flows	The new geography of material/immaterial flows Roads, the locations of flows, are also understood as new geographies for the territorial regeneration of inland areas and for integrated mobility, for a new housing welfare-the right for all to accessibility
	Countering the de-qualification of public spaces, the lack of identity of built-up parts, and physical degradation		B3_Liveable and inclusive public space. Necessary to combine economic growth and social cohesion of an area	"Liveable and inclusive public space". De-fragmentation of the public space system (enhancement, reorganization, and reconfiguration of public spaces with the timing of accessibility and connections with transportation)-revitalization project of urban voids with "zero volume" in suburban and peripheral areas, with greening or creation of "porous areas."
	Creating metropolitan-level urban polarities by intercepting flows	Services to support development and growth. Social services to citizens. Simple and efficient interaction with the P.A. for service delivery and in general for administration/citizen and inter-administration dialogue	B4 The metropolitan endowment system_ Sites of strategic interest ICI	The metropolitan endowment system_Sites of wide area interest (Business park, Attractive Poles, etc.). Reggio and Messina must rediscover a "strategic repositioning" of the city, both outward (Integrated Strait and Mediterranean Area) and toward the provincial and regional hinterland

Table 3. Summary of the strategies underlying the preliminary document for the Strategic Plan (sector C = Environment energy and sustainability). Source: Masterplan and graphics drawn up by the group of 13 experts coordinated by Celestina Fazia.

Affected sector	General objectives	Specific goals	Strategies	
			N. Identifier	***Title Action***
C Environment energy and sustainability	Incentivize climate adaptation measures (including green infrastructure-based solutions)	Improving the organization of the city to reduce consumption and pollution and the management of urban dynamics Protect and enhance environmental, natural and scenic resources, intergenerational of the right to environmental quality…	C1 Resilient city	**Resilient city** Promote individual and collective well-being through the development of environmental sustainability policies and strategies, seeking to ument the resilience of one's area against critical circumstances and changes that play negative effects in relation to the land and environment
	Reduce fragile conditions and exposure to both natural and anthropogenic hazards	Physical, technological and environmental adaptation of new urban contexts, starting precisely from the network of flows and intercepted public spaces, assuming the systemization of criteria for evaluation and control	C2 Healing and design	Healing and urban design Ensuring quality of urban form with a view to improving the perception of safety; a continuous urban mesh, an accessible and hierarchical road system with respect to public spaces improve users' orientation, their perception of safety, facilitate escape routes, vehicle access, and vehicular transit, and reduce consumption, transportation costs, and pollutant emissions
	Making cities smart and resilient	Urban security and new welfare	C3 Secur plan	Secur plan Technological systems designed to protect access, integrate security systems, ensure the soundness of structures. Advanced systems to reduce energy consumption, incentivize slow mobility (bicycles) and energy-saving means of transportation, produce energy from renewable sources (self-generating/solar energy stations and docks). Urban security in new welfare and services, monitored indoor/outdoor connections with remote surveillance system

Table 4. Summary of the strategies underlying the preliminary document for the Strategic Plan (sector D = Cultural Heritage, Protected Areas and Landscape). Source: Masterplan and graphics drawn up by the group of 13 experts coordinated by Celestina Fazia.

Affected sector	General objectives	Specific goals	Strategies	
D Cultural Heritage, Protected Areas and Landscape			*N. Identifier*	*Title Action*
	Conservation and Enhancement of landscape and historical-cultural values		D1 Plot/network/grid	Plot/network/grid Strengthen the texture of historical fabrics and cultural heritage, River ecological and landscape infrastructure network, grid of connections
	Enhancement of landscape areas and tourist attraction Promotion and communication, Tourist information, networking of accommodation offerings	Redefining the governance of marketing interventions (place branding) - Coordinated and unified management of interventions, - Support of certain, automatic and constant funding sources	D2 Tourism, Myths, legends and environmental uniqueness	Tourism, Myths, Legends and Environmental Uniqueness_ Protecting the Straits tourist The organization of local tourism promotion and reception should be based on a series of interventions that promote the desired behaviors. The local tourism organization (or DMO) should be promoted: a public-private partnership sufficiently representative of tourism stakeholders. The entities that to date demonstrate this type of constitution are tourism districts
	Enhancement of ethno-anthropological centers (example Vallata grecanica)		D3 Memory and Identity	Memory and Identity pursue the innovation of material culture, the conceptual place where Arts and Crafts meet technology and scientific research history-cultural identity that characterizes urban and rural dimensions to be preserved and enhanced (Messina Strategic Plan)

(*continued*)

Table 4. (*continued*)

Affected sector	General objectives	Specific goals	Strategies	
	Enhance the ecological network and Natura 2000 network, parks and protected areas		D4 The space of naturalness	The space of naturalness Structuring the local ecological network for the reconstitution of the ecological potential of the area. (PTCP RC)
	Enhancing UNESCO identities and heritage		D5 Widespread heritage	Widespread heritage Encouraging cultural start-ups and craft/cultural workshops in smaller towns and inland areas

Table 5. Summary of the strategies underlying the preliminary document for the Strategic Plan (sector E = Cultural Heritage, Protected Areas and Landscape). Source: Masterplan and graphics drawn up by the group of 13 experts coordinated by Celestina Fazia.

Affected sector	General objectives	Specific goals	Strategies	
			N. Identifier	*Title Action*
E Settlement systems, socio-demographic dynamics, and production realities				
	Counter the fragmentation and abandonment of coastal and mountain centers	Promote the creation of a network of coastal cities (coastal facades) on the two sides, Calabria and Sicily strengthen the attractiveness of mountain and foothill centers	E1 The new coastal and hill polarities	The new coastal and hillside polarities Define urban transformation areas (city ports, water fronts), increase the traction of the most attractive hillside centers
	Reduce social marginality and strengthen the social service system in critical urban areas	Implement policies for social inclusion, for the most fragile segments of the population and for areas and neighborhoods that are deprived Incentivize the use of public transportation and to lower the city's motorization rate	E2 Against Unsustainable Sub-urbanization	Against Unsustainable Suburbanization (Beyond Suburbanization) Toward a new local housing policy: actions for Social Housing; redevelopment of suburbs and smaller centers, with the inclusion of interchange parking

(*continued*)

Table 5. (*continued*)

Affected sector	General objectives	Specific goals	Strategies	
	Reduce the housing hardship of the disadvantaged	Recover the existing building and urban heritage by promoting the energy improvement of buildings and earthquake-proofing	E3 Energy adjustment/optimization	Energy adaptation/optimization improving The relationships between energy consumption and the physical and functional organization of settlements, to establish through guidelines what can be favorable positions through design guidelines for possible redesign of spaces and for new interventions. Improving the relationship between smart building and smart city. Awareness and information actions to citizens and businesses, it is planned to activate an Energy Desk (strategic plan of Messina)
	A system for interactive resource management	Employment and skills for the local economy. Massive investment in agriculture, fisheries, tourism, cultural heritage enhancement, innovative industry, sustainability and green-economy	E4 Circular Economy	Circular Economy System for interactive resource/service management linked to geographic information systems, service providers and service users. Development of a different welfare model based on innovative forms of social enterprise Supporting the transition to a low-carbon economy in all sectors. Accompaniment and start-up for the creation of new social enterprises

(*continued*)

Table 5. (*continued*)

Affected sector	General objectives	Specific goals	Strategies	
	Reduce inequalities, define training needs consistent with the local economy in order to ensure full employability of properly trained human resources	Fostering identity and interculturalism in the contemporary city: analyzing expectations in the space of multi-ethnic infrastructure	E5 Dialogue and multiculturalism	Dialogue and multiculturalism Reorganizing, through related tools such as the PdS Service Plan, the differentiated demand for services with respect to the plural city: multifunctional integration of needs for the purpose of urban and social quality; development of innovative processes in citizen-P.A. dialogue
	Restoring balances of urban ecosystems under pressure due to: uncontrolled urban sprawl and soil sealing	Reduce the spread of low-density settlements, which require public services that are more expensive and difficult to secure	E6 Water Cycle and Waste Climate Change Observatory	Water Cycle and Waste Building zero-waste communities (Messina strategic plan) Create the 'Climate Change Observatory: the Mediterranean area is a focus area in terms of climate change

3 Scenarios for the Redevelopment of the Straits

The strategic plan, specifically, elaborates a reactivation and redevelopment of the Strait starting with the two metropolitan cities-Messina and Reggio Calabria.

Identifying the actions and directions to be pursued to achieve the expected results. Below are the key points of the planning:

1. Define the infrastructure system in terms of efficiency and endowments, implement programming capable of territories and local institutions to build the response to the new instances of change in the integrated infrastructure and urban system; solicit the elaboration of ideas to integrate in the network logic the port system and the SEZs in the most neuralgic Italian hub for the Mediterranean [6] (Fig. 5 and 6);

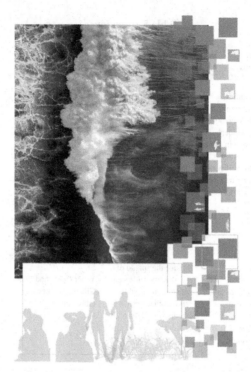

Fig. 5. The Strait of Messina between myth and culture. Source: Image taken from "Land-sea interface and the places of contaminations: the treasures the myths and fears" contribution by Celestina Fazia created for the "Biennale dello stretto" 2022, Graphic processing by Federica Sortino [11].

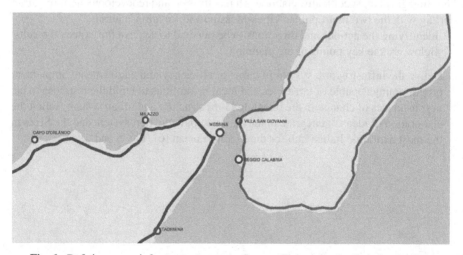

Fig. 6. Defining a new infrastructure system. Source: Elaboration by Federica Sortino.

- define suitable strategies for the reorganization of the supply of metropolitan endowments and services by qualifying and prioritizing them with respect to their strategic relevance, invest in infrastructure in terms of inter-modality, mobility, territorial continuity and safety because the reorganization of networks must be rethought in a system logic in which the Strait Sea is an active part and is not just a "discontinuity element" interposed between the two mainland;
- strengthening and integrating the places of polycentrism, emphasizing the importance of focal nodes: in major urban areas, intermediate urban poles are expected to strengthen their level of connection with the hinterland, "fragile" suburban poles, inland areas and smaller centers, activating a connection between municipalities and cities while also giving rise to a new and denser network of exchanges [7];
- provide a strategic vision of the territories' potential by enhancing the common cultural heritage, landscape and environment. By analyzing the socio-demographic and production reality dynamics, the SP draws new geographies for the territorial regeneration of inland areas including metropolitan areas by promoting the economic and tourism revitalization of the territory, the rediscovery of a landscape heritage and local values for new tourist attractions capable of reconceptualizing, not only locally, but also on a large scale the regional territory.
- laying the groundwork for shared policymaking on some systems of welfare, 'energy' and digital networks, business support, not underestimating citizen and community welfare;
- capturing the specificities and connections of cities, in terms of wide area, in relation to interregional, national and European levels;
- identify new ways to optimize the usability and environmental performance of the territory, in terms of safety, quality of life, accessibility, alternative mobility;
- the Plan incentivizes innovative forms of regeneration for local economic development based on the territory's ability to be a catalyst for new entrepreneurial initiatives linked to cultural and landscape resources; recovery can take place through start-ups of territorial regeneration actions in inland areas, small towns. Provides for the possibility of conveying territorial brands -new centers for territorial economic development, as reward measures for the participation of subjects in the implementation of interventions, for the spread of soft tourism related to the sea and landscape resource, treasures and myths and mirages referable to them [8] (Fig. 7).

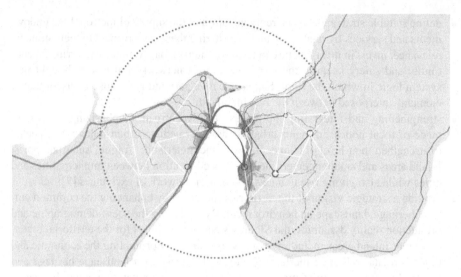

Fig. 7. Defining a new network of connections. Source: Elaboration by Federica Sortino.

4   Conclusions

The Master Plan is closely connected and consistent with the guidelines of the strategic and territorial plans and of the urban planning instruments in force in the municipalities of the two metropolitan cities (Reggio Calabria and Messina). The two urban contexts, which are the result of the still "formal" metropolisation processes, are distinguished by the fragmentation of the settlement systems, with the risk that, by intervening on the pre-existing territorial balances, homogenizing the different cultural landscapes and the different forms of the urban globalized, efforts can be frustrated by encouraging phenomena of environmental impairment and territorial "injustice", with the risk of gaps within the integrated area of the Strait. It is necessary to act on several fronts, perhaps reversing the point of life, starting precisely from the internal areas, marginalized and at risk of a slow recovery.

The Master Plan integrates with the plans for parks and protected areas, the Natura 2000 network and the regional ecological networks. In particular, *the Beach Plans Operational Protocol*[1] *and the Action Plan*, which is a knowledge and guidance tool for the correct management of coastal ambitions affected by Caretta Caretta nestings, identifies

---

[1] The Region of Calabria-Department of National and Community Programming_Cittadella Regionale, Germaneto (CZ)-partner in the Life Caretta Calabria Project, was responsible, among other actions, for the Work Package: the Beach Plans Operational Protocol and Action Plan.

the broad strip of coast of the coast on the Ionian side of Reggio: the Municipalities of Bruzzano Zeffiro, Bianco, Africo, Condofuri, Ferruzzano, Montebello, Melito P.S., S. Lorenzo, Bova Marina [8], according to the timetable of the works, should have received the guidelines of the Action Plan addressed to the sustainable and integrated management of coastal areas.

Compared to numerous ongoing studies, the Master Plan proves to be current and feasible.

Along the same lines is the *LAB Spazio_ Stretto, Permanent Laboratory for the Bridge on the Strait*[2] is conceived as an open construction site and places the territories of the two cities (Reggio Calabria and Messina) [9] in a context of economic and social integration in "progress", defining the identity of the overseas dialogue and the direction of development induced by a possible building, setting up territorial coalitions, new methods of participation with the actors involved on a voluntary basis, favoring the integration of resources for the development of some projects of common interest by reconnecting to some strategic projects that have already started [10].

Contribution Authors

Corresponding authors: although the research is the result of the work carried out jointly by all the authors, which Celestina Fazia is the supervisor, the drafting of the essay is to be attributed differently to each of them:

§ abstract § 1 introduction by Celestina Fazia and Federica Sortino; § 2 by Celestina Fazia 3 by Federica Sortino; § 4 Conclusions by Celestina Fazia and Tiziana Campisi.

Graphics optimization by Federica Sortino.

Essay review: Tiziana Campisi.

References

1. Fazia, C.: Interfaccia Terra-mare e i luoghi delle contaminazioni: i tesori, i miti e le paure, idee dal Piano Strategico dell'Area Integrata dello Stretto, Biennale dello Stretto (2022). https://www.mediterraneiinvisibili.com/la-biennale-dello-stretto/contributors/celestina-fazia/https://www.mediterraneiinvisibili.com/la-biennale-dello-stretto/contributors/celestina-fazia/
2. Moraci, F., Fazia, C.: Nuove orditure territoriali rigenerate per valorizzare il territorio, UI 278 (2018)
3. Moraci, F.: Territorio e infrastrutture resilienti, Relazione in Convegno online Opere pubbliche e territorio: l'importanza dei sistemi di monitoraggio e della loro manutenzione, 25 maggio 2020, CNI, Consiglio Nazionale Ingegneri (2020)
4. Moraci, F.: Il nodo Stretto è questione Nazionale, Gazzetta del Sud 13 marzo (2022)
5. Moraci, F.: Infrastrutture, territorio e futuro. Ripensare al Sud e allo Stretto per abitare il Mediterraneo nella post globalizzazione, In Leotta N. HUB Magna Grecia sulla rotta della Seta, gruppo editoriale Viator (2022)
6. Moraci, F., Errigo, M.F., Bellamacina, D., Fazia, C.: Cities, territories, infrastructures and flows in the Asian and post-pandemic century. the silk road 5.0. In: Ricci, M. (ed.), Medways Open Atlas, LetteraVentidue (2022)

---

[2] LAB Spazio_ Stretto, Unikore Enna 26 April 2023.

7. Moraci, F.: Conclusion: joint governance across the strait, in Piano strategico Studio
8. AAVV, Life Caretta Calabria (2023). https://www.tartarugacaretta.it/it
9. AAVV: La valutazione di soluzioni alternative per il sistema di attraversamento stabile dello Stretto di Messina , Relazione del Gruppo di Lavoro, Struttura Tecnica di Missione per l'indirizzo strategico, lo sviluppo delle infrastrutture e l'alta sorveglianza, Aprile (2021)
10. AAVV: Macro-attività Realizzazione Azione di sistema. Politiche pubbliche e rigenerazione urbana: un quadro ricostruttivo, Formez (2021)
11. Bruttomesso, R.: Città-Porto, in Catalogo per la Mostra Internazionale di Architettura, Marsilio, Venezia (2007)

Scientific Computing Infrastructure (SCI 2023)

Polynomial Neural Layers for Numerical Modeling of Dynamical Processes

Ilya Klimenko(iD), Anna Golovkina(✉)(iD), and Vladimir Ruzhnikov(iD)

Saint Petersburg State University, Saint Petersburg, Russia
a.golovkina@spbu.ru

Abstract. The paper aims to present a description of the tm-flow library for the "flowly" construction and training of polynomial neural networks (PNN) for time-evolving process prediction. The introduced polynomial models have a strong relationship to dynamic systems that can be described by a system of nonlinear differential equations. The paper provides implementation details and an explanation of training strategies, along with a few illustrative numerical examples. The source code is available at https://github.com/PNN-Lab/tmflow/.

Keywords: polynomial neural layers · dynamical processes modeling · neural networks training

1 Introduction

Recently, there has been a lot of focus on sophisticated system modeling methodologies. This is explained by the necessity to address problems related to nonlinear systems and high dimensionality while at the same time providing good accuracy and generalization capabilities. Neural networks take an important place among the different advanced techniques of system modeling. However, most of the existing architecture suffers from poor explainability of the outcomes and extrapolation properties.

Polynomial neural networks (PNNs) are a type of neural network that uses polynomial activation functions to model the non-linear relationships between inputs and outputs. Polynomials are universal approximators that can be used to model all possible feature interactions and provide a rubric for interpretability [4]. PNNs have shown promising results for time-series prediction [2], especially for data with non-linear relationships and complex temporal dependencies. Moreover, polynomial functions have been widely studied by mathematicians and have been shown to have some useful theoretical properties. Polynomial neural networks also link the investigation of generic neural structures to the investigation of polynomial function characteristics [11].

A Group Method of Data Handling (GMDH) is one of the earliest methods for the systematic construction of nonlinear connections with PNN. GMDH was

Supported by Saint Petersburg State University, project ID: 94029367.

developed in the late 1960s by Ivakhnenko [7] to identify nonlinear relations between input and output variables. The GMDH algorithm generates an optimal structure for the model through successive generations of partial descriptions. In comparison to well-known neural networks whose topologies are commonly fixed prior to all detailed (parametric) learning, the GMDH architecture is not fixed in advance but becomes fully optimized (both structurally and parametrically). However, it has drawbacks such as complex polynomials for simple systems and overly complex networks for nonlinear systems.

Another enhancement of PNN can be drawn from [12] where the pi-sigma network is introduced, which is a neural network with a single hidden layer. Improvements include regularization and multiple product units. However, it does not scale well in high-dimensional signals, and its experimental evaluation is conducted only on signals with known ground-truth distributions.

This paper discusses the construction of the architecture and training scheme of a recurrent polynomial neural network for modeling dynamic processes that can be described by stationary or non-stationary systems of ordinary differential equations. This choice is explained by the ability of the Taylor mapping technique to express the solution of an ordinary differential equation (ODE) in the form of a polynomial neural network [5]. According to the deterministic algorithm described in [8], such a PNN can be unambiguously initialized if the ODE corresponding to the modelled process is known. However, even with good initialization, the weight matrices may need to be fine-tuned due to the following factors:

– The ODE can be recovered from the data, but not exactly due to the specifics of the recovery methods;
– ODE can approximately describe the simulated process;
– In real-world conditions, the process can be influenced by various external forces that are not taken into account in the mathematical model, for one reason or another.

During the training, various regularization techniques can be used.

The paper provides the implementation details of different polynomial models and layers as part of the open-sourced library tm-flow available at https://github.com/PNN-Lab/tmflow/.

The rest of the paper is organized as follows: Sect. 2 contains a detailed description of the polynomial layer architecture, differentiating between the basic polynomial implementation and Kroneker's layer. Section 3 introduces different types of polynomial models built based on the described layers. Section 4 shows the main strategies of training and possible enhancements with regularization, masking, and normalization, while Sect. 5 illustrates the proposed architectures in a numerical example that can be found at https://github.com/PNN-Lab/tmflow/tree/main/examples/learn.

2   Architecture of the Polynomial Neural Layer

In this section, we go through the algorithmic specifics and architecture of polynomial layers. Generally, a polynomial layer is defined by three parameters:

1. Dimension of the input vector (`input_dim`)
2. Dimension of the output vector (`output_dim`)
3. Order of nonlinearity (`order`)

The dimension of the input vector usually corresponds to the dimension of the phase vector of a system of ordinary differential equations, but it can also include exogenous variables that can act as control parameters. The dimension of the output vector is determined by the number of measured phase variables, i.e., those for which training data is available (most often, their number coincides with the dimension of the input vector). The order of nonlinearity can be chosen arbitrarily in accordance with the features of the problem being solved and probable information about the dependence's nature.

The polynomial layer belongs to the class of recurrent and transforms the input vector into the output according to the following rule:

$$X\left(t_{i+1}\right) = \text{bias} + \sum_{j=1}^{N} R^j X\left(t_i\right)^{[j]} \tag{1}$$

where $X\left(t_i\right)$ are the values of the input vector measured at time t_i, $X\left(t_{i+1}\right)$ are the predicted values of the output vector at time t_{i+1}, bias is an optional parameter, N is the order of nonlinearity, $[j]$ is the nonlinearity order used to transform the input vector, R^j $(j = 1 \ldots N)$ are the weight matrices of the layer. There is a mechanism for initializing R^j with matrices based on the algorithm given in [8]. In the absence of initializing matrices, all nonlinear orders are first initialized with zeros, while the matrix of the linear order is assigned a unit matrix. Naturally, for complex systems, this situation can cause a considerable increase in network training time and a decline in the neural network model's prediction abilities.

TensorFlow (TF) [1] and Keras libraries for Python were used to develop the polynomial neural layer, which provides a wide variety of built-in tools that facilitate neural layer and model construction and training. Furthermore, TensorFlow allows to leverage a graphics processing unit (GPU) to boost the neural network's learning performance.

Figure 1 shows the classes inheritance implementing polynomial layers derived of `tensorflow.keras.layers.Layer`. `base_polynomial_layer` contains the basic features that are further redefined in two polynomial layers realizations: basic polynomial and Kronecker. The following subsections provide a more extensive description of their differences.

2.1   Polynomial Layer

The polynomial layer (`polynomial_layer`) is derived from `base_polynomial_layer` and overrides the methods `build` and `call` from `tensorflow.keras.layers.Layer`:

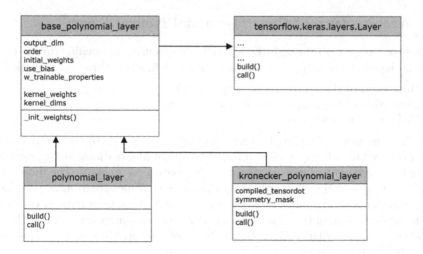

Fig. 1. Inheritance scheme of classes implementing polynomial layers

- (*build*) The dimensions of the weight matrices are computed during the layer construction step for each order of nonlinearity used in the layer. In case of basic polynomials, the dimension of the j-th matrix is $\left[n^j, m\right], j = 1 \ldots N$, where n is the dimension of the input vector, m is the dimension of the output vector. Number of rows in weight matrices relates to the number of combinations of the components of the input vector utilized to generate the j-th order of nonlinearity (repetition included). There is a possibility to initialize the Weight matrices before training.
- (*call*) According to the formula (1), in order to produce the output vector, the input space must be expanded using a polynomial nonlinear transformation of the input vector. This is carried out by calculating the recurrent tensor product with the formula

$$\boldsymbol{X}^k = \boldsymbol{X}^{k-1} \otimes \boldsymbol{X} \tag{2}$$

employing `einsum` function from the TensorFlow library, which applies the Einstein convention on summing the indexes of its arguments.

Thus, the procedure of the output vector calculation consists of two stages:

1. Initialization: $\overline{\boldsymbol{X}} = \text{bias}$;
2. In the cycle (j) from 1 to n:
    (a) Multiply the matrix by a vector and sum the result and $\overline{\boldsymbol{X}}$;
    (b) Raise the vector to the power of $j + 1$ using (2);

It is worth noticing that the polynomial layer implementation does not include any dimension reduction operations. For example, when we elevate an input vector of size 2 to the second power, we get:

$$Y = R^2 \cdot X^2 = \begin{pmatrix} r_{11} & r_{12} & r_{13} & r_{14} \\ r_{21} & r_{22} & r_{23} & r_{24} \\ r_{31} & r_{32} & r_{33} & r_{34} \\ r_{41} & r_{42} & r_{43} & r_{44} \end{pmatrix} \begin{pmatrix} x_1^2 \\ x_1 x_2 \\ x_2 x_1 \\ x_2^2 \end{pmatrix} \tag{3}$$

As seen in (3), when multiplying the matrix by a vector, the second and third components of the vector Y are the same, implying that the vector Y's dimension can be reduced by one. A similar scenario develops when using larger input vectors and higher degrees. A Kronecker layer is developed to actualize the potential of deleting repeating nonlinear components and lowering the dimension of the weight coefficient matrices. The main aspects of Kronecker layer are explained below.

2.2 Kronecker Layer

The main feature of `Kronecker_layer` layer is the implementation of Kronecker exponentiation operations associated with removing duplicate (up to the permutation of the multipliers) elements in the polynomialy transformed input vector. Similarly to `polynomial_layer` it redefines the abstract methods `build` and `call` of `tensorflow.keras.layers.Layer`.

- (*build*) The dimensions of the weight matrices are computed during the layer construction step for each order of nonlinearity used in the layer. In case of Kroneker's polynomials, the dimension of the j-th matrix is $\left[C_j^{n+j-1}, m \right], j = 1 \ldots N$, where n is the dimension of the input vector, m is the dimension of the output vector, $C_j^{n+j-1} = \frac{(n+j-1)!}{j!(n-1)!}$. Number of rows in weight matrices relates to the number of different combinations of the components of the input vector (up to a permutation of factors) utilized to generate the j-th order of nonlinearity. In addition, a set of binary masks is calculated, which is used to eliminate identical components from the formula's exponentiation result (2).
- (*call*) Similarly to the `call` method in the polynomial layer, the input space is extended and duplicates are deleted by employing a polynomial nonlinear modification of the input vector. The following formula, for example, computes the second Kronecker degree for the given input vector of size two:

$$X^{[2]} = X^2 \odot^* mask = \begin{pmatrix} x_1^2 \\ x_1 x_2 \\ x_2 x_1 \\ x_2^2 \end{pmatrix} \odot \begin{pmatrix} \text{True} \\ \text{True} \\ \text{False} \\ \text{True} \end{pmatrix} = \begin{pmatrix} x_1^2 \\ x_1 x_2 \\ x_2^2 \end{pmatrix}.$$

Here $\odot^*$ is the Hadamard product with a decrease in vector dimension (all vector elements with `False` in the appropriate position of the Boolean mask are eliminated). In this scenario, formula (3) will take the following form:

$$Y = \hat{R}^2 \cdot X^{[2]} = \begin{pmatrix} \hat{r}_{11} & \hat{r}_{12} & \hat{r}_{13} \\ \hat{r}_{21} & \hat{r}_{22} & \hat{r}_{23} \\ \hat{r}_{31} & \hat{r}_{32} & \hat{r}_{33} \end{pmatrix} \begin{pmatrix} x_1^2 \\ x_1 x_2 \\ x_2^2 \end{pmatrix}.$$

The matrix $\hat{R}^2$ varies from the matrix $R2$ in that the dimension is reduced.

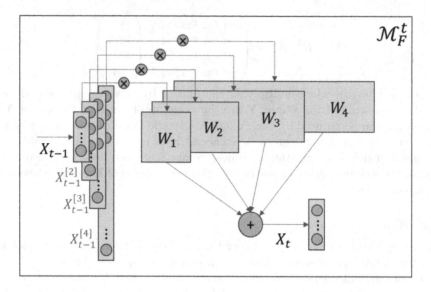

Fig. 2. The scheme of operation of the Kronecker layer in accordance with the formula (1) [5]

3   Polynomial Models

Models for a variety of problems may be created based on the types of polynomial layers covered above (with/without repeats of nonlinear components). The Kronecker layer is a priority building element for the polynomial models discussed below because it reduces the dimensionality of the weight coefficient matrices, reducing the number of free parameters for the optimizer and increasing the speed of output and training of the layer.

We consider two types of polynomial models suitable for describing stationary and non-stationary dynamical processes.

3.1   Polynomial Model with One Output (Single Output Model)

For both stationary and non-stationary systems, a model with a single output may be produced. Because the weight coefficient matrices in the stationary scenario depend only on the discreteness of the time series and not on a given instant in time, such a model has a single Kronecker layer (Fig. 2a)). In the case of a non-stationary system, one can try to bring it to a stationary form by injecting exogenous time-dependent variables into the phase vector, or one can design a multilayer model conforming, for example, to data periodicity (Fig. 2b)). The following procedure is used to train a model with a single output.

I Data Preparation

1. The data obtained as a result of measurement on k trajectories of the simulated dynamic system are given:

$$\boldsymbol{X}_1\left(t_1\right),\ldots,\boldsymbol{X}_1\left(t_{p_1}\right),\boldsymbol{X}_2\left(t_{p_1+1}\right),\ldots,\boldsymbol{X}_2\left(t_{p_1+p_2}\right),\ldots,$$

$$\boldsymbol{X}_k\left(t_{p_1+\ldots+p_{k-1}+1}\right),\ldots,\boldsymbol{X}_k\left(t_{p_1+\ldots+p_k}\right),$$

where, $t_{p_1+\ldots+p_i+J} < t_{p_1+\ldots+p_i+J+1}, \forall j < p_{i+1}, p_i-$, is the number of vectors of the system state measured on the i-th trajectory with the initial vector $\boldsymbol{X}_i\left(t_{p_1+\ldots+p_{i-1}+1}\right)$.

2. Forming a set of training pairs $\{(\boldsymbol{X}_{i+1}\left(t_{p_1+\ldots+p_i+J}\right), \boldsymbol{X}_{i+1}\left(t_{p_1+\ldots+p_i+J+1}\right)),$ $\forall j < p_{i+1}, i = 1, k\}$, where the first vector of the pair is the training input vector, the second vector of the pair is the training output vector

The first vector in the training pair is denoted as $\boldsymbol{X}\left(t_0\right)$, and the second by $\boldsymbol{X}\left(t_M\right)$, where M is the number of Kronecker layers in the model (1 for a stationary system).

II Training

1. The vector $\boldsymbol{X}\left(t_0\right)$ is fed into the input of the Kronecker layer, and the vector $\boldsymbol{X}\left(t_M\right)$ is calculated;
2. The resultant vector $X\left(t_M\right)$ is fed into the input of the Kronecker layer, and the vector $X\left(t_{2M}\right)$ is calculated;
3. This process is repeated a specified number of times.

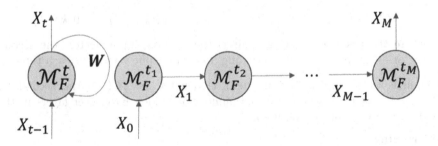

Fig. 3. Polynomial model with one output to describe a) stationary b) non-stationary dynamical process

3.2 Polynomial Model with Multiple Outputs (Multiple Output Model)

A polynomial model with multiple outputs is constructed out of a series of Kronecker layers. The weight matrices in a stationary case are fixed between layers and updated synchronously during the training. For a non-stationary model, the overall architecture does not change, but the output is formed from each hidden layer of the model (Fig. 3b)) [3].

The number of hidden Kronecker layers is usually dictated by the length of the training data (if it is supplied by a sequence of discrete trajectories with varied dynamic system parameters) or by the periodicity/seasonality of the time series used for training.

Figure 4 shows a model with multiple outputs for a stationary system. In this case, a vector $X(t_0)$ is fed into the input, and an array of vectors is obtained at the output, $X(t_1), X(t_2), \ldots, X(t_q)$. Accordingly, a set of training data is prepared for such a model.

I Data Preparation

1. The data obtained as a result of measurement on k trajectories of the simulated dynamic system are given:

$$X_1(t_1), \ldots, X_1(t_{p_1}), X_2(t_{p_1+1}), \ldots, X_2(t_{p_1+p_2}), \ldots,$$

$$X_k(t_{p_1+\ldots+p_{k-1}+1}), \ldots, X_k(t_{p_1+\ldots+p_k}),$$

Here, $t_{p_1+\ldots+p_i+J} < t_{p_1+\ldots+p_i+J+1}, \forall j < p_{i+1}, p_i-$, is the number of vectors of the system state measured on the i-th trajectory with the initial vector $X_i(t_{p_1+\ldots+p_{i-1}+1})$

2. Forming a set of training pairs

$$\{(X_{i+1}(t_{p_1+\ldots}), [X_{i+1}(t_{p_1+\ldots}), \ldots, X_{i+1}(t_{p_1+\ldots})]), i = 0, k-1\},$$

where the first vector of the pair is the training input vector, the second vector of the pair is a list containing a set of output vectors at each time.

The first vector in the training pair is denoted by $X(t_0)$, the second by $[X(t_1), \ldots, X(t_q)]$, where q is the number of hidden Kronecker layers in the model (see Fig. 4 for an example).

II Training

1. The vector $X(t_0)$ is fed into the input to the Kronecker layer, and a set of vectors is calculated $[X(t_1), \ldots, X(t_q)]$;
2. The resulting vector $X(t_q)$ is fed into the input to the Kronecker layer, and the vector is calculated $[X(t_{q+1}), \ldots, X(t_{2q})]$;
3. This procedure is performed a certain number of times.

Because the computation of gradients takes into consideration the mismatch of outputs throughout the full length of the dynamic system's trajectory, rather than only between pairs of nearby locations, training a model with multiple outputs allows for dynamic consistency of predictions.

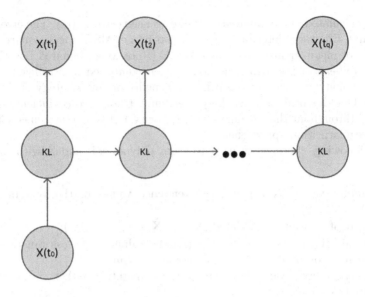

Fig. 4. Polynomial model with multiple outputs

4   Features of Training

This section discusses the possible options that can be employed for training polynomial models. Generally, training can be implemented in two ways:

1. *Training of all weight matrices at once.* This method implies training of all weight matrices simultaneously, i.e. the gradient is computed for all weight coefficients at the same time, and all weight matrices are altered at each step of training. The number of free coefficients can be enormous using this technique, complicating optimization algorithm convergence (particularly in the absence of competent initialization) and can potentially lead to physically incorrect predictions.
2. *Sequential training of matrices, starting from the bias and linear term matrix R^1 to the matrix R^n corresponding to the n-th order of nonlinearity.* Simultaneous weight matrix training ignores a crucial characteristic of the polynomial model: the contribution of weight coefficient matrices to the outcome (see formula (1)) is different. The linear component has the most effect on R^1; but, as the order of nonlinearity increases, the contribution decreases. In this regard, the sequential learning mechanism can be applied:
   - a linear model with a matrix $R1$ is being constructed and trained until the loss function stops decreasing;
   - a second-order model is being built, the linear part of which is initialized by a trained matrix R^1 loaded from the previous model. In this case, R^1 it is fixed, and only the matrix R^2 is trained, etc.

For models with a single output, a basic approach to learning is used, which assumes that a vector $\tilde{X}(t_0)$ is fed into the neural network's input, and a vector

$\tilde{X}(t_1)$ is calculated and compared to the reference vector $\overline{X}(t_0)$. The error function's value $\mathcal{L}$ is then determined, which can be i.e. MSE (mean square error), RMSE (root mean square error), or RMSLE (Root Mean Squared Log Error).

The gradient of the error function is then computed and utilized to alter the weight matrices. One of the primary benefits of this strategy is the rapid learning. One downside is that the placements of non-zero coefficients are not regulated throughout the learning process, however this may be remedied using various regularization approaches.

The following approach is used to train polynomial models with multiple outputs:

1. The input: vector $\tilde{\mathbf{X}}(t_0)$ and the reference values of the vectors $\overline{\mathbf{X}}(t_1)$, $\overline{\mathbf{X}}(t_2), \ldots, \overline{\mathbf{X}}(t_q)$;
2. An array of vectors is calculated, $\tilde{\mathbf{X}}(t_1), \tilde{\mathbf{X}}(t_2), \ldots, \tilde{\mathbf{X}}(t_q)$;
3. For a pair of vectors $\tilde{X}(t_i)$ and $\overline{X}(t_i)$ the value of the loss function $\mathcal{L}$ for each pair is computed at the same moment of time t_i;
4. The average error value is computed; this might be either the average or weighted average error value:

   (a) error $= \frac{1}{Q-1} \sum\limits_{i=1}^{Q} \mathcal{L}\left(\tilde{X}(t_i), \overline{X}(t_i)\right)$,

   (b) error $= \frac{1}{Q-1} \sum\limits_{i=1}^{Q} \alpha_i^* \mathcal{L}\left(\tilde{X}(t_i), \overline{X}(t_i)\right)$,

5. The gradient of the error function is determined using the TensorFlow library's automated differentiation methods;
6. The gradient is used in the optimization of weights.

Additional improvements of the training results can be achieved by applying proper data normalization and regularization. These procedures are outlined below and applicable to both single-output models and multi-output models.

4.1 Regularization of Weights, Masking of Gradients

The usage of masks in the learning process is related to the necessity to keep matrices R^i physical in problems that depict a physical process, as well as the need to shorten the training time of a polynomial neural network. This functionality may be applied during training by zeroing and fixing tiny components of the weight matrix. Simultaneously, by omitting zero elements of the weight matrices from the training process, the number of configurable (trainable) parameters (weights) of the model is decreased.

To obtain a mask, we must first determine which of the coefficients is non-zero. This is only allowed if the matrices' values are received at the startup step. In this example, masks R_m^i of the same dimension as the matrices R^i are built so that there are *True* in place of non-zero elements of the original weights and *False* in place of zeros (or near to zero).

If the matrices Ri were not initialized when the model was built, the regularization L_0 of weights can be used to add to the loss function $\mathcal{L}$ the following value

$$\beta = \lambda \sum g\left(r_{jk}^i\right). \tag{4}$$

Here, *lambda* is the regularizing parameter that must be specified, $g(x) = \begin{cases} 1, x \neq 0 \\ 0, x = 0 \end{cases}$, r_{jk}^i are elements of matrix R^i. The norm L_0 penalizes the number of non-zero elements in the weight matrices, increasing their sparsity.

Because the function's combinatorial nature (4) and non-differentiability make optimization using traditional numerical algorithms impossible, various methods are proposed to weaken the discrete nature of the penalty [6,9,10] and apply optimization methods to smooth functions.

4.2   Normalization of Data and Initializing Weights

The weight matrices and data are adjusted to improve the learning outcomes of a polynomial neural network. The normalizing coefficient is computed using the norm $L_i nfty$ for the vector of the of the initial data.

$$\|X\|_\infty = \max |X_i| \tag{5}$$

At the same time, for normalized data, a relation similar to (1) should be preserved

$$\tilde{X}\left(t_{i+1}\right) = \text{bias} + \sum_{j=1}^{N} \tilde{R}^j \tilde{X}\left(t_i\right)^{[j]},$$

where ˜ means normalization.

The algorithm for normalizing the weight matrices is as follows

1. Calculating the norm by the formula (5)
2. Multiplying all the elements of the matrix R^i by the coefficient $\alpha_i = (\|X\|_\infty)^{i-1}$.

5   Results of the Experiment

Let us consider an example system of ordinary differential equations Lotka–Volterra:

$$\frac{dx}{dt} = (\alpha - \beta y)x,$$
$$\frac{dy}{dt} = (-\gamma + \delta x)y \tag{6}$$

with fixed parameters values $\gamma = \beta = 0.9$, $\alpha = 0.5$, $\delta = 1$. Let us illustrate the ability of PNN to describe this system for initial values not presented in the training data. According to the algorithm, presented in [8], we calculate the weight matrices W_k with low accuracy. We use the system (6) to generate

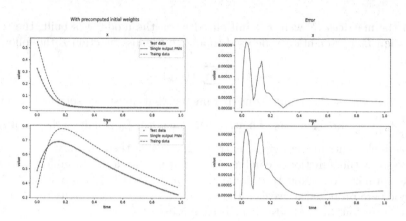

Fig. 5. Training results With precomputed initial weights

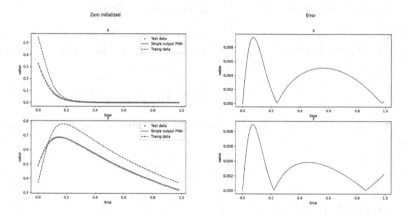

Fig. 6. Training results with zero initialization

the training and test data trajectories. We fit single output model which was initialized by matrices W_k and without initialization.

Figure 5 and 6 depict the results of system's trajectory prediction the integration of the Eq. (6) are presented after training the matrices in two ways compared with the test data. The absolute error at each moment of time is also computed. It can be seen that the maximum absolute error in the case of zero initialization does not exceed 5% and in the case of precomputed initial weights does not exceed 0.01%.

6   Conclusion

The paper contains the description of a learn module of tm-flow library for building and training polynomial neural networks to model dynamical processes. It also explains several learning strategies to increase speed and accuracy or predictions, as well as approaches to keep the weight matrices physical, which allows you to boost the explainability of the outcomes. Such polynomial neural network can represent a general solution of ordinary differential equations, which permits canonical transformations to be preserved across large time periods. The outcomes of tests comparing training with and without initialization are given.

References

1. Abadi, M., Agarwal, A., Barham, P., Brevdo, E.: TensorFlow: large-scale machine learning on heterogeneous systems (2015). https://www.tensorflow.org/
2. Al-Jumeily, D., Ghazali, R., Hussain, A.: Predicting physical time series using dynamic ridge polynomial neural networks. PLoS ONE **9**(8), e105766 (2014)
3. Chollet, F.: Deep Learning with Python. Manning Publications Co., New York (2018)
4. Dubey, A., Radenovic, F., Mahajan, D.: Scalable interpretability via polynomials, June 2022
5. Golovkina, A., Kozynchenko, V.: Neural network representation for ordinary differential equations. In: Dolinina, O., et al. (eds.) AIES 2022. SSDC, vol. 457, pp. 39–55. Springer, Cham (2023). https://doi.org/10.1007/978-3-031-22938-1_3
6. Huang, C.T., Chen, J.C., Wu, J.L.: Learning sparse neural networks through mixture-distributed regularization. In: 2020 IEEE/CVF Conference on Computer Vision and Pattern Recognition Workshops (CVPRW), Seattle, WA, USA, pp. 2968–2977. IEEE, June 2020
7. Ivakhnenko, A.G.: Polynomial theory of complex systems. Trans. Syst. Man Cybern. **4**, 364–378 (1971)
8. Klimenko, I.S.: Implementation of the matrix mapping method for solving a system of differential equations. In: Control Processes and Stability, Saint Petersburg, Russia, vol. 9, pp. 53–57 (2022)
9. Liu, J., Xu, Z., Shi, R., Cheung, R.C.C., So, H.K.H.: Dynamic sparse training: find efficient sparse network from scratch with trainable masked layers, April 2020
10. Louizos, C., Welling, M., Kingma, D.P.: Learning sparse neural networks through L_0 regularization, June 2018
11. Oh, S.K., Pedrycz, W., Park, B.J.: Polynomial neural networks architecture: analysis and design. Comput. Electr. Eng. **29**(6), 703–725 (2003)
12. Shin, Y., Ghosh, J.: The pi-sigma network: an efficient higher-order neural network for pattern classification and function approximation. In: IJCNN-1991-Seattle International Joint Conference on Neural Networks, vol. 1, pp. 13–18 (1991). https://doi.org/10.1109/IJCNN.1991.155142

Deploying Deep Learning Models Using Serverless Computing for Diabetic Retinopathy Detection

Matheus W. Camargo[✉][iD], Cristiano Alex Künas[iD],
and Philippe O. A. Navaux[iD]

Informatics Institute, Federal University of Rio Grande do Sul, Porto Alegre, Brazil
{mwcamargo,cakunas,navaux}@inf.ufrgs.br

Abstract. The incidence of diabetes is increasing at an alarming rate across the world. As a result, cases of diabetic retinopathy (DR) are on the rise, a complication of diabetes that in its most severe form can lead to blindness. The lack of specialized labor for diagnosis, essential for the successful treatment of the disease, brings the need to study alternatives for diagnosis via computational means. Recent research on the use of Deep Learning for the detection of DR proves to be an important alternative to improve the use of specialized labor, by prioritizing the most serious cases. From this context, the work objective is to evaluate the performance and financial cost of alternatives based on serverless computing for the deployment of Deep Learning models for DR classification. Using the Amazon Sagemaker serverless inference service, optimizations and different configuration alternatives were considered, obtaining up to 9.4% of financial cost reduction and up to $2.35\times$ performance boost. Finally, concepts such as containerization and infrastructure as code were used during the solution implementation, to allow the reproduction of deployment and experiments performed.

Keywords: Serverless computing · Cloud computing · Deep Learning · Diabetic Retinopathy · Deployment

1 Introduction

Diabetes has been growing globally at alarming rates. In 2021, it was estimated that around 537 million people suffered from this disease worldwide (Fig. 1). It is expected that 1/3 of these people will develop diabetic retinopathy (DR). DR is a complication of diabetes in which a high level of blood sugar causes damage to the retina, impairing vision and even leading to blindness at its most severe level.

Within this context, diagnosing the disease in its early stages is still the best form of prevention since, after diagnosis, it is possible to prevent DR stage progression by controlling blood sugar levels and blood pressure. An optical coherence tomography makes the diagnosis (OCT) examination, which obtains images of the patient's retina, which a trained ophthalmologist subsequently evaluates.

O. Gervasi et al. (Eds.): ICCSA 2023 Workshops, LNCS 14109, pp. 274–289, 2023.
https://doi.org/10.1007/978-3-031-37120-2_18

Estimates of the global prevalence of diabetes in the 20–79 year age group (millions)   Projections of the global prevalence of diabetes in the 20–79 year age group (millions)

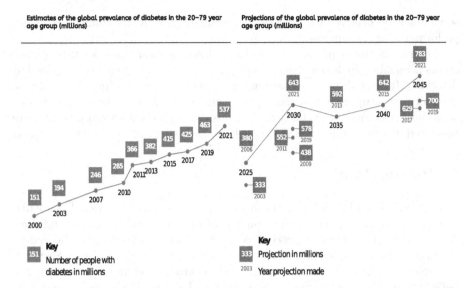

Fig. 1. Estimation and projection of the prevalence of diabetes globally. The left Figure shows the evolution of diabetes prevalence, which was most recently estimated at 537 million people worldwide. The right Figure shows a projection of diabetes until 2045, in which approximately 783 million people will suffer from diabetes [5].

An example of the effectiveness of public policies for diagnosing the disease is the reduction in the number of cases of blindness caused by DR in the United Kingdom. Following the introduction of a comprehensive policy aimed at promoting DR testing on a large scale, the disease lost its position as the leading cause of blindness in adults [13].

Although preventive exams are recognized worldwide as the primary way to combat the disease, this practice is still not widely disseminated due to the shortage of specialized professionals capable of evaluating eye fundus images. In China, the ratio between patients with diabetes and ophthalmologists reaches 1:3000 [4], making applying policies to perform tests at the national level impracticable.

Therefore, it is necessary to apply computational methods capable of evaluating eye fundus images and detecting the presence of diabetic retinopathy in its different degrees of complexity. A very promising approach is the use of *Deep Learning*, in which neural networks are trained in a supervised way to receive eye fundus images and classify the image, interpreting it according to different stages of DR. Such technology, if made available to health professionals, could be used to prioritize the most severe cases, thus providing better use of the limited workforce capable of confirming diagnoses.

Given the current context, this study assesses an alternative approach to deploying two neural network models trained to detect Diabetic Retinopathy on a serverless platform. To achieve this, the Amazon Sagemaker cloud computing service will be utilized, with a focus on evaluating both the financial cost and performance of the proposed solution.

The rest of this paper is organized as follows. Section 2 covers existing work on deep learning deployment on serverless platforms and deep learning for DR detection. In Sect. 3, we describe implementation details, outline the hardware and software setup used, and the experiments' methodology. The results of optimizations' performance evaluations and resources for research reproduction are presented in Sect. 4. Finally, Sect. 5 concludes the paper and outlines future work.

2   Related Work

In this Section, works related to the *deployment* of Deep Learning models are discussed, a fundamental step for making the algorithms available to the end user. As presented in Sect. 2.1, serverless computing presents itself as a compelling alternative due to reduced financial cost and ease of scaling. Finally, in Sect. 2.2, we present works that focus on using Deep Learning techniques to detect diabetic retinopathy. As shown, such techniques have proven to be a promising alternative to the shortage of specialized labor capable of diagnosing DR.

2.1   Serverless Computing for Deep Learning Models Deployment

The usage and popularity of the serverless paradigm are emerging rapidly. This paradigm presents compelling advantages, as pointed out in [1]. For instance, it can significantly reduce financial costs due to the ability to scale compute resources down to zero. Another critical advantage the paradigm offers is the ease of configuration and deployment, resulting in the abstraction of operations and infrastructure configurations.

However, this paradigm also presents significant drawbacks and open problems. For example, resource limitations can exist, such as constraints on maximum memory size and CPU usage. Another critical problem is the cold start latency, a consequence of scaling compute resources down to zero and can significantly hinder application latency.

The use of serverless computing for machine learning and deep learning poses challenges due to these applications' high computational and memory demands, as highlighted in [18]. Despite that, numerous studies have been conducted to overcome these challenges and enable deploying deep learning models in serverless platforms, enabling deploying such models without configuring infrastructure.

In this context, [7] addressed using serverless computing to deploy deep learning models. The authors used Amazon's serverless cloud computing service, AWS Lambda. Although Lambda functions simplify the process of managing the infrastructure on a large scale and even reduces operating costs, their use penalizes the application's performance in the form of cold-starts and warm-starts, as the authors showed.

Furthermore, as shown by the authors of [7], the latency for both cold-start and warm-start cases tends to decrease as the memory increases. However, this decrease is limited, as there are cases where increasing the available memory raises the cost per activation without significant performance gains. Additionally, the size of the model used directly impacts both latencies, making it important to consider models of different sizes when evaluating optimizations and different configurations. These findings inspired our own selection of models to assess how various optimizations impacted the application's overall performance.

Similarly, in [19], the serverless computing paradigm was explored to deploy neural networks for NLP (Natural Language Processing). The models were deployed in a pay-per-request model, with zero ongoing cost for maintaining the service active. Interestingly, as stated by the authors, the system was scalable without any extra engineering effort, restating one advantage of the serverless paradigm.

2.2   Deep Learning for DR Grading

Machine learning has gained prominence in recent decades, showing significant advancements in diverse fields, such as object recognition or disease diagnosis. In [4], the authors presented the DeepDR system, which, based on a residual neural network, showed that it is possible to detect the presence of different degrees of diabetes with an area under the receiver's operational characteristic curve from 0.916 to 0.970 for each degree of DR.

Other neural network architectures can also be used for DR detection. The work of [14] is based on the Inception-V3 architecture. A significant conclusion of the work concerns the impact of image resolution on model training. After an increase in image resolution, it was possible to increase the accuracy of detections by 6%.

Interestingly, even smaller models can successfully detect diabetic retinopathy. In [16], the MobileNet architecture was trained using the APTOS dataset, obtaining a model with accuracy and precision of 95%. As mentioned in the 3.1 section, to analyze alternatives for the deployment of models considering different sizes of neural network architecture, one of the architectures used was MobileNet, due to its reduced size.

The reduced size of the MobileNet architecture has been exploited for DR detection even in mobile applications. In the [3] work, the MobileNet architecture was used so that the models' inference could be performed on cell phones, allowing a complementary diagnosis to be carried out for users who do not have a stable internet connection, such as users who reside in the rural area.

3   Methodology

This section covers the development and implementation details of the solution for the *deployment* of DR classification models using cloud computing. Moreover, we will also address the methodology followed in carrying out the experiments and evaluating the implemented optimizations.

The 3.1 section addresses the development and implementation of the solution, such as the model training method and dataset used, the cloud serverless service used and required interfaces, data extraction, and analysis, as well as the process, followed to deploy endpoint inferences. Finally, the 3.2 section describes the methodology used to carry out the experiments.

3.1   Solution Development

First, we trained and selected models for the detection of DR. For this purpose, a notebook from the Kaggle platform was used, where 27 pre-trained neural network architectures were trained. The dataset used for training is derived from the APTOS 2019 competition dataset, available at [10]. The class distribution of the derived dataset is identical to the competition's original dataset, as shown in Fig. 2.

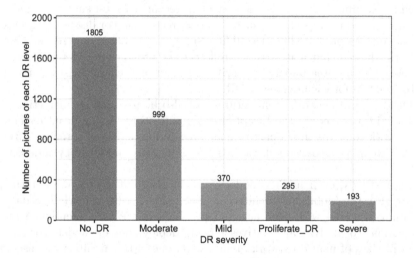

Fig. 2. Distribution of dataset classes used for model training.

All images were resized to 224×224 resolution for different pre-trained deep-learning models. In addition, a Gaussian filter was applied to the images to reduce noise. As shown in Fig. 3, the samples are labeled according to 5 degrees of DR: no DR, mild, moderate, severe, and proliferative.

As shown in [7], model size has a significant impact on both warm-up and cold-start latency. Therefore, to verify the behavior of models of different sizes against different optimizations, the VGG19 and MobileNet models were chosen. The relationship between models, artifact size on disk, and the number of parameters is presented in the Table 1.

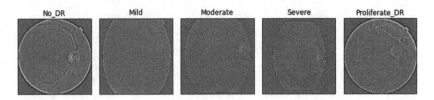

Fig. 3. Images sample from the dataset used for model training. All images are labeled according to 5 degrees of DR: no DR, mild, moderate, severe, and proliferative

After training the models, they were saved in the SavedModel [8] format. So that the models could then be used in the Sagemaker [12] serverless inference service, the model was compacted following the tar.gz format and uploaded to an S3 bucket.

Having the model artifacts hosted in an S3 bucket, it was then necessary to develop a code that loads the model and predicts the classification of diabetic retinopathy from an image. However, given the time taken to load the models from the file system, a *Singleton* class was defined for loading the model and making inference predictions so that the model was kept in memory and reused between different inference requests.

Table 1. Relation between model, number of parameters, and artifact size in the file system. We can notice that the VGG19 is about six times bigger than the MobileNet model.

Model	Number of parameters	Artifact size (SavedModel)
MobileNet	3.377.221	15,7 MB
VGG19	20.107.205	77,7 MB

To satisfy the container interface expected by the Sagemaker serverless inference service, it was necessary to implement an HTTP API using the FastAPI [11] library. Finally, the container's entry point was defined in a file called **serve**, which aims to start sub-processes for the NGINX and Gunicorn services. The NGINX [15] service acts as a proxy to the HTTP API workers, redirecting API calls to Gunicorn [17]. Gunicorn is a pre-fork model Web Server Gateway Interface [6] server that can run and manage multiple workers of an HTTP server.

After starting the processes that will serve the Sagemaker inference requests, the **serve** process continues to wait until the completion of its child processes, also having the responsibility of killing the NGINX processes and the Gunicorn process if it receives a SIGTERM signal indicating that the container will be destroyed. A diagram showing sub-process creation during container initialization is shown in Fig. 4.

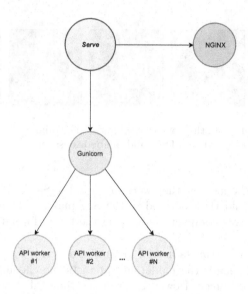

Fig. 4. Diagram of sub-process creation during container initialization. The `serve` process is the main process responsible for creating the NGINX sub-process and Gunicorn sub-process. Then, the Gunicorn sub-process creates N workers, depending on the number of vCPUs of the instance used to run the containers.

3.2 Experiments Methodology

Given that the Sagemaker serverless inference service scales the compute resources down to zero when the application is idle, there are two different latency cases: warm-up and cold-start. The former happens when the compute resources are already initialized, not increasing the application's latency. The latter occurs after a period of application idleness, usually after 10 to 15 min, when the compute resources have been destroyed and need to be re-initialized to serve new requests.

Based on these two types of latency, we then defined two experiments scenarios, each one dedicated to measuring a specific case of latency:

- **Warm-up scenario:** First, we make a warm-up request to initialize the container, and the other requests do not suffer from *cold-start* latency. Then, 25 requests are made in series, with intervals of 5 s between each request.
- **Cold-start scenario:** 10 sequential requests are made, with intervals of 15 min between each request, so that the container is destroyed between executions, resulting in cold-start latencies that we want to measure.

For both scenarios, two metrics related to the application execution time were extracted: total latency and prediction time. Total latency is the time taken between sending the request and the server's response, encompassing both the time for sending the image, model prediction, and server response. The prediction time measures only the time taken to perform the inference of an image.

Using both scenarios, two optimizations were evaluated: docker image optimization and endpoint memory size optimization. The optimizations are further elaborated upon in the subsequent subsections.

Docker Image Size Optimization. To verify the impact of docker image size on the cold-start latency of the application, two optimizations were applied. The first optimization applied was refactoring the docker file to use the concept of multi-stage build [2]. Next, dependencies were reduced, eliminating non-essential dependencies for the application's operation and optimizing the size of existing dependencies, such as replacing the tensorflow-mkl dependency with the Tensorflow dependency. The optimizations and their impact on the size of the resulting Docker image are shown in Table 2.

Table 2. Table of different optimizations applied to the base image and the respective disk image size (without being compressed) and compressed image size (size occupied by the image in image registries, like ECR).

Optimization	Compressed size	Disk size
None	1798.27 MB	4.97 GB
Multi-stage build	923.99 MB	3.32 GB
Dependencies reduction	517.23 MB	2.06 GB

Since the application's container is already running, its initialization time does not influence the application's latency, since the container is only destroyed after some idle time. For this reason, only the cold-start scenario was considered when evaluating the impact of Docker image size optimizations on latency. A total of six experiments were run by combining each optimization and model.

Endpoint Memory Configuration. To verify the impact of the endpoint memory size configuration on the prediction time and the application's total latency, the following memory values were used: 1024MB, 2048MB and 3072MB.

Increasing the memory configuration of a lambda function reflects both the cold-start and the warm-up case, as shown in [7]. For this reason, both the cold-start and warm-up scenarios were evaluated to verify if the same behavior was maintained. On total, twelve experiments were run by combining three memory configurations, two models and two scenarios (cold-start and warm-up).

4 Results

This Section presents the results obtained using the serverless inference service based on the experiments mentioned in Sect. 3.2. We analyzed two optimizations' performance and financial cost: Docker image size and endpoints memory configuration.

The first optimization applied while using the serverless inference service was the Docker image size optimization. Reducing the image size was essential for testing other optimizations and versions of algorithms used in this work since a smaller image leads to lower upload latency for image records and shorter build time. Interestingly, the Docker image optimization also reduced the cold-start latency for both analyzed models, as detailed in the Sect. 4.1.

Optimizing the endpoints' memory size brought significant gains in performance and cost for the execution of the analyzed models, as will be detailed in the Sect. 4.2.

Finally, in the Sect. 4.4 we provide supplementary material for research reproduction.

4.1   Docker Image Optimization

As mentioned in Sect. 3.2, the cold-start latency does not contribute to increasing the prediction time of the models. Therefore, the only fundamental metric to be analyzed is the total latency time of a request.

Analyzing Fig. 5, it can be seen that optimizing the Docker image size increased performance for both models. Comparing the total latency time of the largest Docker image (no optimization - 1798.27 MB) with the smallest Docker image (optimized dependencies - 517.23 MB), there was a speed-up of 1.2864× for the MobileNet model and of 1.3272× for the VGG19 model.

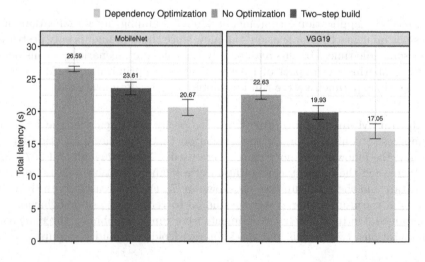

Fig. 5. Total latency time for the MobileNet and VGG19 models for different Docker images. The total latency time is reduced as optimizations are applied to the docker image.

Not limited to the issue of `cold-start` latency time, optimizing the size of the Docker image is essential for reducing the time to deploy, build, and reduce the cost of storing Docker image registries as the ECR service used in this work.

4.2 Endpoint Memory Size

As mentioned in [7], as the memory size configuration of the endpoints increases, there is a decrease in both the total latency and the prediction time of the models.

Next, we analyze the impact of increasing memory for both the `warm-up` and `cold-start` scenarios, described in Sect. 3.2.

Warm-Up Scenario. Analyzing Fig. 6, we noticed a significant reduction in the prediction time and total latency for the VGG19 model. In particular, when comparing the 2048 MB memory configuration with the 1024 MB memory configuration, there was a speed-up of 2.74× analyzing the prediction time.

An exciting case is noticed when evaluating the performance and expense of the different memory configurations for the VGG19 model. As per Fig. 7, the lowest endpoint cost is achieved with 2 GB of memory, even though the cost per second of that endpoint is double the 1 GB endpoint configuration. As the 2 GB endpoint is 2.74× faster than the 1 GB endpoint, we arrive at a case where there is both cost reduction and performance improvement, as the execution cost is directly proportional to the execution time. Therefore, we conclude that an increase in memory configuration does not always imply an increase in the cost per endpoint inference.

By selecting the 2 GB memory configuration for the VGG19 model, we achieved a 9.4% cost reduction, combined with the performance increase mentioned previously.

Analyzing Fig. 8, we noticed a difference in behavior between the VGG19 and MobileNet models. Considering the prediction time of the MobileNet model, there was a considerable performance increase between the 1 GB and 2 GB endpoints, totaling a speed-up of 2.35×. However, when we look at the endpoint's total latency, the speed-up drops to 1.38×.

Since the MobileNet model's prediction time is short compared to the total latency, representing only 37% of the total latency, the performance gains from the memory increase are smaller than larger models such as the VGG19. Due to this fact, for the MobileNet model, every increase in memory meant an increase in cost, as shown in Fig. 7.

Cold-Start Scenario. Similar to the results of the `warm-up` scenario, there were also performance gains in total endpoint latency in the `cold-start` scenario as the endpoint memory used increased.

As shown in Fig. 9, for both the VGG19 and MobileNet models, there was a significant reduction in `cold-start` latency when comparing the 1 GB and 2 GB memory configurations. For the MobileNet model, there was a speed-up of

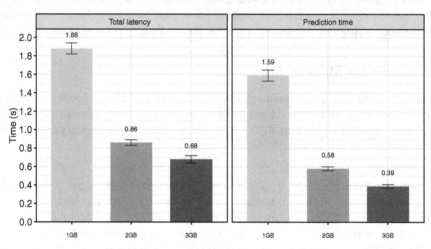

Fig. 6. Prediction time and total latency for the VGG19 model according to memory size. Note that as memory increases, time decreases.

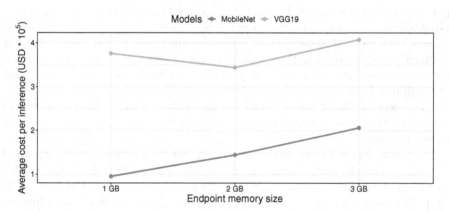

Fig. 7. Average cost per inference by endpoint memory size for MobileNet and VGG19 models.

1.65× between the 1 GB and 2 GB configurations, and for the VGG19 model, the speed-up was 1.54×.

Unlike the `warm-up` scenario, where the total latency reduction was more significant for the VGG19 model, both models showed similar performance gains in the `cold-start` scenario.

As previously mentioned, increasing memory does not translate into improved performance for models whose prediction time is a small fraction of the total latency time. However, the relationship between prediction time and total latency does not impact performance gains for the `cold-start` latency case.

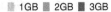

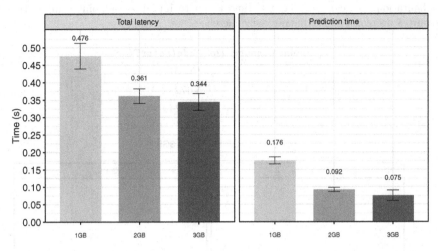

Fig. 8. Prediction time and total latency for the MobileNet model according to memory size. Note that as memory increases, time decreases.

To explain this phenomenon, we can analyze the *ModelSetupTime* metric, which refers to the time required to initialize the computational resources for the execution of the endpoints. According to Tables 3 and 4, we can see that as the memory grows, the *ModelSetupTime* decreases. Since *ModelSetupTime* is a critical additional component for the total latency of a request, this explains the reduction of `cold-start` latency for both models.

Table 3. Average ModelSetupTime of the VGG19 model for each used memory configuration. We can see that the time taken to initialize endpoint computational resources decreases as the memory size increases.

Endpoint memory size	*ModelSetupTime*
1 GB	10.7879 s
2 GB	6.8852 s
3 GB	6.5223 s

Interestingly, there was no considerable difference between the 2 GB and 3 GB memory configurations for both models, as seen in Fig. 9. This observation aligns with what was shown in [7], where the memory configuration of the lambda endpoints affected the `cold-start` latency. However, after a particular memory size, the increase in memory did not increase performance.

Table 4. Average ModelSetupTime of the MobileNet model for each used memory configuration. We can see that the time taken to initialize endpoint computational resources decreases as the memory size increases.

Endpoint memory size	$ModelSetupTime$
1 GB	10.6071 s
2 GB	5.6728 s
3 GB	5.6074 s

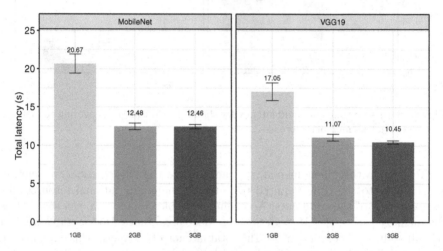

Fig. 9. Total `cold-start` latency for the MobileNet and VGG19 model in the serverless inference service for each used memory size.

4.3 Cold-Start and Warm-Up Latency Comparison

As previously mentioned, using serverless computing for deploying deep learning models presents higher latencies during the initialization of the computational resources dedicated to the execution of the inference, known as `cold-start` latency.

From the combination of Docker image size optimizations and endpoint memory configuration, it was possible to reduce the `cold-start` latency by about 2× for both models used, as shown in Table 5. There was a performance increase of 2.04× for the VGG19 model and 2.13× for the MobileNet model.

Even after applying the optimizations in combination, we noticed a big difference between the latency of the `warm-up` case and the `cold-start` cases' latency. Comparing the `warm-up` latency with the `cold-start` latency of endpoints with a 2 GB configuration, the cold-start latency is 57.42× higher for the MobileNet model and 19.82× higher for the VGG19 model.

Table 5. `Cold-start` latency by the model used before and after optimizations. Note that there was a performance increase of about 2×.

Model	Latency without optimization	Latency with optimization
VGG19	22.63 s	11.07 s
MobileNet	26.59 s	12.48 s

This large difference can be an impediment for solutions that have restrictions on performance. In these cases, there are alternatives to be explored to minimize the impact of cold-start latency, such as the use of requests to warm-up containers during periods of application use. More advanced techniques can be used, such as the use of time series forecasting to determine the periods of use of an application and the appropriate pre-allocation of resources, as studied in [9].

4.4 Resources for Research Reproduction

This work uses tools such as Docker and Terraform to improve research reproducibility. Nevertheless, the following resources are provided as supplementary material to the results:

- Public repository with source code on GitHub: The repository[1] contains code for provisioning infrastructure, building images, and also performing experiments and analyzing them. Additionally, all experiment results are present in the repository as CSV files.
- Public Docker image repository: All images used for the experiments are present in a public repository[2].
- Documentation: In the public GitHub repository, there is a file called `README.md`, containing instructions on how to use tools such as Docker and Terraform for generating images and provisioning the infrastructures used in this work.

5   Conclusion and Future Work

In this work, a solution for deploying deep learning models for detecting diabetic retinopathy in the cloud was implemented. For this, the Amazon Sagemaker serverless inference service was used.

Based on serverless computing, it was possible to deploy the models in a low-cost, on-demand solution without the need to provision and configure instances for the execution of the algorithms. As demonstrated in this work, this alternative suffers from high latencies in cases of cold-start, which can be up to 57× higher than the latency in the warm-up case.

---

[1] Link to GitHub: https://github.com/MatheusWoeffel/dr-detection-deploy.
[2] Link to ECR: https://gallery.ecr.aws/g1e7s9u4/dr-detection-deploy.

To mitigate this problem, it was shown that it is possible to reduce cold-start latency by reducing Docker image size and selecting the correct memory configuration, increasing performance up to 2.13×. Moreover, optimizing the memory configuration of the endpoints also brought performance gains for the normal latency case, improving performance by up to 2.35× and reducing the financial cost by 9.34%.

As demonstrated, the optimizations and alternatives explored behaved differently depending on the models' size. In this sense, a topic for future study is the use of neural network quantization techniques and the analysis of the consequences in terms of performance and financial cost of the solutions studied in this work, evaluated in the optimized models. Given the medical context of the application, it will also be necessary to carefully analyze the impact of quantization techniques on the accuracy and sensitivity of the models.

Another improvement topic is using different architectures to perform model inference. In addition to using CPUs, as researched in this work, it would be interesting to use instances with specific purpose processors destined to optimize the execution of inferences. For example, instances of the `inf1` type stand out, which use *systolic arrays* to optimize the computation of matrix multiplication, an important operation present in the execution of inference models.

Acknowledgment. This study was partially supported by the Coordenação de Aperfeiçoamento de Pessoal de Nível Superior – Brasil (CAPES) – Finance Code 001, by Petrobras grant n.° 2020/00182-5, by CNPq/MCTI/FNDCT - Universal 18/2021 under grants 406182/2021-3, by CIARS RITEs/FAPERGS project and by CI-IA FAPESP-MCTIC-CGI-BR project.

References

1. Baldini, I., et al.: Serverless computing: current trends and open problems. In: Chaudhary, S., Somani, G., Buyya, R. (eds.) Research Advances in Cloud Computing, pp. 1–20. Springer, Singapore (2017). https://doi.org/10.1007/978-981-10-5026-8_1
2. Bhat, S.: Understanding the dockerfile. In: Bhat, S. (ed.) Practical Docker with Python: Build, Release, and Distribute Your Python App with Docker, pp. 61–103. Springer, Cham (2022). https://doi.org/10.1007/978-1-4842-7815-4_4
3. Bidari, I., Chickerur, S., Kulkarni, A., Mahajan, A., Nikkam, A., Abhishek, T.: Deploying machine learning inference on diabetic retinopathy in binary and multiclass classification. In: 2021 International Conference on Industrial Electronics Research and Applications (ICIERA), pp. 1–6. IEEE (2021)
4. Dai, L., et al.: A deep learning system for detecting diabetic retinopathy across the disease spectrum. Nat. Commun. **12**(1), 1–11 (2021)
5. International Diabetes Federation: IDF Diabetes Atlas. International Diabetes Federation, Brussels, Belgium (2021)
6. Gardner, J.: The web server gateway interface (WSGI). In: The Definitive Guide to Pylons, pp. 369–388 (2009)
7. Ishakian, V., Muthusamy, V., Slominski, A.: Serving deep learning models in a serverless platform. In: 2018 IEEE International Conference on Cloud Engineering (IC2E), pp. 257–262. IEEE (2018)

8. Janardhanan, P.: Project repositories for machine learning with TensorFlow. Procedia Comput. Sci. **171**, 188–196 (2020)
9. Jegannathan, A.P., Saha, R., Addya, S.K.: A time series forecasting approach to minimize cold start time in cloud-serverless platform. In: 2022 IEEE International Black Sea Conference on Communications and Networking (BlackSeaCom), pp. 325–330. IEEE (2022)
10. Karthik, Maggie, Sohier Dane: Aptos 2019 blindness detection (2019). https://kaggle.com/competitions/aptos2019-blindness-detection
11. Lathkar, M.: Getting started with FastAPI. In: Lathkar, M. (ed.) High-Performance Web Apps with FastAPI: The Asynchronous Web Framework Based on Modern Python, pp. 29–64. Springer, Cham (2023). https://doi.org/10.1007/978-1-4842-9178-8_2
12. Liberty, E., et al.: Elastic machine learning algorithms in amazon SageMaker. In: Proceedings of the 2020 ACM SIGMOD International Conference on Management of Data, pp. 731–737 (2020)
13. Liew, G., Michaelides, M., Bunce, C.: A comparison of the causes of blindness certifications in England and wales in working age adults (16–64 years), 1999–2000 with 2009–2010. BMJ Open **4**(2), e004015 (2014)
14. Moreira, F., Schaan, B., Schneiders, J., Reis, M., Serpa, M., Navaux, P.: Impacto da resolução na detecção de retinopatia diabética com uso de deep learning. In: Anais do XX Simpósio Brasileiro de Computação Aplicada à Saúde, Porto Alegre, RS, Brasil, pp. 494–499. SBC (2020). https://doi.org/10.5753/sbcas.2020.11546. https://sol.sbc.org.br/index.php/sbcas/article/view/11546
15. Nedelcu, C.: Nginx HTTP Server. Packt Publishing (2013)
16. Pavate, A., Mistry, J., Palve, R., Gami, N.: Diabetic retinopathy detection-MobileNet binary classifier. Acta Sci. Med. Sci. **4**(12), 86–91 (2020)
17. Pretty, D., Blackwell, B., et al.: H1DS: a new web-based data access system. Fusion Eng. Des. **89**(5), 731–735 (2014)
18. Shafiei, H., Khonsari, A., Mousavi, P.: Serverless computing: a survey of opportunities, challenges, and applications. ACM Comput. Surv. **54**(11s), 1–32 (2022)
19. Tu, Z., Li, M., Lin, J.: Pay-per-request deployment of neural network models using serverless architectures. In: Proceedings of the 2018 Conference of the North American Chapter of the Association for Computational Linguistics: Demonstrations, pp. 6–10 (2018)

The Survey of Self-driving Car Challenges in Smart City Infrastructures

Nataliia Kulabukhova[✉]

Independent Researcher, Saint Petersburg, Russia
kulabukhova.nv@gmail.com

Abstract. The article provides an overview of the current situation of interaction between self-driving cars and a smart city. We will look at what successes have been achieved in the adaptation of autonomous vehicle in the context of smart urban mobility. Will speak about unmanned logistic corridors and autodata question. A small comparative analysis of various approaches for solving problems in this direction is given.

Keywords: self-driving cars · autonomous vehicle · smart cities

1 Introduction

This article is primarily aimed to give the reader an idea of what areas for research in the field of autonomous vehicles exist at the moment and how they connect with the smart city infrastructure. To a greater extent, the article deals with problems related to their technical development, and The issues of regulatory and ethical concerns are beyond the scope of the paper, since quite a lot of articles have already been submitted on this topic.

Before speaking about Vehicle-to-Everything communications and Big Data problems of self-driving cars let take a brief view on the connection of different concepts, related to self-driving and its infrastructure. The topics we will speak about in the next subsections shown on the Fig. 1.

1.1 Urban Mobility

Urban mobility refers to the movement of people and goods in urban areas. With the growing population and increasing urbanization, mobility has become a significant issue in cities. Some of the key features of urban mobility are:

Multimodal Transport: Urban mobility is not limited to a single mode of transportation. It involves different means of transport such as walking, cycling, public transport, and personal vehicles. A well-integrated multimodal transport system can improve the efficiency of urban mobility.

Accessibility: Urban mobility aims to provide convenient and easy accessibility to all parts of the city. This includes not only physical access but also ease of payment, information, and communication.

O. Gervasi et al. (Eds.): ICCSA 2023 Workshops, LNCS 14109, pp. 290–301, 2023.
https://doi.org/10.1007/978-3-031-37120-2_19

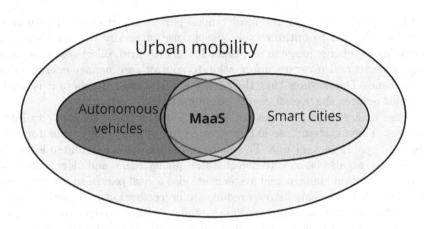

Fig. 1. Connection between Self-driving and Urban mobility

Safety: Urban mobility should ensure safety for all users, including pedestrians, cyclists, public transport users, and personal vehicle users. This includes implementing safety measures such as proper road markings, traffic signals, and pedestrian crossings.

Sustainability: Urban mobility needs to be sustainable to ensure the long-term well-being of the city and its residents. This includes reducing carbon emissions, promoting public transport, and encouraging active modes of transportation such as cycling and walking.

Intelligent Mobility: The use of technology in urban mobility can help improve efficiency and reduce congestion. Intelligent transport systems can provide real-time information about congestion, parking, and public transport schedules, enabling users to make informed decisions.

Overall, urban mobility is a complex and interconnected system that requires integrated planning and coordination to ensure efficient, safe, and sustainable transportation.

1.2   Smart City Infrastructures

Smart city infrastructures are the backbone of the modern cities that cater to the needs of the population in a smart way. The infrastructure consists of various technological interventions such as smart energy grids, water management systems, transportation management systems, and other smart services that make life in the city more sustainable and convenient. The smart city infrastructure is built on a framework of Internet of Things (IoT) devices, sensors, and data analytics.

Smart energy grids are the most crucial part of smart city infrastructures. They are designed to optimize the efficient use of energy by monitoring and controlling the energy usage in real-time. The energy grid collects data on energy usage patterns and uses this information to control and manage energy supply and demand. This ensures that the energy is distributed to where it is needed most and reduces the overall energy consumption.

Water management systems are also an essential part of smart city infrastructures. These systems use IoT devices and data analytics to monitor water usage and quality in real-time. This helps to reduce water loss due to leaks, and the systems can also be used to detect water quality issues and alert authorities.

Transportation management systems are also a vital part of smart city infrastructures. These systems help to reduce traffic congestion and improve public transportation services. Smart parking systems are used to optimize the supply and demand of parking spaces, while smart traffic lights improve the flow of traffic on roads.

Other smart services include waste management systems, which use IoT devices to monitor waste generation and collect data on the waste's composition. This helps to optimize waste collection and disposal and reduce the overall amount of waste generated by the city.

Overall, smart city infrastructures are designed to optimize the use of resources, reduce the impact of the city on the environment, and make life in the city more sustainable and convenient for its residents. As technology continues to advance, we can expect to see even more innovative and efficient solutions being developed to improve the quality of life in the cities of the future.

1.3   Mobility-as-a-Service

Mobility-as-a-Service, also known as MaaS, is a fast-growing transportation concept that offers a range of alternative transport solutions in a single platform. MaaS aims to provide customers with simplified access to various modes of transportation, including public transport, ride-sharing, bike-sharing, car-sharing, and other mobility services.

As the demand for more efficient transportation grows, MaaS has become increasingly popular among commuters, especially in urban areas. Below are the seven steps to MaaS:

1. **Integrating different modes of transportation.** To deliver an efficient MaaS solution, different modes of transportation, including public transit, car-sharing, bike-sharing, ride-hailing, and others, need to be integrated onto a single platform.
2. **Verification of users.** People who use MaaS must be verified to ensure accuracy and security. Users' identity verification is necessary when registering for MaaS services through an app.
3. **Reservation and booking.** MaaS integrates with third-party solutions that offer reservations and booking services across various modes of transportation.

4. **Routing and scheduling.** Real-time routing and scheduling are key components of MaaS solutions. Commuters need to be connected to their ultimate destination or next mode of transportation in the shortest, most efficient way for the mode of transportation they choose.

5. **Payment and billing.** MaaS solutions provide automated payments options for customers via subscription, or per-transaction-basis. By removing the need for separate transactions for each mode of transportation, it reduces the hassle and expense of multiple payments.

6. **Customer service and support.** To provide excellent customer service it's essential that queries and concerns are addressed on time. Customer support and feedback options, along with the provision of emergency safety features, are crucial aspects of MaaS.

7. **Data and analytics.** MaaS solutions use the wealth of transactional data generated by users, which helps maximize efficiency of the overall system by analyzing key metrics such as usage patterns, means of payments, and so on. This is essential in delivering an improved customer experience and minimizing costs.

Overall, Mobility-as-a-Service is revolutionizing how people commute across urban environments. By leveraging technology to integrate multiple transport modes, MaaS offers customers flexibility, convenience, and cost-effective travel.

1.4   Self-driving Cars

Self-driving cars are vehicles that operate autonomously without human input. They use a combination of sensors, cameras, and algorithms to interpret and respond to their environment. There are different levels of autonomy in self-driving cars, ranging from partial automation, where the driver is still responsible for some aspects of driving, to full automation, where the car can handle all aspects of driving without any human intervention.

The potential benefits of self-driving cars include improved safety, increased mobility for people who cannot drive, and reduced traffic congestion. However, there are also concerns about the ethical and legal implications of self-driving cars, as well as the potential loss of jobs for drivers.

Despite some pilot programs and developmental testing, self-driving cars are not widely available for public use yet. There are still many technical and regulatory challenges that need to be addressed before self-driving cars can become a reality for everyday drivers.

- Self-driving cars can potentially increase safety on the road, as they eliminate the human error factor.
- In a smart city, self-driving cars can communicate with each other and with the city infrastructure, optimizing traffic flow and reducing congestion.
- Self-driving cars can also reduce the need for parking, as they can drop off passengers and find a parking spot elsewhere, thus freeing up space in crowded urban areas.

– However, implementing self-driving cars in a smart city requires a significant amount of investment in infrastructure, sensors, and communication technology. It also raises questions about privacy, cybersecurity, and the possible displacement of human drivers.

1.5   Self-driving Projects over the World

There are a number of companies working on self-driving cars today [1, 18–22] (see Fig. 2).

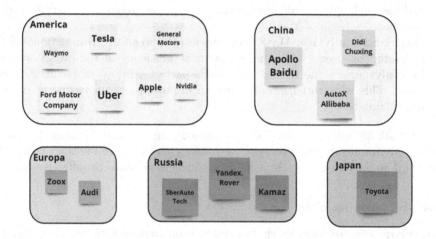

Fig. 2. Self-driving projects over the world

Self-driving car technology has been developing rapidly over the past decade, with major players such as Tesla [2], Google [3], and Uber [4] investing heavily in this field. However, these companies have different approaches and goals for their self-driving car projects.

Tesla's self-driving car technology is based on its Autopilot system, which includes radar, cameras, and ultrasonic sensors. It is designed to assist drivers rather than completely take over the driving experience. Tesla's goal is to develop fully autonomous cars, but the company has faced controversies over the safety of its Autopilot system after multiple accidents.

Google's self-driving car project, Waymo, uses a combination of radar, cameras, and lidar sensors to create a 3D map of the environment around the vehicle. Waymo aims to develop a fully autonomous car that can safely navigate any road condition. The company has been testing its cars in several cities and has already launched a ride-hailing service in Arizona.

Uber's self-driving car project uses a similar system to Waymo, but with an added focus on building a ride-hailing service. Uber's goal is to develop a fleet of autonomous cars that can replace human drivers. However, the program has faced setbacks after a fatal accident involving a self-driving Uber vehicle in 2018.

Other companies such as General Motors, Ford, and Nissan have also invested in self-driving car technology. General Motors' Cruise Automation has been testing its autonomous cars in San Francisco, and the company has plans to launch a commercial ride-hailing service in 2023. Ford is working on its self-driving car technology with Argo AI, and the company has plans to launch a fully autonomous vehicle in 2021. Nissan's ProPilot system [5] is designed to assist drivers on highways and in dense, urban environments.

While each company has its own goals and approaches, the development of self-driving car technology is expected to revolutionize the transportation industry. Fully autonomous vehicles could greatly reduce the number of accidents caused by human error and create new opportunities for ride-sharing services.

2 Challenges of Self-driving Cars in Smart City

As urban populations continue to grow, Smart Cities are emerging as a solution to tackle the rising environmental, social and economic challenges. Smart City infrastructure is built around the idea of using technology to create an efficient and sustainable environment for its citizens. One such technological advancement that has been making waves in recent years is self-driving cars. However, this innovation comes with its own set of challenges that need to be addressed before they can become a common sight in Smart Cities [6].

Several surveys have been conducted to identify the challenges that need to be overcome before self-driving cars can become mainstream in Smart Cities. These challenges range from technology issues to regulatory and ethical concerns. One of the biggest challenges is the need for technology upgrades in existing infrastructure. Smart Cities require high-speed communication networks and real-time data processing capabilities that can support the complex algorithms used by self-driving cars. Without these upgrades, self-driving cars will struggle to operate efficiently in such an environment.

Another key challenge is the issue of cybersecurity [7]. With the amount of sensitive data collected by self-driving cars, there is a real risk of cyber-attacks. It is crucial that cybersecurity measures are put in place to ensure the safety of the passengers and the system as a whole.

Regulatory and ethical concerns are also major obstacles that self-driving cars will face. There is a need for consistent regulations across different cities and countries to ensure the safety and reliability of the technology. Additionally, ethical concerns such as the decision-making process in case of an emergency need to be addressed to ensure that the technology is morally acceptable.

Next we will speak about technical map of communications between self-driving cars and smart city infrastructure.

3   Vehicle-to-Everything Communications

Vehicle-to-everything (V2X) communications is a wireless technology that allows vehicles to communicate with everything around them, including other vehicles, pedestrians, cyclists, and infrastructure such as traffic signals and road signs [17]. The picture 3 shows the main objects of V2X communications. It uses dedicated short-range communication (DSRC) technology to send and receive data between different types of devices.

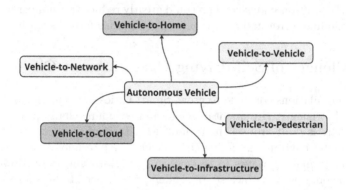

Fig. 3. V2X communications map

There are two types of V2X communications: Vehicle-to-Vehicle (V2V) and Vehicle-to-Infrastructure (V2I). V2V communications enable vehicles to exchange information in real-time to improve safety and efficiency. This includes data on vehicle location, speed, acceleration, and deceleration. V2I communications allow vehicles to communicate with infrastructure such as traffic lights and road signs to provide drivers with real-time information, such as the optimal speed to approach an intersection or the presence of construction or accidents.

Overall, V2X communications can improve road safety and reduce traffic congestion by providing drivers with real-time information and warnings of potential hazards. It is also an essential technology for the development of autonomous vehicles.

Several existing frameworks have been established to assist in the implementation and deployment of V2X technology [23]. These frameworks provide a standardized approach for the development of V2X systems and enable interoperability between different systems. Here are some examples of existing frameworks in V2X technology:

1. Dedicated Short-Range Communications (DSRC): This is a wireless communication technology designed specifically for V2X applications. It operates in the 5.9 GHz frequency band and enables high-speed data exchange between vehicles and infrastructure.

2. Cellular V2X (C-V2X): This is a cellular-based V2X technology that uses existing cellular networks to transfer data. C-V2X has two modes of communication; direct communication (PC5) and network communication. Direct communication allows vehicles to communicate directly with each other, while network communication facilitates communication between vehicles and infrastructure.
3. European Telecommunications Standards Institute (ETSI) ITS: ETSI ITS provides a framework for the development of intelligent transport systems (ITS) in Europe. The framework covers V2V and V2I communication and includes standards for data exchange, network management, and security.
4. IEEE 802.11p: This standard defines a wireless communication protocol for V2X applications. It operates in the 5.9 GHz frequency band and enables high-speed data exchange between vehicles and infrastructure.
5. Society of Automotive Engineers (SAE) J2735: This standard defines a message set for V2X communication. It includes a set of messages for basic safety applications (BSM), such as collision avoidance and emergency vehicle alerts.

These frameworks provide a foundation for the development and implementation of V2X technology. As the technology continues to evolve, it is expected that these frameworks will evolve as well to accommodate new applications and technologies.

Vehicle-to-Everything (V2X) communication is an emerging technology that connects vehicles with infrastructure, pedestrians, and other vehicles through communication systems. V2X communication is poised to not only transform the automotive industry, but also to improve safety, efficiency and functionality in transportation. This review aims to evaluate the current state of the art in V2X communication.

Speaking about recent advances in V2X Communication, according to Elektrobit Automotive GmbH researchers, a new communication network called the Cellular V2X (C-V2X) has emerged recently, which has a high potential to change the existing communication paradigm. C-V2X is based on cellular networks and provides a reliable, low-latency, and high-bandwidth communication for V2X applications. C-V2X has been successfully tested in various countries, especially in China, where the technology has been adopted for use in smart cities.

In addition, in [8–10] conducted a study on cyber-physical vehicle networks. The authors developed a system to analyze and assess the communication link quality between vehicles during platoon movement, which resulted in significant improvements in communication efficiency. The authors proposed a unique encryption method for securing V2X communication, which can ensure the integrity of the message and prevent cyberattacks from malicious users.

Another research articles [11,12] proposed a new approach to vehicle-to-vehicle (V2V) communication using a road-to-vehicle (R2V) communication model. The authors showed that this approach has the potential to reduce the communication overhead of V2V communication, and improve V2V communication performance.

Furthermore, in works [13,14] developed a new communication protocol for V2X communication. The authors performed experimental studies to demonstrate the proposed protocol's increased efficiency in comparison to traditional IEEE802.11p standard, which currently serves as the basis for V2X communication.

Research by [15,16] showed that machine learning algorithms can be used in V2X communication to improve communication efficiency. The authors presented an adaptive modulation and coding scheme that employs machine learning algorithms, and demonstrated that the proposed method improves communication throughput by 25% compared to traditional methods.

In conclusion, V2X communication technology is continuously evolving. The review highlighted the recent advances in V2X communication, such as the use of cellular networks, cyber-physical vehicle networks, R2V communication model, new communication protocols, and machine learning algorithms. These innovations in V2X communication have led to improved communication efficiency, increased reliability, and enhanced cybersecurity, which will ultimately lead to safer and more efficient transportation systems.

4   Data Aspects

Data collection in self-driving cars is essential for their functioning. Self-driving cars collect data from various sensors, such as lidar, cameras, radar, and GPS. The data collected is used to create a real-time 3D map of the car's surroundings. The amount of data collected by self-driving cars is massive, with some cars collecting up to 4 terabytes of data per day. The data collected is used to improve the accuracy and reliability of the car's decision-making process. Data collected from self-driving cars is analyzed using machine learning algorithms to improve their performance. The collected data can help self-driving cars learn from past experiences and avoid mistakes in the future. The data collected is highly sensitive and must be secured to prevent unauthorized access. The collected data can be shared with regulators and researchers to improve the overall safety of self-driving cars. Large tech companies and traditional automakers are investing heavily in collecting and analyzing data from self-driving cars. The accuracy and reliability of self-driving cars are directly proportional to the amount and quality of data collected. Self-driving car companies use simulation to collect additional data to improve their algorithms' performance. Self-driving car companies collaborate with each other to share data and improve each other's technology. The collected data can be used to create detailed maps of roads, including lane markings, traffic signs, and road conditions. Self-driving cars must collect a wide variety of data, including weather conditions and pedestrian traffic. The data collected from self-driving cars is invaluable for improving traffic flow and reducing congestion. Self-driving car companies must comply with laws and regulations governing data privacy and security. The collected data must be stored securely and accessible only to authorized personnel. The data collected can be used to improve other autonomous technologies outside of the automotive industry.

The data collected can also be used to improve urban planning, public transportation, and infrastructure management. The life circle of data shown on Fig. 4.

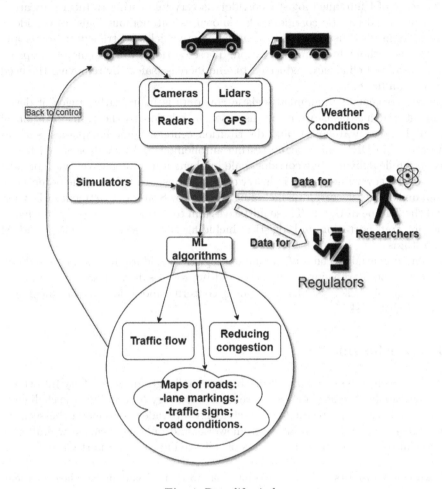

Fig. 4. Data life circle

Autodata is a popular software program used in the automotive industry. It provides information on a wide range of vehicle makes and models, including repair and maintenance procedures, service schedules, wiring diagrams, and technical specifications. Autodata is widely used by mechanics, automotive technicians, and other professionals who work with cars and trucks. It is designed to simplify the access and use of technical data by offering a variety of user-friendly features. Autodata includes thousands of pages of repair and diagnosis information that is continually updated to keep pace with changes in the automotive industry.

5   Future Research - Autonomous Trucks and Delivery

The topic of Unmanned logistic corridors is very interesting to future research.

Unmanned logistic corridors, also known as autonomous logistics corridors, are systems that use intelligent, autonomous vehicles to transport goods and materials without human intervention. These corridors are designed to improve transportation efficiency, reduce costs, and increase safety by removing the need for human drivers.

The concept of unmanned logistic corridors is in its early stages of development and has been primarily discussed in relation to the transportation of goods between warehouses and distribution centers. Some companies, such as Amazon and DHL, have begun testing autonomous delivery drones and trucks for last-mile delivery, but corridor-scale implementation is not yet widespread.

Several governments and industry organizations are exploring the potential of unmanned logistic corridors, including the United States Department of Defense and the European Union. These initiatives aim to develop cutting-edge technologies for transportation and logistics, including advanced sensors, GPS, and AI algorithms.

The potential benefits of unmanned logistic corridors include increased efficiency, reduced transportation costs, and improved safety. However, the implementation of these systems also raises concerns about job displacement and cybersecurity risks.

6   Conclusion

In conclusion, the survey of self-driving car challenges in Smart City infrastructures highlights the need for a comprehensive strategy to overcome the challenges associated with this technology. Technology upgrades, stronger cybersecurity measures, ethical and regulatory frameworks and public education will all play a crucial role in ensuring the success of self-driving cars in Smart Cities.

Acknowledgements. The author would like to thank Vladimir Korkhov for useful advices for the opportunity to work on this theme.

References

1. Chinas Autonomous Driving Industry - An Introduction for Foreign Investors. https://www.china-briefing.com/news/investing-in-chinas-self-driving-car-market/
2. https://www.tesla.com/
3. https://waymo.com/
4. https://www.uber.com/blog/our-road-to-self-driving-vehicles/
5. https://www.nissan-global.com/EN/INNOVATION/TECHNOLOGY/ARCHIVE/PROPILOT/

6. Autonomous Driving Cars in Smart Cities: Recent Advances, Requirements, and Challenges. https://www.researchgate.net/publication/333078814_Autonomous_Driving_Cars_in_Smart_Cities_Recent_Advances_Requirements_and_Challenges
7. Smart Cities: A New Look at the Autonomous-Vehicle Infrastructure. https://medium.com/swlh/smart-cities-a-new-look-at-the-autonomous-vehicle-infrastructure-3e00cf3e93b2
8. Fallah, Y.P., Sengupta, R.: A cyber-physical systems approach to the design of vehicle safety networks. https://doi.org/10.1109/ICDCSW.2012.81. https://www.researchgate.net/publication/261478807_A_Cyber-physical_Systems_Approach_to_the_Design_of_Vehicle_Safety_Networks
9. Guzman, J.A., Nunez, F.: A cyber-physical systems approach to collaborative intersection management and control. https://doi.org/10.1109/ACCESS.2021.3096330. https://www.researchgate.net/publication/353198337_A_Cyber-Physical_Systems_Approach_to_Collaborative_Intersection_Management_and_Control
10. Wan, J., Zhang, D., Zhao, S., Lloret, J., Yang, L.T.: Context-aware vehicular cyber-physical systems with cloud support: architecture, challenges, and solutions. https://doi.org/10.1109/MCOM.2014.6871677. https://www.researchgate.net/publication/264561683_Context-Aware_Vehicular_Cyber-Physical_Systems_with_Cloud_Support_Architecture_Challenges_and_Solutions
11. Hasan, S.F., Siddique, N.: Modelling R2V communications: description, analysis and challenges. https://doi.org/10.1504/IJVICS.2011.044264. https://www.researchgate.net/publication/264438632_Modelling_R2V_communications_Description_analysis_and_challenges
12. Hu, B., Gharavi, H.: A joint vehicle-vehicle/vehicle-roadside communication protocol for highway traffic safety. https://doi.org/10.1155/2011/718048
13. Alnasser, A., Sun, H., Jiang, J.: Cyber Security Challenges and Solutions for V2X Communications: A Survey. https://www.researchgate.net/publication/330185917_Cyber_Security_Challenges_and_Solutions_for_V2X_Communications_A_Survey
14. Wang, T., et al.: Design and performance evaluation of V2X communication protocol based on Nakagami-m outage probability. J. Ambient. Intell. Humaniz. Comput. 12(10), 9405–9421 (2020). https://doi.org/10.1007/s12652-020-02661-0
15. Zhang, L., Wu, Z.: Machine learning-based adaptive modulation and coding design. https://doi.org/10.1002/9781119562306.ch9. https://www.researchgate.net/publication/337931452_Machine_Learning-Based_Adaptive_Modulation_and_Coding_Design
16. Huang, L., et al.: Adaptive modulation and coding in underwater acoustic communications: a machine learning perspective. EURASIP J. Wirel. Commun. Netw. 2020(1), 1–25 (2020). https://doi.org/10.1186/s13638-020-01818-x
17. Improving Self-Driving Car Safety and Reliability with V2X Protocols. https://medium.com/self-driving-cars/improving-self-driving-car-safety-and-reliability-with-v2x-protocols-1408082bae54
18. https://zoox.com/about/
19. https://aurora.tech/company
20. https://www.autox.ai/en/index.html
21. https://sdg.yandex.com/
22. Yandex Introduces Its Fourth-Generation of Self-Driving Cars. https://medium.com/yandex-self-driving-car/yandex-introduces-its-fourth-generation-of-self-driving-cars-9fa2ba7ca7cd
23. Overview and comparison of V2X technologies (in Russian). https://itnan.ru/post.php?c=1&p=477826

New Security Challenges of Internet of Things

Gennady Dik[1,3]([✉]), Alexander Bogdanov[1,2], Nadezhda Shchegoleva[1,2], Jasur Kiyamov[1], and Aleksandr Dik[1]

[1] St. Petersburg University, Saint Petersburg, Russia
{a.v.bogdanov,n.shchegoleva,z.kiyamov,a.dik}@spbu.ru
[2] St. Petersburg State Marine Technical University, Saint Petersburg, Russia
[3] St. Petersburg LLC "System Technologies", Saint Petersburg, Russia
g.dick@systechnologies.ru

Abstract. The paper addresses current security issues of the Internet of Things (IoT), analyzes the most recent and significant violations in this area, proposes a variant of an integrated approach both to protecting the IoT devices themselves and to promising methods organization of interaction using 5G (6G) networks. Particular attention is paid to the process of threat modeling in assessing IoT security, as well as the application of machine learning (ML) principles in order to ensure the protection of the infrastructure of the Internet of things. Practical recommendations are given for organizing measures to improve the security of promising IoT networks.

Keywords: IoT · Smart Habitat · IT-System · 5G · 6G

1 Introduction

In the modern world, IoT devices are not only computers and TVs, tablets and smartphones, smart watches and kitchen appliances, etc. Almost all electronic devices involved in our daily lives can potentially be connected to a single computer network and become part of the Internet of things. The information circulating in this network contains huge amounts of not only information about its owners, but also data of varying degrees of confidentiality, including control signals, status messages, etc. All this data can be either stolen by intruders or distorted for criminal purposes, and IoT devices can be hacked or turned into a non-working "brick". As a result, an increase in the number of IoT devices produced and connected inevitably leads to an increase in the ability of cybercriminals to violate IT security, including the security of the Internet of Things [1].

2 Relevance of IoT Security Threats

The security breach of the Internet of Things can eventually have quite serious and sometimes catastrophic consequences. Attackers can hack and then gain

© The Author(s), under exclusive license to Springer Nature Switzerland AG 2023
O. Gervasi et al. (Eds.): ICCSA 2023 Workshops, LNCS 14109, pp. 302–316, 2023.
https://doi.org/10.1007/978-3-031-37120-2_20

access to a drone or any vehicle controlled via IoT, reconfigure their functionality, security system, etc. Hacking the IoT devices of Smart Homes, Smart Cities and Smart Habitats (SH) will allow cybercriminals to control people's living environment. In medicine and healthcare, in financial institutions (banks) and telephone companies, the access of intruders to the Internet things used in these areas will lead to the disclosure and dissemination of personal (confidential) information about the patient, client, subscriber. In addition, disruption of the functioning of medical devices, banking equipment and equipment of telephone operators leads not only to a deterioration in the quality of life, but also to serious threats to its existence. Cyber attacks on industrial or military Internet of Things systems can lead to a number of irreversible destructive consequences (Fig. 1).

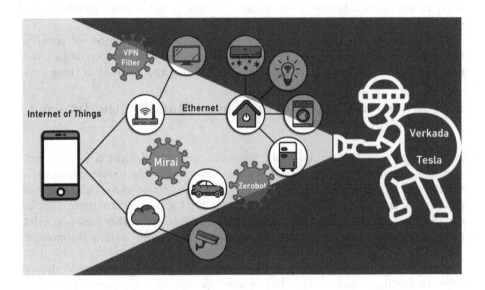

Fig. 1. IoT security breaches

According to a study by Kaspersky Lab JSC, in recent years there have been a number of high-profile cases of compromise of Internet of Things devices by cybercriminals, namely [2]:

- 2016 - Mirai botnet attack, when hundreds of thousands of compromised pluggable devices were involved in the botnet to perform malicious activities such as registration, emulation of "interested client" actions, password theft, and more. The Mirai botnet attack disrupted major services and websites such as Spotify, Netflix and PayPal.
- 2018 - VPNFilter malware infects about half a million routers in more than 50 countries, while VPNFilter malware can be installed on devices connected to the router, and then using malware, collect passing information, block network traffic and steal passwords.

- 2020 - Tesla Model X hack, when a cybersecurity expert hacked a Tesla Model X car in less than two minutes using a Bluetooth vulnerability, which, according to experts, applies to other car models using wireless access.
- 2021 - Verkada video camera hack (Verkada is a surveillance camera company), when Swiss hackers gained access to 150,000 live feeds including cameras at Tesla factories and warehouses, Cloudflare offices, Equinox gyms, hospitals, prisons, schools, police stations and Verkada's own offices.
- 2022 - the attack of the Zerobot botnet, which spreads through the exploitation of almost two dozen vulnerabilities in IoT devices and various software (including F5 BIG-IP, Zyxel firewalls, Totolink and D-Link routers, and Hikvision cameras) [3].

The above list of attacks by intruders on IoT (and this is a very small selective part) clearly demonstrates the seriousness of the possible consequences for all spheres of life in the modern world.

Thus, this is not only a matter of IT security, it is a matter of ensuring the security of all aspects of the life of modern society. To understand it, it is necessary to consider the basic principles of building the Internet of things.

3   Purpose and Basic Principles of Building the Internet of Things

In public opinion there is no exact generally accepted definition for the term "Internet of Things" [4]. At the same time, according to the recommendation of the International Electronics Union (ITU), IoT is understood as a global infrastructure for the information society, which enables the provision of more complex services by connecting (physical and virtual) things to each other based on existing and developing interoperable information and communication technologies (ICT) [5].

Thus, the Internet of Things is a network of things, where the word "things" refers to intelligent objects that have embedded electronics, sensors and embedded technologies for interacting with the external environment with the ability to transmit data about their current state and receive data from outside [5]. To implement their functionality, these "things" are equipped with general software (software), which includes an operating system and other general-purpose software tools that are not focused on solving problems of any particular subject area. They also have special software (SW) installed on them, which includes programs that implement the selected functions of the system, and is developed on the basis of common software. The article deals with the issue of using open source software, since general software is usually standardized and universal. Expanding the capabilities of IoT devices allows us to define the "Internet of Things" as a computer network of physical objects equipped with built-in technologies for collecting and transmitting information in conjunction with devices and technologies for storing and intelligently processing information, as well as devices and algorithms for generating control actions on parts or the entire system generally.

The theory and practice of using the Internet of things shows that their main purpose is to improve the quality of life of the population, to make the process of people's life more dynamic and convenient. These circumstances eventually led to an explosive growth in the use of IoT devices. According to Cisco analysts, by the end of 2023, on average, each person in Russia will have more than six connected devices operating online (for example, a computer, mobile phone, smartphone, phablet and tablet, a smart home control device, a device for monitoring health indicators, etc.) [6, 7].

For the full functionality of IoT, it is necessary to first define (identify) the object, and then involve it in an ever-expanding circle of network connections. The Internet of Things is inherently a continuous flow of data in space, passing through different networks around, which leads to the emergence of the so-called "web of things". The functioning of this "web" is possible under the following two conditions [8]:

1. mandatory identification of each specific object from the IoT;
2. continuous switching of the growing volume of information and objects in the network, which, in turn, will also be combined in the network.

At the same time, the implementation of IoT technology is carried out by the following functional components (ABCDE-components) [9] (Fig. 2):

1. **Analytics** – is designed to analyze information coming from data collection devices (sensors, controllers, video cameras, etc.). Based on the processing results, control signals are generated for IoT devices. Analytical platforms (SSW modules), depending on the complexity of information processing and its volume, can be installed locally, in the cloud, or have a hybrid version of their placement.
2. **Big Data** – in this context, it is a distributed database designed to organize the storage of all primary (raw) and processed information on the involved IoT [10].
3. **Connection** is a combination of ICT options necessary for the functioning (all kinds of wired and wireless networks, various physical methods of connecting IoT devices, SPD protocols, switching devices, routing, signal amplification, etc., as well as switching open source software).
4. **Devices** – this is a set of devices designed for retrieving information, displaying it, issuing a control action, etc.
5. **Experience** – in the context of application for the Internet of things, it is considered as an option for using knowledge to build and improve IoT devices based on the accumulated "baggage" and further moving forward.

Based on the presented principles of functioning of the technology of the Internet of things (according to the designated functions and component construction), it is possible to determine the basic components of the IoT and the main ways to combine them into a single "web" or data transmission system (DTS). Then it is advisable to include the following main elements in the infrastructure construction of the Internet of Things (Fig. 3):

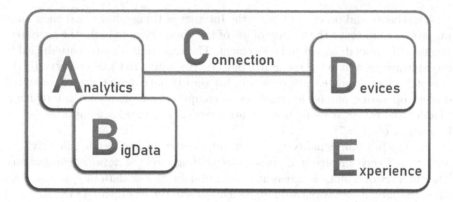

Fig. 2. Components of the implementation of the technology of the IoT

1. IoT devices - various types of sensors and various electronic devices connected to the DTS [11,12].
2. Information storage and processing systems - computer systems for collecting, processing, generating recommendations, reports, control actions, etc. [13].
3. Communication systems - wired and wireless networks, including equipment for their operation [8,14,15].
4. SSW - software designed to ensure the performance of IoT [16].

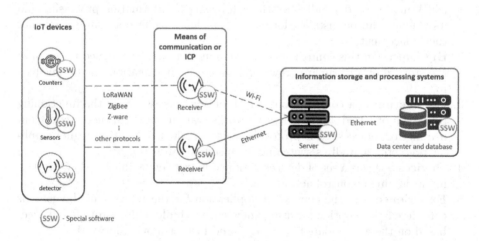

Fig. 3. IoT infrastructure

At the same time, possible integrations and combinations of the above-defined basic elements of the Internet of things should be taken into account (for example, modern video cameras may contain SSW for analytics and critical situations recognition and independently generate alarm signals and control actions). But it is precisely these basic elements of the IoT infrastructure that represent a "tasty" world of opportunities for attackers (hackers, cybercriminals) [17,18]. For this reason, further in the article, an analysis of possible security problems and existing IoT threats will be given in order to subsequently determine a set of measures to protect the Internet of Things.

4   Problem Analysis of Internet of Things Security Issues

Consideration of IoT security issues starts with the model of the Internet of Things. In accordance with the previously defined infrastructure for the interaction of smart things, a variant of the IoT reference model is presented in Fig. 4. This model contains four infrastructure layers:

- application layer;
- service support and application support layer;
- network layer;
- the level of IoT devices.

The process of functioning of the proposed levels provides managerial impacts, and the process of ensuring the security of the Internet of things: general in software and hardware.

The overall security of the Internet of things is aimed at solving current administrative, legal and other issues, that decrease in the security of IoT:

1. Lack of legislative acts, norms, as well as uniform standards, rules and instructions for IoT.
2. Saving of manufacturers on safety in the development and further implementation (release for sale) of smart things [19].
3. Lack of clearly defined physical or legal liability in the operation of the Internet of things [20].
4. The presence of "staff shortage" or a significant lack of experienced specialists in the field of IoT [21].
5. Dissemination (unintentional) of confidential information by users or maintenance personnel during operation, as well as employees during the creation of IoT.

There are known cases of publication in wide circles of technical information about IoT devices that have not yet switched to service. Employees fired or moving to other companies often become a source of "secrets".

As for the software and technical issues of ensuring the security of the Internet of things, they should include:

1. Compliance with security requirements at the stages of development, testing and implementation (release for sale) of software and hardware of IoT devices.

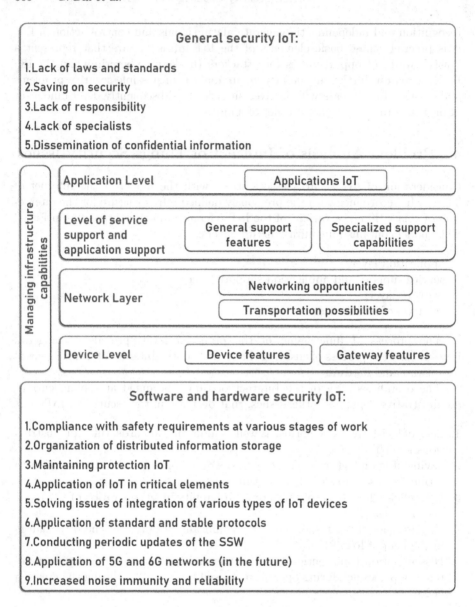

Fig. 4. Variant of the IoT Reference Model

2. Organization of distributed cloud, edge and hybrid storage of information on virtual machines for various IoT service providers so that data is not inaccessible or completely lost for everyone in the event of an attack by intruders on one service provider or IoT device.

3. Maintaining the protection of the Internet of Things in the face of an ever-expanding area of attacks on smart things, taking into account the improvement in the methods and speed of attacks on the IoT infrastructure.

4. Fulfillment of security requirements when using IoT in critical infrastructure elements of the industrial Internet of things (IIoT), in military systems (Battle IoT or BIoT), etc.

5. Compliance with security requirements when solving the issues of integration of various types of IoT devices, taking into account the complexity of the infrastructure construction and the diversity of the Internet of things.

6. The use of standard and stable developments in the construction of ICT, to exclude the use of both proprietary or less well-known protocols that do not meet security standards, and various methods of connecting devices through "crutches", etc.

7. Periodic updating of SSW, IoT "firmware" and ICT equipment (outdated software may contain not only errors and "security holes", but also has a high probability of being hacked by cybercriminals).

8. Improving the noise immunity and reliability of software and hardware in order to counter planned actions by intruders (crashes, failures, etc.).

9. Building ICT based on 5G networks, as well as working out the issue of using 6G networks as options for promising means of communication (hereinafter, the 5G communication standard is mainly considered).

Moreover, taking into account the peculiarities of the architecture and landscape of 5G (6G) networks, which include a large number of connections and high bandwidth, serious consequences of failures and abuses (cloud technology and a variety of services) and placement of equipment outside the protected circuit, it is necessary to plan the organization of protection at three levels [9]:

- The first level is protection at the level of implementing technical solutions, building network infrastructure and equipment placement options:
  • use of a powerful firewall between users and the outside world, multi-level isolation and integrity protection of SDN (Software-defined Networking) and VNF (Network Functions Virtualization) components - hypervisor, virtual machines, OS, controllers and containers;
  • application authentication in Mobile Edge Computing (MEC), use of an additional authentication factor when accessing the corporate network, whitelisting of devices and services, authorization of requests in the application programming interface (API);
  • ensuring high availability of virtual machines for fast recovery after attacks;
  • trusted hardware environment – safe booting of devices, application of TEE (Trusted Execution Environment) technology;
  • real-time attack detection on network nodes and virtual infrastructure elements using artificial intelligence algorithms.
- The second level is protection at the level of network infrastructure management:

- secure management of not only user data, but service, technical, analytical and other types of information involved in ensuring the functioning of the Internet of things (the so-called attack on the subscriber and attack on the mobile operator), using encryption, anonymization, depersonalization and etc.;
- centralized management of identified vulnerabilities, as well as policies and levels of information security, use of information in the course of ongoing analysis of big data to detect anomalies and promptly respond to attacks;
- comprehensive use of counterfeit base station detection tools based on real-time monitoring of operational and maintenance events;
- application of multi-factor authentication algorithms and organization of access differentiation to segments by O&M (Operations & Maintenance or Operation and Maintenance).
- Third level - protection at the level of the standard:
  - separation of the layers of the data transmission and reception protocol into three planes: User Plane, Control Plane, Management Plane. With complete isolation, encryption (of subscriber and signal traffic), and control of the integrity of these planes;
  - use of encryption methods for subscriber and technological traffic with an increase in the length of the encryption key up to 256 bits;
  - application of a unified subscriber authentication mechanism for various types of wireless communications;
  - support for flexible security policies for segments;
  - use of unified standards, etc. [9].

The implementation of the presented set of measures is a rather complicated and time-consuming task. This article proposes to consider the use of machine learning methods, which, as you know, can do what humans cannot, providing automation for large-scale analysis of possible threats and ways to protect. Thanks to ML, it is planned to solve a growing number of problems in the field of cybersecurity: scaling security solutions, detection of unknown attacks and detection of complex attacks, including polymorphic malware and other tasks [22]. When applying machine learning methods in the tasks of ensuring the protection of the Internet of Things infrastructure, it is proposed to carry out threat modeling in order to assess IoT security (according to one of the threat classification models).

5 Ways to Model IoT Threats

It should be noted that in the course of threat modeling, it is possible not only to identify attacks on IoT devices and rank risks according to their severity, but also to consider options for using machine learning methods to ensure the security of Internet of things. To do this, it is proposed to apply a software-oriented approach that targets the vulnerabilities of each application component, based on the STRIDE threat classification model [18], which focuses on identifying weaknesses in software and hardware, rather than modeling vulnerable Internet of Things assets, risk assessment (DREAD) or analyzing the behavior of likely attackers [23].

The STRIDE threat classification model, developed by Prairite Garg and Lauren Confelder (Microsoft), is one of the most popular threat classification systems [24]. The abbreviation STRIDE stands for the following types of threats:

1. Spoofing - bypassing the access control system by disguising it as another system;
2. Tampering - the subject violates the integrity of the system or data;
3. Repudiation - the user can hide that he has taken certain actions in relation to the system;
4. Information disclosure - the confidentiality of data in the system has been violated (data is leaked, intercepted);
5. Denial of Service (D.o.S) - an attacker creates conditions under which legal users of the system cannot access its resources;
6. Elevation of privilege - a user who has only limited access to the system can independently expand the accessibility.

The STRIDE model includes three steps: defining the architecture, breaking it down into components, and identifying threats for each component.

Let us consider the operation of the STRIDE model using the example of the functioning of a fragment of the data transmission subsystem in IoT based on new generation 5G (6G) cellular networks (hereinafter referred to as diagrams) [25]. This choice is based on the fact that every day people, companies and government bodies exchange data arrays, often in unencrypted form, without assuming that an outsider can access this data, because by default they trust the protection of their data to the transmission medium of this data [26], and cellular networks of the 5G (6G) standard are promising networks of the future.

The simplified diagram shown in Fig. 5 consists of User Equipment (UE) which is a smartphone, tablet, etc. (usually called an IoT device), a complex of receiving and transmitting antennas (Radio access network (RAN)) and a distributed software and hardware complex - the 5G core.

A more detailed division of the system into components (according to the algorithm of the STRIDE model) makes it possible to identify the main software modules and network functions (Network Function (NF)) of the basic architecture of the 5G network (Fig. 6) [27]:

- User Plane Function (UPF) module for implementing user plane functions;
- Data Network (DN) for organizing operator services, Internet access, etc.;
- Access and Mobility Management Function (AMF - Access and Mobility Management Function);

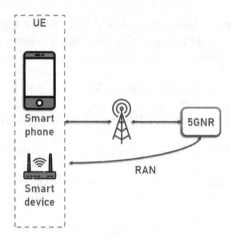

Fig. 5. Simplified diagram of 5G

- Session Management Function (SMF) module;
- Policy control module (Policy Control Function (PCF));
- Unified Data Management (UDM) module;
- Application Function (AF) module.

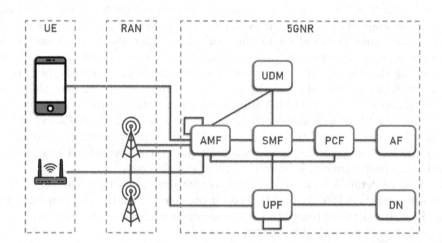

Fig. 6. Detailed diagram of 5G architecture

To make it more effective, the following security management features need to be added [27]:

- Anchor function of safety (Security Anchor Function (SEAF));

- The Authentication Function (AUSF) that acts as an authentication server, terminating requests from SEAF and translating them to the Authentication Credential Repository and Processing Function (ARPF);
- Authentication credential or ARPF repository and processing function;
- Subscription Identifier De-concealing Function (SIDF) function;
- Security Context Management Function (SCMF) function;
- Security Policy Control Function (SPCF) function;

These schemes determine not only information transfer flows between system components, but also provide an opportunity to analyze the process of confidential information circulation in order to understand which components can be attacked. In addition, identifying the boundaries of trust (red dashed line) will help to find possible entry points to potentially vulnerable information flows (Fig. 7).

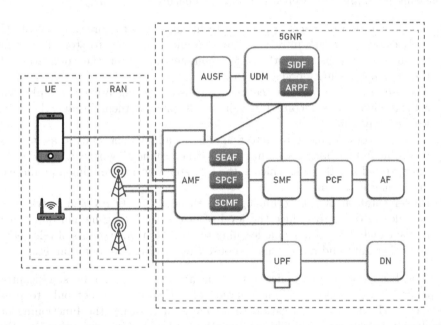

Fig. 7. Detailed 5G Architecture Diagram with Trust Boundaries and Security Modules (Color figure online)

As a result of the detailing and application of the STRIDE model to the components of the 5G network architecture, it is possible to determine a fairly complete list of possible threats to a given fragment of the IoT data transmission network. As for the general requirements for the security of IoT devices, they should be eliminated during development or specified in the documentation.

6   Using ML to Secure the Internet of Things

As noted earlier, machine learning can do things that humans cannot. ML capabilities include providing automation of large-scale analysis, predicting future events, converting raw data into a human-understandable format, developing a real-time recommendation system, device maintenance (IoT), etc. Based on ML, information processing devices that are part of The Internet of Things can detect trends, anomalies, carry out informational and advisory preparation of solutions, and, ultimately, perform the necessary targeted actions for the functioning of IoT devices. A clear example of the effectiveness of ML is the fight against malware that can change shape to avoid detection, and using the traditional signature-based approach makes it very difficult to detect such sophisticated attacks [22].

The analysis based on the results of threat modeling, taking into account the specifics of new generation 5G (6G) cellular networks, allows us to identify the following main areas of application of ML to ensure IoT security:

1. Implementation of machine learning technology into the firewall core of 5G (6G) cellular network infrastructure equipment in order to stop threats in advance, as well as promptly issue recommendations on the application of the necessary security policy for IoT.
2. The use of built-in machine learning models to prevent previously unknown attacks. Signatures become less valuable to prevent them (using ML's self-learning capability).
3. Using ML development to detect anomalies and vulnerabilities, as well as providing full visibility and transparency when connecting new and previously unregistered IoT devices, which is the first step towards building a predictive maintenance system.
4. Implementation of ML technologies in the core of 5G (6G) infrastructure modules in order to reduce the level of errors (including human ones) due to the capabilities of machine learning to analyze huge amounts of telemetry and other data and reduce the response time to threat recognition, etc.

The list of areas of application of machine learning can be significantly expanded if we consider the introduction of ML technology not only to protect the IoT, but also in relation to all levels of ensuring the functioning of the Internet of things, including identification, classification, forecasting, etc. By definition, IoT deals with the interconnection of devices with the primary purpose of exchanging information (data). At the same time, it is this data that is the standard reason that makes machine learning more powerful, increasing the efficiency of IoT [28].

7   Conclusions

The rapidly evolving technologies of the Internet of Things require constant attention to security issues, especially given the serious catastrophic consequences of breaching their protection. To carry out measures to protect IoT, it is necessary to complete a whole complex, starting with the analysis of possible attacks and building a classification model for possible threats. Considering the trend of further development of IoT devices, it is advisable to focus on ensuring the security of promising information transmission systems based on cellular networks of the 5G (6G) standard, as well as the use of machine learning technology to ensure the security of the Internet of things. In this paper, we have formulated a sequence of steps and a set of technologies that should provide sufficient security for promising IoT systems.

The article was prepared as part of the implementation of the program of strategic academic leadership "Priority-2030", Strategic project No. 2 "Digital transformation of the university and industrial enterprises based on the Intelligent Cyber-Physical Platform".

References

1. "2020 Unit 42 IoT Threat Report," Palo Alto Networks, 10 March 2020. https://unit42.paloaltonetworks.com/iot-threat-report-2020. Accessed 04 Apr 2023
2. Electronic resource. https://www.kaspersky.ru/resource-center/preemptive-safety/best-practices-for-iot-security?ysclid=lg2357k9zr450745102. Accessed 04 Apr 2023
3. Nefedova, M.: Zerobot botnet attacks vulnerable IoT devices Zyxel, D-Link, BIG-IP and more 08.12.2022. https://xakep.ru/2022/12/08/zerobot. Accessed 04 Apr 2023
4. Vereshchagina, E.A., Kapetsky, I.O., Yarmonov, A.S.: 317 Security Issues of the Internet of Things. World of Science, Moscow (2021). Online edition. ISBN: 978-5-6045771-9-6. https://izd-mn.com/PDF/20MNNPU21.pdf. Accessed 27 Mar 2023
5. Global Information Infrastructure, Internet Protocol Aspects and Next Generation Networks: Overview of the Internet of Things, 22 p. ITU (2012). (ITU-T Recommendations; Y. 2060). https://iotas.ru/files/documents/wg/T-REC-Y.2060-201206-PDF-R.pdf. Accessed 27 Mar 2023
6. Tsvetkov, V.: Information interaction. European Researcher. Series A. **62**(11-1), 2573–2577 (2013). http://www.erjournal.ru/journals_n/1386019866.pdf. Accessed 29 June 2023
7. Grammatchikov, A.: In three years, each Russian will have six devices connected to the network. CNews.ru, 21 April 2020. https://www.cnews.ru/articles/2020-04-21_cherez_tri_goda_na_kazhdogo_rossiyanina?ysclid=lfsrgtbgdy268814557. Accessed 29 June 2023
8. Prieto, R., Hunt, E., Cromwell, C.: Cisco Visual Networking Index Predicts Global Annual IP Traffic to Exceed Three Zettabytes by 2021. The Newsroom: Cisco's Technology News Site, 08 June 2017. https://newsroom.cisco.com/press-releasecontent?type=webcontent&articleId=1853168. Accessed 28 Mar 2023
9. Bogdanov, A., Shchegoleva, N., Dik, G., Khvatov, A., Dik, A.: "Smart habitat": features of building it infrastructure, main problems of building data networks using 5G (6G) technologies. In: Gervasi, O., Murgante, B., Misra, S., Rocha, A.M.A.C., Garau, C. (eds.) ICCSA 2022. LNCS, vol. 13380, pp. 628–638. Springer, Cham (2022). https://doi.org/10.1007/978-3-031-10542-5_43
10. Kupriyanovskiy, V.: On standardization of smart cities, Internet of Things and big data. The considerations on the practical use in Russia. Int. J. Open Inf. Technol. **4**(2), 34–40 (2016)

11. Just like ABCDE: how the Internet of Things works. Electronic Resource. https://trends.rbc.ru/trends/industry/5f7ca9f89a79471a3d36cb2c. Accessed 29 Mar 2023
12. Rayes, A., Salam, S.: The things in IoT: sensors and actuators. In: Rayes, A., Salam, S. (eds.) Internet of Things From Hype to Reality, pp. 57–77. Springer, Cham (2017). https://doi.org/10.1007/978-3-319-44860-2_3. Accessed 31 Mar 2023
13. Minerva, R., Biru, A., Rotondi, D.: Towards a definition of the Internet of Things (IoT). IEEE (2015)
14. Veretennikov, A.V.: BigData: big data analysis today, No. 32 (166), pp. 9–12 (2017). https://moluch.ru/archive/166/45354/. Accessed 04 Apr 2023
15. Lee, P.: Architecture of the Internet of Things, 454 p. DMK Press, Moscow (2020). Lee P., trans. from Eng. M. A. Reitman. ISBN: 978-5-97060-784-8
16. Letichevsky, A., et al.: Basic protocols, message sequence charts, and the verification of requirements specifications. Comput. Netw. **49**(5), 661–675 (2005). https://doi.org/10.1016/j.comnet.2005.05.005. Accessed 31 Mar 2023
17. Baseline Security Recommendations for IoT in the Context of Critical Information Infrastructures, 103 p. European Union Agency For Network And Information Security, ENISA, Hague (2017). https://doi.org/10.2824/03228
18. Chantsis, F., Stais, I., Calderon, P., Deirmenzoglu, E., Woods, B.: Practical Hacking of the Internet of Things, 480 p. DMK Press, Moscow (2022). Transl. from English. L. N. Akulich
19. Ubozhenko, E., Kruteeva, O., Vdovin, S.: Economic justification for the introduction of digital technology "Internet of Things" in the company's activities. Bull. Altai Acad. Econ. Law **11**(1), 92 (2021)
20. Vlasenko, A.V., Kiselev, P.S., Sklyarova, E.A.: Security of the Internet of Things, No. 21 (363), pp. 86–89 (2021). https://moluch.ru/archive/363/81232/. Accessed 05 Apr 2023
21. Vlasova, Y., Kireev, V.: Review of the Russian market of IoT-technologies. Mod. Sci. Intensive Technol. (8), 48–53 (2018). https://top-technologies.ru/ru/article/view?id=37118. Accessed 05 Apr 2023
22. Glonass, V.: The future of machine learning in cybersecurity. Intersectoral J. Navig. Technol. (2022). http://vestnik-glonass.ru/news/tech/budushchee-mashinnogo-obucheniya-v-kiberbezopasnosti/?ysclid=lgamagzbr866573019. Accessed 10 Apr 2023
23. Riad, R., et al.: Learning strides in convolutional neural networks. arXiv preprint arXiv:2202.01653 (2022)
24. Threats included in the Microsoft Threat Modeling Tool, 27 September 2022. https://learn.microsoft.com/ru-ru/azure/security/develop/threat-modeling-tool-threats. Accessed 10 Apr 2023
25. Tong, W., Zhu, P. (eds.): 6G Networks. The Path From 5G to 6G Through the Eyes of Developers. From Connected People and Things to Connected Intelligence, 624 p. DMK Press, Moscow (2022). per. from English. V. S. Yatsenkova
26. Smelyansky, T. https://cipr.ru/news/kakoe-oborudovanie-neobhodimo-dlya-rossijskih-setej-5g/?ysclid=lgdpc73kar778720058. Accessed 13 Apr 2023
27. What is the 5G network architecture. https://www.shunlongwei.com/ru/what-is-5g-network-architecture/. Accessed 12 Apr 2023
28. Antipko, A.: What tasks can be solved by machine learning, No. 5 (452), pp. 4–6 (2023). https://moluch.ru/archive/452/99591/. Accessed 13 Apr 2023

K-Anonymity Versus PSI3
for Depersonalization and Security
Assessment of Large Data Structures

Alexander Bogdanov[1,2(✉)], Nadezhda Shchegoleva[1,2], Valery Khvatov[3],
Gennady Dik[1,4], Jasur Kiyamov[1], and Aleksandr Dik[1]

[1] St. Petersburg University, Saint Petersburg, Russia
{a.v.bogdanov,n.shchegoleva,z.kiyamov,a.dik}@spbu.ru
[2] St. Petersburg State Marine Technical University, Saint Petersburg, Russia
[3] DGT Technologies AG, Ottawa, Canada
[4] St. Petersburg LLC "System Technologies", St. Petersburg, Russia
g.dick@systechnologies.ru

Abstract. The article presents a modern approach to protecting personal data from de-anonymization. Descriptions of the k-anonymity model using entropy, with one-way publication of information, and the PSI3 technique using homomorphic encryption, with bilateral or multilateral information exchange, examples of the use of metrics for assessing the quality of depersonalization and their improvement, recommendations for using methods in the current activities of personal data operators are given.

Keywords: information protection · personal data · k-anonymity · entropy · PSI3

1 Introduction

Information systems supports the big data ecosystem process personal data everywhere. Processing of personal data is a set of actions (operations) performed with or without the use of automation tools with personal data, including collection, recording, systematization, accumulation, storage, clarification (updating, changing), extraction, use, transfer (distribution, provision, access), depersonalization, blocking, deletion and destruction.

Protection of personal data is a measures set of technical, organizational and organizational-technical nature aimed at protecting information related to a certain or determined on basis of an individual information (subject of personal data). As with any other information, personal data security breaches falls into three categories:

1. confidentiality (inaccessibility of information to be available to unauthorized persons);

2. integrity (preservation of completeness and consistency of information);
3. availability (information is available and ready for use by authorized participants in the information exchange).

There are few of key examples of personal data protection:

- Individuals have the rights to control how their personal data is used. Operators must obtain explicit and informed consent from individuals before collecting, using or disclosing their personal data;
- Operators must only collect personal data for specific, legitimate purposes and do not use it for other purposes without obtaining the consent of the individual;
- Operators must only collect and process the minimal amount of personal data necessary to achieve their legitimate purposes;
- Personal data operators must take reasonable steps to ensure that personal data is accurate, complete and up-to-date;
- Operators must implement appropriate technical and organizational measures to protect personal data from unauthorized or unlawful processing of accidental loss, destruction or damage;
- Individuals have certain rights in relation for their personal data, including the right to access, correct, delete and restrict the processing of their personal data;
- Operators are responsible for complying with applicable data protection laws and regulations, taking appropriate steps to ensure that their employees and third party service providers also comply with laws and regulations.

At the same time, an important point in risk assessment is not the fact of gaining access to an array of anonymized data (developers, system administrators have a significant amount of access to data), but the fact that attack is completed. If the organization has mechanisms for detecting an attack and preventing it before the attack is completed, i.e. the attack began, but did not end and reach the goal, then the risk was not realized, since the result - depersonalization - was not achieved. Such mechanisms are included in the technical and administrateve aspects of the organization. To determine contextual risks, this criterion of completeness is important - the data must be de-anonymized, which creates the possibility of causing damage to the personal data (PD) subject.

In general, the specific measures required to protect different types of personal data will be depend of the context and information confidentiality [1]. In general, the protection of personal data requires an integrated approach that includes strict access control, encryption, authentication measures, and strict protocols for data processing (anonymization) and storage. In addition, organizations must comply with applicable laws and regulations, regarding the collecting, using and disclosuring of personal data.

This article continues and improves the approach described in [2], based on calculated value of the re-identification risk.

The risk approach to personal data security is a proactive and systematic approach that enables organizations to continuously assess and manage the privacy risks associated with personal data. By following this approach, organizations can ensure that their customers personal data is protected, employees and other stakeholders can be confident that their personal data is handled.

2   Modern Approach to Data Protection

PD security differs from the classical concept of information security [3,4], the focus of which is unauthorized activity (which actually leads to loss of confidentiality, integrity or availability). When processing PD for the purpose of depersonalization, we are talking about planned activities, which, however, may create consequences for the private life of individuals. PD confidentiality threats arises as a result of authorized data processing and as a result of unauthorized access (actions of an attacker):

- As a result of unauthorized access to data - emotional suffering of individuals, economic losses from identity theft, as well as physical or psychological harm due to persecution;
- As a result of a decrease in the quality of information processing (decrease in it's value) within the framework of planned processing - a decrease in the quality of services provided, failures in the operation of systems, incorrectly made or delayed decisions, which may also affect the health of individuals or entire population groups.

The key provisions of the proposed risk model depersonalization procedure take into account confidentiality issues that arises as a result of unauthorized access and planned data processing:

- The risk of publishing (exchanging) anonymized data is a measure of the extent where the subject is threatened by potential circumstances or events and remains as a probability function P of the occurrence of such events and the adverse consequences violation of the personal data confidentiality - I, Impact:

$$R = P * I \tag{1}$$

- The construction of completely anonymized data sets that store useful information is an idealized hypothesis that is not feasible in practical solutions. The proposed approach based on the likelihood of re-identification attacks and setting an acceptable risk;
- The process by identified risks, according to [4] is called risk assessment;
- Risk assessment requires a risk model that defines risk factors and the relationships between them:
  - Risk factorization (set selection of individual risk components and establishing a relationship between them);
  - Release model of data;
  - Set quantitative risk thresholds;
  - The required usefulness level of the received depersonalized data;

- Building a risk model procedure for a specific depersonalization procedure, including the possibility of reassessing the risk when using various depersonalization methods

Damage may include:

- Compliance costs associated with privacy concerns for individuals;
- Direct costs of fines and legal fees;
- Business loss, refusal of using products or services;
- Reputational costs leading to loss of trust from users;
- Decreased performance or inability to achieve the organization's mission.

Specific damage can be assessed for each specific situation; within the framework of this model, proposed to confine ourselves vector of values:

$$I = [Minor Damage = I_1; Medium Damage = I_2; High Damage = I_3] \quad (2)$$

Thus, the risk assessment proposed in this model contains damage as a parameter; in what follows that risk assessment is understood as an assessment probability of occurrence events $P \in [0; 1]$.

The general factorization formula is the probability of the re-identification risk:

$$P_{re-id} = P_{context} * P_{data} \quad (3)$$

Here: P_{re-id} - general risk of re-identification, $P_{context}$ - contextual risk, defined by a set of organizational and technical risks, P_{data} - data risks

Data risks are associated with a specific data set and should be calculated taking into account the characteristics of the data set - in particular, the allocation of direct identifiers and quasi-identifiers. Direct identifiers and their substitution are the smallest problem in solving the reidentification risk problem. Correct quasi-identifiers identification and depersonalization application methods taking into account their structure and type, is a much more difficult task, bearing in mind the probabilistic approach to risk assessment.

Transformation of PD (depersonalization), taking into account the risk model, requires a balance between the usefulness data obtained as a result of depersonalization and the acceptable level of risk. The acceptable threshold for the risk of re-identification personal data depends on various factors, including the data confidentiality, context of its use, applicable laws and regulations. Generally, the risk threshold for re-identification is considered being very low, since any re-identification of personal data may lead to a breach of confidentiality and security. Thresholds risk is setting according to use cases.

The acceptable risk threshold quantification for the personal data re-identification might vary depending of the specific context and requirements for data use. In some cases, a certain percentage value, such as 3%, 10%, or 20%, may be used to determine threshold. These percentage meanings represent the acceptable probability of re-identifying individual from the dataset.

For example, some countries regulations requires that personal data must be anonymized in the point where the risk of re-identification is below a certain percentage, such as 3% or 5%. In other cases, a threshold may be set based on the data confidentiality and the potential harm that may result breach of confidentiality. A general idea orders of the risk can be drawn from the Table 1 below [5]:

Table 1. Applying k-Anonymity

Impact on PD privacy	Acceptable vice of risk	Equivalence class size for aggregated data
Low	0.1	10
Medium	0.075	15
High	0.05	20

The acceptable level of risk is determined taking into account the following parameters:

- Likelihood of a threat to confidential data ($P_{context} * P_{data}$);
- Potential damage I (assessed in terms of "low", "medium", "high" or through points) - see [6,7]. The damage is also determined taking into account the volume of published data and the sensitivity of the attributes;
- Publication scenarios (data dissemination scenarios) - influences the recommended equivalence classes and therefore data risk;
- The business model of the organization publishing the data ("risk appetite"). This parameter describes risk tolerance taking into account the characteristics of the business (industry), the value of assets (data containing private characteristics), management preferences;

3 Risk Assessment Metrics

Although, calculation metrics risk may be differ by depending of used methods. Here are general approaches that allow quantifying the probability based on data behavior (homogeneity, difference between the original data and ones anonymized, etc.).

The metrics are calculated in consideration with the attributes (fields) of the sets, which classification is shown in the Fig. 1 below [6].

According with accepted approach [7], the greatest influence on metrics is exert by quasi-identifiers, which combination makes possible to indirectly determine the individual and compare his sensitive attributes. The main idea of risk calculation which based on attribute selection is to form a group of similar records (equivalence classes), where impossible to match only one individual and his sensitive attributes. Then probability of re-identification is directly related with the size of equivalence classes (inversely proportional to equivalence class), and also depends of distribution of sensitive attributes in such equivalence classes. The Table 2 provides summary information of the various metrics with specified subject dependencies.

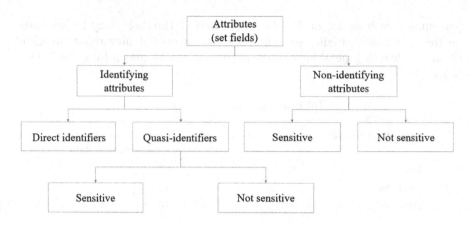

Fig. 1. Classification of attributes

Table 2. Evaluation of entropy by attributes for the choice of quasi-identifiers

№	Metrics	Explanation and calculation method
1	k-Map	Measures degrees anonymity achieved by anonymized dataset, based on smallest size of records group that share same Quasi-Identifier (QI) values. In other words, the metric measures have minimal number of records, needed for attacker to re-identify a person in a dataset.
2	k-Anonymity	Anonymity degree measure in dataset. Dataset is called to be k-anonymous if each entry in dataset is indistinguishable from at least other k-1 entries.
3	L-Diversity	A measure of sensitive diversity attributes values in a group of k-anonymous records. It measures probability that an attacker will be able to re-identify a person based on quasi-identifiers combination and sensitive attributes.
4	t-Closeness	A measure of similarity between distribution of sensitive attribute values in the original dataset and anonymous dataset. This measure extends which anonymized dataset retains the statistical properties from the original dataset

The calculated metrics makes possible to evaluate numerical probabilities of re-identification risks by using formulas from the form.

$$P_{data} = \frac{1}{f} \qquad (4)$$

where f - one of the metrics meanings, listed in the table above.

In accordance with these descriptions, depersonalization calculation metrics is applies for specific datasets, both determined by their attributes (columns), and directly by the records in set - the match frequency for individual attributes. For example, to calculate k-anonymity metric (i.e. ensure that each record in data sets is indistinguishable from at least another k-1 records), must be taken these following steps:

- Conduct identification of quasi-identifiers (Qi) in data set (fields or attributes in dataset that could be used to associate a person with his confidential information). For example, Qi include demographic information such as age, gender, and a zip code;
- Group the records in data set according with the key interfaces values. This creates a set of groups, in which each group contains entries that have the same values for Qi identifiers;
- Generalize or suppress Qi."Generalization" means replacing a specific value with more general value, such as replacing a date of birth with an age range."Suppression" means complete value removal;
- Make sure that each group has at least k-entries. If group contains less k-records, it is necessary to merge it with another group and generalize, or suppress Qi until the group satisfies the k-anonymity requirement;
- Repeat the previous steps until all groups meet k-anonymity requirement.

4 Practical Implementation of Risk Assessment

4.1 Using the Models K-Anonymity

When unilaterally information is publishing (for example, generating machine learning data), it's convenient to use classical depersonalization, developed by k-Anonymity model. The k-Anonymity model is based on quasi identifiers allocation in the set attributes (columns). There is practical algorithm implementation. Main method steps are include:

1. Identifier highlighting - attributes defining or their combinations that can potentially identify individuals in dataset;
2. Records grouping (finding equivalence classes) - removing direct identifiers and clustering records, bases on their quasi-identifiers values. Each group must obtain at least k-quantity entries to achieve k-anonymity (other metrics may also be used);
3. Quasi-identifiers generalization - summarizing the meanings of quasi-identifiers in each group to make them less specific and more similar. Generalization degree depends on confidentiality requirements and information loss level, which is acceptable to solve the problem;
4. Suppression of sensitive values - suppressing or removing sensitive attributes or values that may be associated with specific users in each group (suppression can also be done by randomizing values);

5. Depersonalization level evaluation - level assessment of depersonalization is determined by used metric. In this case, probability of re-identification is estimated as inversely value, proportional to metric value. Each entry in dataset has its own value equal to the size of corresponding equivalence class, depending on used offender model selected the smallest metric (highest probability), and the average metric for the entire set;
6. Checking the level of information loss - using depersonalization techniques (step 3.4) inevitably leads to information loss. Numerical value of corresponding metric gives a relative loss estimate, which acceptability is ultimately determined by testing problem application being solved during publication;
7. Reapplying Depersonalization Techniques - if assessment metrics risk (depersonalization level) does not provide the required security level (comparison with threshold risks) or information loss level is high, corresponding depersonalization parameters (the "blurring" level) could be changed. In this case, new iteration is carried out, starting from step 2;
8. Total Risk Calculation - when we considering contextual risk, overall probability is calculated by using a formula, which compares probability threshold;
9. Re-identification risks monitoring - tracking and assessing re-identification risks of given information set is adds over time as a new data, or new available becoming information.

Below is the pseudo-code implementation sample of the k-Anonymity method (Algorithm 1) according to the algorithm.

The algorithm consist next following steps:

1. Collect the data from given columns by using the group method and count the number of records in each group;
2. Determine minimal number of records in each group by using lambda function method;
3. Count the number of groups with a certain minimal number entries by using the Counter function;
4. Select 5 smallest values for minimal number of entries;
5. Find the unique number values in "Account" column;
6. Calculate k-anonymity as ratio records number in the dataset to number of unique values in "Account" column;
7. Return consisting pairs of values list (k, the percentage of groups with the minimal number of entries), where k takes the values chosen in step 4;
8. In the output, the function returns a pairs of values list representing k values, and percent the groups with the minimal number of records in the data. These values allow you to assess degree anonymity data.

The function takes two input arguments:

– data - is a data set, in which k-anonymity parameter should be calculated;
– columns - is a list of columns, in which data should be grouped.

Algorithm 1. calculating the k-anonymity metric

1: **function** K_ANONYMOUS(data, columns)
2:      aggregrate ← data.groupby(columns).count().apply(lambda x : set(x) - set({0}),axis = 1)
3:      aggregrate ← aggregrate.apply(lambda x : 0 if x == set() else min(x))
4:      count ← dict(Counter(aggregrate))
5:      sort_arg ← sorted(set(aggregrate))[:5]
6:      dub_data ← data["Account"].drop_duplicates()
7:      nyu ← round(len(data)/len(dub_data))
8:      print(len(dub_data))
9:      **return** [[arg*nyu,round(count[arg]/len(aggregrate) * 100,3)] **for** arg **in** sort_arg]
10: **end function**

The k-Anonymity model is a privacy preservation technique that protects to identity people in dataset by grouping them into anonymous groups, based on their quasi-identities. Quasi-identifiers are attributes (or attributes combinations) which potentially identify individual in a dataset. Algorithm 1 above is assumes a "manual" choice of quasi-identifiers, which represents as complex structure. Within of the k-anonymity model, various metrics could be used, making possible to quantify the re-identification probability. Some approaches allows automating:

- Entropy-based approach: this approach involves calculating the entropy of each attribute in the dataset and selecting features with the highest entropy values as quasi-identifiers. Attributes with high entropy have more unique values, making them more likely to distinguish between people.
- Correlation-based approach: the approach involves identifying attributes that are highly correlated with each other since they may reveal sensitive information when combined. Then, highly correlated attributes are selected as quasi-identifiers.
- Domain knowledge-based approach: this approach is similar to "hand-picked" selection, involves using domain knowledge and expert judgment to determine which attributes are likely to be quasi-identifiers. This approach can be useful in work with datasets containing sensitive or confidential information.
- L-diversity-based approach: this approach involves selecting quasi-identifiers, based on their ability to achieve l-diversity which represents as a measure of sensitive diversity attributes in each group. The approach idea lies that each group of selected attributes has a sufficient level of diversity in sensitive values, what makes difficult to identify people.
- Outlier-based approach: the approach involves identifying outliers in the dataset and using outlier-related attributes as quasi-identifiers. Within some sets, outliers are individual related records that have unique different attribute values against to other records in terms of selected attributes, making them more likely being identified.

Below is the algorithm pseudocode (Algorithm 2) that calculates the entropy [10,11] for each column of the quasi-identifier in the dataset. Algorithm consists these following steps:

- Create an empty list ent_array to store entropy values for each quasiidentifier;
- Pass through each quasi-identifier in QI (set of quasi-identifiers);
- Group the data by current quasi-identifier and count the number of occurrences;
- Calculate the total number of occurrences;
- Initiate entropy in the current quasi-identifier aims to 0;
- Pass through each count and calculate the probability contribution into entropy;
- Add the entropy value into the ent_array list;
- Print the entropy value for the current quasi-identifier.

Algorithm 2. Attribute entropy calculation

1: $ent\_array \leftarrow []$
2: **for** each qi in QI **do**
3:     $counts \leftarrow df.groupby(qi).size()$
4:     $total \leftarrow counts.sum()$
5: **end for**
6: $entropy \leftarrow 0$
7: **for** each $count$ in $counts$ **do**
8:     $probability \leftarrow count/total$
9:     $entropy \leftarrow entropy - probability * \log_2(probability)$
10: **end for**
11: ent_array.append($entropy$)
12: **print**("Entropy of ", qi, ": ", $entropy$)

4.2   Using the PSI3 Algorithm

Some information exchange scenarios involve bilateral or multilateral data exchange in order to form a common data array (intersection set). Such data set can be formed by using the Private Set Intersection (PSI) [12] technique.

For example consider the information exchange between A organization (advertising platform) and B organization (bank, financial institution). Organization A has a list of customers with phone numbers and additional information (such as number of viewed ad times). Organization B (bank) also has a list of customers with phone numbers and banking information (who, when and how much they spent). To solve the problem you need to form total set of ad views against costs that gives advertising effectiveness (advertising touch, marketing attribution). Both organizations have a number of restrictions in phone numbers transfer, therefore using of hashing schemes is not acceptable due to significant sensitive information amount. To solve the problem of constructing confidential intersection sets (which hides phone numbers) can be used various approaches:

- Homomorphic encryption scheme [9]: an encryption scheme that allows calculations to be performed on encrypted without decrypting this data. Example of homomorphic encryption scheme lays in Payet cryptosystem;
- Invisible/forgetful transmission: this protocol allows one party send a message to another party without knowing anything about its content, so sender receives recipient message without knowing anything about his choice. Example of a forgotten transfer protocol is 1-of-2 Oblivious Transfer, as well as Bloom filters.

Confidentiality-preserving intersection of data sets can be arranged by using the PSI3 approach. PSI3 [13] (Privacy-Preserving Sequential Subgroup Summation and Intersection) is a privacy preservation algorithm for calculating subgroups intersection within larger group, providing differential privacy in combination with confidential computing mechanisms.

The PSI3 algorithm works by dividing a large group into smaller subgroups and calculating the sum of each. Then it adds Laplace noise into each of these subgroup sums to preserve differential privacy. After that, algorithm computes the subgroup intersection by comparing the sums of the noise in subgroups. Finally, it adds more Laplace noise to intersection result for better protection privacy of the people in subgroups.

Key advantage of PSI3 algorithm is about allowing intersection queries to be computed over subgroups without exposing any individual level information. This makes it useful for scenarios with issue privacy, such as healthcare, finance, or government data sharing. Although, the PSI3 protocol can be used in industrial implementations, there are some use restrictions:

- Computational complexity: the PSI3 algorithm involves several rounds of communication and computation, which can be computationally intensive and consuming time. This can be especially tricky when dealing with large datasets.
- Difficulty in communication: the PSI3 algorithm includes multiple rounds of communication between the parties, which can be a significant barrier in situations where the parties are geographically dispersed or communication channels are unreliable.
- Errors accumulation: each PSI3 algorithm round introduces some error degree into computation of subgroup intersections. This error can accumulate over several rounds. Care must be taken to ensure that error lies within acceptable limits.
- Sensitivity to outliers: the PSI3 algorithm assumes that the data is distributed according to a normal distribution, which may not always be in the case. In particular, the algorithm may be sensitive to outliers in the data, which may affect the accuracy of the results.
- The need for trust: the PSI3 algorithm requires parties to trust each other to follow the protocol, and not deviate from agreed procedures. This can be challenging in situations where is no trust, or where the parties have competing interests.

Below generalized implementation method in pseudocode (Algorithm 3).

Algorithm 3. PSI3 algorithm

```
 1: public_key, private_key ← paillier.generate_pailier_keypair()
 2: function ENCRYPT-RECORDS(records)
 3:     encrypted-record ← public_key.encrypt(records)
 4:     return encrypted-record
 5: end function
 6: function INTERSECT
 7:     bank_records ← bank.records
 8:     ad_records ← advertisement_hub.records
 9:     result ← []
10:     for each bank_record in bank_records do
11:         for each ad_record in ad_records do
12:             if bank_record[0] ← ad_record[0] then
13:                 result.append((encrypt_records(bank_record[0])
14:             end if
15:         end for
16:     end for
17:     return bank_records
18:     return risk_level
19: end function
20: function CALCULATE-RISK(epsilon)
21:     intersection_size ← len(intersect())
22:     bank_size ← len(bank.records)
23:     advertisement_hub_size ← len(advertisement_hub.records)
24:     privacy_budget ← bank_size * advertisement_hub_size / intersection_size
25:     risk_level ← ε / privacy_budget
26:     return risk_level
27: end function
```

The algorithm describes PSI3 class, which is using to analyze data privacy risks in two data sources: bank records and advertising hub. The class includes these following methods:

- constructor PSI3 (bank, advertisemen_hub, public_key): this method initializes PSI3 class and sets the values for bank records, ad hub and public key, which are passed as parameters;
- function encrypt_records (records): this method is used to encrypt the input record data with the public key and returns the encrypted record;
- function intersect: this method finds an intersection between the bank records and the ad hub by using the encrypted values of the bank records and matching them with the corresponding values in the ad hub. If the values match, they are added to the result;
- function calculate_risk (epsilon): this method calculates the level of data privacy risk. It determines the size of the intersection between the bank records

and the ad hub and calculates the privacy budget based on the size of the bank records and the size of the ad hub. The result is used to calculate the data privacy risk level based on the epsilon parameter.

5   Results of Testing on Conditionally Real Data

Consider a typical data set (dataset), which often uses in organizations and contains information about the client (what, where, how and through what he purchased or viewed). The most common method for anonymization is using micro segments and masking.

Checking for dataset re-identification, based on information about purchases and viewing advertisements for useful and safe report at each processing step, using the k-anonymity model (When $K \geq 10$ - data is protected) During the conversion process, data converts several times - at the source level, through depersonalization (formation of micro-segments), and final depersonalization by micro-segments. There are key features of data storage organization:

- The object is used to solve analytical problems characterized by large data samples for machine learning and other advanced analytical tools. The data flow profile tends to be batch-oriented, the main users are internal analysis;
- The organization has a developed security system, the contextual risks calculated on the basis of calculators is 40% (0.4);
- Used depersonalization methods should allow protecting data in a recurrent manner (serial protection, repeated procedures) and make it possible to adjust the algorithm depending on attribute composition of the protected data and their volume;
- In fact, in exchange process three sets of data are processed and published: A (purchase data) - contains data tied to the phone number of an individual, B (advertising view data) - ad views data, also tied to the phone number, C (summary report) - formed by the merger of A and B, comparing purchases and ad views. The problem to be solved belongs to SMPC / PSI (Secure Multi-Part Calculation / Private Set Intersection) class;

In the data preparing process, they are anonymized: sets A - forms microsegments, then data is aggregated by purchases relative to the brand and product category; sets B - by ad views. Before sending formation of summary report, pointers to micro-segments are pseudonymised (reduced to abstract numbers). Further, combining reports A and B allows us to form set C, in which references microsegment aliases are also removed.

To create synthetic data (dummy data), uses an algorithmic data generator, tunes each attributes in the test set (7 sheets (A1, A2, A3, B1, B2, C1 and C2) with 500,000 data lines each). After choosing the degree of data blurring (degree of generalization), the results are:

- $k - anonymity = 1[94.39\%]$
- $k - anonymity = 2[5.61\%]$

After suppressing the rows $k - anonymity \leq 2$, the desired re-identification probability from the data is:

$$P_{data} = \frac{1}{1 * 2} = 0.5 \rightarrow P_{re-id} = 0.5 * 0.5 = 0.2 > 10\% \tag{5}$$

Thus, testing on synthetic data did not reach the safety threshold of 10%, which required refinement of the generalization parameters for testing on conditionally real data.

- The applied algorithm contains protective functions in relation to personal data;
- In terms of depersonalization procedures, other fields that are not depersonalized according to the proposed algorithm, such as the time of purchase, provide unique data accurate to the second;
- The overall k-anonymity metrics are low, mostly in the range of 1–4 and do not allow reducing the probability of re-identification below the threshold of 10%.

The depersonalization algorithm based on conditionally real data was largely based on the results obtained during the preliminary testing round. Key features of the approach used. The PSI3 algorithm works by dividing a large group into smaller subgroups and calculating the sum of each subgroup. It then adds Laplace noise to each of these subgroup sums to preserve differential privacy. It then computes the subgroup intersection by comparing the sums of the noisy subgroups. Finally, it adds more Laplace noise to the result of the intersection to further protect the privacy of the people in the subgroups. As a result of testing on conditionally real data, the following results were obtained:

- $k - anonymity = 8[98.239\%]$
- $k - anonymity = 16[1.727\%]$
- $k - anonymity = 24[0.035\%]$

After suppressing the rows $k - anonymity \leq 8$, the desired probability of re-identification from the data was:

$$P_{data} = \frac{1}{8} = 0.125 \rightarrow P_{re-id} = 0.125 * 0.4 = 0.05 \leq 10\% \tag{6}$$

Taking the data set and the k value as the k-anonymity metric of the input data, and first calculates the entropy of each attribute. If an attribute has non-zero entropy, it generalizes it using a masking method: replacing the last characters with wildcards (asterisks) until its entropy is less than or equal to the logarithmic base 2 of the value of k. If the attribute has high entropy (entropy greater than or equal to base 2 logarithm of k), it is added to the list of high entropy attributes that are potential quasi-identifiers Qi. (Fig. 2)

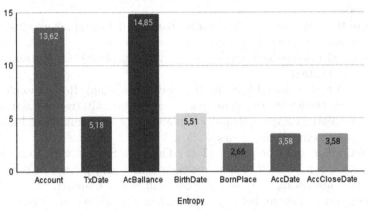

Fig. 2. Graphical interpretation of entropy on the original data

In a multi-threaded scenario using homomorphic encryption, this level of risk is reduced to a new level, namely

– $Intersectionsize = 49998$
– $Risklevel = 1.0002000400080017e - 05 = 0.0000100020$

$$P_{data} = 0.00001 \rightarrow P_{re-id} = 0.00001 * 0.4 = 0.000004 \le 10\% \tag{7}$$

Thus, the use of additional degrees of generalization for conditionally real data made it possible to achieve the necessary threshold for the risk of re-identification.

6 Conclusions

The conducted testing allows us to formulate the following general conclusions on the use of depersonalization methods for large data structures:

1. Assessing the effectiveness of anonymization methods: It is important to evaluate the effectiveness of anonymization methods before publishing data. This can be done by measuring the degree of anonymization achieved using metrics, as well as checking whether it is possible to re-identify the individual from previously anonymized data.
2. Factoring the probability of reidentification: Explicit allocation of contextual risks reduces the probability of reidentification by protecting against multilevel attack vectors
3. Include in the depersonalization procedure all attributes of the set, including time, geolocation, and product categories. Because the sensitive attribute (representing the subject matter) is the purchase amount, which represents the aggregated value. This blurring of time and geo-location in a small range

will significantly improve risk indicators and will not affect the usefulness of the model.

4. Change the procedure for integrating banking data and ad viewing data to use advanced integration models:
   - Trusted intermediary model (for testing purposes). Limitation: Cannot be generalized.
   - Model of distributed learning (Federated Learning). Restriction: does not provide the ability to calculate metrics and quantitative risk assessments.
   - Confidential computing model combined with anonymization. Limitation: requires computational costs.

5. In the Confidential Computing Model The PSI3 Scheme with Homomorphic Encryption can be used to improve the security and privacy of communications over marketing attribution phone numbers. Compared to using microsegments on phone numbers, the PSI3 scheme provides greater accuracy and significantly better privacy. However, this is relatively slow and difficult to implement.
   - The PSI3 scheme allows financial institutions and marketing platforms to exchange customer phone numbers to determine the intersection of their respective sets without disclosing any additional information. This approach ensures the confidentiality and security of customer data, preventing any unauthorized access to confidential information.
   - Compared to using phone number microsegments, which generalize to the last two digits of the number, the PSI3 scheme provides greater accuracy in identifying common customers between two sets. The use of homomorphic encryption also ensures that the transmitted data remains confidential, further enhancing the privacy of customer information.
   - However, the PSI3 scheme can be relatively slow and complex to implement, requiring a significant amount of computational time and technical knowledge. Despite this, the accuracy and privacy advantages of this approach make it a promising solution for exchanging phone number data in marketing attribution

The article was prepared as part of the implementation of the program of strategic academic leadership "Priority-2030", Strategic project No. 2 "Digital transformation of the university and industrial enterprises based on the Intelligent Cyber-Physical Platform".

References

1. Bogdanov, A.V., et al.: Protection of personal data using anonymization. In: Gervasi, O., et al. (eds.) ICCSA 2021. LNCS, vol. 12956, pp. 447–459. Springer, Cham (2021). https://doi.org/10.1007/978-3-030-87010-2_33
2. Bogdanov, A.V., et al.: Risk model of application of lifting methods. In: Proceedings of the 9th International Conference Distributed Computing and Grid Technologies in Science and Education. RWTH Aahen University, vol. 3041. pp. 369–374, December 2021. (CEUR Workshop Proceedings)

3. NISTIR 8062. An Introduction to Privacy Engineering and Risk Management in Federal Systems

4. ISO/IEC27701. Security techniques - Extension to ISO/IEC 27001 and ISO/IEC 27002 for privacy information management - Requirements and guidelines

5. De-identification Guidelines for Structured Data, IPC Ontario (2016)

6. General Data Protection Regulation (REGULATION (EU) 2016/679 OF THE EUROPEAN PARLIAMENT AND OF THE COUNCIL of 27 April 2016 on the protection of natural persons with regard to the processing of personal data and on the free movement of such data, and repealing Directive 95/46/EC)

7. Anonymization: managing data protection risk code of practice. Information Commissioner's Office, Wycliffe House, Water Lane, Wilmslow, Cheshire SK9 5AF. November 2012

8. ISO/IEC 20889:2018. Privacy enhancing data de-identification terminology and classification of techniques

9. Ito, K., Kogure, J., Shimoyama, T., Tsuda, H.: De-identification and encryption technologies to protect personal information. Fujitsu Sci. Tech. J. **52**(3), 28–36 (2016)

10. Shannon, C.: A mathematical theory of communication. Bell Syst. Tech. J. **27**, 379–423 (1948)

11. Baez, J.C., Fritz, T., Leinster, T.: A characterization of entropy in terms of information loss. Entropy **13**, 1945–1957 (2011)

12. Wang, Z., Banawan, K., Ulukus, S.: Private set intersection: a multi-message symmetric private information retrieval perspective. IEEE Trans. Inf. Theor. **68**(3), 2001–2019 (2021)

13. Gómez-Sanz, Jorge J.., Pavón, Juan, Díaz-Carrasco, Áureo.: The PSI3 agent recommender system. In: Lovelle, Juan Manuel Cueva., Rodríguez, Bernardo Martín González., Gayo, Jose Emilio Labra., del Puerto Paule Ruiz, María, Aguilar, Luis Joyanes (eds.) ICWE 2003. LNCS, vol. 2722, pp. 30–39. Springer, Heidelberg (2003). https://doi.org/10.1007/3-540-45068-8_5

Continuous Authentication Methods for Zero-Trust Cybersecurity Architecture

Iurii Matiushin🆔 and Vladimir Korkhov(⊠) 🆔

St Petersburg State University, 7-9 Universitetskaya Embankment, 199034 St Petersburg, Russia
v.korkhov@spbu.ru

Abstract. Zero-trust architecture (ZTA) is a new approach to distributed systems cybersecurity which both provides better data protection and reflects the structure of modern information systems more accurately. Unlike the traditional perimeter-style approach, ZTA views each part of the system as a potential threat, and continuously authenticates it to detect possible threats. This article presents a comparative analysis of the most common continuous authentication methods, and evaluates their viability for use in ZTA systems. Comparison criteria are introduced, most prominent authentication methods found in literature are listed, and their thorough evaluation is carried out. We conclude that, first, most continuous authentication approaches are not universal and can only be used with certain specific input methods; second, that face recognition, while a theoretically universal approach, has several issues of its own according to our criteria; third, that hybrid methods that combine several approaches are a potentially viable way of authentication in ZTA context; and fourth, that machine learning is essential to all of the present approaches.

Keywords: Cybersecurity · distributed systems · continuous authentication · zero-trust architecture

1 Introduction

1.1 The Need for a New Cybersecurity Approach

With each passing year, the issue of providing security for distributed systems is becoming more and more urgent. As the number of such systems and their complexity both increase, so does the amount of various cyberattacks on them, from within as well as from without. It is becoming increasingly clear that in many cases, most common security methods and paradigms are no longer sufficient for protecting one's systems and one's data [1]. Furthermore, the widespread shift to remote work, motivated in large part by the COVID-19 pandemic, has made its mark on the physical layout of many systems – no longer are their parts concentrated in a single location, instead being spread out among different buildings, cities, or even countries. Finally, the development of new technologies and approaches such as blockchain and IoT also call for novel methods of protecting the emerging systems. Thus, it becomes necessary to uncover new approaches to cybersecurity, ones that would provide protection against the latest threats and take into account the new realities of the world of computer systems.

O. Gervasi et al. (Eds.): ICCSA 2023 Workshops, LNCS 14109, pp. 334–351, 2023.
https://doi.org/10.1007/978-3-031-37120-2_22

Zero-trust architecture (ZTA), also known as zero-trust security model, is an example of such an approach. While relatively recent, the concept of zero-trust security has quickly become very prominent, with 76% responders of a 2021 Microsoft poll among organizations claiming they have either implemented it or are interested in doing so [2]. Moreover, both companies and governments all over the world increasingly begin to consider ZTA to be one of the best choices when it comes to developing security strategy.

1.2   A Brief History of ZTA

To understand the meaning of zero-trust architecture, as well as the reason for its growing popularity, one should first consider the "traditional" approach to computer system security. This approach largely relies on a notion of a "security perimeter"; essentially, it treats the network as being divided into "outside" and "inside" zones. The outside zone – which is to say, the network outside the organization – is treated as inherently hostile and compromised, while the inside zone, being the part of the network that connects the organization's computational systems and data storage devices, is treated as safe. To separate the two, measures such as firewalls are used.

The approach described above is simple and intuitive, with clear separation of "safe zones" from potentially dangerous outside world. However, while it was the basis of computer system security for decades, certain recent developments have forced organizations to reconsider it.

Among such developments was the rise of concepts like cloud computing, Internet of Things, blockchain, and remote work policies. All these concepts meant that the perimeter itself was slowly disintegrating, as corporate systems grew more and more widespread and heterogeneous. In the past, connecting to a corporate network from the outside was the exception, whereas in recent years, it can often be the rule. Thus, drawing a line between the "inside zone" and the "outside zone" becomes harder and harder.

Another development was the recognition of an inherent vulnerability in the "security perimeter" concept. Namely, the fact that an entity that has managed to get past the perimeter security essentially has free reign inside the system. It effectively banks on the belief that the firewalls and other security systems can stop any threat from gaining access to the system; but if that belief proves to be incorrect, the entire system can become compromised as the result.

Starting from mid-2000s, security professionals began attempting to move away from the perimeter-based approach. In 2004, Paul Simmonds coined the term "deperimeterization", noting the need for a new data security model in his Jericho Forum presentation. In 2010, Forrester Research analyst John Kindervag popularized the term "zero trust" [3]. A year later, Google's zero-trust-based system called BeyondCorp was unveiled as a response to increasing cyberattacks; the company's articles on the subject also brought zero trust to the attention of many. In 2018, NIST released SP 800–207, the first specification for ZTA. By 2021, both US and British government cybersecurity organizations were recommending zero-trust approach for new IT deployments.

1.3 The Main Principles of ZTA

In the previous subsection, we described the traditional "security perimeter" approach, and indicated that zero-trust means abandoning it for something different. Essentially, if the traditional method can be summarized as "trust, but verify", then zero-trust can be summed up as "never trust, always verify". It basically does away with the division of network into "safe" and "unsafe" zones, and treats each and every entity as a potential threat. Thus, each interaction involves some sort of verification, in order to make sure that the entity has not been compromised since the last time.

In Fig. 1, the difference between the classic approach to system security and the zero-trust approach is shown [4].

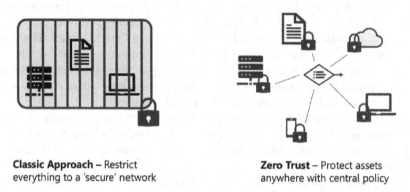

Classic Approach – Restrict
everything to a 'secure' network

Zero Trust – Protect assets
anywhere with central policy

Fig. 1. Classic approach to security versus zero-trust approach.

Zero-trust architecture is built on three main principles: risk awareness, least privileged access, continuous authentication.

Risk awareness can be summarized as good knowledge of your system's vulnerabilities and possible threats. Security specialists need to be aware of all the assets that comprise the system – be it servers, personal computers, mobile devices, laptops, or anything else – and the ways users interact with them, all well as possible ways the security of each asset might be compromised.

The principle of least privilege means that each entity only gets as much access rights as necessary for its work and nothing more. This way, even if it is compromised, the possible damage is minimized.

Continuous authentication is a crucial part of zero-trust architecture. In a traditional perimeter-based model, authentication is carried out only once, at the beginning of the session; for ZTA, however, this is not acceptable. According to the "never trust, always verify" principle, the user's authenticity should be checked multiple times throughout the entire session, since it is possible that the user's credentials, or the device they are using to access the system, become compromised. So, the authentication mechanism must be capable of preventing unauthorized access not just once per session, but at any time.

This article examines various continuous authentication methods and determines their advantages and disadvantages as applied to their possible use in a zero-trust security mechanism. We consider various factors that could influence a decision on whether to adopt any given method, and use them for a comprehensive comparative evaluation of different classes of methods. We also investigate the possibility of further development of certain methods, or using them in combination with one another.

The remainder of this paper is organized as follows. In Sect. 2, we provide an overview of relevant works on the topic of zero trust and continuous authentication. In Sect. 3, we introduce our comparison framework, listing the factors used for comparative analysis and explaining their significance. In Sect. 4, we enumerate the methods that will be compared, including their basic principles and existing implementations. In Sect. 5, the comparative analysis is carried out, and the methods are evaluated based on both quantifiable and non-quantifiable characteristics. Section 6 concludes the article, discusses the results of the previous sections, and lists possible directions for future work.

2 Literature Review

In this section, we investigate several articles that are relevant to our work, or have a similar topic.

In NIST Special Publication 800–207 "Zero Trust Architecture" [5], the standard for ZTA is described in detail. It details the requirements for a zero-trust security system, its necessary components, possible implementations, etc. Among other things, it also deals with authentication in such systems. In particular, it states that an authentication system must be strong, continuous, and yet unobtrusive to the user, lest it causes serious usability issues. The requirements set in the standard are used in this article to develop a comparison framework.

In "Zero Trust Architecture: Does It Help?" [6], E. Bertino discusses some challenges in implementing a zero-trust security system. In particular, it is stated that the zero-trust security policies must be correct, consistent, minimal, and complete; that is, they must align with the organization's goals, minimize and resolve permission conflicts, include no redundancies, and yet cover every possible situation when a user interacts with the system. Not fulfilling these requirements means that either the system's security, its usability, or both suffer; thus, they must be taken into account when designing a ZTA system.

In "A survey on continuous authentication methods in Internet of Things environment" [7], F. Hussain Al-Naji and R. Zagrouba provide a comprehensive analysis of continuous authentication algorithms that can be used in an IoT system. Their investigation is extensive and thorough, although centered mainly on the topics of IoT and using blockchain for authentication.

In "Security, Privacy, and Usability in Continuous Authentication: A Survey" [8], A. F. Baig and S. Eskeland present an overview of various continuous authentication methods, focused on three main factors – security, privacy, and usability. They discuss several methods, identify their issues and possible threat directions, and finally propose directions for future research. The authors list a number of possible approaches to authentication; they do not go into detail on each, preferring rather to provide a general overview and comparison.

In "Examining the Current Status and Emerging Trends in Continuous Authentication Technologies through Citation Network Analysis" [9], J. Jeong, Y. Zolotavkin, and R. Doss analyze the most frequently referenced works on the topic of continuous authentication; they use this analysis to investigate the current trends in this field. They discover that keystroke dynamics, mouse movement, and mobile device touch are three most popular approaches at the moment. Furthermore, they point out that there is a need for a consensus on how to evaluate the algorithms' application, utility, and feasibility.

In "Continuous authentication by free-text keystroke based on CNN and RNN" [10], X. Lu et al. propose a method for keystroke dynamics-based continuous authentication that uses neural networks to determine legitimate users. Unlike many other methods, the authors' algorithm is free-text, that is, it does not require the user to enter the exact same text (e. g. a password) to be authenticated. This makes it especially fitting for continuous authentication, since one of the goals is to be unobtrusive while keeping checking the user's authenticity throughout the entire session.

In "Continuous face authentication scheme for mobile devices with tracking and liveness detection" [11], M. Smith-Creasey, F. A. Albalooshi, and M. Rajarajan propose a continuous authentication algorithm based on face recognition. It is intended for use in mobile devices. The novelty is that instead of periodical re-authentication, the system tracks the user's face and only restarts when the face is lost. According to the authors, this approach is more secure, since it eliminates certain attack windows.

In "Continuous Authentication Using Mouse Movements, Machine Learning, and Minecraft" [12], N. Siddiqui, R. Dave, and N. Seliya discuss a dynamic biometrics continuous authentication method based on the user's mouse movement patterns. They note that the most common mouse movement dataset at the moment is too homogeneous and not representative of real-world applications. To gather heterogeneous data from the users for the authors' proposed dataset, a video game is utilized; machine learning, binary random forest in particular, is used to determine a user's authenticity.

In "Touch-based continuous mobile device authentication: State-of-the-art, challenges and opportunities" [13], A. Zaidi et al. provide a comprehensive review of authentication methods based on analyzing the user's touch behaviour pattern while using a mobile device. They propose it as a viable continuous authentication method, analogous in some ways to keystroke recognition; that said, the authors also recognize that certain challenges and obstacles still remain.

In "Continuous Authentication Based on User Interaction Behavior" [14], L. Chen et al. introduce a hybrid system that combines keystroke dynamic and mouse dynamic-based authentication methods. Furthermore, their system also takes into account the overall context and whether the user's interaction with the system deviates from the norm. This makes their work stand out from many other algorithms that only rely on biometrics, and provides a possibility to further look into combining various metrics in a continuous authentication system.

In "Secure Path: Block-Chaining IoT Information for Continuous Authentication in Smart Spaces" [15], L. Bracciale et al. propose another approach to user behaviour-based authentication. Their algorithm uses smart devices worn by users to determine their physical location and other relevant characteristics, which are then used by a distributed "trust committee" to determine if a user can be trusted.

In this section, we have reviewed various existing works on the topic of continuous authentication. The information about the most relevant qualities of such systems, as well as the most common approaches and their characteristics, will be used in the remainder of this article.

3 Method Comparison Framework

3.1 Introducing the Comparison Criteria

The methods we investigate in this article vary considerably. They are based on different principles and have different requirements; as such, meaningfully comparing them is no easy task. So, in order to carry out comparative analysis of various continuous authentication methods, suitable comparison criteria must first be identified.

In [6], Bertino discusses a similar topic, and introduces several requirements a ZTA system must meet in order to be useful. Based on this, as well as other considerations, we have decided to base our analysis on a list of factors that we consider to be essential for any authentication system.

The factors are as follows:

1. Accuracy
2. User convenience
3. Feasibility
4. Universality

Let us explore each criterion in more depth.

3.2 Accuracy

The importance of accuracy is obvious. Any authentication mechanism, in order to do its job effectively, must be good in telling the difference between the legitimate users and those who do not possess the necessary credentials, yet try to gain access to the system or its components anyway (whether with malicious intent or as mere error). The two most common parameters used to determine the authentication system accuracy are usually referred to as FRR and FAR.

FRR stands for False Rejection Rate. It refers to a percentage of times the system does not grant access to a legitimate user. It is also sometimes called a Type I error.

FAR stands for False Acceptance Rate. It refers to a percentage of times the system grants access to the user not possessing the necessary credentials. It is also sometimes called a Type II error.

Obviously, an ideal system will always grant access to legitimate users and will always deny it to everyone else. In the real world, however, neither FRR nor FAR can be totally excluded from the equation. What determines an accurate system, then, is whether both FRR and FAR are low enough.

Another obvious consideration is that minimizing FRR and minimizing FAR are often somewhat opposite goals: a stricter system would likely have lower FAR and higher FRR, and vice versa for a more permissive one. We can imagine a system that always grants access to everyone and would thus have 0% FRR, or, on the other hand, a system that never grants access to anyone and would thus have 0% FAR. Both would, of course, be utterly useless in practice. Thus, it is necessary to find some balance between the two.

3.3 User Convenience

Unlike accuracy, user convenience is something that is often overlooked by security professionals, but is arguably just as vital. Any system must, in the end, serve its users, and if the security mechanism is too onerous for most users, it will seriously interfere with their experience. In a commercial context, it will likely lead to users and organizations abandoning the system altogether; in a work context, it will negatively affect the employee performance. Only when the data being protected is of utmost importance can the considerations for the user convenience be discarded.

Besides, low user convenience can lead to lapses in security as well. A simple example would be a company's employees (especially those not in IT or technical professions) being forced to memorize long and complicated passwords. Oftentimes, in practice the passwords are simply written down, which presents a serious security risk if a malicious party can gain physical access to the company's facilities.

For continuous authentication, user convenience is especially important. Using a secure yet somewhat onerous method like multi-factor authentication (MFA) once in the beginning of a work day would be acceptable to most people; however, the entire point of continuous authentication is that the entities in the system are authenticated much more often than that. Naturally, having to go through MFA many times per day is not something a lot of users would find acceptable.

3.4 Feasibility

By feasibility, we mean a number of factors that determine how easy and convenient an authentication method would be for an organization to implement. It includes various associated costs (for instance, if the method requires any special equipment to be installed), as well as how easy a method is to set up in an existing system.

Feasibility is another factor that should not be discarded from any analysis. For any organization, adopting a new technology is no easy task, and in many cases, it would not be done unless the organization understands the innovation, its importance, and how adopting it will be a benefit. In the field of authentication, passwords are a clear example – multiple security experts have proclaimed password-based authentication to be no longer effective, and plenty other methods have been developed; yet passwords remain the most popular method bar none. It is their simplicity and cheapness of implementation that contribute to them still being popular, as well as the fact that they are the "default option", and many organizations do not consider anything else.

Another example is continuous authentication in the IoT environment. As pointed out in [16], many IoT devices do not have the computational resources necessary for such a task; the authors suggest using blockchain technology to bypass this limitation.

Thus, in order for an authentication mechanism to be adopted in practice, it must be feasible for an organization to do so. Of course, like with user convenience, reasoning may differ depending on the nature of the organization and the data it is trying to protect – government entities would have a different set of goals and values compared to commercial ones. Still, the importance of feasibility should not be underestimated.

3.5 Universality

We also list universality as a criterion, by which we essentially mean whether an authentication method is platform independent. The inclusion of this factor is motivated by the fact that modern distributed systems are increasingly becoming more heterogeneous. Their components might include mobile devices, laptops, personal computers, servers, etc. So, for instance, if the authentication method only works for mobile phones, it will be a serious limitation in any other context.

3.6 Other Criteria

Aside from the four main criteria listed above, other miscellaneous factors and concerns may also be addressed if necessary.

3.7 Framework Summary

The framework for comparative analysis is summarized in Table 1.

Table 1. Authentication methods comparison framework.

No	Criterion	Meaning
1	Accuracy	FRR (false rejection rate) and FAR (false acceptance rate)
2	User convenience	Whether the method interferes with the users' normal experience
3	Feasibility	Possible complications that can arise during the method's implementation
4	Universality	Whether the method has any limitations regarding devices it can be used with
5	Other criteria	Any other concerns not addressed by the aforementioned sections

4 Continuous Authentication Methods

4.1 Overview

Continuous authentication can be implemented through use of various methods. The basic idea, however, remains the same: instead of authenticating a user once at the beginning of their session, the system keeps checking their authenticity throughout the entire session. The checking consists of comparing the user's current behaviour – as measured by some metric or algorithm – to their normal behaviour. If it is similar enough, the authentication algorithm considers the user to still be legitimate, otherwise, a more explicit check is used (e. g. MFA). In this way, continuous authentication works in tandem with existing user authentication methods, instead of replacing them completely.

Consider, for instance, an example where a user connects to the system through a mobile phone (e. g. opening a blockchain wallet application). If the user is successfully authenticated through a standard method, and then a third party gets their hands on the user's phone, this third party then gains access to the system for the duration of the session, and possibly indefinitely. Other similar cases include using keyloggers or social engineering, users connecting to unsafe third-party websites, etc. Continuous authentication helps prevent breaches in such instances – it is believed that a new entity using the existing entity's credentials will still behave in a sufficiently distinct way for the system to raise an alarm and investigate.

So, in order for the continuous authentication to work, it needs a way to distinguish one user's behaviour from another one's. There are multiple ways to achieve this; when it comes to human users, one of the most common approaches is to use static or dynamic biometrics.

Biometric authentication is based on a person's unique biological properties. The most common variety is static biometrics, including fingerprint scanning, facial recognition, retina scanning, etc. It analyzes some property of the user's body that is both unique and unchanging, converts it to a convenient data format, and compares it with the expected value of data. Dynamic biometrics, on the other hand, analyze some aspect of the user's behaviour – the way they type, move their mouse, walk, talk, etc.

Another way is to analyze the entity's actions in the system. For instance, if an entity starts requesting access to multiple files and locations it did not need before, sending or receiving larger-than-usual amounts of data, or performing other atypical actions, the zero-trust system can flag this as suspicious behaviour and act accordingly.

4.2 Keystroke-Based User Recognition

Keystroke biometrics is one of the oldest and most common types of dynamic biometric authentication. It is based on the principle that just as each person has their own distinct handwriting, the way different people type is also different.

There are many different features that can be used to establish a user's "signature". These include the time it takes to press or release a key, the time between key taps, the way a user enters certain common combinations of symbols (words like "the", "and", etc.), and many others.

The usual way to utilize keystroke recognition for user authentication purposes is to have the user enter some predetermined text. This can be used as a one-off security mechanism in the beginning of a session, but it does not particularly fit the requirements of continuous authentication. To authenticate the user throughout the session, it would require them to enter the same text multiple times at some time interval, which goes against our user convenience criterion. On the other hand, some of the newer algorithms use the so-called "free-text" keystroke recognition: the user does not have to enter any specific words or sentences, any text input will do.

Machine learning is a very useful tool for keystroke biometrics. A neural network can learn the keystroke patterns of a certain users, and then use them to verify if the input comes from a certain user or an impostor. For the free-text method, using neural networks seems to be the most efficient approach.

4.3 Face Identification

Face identification is one of the most common forms of biometric authentication. Unlike keystroke recognition, face identification is a type of static biometric algorithm, analyzing not user behavioral patterns, but rather some immutable characteristic unique to each user – in this case, the shape of their face and facial features.

Face recognition algorithms began their development in the 1960s, and have gradually grown more and more sophisticated and usable in real-world scenarios. Nowadays, they are used for an extremely wide variety of tasks, user authentication in various systems being one of the most common uses.

The main principle face recognition algorithms rely upon is that each human face has a large number of distinguishable characteristics, or landmarks: distance between the eyes, width of the nose, the shape of the cheekbones, etc. Taking these characteristics from an image and transforming them into digital format, an authentication algorithm gets some piece of data, which it then compares with the corresponding entry in its database. If it gets a fit – if the user's features correspond to those the one who currently claims to be the user possesses – then the authentication is successful.

4.4 Mouse Movement Recognition

Mouse movement recognition is another type of dynamic biometrics authentication algorithm. As the name suggests, it is based on recognizing unique patterns in the way a user moves their mouse and clicks the mouse buttons. It is more recent and less common compared to the algorithms described above; however, there is still a not-inconsiderable number of works on this topic.

Like with keystroke recognition, mouse movement recognition algorithms generally come in two types. One type deals with specific types of mouse movement, and gives the user certain tasks to fulfill in order to authenticate them. The other type uses general mouse movement, using the data generated by the users as they go about their daily activities on their computer. Once again, for continuous authentication purposes, the latter type is vastly more preferable.

Machine learning is as useful here as it is with other types of dynamic biometrics; in Sect. 5, ML-based mouse movement recognition algorithms are investigated.

4.5 Touch Gesture-based Authentication

Touch gesture-based authentication is yet another type of dynamic biometric authentication method that is currently gaining traction. The increasing popularity of mobile devices, as well as other types of equipment using touchscreens as an alternative or in addition to keyboard and mouse, makes this class of authentication algorithms more and more relevant.

Broadly, the similar principles apply here as with other user behaviour-based methods. In gesture-based authentication, the main point of interest is the swipe – a singular gesture made while interacting with a touchscreen. Such characteristics as the swipe's starting position, its trajectory, the average pressure, etc. can be taken into account. Some algorithms consider not just the individual swipes, but also the data from the entire session, like the average number of swipes and the average time between swipes. As with other algorithms, machine learning is the main tool utilized for confirming a user's authenticity based on their interaction with a touchscreen.

4.6 User Behaviour-Based Authentication

User behaviour-based authentication, unlike the majority of continuous authentication, algorithms, does not necessarily have to be based on biometrics. Rather, it analyzes the actions the user usually performs during a session, such as their interaction with various system components and applications, the requests they make from the system, etc., and then, based on this data, makes the decision on whether the user's actions in any given session are unusual and should be investigated further.

However, biometrics can also be a part of the authentication system, being one of the characteristics considered in order to determine whether the user behaves "as usual." So, some of the algorithms mentioned above can also be a part of a user behaviour-based method.

4.7 Authentication Methods Summary

The continuous authentication methods that we have described above are summarized in Table 2.

Table 2. Continuous authentication methods.

Method	Based on	Source
Keystroke-based	How the user presses the keys, enters certain combinations, etc	[10]
Face recognition	Continuous observation of the user's face via a camera	[11]
Mouse movement	How the user moves the mouse, clicks the mouse buttons, etc	[12]
Touch gesture	How the user interacts with a touchscreen device, presses, swipes, performs multi-touch gestures, etc	[13]
User behaviour	The patterns of the user's interactions with the system, possibly combined with other methods	[14]

5 Comparative Analysis

5.1 Methods Evaluation

Accuracy. Here, the accuracy of each method is considered, based on the results presented in existing literature.

Keystroke-based recognition's accuracy was evaluated in [10]. Depending on the dataset, FRR ranged from 1.89% to 6.61%, and FAR ranged from 2.83% to 5.31%.

Face identification's accuracy was evaluated in [11]. Depending on the dataset and the specific features used, FRR ranged from 1.49% to 37.89%, and FAR ranged from 1.05% to 60.81%.

Mouse movement recognition's accuracy was evaluated in [12]. A slightly different terms were used (false negatives rate and false positives rate), but overall, FRR ranged from 0% to 77.04%, and FAR ranged from 11.86% to 28.73%.

Touch gesture-based authentication's accuracy was evaluated in [13]. Multiple different approaches were mentioned, each with accuracy data from the relevant studies. Across different studies, FRR ranged from 1.65% to 28.52%, whereas FAR ranged from 0.04% to 22.45%.

User behaviour-based authentication's accuracy was evaluated in [14]. The authors claim FAR of 0% for all cases of their scenario, whereas FRR ranged from 0% to 5.88%. Other studies were mentioned as well, with maximum FRR of 2.10% and FAR of 5.7% across three different studies.

The distribution of FAR and FRR across different methods is shown in Fig. 2.

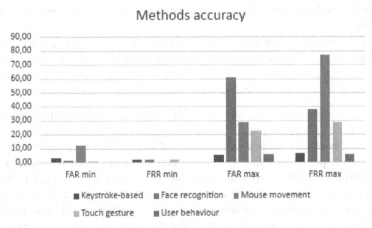

Fig. 2. Methods accuracy distribution.

User Convenience. Here, we investigate how convenient each method is for the end user, given that it will need to be used continuously throughout every session in the system.

Keystroke-based recognition is very convenient for the user if two conditions hold: first, that text-based input is used as the main method of interacting with the system (as opposed to, for instance, mainly using a cursor), and second, that the recognition method is free-text: that is, *any* input text is acceptable to determine the user's authenticity. If the user does not use their keyboard while interacting with the system, it will need to prompt them to enter some text, which would interrupt the normal workflow. And, of course, if a user is forced to enter the same text several times throughout the session, there can be no convenience to speak of. However, if both of these conditions can be ensured, keystroke-based recognition would be one of the most unobtrusive methods to currently exist.

Face identification's convenience depends greatly on technology used. Some methods might not recognize the user's face from certain angles, or if the lighting is insufficient, or if a part of their face is obscured, or in some other cases. This is even more pronounced in mobile-based identification, where the device's camera has to be pointed at the user's face for the majority of the time. All in all, while this method cannot be called absolutely inconvenient per se, it still has certain inherent challenges the other approaches lack.

Mouse movement recognition is generally similar to keystroke-based recognition, with the necessary caveat that the user needs to chiefly use their cursor over their keyboard. Other than that, the same two conditions hold, and which method of the two is preferable depends on how an average user is projected to interact with the system.

Touch gesture-based authentication has the advantage that when it is used, there are generally no other alternatives, so there are less problems with users having to prioritize one method of input or the other. Devices with combined touch-based and keyboard/mouse-based input do exist, but they are less common. The other condition from above still holds – as long as the user does not have to fulfill a predetermined task, but can just be authenticated while working with the system, the convenience level will be sufficiently high.

User behaviour-based authentication is convenient if the user is expected to carry out similar actions during each session. If, however, the actions can differ in a significant manner, an alarm can be raised, even though the user is legitimate; this possibility can be considered as a negative for user convenience.

Feasibility This part looks into how cheap and simple the authentication method is to implement in an existing system.

Keystroke-based recognition has certain challenges when it comes to its practical implementation, particularly free-text recognition – which, as we have established earlier, is a must for a usable continuous authentication mechanism. Firstly, it is necessary to build up a considerable database of keyboard input samples for each user, so that it can be used to determine whether any given text input was typed by the user in question. Also, training the neural network – given that the most common approaches involve deep learning, CNNs, and RNNs – can take a non-inconsiderable amount of time and computational resources. So, the added requirements for data storage space and necessary computations should be taken into consideration, as well as the fact that the method needs to learn the user's "signature" before working properly.

Face identification requires that each device is outfitted with a video camera. This is not much of a problem for mobile devices, but can be an additional expense when it comes to desktop-based devices. If the distributed system is large enough, the financial requirements would not be inconsiderable. Besides, a database of faces should also be created, though the mechanism to do so is older and more developed compared to other methods mentioned in this article, and the overall method would likely be more familiar to the majority of system owners and administrators.

Mouse movement recognition faces many of the similar problems to keystroke-based recognition. Namely, it needs to be free-form, so a database of mouse movement patterns must be built, and a neural network must be trained. The authors of one article [12] suggest a video game-based format to do so, but it might not be a good fit for every system.

Touch gesture-based authentication is also similar to keystroke-based recognition – in fact, many of the earlier methods were adapted from keystroke-based methods. That said, using a touchscreen adds certain peculiarities of its own; for instance, the fact that multi-touch is possible (unlike with a keyboard or a mouse) should also be taken into account.

User behaviour-based authentication faces many of the same issues other methods do, particularly if biometric algorithms are implemented as a part of it. In addition, a database of typical behavioural patterns for each user needs to be built up. For instance, in [14], the volunteers worked on data collection for 30 days before sufficient amount of user behaviour data was collected.

Universality. Here, we see how universal the method is – that is, whether it can be used with various types of devices that can be a part of a heterogeneous distributed system.

Keystroke-based recognition can be applied to systems that utilize a keyboard as an input mechanism. This is a rather broad category – including personal computers, laptops, mainframes, etc. – but it does exclude most mobile devices, which are becoming more and more common. Thus, this method cannot be called universal.

Face identification can be used with any device that has a camera. This includes most modern mobile devices, but it is less of a certainty when it comes to personal computers. Nevertheless, under the condition that a camera is either a part of the device a user is expected to use or can be installed separately, this authentication method can be used for a wide range of devices.

Mouse movement recognition broadly has the same limitations as keystroke-based recognition, since most modern devices that use a keyboard also use a mouse. It is also limited to such devices, and so is not universal.

Touch gesture-based authentication is, naturally, limited to devices that use a touch screen. As noted before, some of these devices also utilize a keyboard and a mouse; however, for such devices, touch screen is usually not the main input method, so a continuous authentication algorithm for them cannot be reasonably based on touch gesture recognition. This approach is also not universal.

User behaviour-based authentication's universality can vary, since this category is rather broad and can include other approaches in turn. In general, though, the idea of authenticating a user based on their behaviour in the system is not inherently limited to any one type of device or input method; therefore, this approach can generally be considered to be a more universal one.

Other Criteria. The one thing that is usually either absent from comparative analysis or is mentioned only in passing would be possible privacy concerns from the prospective users. This is especially relevant since most methods we list involve biometrics – that is, the users will have to consent to having some of their features recorded, stored, and used for authentication, with the understanding that this data might be compromised in an attempt to gain access to the system.

We believe that face identification in particular can lead to such concerns. Face recognition technology is widely associated with biometrics, and, despite becoming more widespread in the recent years, has drawn both criticism and governmental restrictions in multiple countries [17]. Other methods discussed, on the other hand, are more obscure among the general public, and would likely lack such associations. That said, more in-depth research about public perception of different biometric authentication methods would be necessary to examine this issue in more detail.

5.2 Final Results

In this subsection, we sum up the results of our comparative analysis.

Overall, keystroke-based recognition was found to be the most consistently accurate approach, whereas for most other methods, both FRR and FAR can vary greatly, depending on the input data, the specific algorithms used, the usage scenarios, etc.

Most of the methods discussed above can be considered convenient for the end users, since they do not usually interrupt their normal workflow. Face recognition is likely the least convenient for the purposes of continuous authentication, since it needs the user to constantly look at the camera. User behaviour-based methods, meanwhile, need the user to interact with the system in a consistent, repetitive manner.

As for feasibility, most methods can be considered feasible to implement, since they do not require any additional hardware to be installed; face recognition is the exception, since it does need a camera for each device a user can utilize to connect to the system. All methods do, however, need to collect data on user input and/or behaviour patterns, and use it to train a neural network, which means additional storage and computational resources requirements.

Most of the methods cannot be considered universal, since they need specific input methods to work; once again, face recognition is an exception. Whether user behaviour-based authentication is universal depends on whether other biometric methods are a part of its implementation.

Finally, since most methods are biometric, possible privacy concerns should be taken into consideration, especially in case of face recognition.

The results are summarized in Table 3.

Table 3. Comparative analysis final results.

Method	Keystroke-based	Face recognition	Mouse movement-based	Touch gesture-based	User behaviour-based
FAR, %	2.83–5.31	1.05–60.81	11.86–28.73	0.04–22.45	0–5.7
FRR, %	1.89–6.61	1.49–37.89	0–77.04	1.65–28.52	0–5.88
Convenience	Convenient for free-text methods	Needs constant observation of the user	Convenient for free-input methods	Convenient for free-input methods	Needs stable user action patterns
Feasibility	Needs a neural network and a database of keystroke patterns	Needs a neural network + database + camera for each device	Needs a neural network and a database of mouse movement patterns	Needs a neural network and a database of touch gesture patterns	Needs a neural network + database for behaviour patterns and additional biometric methods
Universality	No, needs a keyboard	Possibly, needs a camera	No, needs a mouse	No, needs touchscreen	Possibly, depends on implementation
Other concerns	Minor privacy concerns	Major privacy concerns	Minor privacy concerns	Minor privacy concerns	Privacy concerns (if using biometrics)

6 Conclusions and Future Work

Continuous authentication is an essential part of zero-trust security – a new paradigm that can make for a much better protection of distributed systems in the age of blockchain, cloud computing, and remote work. In this article, we have carried out a comprehensive comparative analysis of five approaches to continuous user authentication in the context of a zero-trust security system – keystroke recognition, face recognition, mouse movement recognition, touch gesture recognition, and user behaviour analysis.

We have developed a framework for comparing different methods, and then used it to evaluate the most promising continuous authentication methods. Various factors were considered as a part of the framework – from recognition accuracy to user convenience and privacy concerns.

Most of the methods we have considered require some specific input method to work, so they cannot be universally applied to any devices in a heterogeneous system. Face recognition can be considered universal, but it has other limitations when it comes to feasibility, user convenience, and possible privacy concerns. User behaviour-based methods can be universal as well (depending on implementation specifics), and show good results in regard to authentication accuracy, but they need additional data about the user behaviour patterns, and besides, they require the user to interact with the system in a predictable manner.

As for accuracy, keystroke-based recognition and user behaviour-based methods show the best consistent results.

Also, as we have seen, there is no need to limit ourselves to using just one method. Hybrid approaches, combining two or more various metrics, are present in the literature. They allow the security system to become more universal – allowing it to be used for users with various devices with various input types – as well as more flexible, taking into account multiple factors that help determine the user's authenticity. On the other hand, such systems can also be more complicated and difficult to implement compared to using a single metric.

Regarding the hybrid methods' accuracy, it can be estimated to be similar or higher compared to the methods using a single authentication factor. In particular, a method evaluated in this paper, combining user behaviour, keyboard, and mouse-based authentication, has demonstrated one of the best results in both FAR and FRR.

The field of continuous authentication is currently actively developing. New methods, or new variations of older methods – like free-text keystroke recognition, for instance – are being invented and put into practice. Of course, this means that many approaches are quite imperfect, and while they might not show the best results now, it is reasonable to expect notable improvements in the near future. Mouse movement recognition can serve as an example – the datasets existing now are for the most part limited and not representative of practical everyday use, but works are now appearing that seek to change that.

Machine learning is an essential tool for all methods of continuous authentication. As we have seen, every approach investigated is likely to involve neural networks in some way, shape, or form; the most common approach is to create a database of patterns associated with each user (ways of inputting data, face shape information, system interaction patterns) and then use it to determine whether the user is who they claim to be.

Based on the above, the following directions for future work present themselves:

- Further development of dynamic biometric methods suitable for use in zero-trust systems, i. e., continuous authentication methods. Examples include free-text keyboard recognition and non-specific mouse movement recognition.
- Discovering approaches in the field of machine learning most suitable for our task, based both on accuracy and other factors, such as feasibility and usability.
- Addressing the user privacy concerns, since most of the methods currently in use employ the users' biometric information. Depersonalizing the biometric data is one possible way to address these concerns.
- Considering hybrid continuous authentication methods.

Acknowledgment. This work was supported by Saint-Petersburg State University, project ID: 94062114.

References

1. Verizon 2022 data breach investigations report. https://www.verizon.com/business//resources/reports/dbir/2022/master-guide/. Accessed 02 Apr 2023
2. Microsoft security zero trust adoption report. https://query.prod.cms.rt.microsoft.com/cms/api/am/binary/RWGWha. Accessed 05 Apr 2023
3. Higgins, K.J.: Forrester pushes 'Zero trust' Model for security. https://www.darkreading.com/perimeter/forrester-pushes-zero-trust-model-for-security. Accessed 05 Apr 2023

4. Davis, J., Simos, M., Skoniecki, J.: Back to the future: what the Jericho forum taught us about modern security. https://www.microsoft.com/en-us/security/blog/2020/10/28/back-to-the-fut ure-what-the-jericho-forum-taught-us-about-modern-security/. Accessed 05 Apr 2023

5. Rose, S., Borchert, O., Mitchell, S., Connelly, S.: Zero trust architecture. https://doi.org/10. 6028/NIST.SP.800-207. Accessed 06 Apr 2023

6. Bertino, E.: Zero trust architecture: does it help? IEEE Secur. Priv. 5(19), 95–96 (2021)

7. Hussain Al-Naji, F., Zagrouba, R.: A survey on continuous authentication methods in internet of things environment. Comput. Commun. 163, 109–133 (2020)

8. Baig, A.F., Eskeland, S.: Security, privacy, and usability in continuous authentication: a survey. Sensors 21(17), 59–67 (2021)

9. Jeong, J., Zolovatkin, Y., Doss, R.: Examining the current status and emerging trends in continuous authentication technologies through citation network analysis. ACM Comput. Surv. 56(4), 31 (2022). Article 111

10. Lu, X., Zhang, S., Hui, P., Lio, P.: Continuous authentication by free-text keystroke based on CNN and RNN. Comput. Secur. 96, 101861 (2020)

11. Smith-Creasey, M., Albalooshi, F.A., Rajarajan, M.: Continuous face authentication scheme for mobile devices with tracking and liveness detection. Microprocess. Microsyst. 63, 147–157 (2018)

12. Siddiqui, N., Dave, R., Seliya, N.: Continuous authentication using mouse movements, machine learning, and Minecraft. In: Proceedings of the International Conference on Electrical, Computer and Energy Technologies (ICECET). IEEE, Cape Town, South Africa (2021)

13. Zaidi, A.Z., Chong, C.Y., Jin, Z., Parthiban, R., Sadiq, A.S.: Touch-based continuous mobile device authentication: state-of-the-art, challenges and opportunities. J. Netw. Comput. Appl. 191, 103162 (2021)

14. Chen, L., Zhong, Y., Ai, W., Zhang, D.: Continuous authentication based on user interaction behavior. In: 7th International Symposium on Digital Forensics and Security (ISDFS), pp. 1–6. IEEE, Barcelos, Portugal (2019)

15. Bracciale, L., Loreti, P., Pisa, C., Shahidi, A.: Secure path: block-chaining IoT information for continuous authentication in smart spaces. IoT 2(2), 326–340 (2021)

16. Hussain Al-Naji, F., Zagrouba, R.: CAB-IoT: continuous authentication architecture based on Blockchain for internet of things. J. King Saud Univ. Comput. Inf. Sci. 6(34), 2497–2514 (2022)

17. Facial recognition technology and privacy concerns. https://www.isaca.org/resources/news-and-trends/newsletters/atisaca/2022/volume-51/facial-recognition-technology-and-privacy-concerns. Accessed 07 Apr 2023

Spatial Cognition in Urban and Regional Planning Under Risk (SCOPUR23)

Mapping Citizens' Knowledge and Perception. What Support for Flood Risk Planning? Some Tips from Brindisi Case Study

Stefania Santoro[1], Vincenzo Totaro[2], Giulia Mastrodonato[2](✉), and Pasquale Balena[2]

[1] Water Research Institute of National Research Council (IRSA, CNR), Bari, Italy
[2] Polytechnic University of Bari, Bari, Italy
`giulia.mastrodonato@poliba.it`

Abstract. Flood risk management strategies are of paramount importance in ensuring the safeguard of people and assets. It is now widely recognized the importance of defining adequate nonstructural measures in coping with flood risk to be implemented in urban planning tools. The importance of evaluating citizens' knowledge and perception of risk represents a key factor in order to support the decision-making process of planning mitigation activities. However, attempts to map this information are still far from a complete formalization. In this study an integrated approach combining historical events news and survey-collected information about flood risk perception for the city of Brindisi (southern Italy) is described. Collected information has been analyzed and georeferenced in order to define and provide three different layers of maps, each highlighting a peculiar aspect of flood risk. The mutual analysis of these layers allows to detect interactions between different aspects of risk management and can constitute a precious source of information for implementing flood risk mitigation strategies in urban context.

Keywords: Flood Risk Mapping · Non-structural Mitigation Measures · Urban Planning

1 Introduction

It is estimated that the continued increase in population and economic resources in flood-prone areas, could increase global flood exposure by a factor of three by 2050 [1]. Traditional spatial planning policies such as zoning and building codes do not seem sufficient to reduce the exposure and vulnerability of people and assets [2]. In this context, synergies between urban planning and flood risk management become essential.

Structural and non-structural measures can be adopted in order to substantially reduce the incidence of the resulting damage in case of flood events. These include actions aimed at rational and sustainable urban planning, more effective emergency management strategies and the adoption of preventive behavior to mitigate flood risk from a socio-psychological perspective. [3]. As reported in *A Whole Community Approach to*

O. Gervasi et al. (Eds.): ICCSA 2023 Workshops, LNCS 14109, pp. 355–367, 2023.
https://doi.org/10.1007/978-3-031-37120-2_23

Emergency Management: Principles, Themes, and Pathways for Action [4], the involvement of local communities represents an indispensable basis during the emergency planning phase of risk. Their contribution helps in building a deeper knowledge deriving from their experiences, composite background, expectations and the proposed hypotheses of behavior in case of risk. It allows to elicit weaknesses and vulnerabilities that would not emerge through analyzes based on traditional tools and methods and increase citizens' sense of responsibility. Therefore, an accurate characterization of risks and a better evaluation of the effectiveness of risk management strategies should consider the integration of community behavior and behavioral adaptation dynamics in complete flood emergency management strategies. In this sense, a challenge in quantitative risk assessment is represented by the need to introduce the interpretation of the role of individual risk perceptions and understand how these perceptions influence risk reduction behaviors. Undoubtedly some factors such as previous direct/indirect experiences of flooding, level of education, socioeconomic status, frequency and severity of catastrophic events influence the choices of individuals to adopt precautionary measures against natural and flood risks. Furthermore, the scientific community put the reduction of social vulnerability as another key element in the mitigation of flood damage. As a matter of fact, the behavioral attitudes of citizens, companies and government agencies can heavily influence the impact and recovery time both before, during and after a disaster [5].

In this context, an important role is attributed to the knowledge of the places offered by inhabitants or people so familiar with the area to be defined as "local experts". Therefore it becomes essential to access the knowledge of 'expert' agents in the traditional sense [6], i.e. agents who have formal knowledge, even partial, in relation to their specific skills, able to read "the place from the inside" thanks to the time spent there, the life experience accumulated there, the knowledge of the places handed down from previous generations, the possibility of observing the trend of the dynamics of urban transformation over time. Often, they are not experts in urban planning and regulatory techniques but can contribute to the construction of the general knowledge framework [6].

This informal, non-expert knowledge must be brought into play alongside the expertise of emergency planners and managers. Therefore, emergency plans should represent the result of multidisciplinary and multi-actor processes that aim to anticipate, with the available resources, urgent needs that cannot be satisfied during the emergency phase. In this sense, the preparatory process to support flood risk planning must be coordinated and cooperative and must include the elaboration of general plans and procedures also aimed at specific sectors such as education, health, industry and commerce. Procedures that must involve the participation of a wide variety of first responders, technicians and citizens. A further complication of emergency planning is the need to integrate different dimensions also in governmental terms, allowing the overlapping of plans and measures to different hierarchies in response to local, regional, up to national and international emergencies. In fact, first aid begins at the local level and when local resources become insufficient, inter-municipal, regional, national or even international scales come into play. Emergency and territorial planning tools often overlap, acting on different geographical scales, involving different and not always coherent actors [7]. However, it is noteworthy that natural hazards still remain multidimensional phenomena with a strong spatial component.

Based on these premises in this work, local knowledge and risk perception have been spatialised in order to build a multi-layers map to support flood risk planning with some remarks regarding the implications for urban planning. The innovative character can be glimpsed in the attempt to spatialize data relating to the social sphere and combine them with some of the existing physical information of the territory, such as data deriving from geographic information systems (GIS).

Their use allows cartographic approaches to physical risk mapping, integrative spatial risk modeling and disaster response planning [8]. They offer the advantage of representing a huge variety of climatic, demographic, economic and sociological data by making information on places, buildings, services and resources available to users and at the same time allowing their punctual and specific localization throughout the territory [9].

Testing the effectiveness of using maps of a social nature could open up an implementation perspective in the current Territorial Information Systems (SIT) used by public administrations for the planning, management and use of risks and of the land management.

A multistep methodology has been used and experimentally applied to the case study of the city of Brindisi.

2 Materials and Methods

Data exploited in this study were collected at the same time as those exploited in Santoro et al. (2022) and properly updated for this study. Further details and descriptions can be found in [12].

2.1 Study Area

Brindisi is an Italian municipality with 82,773 inhabitants [10]. It lies on a natural harbour on the Adriatic coast of Puglia (Fig. 1).

From a hydraulic point of view, the city is crossed by several streams, Canale Cillarese (Fig. 1, a), characterized by the presence of an embankment dam; Canale Patri (Fig. 1, b), the stream mainly interacting with the urban fabric, Fiume Piccolo (Fig. 1, c) and Fiume Grande (Fig. 1, d).

The presence of these streams, combined with the hydrogeological characteristics of the area and the dense urban network have caused several flooding events over the years, analysed below. High flood hazard areas identified in this areas are illustrated in Fig. 2 [11].

Fig. 1. Stream network of the city of Brindisi (a: Canale Cillarese; b: Canale Patri; c: Fiume Piccolo; d: Fiume Grande).

Fig. 2. Flood hazard map for an event with a return period of 30 years (in blue) (PAI, 2019).

2.2 Mapping the Risk

In the field of flood risk planning, it is not enough to focus on goods at risk but local perceptions, traditions, economies, the safety of vulnerable people, their social reactions, inclusion activities and participation in emergency planning processes come into play. It is necessary to overcome the physical dimension of the disaster and ensure greater integration between specialist knowledge and local knowledge, favoring shared solutions with the local community [13]. Although integrating community responses and behavioral adaptation dynamics into disaster planning is known to improve management strategies, efforts in social vulnerability research [14] are still heavily overlooked.

To deal with these additional elements of complexity, currently one of the key challenges in quantitative risk assessment is represented by the introduction of the role of individual risk perceptions and the influence they exert on risk reduction behaviors [15]. Obviously, the qualitative approaches to the definition of disaster risk reduction must be accompanied by quantitative assessments capable of estimating the extent and frequency of natural hazards, the exposure and vulnerability of goods and people in those specific conditions of danger [2]. This multiplicity and complexity of elements requires the use of more specific skills and sophisticated tools capable of collecting and processing information from different and detailed sources.

A valuable support in emergency planning comes from the introduction of Information Systems (GIS) capable of managing and implementing a more in-depth knowledge of the multi-faceted elements not only in terms of exposure but also of vulnerability. In this sense, the spatial dimension should be considered together with the functional, social and economic one both in the emergency phase and in the post-event phase, which is often very critical [7].

However, GIS practitioners, being experts in software and spatial data manipulation and modelling problems, focus fundamentally on technological aspects, often neglecting user perceptions, cognitive responses and their own perceptions [16]. A general neglect of human interaction problems often appears in their applications. This is most likely due to the fact that human behaviour and risk perception represent an extremely and intrinsically complex topic to understand and quantitatively integrate into their methodologies. Indeed, in these circumstances human behaviour is often unpredictable probably because, according to one branch of the literature, populations in high risk areas are often unaware of the dangers of flooding. This results in a low perception of risk and, consequently, they maintain a low level of concern, not adopting appropriate protective measures [2].

However, this data is challenging to be implemented in GIS systems. On the other hand, the lack of awareness of the risk or its underestimation due to lack of recent experience of the danger, or due to a lack of information provided by risk managers [17] results in underinvestment by households in flood protection of their assets, even when such measures are cost-effective [18].

In an emergency, a series of complex individual and group interactions occur. The key factor becomes the speed of spatial movement of people, assets and services. Maps allow for such representations, but the way in which the elements of a map are organized is critical to enabling fast communication of the message. In fact, under evacuation conditions, under time constraints the map must be able to provide the user with a complete photograph already after a quick glance. Alternatively, if poorly designed, it could leave the reader both visually and intellectually confused and disoriented [19, 20]. Negatively influencing his behaviour. A clear hierarchy of maps is, therefore, the most important cartographic element [19]. Dymon and Winter [19] demonstrated that a clear hierarchy of maps allows users to quickly extract relevant information. Crossland [25] argues that users' decision times are reduced after studying a GIS display when compared with the times deriving from the use of paper maps, also improving the accuracy of the choices made. The design of cartographic presentations must, therefore, be carefully studied.

During emergencies, maps provide vital geographic information and facilitate preventive evacuation processes. They are therefore powerful tools for communicating risk analyzes and the results of their assessment. In this way they favour the decision-making process both in the preliminary investigation phase and in the definition of risk management strategies, becoming a fundamental element both in the coordination phase of preventive activities and during evacuation, protection and rescue operations. For these reasons they should become an integral part of emergency plans [19]. The purpose of risk analysis is to spatially identify where the risk is greatest and to indicate possible escape routes, allowing for the rapid spatial movement of people, goods and services.

Maps address different audiences and play a critical role. Therefore, it would be appropriate, in the design phase, to consider not only the choice of data to be collected, but also the cultural, educational, socio-economic factors that influence people's ability to use maps effectively [21]. The adoption of the cognitive and social approach would make it possible to implement the spatial behaviours adopted by the users, the daily routines, the public conceptions of the local geography, the knowledge of the local tradition, thus favouring the development of flexible plans. In fact, it is known that, in the event of an emergency, people tend to choose their own evacuation routes rather than using the planned ones [19]. These sociologically recognized spatial behaviours should be integrated into risk planning tools and consequent representations. Such diverse and multiple data can only be managed by a GIS tool capable of choosing the elements to represent, sourcing from numerous databases.

Starting from these premises in this work, local knowledge and risk perception have been spatialised in order to build a multi-layers map to support flood risk planning.

2.3 Multi-layers Maps Design

The methodology adopted to create the multi-layers map to support flood risk planning in the city of Brindisi involved three main steps (Fig. 3).

1. collection of historical event data;
2. analysis of floodable roads in accordance with citizens' local knowledge;
3. analysis of districts perceived at risk in accordance with citizens' flood risk perception.

The results from the above-mentioned analyses were geolocated in GIS maps, constituting what is referred to as *layers*.

STEP	HISTORICAL FLOOD DATA COLLECTION	ASSESSMENT OF THE MOST FLOODED ROADS according citizens' knowledge	ASSESSMENT OF THE MOST FLOODED DISTRICTS according citizens' perception
METHOD	Qualitative analysis from AVT dataset 2021 and local newspapers (from 1950 to 1999)	Qualitative analysis from on-line interviews	Risk perception analysis from on-line interviews
OUTPUT	Layer 1	Layer 2	Layer 3

Fig. 3. Methodology process

The first step involves a preliminary collection of flood events from the AVI dataset, available until 1999 [3]. Therefore, a newspaper-based analysis allowed to deepen and verify the data collected of occurrences of floods, allowing to retrieve also affected streets and neighborhoods, as well as notices about hydrological and hydraulic dynamics of events. Analysis has been focused during the years 1951–1999 and an amount of sixty-four events has been identified.

In order to extend this investigation to recent years, a further study using online newspapers was conducted finding on average a couple of flood events per year. Nevertheless, it has not been possible to verify the robustness of the available online information due to the different nature of references.

It should be remarked that not for all of them the information about streets or neighborhoods was available. For the purpose of this analysis, we decided to focus only on affected streets, and the localisation of the information about the number of flood events gave rise to *layer 1* (Fig. 4).

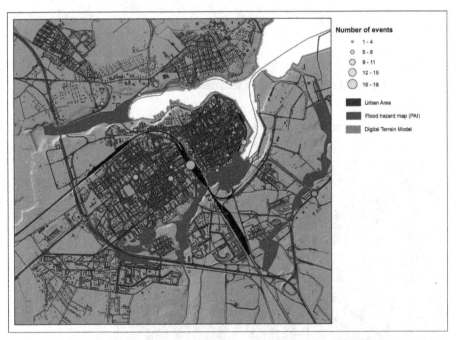

Fig. 4. Layer 1: geolocalised historical flood event. The size of the sphere indicates the number of events recorded [4].

The analysis of roads and districts susceptible to being flooded in accordance with citizens' knowledge has been possible from analysis of data collected during online interviews, took place from November 2019 and May 2020 and involved 301 citizens.

Specifically, as part of work defined in more detail in [12], citizens have been asked through an open-ended question, which road would be most at risk of flooding in the case of heavy rainfall.

The street names have been recorded and structured according to the histogram below (Fig. 5).

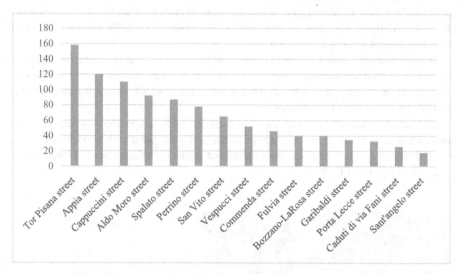

Fig. 5. The flood risk roads in accordance with citizens' knowledge

The geolocalisation of this data gave rise to *layer 2* (Fig. 6).

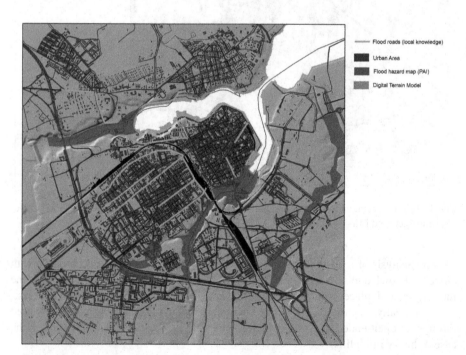

Fig. 6. Layer 2: geolocalised flood risk roads in accordance with citizens' knowledge

With respect to the evaluation of districts perceived to be subject to flood risk, an online semi-structured interview (SSIs) has been built in order to collect data regarding citizens' flood risk perception. The questions of SSIs were structured according to a Likert scale (from 1 to 7) and investigated five items of perception according to the theoretical framework of [22–24], as Cognitive, Awareness, Knowledge, Risk Communication and Trust.

In this work, the perception dimension has been measured by taking into consideration the resident population, without any distinction between gender, age and other socio-demographic characteristics analyzed in the above-mentioned study. The reason for this choice lies in the fact that the above-mentioned study showed that there is little difference in perceived risk between those living in a flood-risk area and in a non-risk area. Therefore, the subdivision would be irrelevant.

The assessment of flood risk perception was carried out instead by using the Mann-Whitney test (MWT).

The geolocalisation of this data gave rise to *layer 3* (Fig. 7).

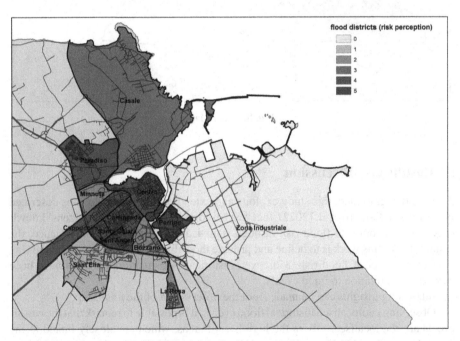

Fig. 7. Layer 3: geolocalised flood risk district in accordance with citizens' perception

The overlap of the three layers give rise to the final map (Fig. 8).

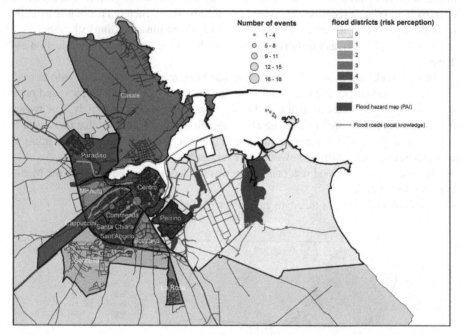

Fig. 8. Final Map

3   Results and Discussion

As already highlighted, this study exploits and extends data and conclusions described in the work of Santoro et al. (2022), that was based on the structuring of citizens' knowledge and perception of flood risk through statistical methods. As a consequence, the assumption of this work is to define and provide three different layers, each highlighting a peculiar aspect of flood risk. Moreover, historical investigation activities have been carried out in relation to flood events.

Interesting insights can be made from the observation of the final Map.

Observing geolocalised historical flood events, it is possible to remark that the census events are not localised only in the high hazard areas, which are closely linked to the presence of the stream network. This result may trigger new considerations useful for decision-makers responsible for adopting policies and strategies to cope with flood risk that are based on the identification of the nature of floods and their potential effects. For example, it may support the identification of problems related to under-dimensioning or mismanagement of urban drainage systems.

Furthermore, progressive urbanization and population of residential districts can explain the temporal inhomogeneity in the noticing of flooded streets. The hydrogeomorphological characteristics of the area where the city of Brindisi is located make the situation more complex, as already documented by Santoro et al. [12].

Observing geolocalised flood risk roads in accordance with citizens' knowledge it is possible to remark that it confirm the results emerging from data regarding historical flood event. The citizens' knowledge coincides with the historical occurrence of the events. This is an important point to highlight, because of the historical analysis carried out stops at 1999. The reasons could be twofold: (i) either there has been memory transmission of the effects caused by the flood events, (ii) or the roads are still being damaged by heavy rainfall.

From the point of view of emergency planning and related correlation on urban strategies, interesting suggestions could be defined, as detailed investigation to carry out on streets perceived to be at risk, in order to adequately implement mitigation and prevention strategies. Prevention and mitigation here are intended not only limited to structural measures but, in a broader sense, involving awareness-raising activities and increasing citizens' information (soft measures).

Another element in agreement with the findings of *layer 1* is the presence of roads at flood risk, far from high hazard areas. Other roads, on the other hand, were not detected by the historical collection of events. This may probably be due to the fact that historical analysis has not been carried out to date due to a lack of data, but this result should invite decision-makers called upon to investigate the nature of flooding in these areas to reflect and make more in-depth assessments.

Finally, observing geolocalised flood risk district in accordance with citizens' perception highlights that the highest perception is detected in the Perrino, Centro and Commenda districts. For the first two districts this result is easily interpretable due to the presence of the Canale Patri, whose floods have had significant effects on the ground over time. Deeper and detailed investigations are instead required for the Commenda district. A similar distinction and homogeneous reasons can also explain the high value of risk perception for Cappuccini and Santa Chiara districts.

The risk perception detected in the industrial area is equal to zero as the questionnaire was not administered. This result represents a limitation of the tool used (online survey) and shows that the study should be deepened considering the effects that the 2003 flood caused in this area.

As can be seen, the overlap of only three layers built a map in which a lot of useful insights for decision-makers in the field of risk planning. At this time, this study is purely explorative. The future goal is to continue working on structuring other social aspects related to flood risk and geo-referencing them. These results represent a starting point for studying methods of mapping the qualitative aspects that contribute to the definition of flood risk in urban areas.

4 Conclusions

The importance of considering the citizens' knowledge and perception of risk in order to support the decision-making process of planning mitigation activities is now widely recognized in the literature, however, attempts to map this information are still far from a complete formalization. In fact, while on the one hand maps containing qualitative elements, implemented in physical maps, could facilitate risk classification in a specific area and could help policy makers and planners to plan more timely interventions, on the other hand it is true that the formalization of knowledge and perception of risk is very complex and uncertain.

In the event of a preventive or protective evacuation, the maps provided to the public are an integral part of the emergency plans. Map design is a rather complex task due to the multiplicity of elements to consider and the need to transfer clear and easily readable information to most users. The aim should be to design optimal maps that, in the preventive phase, help potential risk managers to study correct prevention/mitigation measures that bring into play all the aforementioned elements and, during the event, help users navigate towards the exit area. A challenge is represented by the issue that the risk scenarios evolve constantly as for the characteristics of the hazard and the characteristics of the potentially affected areas changes [26]. To deal with the uncertainties related to the available knowledge of the risks or to unforeseen impacts, maps and planned measures should be flexible and adaptable too.

In this context, the present study tries to construct a multi-layers map based on qualitative elements. According to the results of a previous study, a methodology was built which envisaged three main phases: the collection of historical data of the events; the analysis of flood-prone roads based on citizens' local knowledge and the analysis of flood-prone districts based on citizens' perception of risk.

The output of this study is the construction of a multi-layers map. Such a tool obviously brings along an interesting potential in terms of supporting flood risk planning. Such support can integrate traditional flood hazard mapping strategies and could represent a possible future outlook of this study.

Given its exploratory nature, the presented methodology represents a starting point for investigating ways of mapping the qualitative aspects that contribute to the definition of flood risk in urban areas.

References

1. Rentschler, J., Salhab, M., Jafino, B.A.: Flood exposure and poverty in 188 countries. Nat Commun **13**, 3527 (2022). https://doi.org/10.1038/s41467-022-30727-4
2. Aerts, J.C.J.H., Botzen, W.J., Clarke, K.C., et al.: Integrating human behaviour dynamics into flood disaster risk assessment. Nat. Clim. Chang. **8**(3), 193–199 (2018)
3. Andjelkovic, I.: Guidelines on non-structural measures in urban flood management. International Hydrological Programme (IHP), United Nations Educational, Scientific and Cultural Organization (UNESCO) (2001)
4. FEMA. A whole community approach to emergency management: principles, themes and pathways for action. FDOC 104-008-1 (2011). https://www.fema.gov/sites/default/files/2020-07/whole_community_dec2011__2.pdf
5. Lee, Y.J.: Relationships among environmental attitudes, risk perceptions, and coping behavior a case study of four environmentally sensitive townships in Yunlin county Taiwan. Sustainability **10**(8), 2663 (2018). https://doi.org/10.3390/su10082663
6. Khakee, A., Barbanente, A., et al.: Expert and experiential knowledge in planning. J. Oper. Res. Soc. **51**, 776–788 (2000)
7. Alexander, D.: Disaster and emergency planning for preparedness, response, and recovery. Oxford Research Encyclopedia of Natural Hazard Science, pp. 1–20. Oxford University Press, Oxford (2015)

8. Zografos, K.G., Douligeris, C., Tsoumpas, P.: Using a GIS platform for design and analysis of emergency response operations. In: Sullivan, J.D. (ed.), The International Emergency Management and Engineering Conference, Hollywood, FL, pp. 14–19 (1994)

9. Denis, M.: Space and Spatial Cognition. A Multidisciplinary Perspective. Routledge. London and New York (2018)

10. Bilancio demografico mensile anno 2022 (dati provvisori), su demo.istat.it, ISTAT (2022)

11. PAI (Piano di Assetto Idrogeologico, Puglia Basin Authority, 2005). http://webgis.adb.puglia.it/gis/map_default.phtml. Accessed 21 Mar 2023

12. Santoro, S., Totaro, V., Lovreglio, R., Camarda, D., Iacobellis, V., Fratino, U.: Risk perception and knowledge of protective measures for flood risk planning. Saf. Sci. **153**, 105791 (2022). ISSN 0925–7535,https://doi.org/10.1016/j.ssci.2022.105791

13. Galderisi, A., Guida, G., et al.: Emergency and spatial planning towards cooperative approaches. TeMA J. Land Use Mob. Environ. Spec. Issue **1**, 73–92 (2021)

14. Jongman, B., Ward, P.J., Aerts, J.C.J.H.: Global exposure to river and coastal flooding: long term trends and changes. Global Environ. Change **22**, 823–835 (2012)

15. Kunreuther, H.C., Michel-Kerjan, E.O.: At War with the Weather. MIT Press, Cambridge (2011)

16. Nyerges, T.L: Cognitive issues in the evolution of GIS user knowledge. In: Nyerges, T., Mark, D.M., Laurini, R., Egenhofer, M.J. (Eds.), Cognitive Aspects of Human–Computer Interaction for Geographic Information Systems, vol. 83. Kluwer, Dordrecht, pp. 61–74. (1995)18

17. Kellens, W., Terpstra, T., et al.: Perception and communication of flood risks: a systematic review of empirical research. Risk Anal. **33**, 24–49 (2013)

18. Bubeck, P., Botzen, W.J.W., et al.: Long-term development and effectiveness of private flood mitigation measures: an analysis for the German part of the river Rhine. Nat. Haz. Earth Sys. Sci. **12**, 3507–3518 (2012)

19. Dymon, U.J., Winter, N.L.: Evacuation mapping: the utility of guidelines. Disasters **17**(1), 12–24 (2007)

20. Dent, B.D.: Visual organization and thematic map communication. Assoc. Am. Geogr. Ann. **62**, 79–93 (1972)

21. Gould, P., White R.: Mental Maps. 2nd (ed.) Routledge, Milton Mark (1986)

22. Renn, O., Rohrmann, B.: Cross-cultural risk perception: state and challenges. In: Renn, O., Rohrmann, B. (eds.), Cross-Cultural Risk Perception. Technology, Risk, and Society (An International Series in Risk Analysis), vol. 13. Springer, Boston (2000). https://doi.org/10.1007/978-1-4757-4891-8_6

23. Renn, O.: Risk communication: insights and requirements for designing successful communication programs on health and environmental hazards. In: Robert, L. (ed.), Handbook of Risk and Crisis Communication. Heath and Dan O'Hair, pp. 80–98. Routledge Communication Series. Routledge, New York (2008)

24. Lechowska, E.: What determines flood risk perception? A review of factors of flood risk perception and relations between its basic elements. Nat. Hazards **94**, 1341–1366 (2018). https://doi.org/10.1007/s11069-018-3480-z, http://dx.doi.org/10.1016/j.ijproman.2013.09.002

25. Crossland, M., Scudder, J.N., Herschel, R.T., Wynne, B.E.: Measuring the relationships of task and cognitive style factors and their effects on individual decision-making effectiveness using a geographic information system. In: Nunamaker, J.F., Sprague, R.H. (Eds.), Proceedings of the 26th Annual Hawaii International Conference on Systems Sciences, vol. 4. IEEE Computer Society Press, Hawaii, pp. 575–584 (1993)

26. Di Lodovico, L., Di Ludovico, D.: Limit condition for the intermunicipal emergency. Tema. J. Land Use Mob. Environ. **11**(3), 305–322 (2018). https://doi.org/10.6092/1970-9870/5845

Advancing Urban Science with Multi-Agent Systems: Prospects for Innovation and Sustainability in Spatial Planning and Urban Governance

Dario Esposito[✉] and Miriam Ruggiero

Polytechnic University of Bari, 70126 Bari, Italy
dario.esposito@poliba.it

Abstract. The paper explores the potential of Multi-Agent Systems (MAS) to enhance urban and regional planning. It provides background on the importance of understanding the complex and dynamic nature of cities and the limitations of established planning methods, which struggle to meet the increasing demands for improved quality of life and address social and environmental challenges. Through a comparative analysis of relevant studies, the paper illustrates how MAS can overcome the limitations of purely technical-operational application by providing a more comprehensive conceptualization, understanding, and decision-making in the anthropized environment. Despite the need for multidisciplinary teams and effective integration into the planning process, MAS can challenge partial viewpoints, ineffective decision-making, and implementation approaches. Moreover, MAS can inform public policies and support more efficient and equitable planning processes by assisting decision-makers in developing paradigmatic reasonings. Consequently, MAS can aid in designing innovative possibilities that are more sustainable and resilient by mirroring the complex interactions among individuals, organizations, and systems within territories and the communities that inhabit them. Ultimately, the paper highlights new perspectives for urban science inspired by the multi-agent methodology, emphasizing the advantages it offers in recognizing distinctive relational qualities within complex socio-technical ecosystems, enhancing understanding of the dynamic process of territorialization, and contributing to the cultural advancement needed for revitalizing the spatial planning discipline and guiding policymaking towards strategic perspectives.

Keywords: Multi-Agent Systems · Agent-Based Modelling · Spatial Planning · Urban Governance · Urban Science

1 Introduction

The anthropized environment is a multidimensional socio-technical ecosystem that is complex, open, and dynamic. With the systemic increase in the quantity and diversity of interaction of its constituent elements such an ecosystem becomes increasingly complex, giving rise to emergent properties that are qualitatively new. These properties allow complex systems to develop innovations, recognize and exploit new resources, and reorganize the network of agents to embrace change. Thus, enabling them to adapt or transform to overcome cyclical instabilities, unexpected crises and to reach new states of dynamic equilibrium (Meena et al. 2023).

For human civilization, culture and scientific knowledge are key to enabling this evolutionary mechanism, which ensures the persistence of society. Ecological and community dynamics including temporal fluctuations in species population is a consequence of the information processing (Ushio et al. 2021). However, knowledge in complex socio-technical ecosystems is also emergent and divergent future scenarios grows exponentially with time, making it difficult to accurately predict outcomes. Quoting Zadeh: "As the complexity of a system increase, our ability to make precise and yet significant statement about its behaviour diminishes until a threshold is reached beyond which precision and significance become almost mutually exclusive characteristics" (Zadeh 1996). Therefore, communities shaping and shaped by their living environment cannot fully anticipate the impacts of innovations.

Cities serve as the connecting medium for human communities. In this place agents live, produce knowledge, organize and form institutions (Glaeser 2011). Thus, they are the pivotal factor in understanding and orienting cities. This to the extent that their sustainable and innovative potential depends on the cognitive reach of their agents and the density of form and structure of the network of relations and interactions between them, which allows for certain social and spatial behaviours, but not others. Urban communities are composed of numerous agents who interact with one another, organize themselves into social networks, and make decisions about how to operate in the territory. Each agent makes decisions based on their partial knowledge, and these decisions, when implemented, can change the local context. The complex set of decisions and actions taken by all agents influences the organization of the entire system, resulting in emergent phenomena at the macro-level that are more than the sum of lower-level actions and provide feedback to individual agents, inducing adaptation at the micro-level.

Understanding this tripartite framework of complex multilevel and nested systems, formed by cities, communities, and knowledge, is critical to addressing challenges such as environmental and climate change in a sustainable manner. However, the uncertainties of domain knowledge and the plurality of perspectives and values underlying them, despite being not only unavoidable features, but also required aspects of the diversity that ensure innovation, present significant challenges to conventional linear approaches to spatial planning and urban governance.

The human component in spatial analysis introduces multiple and highly variable meanings, in terms of cultures, traditions, roles, and capacities that challenge those who study the territory to justify decisions supporting government choices. However, if the planning approach in practice is distant from reality and incapable of achieving desired effects, it is due to the clash between increasingly strategic objectives and the limitations of the methods adopted to study and govern the territory, affecting decisions at all levels. These limitations hinder the possibility of concretely realizing what has been imagined and postulated in line with the core principles and values of the discipline, such as democracy, equity, justice and sustainability.

Indeed, experts face the paradox whereby they believe they can shape and exploit the tools at their disposal to justify their point of view, but they remain trapped of the limitations of such tools and the organizational and regulatory frameworks within which they can be used. Consequently, the possibilities for effective change remain confined within narrow spatial and temporal perspectives. The ordinary approach is static and linear, following a knowledge path from data acquisition to analysis through information processing algorithms, to the explicit representation of results for decision support, which are often implemented through a series of hierarchical plans and sequential and controllable interventions, in the hope of reaching a compromise of interests and ends that is ameliorative (Porqueddu 2018). However, this process harshly reveals its precariousness when applied to study and manage complex and dynamic systems that are nonlinear, far from equilibrium, and unpredictable (Batty 2009) and where top-down imposition of decisions will likely produce unexpected and unintended consequences that generate problems more challenging than the issues they were intended to address (Lovins 1995).

Evidently, because the object of urban policies is such a complex socio-technical ecosystem, there is a need to go beyond the collection and analysis of data to try to discover the mechanisms that generated them. Thus, to move from data to meanings and new knowledge it is essential to refer to a paradigm capable of capturing flows of interactions, internal and external to the system, of the multitude of cognitive agents that generated those data. Indeed, there is a growing recognition of the need to rethink the traditional urban planning paradigm based on linear and deterministic models, with a more flexible, adaptive, and interactive approach, capable of embracing the complexity and uncertainty of urban systems. The multi-agent systems (MAS) approach offers interesting possibilities in this direction and can provide the preconditions for developing broader and more informed reflections for the renewal of the fundamentals of the discipline. The potential of MAS for urban planning has been recognized in a growing body of literature that has explored their use for a range of applications, such as transportation, land use, environmental management, and social simulation. However, most of these studies have focused on technical and operational aspects of MAS, without exploring their broader theoretical implications for urban science and spatial governance.

This research aims to explore the potential of MAS to update spatial planning theory and practice towards more strategic and participatory perspectives. The approach's flexibility can adapt to structure multiple spatial issues, situations, and phenomena, such as wicked problems and better represent the dynamic relationships between components characterizing the territory (Rittel and Webber 1973). Nevertheless, usually policymakers dismiss academic research as too theoretical, unrelated to the actual problems they are wrestling with, or in other ways irrelevant to their concerns (Gilbert 2002). The difference in perspectives poses an immediate difficulty in identifying a direct correspondence of the results obtained with the multi-agent analyses and the technical-design requirements, regulatory constraints, etc., that are the languages of applied urban planning. For this reason, the approach is often exploited only limitedly in circumscribed areas of research and case studies and is generally underutilized. Whereas considering the growing inadequacy of the discipline and the crisis due to the gap between values, competencies and real possibilities of impacting at both environmental and social levels,

MAS could lead the renewal of the conceptual paradigm of spatial governance and help to pursue strategic planning.

The study is guided by the following research questions: (i) What are the advantages of the agent-based approach for recognizing distinctive relational qualities in complex socio-technical ecosystems? (ii) What opportunities does it offer for a better understanding of the dynamic process of territorialization? (iii) What is its contribution to the cultural advancement needed to renew from the ground up the discipline of spatial governance and innovate policymaking toward strategic perspectives?

Hence, this research offers insights into how the use of the MAS approach for the understanding of phenomena from the bottom-up is not only beneficial for improving outcomes in various application contexts but also crucial for fostering an innovative approach to how spatial planning is conceptualized, implemented, and assessed. Additionally, these reflections demonstrate how MAS offers a new perspective on urban science, emphasizing the importance of cultural advancement in spatial planning and strategic policymaking.

The remaining of the article is organized as follows. Section 2 provides a background on theoretical foundation of MAS. Section 3 present a review of the case studies form literature on the use of MAS for spatial planning and urban governance. Section 4 discusses implications for urban science and spatial governance, illustrating the potential of MAS for addressing the research questions. Section 5 concludes the article by summarizing the main contributions and implications of the research, as well as its limitations and future directions.

2 Background

The dynamics of socio-technical ecosystems are too complex to understand analytically by studying the overall effects of phenomena, while a problem that is difficult to describe globally with hypotheses that cannot be proven mathematically can be described locally from the individual participating entities and through the operation of the MAS the emergent systemic effects can be captured. Definitely, by appropriately calibrate the simulated model, MAS can help answer questions about the dynamics of the real system.

Multi-agent systems (MAS) originated in computer science and engineering to model and simulate complex, distributed phenomena that occur in the real world and involve living systems characterized by different levels of intelligence and/or coupled with artificial intelligence. Thus, a MAS is a system of multiple agents that interact in a common environment and modify themselves and the environment. This cyclically and dynamically impacts and transforms the activities and behaviours of the agents that populate it. MAS is a broader term that encompasses the design and implementation of multi-agent systems, while agent-based modelling (ABM) specifically refers to modelling complex systems using a bottom-up, agent-based approach.

In ABM, each individual in the system is modelled as an autonomous decision-making entity with a set of properties, and action capabilities. Then several agents relate, communicate and interact autonomously in a shared, virtually represented environment and the system behaviour emerges from multiple local interactions. Agents with different characteristics, capabilities, and decision-making logic, starting from any initial conditions and constraints, make autonomous and adaptive decisions, can improve their performance learning from experience, and act consistently to solve problems and pursue individual goals, but also can coordinate to achieve common or collective goals. Agents can be anything: animals, cities, nations, organisms, humans, businesses, organizations, institutions, and any other entity for which at least one purpose can be recognized or attributed. The environment can be described as an agent rather than as the background where agents operate.

MAS are used for understanding how the emergent behaviours of complex systems is related to the characteristics and behaviours of individual components and vice versa. For Railsback and Grimm, this is a cross-sectional and transcalar approach, simultaneously representing both what happens to the system because of what the agents do and what happens to the agents because of what the system does, as well as reciprocal influences between these levels (Railsback and Grimm 2019).

MAS are widely used for modelling and simulation of complex adaptive systems. It helps to capture when individual behaviour, ranging from reactive or proactive and from finalistic to conscious, produces the best outcome for the individual agent or for the entire community of agents, e.g. maximizing personal utility, improving the quality of life or safeguarding non-renewable resources. It is used to model social behaviour with game theory, to study the conditions under which mutualism and cooperation can emerge in a competitive social system. It figures out how to provide agents with adequate decision flexibility to readily change behaviour, so that they can adapt as needed to others and the environment to solve problems and overcome states of crisis. Moreover, MAS are useful for studying the effect of hypothetical external impacts on the overall development of the system. For instance, they can help understand the local response to unexpected global phenomena or assess the impact of high-level decisions on operational actions. An interesting case is the one of the spread of infections in an environment, which can help decision-makers in evaluating alternative measures and determining the most appropriate ones, such as assessing whether closing schools or cancelling flights is sufficiently effective in curbing the spread (Esposito et al. 2020a).

However, MAS has not only to do with specific quantitative conditions that must be met for some dynamic of interest to emerge, e.g. prerequisites and thresholds for something to activate or happen in the system according to if-then type logic. They are also used to understand how certain preconditions and critical quantities, through phase transitions, can lead to the spontaneous emergence of novel desirable qualities and properties in the system, or to identify dangerous tipping points toward which the system needs to be restrained (Rockström 2009). Thus, a MAS simulates the system of interest to capture its behaviour that is not necessarily an optimal strategy to reach an equilibrium, but rather a flexible process capable of producing a novel systemic change that can lead to discover a new dynamic equilibrium.

Although the multi-agent approach is still underutilized in town and regional planning compared to its real potential, according to this logic it is possible to use MAS to define the best policy for many different and varied decision-making scenarios. The present contribution evaluates the potential and limitations of MAS for the analysis and management of land and local communities through the identification of the methodology's peculiar characteristics, which are discussed with the analysis of example cases and the evaluation of the advantages of their application in a paradigmatic dimension and with respect to the cross-cutting and dynamic qualities and beyond their specific purposes. In the following section, starting with the study of a range of relevant applications for decision support, a comparative analysis of the features of greatest interest for spatial planning strategies and urban governance is proposed.

3 Agent-Based Modelling in Spatial Planning and Urban Governance

Agent-based modelling (ABM) has become an important tool for the study of cities and regions. ABM enables the modelling of individual and social decisions and interactions that drive spatial dynamics, making it useful for decision-making, design, and management of urban systems and infrastructure. Indeed, ABM has been applied to understand the relationship between humans and space, ranging from the micro-movements of pedestrians to the growth of cities (Crooks et al. 2021).

ABM applications can simulate scenarios that consider the spatial perception and social and physical interaction capabilities of agents, and accurately foresee how the system will function, even during disasters (Esposito et al. 2021). These have been used to represent specific human and group behaviours, such as the emergence of crowds, evacuation in emergencies, pedestrian flows, vehicular traffic, and crowding. ABM have also been used to test hypotheses on topics such as wayfinding, queue formation, territoriality, conflict, and emotional contagion.

In spatial analysis applications, agents are endowed with capabilities for decision, action and movement, which are more or less simplified. The possibility to represent the location of agents and their context is crucial to replicate human spatial behaviour together with the decision-making process that drives it and as it is influenced by the characteristics of the surrounding environment through affordances (Golledge 2003), functions that enables certain activities and because of the presence of other agents (Gehl 1987).

To validate ABM, it is possible to modify rules, parameters and conditions in order to compare results of simulated dynamics with data collected in reality. ABM simulations of specific situations are developed with many agents expressing approximately linear behaviour, limiting the need to introduce assumptions about variability due to different cognitive abilities or social preferences, cases that are more difficult to validate. However, a few assumptions applied to many agents can generate complex and counterintuitive macro-phenomena, giving rise to unexpected outcomes that constitute the factor of greatest interest in the study of socio-technical ecosystems with ABM. Although many models still assume that agents have perfect spatial knowledge and can optimize their choices, a promising route forward could be to develop behaviour-based intelligence that allows agents to learn their environment for themselves and develop cognitive frameworks within the modelling package.

Table 1. Relevant features of illustrative use cases for different types of applications.

Subject	Time scale	Spatial scale	Agent capacities	Environmental role	Types of agents	Number of agents	Type of space	Reference	Application
Pedestrian movement	minutes	neighbourhood	reactive		pedestrians	100 000		Rose et al. (2014)	pedestrian flow in the city centre
Migration	months	regions	reactive	background	groups	22 millions	geographic	Groen et al. (2017)	effect of conflicts
Evacuation	minutes	city	reactive coordinated	active background	pedestrians buildings	37 000	geographic	Iskandar et al. (2020)	earthquake
Evacuation	minutes	city	reactive cooperative	active	pedestrians vehicles	40 000	grid topologico	Aguilar, Lalith (2016)	earthquake tsunami
Crowd safety	hours	neighbourhood	reactive proactive	background active	pedestrians	260 000	grid	Batty (2003)	crowding at events
Crime	hours	city	proactive	background active	buildings individuals and groups	273	geographic	Malleson (2012)	crimes and residential burglaries
Public health	days	city	reactive reflexive		individuals	1000	geographic	Perez, Dragicevic (2009)	spread of diseases
Disasters	minutes	neighbourhood	reactive		groups	1000		Barnes et al. (2021)	study of behaviour
Housing market	months	city	reactive		individuals bank	1,6 millions		Geanakoplos et al.(2014)	real estate bubble
Traffic	minutes	neighbourhood			vehicles	15 000	geographic	Manley, Cheng (2018)	traffic flow forecast

(continued)

Table 1. (*continued*)

Subject	Time scale	Spatial scale	Agent capacities	Environmental role	Types of agents	Number of agents	Type of space	Reference	Application
Land use changes	years	city	motivated proactive	background	territory areas		grid	Liu et al. (2013)	urbanisation of rural settlements
Spread of diseases	hours	building	reactive motivated	background active	individuals	50	geographic	Esposito et al. (2020b)	contamination and contagion
Energy demand	months	regions		background	Individuals groups	households housing drives	geographic	Muñoz H. (2016)	energy requirements for heating
Urban growth	years	city	reactive	background	groups	1668 slums	geographic grid	Patel et al. (2018)	formation of slums

Some MAS applications of interest with reference to typical use cases drawn from the literature are taken up and elaborated upon below in a non-exhaustive guideline list. Table 1 provides schematic details of selected example applications of ABM, with classification of the most prominent features and reference to the research from which they are taken. Specifically, the definition of the type of space follows the taxonomy proposed by Macal and North (2014) and Crooks et al. (2018), the one relating to agent capability refers to the classification proposed by Weiss (1999) and Gershenson (2001), and the role of the environment is alternatively evaluated as a background with the mere function of a physical constraint or as an active element able of influencing agents states, capabilities or choices.

Table 2. Problems, limits and advantages of using MAS for each type of application.

Subject	Problem	Limits	Advantages
Pedestrian movement	include pedestrians' spatial preference for exploring city streets and places in the model	need to simplify complexity with assumptions about preferences such as time budgets, routes, destination, etc. for each agent	the model allows the testing of various scenarios, even hypothetical ones
Migration of populations	predicting the distribution of refugees fleeing as involuntary migration	much more time is needed to develop the model than the rapid response required by the crisis	it is possible to predict the distribution of refugees in destination camps
Emergency evacuation	include human behaviour and the anthropogenic impact it has on the disaster	need to consider actions taken during and immediately after a disaster event	social behaviour can be simulated, which is the key to security
Crowd safety	merging a traditional processing model with a dynamic model	complexity is given by the unpredictable stimuli in the agents' movements	testing alternative routes to reduce crowding
Crime	capture the bottom-up dynamics of the criminal system like human behaviour	irrational behaviour and complex psychology lead to computational difficulty	captures emerging phenomena related to interactions between individuals and space
Public health spread of diseases	the spatial effects of diffusion, the individual contact process and the effects of individual behaviour are ignored	computational limitation; the simulation does not take prevention measures into account	increases the flexibility of the model; subdivision by age, gender, etc.; simulate any other communicable diseases by modifying the time line and the transmission process

(continued)

Table 2. (*continued*)

Subject	Problem	Limits	Advantages
Disasters	Not rely only on the routes given by emergency plans. Make sure that the agents do not all move in the same way	if we do not enter the characteristics of the agents we have a knock-on; not all complexity can be entered	inclusion of human behavioural characteristics (gender, age, mobility)
Housing market	including heterogeneity in real estate market variables	seasonality; lending constraints and boom characteristics; role of real estate, mortgage brokers, developers	excellent results in reproducing the data history; it is suitable for economic processes
Traffic	incorporate the results of cognitive science	it is not easy to capture the heterogeneity of driver behaviour	introduces both heterogeneous spatial knowledge and the choice of preferred route
Land use changes	incorporate agents' behaviour	only considers conversion from other types of land to communal land, and not vice versa	understanding of land development
Energy demand	use not only high-level aggregated data and capture the complexity	data at a low level of aggregation are difficult to obtain; calculation of domestic heating energy needs only	micro-scale representation and monthly resolution
Urban Growth	explore links between individuals and aggregated data	requires data that are very often not available in developing countries	predicting the location of slums and exploring the interactions between human behaviour, environment and policies

Table 2. Shows schematically for each type of application considered: the problem which the analysed study seeks to address, the advantages of using ABM for the specific case study, and any limitations encountered.

Figure 1. Represents the spatial, temporal, and quantitative dimensions of the types of applications considered.

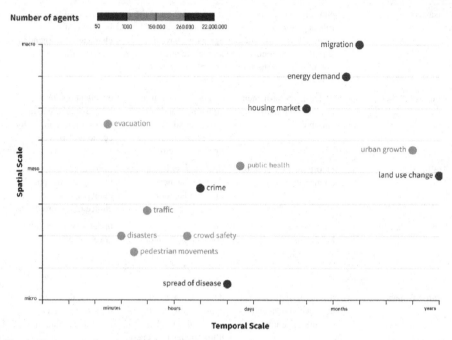

Fig. 1. Representative graph of the spatial, temporal, and dimensional dimensions of the various applications considered.

4 Discussion

Based on the case studies analysed, we can draw cross-cutting assessments of the potential and limitations of applying MAS for analysing and managing the land and man-made environment.

The complete development of a multi-agent model involves several steps, which can be condensed into three main stages in a cyclic process: (i) conceptual modelling of the phenomenon or problem to be analysed, (ii) computational simulation of what-if scenarios, and (iii) analysis of results to confirm or disprove assumptions and update the formulated model. However, it is not always necessary to go through all three stages. In fact, formalizing issues according to the logical architecture proposed by the MAS paradigm may be sufficient to significantly improve understanding (Esposito et al. 2020c).

Leveraging MAS main strength, which consists in recognizing the elements under study on the basis of the qualities derived from the relationships among them, offers experts an opportunity to rethink the established methods. Since these, still today, mostly look at static and intrinsic properties of the elements involved, such as physical-geometric characteristics and market values. Thus, ABM are not only useful for the specific purpose for which they are built; they also allow us to examine organizations and the relationships between people and space.

While spatial planning is primarily concerned with the "where" (Abbott 2020)– i.e., norming, regulating, and deciding where to realize the infrastructure that society intends to build, and constraining geometric and dimensional aspects at most – the MAS approach forces us to consider "when" and "for how long." This has the great advantage of spurring us to think about what we intend to accomplish in terms of its implications for development, and to read spatial governance decisions as part of a dynamic and open-ended process of territorialization, both spatially and temporally. Through simulation in the virtual environment of the MAS, we can observe the mutual influences between these two levels. Being able to grasp and evaluate the effects of spatial choices in the temporal dimension is crucial to effectively manage any complex territorial living system. This is important for socio-technical ecosystems, as they structurally exploit scientific innovations and their technological applications to cyclically postpone the moment of systemic collapse (Bettencourt et al. 2007). From a broader perspective, given the increasingly frequent and dramatic emergencies predicted in the near future, being able to grasp the conditions and requirements imposed by the pace of change necessary to target societal adaptation for resilience can make all the difference in ensuring the survival of the human species on the planet. The possibility to model together different temporal and spatial scales is also crucial for urban-scale dynamics.

Furthermore, the MAS approach helps us think in terms of who is involved, since is inherently suited to considering active agents in the area and their characteristics, i.e. it forces us to recognize that these agents are not static, but change dynamically. Moreover, it allows us to capture the overall effects resulting from the decisions of many agents, which is beyond the rational capacity of an expert. From a problem-solving perspective, MAS help to identify adaptive solutions that take advantage of the natural and instinctive propensities and behaviors of agents of the systems, as well as the actual conditions offered by the environmental and cultural context. This is preferable to opposing these tendencies by proposing solutions. As is the case with the imposition of rules and constraints, that result inadequate. Moreover, because they allow agents of different types to be included within the same model and aggregated into phenomena that serve as the building blocks for higher-level or larger-scale complex systems at different scales, multilevel effects through nested systems can be represented simultaneously.

Additionally, the logic behind MAS allows for the focus of studies on the relationships between elements rather than solely on their intrinsic properties. In spatial and environmental issues, it is becoming increasingly evident that it is not essentially the nature of the agents or their properties that unite or differentiate them, but rather how they relate and interact with one another. In fact, even if the number of relationships increases exponentially with the number of agents involved, just a handful of agents can connect in hundreds of different ways. By paying attention to the connectivity among agents, we can examine a specific feature of the spatial complexity of environmental systems. The network of connections serves as an organization of interconnections among agents, and it is through this that agents continuously exchange flows of energy, goods, information, capital, waste, up to the point that choices and actions of one agent somehow influence or have implications for another agent connected to the network, even at great distances (Batty 2013).

MAS allow us to abstract from the dimensionally measurable spatial instance alone and look at the complex system composed of the relationships among agents, which are organized into networks that give rise to spatial phenomena (Esposito and Abbattista 2020d). Indeed, ABM can also be designed in a way that agents connect through links and space is ignored, closing to network analysis. As the degree of connectivity between agents increases, it becomes more and more the quantity, nature, pattern, and properties of connections that define the system, rather than the properties of individuals. Once a critical level of connectivity among agents is reached, the system stops being a set of parts and becomes a single complex system, and its development depends on how things flow in the network.

This consideration is especially useful for complex systems that exhibit high levels of interdependence and is, therefore, of interest in dealing with the urgent and current problems peculiar to a globalized society in a highly connected world. The space of these complex systems, such as global systems of transportation, of people and exchange of goods, social networks, and the financial system, is redefined in terms of the topology created by connectivity that replaces the Euclidean conception of space. What matters in defining the importance, role, and development prospects of an agent in the network, as well as the territory it physically inhabits, is its position in the network structure and its degree of connectivity. This interpretation allows us to understand how the anthropic environment functions from the shape of the network and the relative position of each agent. For example, it enables us to identify key agents in the network who can leverage phenomena to activate change and assess the implications of a certain structure of the existing connection. Indeed, if an agent lives in a central node of the network, it will shape the context in which the agent exists and may have more or different information and possibilities, living in a very different world from those who inhabit the margins. Megacities, for instance, serve simultaneously as nodes of different types of global networks, whereas medium-sized cities may need to develop strategies to become access nodes of at least specialized global networks. Each city always acts as the place where global and local networks meet and serves as an access point for people to communicate and work with each other from there.

Lastly, it is important to underline that many agent-based models tend to look at only one aspect of a spatial system at the time. If we want to address larger societal issues, such as climate change or urban change, specific models need to be integrated to couple various processes together.

5 Conclusion

The paper examines how Multi-Agent Systems (MAS) can enhance urban and regional planning by addressing the limitations of traditional methods that struggle to manage the complex and dynamic nature of cities. It presents a comparative analysis of studies demonstrating how MAS can support decision-making by providing a more comprehensive conceptualization of the urban environment, as well how MAS can improve sustainability and resilience by understanding the interactions between individuals, organizations, and systems within communities.

The developed reflection is supported by an analysis of relevant cases, focusing on the characteristics, advantages, and limitations of applying Multi-Agent Systems (MAS) to urban and regional planning. Considerations allow us to define dimensions by which MAS can improve urban science, contributing to a more complete and accurate understanding and representation of the object of study and thus to a more effective governance of the territory. Indeed, ABM are a powerful tool that make it possible to simulate what-if scenarios to explore systems and processes they cannot directly manipulate and through which it is possible to improve understanding of the physical and social impact of the built environment on communities and vice versa. Emblematic is the case of worst-case scenarios, which are impossible to reproduce in the real environment because of the logistical, economic and safety implications of in vivo experiments. Best practices demonstrate that for policymakers, the use of these computational tools can be critical to the success of solutions and initiatives to plan and manage infrastructure, territories, and communities. MAS approach activate iterative processes in which alternative solutions and information obtained from the analysis of what-if scenarios are used to reason about and formulate new hypotheses to be tested. This is a dynamic and flexible process that aims to recursively minimize the gap between the unfolding reality and the expert assumptions made in adaptation to it.

They can support urban and spatial planning by simulating complex interactions between individuals, organizations, and systems within a city. Their flexibility means that it is the phenomena of interest that determine the most appropriate scale for representation, not the limitations of the methodology adopted for modeling. Thus, they can help planners predict and understand the impacts of different planning scenarios and policies, taking into account factors such as land use, transportation, demographics, and economics. By providing a virtual test bed for planning, these tools can support more informed, efficient, and equitable planning processes. This information can support decision making, help identify potential issues and conflicts, and evaluate effects and effectiveness of alternative policies.

Their challenge is to advance the level of knowledge of anthropogenic systems at all scales and to develop useful processes to support experts in dealing with the innate variability and uncertainty of socio-technical ecosystems. In terms of the connections between the technical-application aspects of the method and the implications at the theoretical level, the potential of MAS exceeds the expressive scope of simulations applied to solve contingent shorter-term technical management problems. Indeed, at the end of the analysis it is possible to detect a high degree of results variety with the introduction of small variations in the starting data, thus exactly mimicking what happens in complex socio-technical ecosystems for which small variations in the starting conditions to rapid divergences.

Rather than arriving at certain and reassuring predictions, MASs serve as flight simulators to train experts to deal with the unexpected by failing repeatedly in virtual mode, rather than when making choices in the real world. In fact, its greatest value lies in its ability to project those who use them onto a level of paradigmatic reasoning capable of challenging partial viewpoints and established ways of doing things. Making human systems sustainable, encouraging innovation in society, promoting community disaster resilience and a circular economy for better resource use, and many other issues, are all largely dependent on a proper understanding and representation of decisions and interactions among agents in complex spatial systems. MASs are a metaphor by which it is possible to understand how simple things produce complex phenomena, in that they function not to offer a snapshot of the situation, but to capture the development of a dynamic process for which we have the instructions, but not the description of its development. MAS help decision-makers invent innovative perspectives that are more sustainable and resilient precisely because they are more adherent to the complex nature of territories and the communities that inhabit them.

Despite these envisaged benefits, the use of ABM tools may have limited impact if they are not integrated effectively into the broader planning process and if decision makers do not have the necessary technical skills to understand them. Only in rare cases is this methodology included in the planner's training, and thus multidisciplinary teams are needed for its implementation. This is also why ABM are not widely used and are hardly officially recognized in professional practice. As these tools become more accessible and user-friendly, they are likely to be adopted by a wider range of planners, stakeholders, and citizens and become increasingly integrated into the broader planning process, serving as a central tool for understanding, communicating, and evaluating.

Nowadays, typical evaluation of public policies is steadily based on a definition of a plan that can be easily tracked and measured upon indicator that are known a priori. This assumption leaves no room for socio-technical ecosystems that adapt, evolve and learn which are exactly what objects of public policies, such as the economy, the environment, the society and the cities. Indeed, spatial plans and projects based on norms and laws could be the strangest as long as they are justified by causes and preconditions and meet pre-established requirements, resources and budgets. In truth, objectives are easily lost in the face of the race to meet regulations and constraints on time. Therefore, they often offer no assurances on how clear and useful goals will be achieved fulfilled and who will be responsible for them, and people needs satisfied. Ultimately these are often self-referenced to meet the expectations of decision makers and therefore although they are very reassuring for them, at the same time they are not also effective for others in view of sustainability and innovation.

In contrast, strategy development has to do with a set of win-win choices that are also feasible because they analyse the agents involved and their network of relationships over time to achieve a clear end strictly related to the welfare of other agents, citizens and the environment for example, who are external to the decision maker and over whom the decision maker has no control or guarantee of success. In line with this wisdom, the MAS approach proves to be not only useful addressing specific technical-operational issues, as much as in creating conditions such that the decision maker can build informed visions, teaching him or her to think about the right questions to ask and why to ask them, and finally to develop the ability to make dynamic an flexible choices that can be readily modified in the process. All these issues are at the hedge for renewed strategic spatial planning and sustainable city and community governance.

6 Contribution

Conceptualization, methodology, writing and revision D.E.; figures and editing M.R. All authors read and approved the published version of the manuscript.

References

Abbott, C.: City planning: a very short introduction. Oxford University Press, USA (2020)

Aguilar, L., Lalith, M.: On a mass evacuation simulator with complex autonomous agents and applications. J. Earthquake Tsunami **10**(05), 1640021 (2016)

Barnes, B., Dunn, S., Pearson, C., Wilkinson, S.: Improving human behaviour in macroscale city evacuation agent-based simulation. Int. J. Disaster Risk Reduction **60**, 102289 (2021)

Batty, M.: Agent-based pedestrian modelling, Advanced spatial analysis: the CASA book of GIS **81**, 81–106 (2003)

Batty, M.: Cities as complex systems: scaling, interaction, networks, dynamics and urban morphologies (2009)

Batty, M.: The New Science of Cities, MIT Press, Cambridge (2013)

Bettencourt, L.M., Lobo, J., Helbing, D., Kühnert, C., West, G.B.: Growth, innovation, scaling, and the pace of life in cities. Proc. Natl. Acad. Sci. **104**(17), 7301–7306 (2007)

Crooks, A., Malleson N., Manley E., Heppenstall A.: Agent-based modelling and geographical information systems: a practical primer, Sage (2018)

Crooks, A., Heppenstall, A., Malleson, N., Manley, E.: Agent-based modeling and the city: a gallery of applications. In: Shi, W., Goodchild, M.F., Batty, M., Kwan, MP., Zhang, A. (eds.) Urban Informatics. The Urban Book Series. Springer, Singapore, pp. 885–910 (2021). https://doi.org/10.1007/978-981-15-8983-6_46

Esposito, D., Schaumann, D., Camarda, D., Kalay, Y.E.: Decision support systems based on multi-agent simulation for spatial design and management of a built environment: the case study of hospitals. In: Computational Science and Its Applications – ICCSA 2020a. ICCSA 2020a. LNCS, vol. 12251, pp. 340–351. Springer, Cham (2020a). https://doi.org/10.1007/978-3-030-58808-3_25

Esposito, D., Schaumann, D., Camarda, D., Kalay, Y.E.: Multi-agent modelling and simulation of hospital acquired infection propagation dynamics by contact transmission in hospital wards. In: International Conference on Practical Applications of Agents and Multi-Agent Systems, Springer. Cham, pp. 118–133 (2020b)

Esposito, D., Abbattista, I., Camarda, D.: A conceptual framework for agent-based modeling of human behavior in spatial design. In: Jezic, G., Chen-Burger, J., Kusek, M., Sperka, R., Howlett, R., Jain, L. (eds.) Agents and Multi-Agent Systems: Technologies and Applications 2020c. Smart Innovation, Systems and Technologies, vol. 186, pp. 187–198. Springer, Singapore (2020c). https://doi.org/10.1007/978-981-15-5764-4_17

Esposito, D., Abbattista, I.: Dynamic network visualization of space use patterns to support agent-based modelling for spatial design. In: Luo, Y. (ed.) Cooperative Design, Visualization, and Engineering. CDVE 2020d. LNCS, vol. 12341, pp. 260–269. Springer, Cham (2020d). https://doi.org/10.1007/978-3-030-60816-3_29

Esposito, D., Cantatore, E., Sonnessa, A.: A multi risk analysis for the planning, management and retrofit of cultural heritage in historic urban districts. In: La Rosa, D., Privitera, R. (eds.) Innovation in Urban and Regional Planning. INPUT 2021. LNCE, vol. 146, pp. 571–580. Springer, Cham (2021). https://doi.org/10.1007/978-3-030-68824-0_61

Geanakoplos J., Axtell R., Farmer D., Howitt P.: An agent-based model of the housing market bubble in metropolitan Washington, DC (2014)

Gershenson, C.: Artificial societies of intelligent agents, Fundacion Arturo Rosenblueth Unpublished Thesis (2001)

Gehl, J.: Life between buildings, Van Nostrand Reinhold, New York, vol. 23 (1987)

Gilbert, N., Maltby, S., Asakawa, T.: Participatory simulations for developing scenarios in environmental resource management. In: Third workshop on agent-based simulation, pp. 67–72, SCS-European Publishing House, Ghent, Belgium, April 2002

Glaeser, E.: Triumph of the City: How Urban Spaces make us Human. Pan Macmillan (2011)

Golledge, R. G.: Human wayfinding and cognitive maps. In: The Colonization of Unfamiliar Landscapes, pp. 49–54. Routledge (2003)

Groen, D., Suleimenova, D., Bell, D.: Towards an automated framework for agent-based simulation of refugee movements. In: Winter Simulation Conference (WSC) (2017)

Iskandar, R., et al.: Agent-based simulation of pedestrians' earthquake evacuation; Application to Beirut, Lebanon (2020)

Liu, Y., Kong, X., Liu, Y., Chen, Y.: Simulating the conversion of rural settlements to town land based on multi-agent systems and cellular automata. PLoS ONE 8(11), e79300 (2013)

Lovins, L.H., Lovins, A.: How not to parachute more cats. Rocky Mountain Institute, Snowmass, Colorado. Published online at www.rmi.org (1995)

Macal, C., North, M.: Introductory tutorial: agent-based modeling and simulation. In: Proceedings of the Winter Simulation Conference, pp. 6–20. IEEE (2014)

Malleson, N.: Using agent-based models to simulate crime. In: Heppenstall, A., Crooks, A., See, L., Batty, M. (eds.) Agent-Based Models of Geographical Systems, pp. 411–434. Springer, Dordrecht (2012). https://doi.org/10.1007/978-90-481-8927-4_19

Manley, E., Cheng, T.: Exploring the role of spatial cognition in predicting urban traffic flow through agent-based modelling. Transp. Res. Part A: Policy Pract. 109, 14–23 (2018)

Meena, C., Hens, C., Acharyya, S., et al. Emergent stability in complex network dynamics. Nat. Phys. (2023). https://doi.org/10.1038/s41567-023-02020-8

Muñoz Hidalgo, M.E.: A national heat demand model for Germany. In: Namazi-Rad, MR., Padgham, L., Perez, P., Nagel, K., Bazzan, A. (eds.) Agent Based Modelling of Urban Systems. ABMUS 2016. LNCS, vol. 10051, pp. 172–188 (2017). Springer, Cham. https://doi.org/10.1007/978-3-319-51957-9_10

Patel, A., Crooks, A., Koizumi, N.: Spatial agent-based modeling to explore slum formation dynamics in Ahmedabad, India. In: Thill, J.C., Dragicevic, S. (eds.) GeoComputational Analysis and Modeling of Regional Systems. Advances in Geographic Information Science, pp. 121–141. Springer, Cham (2018). https://doi.org/10.1007/978-3-319-59511-5_8

Perez, L., Dragicevic, S.: An agent-based approach for modeling dynamics of contagious disease spread. Int. J. Health Geogr. 8(1), 1–17 (2009)

Porqueddu: Detecting and directing emergent urban systems. A multi-scale approach. Cosmos+ Taxis. Stud. Emergent Order Organ. 5(3+4), 32–49 (2018)

Railsback S. F., Grimm V.: Agent-Based and Individual-Based Modeling: a Practical Introduction. Princeton University Press, Princeton (2019)

Rittel, H.W., Webber, M.M.: Dilemmas in a general theory of planning. Policy Sci. 4(2), 155–169 (1973)

Rockström, J., et al.: Planetary boundaries: exploring the safe operating space for humanity. Ecol. Soc. 14, 1–33 (2009)

Rose J., Ligtenberg A., Spek S. V. D.: Simulating pedestrians through the inner-city: an agent-based approach, Bellaterra, Cerdanyola del Vallès. In: Social Simulation Conference (2014)

Ushio, M., Watanabe, K., Fukuda, Y., Tokudome, Y., & Nakajima, K. (2021). Computational capability of ecological dynamics. bioRxiv, 2021–09

Weiss, G.: Multiagent Systems: a Modern Approach to Distributed Artificial Intelligence, MIT Press, Cambridge (1999)

Zadeh, L.A., Klir, G.J., Yuan, B.: Fuzzy Sets, Fuzzy Logic, and Fuzzy Systems: Selected Papers (vol. 6). World scientific (1996)

Socio-Economic and Environmental Models for Land Use Management (SEMLUM 2023)

The Student Housing as a Catalyst for Virtuous Processes of *"win-win"* Revitalization of Property Assets in Disuse

Francesco Tajani[1], Benedetto Manganelli[2]([⊠]), Giuseppe Cerullo[1], Pierluigi Morano[3], and Melania Arenas Morente[2]

[1] Department of Architecture and Design, "Sapienza" University of Rome, 00196 Rome, Italy
[2] School of Engineering, University of Basilicata, 85100 Potenza, Italy
benedetto.manganelli@unibas.it
[3] Department of Civil, Environmental, Land, Building Engineering and Chemistry (DICATECh), Polytechnic University of Bari, 70126 Bari, Italy

Abstract. Higher education has been becoming increasingly globalized as a business. Currently, there are approximately 200 million University students worldwide, which is more than double the number from twenty years ago. According to several studies, this number will reach 263 million by 2025. In Italy, the structural shortage of beds barely covers 12% of the total, and there is a lack of around 100,000 beds to reach the European average. To face this emergency, the National Recovery and Resilience Plan (PNRR) has allocated 960 million Euros for new facilities for student housing, also through the enhancement of property assets in disuse. The present research addresses the issue outlined, by analyzing a case study on the economic feasibility of an investment in the recovery of a disused building for student housing.

Keywords: PNRR · Student housing · property enhancement · property valuation

1 Introduction

The scarcity of housing, the proliferation of a black market for exorbitant rents, and the growing demand for students have been leading to an increasingly difficult situation for students living away from home [1]. According to a study by the HousingIngBo project, on average, a student takes about seven weeks to find housing and about 30% of them take more than two months [2]. These issues, which have been evident for some time, have been exacerbated by the pandemic period, as many students have abandoned online classes to return to the cities [1].

A concrete response to the housing emergency for University students comes from the National Recovery and Resilience Plan (PNRR), with a budget of 960 million Euros to triple the number of available beds for students living away from home, increasing from 40,000 to 105,500 by 2026 [3]. The resources made available, according to the

O. Gervasi et al. (Eds.): ICCSA 2023 Workshops, LNCS 14109, pp. 387–400, 2023.
https://doi.org/10.1007/978-3-031-37120-2_25

predictions of the Ministry of University and Research, are outlined into the two phases described below.

The first phase is described by the Decree No. 152/2021, whose aim was to facilitate and simplify, even in terms of timing, the restructuring and renewal of existing structures and pushing for new green-field buildings [4].

The second phase, which instead aims to more extensively involve the private sector, is described by the Decree No. 144/2022 [5] which intervenes on the regulations regarding housing and residences for University students, by inserting a new article 1-bis in Law 338/2000, entitled "New University housing", in order to create a fund for University housing of 660 million Euros. The privileged beneficiaries of the funds are private investors in agreement with universities and public entities, who will have to bind their properties for twelve years [6]. University housing will be substantially assimilated to social housing, hoping that this will be enough to convince investors [4].

Student housing is recognized as a type of construction that has social significance and for which the government provides incentives for private investors and funding for public operators. The right to University education is a significant cost for the public sector, and student housing is the function that consumes the largest share of funding for this service. The development of student housing is an important area of growth, and a viable means of revitalizing existing real estate assets [7] through government funding and induced environmental impacts on the surrounding area.

2 Aim

This research aims to analyze the main aspects related to the student housing sector. It focuses on the increasing number of University students, particularly those living away from home, who generally have to face a shortage of student housing at agreed-upon rents and a free market with rents above average. Also, it focuses on analyzing the demand and the supply present in Italy through the current dynamics and investment opportunities. In this sense, an economic evaluation case study is presented, in order to highlight the most significant aspects regarding the management of University housing initiatives by relating cost items and revenues, focusing on a business plan that is decisive in the economic return for the private investor.

The work is divided as follows. In Sect. 3, an overview of the growing number of University students is presented; the attention is focused on the Italian context, analyzing the demand and the supply, the shortage of beds and the possible future scenarios. In Sect. 4, a case study of a disused building located in Perugia (Italy) is illustrated and the financial analysis of the enhancement investment is developed. In Sect. 5, the conclusions are discussed.

3 Framework

In recent years the student housing sector has taken a prominent place among the interests of investors, also thanks to the continuous growth of the number of students, which is currently a global phenomenon [8]. Worldwide, there is a growing tendency towards the massification of higher education [9]. The number of tertiary students globally has more than doubled over the last two decades, rising from 100 million in 2000 to 235 million in 2020 [10]. The tertiary systems in many high-income countries achieved *universal* access, prior to the turn of the millennium [11].

As identified by Oliveira B. (2016), there are pull factors that drive the student to seek education abroad in order to satisfy their own needs and preferences [12]. Throughout the world, with the progressive growth of the student's population that has started to migrate to new cities in order to obtain higher education opportunities, an impressive shortage in the housing supply has emerged, since the demand for housing from students has far exceeded the capacity of higher education institutions (HEI) to supply [13]. In many parts of the world, the growth of housing supply for students has widened with the expansion of higher education, causing concerns in both developed and developing countries [14].

3.1 Student Housing in the Italian Context

Italy counts a total of 257 schools for tertiary education: 98 are universities, while the remaining are AFAM ("Alta Formazione Artistica e Musicale") institutions legally recognised. Rome is the city with the highest number of schools (=32), followed by Milan (=21) and Firenze (=12) [15]. In addition, the top 10 Italian universities are also present in the ranking of the world's 500 best universities, making Italy an attractive location for the education.

Demand. In the academic year 2020/2021, despite the Covid-19 pandemic, the number of University students registered a 4% increase compared to the previous year [16]. Italian universities counted 1,822,141 enrolled students, and just 83,613 of them in AFAM institutions [17]. In detail, the trend of enrollment in the last decade shows a decrease until the academic year 2015/2016, and then a subsequent growth with the highest peak of 1,839,846 in the academic year 2020/2021 [17]. Analyzing the current year, 2022/2023, for the second year in a row, University enrollment is decreasing. Compared to 12 months ago, the overall data is negative by 2% [18]. The reasons for this decline can be attributed to the high costs of Italian universities, which for off-site students reach prohibitive costs that include rent, transportation, and living expenses [19].

For a general overview of which regions are most populated in terms of students and where they are located, public data shows that in the academic year 2021/2022, Lombardia, Lazio, and Campania are the regions with the highest number of enrollments. The most populated regions are mainly located in the central-northern part of the country [17]. Italy, with its geographical gap, the common North-South divide, and its experience of brain drain, constitutes an interesting case in mobility analysis [20]. Student flows primarily move along the South-North direction: 20% of students who change regions move to the north and another 17% stay in the center [21]. Southern regions are structurally characterized by intense outflow mobility. In 2018, among enrollments from residents in the South, about a quarter enrolled in a University in the North-Center. The data is slightly declining compared to the peak reached in 2016 [22].

As emerged from the latest report of *'immobiliare.it insights'* the commuter student, representing about 50% of students in Italy [23], has become the dominant trend among off-site students. It is primarily the result of a combination between the good quality of education offered by some institutions [24] and the difficulty of obtaining housing due to the high rent [25], especially in the most popular cities.

In Italy, 68% of University students live with their parents, compared to the European average of 34%. Only 5% have housing in a University residence, compared to a European average of students with a bed in a residence of 17% [24]. Despite this, according to the annual Erasmus + report, Italian students are the ones who have participated the most in mobility experiences for study and training in Europe. In 2021, there were almost 74,000 participants [26]. In 2022, as an incoming mobility flow, 188,000 chose Italy for a period of study and training, 7,000 of them from non-EU areas [27].

Public Supply. In Italy, institutional housing supply can be divided into three subgroups: residences affiliated with regional organizations for the Right to Study (DSU), residences at the Universities Colleges of Merit, and residences of the Italian Association of Colleges and University Residences.

Currently, the bed supply is over 62,000 units [28]. The beds in student housing facilities are mainly located in University residences managed by the regional entities for the DSU, which constitute for the 66% the majority of the bed supply for students in our country, another 15% is made up of beds managed by private operators, another 11% is made up of beds managed directly by universities, while the remaining 8% is made up of private and public housing for students legally recognized [29].

Private Supply. University residences managed by affiliated entities provide housing solutions aimed only at a portion of the demand with well-defined socioeconomic and academic merit characteristics [30]. Consequently, the portion of students who are unable to intercept this offer is forced to resort to individual private operators, often in an unorganized form, who substitute the void created in the supply by institutional and structured private operators, offering on the free market housing solutions that are not suitable for the needs of University students and with often high tariffs, especially in recent years.

The latest report by *immobiliare.it* has confirmed Milan's primacy as the most expensive city in Italy with the price of a single room that, for the first time, has exceeded 600 Euros, with an increasing at a rate of 20% from last year and 8.2% from pre-pandemic. The price difference with Rome, which is the second one in the ranking, is significant. In fact, in the capital, an average of 465 Euros is paid for a single room, 248 Euros for a double [31].

Demand/Supply Consistency. Between 2015 and 2019, there has been a steady growth of off-site students (5.54%), driven in particular by universities in the North such as Milan, Turin, and Bologna. The increase in off-site students is counterbalanced by the structural shortage of beds: only 12% of the total is hardly covered and 29.8% of students are beneficiaries of housing [32].

This value is clearly lower than that recorded in France (23%), Germany (14%), and Spain (11%) [28], whose student housing supply is much more substantial.

To bring the student housing supply to the levels of the best European peers, and therefore to at least 20% of the number of off-site students [28], it would be necessary to add about 260,000 beds to the existing stock [33]. Considering the structures already under construction, by 2025, it is believed that they will not be sufficient to close the gap with potential demand [15].

4 Case Study

The case study of present research concerns a building located in the central area of the Municipality of Perugia. The predominantly office use asset is currently vacant. The building, about $4,000\,m^2$, built with a mixed structure (reinforced concrete and masonry), underwent a significant renovation in the late 1990s. It develops over five floors above street level and two floors below street level, connected by an internal staircase and elevator (Fig. 1).

Fig. 1. Type plan of the floor below street level (above) and type plan of the floor above street level (below).

In order to enhance the property by changing its use from office to student housing, the economic feasibility is evaluated through the Discounted Cash Flow Analysis (DCFA) technique. The second semester of 2021 is the reference date of the valuation. The final result was achieved by evaluating a series of critical factors, useful for the implementation of student housing interventions, which can be traced back to: the location of the intervention, market analysis and management, economic and financial aspects.

The redevelopment of the building took place in accordance with what is provided by the current urban planning tools in the municipality of Perugia. In particular, the area subject to a landscape constraint, letters c) and d) of Decree No. 42/2004, - buildings and areas of significant public interest, characteristic complexes, and panoramic beauties, which allows for building transformation activities and interventions for the recovery of existing building heritage.

4.1 Market Analysis

Demand. In the city of Perugia, in addition to the two well-known universities - the University of Perugia and the University for Foreigners of Perugia - there are other HEI, perhaps less well-known, but significant for their ability to represent a range of educational offerings available to a national and international audience. According to public data, in the 2020/2021 academic year, University students are a total of 27,193, increasing in the last 5 academic years, as a result of new enrollments. The growth particularly affected the last year, + 10.5%, confirming the attractiveness of the University institution. In the current academic year, the number continues to increase, currently there are 28,655 enrolled. Off-site students enrolled in the universities of Perugia in the 2019/2020 academic year are 11,490. In the 2020/2021 academic year, Umbria welcomed, on the total number of students that came from Italian universities, 3.7% of off-site students, with an increase over the previous year of 1.8% [17].

Supply. From the supply perspective, the positive growth of the number of enrolments has not been matched by an increase in the number of beds offered by the regional right-to-study system. Various colleges have undergone important but necessary renovations. Due to delays caused by changes in the political and economic context (such as the "Superbonus 110%" Law, the Ukraine conflict, the Covid19 pandemic), these residences are still under renovation and therefore, at the beginning of the 2022/2023 academic year, the number of beds in the DSU residences is only 696, which is about 40% less than before the pandemic.

According to data from the Umbria Agency for University Rights, for the 2022/23 academic year, there are about 1700 eligible applications for a bed, compared to only 696 available beds, alarming numbers [34].

Perugia, with its century-old University tradition, offers various University housing solutions: for those attending classes in the historic center, in the suburbs, walking, or with their own transportation. It offers options for students in both private and public facilities (Table 1).

4.2 Design

The general strategy of the intervention on the existing building favors the transition from old to new, avoiding morphological transformations that alter the external perception of the image of the existing building. Inside the new building there are 114 rooms divided into 46 single and 68 double rooms for a total of 182 beds, organized in hotel-type housing units (Fig. 2).

Table 1. Private and public student housing supply in Perugia.

DSU structures	Location	Beds
Student housing	Z. Faina Street, 6	180
Ruggero Rossi College	Trasimeno West Street, 116/ter. 5	170
F. Innamorati College	F. Innamorati Street, 4	225
College of Agraria	Romana Street, 4/B	250
G. Ermini College	Benedetta Street, 42	251
Favarone College	Favarone Street, 26	116
Fatebenefratelli College	Fatebenefratelli Street, 4	23
Monteluce University Residence	Giochetto Street, 25	50
Total		1365
Private structures	Location	Beds
Antinori College	Garibaldi Avenue, 226	25
Monteripido house	Monteripido Street, 8	50
Monteluce University College - Teresian Institution	Massari Street, 1/a	30
Saint Clare House	Clarisse Street, 8	22
Don Bosco University Residence	Don Bosco Street, 5	35
Total		162

Individual living units are designed to accommodate one or a maximum of two individuals. In accordance with regulations, in order to minimize the overall expenses of the housing facility, rooms located on upper floors are furnished with a shared bathroom.

In compliance with Law No. 13/89, measures have been taken to ensure accessibility for disabled individuals within the residence. Additionally, as per the requirements set forth by Law No. 338/2000, a minimum of 5% of the total beds have been allocated for disabled students. Rooms designated for disabled individuals, which meet the regulatory requirement of at least a 10% increase in net surface area, are located on the lower floors of the building.

The rooms have been designed in compliance with the dimensional standards outlined in Annex A of Decree No. 1252, dated December 2nd, 2022. The double rooms have an area of approximately 12.8 m^2, while the single rooms have an area of approximately 8.8 m^2 [35]. Each room is equipped with essential furniture including a bed, bedside table, large desk, and wardrobe. All rooms feature either a window door leading to a balcony, or windows that ensure adequate lighting throughout the space.

The building also features a variety of additional services including: a lobby, a concierge desk, toilets, a laundry facility, and outdoor green space. These spaces ensure a minimum area of 2.0 square meters per bed. The remaining space can be allocated according to individual needs and priorities [36].

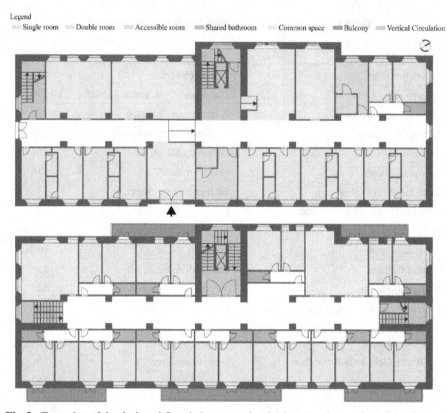

Fig. 2. Type plan of the designed floor below street level (above) and type plan of the designed floor above street level (below).

4.3 Valuation

The evaluation of the enhancement investment on the case study property was developed using the DCFA technique. This monetary evaluation does not consider the intangible social impacts of the project, therefore the perspective is strictly private, meaning that for the investor the optimal behavior is to seek the maximum earning from the investment.

The analysis period was determined as a balance between the specific characteristics of the property and the ability to predict market fluctuations. In this case, the DCFA was carried out over a period of twenty-one years, by considering a lease period equal to eighteen years (9 + 9 contract), as provided by Law No. 392/1978, and three years for the sale of the entire property.

Costs. In order to determine the expected costs, the following unit parameters were adopted.

Fixed costs incurred by the property:

– administrative expenses: 1.50% of gross actual revenues, pertaining to property management cost, annually paid and variable according to the revenues;

- reserves for extraordinary maintenance: 1% of the cost of new construction of the entire property. This expense item is intended for the creation of a fund for renovation, necessary for the periodic renewal of the property. An annual down payment equal to 70,000 Euros has been assessed;
- property insurance: 0.10% of the cost of new construction, determined by borrowing parametric costs from the DEI price list [37], for similar typologies. An annual cost equal to 7,000 Euros has been assessed;
- property taxes: equal to 42,711 Euros annually, estimated by considering the Italian property taxation system and in proportion to the property's cadastral value;
- registration taxes of the lease contract: 0.50% of the annual revenues, to be paid annually and variable according to the revenues;
- lease commission: 10% of the first annual revenues, as a commission on rentals for the commercialization activities of property agents, to be paid only upon formalization of the related contracts. This cost is equal to 37,527 Euros and occurs in the second year of the analysis period.

Construction costs: borrowing the data of the DEI price list [37], a parametric cost of 683.73 Euros/m^2 was assessed. This value has undergone adjustments and has been found to be in line with the national average [38]. The total construction costs amount at 3,290,473 Euros and are referred to the first and the second years of the analysis period.

FF&E Acquisition: equal to 3,800 Euros per bed, This item refers to the cost of purchasing furniture, fixtures, and equipment for the student housing units. These may include items such as beds, wardrobes, desks and chairs. This cost is equal to 691,600 Euros and occurs in the second year of the analysis period.

Design and construction management: equal to 6% of the construction costs, amounting to 197,428 Euros, and it is referred to the first and the second years of the analysis period.

Urbanization charges: this cost includes two shares, determined according to Municipality's resolutions [39]: the first share, the construction cost contribution, is equal to 5% of construction costs, which amounts to 164,524 Euros. The second share, that constitutes the primary and secondary urbanization fees, has been assessed according to specific annexes of the Municipality's resolution, and they are equal to 70,000 Euros. Both the shares are referred to the first and the second years of the analysis period.

Contingency: this item is equivalent to 5% of the amount related to direct construction costs, amounting to 164,524 Euros. It occurs in the first and the second years of the analysis period.

Operational costs: these costs can significantly fluctuate based on the scope and quality of the services provided. In the scenario under examination, they include cleaning of common areas and rooms, bed linen change, reception service, and maintenance of garden. These services are estimated to be equal to 210,000 Euros per year. It is essential to recognize that the implementation of measures aimed at promoting student accountability and adherence to established protocols can result in a significant reduction of operational costs [40].

Financial charges: it has been considered that for the entire initiative, the investor activates a bank credit line at an annual rate of 5.0%, resulting in consequent differential financial charges, determined on the progressive positive cash flows, spread in the considered analysis period.

Revenues. They are primarily comprised of rental income derived from long-stay accommodations for the "Autumn/Spring" period, spanning a duration of ten months, as well as from short-stay accommodations for the "Summer" period, spanning a duration of eight weeks. Additional revenue is derived from the "ancillary" section, which represents a marginal percentage, approximately 2.9% of total revenue in the stabilized year.

The unit rent tariffs, categorized by bed type, have been determined through the application of a pluri-parametric market approach method, in order to estimate the monthly prices for single and double rooms, by making adjustments based on the differences between the factors of property competitors found in the territorial context (Fig. 3) and those of the subject property being evaluated (Table 2).

The implementation of the pluri-parametric market approach method has led to the following values: the unit rental tariff for double rooms has been assessed equal to 302.25 Euros per month, whereas for single rooms it is equal to 361.12 Euros per month.

Furthermore, the terminal value is estimated by capitalizing the cash flow in the last year of the analysis period using a rate of 5.0%. This results in a value of 14,235,705 Euros.

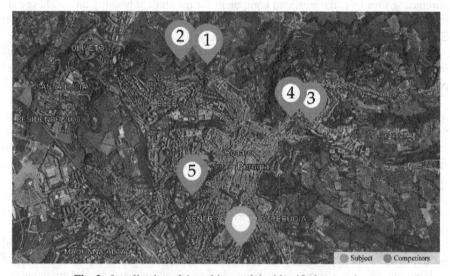

Fig. 3. Localization of the subject and the identified competitors.

The discount rate has been assessed equal to 6.5%, by taking into account the ordinary expected returns in the relevant sector and the various risk factors (context, property, tenant, etc.) that are specific to the case under analysis.

The Net Present Value (NPV) of the investment before taxes is positive, amounting to 2,182,927 Euros. The post-tax NPV, estimated by considering taxes of approximately

30% on the positive cash flows, is equal to 107,492 Euros, and the corresponding Internal Rate of Return (IRR) is equal to 6.66%. As the NPV is higher than zero and the IRR exceeds the established threshold (i.e. the discount rate used for the implementation of the DCFA), the project is financially viable.

Table 2. Factors considered in the pluri-parametric market approach method and differential adjustments applied to the competitors' tariffs compared to the property subject.

In-room kitchen							
Yes	−5%	No	0%	Absent (in the entire property)	5%		
Garden							
Yes	0%	No	5%				
Private bathroom							
Yes	−3%	No	0%				
Reception							
Day-time and night-time	0%	Absent	5%				
Proximity to airport							
>13 km	3%	Approximately 13 km	0%	<13 km	−3%		
Balcony room							
Yes	−3%	Partial (on the facades of the entire property)	0%	No	3%		
Presence of disabled toilets							
Yes	0%	No	5%				

5 Conclusions

Despite efforts made in Italy in recent years to balance the supply and demand of housing solutions for students, a structural shortage of beds remains a significant issue. The market for student housing is far from saturated and requires efforts from both public and private entities to achieve a satisfactory and coherent ratio of beds to students, consistent with the internationalization expectations of Universities in the coming years. From an environmental perspective, Italian cities are characterized by the presence of numerous buildings in disuse, with University locations primarily situated in historic centers. Thanks to the funds allocated by the PNRR, it is now possible to concretely consider the recovery of existing real estate heritage [41, 42], also favoured by the strong involvement of the private sector [43–45].

In this perspective, the case study of the construction of a new University residence that involves the recovery and enhancement of an abandoned building has been dealt with. In addition to generating a positive environmental impact on the intervention context, this operation also entails an appropriate earning for the investor that has been specifically assessed [46].

Starting from student housing as an asset class with a strong social vocation, putting young people and their future at the center, creating sustainable residences from an environmental, social and economic point of view thanks also to the resources allocated by the PNRR, are the springboard towards a radically different housing future for students who live away from home. The challenge is to combine the quality of design with financial convenience, by developing a new culture of design and construction of these structures, that i) pursues how to seek innovative solutions, ii) does not flatten out on "housing containers", iii) is able to generate "win-win" initiative from an environmental, social and economic points of view.

References

1. Gennari, C.: Universitari, c'è carenza di alloggi e servizi. Il Resto del Carlino (2022)
2. Affitti a Bologna: un'odissea per tutti gli studenti. Available online: Affitti a Bologna, un'odissea per tutti gli studenti. Accessed 26 Jan 2023
3. Zaccardi, M.: Pnrr, errore nel bando dell'ex ministra Messa per 7.500 posti letto per universitari. Il Fatto Quotidiano (2022)
4. Bruno, E.: Università, 660 milioni per i posti letto. Il Sole 24 Ore, 19 (2022)
5. Bruno, E.: Pronti i primi 6.500 alloggi universitari. Il Sole 24 Ore, 12 (2022)
6. Bruno, E.: A Roma -6.900 posti letto universitari, a Milano -16mila. Il Sole 24 Ore (2023)
7. Fecchio, A., Casara, E.: Facility management in social housing, integration of services for management of college student housing as an opportunity for supply development in Italy. Tech. J. Technol. Archit. Environ. 4, 118–123 (2012). https://doi.org/10.13128/Techne-11510
8. Voltolin, C.: Student Housing, Secondary Cities e nuove forme di residenzialità. CBRE (2019)
9. Özoğlu, M., Gür, B., Gümüs, S.: Rapid expansion of higher education in turkey, the challenges of recently established public universities (2006–2013). High Educ. Policy 29, 21–39 (2016). https://doi.org/10.1057/hep.2015.7
10. UNESCO: Higher education global data report. In: World Higher Education Conference 2022. Barcelona, Spain (2022)
11. Durak, T., Uzan, M.F., Robert, V.R.: Higher education expansion in emerging economies: examples from Turkey and Chile. High. Educ. Govern. Policy 3(1), 45–58 (2022)
12. Oliveira, D.B., Soares A.M.: Studying abroad. Developing a model for the decision process of international students. J. High. Educ. Policy Manag. 38(2), 126–139 (2016). https://doi.org/10.1080/1360080X.2016.1150234
13. Rugg, J., Rhodes, D., Jones, A.: The nature and impact of student demand on housing markets. Joseph Rowntree Foundation, York (2000)
14. Ghani, Z.A., Suleiman, N.: Cash-cow into the purse of Malaysian property investors: students housing investment. Path Sci. 3(8), 1013–1022 (2017). https://doi.org/10.22178/pos.25-5
15. Savills: Italian Student Housing Market Overview. https://www.savills.it. Accessed 26 Jan 2023
16. Bellini, O.E., Gullace, M.T., Mocchi, M.: Re-start: student housing polycrisis post-coronavirus. Tech. J. Technol. Archit. Environ. 23, 94–103 (2022). https://doi.org/10.36253/techne-12155
17. Portale dei dati dell'istruzione superiore. http://dati.ustat.miur.it/organization/miur. Accessed 26 Jan 2023

18. Bruno, E.: Università, matricole ancora in calo: a dicembre sono 295mila, -2% rispetto a un anno fa. Il Sole 24 Ore (2022)
19. Gazzettino del Golfo. https://www.gazzettinodelgolfo.it/universita-numeri-in-calo-per-lit alia-dopo-20-anni. Accessed 26 Jan 2023
20. Vittorietti, M., Giambalvo, O., Genova, V.G.: A new measure for the attitude to mobility of Italian students and graduates: a topological data analysis approach. Stat. Methods Appl. (2022). https://doi.org/10.1007/s10260-022-00666-x
21. Bruno, E.: Studenti fuori sede al 50%. In manovra solo 4 milioni. Il Sole 24 Ore, 13 (2023)
22. Mariani, V., Torrini, R.: Il sistema universitario: un confronto tra Centro-Nord e Mezzogiorno. Questioni di Economia e Finanza 675 (2022)
23. Polizzi D., Ravizza, S.: Università, perchè in Italia gli studenti sono obbligati a stare in famiglia. Corriere della Sera (2019)
24. Gwosć, C., Schirmer H., Hauschildt, H.: Social and Economic Conditions of Student Life in Europe. EUROSTUDENT VII Synopsis of Indicators 2018–2021 (2021)
25. I fuorisede diventano pendolari? si cercano singole anche fuori da milano e firenze, https:// www.immobiliare.it/news. Accessed 26 Jan 2023
26. European Commission, Directorate-General for Education, Youth, Sport and Culture: Erasmus+ annual report 2021. Publications Office of the European Union (2022). https://doi.org/ 10.2766/635340
27. Maddalena, E.: Erasmus+, nel 2022 cresce la partecipazione italiana al Programma. Istituto Nazionale Documentazione Innovativa Ricerca Educativa (INDIRE) (2022)
28. Student housing: quale futuro tra pubblico e privato?, https://www.cdp.it/sitointernet/page/it. Accessed 26 Jan 2023
29. JLL: Student housing snapshot H2 2021. https://www.jll.it/it/tendenze-e-ricerca/research/stu dent-housing-snapshot-h2-2021. Accessed 26 Jan 2023
30. Laudisa, F.: Le residenze universitarie in Italia. In: Catalano, G. (ed.) Gestire le residenze universitarie. Aspetti metodologici ed esperienze applicative. Bologna (2013)
31. Immobiliare.it: Posti letto nelle città universitarie, i prezzi per le singole tornano a salire (+11% in un anno). https://media.immobiliare.it/News-2358.pdf. Accessed 26 Jan 2023
32. Lavoce.info: Per gli studenti fuori sede una casa dal Pnrr. https://www.lavoce.info/archives/ 95929. Accessed 26 Jan 2023
33. L'Economia: Alloggi per studenti, 20 mila nuovi posti letto in Italia entro il 2025. https:// www.corriere.it/economia. Accessed 26 Jan 2023
34. Umbria Journal: Crisi abitativa, 10mila studenti non sapranno dove andare a dormire. https:// www.umbriajournal.com/istruzione. Accessed 26 Jan 2023
35. MUR: Ministerial Decree No. 1252 of December 2, 2022. https://www.mur.gov.it/it/atti-e-normativa. Accessed 26 Jan 2023
36. Italian Ministry of Economic Development: Ministerial Decree 28/11/2016. Standard minimi dimensionali e qualitativi e linee guida relative ai parametri tecnici ed economici concernenti la realizzazione di alloggi e residenze per studenti universitari. http://attiministeriali.miur.it/ anno-2016/novembre/dm-28112016.aspx. Accessed 26 Jan 2023
37. DEI tipografia del Genio civile: Prezzi Tipologie Edilizie. DEI, Milan (2019)
38. Piferi, C.: I costi standard di costruzione delle residenze per studenti universitari: l'esperienza italiana della legge n. 338/2000. Residenze e servizi per studenti universitari, pp. 69–78 (2016)
39. Città di Perugia: Edilizia ed urbanistica. https://www.comune.perugia.it/resources/Moduli stica/Edilizia_Urbanistica/DeliberazioneCC103-11072016. Accessed 26 Jan 2023
40. Bellini, O.E., Bellintani, S., Ciaramella, A. Del Gatto, M.L.: Learning and living. Abitare lo Student Housing. Franco Angeli, Milano (2015)
41. Trovato, M.R., Clienti, C., Giuffrida, S.: People and the city: urban fragility and the real estate-scape in a neighborhood of Catania Italy. Sustainability 12(5409), 1–35 (2020). https://doi. org/10.3390/su12135409

42. Spatari, G., Lorè, I., Viglianisi, A., Calabrò, F.: Economic feasibility of an integrated program for the enhancement of the byzantine heritage in the Aspromonte national park. The case of Staiti. In: Calabrò, F., Della Spina, L., Piñeira Mantiñán, M.J. (eds.) New Metropolitan Perspectives. NMP 2022. LNNS, vol. 482, pp. 313–323. Springer, Cham (2022). https://doi.org/10.1007/978-3-031-06825-6_30

43. Morano, P., Tajani, F., Anelli, D.: Urban planning decisions: an evaluation support model for natural soil surface saving policies and the enhancement of properties in disuse. Prop. Manag. **38**(5), 699–723 (2021)

44. Massimo, D.E., Del Giudice, V., Malerba, A., Bernardo, C., Musolino, M., De Paola, P.: Valuation of ecological retrofitting technology in existing buildings: a real-world case study. Sustainability **13**(13), 7001 (2021)

45. Locurcio, M., Morano, P., Tajani, F., Di Liddo, F.: An innovative GIS-based territorial information tool for the evaluation of corporate properties: an application to the Italian context. Sustainability **12**(14), 5836 (2020). https://doi.org/10.3390/su12145836

46. Calabrò, F., Mafrici, F., Meduri, T.: The valuation of unused public buildings in support of policies for the inner areas. The application of SostEc model in a case study in Condofuri (Reggio Calabria, Italy). In: Bevilacqua, C., Calabrò, F., Della Spina, L. (eds.) New Metropolitan Perspectives. NMP 2020. Smart Innovation, Systems and Technologies, vol. 178, pp. 566–579. Springer, Cham (2021). https://doi.org/10.1007/978-3-030-48279-4_54

A Logical-Perequative Methodology to Define the Social Discount Rate for the Cost-Benefit Analysis Application

Felicia Di Liddo[1] (ID), Debora Anelli[1(✉)] (ID), Pierluigi Morano[1] (ID), Francesco Tajani[2] (ID), and Carmelo Maria Torre[1] (ID)

[1] Department of Civil, Environmental, Land, Building Engineering and Chemistry (DICATECh), Polytechnic University of Bari, 70126 Bari, Italy
debora.anelli@poliba.it
[2] Department of Architecture and Design, "Sapienza" University of Rome, 00196 Rome, Italy

Abstract. The need to define effective interventions for the urban sustainable development goals is always growing and recognized by the central governments. In the current economic situation, the adequate use of EU-funds for the investments to be carried out on the territory requires a targeted and valid implementation of the economic evaluations of the projects. In this framework, in the Cost-Benefit Analysis the Social Discount Rate (SDR) is ordinarily assessed by empirical approaches that neglect the main environmental, social and economic aspects of the nation in which the intervention will be realized. In this sense, in the present research an innovative logical-perequative methodology is proposed, able to take into account the specificities of the country through the detection of the main indicators related to the environmental, social and economic sustainability issues. The main advantage of the proposed methodology is the ability to determine the adequate corrective coefficient able to adjust the official SDR values, according to the real current sustainability levels of each country.

Keywords: Social Discount Rate · Cost-Benefit Analysis · sustainable development goals · equitable growth · multi-criteria assessment technique · composite indicator

1 Introduction

The awareness of the fundamental role played by the social cohesion for the achievement of the Sustainable Development Goals is growing, especially with reference to the key objective "to leave no one behind" expressed by the 2030 Agenda and to achieve a greater well-being for everyone [1].

The territorial disparities not only between regions and areas of each nation, but above all among the different European countries and between the European countries and the rest of the world, constitute the focus of the goal No.10 of the 2030 Agenda [1], which aims to reduce the inequalities within and between nations. In this sense, the access to essential services and infrastructures (transport, broadband, healthcare,

O. Gervasi et al. (Eds.): ICCSA 2023 Workshops, LNCS 14109, pp. 401–413, 2023.
https://doi.org/10.1007/978-3-031-37120-2_26

schools, etc.) is unequally distributed among the collectivities, with remote, rural and disadvantaged regions that are increasingly late and missing basic facilities.

In theoretical terms, the accentuation and persistence of inequalities between the various growing territories undermines the economic strength of the European Union (EU), not allowing a fair and long-term sustainable development. The issue of the nations well-balanced growth is closely connected to the social inclusiveness target, which constitutes an important question debated in the recent decades by central and local governments. Therefore, the progressive achievement of a greater equality of and between nations should start from the adoption of fiscal, wage and social protection policies capable of highlighting the needs of disadvantaged and marginalized populations and of determining a countries economic growth that includes the quality of life improvement, in social, cultural and environmental terms.

According to the art. 174 of the consolidated versions of the treaty on the functioning of the European Union [2], the harmonious development of nations and the strength of economic, social and territorial cohesion are promoted, by paying particular attention to the rural areas, to the regions involved in industrial transition processes and to the zones with relevant and permanent natural or demographic minuses (e.g. the regions with very low population density as well as the island, cross-border and mountain regions) [3].

Within the urban transformation initiatives for the construction of new infrastructures and/or services and for the adaptation of existing ones, the need to increase the public investments is associated with the ever more pressing cogence to implement quality interventions. In the mentioned framework, it is essential to rationalize the entire planning, evaluating and monitoring public works process, in order to define urban initiatives that are able to lead to a balanced nations growth.

In the recent decades, the European programs (European Regional Development Fund (ERDF), European Social Fund Plus (ESF +), Cohesion Fund (CF), etc.) aimed at developing a structured set of strategies and reforms, that the Member States must follow for the robust recovery of the global economy and of each individual geographical context, include the reduction of gender, generational and territories inequalities among the priorities to be achieved [4–6].

In the current Italian context, the Mission No. 5 of the National Recovery and Resilience Plan (NRRP) [7] is in line with the main European purposes, as it is mainly focused on the cohesion goals to support the gender equality, the fight against discrimination, the increase in youth employment, the development of the South and inner areas. In particular, the component 2.2 of the Mission No. 5 – so-called M5C2.2 "urban regeneration and social housing" - defines a specific interventions cluster aimed at reducing marginalization and social degradation situations through the redevelopment of public areas and the promotion of cultural and sporting activities. Furthermore, the component 3 of the same Mission – named M5C3 "special interventions for territorial cohesion" - benefits from almost 2 billion euro for strengthening the national strategy in policies for the South and inner areas, with measures to improve the education, health and social services quality. Further interventions included in this target concern the economic and social enhancement of assets confiscated from the mafia and the improvement of the special economic zones service infrastructures, to increase the competitiveness and attractiveness of the existing activities. However, it should be pointed out that the social inclusion strategic axis, defined primarily at European level, constitutes a cross-cutting goal in all components of the NRRP (in terms of essential public services provision, in the education and training sector, for the labor market, etc.). In fact, a complete social inclusion is fundamental i) to improve the territorial cohesion, ii) to help the economy growth and iii) to overcome the relevant gender and generational inequalities - often also accentuated by the Covid-19 pandemic.

In general terms, the NRRP aims to support the redevelopment of the most vulnerable urban tissues (suburbs, inner areas of the country) and to promote inclusion policies, mainly focused on the socially marginalized community groups, also through interventions to enhance the social housing, the temporary housing (such as the temporary reception facilities for the homeless or financially distressed individuals) and the subsidized housing to provide students or single-income families with accommodation at reduced rents.

At a wider European scale, the definition and execution of the social projects, in the same way, should be consistent with the six pillars of the Next Generation EU financial tool [8], on which each national reform and investment program up to 2026 is based. The social and territorial cohesions represent the fourth sector on which each national plan has been defined, after those related to the green transition, the digital transformation, the smart, sustainable and inclusive growth. Moreover, this sector is primary than the health and economic, social and institutional resilience and the policies for the next generation, including the education. Therefore, the social and territorial cohesion goal - at different scales (i. national, with reference to the gap between the different regions and macro-areas; ii. European, between the different EU Member States and iii. Global, between the different EU nations and the rest of the world) - is strongly connected to the homogeneous and equitable growth of nations scope, which intrinsically includes the sustainable development of countries issue. Within the framework of the CF (2014–2020 and 2021–2027) [9–11], established in order to strengthen the economic, social and territorial cohesion of the EU, the economic growth, the creation of jobs, the enterprises competitiveness and the environment protection represent the crucial measures to be promoted. Specifically, the allocation of the Union's funding for the cohesion policies is focused on two main purposes: the first is related to the investments for the employment for the labor market improvement; the second concerns the European territorial cooperation level in order to achieve a balanced development of each Member State.

2 The Economic Analysis for the Assessment of the Cohesion Policy-Funded Investments

In order to ensure the sustainable (in the three economic, environmental and social components), uniform and equitable growth for all EU Member States and, in a broader perspective, of Europe with respect to the rest of the world, the need to implement effective territorial investments, in line with the specificities of each geographical context and with the global goals of the inclusive development of the countries, is significant.

In this sense, the tools for assessing the projects feasibility should be able to provide reliable and appropriate results, according to the characteristics of the urban context in which each initiative, is included. Thus, the evaluations should be flexible (as well as the techniques to be used) and carried out *ad hoc* according to the nature and size of the intervention and the surrounding urban area.

For the *ex-ante* verification of the economic feasibility of a project, the Cost-Benefit Analysis (CBA) is the main technique for evaluating the investments [12]. The core of the CBA concerns the determination of economic performance indicators (Net Present Value, Internal Rate of Return, Pay-back Period, etc.), starting from the results of a multi-year development of estimated costs and benefits associated with the analyzed investment (always considered compared to the alternative scenario referred to the *status quo*) [13, 14]. According to the art. 101(e) of Regulation No. 1303/2013 [15], the CBA – including an economic and financial analysis and a risk assessment – is mandatory in order to get the approval of large projects (i.e. whose construction costs is higher than 50 million euro) included within the EU Cohesion Fund 2014–2020. Depending on the investment type, sector, size and complexity, a set of economic appraisal methodologies could be considered for the assessment of projects included the EU 2021–2027 policy framework: the CBA is the preferred approach, even if, the Least-Cost Analysis (LCA) or the Cost-Effectiveness Analysis (CEA) are proposed for voluntary use and could be adopted as alternatives. A Multi-Criteria Analysis (MCA) could also be implemented, even though it is more often used as a complement to the other tools [16].

With reference to the input data to be included in the economic analysis carried out by using the CBA, the investment costs and, possibly, the operating costs (if the operativity phase regards the direct activity management) and the benefits deriving from the financial revenues appropriately turned by using the conversion factors, are estimated considering the prices charged on the local market. The Social Discount Rate (SDR) assumes a relevant role in the CBA context, since the determined costs and benefits - and subsequently attributed in the different years of the considered period of analysis - occur in different times and have to be homogenized, in order to be compared with each other. In theoretical terms, the SDR reflects the social point of view about the preference level of future costs and benefits compared to the present ones. Moreover, the value of the SDR is crucial for the analysis effectiveness, as it is strictly connected to the riskiness of the investment and it is defined taking into account the sacrifice that the community is willing to bear in order to renounce the current benefits for future ones (i.e. the cost/opportunity for the community principle) [17–19].

For the Cohesion Fund 2014–2020, the European States have ordinarily used the official SDR reported by the Guidelines for CBA implementation developed by local governments (5% for large projects promoted in the CF beneficiary countries and 3% for other Member States) [12]. For EU-funded projects in 2021–2027, Member States can independently establish and use their own country-specific SDR. In this sense, the Economic Appraisal Vademecum 2021–2027 sets that, in the absence of national values, 3% can be used [16]. In the reference literature, different approaches have been proposed to estimate the SDR, even if that generally recommended is the Social Rate of Time Preference (SRTP = $p + e \times g$, where p is the pure time preference, e is the elasticity of the marginal utility of consumption - i.e. the percentage change in individuals' marginal utility corresponding to each percentage change in consumption - and g is the expected growth rate of per capita consumption) [20]. The country-specific SDR empirical determination should be carried out, by taking into account that i) the systemic risk and optimism bias should be reflected not in the SDR but in the risk assessment, ii) the SDR can decline over the reference period in projects with very long-term impacts, e.g. beyond 50 years, as they involve intergenerational equity considerations, iii) the SDR should not vary across sectors based on policy considerations [16].

Within the outlined framework, the differentiation of the SDR to be used according to the nation in which the initiative is to be implemented would allow a reduction of the risks associated with incorrect evaluations and a greater ability of the analysis to take into account the context specificities. In order to pursue the mentioned goals of inclusive and equitable sustainable growth of the European nations, the adoption of different rates would allow to reward projects characterized by positive long-term effects and to provide a lower coefficient for projects in countries in which higher need for interventions for the community is detected. In particular, the specificities of each nation could be summarized by a set of measurable indicators and reported by official sources, which allow to analyze the different characteristics of the countries to be compared in economic, environmental and social terms. The reference literature includes several contributions aimed at i) highlighting the role of indicators for the description of different contexts [21–23] and ii) identifying the main indicators able to measure the environmental, cultural, educational, social and economic level of the country [24–27].

It should be highlighted that the need to determine specific SDR according to the nations characteristics is also associated with the requirement of transparent methodological approaches to be used for this parameter estimation. Currently, the two issues assume a key role that is still poorly pointed out by governments, which rely on standard and often unique values for different countries, by neglecting, however, their different specificities. In addition, the cogence for constant updating of SDR to be used in the economic analysis is relevant, in order to avoid the use of obsolete and unreliable data, by remembering that too high SDR setting may mean that socially desirable projects are rejected and, conversely, too low SDR setting may result in resources being wasted on economically inefficient projects [28].

3   Aim

Within the economic evaluations implemented through the CBA, the current official SDR values totally neglect environmental aspects that assume a crucial role within the Sustainable Development Goals of the 2030 Agenda. Furthermore, the SRTP empirical approach - recommended by the Vademecum for the determination of SDR - is based on very often difficult computation processes aimed at calculating the different parameters included in its algebraic formula. Therefore, the aim of the present research is to define a logical-perequative methodology for the definition of the SDR that is able to take into account the environmental, social, economic specificities of the EU countries. In particular, the methodology is articulated in six ordered and sequential phases and involves the integration of the Analytic Hierarchy Process (AHP) and Data Envelopment Analysis (DEA).

Starting from the identification of a set of indicators that represent the existent environmental, social and economic issues at the time of the evaluation, the proposed methodology provides for a corrective coefficient of the SDR reference values to be used for the "adjusted" SDR determination. This obtained SDR value can be adopted in the CBA applications aimed at the economic evaluation of the projects within each EU nation.

For an effective determination of the corrective coefficients or the "adjusted" SDR values, the identification of a "benchmark State" is necessary for the comparison among the nations, by considering the detected indicators data.

The developed methodology could be implemented in any territorial context that requires the CBA application for the economic evaluation of the investments to be carried out for the urban sustainable development goals. Due to this feature, it appears flexible and user-friendly and it constitutes a valid tool with reference to the assessment of effective interventions on each country.

The Sections contents included in the paper are described below: in Sect. 4 the proposed methodology is illustrated and the main steps that constitute the logical-perequative procedure to be implemented in order to determine the "adjusted" SDR value are described. In Sect. 5 the conclusions are introduced, and the further insights of the research are listed.

4   Methodology

The proposed methodology consists into six ordered and sequential phases by involving the integration of the AHP multi-criteria technique and the DEA for, respectively, firstly determining the level of the economic, social and environmental conditions, based on the existent disposable set of indicators that are collected as able to represent each aspect, and for secondly, defining the corrective coefficient of the SDR values officially used as references, according to the guidelines provided by the European Commission for the period under analysis.

In Fig. 1 the phases of the proposed methodology are shown.

It could be useful to highlight that the proposed methodology doesn't have limits of application related to the EU territorial context, because the sole required conditions of its adoption are: i) the use of the CBA requirement for the economic evaluation of the investment decisions; ii) there are known SDR values provided by official sources and iii) there is a sufficient number of States under analysis that allow to identify the features of the so-called "benchmark State".

4.1   Phase 1. Analysis of the Social, Environmental and Economic Issues Related to the CBA Field for Identifying the Sample of n Indicators that are Able to Represent Each Issue for the States

The analysis of the social, environmental and economic issues that characterize the economic evaluation of the CBA applications is important to identify the specific set of indicators that can represent the aspects for each of the State. This initial phase, in fact, is aimed at carefully defining the most influential socio-economic and environmental parameters that affect the CBA economic evaluation, according to the national and international literature on the matter and also by considering the main official guidelines. Therefore, in order to take into account the conditions of the States on the social, environmental and economic points of view, the identification of a unique set of n indicators

PHASE 1

Analysis of the social, environmental and economic issues that affect the CBA economic evaluation and identification of a sample of *n* indicators that are able to represent each issue for the States

PHASE 2

Normalization and correlation analysis applied to the sample of *n* initial indicators for the construction of the final set of indicators to be aggregated

PHASE 3

Determination of the local weights of each indicator, different for each of the EU State under analysis, through the construction of pairwise comparison matrices

PHASE 4

Application of the Weighted Sum Model for aggregating the EU States indicators into the so-called "actual performance index"

PHASE 5

Identification of the "benchmark State" indicator's values and determination of the local weights and the "benchmark index"

PHASE 6

Determination of the corrective coefficient through the DEA application and the "adjusted" SDR values

Fig. 1. Phases of the proposed methodology

for all the States is carried out. The indicators must be characterized by availability, scientific robustness, readability and coherence with the related aspect that are intended to represent.

4.2 Phase 2. Normalization and Correlation Analysis Applied to the Sample of n Initial Indicators for the Construction of the Final Set of Indicators to be Aggregated

After having identified a sample of indicators that, in an adequate way and for all the EU States, allow to represent the social, environmental and economic conditions of each of them at the time of the reference year, in the case for which different unit of measure can be observed, the normalization is necessary to facilitate the comparison and the aggregation of the indicators. The normalization can be achieved through the use of different existent techniques such as the min-max technique or the z-score ones. It is a decision that can be affected by the purposes of highlighting the main critical values of the indicators or, differently, provide an average framework of them. Subsequently, the correlation analysis is aimed at removing the high-correlated indicators for the sample initially identified by carrying out a Pearson's matrix of order n, where n is equal to the number of the indicators.

At the end of this phase, the final sample of indicators from which the corrective coefficient of the SDR values officially used as references will be determined, is constituted.

4.3 Phase 3. Determination of the Local Weights of Each Indicator, Different for Each of the EU State Under Analysis, Through the Construction of Pairwise Comparison Matrices

In this phase the AHP is utilized for determining the relative importance that each indicator of the final sample has for each of the different EU State. It is important to note that the differentiation of the importance that each indicator can play for the States is related to the real role and relevance covered by each sector within the specific State: the environmental issues may be very important for some States, but for others they may be less important and the social or economic issues may prevail. For this reason, for each EU State a pairwise comparison matrix of order n is realized. In this case, a panel of experts that comprises professional and specialist profiles with a knowledge in the CBA economic evaluation field is involved. Pairwise comparisons tell how much more important one indicator is compared to the others by formulating the following question "how important is the indicator x to the indicator y?" to each member of the panel of experts. The collection of all the verbal judgments provides for the analysis of the transformed values through the use of the Saaty scale [29] and the subjectivity level analysis is given by the calculation of the Consistency Ratio (CR), as the ratio of the Consistency Index and the Random Index as shown in Eq. (1).

$$\text{Consistency Ratio} = \frac{Consistency\,Index}{Random\,Index} = \frac{[(\lambda_{max} - n)/(n - 1)]}{Random\,Index} \qquad (1)$$

where λ_{max} is the maximum eigenvalue of the matrix, n is the order of all the pairwise comparison matrices and the Random Index is chosen from the pre-established table of values, according to the order n of all of them. If the Consistency Ratio is minor than 0.1, the consistency of the local weight's determination process is verified.

4.4 Phase 4. Application of the Weighted Sum Model for Aggregating the Indicators into the So-Called "Actual Performance Index"

A Weighted Sum Model (WSM) is applied in this phase for two reasons: the first one is the aggregation of the n social, environmental and economic indicators into a synthetic index, specifically called "actual performance index". The second one, is the verification of the presence of critical issues by comparing the performances index. This, in fact, represents the specific conditions of the States at the time of the evaluation and the reference years of the indicators.

4.5 Phase 5. Identification of the "Benchmark State" Indicator's Values and Determination of the Local Weights and the "Benchmark Index"

Once having analyzed the existent conditions of all the considered EU States, in Phase 5) the profile of the "benchmark State" is defined according to the optimal values that the n processed indicators could assume among the ones already detected for the States. In this way, the elementary indicators of the "benchmark State" have the maximum values if the indicator has a positive influence on the overall performance, otherwise minimum values are attributed to the "benchmark State" if elevated values of the indicators raise the criticalities of the related issues (e.g. occupational rate for the social sphere, public debt for the economic one and pollution level for the environmental one). The ranges of the collected indicators' values will guide the features' profile of the "benchmark State", in order to have the best possible combinations of the socio-economic and environmental conditions, ideally achievable by the EU States. The adoption of this "ideal" State is useful for comparing the obtained performances of the previous phase 4) and identify the State for which effective efforts are more or less required for an equitable growth. The determination of the local weights of the n indicators of the benchmark State is carried out in the same way as the other EU States, therefore by applying the AHP multi-criteria technique and with the support of the same panel of experts used in the Phase 3). A pairwise comparison matrix of order n is realized, and the CR of the judgments is verified with the Eq. (1) application. Subsequently, for determining the so-called "benchmark index" that refers to the "benchmark State" as the optimal target for all the EU States, a WSM is used, as in the Phase 4).

4.6 Phase 6. Determination of the Corrective Coefficient Through the DEA Application and the "Adjusted" SDR Values

The final step of the proposed logical-perequative methodology consists with the application of the DEA, in particular the Benefit of Doubt (BoD) approach that determines the corrective coefficients as the ratio between the i-th "actual performance index" associated to the European State - obtained in the Phase 4) – and the "benchmark one" or the "benchmark State"- obtained in the Phase 5) – by applying the following Eq. (2):

$$\text{Corrective coefficient} = \frac{performance\ index\ of\ the\ i - th\ European\ State}{target\ performance\ of\ the\ benchmark\ State} = \frac{CI_i}{CI_{bs}} \quad (2)$$

After having obtained, by using the Eq. (2), the real corrective coefficients pertaining to each of the EU States under analysis, the "adjusted" SDR values are calculated as the product between the obtained corrective coefficient of the EU State and the SDR value officially used as reference in the period of analysis. In this way, an abacus where for each considered EU State corresponds the "official" SDR, the obtained corrective coefficient and the "adjusted" SDR can be provided.

5 Conclusions

The social and territorial cohesion goals - at different scales - are strongly connected to the scope of a homogeneous and equitable growth of nations, and they intrinsically include the issue of the sustainable development of countries [30–35]. For guaranteeing uniform economic, environmental and social growth, the need to define effective tool for supporting efficient territorial governance, consistent with the Sustainable Development Goals of the 2030 Agenda [1], is often central. Within the economic evaluations of the urban projects carried out through the adoption of the CBA, the SDR constitutes a fundamental parameter that reflects the social point of view about the preference level of future costs and benefits compared to the present ones and often is linked to the political targets set by each local and central government. The appropriate use of the SDR affects the results of the analysis, because a low SDR value may cause undesirable projects to be approved and public organizations to allocate a larger share of tax revenues to the long-term intergenerational projects, whereas a high SDR value can discriminate future generations and it may result in a possible rejection of desirable projects. For these reasons, the SDR to be used in the CBA for the decision-making process for selecting investments capable of ensuring sustainable and equitable development of all the States plays a fundamental role, in determining an adequate assessment of the aspects on which fair and inclusive growth depends.

This research is part of the framework outlined. The aim was to provide an innovative logical-perequative methodology for the assessment of the "adjusted" SDR according to the influencing socio-economic and environmental specificities on the sustainable development of each EU State. In specific terms, the proposed methodology differs from the generally used SRTP approach for the inclusion of the environmental issues, associated with the socio-economic aspects that characterize each nation. These parameters, in fact, are fundamental in the economic analysis of the projects, due to their capacity to affect the results, and therefore the investment decisions, in the CBA process.

The main advantages of the methodology regard:

i. the flexibility to be used in different territorial contexts;
ii. the simple structure and computational operative procedure;
iii. the possibility to take into account both qualitative and quantitative sustainability aspects;

iv. the ability to obtain a comprehensive framework for the current equitable growth of all the States.

However, it is necessary to highlight that, among the methodology limits, there is the cogence to detect valid, update and robust indicators for all the EU States that, at the same time, are consistent with the assessed sustainability's issues. For these reason, official sources or guidelines are required to be used.

Future developments of this research may concern the application to a real case study that regards the 27 EU States in order to test and verify the validity of the proposed logical-perequative methodology and to grasp the effects that the different environmental, social and economic conditions generate on the corrective coefficient and, therefore, on the reference SDR values of each State.

Note

The research has been developed within the project "MISTRAL - a toolkit for dynaMic health Impact analysis to predicT disability-Related costs in the Aging population based on three case studies of steeL-industry exposed areas in Europe"- HORIZON-HLTH-2022-ENVHLTH04 - Grant Agreement Project n. 101095119 of the Polytechnic University of Bari (Italy).

References

1. United Nations: Agenda 2030 (2015). https://unric.org/it/agenda-2030. Accessed 12 Nov 2022
2. Official journal of the European Union: consolidated version of the treaty on the functioning of the European Union, C 326, 26 October 2012. https://eur-lex.europa.eu/. Accessed 05 Jan 2023
3. European parliament: economic, social and territorial cohesion. https://www.europarl.eur opa.eu/. Accessed 25 Jan 2023
4. European commission: EU funding programmes. https://commission.europa.eu/. Accessed 08 Feb 2023
5. European commission: communication from the commission to the European parliament, the council, the European economic and social committee and the committee of the regions, a union of equality: gender equality strategy 2020–2025 (2020). https://eur-lex.europa.eu/. Accessed 18 Jan 2023
6. European commission: strategic engagement for gender equality 2016–2019 (2016). https://commission.europa.eu/. Accessed 20 Dec 2022. ISBN 978-92-79-53451-5
7. National recovery and resilience plan (NRRP). www.mef.gov.it. Accessed 10 Jul 2022
8. Next generation EU (NGEU) - Recovery fund. www.ec.europa.eu.it. Accessed 17 Jul 2022
9. European commission, cohesion policy legislation 2014–2020. https://ec.europa.eu/. Accessed 04 Dec 2022
10. European commission: european structural and investment funds 2014–2020: Official texts and commentaries (2015). https://ec.europa.eu/. Accessed 14 Nov 2022. ISBN (PDF): 978-92-79-39433-1
11. European commission, New cohesion policy. https://ec.europa.eu/. Accessed 07 Dec 2022
12. European commission, Directorate-general for regional and urban policy: guide to CostBenefit analysis of investment projects. Economic appraisal tool for cohesion policy 2014–2020 (2014)
13. Hwang, K.: Cost-benefit analysis: its usage and critiques. J. Public Aff. **16**(1), 75–80 (2016)

14. Priemus, H., Flyvbjerg, B., van Wee, B. (eds.): Decision-Making on Mega-Projects: CostBenefit Analysis, Planning and Innovation. Edward Elgar Publishing, Cheltenham (2008)

15. official journal of the European Union: regulation (EU) No. 1303/2013 of the European parliament and of the council of 17 December 2013 laying down common provisions on the European Regional development fund, the European social fund, the cohesion fund, the European agricultural fund for rural development and the European maritime and fisheries fund and laying down general provisions on the European regional development fund, the European social fund, the cohesion fund and the European maritime and fisheries fund and repealing council regulation (EC) No. 1083/2006. https://eur-lex.europa.eu/. Accessed 27 Nov 2022

16. European commission: economic appraisal vademecum 2021–2027 - General Principles and sector applications (2021). https://jaspers.eib.org/LibraryNP/EC%20Reports/Economic% 20Appraisal%20Vademecum%202021-2027%20-%20General%20Principles%20and%20S ector%20Applications.pdf

17. Zhuang, J., Liang, Z., Lin, T., De Guzman, F.: Theory and practice in the choice of social discount rate for cost-benefit analysis: a survey. Working paper No. 94, Economics and research department, Asian development bank, May 2007. http://hdl.handle.net/10419/ 109296. Accessed 11 Dec 2022

18. Tajani, F., Morano, P., Ntalianis, K.: Automated valuation models for real estate portfolios: a method for the value updates of the property assets. J. Property Invest. Finan. 36(4), 324–347 (2018)

19. Burgess, D.F., Zerbe, R.O.: Calculating the social opportunity cost discount rate. J. Benefit-Cost Anal. 2(3), 1–10 (2011)

20. Ramsey, F.P.: A mathematical theory of saving. Econ. J. 38(152), 543–559 (1928)

21. Boyko, C.T., et al.: Benchmarking sustainability in cities: The role of indicators and future scenarios. Global Environ. Change 22(1), 245–254 (2012)

22. Ibrahim, R., Abdelmonem, M.G., Mushatat, S.: The role of urban pattern indicators for sustainable urban forms in the developed countries: a pragmatic evaluation of two sustainable urban contexts. In: Proceedings of the 1st International Conference on Engineering And Innovative Technology (SU-ICEIT 2016), Engineering College at Salahaddin University, Erbil, Kurdistan, Iraq, 12–14 April 2016. CEIT, Erbil (2016)

23. Button, K.: City management and urban environmental indicators. Ecol. Econ. 40(2), 217–233 (2002)

24. Can, A., Michel, S., De Coensel, B., Ribeiro, C., Botteldooren, D., Lavandier, C.: Comparison of noise indicators in an urban context. In: Inter-noise and Noise-con Congress and Conference Proceedings, vol. 253, no. 8, pp. 775–783. Institute of Noise Control Engineering (2016)

25. Abualhagag, A., Valánszki, I.: Mapping indicators of cultural ecosystem services: review and relevance to urban context. J. Landscape Ecol. 13(1), 4–24 (2020)

26. Popovic, T., Barbosa-Póvoa, A., Kraslawski, A., Carvalho, A.: Quantitative indicators for social sustainability assessment of supply chains. J. Clean. Prod. 180, 748–768 (2018)

27. Diaz-Chavez, R.: Indicators for socio-economic sustainability assessment. Socio-economic impacts of bioenergy production, pp. 17–37 (2014)

28. Castillo, J.G., Zhangallimbay, D.: The social discount rate in the evaluation of investment projects: an application for Ecuador, CEPAL Review No. 134 (2021). https://hdl.handle.net/ 11362/47523. Accessed 18 Oct 2022

29. Saaty, T.L.: Decision making—the analytic hierarchy and network processes (AHP/ANP). J. Syst. Sci. Syst. Eng. 13, 1–35 (2004)

30. Morano, P., Tajani, F., Di Liddo, F., Amoruso, P.: The public role for the effectiveness of the territorial enhancement initiatives: a case study on the redevelopment of a building in disuse in an Italian small town. Buildings 11(3), 87 (2021)

31. Morano, P., Tajani, F., Anelli, D.: Urban planning variants: a model for the division of the activated "plusvalue" between public and private subjects. Valori e Valutazioni **28**, 31–48 (2021)
32. Tajani, F., Anelli, D., Di Liddo, F., Morano, P.: An innovative methodology for the assessment of the social discount rate: an application to the European states for ensuring the goals of equitable growth. Smart and Sustainable Built Environment (2023). (In press)
33. Anelli, D., Tajani, F., Ranieri, R.: Urban resilience against natural disasters: mapping the risk with an innovative indicators-based assessment approach. J. Clean. Prod. **371**, 133496 (2022)
34. Locurcio, M., Tajani, F., Morano, P., Anelli, D., Manganelli, B.: Credit risk management of property investments through multi-criteria indicators. Risks **9**(6), 106 (2021)
35. Spatari, G., Lorè, I., Viglianisi, A., Calabrò, F.: Economic feasibility of an integrated program for the enhancement of the byzantine heritage in the Aspromonte National Park. The case of Staiti. In: Calabrò, F., Della Spina, L., Piñeira Mantiñán, M.J. (eds.) New Metropolitan Perspectives. NMP 2022. LNNS, vol. 482, pp. 313–323. Springer, Cham (2022). https://doi.org/10.1007/978-3-031-06825-6_30

The Real Estate Risk Assessment: An Innovative Methodology for Supporting Public and Private Subjects Involved into Sustainable Urban Interventions

Pierluigi Morano[1] , Debora Anelli[1]([⊠]) , Francesco Tajani[2] ,
and Antonella Roma[2]

[1] Department of Civil, Environmental, Land, Construction and Chemistry Engineering,
Polytechnic University of Bari, 70126 Bari, Italy
debora.anelli@poliba.it

[2] Department of Architecture and Design, "Sapienza" University of Rome, 00196 Rome, Italy

Abstract. Projects carried out under Public-Private Partnership (PPP) forms are increasingly being used for construction, new infrastructure implementation, urban redevelopment operations and more general land interventions. PPP projects, due to their complexity, are characterized by risks that undermine their success, for this reason risk assessment models for PPP projects are essential to their successful implementation. In this context, the research proposes an innovative real estate risk assessment methodology for supporting the Public Administration and the Private Entrepreneur involved into PPP projects. The research proposes an *ex-ante* real estate risk assessment methodology, based on the multi-criteria Analytic Hierarchy Process (AHP) technique that can be used at different territorial scales and by both public and private parties involved in urban transformations projects. The construction of the risk index is obtained through the logical-operative framework that consists into a protocol of 7 ordered and sequential phases. The methodology turns out to be flexible and reproducible and allows for parallel analysis of qualitative and quantitative aspects that in terms of risk undermine the success of projects.

Keywords: real estate risk assessment · PPP · risk index · assessment methodology · composite indicator · flexible evaluation

1 Introduction

In recent decades, the attention paid to environmental, economic and social sustainability together with the containment of land consumption has been at the center of public debates related to urban development processes. Urban regeneration is one of the main strategies to be conducted to achieve resilient urban paradigms and innovative housing models. In particular, the aim of current governments is to promote urban transformation interventions aimed at both the redevelopment of disused or abandoned buildings and the redevelopment of degraded areas. In order to achieve an adequate match between the functions to be settled and the actual changing needs of local communities, the recent development programs aim to define safer and greener cities, consistent with the international purposes of the 17 Sustainable Development Goals set out in the 2030 Agenda [1] and the recent strategies financed within the EU Next Generation and the European Green Deal programs, received in the National Plan of Recovery and Resilience (PNRR) [2].

For these reasons, there is an increasingly important need to develop tools that implement effective urban regeneration strategies for which land use governance policies must give priority to the rehabilitation of existing built and underused urban spaces. In this way, therefore, the traditional physical transformations of the land should be replaced by the general improvement of the community's quality of life, in terms of social wellbeing, environmental value and economic inclusive cities.

However, the complexity that characterizes the overall urban regeneration interventions, and more generally the land transformations, requires the use of appropriate methodologies that are able to efficiently support the management of the entire process, guarantee the stakeholder's interests and the achievement of the projects' established goals. Given these needs and the scarcity of public financial resources that can cover the entire costs of the transformations, urban regeneration practices have largely been carried out through partnerships between the public and the private sectors [3]. The Public-Private Partnership (PPP) form is often adopted for its advantages of sharing, in the most suitable way, not only the benefits related to the projects, but in particularly, the several risks that can occur in all the phases of the procedure. In fact, according to Grimsey et. Al, 2004 [4], there is evidence of numerous European projects implemented with the adoption of the PPP for different sectors, such as wastewater treatment and management, public highways and railways or subways, power plants and telecommunications infrastructure, school buildings, airport facilities, public offices, prisons, light rail systems, parking stations, harbors, pipelines, cultural properties like museum, health services. Due to its flexibility, it is possible to identify numerous adoptions of the PPP, whose broad-spectrum analysis allows to identify its main advantages and, at the same time, to highlight the most critical issues related to its implementation. Among the advantages, there are: i) the compensation of the government's shortage of financial resources; ii) the possibility to ensure the success of the project through the specific entrepreneurial skills of the private subject involved; iii) the ability to provide the community's facilities by reducing the pressure of the economic development on the public sector; iv) the creation of a cooperation that can ensure the private sector development with the use of innovative technological profiles for the works; v) the distribution of the risks associated with the execution of the works [5–7].

Despite the many advantages, the PPP may be difficult in the phase of correct allocation of risks to the appropriate subject who, involved in the procedure, is able to manage it better. Several types of risks can occur during the phases of the project, from its programming to its possible dismissal, passing through the phases of planning, realization and eventual management [8]. The risk is defined in economics as "the probability that a damage or loss may occur at some instant" and therefore requires appropriate assessment methodologies to quantify, manage and reduce it. With special attention to urban interventions, property risk assessment assumes considerable importance in order to safeguard the economic interests of the private sector that is often the main driving force of the interventions. Estimating the likelihood that damage or loss will occur at a certain instant of time depends on a number of factors attributable to the magnitude of the intervention, the legal status of the sites, the entrepreneurial capacity and individual risk aversion to which the risks are attributed. It is also essential to know the economic, physical and social conditions of the context in which the operation takes place.

In these terms, the complexity of the assessment of all risks appears evident, but the accurate identification of all the risks of the operation and then the allocation of the different types of risk among the parties involved in the real estate initiative, placed in the hands of the party(ies) with the greatest capacity, are the fundamental operations to ensure the success of projects.

2 Aim of the Work

The work is part of the outlined framework. In particular, the research is aimed at developing an innovative real estate risk assessment methodology intended for supporting the Public Administration and the Private Entrepreneur involved into PPP urban transformation intervention through the determination of a composite indicator, namely the Real Estate Risk Index (I_{RER}). The proposed methodology consists of a protocol of sequential and ordered phases that, based on an adequate socio-economic and real estate spatial data, is able to assess the level of the real estate risk that pertains to a specific territorial scale chosen for the analysis, according to the goals, the requirements, the data or the point of view (if public or private). Due to the capacity of the Analytic Hierarchy Process (AHP) multi-criteria technique for processing and aggregating both qualitative and quantitative risk indicators and the spatial distribution visualization offered by the Geographic Information Systems for the obtained risk levels, a conceptual framework and operative procedure for the ex-ante risk assessment is proposed. In this way, it is performed a rigorous decomposition of the real estate risk factors into hierarchical and clear levels that, at the same time, is simply reproducible because it doesn't require specific or high calculating and knowledge skills, with the exception of the knowledge of the socio-economic characteristics of the urban fabric under analysis and those of the real estate market.

The composite indicator determinable through the seven sequential and ordered phases allows to analyze the local real estate market features known at the moment of the evaluation, and that could affect the feasibility of a urban PPP development project.

The paper is structured as follows: in Sect. 3 an overview of the main real estate risk factors affecting PPP initiatives is carried out. In Sect. 4 the structure and the phases that characterize the proposed composite indicator methodology is explained. In Sect. 5 the advantages and limits, nor the practical implications of the proposed risk assessment methodology with the future insights of the research are discussed.

3 Background

The PPP projects are widely debated internationally. Many researchers have conducted studies aimed at understanding recurring risk factors in projects execution due to the evidence that identifying risks and assigning their responsibility represents the winning strategy for successful and effective projects.

Yelin et al. [9] analyze 9 projects related to the construction of water facilities in China to identify risks that undermine the success of projects implemented in PPP. The authors conduct a review of literature and then they proceed by studying 9 projects with the aim of conducting a data collection on the main risk factors, principally related to political, legal profiles, government conditions and local/global market dynamics. The analysis identified 11 critical risks that undermine the success of water projects in China. Poor ability to manage these risks causes consequences such as: poor project quality, delivery delays, un-respected budgets and contract disputes. The authors show that proper risk allocation strategies turn out to be essential for the success of projects.

Similarly Chan et al. [10], following the literature review, identify 34 recurrent risk factors in construction projects in China, that often cause schedule delay or/and cost over-run. The risks identified can be associated with two main categories: systematic/country risks and specific projects risks. The authors develop a questionnaire to understand industrialists' and academics' perceptions of these risks and to understand the responsibility for these risks among the parties, in PPP projects in China. The research findings showed that a key problem in China is the lack of a model for risk assessment and equitable sharing of the risks associated with the project.

Hwang et al. [11] identify 42 risk factors in PPP projects from a literary review, in the context of the implementation of road projects and public facilities. They develop a questionnaire that is submitted to contractors in Singapore. The authors obtain 48 valid questionnaires that they process using the Mean Score technique, through which they obtained a criticality ranking of risk factors in the execution of PPP projects in Singapore, in particular the risks considered most critical were found to be: lack of government support, inexperience in the execution of PPP projects, and construction delays.

Rybnicek et al. [12] develop a review analyzing the recurring risks factors in international PPP projects, without reference to a specific project or project area. The authors develop a model that consists of three steps: risk identification, risk assessment and risk mitigation. They analyze these aspects for the 8 risks most cited in the literature including: contractual issues, resources, and objectives pursued by the parties.

Carbonara et al. [13] affirms that one of the critical aspects of a successful project is risk management. This is possible by identifying the different risks associated with the project, which will differ from sector to sector. Based on a Delphi survey, they propose a list of significant risks in PPP highway projects and define the allocation of each risk. In this way the involved parties can establish effective resolution strategies.

Zou et al. [14] analyze three PPP infrastructure projects, two from Australia and one from China. They analyze financial risks, public acceptance/rejection risks, political risks, corruption risks and construction risks of each projects. The authors, from their study of the 3 projects, show how the identification of risks in the early stages and the subsequent allocation of risks to the parties that demonstrate the greatest capacity to manage it, is a key operation. In order to preserve the interests of both the public and the private sector, while preserving the project's value for money, risk management must be defined over the entire project life cycle.

Fischer et al. [15] develop interviews, questionnaires and a literature review from which they deduce a standardization of risk types in PPP infrastructure projects such as site risk, contractual risk, financial risk. They develop a risk management process model: an Integrated Risk Management System (IRMS). Risk management processes are structured as an IRMS on four levels. The system developed serves all parties involved in projects by enabling a range of benefits including the identification of appropriate risk management strategies during all phases of the project life cycle.

Jin X.-H. et al. [16] propose an Artificial Neural Network model (ANN) to support risk allocation decision making in construction PPP projects, developed on the basis of transaction cost economics. The research shows how ANN is a satisfactory model to be used to support decision-making processes and how it is appropriate to utilize transaction cost economics and resource-based view of organizational capability to interpret risk allocation decision-making process.

Identification processes of recurring risks in the execution of PPP projects is a preliminary operation to risk assessment. The implementation of PPP projects requires the use of substantial capital resources; however, incorrect risk assessment leads to increased project costs. The use of correct risk assessment techniques allows the most critical issues of projects to be managed and allocated in the correct manner, ensuring their success.

Kumar et al. [17] analyze the investment risk of projects related to highway construction in India. The authors apply a standard risk analysis model, that is Net Present Value (NPV)-at-risk tool supported by Monte Carlo Simulation to 30 highway projects (built and under construction) in India. The analysis shows that the factors that most influence NPV in the projects considered are the discount rate and construction cost. The authors propose NPV-at-risk tool to support private investors and public entities, because the analysis of different settings permits more informed investment choices.

Valipour et al. [18] use different types of Multi-Attribute Decision-Making (MADM) methods to examine the performance of methods applied to the same case. The authors identified the top 10 recurring risks in the implementation of highway projects in Iran, such as problems in project design, limited capital, delays in resolving contractual disputes, and environmental issues. From this, a decision-making group defined 5 risk assessment criteria: impact of risk, consequence, risk predictability, risk uncertainty and detectability. The study inferred that the Step-Wise Weight Assessment Ratio Analysis (SWARA), Complex Proportional Assessment (COPRAS) and Evaluation based on Distance from Average Solution (EDAS), show the highest potential for risk assessment in PPP projects.

4 Methodology

The research proposes a methodology aimed at defining a real estate risk index able to assess - in the *ex-ante* situation – the level of the real estate risk that could derive from the dynamics of the local real estate markets. It is obtained through the logical-operative framework that consists into a protocol of 7 ordered and sequential phases. In Fig. 1 all the sequential phases of the methodology are shown.

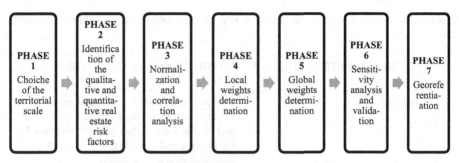

Fig. 1. Phases of the proposed assessment methodology

The high flexibility that characterizes the proposed methodology gives the opportunity to use it for constructing a real estate risk index for both public and private specific requirements, for several territorial scale (e.g. national, regional, municipal, sub-urban etc.) and for different purposes regarding the risk assessment (e.g. ranking the areas, compare the risk levels etc.). For these reasons, the description of each phase is done also by referring to some possible applications of the methodology, in order to better specify its operative usefulness.

4.1 Phase 1. Choice of the Territorial Scale According to the Final Utilization

The first step of the methodology is the definition of the uses for which the real estate risk index is intended and, therefore, the choice of the territorial scale of analysis that will influence the subsequent phases of collecting data and the real estate risk typologies to consider in the final synthetic value of the index. In other words, the different uses that the index could have directly affect the choice of the territorial scale to which the index should refers. In fact, the territorial scale must be carefully chosen in order to be adequate for the purposes of the assessment. This link between the risk index, the territorial scale and the final utilizations is better explained in Table 1.

As can be seen in Table 1, due to the high flexibility of the proposed methodology, there are 5 different territorial scales to which the protocol could allow to obtain a real estate risk index, according to the different goals. However, it is important to highlight that the present research is intended to take account also the spatial component related to the real estate data georeferentiation. This does not imply that the methodology for creating the index cannot ignore this question and directly be aimed at taking into account the point of view of the public or the private sector or changing the period of the evaluation passing from an *ex-ante* assessment to an *itinere* or *ex-post* ones and so on.

Table 1. Synthesis of the different territorial scales and possible goals related to the risk index use

N.	POSSIBLE TERRITORIAL SCALE	POSSIBLE GOALS/USES OF THE RISK INDEX
1	Building	It refers to the individual building and could be implemented for giving a synthetic preliminary and general view of the real estate risk based on the intrinsic and positional features or the transformation to be considered
2	Sub-urban	It can be used for providing an ex-ante risk assessment based on the local real estate risk factors that characterize a neighborhood
3	Urban area	It can be used for providing an ex-ante risk assessment based on the local real estate risk factors that characterize a neighborhood
4	Municipal	It involves the entire city and could be useful for comparing the ranking of the different cities and provide a more comprehensive vision
5	Extra-urban	It includes all the urban communities within a region or a nation and it can be chosen for carrying out an analysis for the global market

4.2 Identification of the Risk Typology to Assess

After the selection of the territorial scale to which the risk index will belong according to the specific purposes, the Phase 2) requires the identification of the specific real estate risk typology to consider. This phase, in fact, generally refers to the well-known subdivision of the real estate risk components into "systematic" and "specific". The first one is caused by global market's factors and affects all the different type of investments, therefore is extremely susceptible to the fluctuations of the general financial market: it is uncontrollable for the real estate redevelopment process, because it cannot be avoided through the diversification. The second one includes all the critical factors that characterizes a precise investment decision and it largely affects the feasibility of the projects. It appears to be more controllable than the "systematic" one and numerous typologies can be retrieved, such as property, insurance, administrative, construction, technical testing, tenant, geopolitical, location etc. Into this phase of the methodology, therefore, it is important to clearly identify the type of real estate risk that can be assessed according to the territorial scale chosen for the construction of the index. In particular, the "specific" type will guide the choice and, for example, for the building scale the risk will refers to the intrinsic and extrinsic variables, for the sub-urban scale the main risk drivers of the local demand and supply, as also for the urban area. A different behavior can be recognized for the major territorial scale, or the regional and national ones, where the geo-political issues and other main relevant global market dynamics may be considered in the real estate risk index for their influences.

4.3 Phase 3. Identification of the Qualitative and Quantitative Indicators Related to the Considered Risk Factors

The real estate risk index represents the synthesis of a sample of data and information useful for the analysis of the real estate risk typologies related to the chosen territorial scale. It derives from the aggregation of a set of n qualitative and quantitative indicators that are adequality able to represent each type of the real estate risk associated to the territorial scale. In this phase, the analysis of the real estate dynamics is essential for understanding what are the most suitable indicators that are able to represent each of the risk types considered. It could be assumed as a contextualization phase, where the indicators retrieved by the reference literature and professional practices, or *grey* documents, are fitted with the features of the urban tissue and the typology of available data on the real estate assets. For example, if the sub-urban scale is chosen according to the final utilization of the risk index, the market, context and tenant risk factors define the level of risk of each considered sub-urban area within the municipal territory therefore the qualitative and quantitative indicators should be identified in order to explain each of them. It is important to collect indicators due to their readability, availability, scientific background and coherence with the process and the territorial scale's peculiarities.

4.4 Phase 4. Normalization and Correlation Analysis of the Indicators Set

The sample of n qualitative and quantitative real estate risk indicators could be characterized by different units of measurement that don't allow to immediately compare the data and aggregate them into the synthetic risk value. If this happens, the normalization is necessary to bring all the collected data into a single and unambiguous measurement scale for comparing and aggregating purposes. The normalization techniques that could be applied is differently identified due to the several effects that the technique can induce on the final risk index's values.

The obtained normalized sample of n indicators should avoid the appearance of redundancy in the aggregation subsequent phase, therefore the determination of the correlation levels among all the considered indicators is important. The correlation analysis is required for eliminating the indicators with high overlapping of data in order to obtain a more robust and efficient real estate risk index and acquire a final sample of the indicators that contains only the ones that will determine the synthetic risk index. The Spearman and Pearsons methods are generally the most used for determining the correlation levels. In this phase the AHP can be utilized for structuring all the indicator's data into tree hierarchical levels as follows: the first one relates to the goal, or the creation of the real estate risk index, the second one contains the typologies of real estate risk considered after having carried out the Phase 2 of the proposed methodology and then the third and the fourth ones, respectively involve the n qualitative and quantitative final sample of indicators related to each of the risk types and the so-called "intensity ranges" that are defined according to the indicators values sensibility among the territorial units under analysis.

4.5 Phase 5. Local Weights Determination

Each of real estate risk factors represented by the set of the indicators differently affects and influences the final real estate risk level of the territorial unit because each of them has its importance, mathematically translated into a local weight. For all the elements of the AHP structure realized into the previous Phase 4), comparison matrices must be constructed for determining the importance, in terms of local weight, of intensity ranges, indicators and risk typology. Consultation with a panel of experts composed of several subjects, both form public and private sphere, that have a professional profile or level of knowledge adequate for the analysis and the territorial scale dynamics, can be identified for this phase for formulating the preference judgments for each comparison matrix, transformed into values through the adoption of the Saaty scale, as follows (Fig. 2).

Rating Scale	Definition	Explanation
1	Equal importance	Two elements contribute equally to the objective
2	Weak	Between equal and moderate
3	Moderate importance	Experience and judgment slightly favor one element over another
4	Moderate plus	Between moderate and strong
5	Strong importance	Experience and judgment strongly favor one element over another
6	Strong plus	Between strong and very strong
7	Very strong or demonstrated importance	An element is favored very strongly over another; its dominance demonstrated in practice
8	Very, very strong	Between very strong and extreme
9	Extreme importance	The evidence favoring one element over another is one of the highest possible order or affirmation

Fig. 2. Saaty scale used for the rating of the verbal judgments

It is important to note that if the indicator has a direct proportionality with the real estate risk index, the classes with the highest value of the intensity ranges will have a greater weight than those with the lowest one. For the elementary indicators for which their increasing values generates a reduction in the real estate risk level, the lower value ranges will have greater weight than the higher value ranges. The consistency of the panel of experts' judgments is verified through the calculation of the Consistency Index (CI), a control parameter proposed by Saaty that is based on the maximum eigenvalue of the matrix λ_{max} and the order n of the same, as Eq. (1) follows:

$$CI = [(\lambda_{max} - n)/(n - 1)]/RandomIndex \tag{1}$$

The Random index is a predefined table value depending on the order n of the comparison matrix. In order for the judgments expressed by the panel of experts to be used for the determination of the weights, the CI of each comparison matrix is less than 0.1.

4.6 Phase 6. Global Weights Determination

All the samples of real estate data considered in the set of final indicators are used to determine the real estate risk index by aggregating them through the implementation of a Weighted Sum Model. In particular, the proposed methodology provides for the adoption of the following formula (Eq. 2) for the determination of the real estate risk level pertaining to the territorial units under analysis.

$$I_{RER} = p_1(\Sigma_n^n v_{n,1} * w_{n,1}) + p_2(\Sigma_n^n v_{n,2} * w_{n,2}) + p_3(\Sigma_n^n v_{n,3} * w_{n,3}) + ..p_i(\Sigma_n^n v_{n,i} * w_{n,i})$$

(2)

where:

- p_1, p_2 and p_3 are the local weights of the risk types (systematic or specific according to the territorial scale of analysis);
- $v_{n1}, v_{n,2}$ and $v_{n,3}$ are the local weights determined through the pairwise comparison matrices for the n-th indicators of the final sample associated to each type of risk;
- $w_{n,1}, w_{n,2}$ $w_{n,3}$ are the weights of the defined m-th intensity range associated to the n-th indicator.

The obtained index value, normalized within the range 0 (minimum) and 1 (maximum) in order to be easily comparable, refers to the i-th territorial unit considered in analysis. The higher the index value the greater is the real estate risk associated with it on the basis of the considered indicators. This operation must be carried out for each of the examined territorial units within the chosen scale of analysis.

4.7 Phase 7. Sensitivity Analysis, Validation and Georeferentiation

A combination of uncertainty and sensitivity analysis can help to gauge the robustness of the proposed risk index, to increase its transparency and to help framing a debate around it. In particular, the analysis is focused on the possible sources of uncertainty, which can arise from the:

  i) selection of sub-indicators,
 ii) data quality,
iii) data normalization technique,
 iv) weighting scheme,
  v) aggregation formulas.

There are several operations to be taken, such as the inclusion/exclusion of some indicators; the modelling of data error; the alternative intensity ranges schemes; the alternative data normalization schemes; the several weighting schemes, i.e. two methods in the participatory family (budget allocation and AHP), and one based on endogenous weighting (Data Envelopment Analysis). In particular, the disposable data with the territorial scale of analysis could guide this final phase that is aimed at testing the robustness of the obtained results of the index and also its consistency with the effective expected results derived from the real values of the indicator's set. The validation may be carried out by comparing the real estate risk levels with the ones of other studies or analysis conducted by other robust research or studies. Moreover, in order to immediately identify the distribution of the real estate risk levels among the territorial scales considered, the geographic information systems - such as for example "My Maps" (provider: Google), can help the final users to arise the knowledge on the matter and support the negotiation phase, or the sustainable planning choices.

5 Conclusions

The PPP projects turn out to be an effective strategy in approaching the complexity that characterizes urban regeneration interventions, the implementation of services and infrastructure, but more generally, any type of intervention on the territory [19–26]. The form of PPP is adopted for the implementation of many interventions on an international scale, since its advantage lies in sharing both the benefits but also the many risks associated with projects between the public and the private subjects. However, the main delicate points associated with the implementation of PPP forms relate to the identification and subsequent assessment of risks. The management of risks and their allocation among the parties involved in real estate initiatives, is the key step to ensure the success of PPP projects.

In this framework, the research aims to develop an innovative method of real estate risk assessment through the determination of a composite indicator, namely the Real Estate Risk Index (I_{RER}), in order to support the decision-making processes of Public Administration and private entrepreneurs regarding possible investments for real estate initiatives. The critical contribution of the paper consists in the development and definition of a real estate risk assessment methodology. The method developed is easily reproducible because it does not require complex computational analysis and is flexible because it can be applied at different territorial scales, (e.g. national, regional, municipal, sub-urban etc.) depending on the goals to be pursued. The proposed methodology consists of a protocol of 7 sequential and ordered phases that is able to assess the level of the real estate risk, enabling an *ex-ante* evaluation procedure for real estate interventions.

The developed operational risk assessment procedure takes advantage of the capability of the multi-criteria technique AHP, which processes and aggregates qualitative and quantitative risk indicators, and the visualization of the spatial distribution offered by Geographic Information Systems for the risk levels obtained.

The developed method allows to weigh the investment decisions in the bidding phase through an overall risk assessment. The real estate valuation risk index can thus be used by both entrepreneurs and the public administration, who can identify high-risk projects from before implementation and monitor critical factors. Research developments involve the application of the methodology to real project cases, at different territorial scales, in order to verify the efficiency of the developed risk index.

References

1. Organizzazione Nazioni Unite, Trasforming the World: The 2030 Agenda for Sustainable Development (2015). https://unric.org/it/agenda-2030/. Accessed 06 Apr 2023
2. Ministry Of Economy and Finance (MEF). https://www.mef.gov.it/focus/Il-Piano-Nazionale-di-Ripresa-e-Resilienza-PNRR/. Accessed 06 Apr 2023
3. De Paula, P.V., Marques, R.C., Gonçalves. J.M.: Public–private partnerships in urban regeneration projects: a review. J. Urban Plan. Dev. **149**(1), (2023)
4. Grimsey, D., Lewis, M.K.: Public Private Partnerships: The Worldwide Revolution in Infrastructure Provision and Project Finance. Edward Elgar, Cheltenham (2004)
5. Anelli, D., Tajani, F.: Valorization of cultural heritage and land take reduction: an urban compensation model for the replacement of unsuitable buildings in an Italian UNESCO site. J. Cult. Herit. **57**, 165–172 (2022)

6. Cheung, E., Chan, A.P.C., Kajewski, S.: Reasons for implementing public private partnership projects. J. Property Investment Finan. **27**(1), 81–95 (2009)

7. Cheung, E., Chan, A.P.C.: Evaluation model for assessing the suitability of public-private partnership projects. J. Manag. Eng. **27**(2), 80–89 (2011)

8. Chinyio, E., Fergusson, A.: A construction perspective on risk management in public-private partnership. In: Public-Private Partnerships: Managing Risks and Opportunities, pp.93–126. John Wiley & Sons, Hoboken (2003)

9. Yelin, X., Yunfang, Y., Albert, P.C.C., John, F.Y.Y., Hu, C.: Identification and allocation of risks associated with PPP water projects in China. Int. J. Strateg. Prop. Manag. **15**(3), 275–294 (2011)

10. Chan, A.P.C., Yeung, J.F.Y., Yu, C.C.P., Wang, S.Q., Ke, Y.: Empirical study of risk assessment and allocation of public-private partnership projects in China. J. Manag. Eng. **27**(3), 136–148 (2011)

11. Hwang, B.-G., Zhao, X., Gay, M.J.S.: Public private partnership projects in Singapore: factors, critical risks and preferred risk allocation from the perspective of contractors. Int. J. Project Manage. **31**(3), 424–433 (2013)

12. Rybnicek, R., Plakolm, J., Baumgartner, L.: Risks in public-private partnerships: a systematic literature review of risk factors, their impact and risk mitigation strategies, public performance & management review. Public Perform. Manag. Rev. **43**(12), 1–35 (2020)

13. Carbonara, N., Costantino, N., Gunnigan, L., Pellegrino, P.: Risk management in motorway PPP projects: empirical-based guidelines. Publ. Private Partnerships Transp. **35**(2), 162–182 (2015)

14. Zou, P.X.W., Wang, S., Fang, D.: A life-cycle risk management framework for PPP infrastructure projects. J. Financ. Manag. Prop. Constr. **13**(2), 123–142 (2008)

15. Fischer, K., Leidel, K., Riemann, A., Wilhelm Alfen, H.: An integrated risk management system (IRMS) for PPP projects. J. Finan. Manag. Property Constr. **15**(3), 260–282 (2010)

16. Jin, X.-H., Zhang, G.: Modelling optimal risk allocation in PPP projects using artificial neural networks. Int. J. Project Manage. **25**(5), 591–603 (2011)

17. Lakshya, K., Apurva, J., Nagendra, R.V.: Financial risk assessment and modelling of PPP based Indian highway infrastructure projects. Transp. Policy **62**(4), 2–11 (2018)

18. Valipour, A., Sarvari, H., Tamošaitiene, J.: Risk assessment in PPP projects by applying different MCDM methods and comparative results analysis. Adm. Sci. **8**(4), 80 (2018)

19. Anelli, D., Tajani, F.: Spatial decision support systems for effective ex-ante risk evaluation: an innovative model for improving the real estate redevelopment processes. Land Use Policy **128**, 106595 (2023)

20. Locurcio, M., Tajani, F., Morano, P., Anelli, D., Manganelli, B.: Credit risk management of property investments through multi-criteria indicators. Risks **9**(6), 106 (2021)

21. Tajani, F., Morano, P., Salvo, F., De Ruggiero, M.: Property valuation: the market approach optimised by a weighted appraisal model. J. Property Investment Finan. **38**(5), 399–418 (2020)

22. Morano, P., Guarini, M.R., Sica, F., Anelli, D.: Ecosystem services and land take. a composite indicator for the assessment of sustainable urban projects. In: Gervasi, O., et al. (eds.) ICCSA 2021. LNCS, vol. 12954, pp. 210–225. Springer, Cham (2021). https://doi.org/10.1007/978-3-030-86979-3_16

23. Sessa, M.R., Russo, A., Sica, F.: Opinion paper on green deal for the urban regeneration of industrial brownfield land in Europe. Land Use Policy **119**, 106198 (2022)

24. Tajani, F., Morano, P., Di Liddo, F.: The optimal combinations of the eligible functions in multiple property assets enhancement. Land Use Policy **99**, 105050 (2020)

25. Di Liddo, F., Morano, P., Tajani, F., Torre, C.M.: An innovative methodological approach for the analysis of the effects of urban interventions on property prices. Valori e Valutazioni, (26) (2020)
26. Anelli, D., Tajani, F., Ranieri, R.: Urban resilience against natural disasters: mapping the risk with an innovative indicators-based assessment approach. J. Clean. Prod. **371**, 133496 (2022)

(Con)temporary Housing: The AirBnb Phenomenon and Its Impact on the Naples Historic Center's Rental Market

Pierfrancesco De Paola[1]([✉]) [iD], Elvio Iannitti[1], Benedetto Manganelli[2] [iD], and Francesco Paolo Del Giudice[3] [iD]

[1] Department of Industrial Engineering, University of Naples Federico II, Vincenzo Tecchio Sq. 80, 80125 Naples, Italy
`pierfrancesco.depaola@unina.it`
[2] School of Engineering, University of Basilicata, Ateneo Lucano Av., 85100 Potenza, Italy
`benedetto.manganelli@unibas.it`
[3] Department of Architecture and Design, Sapienza University of Rome, Borghese Sq. 9, 00186 Rome, Italy
`francescopaolo.delgiudice@uniroma1.it`

Abstract. Some significative historical events have contributed to radical changes in people life (industrial revolution, great depression of the 1920s, world wars, digital revolution, American subprime crisis of the 2000s, COVID-19 pandemic, war in Ukraine). All this at the same time as the unprecedented acceleration of digital technological development. This has led to the birth of new forms of economy, which have made it possible in many cases to fill the income gaps caused by the post-crisis aftermath. The study aims to provide a general overview of "home sharing", and subsequently focusing on the real estate market of Naples by comparing, through geoadditive statistical models, the spatial distributions related to the real estate incomes of two forms of distinct rent: short-term, traditional long-term. The analysis is conducted with reference to the latest data available for 2020, before the COVID19 pandemic, as for about two subsequent years the tourism sector was overwhelmed by uncontrollable and non-ordinary dynamics. Preliminarily, the paper deals aspects linket to urban changes, gentrification, touristification, rent gap, home sharing and Airbnb phenomenon and the influence it has had on the most relevant turistic realities.

Keywords: Gentrification · Touristification · Rent Gap theory · Short and long-term rental · AirBnB · Geoadditive models

1 Introduction

Man, by his nature, is the living being with the greatest ability to adapt to new situations, to unknown and often not easily modifiable problems, to environmental conditions of all kinds. Certainly not only for his potential and biological and physical characteristics, but rather for the great variety of behavioral responses that he can implement and for the high dynamism by nature intrinsic in the behavior of the human being.

© The Author(s), under exclusive license to Springer Nature Switzerland AG 2023
O. Gervasi et al. (Eds.): ICCSA 2023 Workshops, LNCS 14109, pp. 427–443, 2023.
https://doi.org/10.1007/978-3-031-37120-2_28

In 1927 Scheler considers man as a being different from all other animals due to his ability to escape from environmental enclosure [1]. According to Scheler, man differs from animals not in intelligence, which animals also possess to a greater or lesser extent, but in being a creature open to the world without a predefined essence; while the animal lives entirely within its environment, like a snail in its shell, man possesses a world and not an environment. In this world, man has adapted in order to satisfy his needs, which in turn have evolved over time due to historical, anthropological and economic changes.

We can identify multiple historical events that have contributed to radical changes in society and therefore in the individual; the industrial revolution, the great depression of the 1920s, the world wars, the digital revolution, the American subprime crisis in the end of the first decade of the 2000s, the COVID-19 pandemic, the war in Ukraine with the consequence of crises both energy (supply of natural gas) and economic (inflation linked to the increase in the cost of raw materials and fossil resources). Events that, in one way or another, have radically influenced the world economy and, in detail, the way of life of the individual [2].

All this at the same time as the unprecedented acceleration of digital technological development.

This has led to the birth of new forms of economy, which have made it possible in many cases to fill the income gaps caused by the post-crisis aftermath. This is the case of the sharing economy, more specifically of "home sharing", and this study focuses also on this.

The study aims to provide a general overview of this phenomenon, certainly by the best known but rarely explored, and subsequently focus on the real estate market of Naples by comparing, through a geo-additive statistical model, the spatial distribution related to the incomes of two forms of distinct leases: short-term rental (STR) and the traditional lease, or long-term rental (LTR). The analysis is conducted with reference to the latest data available for 2020, before the COVID19 pandemic, as for about two subsequent years the tourism sector was overwhelmed by uncontrollable and non-ordinary dynamics.

As a preliminary point, however, it is necessary to analyze the phenomenon in its generality, focusing on the effects of the new market on urban, anthropological and economic spatial systems, maintaining a reference system on a metropolitan scale. We want to refer on the phenomenon of gentrification, of how urban and socio-cultural changes influence city centres, alienating the traditional inhabitants in favor of a more affluent social class with a consequent loss of tradition in the neighborhoods in question. We want to put a magnifying glass on tourism, therefore on the influence of unbridled low-cost tourism on the historic city centers and how it has inevitably conditioned the real estate market. Subsequently, the investigation scale of home sharing narrows down to the Airbnb phenomenon, the giant of the short-term rental market, and the influence it has had on the most relevant italian and global urban realities.

2 Urban Changes

2.1 What Social and Sharing Phenomena?

The city can be defined in many ways, and every definition can be correct.

The multiplicity of definitions derives from the possibility of highlighting only some of the many features characterizing the city. By highlighting, for example, the dimension and physical density, a settlement can be defined considering as buildings set placed close to each other, or the place where have men transformed spaces more and more densely to improve their living conditions. Therefore, the city has become an exchange place for relationships, as well as for commercial, cultural, productive, and social links [3].

It is an open, dynamic and highly complex system, made up of a set of related components. To say that it is a dynamic and complex system means to affirm that the city can be traced back to a set of components in relation to each other, that the processes of the system are not manageable and controllable with deterministic tools and, lastly, that the future evolution of the system city is not predictable linearly on the basis of knowledge of the initial conditions.

The city changes: from the "polis" of ancient world, passing from the static organizational structure of medieval walled city and from the ideal city theory in the 18th century, understood as possible alternatives to pre-existing cities. Furthermore, from the end of eighteenth century the changes become dynamic due to the revolutions that affect all aspects of city life: economic, political, scientific, industrial, and demographic (it is in this period that the European population passes from 180 million in 1800 to 400 million of 1900). And it is precisely from the industrial revolution onwards that the city begins to take on the appearance of modern city, the one we live today. And the changes that invest it become more and more sudden, becoming uncontrollable and unpredictable. Globalization and digitalization are the phenomena that have upset the city in recent decades and that have contributed most to accelerating the dynamics of change of all the components of which the city system is composed, also giving rise to the phenomena of "gentrification" and "touristification".

2.2 Gentrification

In sociology, the term gentrification indicates the set of urban and socio-cultural changes in an urban area traditionally popular or inhabited by the working class, resulting from the purchase of properties by more rich people [4].

The term gentrification was introduced by the English sociologist Ruth Glass in 1964 to describe the physical and social changes in a London neighborhood following the settlement of a new middle-class social group [5]. Ruth Glass identified gentrification as a complex process involving the physical improvement of housing stock, the change of housing management from rental to ownership, rising prices, and the removal or replacement of the existing working-class population by the middle-classes. These changes do not occur only in the urban suburbs, but above all in historic centers and central districts, in areas with a visible deterioration from a building point of view and with low housing costs. As these areas undergo redevelopment and urban improvement, they tend to bring in new high-income residents and expel old low-income residents,

who can no longer afford to reside there. It is a process of progressive socio-spatial transformation, which can take several years to produce a new image of the place on which
it insists. Furthermore, its effects on the urban fabric and on the resident population can
vary greatly according to the contexts and the type of "gentrifiers" involved (university
students, artists, highly skilled workers, etc.).

Rents and house prices soar, large chain stores and sophisticated restaurants begin
to crowd the area, gradually replacing the popular neighborhood shops. The result is
a generalized increase in the cost of living which makes it very difficult for the old
inhabitants of the neighborhood to continue to reside there.

When we refer to gentrification, we must also consider another fundamental aspect:
that of displacement of the less well-off residents of the neighborhood, usually towards
the suburbs.

A series of effects are therefore created, which can be traced back to the phenomenon
in question, which depend on the characteristics of the new inhabitants, the connota-
tions of the neighborhood and the relationships that are established between these two
elements. Certainly, a common effect of gentrification is the aesthetic and functional
improvement of the area concerned [4]. The neighborhood is redeveloped through the
action of private individuals, through specific public projects or through public-private
partnerships. The fight against degradation, architectural improvement, the orientation
towards greater urban decorum are topics that develop in many political contexts, and
which generate a series of institutional responses.

It is a process that develops on a neighborhood scale and which involves its physical
(through the rehabilitation of the built environment), social (through the replacement of
the population) and economic (following the change in prices in the real estate market)
transformation. Hence the interest in the phenomenon on the part of various scholars,
such as urban planners, sociologists, economists and geographers.

In 1987, Smith defined it as a process of urban transformation that involves changes
in the structural characteristics of buildings, variations in the real estate market and the
replacement of the original residents with new residents belonging to another social class
[6]. With reference to the aesthetic improvement of neighborhoods in order to satisfy
the taste of the new middle-class that settles there, gentrification has also been defined
as "trendification" [7] or "yuppification" [8].

2.3 Touristification

By touristification we mean the phenomenon that is taking hold in many cities of the
world, closely related to gentrification, through which cities, or more specifically the
historic centers of cities, are literally invaded by the tourist flow causing a series of
problems connected to the inability of the neighborhoods themselves to cope with this
situation. It is a process by which a place becomes an object of tourist consumption, thus
bringing about profound changes to the morphology and economy of that place [9].

In the last decades, many cities have opted for growing tourism as a way to cope
with the growing economic decline and to intensify competitiveness in a context of
economic globalization. Growing masses of visitors arrive in the cities, especially in the
high season and, consequently, the negative perception that residents produce towards
tourism is growing. Among the positive effects of this phenomenon there is certainly

the strong contribution to the economy of the cities concerned through the creation of employment in terms of work, in fact, tourism is very often the major or even the only source of local economic development in many cities and is the driving force behind significant urban renewal. But, despite the positive contributions, in recent years the debate has grown regarding the negative consequences of mass tourism in certain places, surrounded by demonstrations of intolerance by the locals towards unbridled tourism.

Many of the criticisms of urban tourism are related to the fact that the concentration of this phenomenon is often enclosed in very small areas of the city, overloading the services present in these areas and creating inconvenience for the population, especially during the high season. During which the infrastructures become saturated, and the traffic becomes congested, causing severe problems for the livability in the areas concerned. In addition, very many visitors also have a significant impact on the environmental sustainability of the place.

From a social point of view, tourism can cause strong economic imbalances between the city center and its hinterland, and this can lead to the initiation of a migratory phenomenon from rural areas and an important loss of the specific traditions of that place.

These imbalances are related to the new forms of dependency between centers and peripheries.

Mass tourism contributes to an increase in the demand for accommodation, which can be addressed both by the presence of large hotel chains and by the conversion of apartments into short-term rental adverts and all of which we know is the cause of gentrification. Tourist interest in city centers and especially in the architectural heritage contained therein is also related to the growing tendency, in a situation of global capitalism, of exploitation of cultures. This "mass cultural consumption" is connected to urban tourism since cities are places where "cultural products" are developed.

Some cities have tried to mitigate the negative effect of "overtourism" through urban planning which, together with a correct management of "intended uses", is the most useful tool for being able in some way to counter the incessant advance of the phenomenon concerned in urban centres.

Most tourists look for accommodation that is not far from the major historical points of interest and this does nothing but favor the accommodation facilities located within the city center to the detriment of those located in the peripheral suburbs.

When urban planning does not take into account this type of analysis and is focused solely and exclusively on short-term profit, rapid changes in the central areas of the city can lead to a degenerative vicious circle and potentially, due to overcrowding, negative change the feelings of the resident population towards tourism.

The dramatic increase in the number of tourist apartments is a particularly controversial topic also due to the problems that can exist between residents and short-term visitors, such as noise, anti-social behaviour, use of common facilities, etc. Studies on this topic show that the major dissatisfactions from the point of view of residents are excessive property prices and rents, shop prices, lack of hygiene, urban decay, lack of human respect, insecurity, noise, without neglecting the loss of the historical identity of the place [9].

2.4 Rent Gap

The concept of rent gap is closely related to that of urban gentrification. In contrast to other hypotheses on this question, which explain the phenomenon in terms of demand and preferences of users who opt to return to the city after a disappointing life in the peri-urban countryside, in 1979 Neil Smith assumes a logic of offer according to which it is the capital invested in the degraded areas that triggers the process on the basis of the growing gap between the current rent, depreciated by the degradation, and the potential rent that could be realized after the intervention [10]. Classical theory, especially the contributions of Ricardo and Von Thunen, has always considered land rent as essentially generated only by the demand for accessibility [11]. Proximity to the urban center therefore, maximizing the "position value" indicated by Marshall [12] and minimizing transport costs [13], would represent a certain advantage capable of guaranteeing the stability or growth of real estate values over time. The classical theory, however, is unable to explain the presence of deteriorated neighborhoods in central areas of the city, nor the fluctuations of rent values in comparative terms between the various parts of the city having the same distance from the centre [14]. In various Italian cities, in central areas, highly degraded neighborhoods are found both from a social and an economic/environmental point of view. Obsolescent buildings welcome increasingly poor and marginalized inhabitants, commercial services close or move; degradation advances in public places and increases the level of crime and vandalism and, as result of all this, real estate values collapse [15–17].

However, it may happen that signs of improvement begin to appear with a gradual positive transformation of both public spaces, which begin to be exploited for innovative activities, and private spaces through increasingly frequent renovations. This turnover begins to attract a younger and more socially inclusive population, able to cope with the price increase in the neighborhood under analysis.

The phenomenon does not manifest itself in flashes and in reference to a single building or block but concerns entire neighborhoods. The whole process appears as the result of the interaction of many individual decisions that influence each other within a given spatial limit. For years, the question has been whether the gentrification process is a demand-driven or a supply-driven process. The debate has always taken one side or the other, with the supporters of the question essentially represented by exponents of sociological studies, such as Ley [18] or Lipton [19], who claim that the cause is the desire to return to live in the city center of the middle class, which moves again from suburban villas to urban centres (demand). The supporters of the offer mechanism, of which Smith is the spokesman [6], state that it is capital which, under certain conditions, can find it convenient to invest in degraded districts of the city and subsequently promote a redevelopment of these areas to favor a turnover population of the highest social class and therefore make a profit on the investments made.

2.5 Home Sharing

The digital economy is closely linked to the diffusion of information and digital technologies. These new technologies are the means by which the so-called digital revolution began, which has radically and rapidly changed not only our daily life, but also some of the founding concepts of cultural tradition.

E-commerce, social networks, crowdfunding and sharing economy are now terms permanently present in our vocabulary, but if they are analyzed ex-ante it is immediate to understand how these have had such a sudden development, adapting perfectly to the socio-economic changes of the third millennium, going to fill the needs of the individual, fitting perfectly with the progressive liberal wave of today, albeit contradicting the anti-capitalist principles of which the latter is characterized.

Home sharing is the short-term practice of renting one's home to tourists and travellers, an economic model spread through various digital platforms that act as intermediaries in the market between private individuals in exchange for an economic consideration paid in the form of a commission. It represents a way for owners to supplement their income and for travelers to save on accommodation (compared to an authorized structure).

However, to better understand the phenomenon and the meaning of home sharing, it is appropriate to deepen the concept of sharing economy. In particular, the sharing economy can be defined as an economic system based on the sharing, free of charge or with fee, of underutilized services or properties directly by private individuals [20].

It is a term applicable to various economic sectors and can be explained in many words: gig economy, on demand services, peer to peer economy, sharing mobility and, obviously, home sharing. It is a concept that has been gaining ground in recent years, declined in various ways and applied to various economic and social sectors. Thus, a series of contiguous, analogous, or parallel definitions have developed, differing from each other only in the type of service or product offered. The sharing economy can be defined as a new economic approach that promotes more conscious forms of consumption based on reuse instead of purchase and access rather than ownership, therefore it indicates an emerging economy based on the sharing of private resources, both material (such as the apartment, car, bike, desk), and intangible (provision of services, jobs, etc.). The form of innovation of these activities lies in the scale on which it operates, which is not limited to a more or less wide geographical context, but extends to cover the entire globe, putting completely strangers who live in distant places that do not know each other, thanks to the development and diffusion of new digital technologies, via computers, smartphones and tablets. This model aims to make itself an alternative to classic consumption by reducing the impact it produces on the environment around us.

The term was originally coined by Felson and Spaeth in a 1978 [21], even if their definition underwent changes as little related, due to the lack of perspective of new technologies, to what is currently provided. The advent of new technologies was the factor that had the most weight in the birth of this new type of economy. The birth of social networks has made it possible to facilitate communication, but also transactions and exchanges, in revolutionary way. These platforms, from places in which to communicate and share one's opinions, have transformed into real commercial places, where users become consumers, but also offerers of goods or services, which can be exchanged at a "click" in simplified and immediate way. Environmental aspects have also contributed to the development of the sharing economy model. Climate change, the unstoppable depletion of resources, the increase in population, highlight the need to set limits on the unbridled consumption of newly manufactured goods or services and therefore to adopt more sustainable behaviours [22–24].

2.6 The AirBnb Phenomenon

Multinational born in San Francisco in 2008, Airbnb is the first digital platform aimed at connecting people looking for a shared accommodation or a room for short periods. In the short-term rental sector, Airbnb is certainly the pioneer and the most successful case. In 2011, Airbnb had already reached 50,000 listings and registered bookings for one million nights, mainly through listings in New York and San Francisco. In 2018, the site boasted nearly 5 million listings worldwide, rising to 6 million in 2019, in nearly 100,000 cities and 191 countries [25].

If San Francisco is the birthplace of Airbnb, New York is its first market. New York was one of the first cities to adopt gentrification as an economic strategy, as a true urban policy, at least starting from 1929, when the approval of the Regional Plan initiated the conversion of the industrial fabric into commercial and residential areas in all areas along the East River, i.e. Manhattan and Brooklyn.

Research by the Boston University Department of Economics has highlighted a causal relationship between the proliferation of Airbnb and house prices: every 12 listings on Airbnb by area corresponds to a loss of houses on the ordinary market of 5.9%, an increase rents by 0.4% and an increase in real estate values by 0.76%. Nationwide, researchers estimated that Airbnb contributed in U.S.A. to a 1% increase in rents and a 2% increase in house prices between 2012 and 2016. A further study based on the same metrics concluded that in New York Airbnb's growth between 2014 and 2017 resulted in an average rent increase of $ 380 per year [26].

According to Wachsmuth and Weisler [27], a house on Airbnb affects the cost of ordinary rent by creating a rent gap, as a tool for increasing real estate income, and then fills it with the increase in values throughout the area. Wachsmuth and Weisler concluded their study, which focused on New York City, by establishing that Airbnb facilitates gentrification and the expulsion of residents through the creation and then "closing" of rent differentials. Furthermore, unlike the traditional rent gap, AirBnB triggers gentrification dynamics even in the absence of an initial disinvestment situation, such as in already gentrified and touristized urban centers. In fact, to increase the real estate income with Airbnb, there is no need for large initial investments, but a change of use of the house and the possible eviction of the previous tenant is enough [25].

Italy is the third market in the world after the USA and France for short-term rentals [28, 29].

The historical connotation and the urban morphology of the cities has led to a greater density of advertisements in the italian historical centres. The scale of the concentration of advertisements in Italian historical centers has no equal in the world. In the urban area of the historic center of Rome, 8% of the apartments are rented on Airbnb. In Florence, 18% of the entire homes in the historic center are on the platform, but it is in Matera that the highest percentage of homes located in the STR is reached, even reaching 25% in the Sassi area. Matera is probably the most fitting example of what is happening to Italian historic centers which are literally emptying themselves of the original inhabitants to make way for the tourist swarm, attracted by the characteristic European capital of culture 2019.

In recent years, the city of Naples has recorded the greatest increase in tourist presences in Italy (91.3%) after Matera. From 2017 to 2019, the listings more than doubled, reaching 7,169 in the latest Inside Airbnb registration, with the greatest concentration in the Montecalvario, San Ferdinando and San Lorenzo districts. Of the 7169 total listings in Naples, 58.9% are entire houses or apartments (4223), 40.4% private rooms (2897) and 0.7% shared rooms (49). Since there are no legislative limits in the municipal regulation, each host can decide to extend the availability of their home up to 365 days a year, so there is 92.2% of homes with high availability (>60 days/year), the 7.1% advertisements with low availability and a territorial average of 259.8 nights a year, i.e. 71.2%. The estimated number of nights per year booked on average per listing is 82, with an estimated occupancy rate of 22.6% and an estimated monthly turnover of 376 euros.

It is important to note that some Airbnb hosts may have more than one listing. A host can list more than one room in several listings, or more than one fully available house or apartment. It is likely that hosts with multiple listings are run as a real business and that the hosts do not live on the property itself, thus violating the terms of short-term rental regulations designed to protect affordability in the residential market. 58.7% of multiple announcements were detected in Naples. The growing success of the platform in the Neapolitan area is evidenced by the tourist boom in the years from 2017 to 2018, with a 46% increase in announcements, for an average length of stay per person of 3.2 nights.

3   Materials and Method

The most relevant areas of the city of Naples, in terms of number of real estate sales offers published, are the Vomero, Chiaia, Arenella, Posillipo, Fuorigrotta, Pendino, San Giuseppe, Bagnoli, and Pianura districts.

By far, the area most present in real estate sales offers is Vomero with over 2,678 total real estate sales offers among rent and sale. In total, as of 2020, there are 31,843 real estate sales offers in the city, of which 22,338 are for sale and 9,505 for rent, with an overall index of 33 sales offers per thousand inhabitants [30].

According to O.M.I. data [31], the price of apartments in the different areas of Naples is between 850 €/m^2 and 5,550 €/m^2 for the sale, and between 2.3 €/m^2 month and 13.4 €/m^2 month for long-term rent. The average price of the apartments for sale (2,800 €/m^2) is approximately 55% higher than the regional average quotation, equal to 1,800 €/m^2 and is also approximately 28% higher than the provincial average quotation (2,150 €/m^2). The asking price for individual apartments in Naples is extremely uneven throughout the city and in 40% of cases it is lower than €1,450/m^2 or higher than €4,000/m^2. As far as a long-term framework is concerned, the O.M.I. from 2006 to 2019 shows a strong decrease in both market values and rental values, for each building typology and for each area analyzed in this work.

All data relating to the Airbnb platform in this work was retrieved from the Inside AirBnb site [28]. The information that can be inferred from this portal is processed by data scraping, an IT technique for extracting data from a website by means of special software programs. With Inside AirBnb you can easily access a series of detailed information such as: exact number of listings present in a city, with the relative typological distributions in percentage and in detail; an estimated average of the annual occupancy of individual advertisements, of the selected neighborhood or of the entire urban context; the average price per night; the employment rate estimated as a percentage; the estimated turnover per month; the annual availability of the posted ads; the percentage and detail of multiple ads. This information is assisted by an interactive map of the area containing each single advert which can be filtered by type, booking frequency, availability, multiple or single adverts and, of course, by neighbourhood.

The information sources used to collect information on the trend of long-term rent values in the Naples area are instead constituted by the Observatory of the Real Estate Market of the Revenue Agency (public law body controlled by the Italian Ministry of Finance), as well as by one of the main digital real estate portals on the national internet (www.immobiliare.it) [30, 31].

In our case, 54 rental announcements of residential properties located in Naples in the areas of San Ferdinando, Montecalvario and Chiaia were taken into consideration. Each advertisement contains: indication of the neighbourhood, exact address, monthly rental price, surface area in sqm, floor level, number of rooms, presence of lift, latitude and longitude.

It should be emphasized that the study carried out here refers, as far as AirBnb announcements are concerned, only to the data of entire homes, recovered as we know from the Inside AirBnb site, ignoring the rooms in apartments and clearly the shared rooms.

The intention is to highlight the differences between STR and LTR in terms of yield, and what influence the former have on the latter on the selected districts of the municipality of Naples.

Only announcements of entire apartments with an annual availability of no less than 300 days have been considered.

The occupancy rate used is the average recorded for each neighbourhood.

Therefore, by multiplying the occupancy rate with the number of days in which an ad is available, we obtain the estimate of the days in which the apartment is actually booked. By multiplying the latter with the price per night we obtain the annual gross income, which divided by 12, gives us the monthly gross income per advertisement (estimated). On this basis, for the most important listings, an estimate of what the gross revenue can be for each listing is obtained.

The relationship between geographical location and rental values of the STRs and LTRs are analyzed using a semi-parametric approach, based on a geo-additive model. These models consist of the sum of a semiparametric component in the form of an additive model, which serves to express the non-linear link between the response and the explanatory variables, and a linear mixed-effects model, with which the spatial correlation of the observed values [32, 33].

If s_i e y_i ($i = 1, ..., n$) are, respectively, the observed values of an antecedent variable and of the response variable corresponding to the spatial location x_i, ($x \in \Re^2$), a geo-additive model can be defined through the following general formulation:

$$y_i = \beta_0 + f(S_i) + \beta_1^T x_i + S(x_i) + \varepsilon_i \qquad (1)$$

where $f(.)$ is a smooth function, $S(x)$ is a stationary Gaussian stochastic process of the second order with zero expected value and constant variance equal to σ_x^2. In relation (1) the additive component, the mixed effects one and the erratic one ε, are mutually independent.

In order to obtain a version of (1) that can be estimated using the procedures related to mixed effects models implemented in standard statistical software, a low rank version of both the additive and mixed effects components has been considered.

For the first component a penalized spline function of the form was used:

$$f(s_i) = \beta_s s_i + \sum uk(s_i - k_k)+ \qquad (2)$$

Considering the coefficients u_k of the nodes κ_k as random effects.

The fundamental advantage of this formulation consists in the possibility of obtaining the estimates of the model parameters through R.E.M.L., using the spm function of the *SemiPar* library of *R* software [34]. Furthermore, the low rank representation means that the number of basis functions used does not increase with the sample size.

The amount of smoothing of the model with reference to the additive and spatially correlated components is quantified on the basis of the ratios $\sigma^2_\varepsilon / \sigma^2_s$, e $\sigma^2_\varepsilon / \sigma^2_x$, computable using REML estimated variances.

These smoothing parameters are involved in the determination of freedom degrees for non-linear component and make possible to control the trade-off between the adaptation of the model to the observed values (values close to zero of the smoothing parameters) and its smoothness (high values of the aforementioned parameters) [32, 33].

4 Results and Discussions

This section presents the results of the model previously described in relation to the data sample collected for traditional LTR and that for STR.

The sample relating to the LTR it is made up of 54 residential units located in Naples in the areas of Montecalvario, San Ferdinando and Chiaia. The variables taken into consideration for this sample are floor level (*lev*), presence of lift (*lift*), geographical coordinates (longitude and latitude, or *Xcoord* and *Ycoord*).

The reference function for this sample, about the unitary sale price for LTR, is the following:

$$Uprice_{LTR} = lev + lift + f(Xcoord, Ycoord)$$

For STR the main variables available are the geographic coordinates only (*Xcoord* and *Ycoord*), considering a number of real estate rental offers equal to 219:

$$Uprice_{STR} = f(Xcoord, Ycoord)$$

Subsequently, from the availability of rooms number for each real estate sale offer, the indicative sqm of each unit was obtained considering the following indications: up to 35 sqm no rooms, 35–50 sqm equal to 1 room, 50–65 sqm equal to 2 rooms, 65–80 sqm equal to 3 rooms, 80–95 sqm equal to 4 rooms, 95–120 sqm equal to 5 rooms, over 120 sqm equal to 5 rooms.

Furthermore, from the price per night of the apartment, the annual availability of the announcement on the Airbnb portal and the average occupancy rate of the reference neighborhood, the estimated annual turnover was obtained which, divided by 12, returned the estimated monthly turnover.

The graphical results of models are presented in Figs. 1 and 2, while the distribution of LTR and STR data in the districts considered is shown in Fig. 3.

The effect estimates in the nonlinear model were significant, as shown by the values of the degrees of freedom and the smoothing parameters. The values of the predictions obtained are consistent with the observed data, furthermore the analysis of the residuals did not show any anomaly in its structure.

In the area examined, the spatial distribution of unitary property rents clearly shows how the geographic component affects the rents of the sampled properties. The main result of the interpolation, for each of the two cases, is a thematic map which depicts the unitary values of the real estate rents in the considered urban context, in which the blue and red colors represent the unitary rents respectively, the lowest and the highest.

Basically, the values resulting from the analysis of LTR collected coincide with the data of the O.M.I. Observatory relating to the areas analyzed (Montecalvario, Chiaia, San Ferdinando).

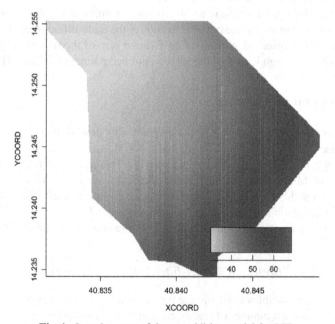

Fig. 1. Isovalue map of the geoadditive model for LTR

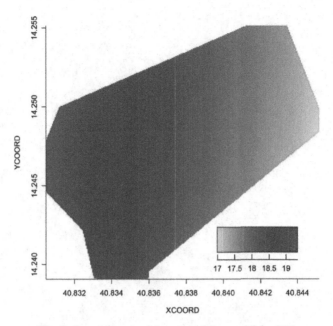

Fig. 2. Isovalue map of the geoadditive model for STR

In the Naples area, with the same qualitative characteristics and accessibility, the income that can be drawn from short-term leased real estate units is approximately double that of traditional leases. The range of price variation for STR varies from 30 €/sqm to 70 €/sqm, while for traditional LTR the variation is contained in a range that goes from 17 €/sqm to 20 €/sqm.

The geoadditive analysis shows that, as regards the STR (Fig. 2), the highest values are concentrated on the coastal strip, i.e. in reference to those solutions that have characteristics of proximity to the sea, panoramic or semi-panoramic. The lowest values are found in the vicinity of the Quartieri Spagnoli, where multiple rental solutions adapted to the classic Neapolitan "bassi" (cellars) have been identified, traditional social housing located on the ground floor or in the basement. The practice of renting these basses is connected to the desire to attract tourists in a typically Neapolitan traditional context, but also to the need to make the most of otherwise unused or underestimated living spaces for the purpose of a long-term lease and maximize their income. This practice is conceptually similar to that adopted in the historic center of Matera, with the short-term rental of houses in the "sassi".

As regards the analysis of the geoadditive model referring to traditional or LTR locations (Fig. 1), the highest values are recorded for the area that goes from via Toledo towards Mergellina, while they decrease in the direction of Corso Umberto I.

The values agree for the area of via Partenope and via Caracciolo, where in both cases they are very high. Based on these considerations, we can state that, for the same type of property, the dynamics between STR and LTR are completely different from each other, both in terms of profitability and in terms of space.

Fig. 3. Data distribution for LTR (blue dots) and STR (orange dots)

The results obtained are valid for the territory of Naples, a city that structurally has a relatively limited historic center in terms of space and an urban distribution with multiple outlets to the sea, which are probably not found in other provincial capitals [35–39].

5 Conclusions

The fact that the short-term rent sector in Italy is not definitively regulated makes this practice in some cases convenient for property owners from an income point of view, but also less binding in contractual terms.

Nowadays, renting your property on a long-term basis to a private individual can in practice lead to a series of problems relating to the management area and the constraints that follow from signing the contract, as well as being in most cases less profitable than a short-term rental. It must be emphasized that the management of a fully operational STR requires a considerable amount of time, necessary to carry out all those activities aimed at welcoming tourists, a fundamental qualitative characteristic for a successful accommodation business. And precisely for this reason, many hosts entrust the management of their property to third parties, generally agencies aimed at this purpose, placing themselves in competition with the authorized accommodation businesses and in some cases contributing to increasing the phenomenon of tax evasion.

Finally, we do not want to overlook the issue relating to the phenomenon of gentrification in historic centres. Unlike some districts of Rome, Venice, Florence and Matera, in

Naples this phenomenon does not seem to have affected the housing dynamics of the historic centers yet, influencing real estate values and distancing the traditional inhabitants from their place of birth.

References

1. Scheler, M.: On the Eternal iIn Man, 1st edn. Routledge, London (2009)
2. Del Giudice, V., De Paola, P., Del Giudice, F.P.: COVID-19 infects real estate markets: short and mid-run effects on housing prices in Campania region (Italy). Soc. Sci. **9**, 114 (2020). https://doi.org/10.3390/socsci9070114
3. Saaty, T.L., De Paola, P.: Rethinking design and urban planning for the cities of the future. Buildings **7**, 76 (2017). https://doi.org/10.3390/buildings7030076
4. Forte, F., De Paola, P.: How can street art have economic value? Sustainability **11**, 580 (2019). https://doi.org/10.3390/su11030580
5. Glass, R.: London: Aspects of Change. MacGibbon & Kee edn., London (1964)
6. Smith, N.: Gentrification and the Rent Gap. Annals of the Association of American Geographers, pp. 462–465. Taylor & Francis, Ltd. (1987)
7. Smith, N. Gentrification and Uneven Development. Economic Geography, vol. 58, no. 2, pp. 139–155. Taylor & Francis, Ltd. (1982)
8. Van Criekingen, M., Decroly, J.M.: Revisiting the diversity of gentrification: neighbourhood renewal processes in Brussels and Montreal. Urban Stud. **40**(12), 2451–2468 (2003). https://doi.org/10.1080/0042098032000136156
9. Barrera-Fernandez, D., Garcia-Bujalance, S.: Touristification in historic cities: reflections on Malaga. Revista de Turismo Contemporâneo **7**(1), 93–115 (2019). https://doi.org/10.21680/2357-8211.2019v7n1ID16169
10. Smith, N.: Toward a theory of gentrification a back to the city movement by capital, not people. J. Am. Plann. Assoc. **45**(4), 538–548 (1979). https://doi.org/10.1080/01944367908977002
11. Kellerman, A.; Jones, D.W.: Does Von Thunen Meet Ricardo? Annals of the Association of American Geographers, vol. 69, no. 4, pp. 639–642. Taylor & Francis, Ltd. (1979)
12. Marshall, A.: Principles of Economics, 9th variorum edition, vol. 1. Macmillan, London (1961)
13. Alonso, W.: Location and Land Use: Toward a General Theory of Land Rent. Harward University Press, Cambridge (1964). https://doi.org/10.4159/harvard.9780674730854
14. Hoyt, H.: One Hundred Years of Land Values in Chicago. University of Chicago Press, Chicago (1933)
15. Del Giudice, V.; De Paola, P.; Morano, P.; Tajani, F.; Del Giudice, F.P.; Anelli, D.: Depreciation of residential buildings and maintenance strategies in urban multicultural contexts. In: Napoli, G., Mondini, G., Oppio, A., Rosato, P., Barbaro, S. (eds.) Values, Cities and Migrations. Green Energy and Technology, pp. 217–232. Springer, Cham (2023). https://doi.org/10.1007/978-3-031-16926-7_16
16. Manganelli, B., Tataranna, S., De Paola, P.: A comparison of short-term and long-term rental market in an Italian city. In: Gervasi, O., et al. (eds.) ICCSA 2020. LNCS, vol. 12251, pp. 884–898. Springer, Cham (2020). https://doi.org/10.1007/978-3-030-58808-3_63
17. Morano, P., Tajani, F., del Giudice, V., De Paola, P., Anelli, D.: Urban transformation interventions: a decision support model for a fair rent gap recapture. In: Gervasi, O., et al. (eds.) ICCSA 2021. LNCS, vol. 12954, pp. 253–264. Springer, Cham (2021). https://doi.org/10.1007/978-3-030-86979-3_19

18. Ley, D.: Alternative explanations for inner-city gentrification: a Canadian assessment. Ann. Assoc. Am. Geogr. **16**, 521–535 (1986)
19. Lipton, S.: Evidence of central revival. J. Am. Inst. Plann. **43**, 136–147 (1977)
20. Sundararajan, A.: The Sharing Economy: The End of Employment and the Rise of Crowd-Based Capitalism. MIT Press, Cambridge (2016)
21. Felson, M., Spaeth, J.L.: Community structure and collaborative consumption: a routine activity approach. Am. Behav. Sci. **21**, 23 (1978). https://doi.org/10.1177/000276427802 100411
22. Massimo, D.E., De Paola, P., Musolino, M., Malerba, A., Del Giudice, F.P.: Green and gold buildings? detecting real estate market premium for green buildings through evolutionary polynomial regression. Buildings **12**, 621 (2022). https://doi.org/10.3390/buildings12050621
23. Massimo, D.E., Del Giudice, V., Malerba, A., Bernardo, C., Musolino, M., De Paola, P.: Valuation of ecological retrofitting technology in existing buildings: a real-world case study. Sustainability **13**, 7001 (2021)
24. Forte, F., Antoniucci, V., De Paola, P.: Immigration and the housing market: the case of castel Volturno, in Campania Region, Italy. Sustainability **10**, 343 (2018). https://doi.org/10.3390/su10020343
25. Gainsforth, S.: Airbnb città merce. Storie di resistenza alla gentrificazione digitale, Deriveapprodi edn., Rome, Italy (2019)
26. Benner, K.: Airbnb Proposes Crackdown on New York City Hosts. New York Times, pp. B2, 28 October 2016
27. Wachsmuth, D., Weisler, A.: Airbnb and the rent gap: Gentrification through the sharing economy. Environ. Plan. A: Econ. Space **50**(6), 1147–1170 (2018). https://doi.org/10.1177/0308518X18778038
28. Inside AirBnb. http://www.insideairbnb.com. Accessed 21 Nov 2021
29. AirBnb. http://www.airbnb.it. Accessed 01 Dec 2022
30. Immobiliare. http://www.immobiliare.it. Accessed 01 Dec 2022
31. Revenue Agency of the Italian Government - Observatory of Real Estate Markek. https://www.agenziaentrate.gov.it. Accessed 01 Dec 2022
32. De Paola, P., Del Giudice, V., Massimo, D.E., Forte, F., Musolino, M., Malerba, A.: Isovalore maps for the spatial analysis of real estate market: a case study for a central urban area of Reggio Calabria, Italy. In: Calabrò, F., Della Spina, L., Bevilacqua, C. (eds.) ISHT 2018. SIST, vol. 100, pp. 402–410. Springer, Cham (2019). https://doi.org/10.1007/978-3-319-92099-3_46
33. De Paola, P., Del Giudice, V., Massimo, D.E., Del Giudice, F.P., Musolino, M., Malerba, A.: Green building market premium: detection through spatial analysis of real estate values. a case study. In: Bevilacqua, C., Calabrò, F., Della Spina, L. (eds.) NMP 2020. SIST, vol. 178, pp. 1413–1422. Springer, Cham (2021). https://doi.org/10.1007/978-3-030-48279-4_132
34. R software. https://www.r-project.org. Accessed 01 Dec 2022
35. Del Giudice, V., De Paola, P., Bevilacqua, P., Pino, A., Del Giudice, F.P.: Abandoned industrial areas with critical environmental pollution: evaluation model and stigma effect. Sustainability **12**, 5267 (2020). https://doi.org/10.3390/su12135267
36. Del Giudice, V., De Paola, P., Forte, F.: The appraisal of office towers in bilateral monopoly's market: evidence from application of newton's physical laws to the directional centre of Naples. Int. J. Appl. Eng. Res. **11**, 9455–9459 (2016)
37. Acampa, G., Forte, F., De Paola, P.: B.I.M. Models and evaluations. In: Mondini, G., Oppio, A., Stanghellini, S., Bottero, M., Abastante, F. (eds.) Values and Functions for Future Cities. GET, pp. 351–363. Springer, Cham (2020). https://doi.org/10.1007/978-3-030-23786-8_20

38. Del Giudice, V., De Paola, P.: Undivided real estate shares: appraisal and interactions with capital markets. Appl. Mech. Mater. **584–586**, 2522–2527 (2014). https://doi.org/10.4028/www.scientific.net/AMM.584-586.2522
39. Morano, P., Tajani, F., Anelli, D.: Urban planning variants: A model for the division of the activated "plusvalue" between public and private subjects. Valori e Valutazioni (28) (2021)

Endogenous vs. Exogenous Leadership in Teamwork: An Socio-Economic Experimental Study

Carlos Eduardo Jijena Michel[1] (iD), Natalie Olmos Paredes[1] (iD), Marcelo León[2(✉)] (iD),
Paulina Tapia[3] (iD), and Fernando Calle[4] (iD)

[1] Universidad Privada Boliviana, La Paz, Bolivia
[2] Universidad ECOTEC, Samborondón, Ecuador
marceloleon11@hotmail.com
[3] Universidad de Otavalo, Otavalo, Ecuador
[4] Universidad Católica de Santiago de Guayaquil, Guayaquil, Ecuador

Abstract. This paper presents the results of laboratory experiments designed to study the effectiveness of leadership as a way to improve efficiency in team production. In a three-player minimum effort game framework, the research compares either endogenous or exogenous leadership (in the former, the leader is chosen in an auction, and in the latter, the leader is randomly selected) with a control treatment where no leadership is considered. Although contributions do not seem to be significantly different between both leadership treatments, the effort levels found are in fact higher with exogenous (random) leadership than in the control treatment. Conversely, this effect is not found with endogenous (intentional) leadership.

Keywords: Leadership · Productive resources · Teamwork · Organizational designs · Control treatment

1 Introduction

When firms or organizations are stuck in a performance trap or free riding, the need for coordination is strongly required (Brandts, Cooper, Fatas, & Qi, 2015). Such mechanisms have been widely studied by game and behavioral theorists from several perspectives (C. Camerer, 2003). In team production, Holmstrom (1982) concludes that optimal outcomes cannot be achieved due to moral hazard problems under the following assumptions: (1) there exists a 'team' production technology; (2) productive resources belong to different owners; and (3) the value of the resource devoted by a member to the team is unobservable. In this framework, "there is no function of output distribution, differentiable, that induces individuals to achieve efficient team balance" (Holmstrom, 1982). Consequently, team members are not willing to supply the efficient level of their resources because the outcome of the team is shared among members, but the cost of the input is individually borne.

O. Gervasi et al. (Eds.): ICCSA 2023 Workshops, LNCS 14109, pp. 444–460, 2023.
https://doi.org/10.1007/978-3-031-37120-2_29

At that point, organizational designs based on alternative conditions had been proposed as ways to improve team efficiency. For example, when the team is organized as a 'classical capitalistic firm' collective production activity can reach higher efficient levels (Alchian & Demsetz, 1972). From this view, efficiency can be restored under several assumptions: 1) the existence of a 'monitor', who has the right to agree with the members of the former team on their respective contributions as well as on their earnings; 2) this 'monitor' holds the residual claim as an incentive to guarantee the optimal design of the contracts with the owners of the inputs. Different solutions have been proposed to the inefficiency problem in teams through the implementation of optimal incentive systems (Holmstrom, 1982), contracts (Milgrom & Roberts, 1987), and leadership (Hermalin, 1998).

Leadership is a prominent alternative for solving coordination problems (Arce M, 2001; R. Cooper et al., 1994; Foss, 2001). Nevertheless, previous studies in leadership focused on corporate culture (Kreps, 1990) and the role of environmental contingencies in leadership styles (Rotemberg & Saloner, 1993), among others.

2 Antecedents

Previous studies reveal the relevant role of leadership in team performance (Bass & Stogdill, 1990). Effective leaders are characterized by their ability to coordinate the actions of team members through the successful communication of common goals (Bolton, Brunnermeier, & Veldkamp, 2010). Effective leadership processes represent one of the most critical factors in the success of organizational teams (Zaccaro, Rittman, & Marks, 2001). These findings encourage us to look into organizational designs based on leadership viewed as a potential solution to the inefficiency of teams that relies more on the leader's 'informal authority' (Aghion & Tirole, 1997; Gerth & Mills, 1946) than on hierarchical structures that could lead team members to substitute their criterion of individual utility for collective utility.

Leadership and teamwork are strongly related. On the one hand, leadership is about selecting a goal and making others follow this goal (Gardner, 1993), and its effectiveness depends heavily upon how much "*a leader convinces followers that she is not misleading them*" (Kotter, 1996). On the other hand, teamwork is positively related to performance and particularly to productivity (Delarue, Van Hootegem, Procter, & Burridge, 2008). The leader may also be viewed as a "coach" in teamwork (Rosner, 2001).

Experimental methodology has contributed to testing a wide variety of theories on economic behavioral issues, like the analysis of individual decisions (Von Neumann & Morgenstern, 1944), prospective theory (Kahneman & Tversky, 1979), theory of the generalized expected utility (Ormiston & Quiggin, 1993), among others. However, as its known, the effect of elected leadership on teamwork and its effects regarding coordination issues have been ignored in experimental studies.

This paper fills this gap by suggesting an experimental design based on the so-called Minimum Effort Coordination Game (MECG) agent's utility functions. Next, its defined the model proposed to test the differential effects of random versus intentional leadership on team production.

3 Theoretical Results

This section reviews the model of team production and its theoretical predictions, according to Holmstrom's definition of team production. The theory is summarized by the following assumptions: (1) The feasible production set is represented by a production function, $y = F(\vec{a})$, where y is the output value and $\vec{a} = (a_1, a_2, .., a_N)$ the vector comprising each member's contribution; (2) Production function $F(\cdot)$ holds the property of 'team technology', which implies that individuals, given the same level of input, can obtain a higher level of output if they participate in the team than if they do not; (3) each member owns one and only one input and hence, a_i is the contribution of member i; (4) each member bears the cost to allocate his resource to the productive activity of the team, $V_i (ai)$, where $Vi (\cdot)$ is an increasing and convex function in ai for all i. Therefore, the net profit or surplus of the team will be given by $U(\vec{a}) = F(\vec{a})-$; (5) the utility function of the member i of the team is $U_i = S_i(y) - V_i(a_i)$ for $i = 1, 2, ..., N$, where $S_i(\cdot)$ is a rule on the output distribution or, in other terms, the compensation function that depends exclusively upon the output of the team (y); (6) any member can obtain a utility of zero if she leaves (or she does not join) the team.

Given the above assumptions, efficient and Nash-equilibrium solutions are described as follows.

3.1 Efficient Solution and Nash Equilibrium with no Leadership in the Team

Pareto-efficient solution to the team problem is given by:

$$\max_{a_i} \sum_{i=1}^{N} U_i = y - \sum_{i=1}^{N} V_i(a_i) \tag{1}$$

such that: $U_i = S_i(y) - V_i(a_i) \geq 0, \quad for\ i = 1, 2, \ldots, N$

$$y = F(a_1, a_2, .., a_N)$$

$$a_i \geq 0, \ for\ i = 1, 2, \ldots, N.$$

The first order conditions (FOC) of the above problem are:

$$\frac{\partial F}{\partial a_i} - \frac{dV_i}{da_i} = 0 \ for\ i = 1, 2, \ldots, N. \tag{2}$$

Thus, the efficient solution to the team problem is achieved when the marginal revenue of each productive resource equals its marginal cost.

However, the maximizing problem of an individual member is quite different from the above since each (selfish) individual would seek to maximize her own utility, given the contributions of the other team members, i.e.:

$$\max_{a_i} U_i = S_i(y) - V_i(a_i)$$

s.t.: $U_i = S_i(y) - V_i(a_i) \geq 0, \ for\ i = 1, 2, \ldots, N$

$$\sum_{i=1}^{N} S_i(y) \leq y$$

$$y = F(a_1, a_2, .., a_N)$$

$$a_i \geq 0, \;\; for \; i = 1, 2, \ldots, N.$$

The FOC to the above problem are:

$$\frac{dS_i}{dy} \frac{\partial F}{\partial a_i} - \frac{\partial V_i}{\partial a_i} = 0 \; for \; i = 1, 2, \ldots, N. \tag{3}$$

The inefficiency of the above Nash equilibrium becomes clear as the term $\frac{dS_i}{dy}$ is always positive but lower than one.

3.2 Nash Equilibrium with Leadership in the Team

Let us assume now that team members take into account the information delivered by the member i of the team, will be called 'the leader'. The leader decides her own contribution in order to maximize her utility. She also knows that her decision will determine the contributions of the remaining members, or 'followers' which are determined by a $N - 1$ vector of 'reaction functions' that characterizes the contribution of member j ('follower') as a deterministic response to the leader's choice, namely, $a_j = \phi_{ij}(a_i)$. Other assumptions of the model remain unchanged. Then, the variation in subject j ('follower') contribution due to changes in the contribution of subject i (the leader) contributions is:

$$\frac{da_j}{da_i} = \frac{d\Phi_j}{da_i} \; for \; j = 1, 2, \ldots, i-1, i+1, \ldots, N \tag{4}$$

where $da_j/da_i \neq 0$.

Hence, the production function can be expressed as:

$$y = F(\phi_1(a_i), \phi_2(a_i), \ldots, \phi_{i-1}(a_i), a_i, \phi_{i+1}(a_i), \ldots, \phi_N(a_i)) \tag{5}$$

Notice that the only team member who faces a problem of choice is the leader, since followers' choices depend deterministically upon the leader's decision.

The problem faced by leader is:

$$\max_{a_i} U_i = S_i(y) - V_i(a_i)$$

s.t.: $U_i = S_i(y) - V_i(a_i) \geq 0$

$$\sum_{j=1}^{N} S_j(y) \leq y$$

$$S_j(y) - V_j(a_j) \geq 0$$

$$y = F(\phi_1(a_i), \phi_2(a_i), \ldots, \phi_{i-1}(a_i), \phi_{i+1}(a_i), \ldots, \phi_N(a_i))$$

$$a_j \geq 0 \; for \; j = 1, 2, \ldots, N$$

The first-order condition for the above problem is:

$$\frac{dS_i}{dy}\left[\frac{\partial F}{\partial a_i} + \sum_{j=1, j\neq i}^{N} \frac{\partial F}{\partial a_j}\frac{d\phi_j}{da_i}\right] = \frac{\partial V_i}{\partial a_i} \tag{6}$$

This solution to the team problem with leadership will be efficient if the following conditions hold:

$$\frac{\partial F}{\partial a_i} = \frac{dV_i}{da_i} = \frac{\sum_{j=1, j\neq i}^{N}\frac{dV_i}{da_j}\frac{d\phi_j}{da_i}}{1 - \left(dS_i/dy\right)} = \frac{\sum_{j=1, j\neq i}^{N}\frac{dV_i}{da_j}\frac{d\phi_j}{da_i}}{\sum_{j=1, j\neq i}^{N}\frac{dS_j}{dy}} \tag{7}$$

Therefore, the optimality of the solution of the leader choice will depend upon the ratio defined as the sum of the marginal costs (dV_i/dy) multiplied by the derivatives of the reaction functions $(d\phi_{ij}/da_i)$ divided by the sum of the derivatives of the compensation functions of (dS_j/dy) of the followers. Condition 7 is trivially met under the following assumptions: (1) reaction functions are defined so that each follower equals the leader's contribution, i.e. $a_i = a_j$ for $j = 1,2,...,N$; (2) the output share is egalitarian, i.e. $S_i = S_j = 1/N$; and (3) marginal costs are also equal between team members, namely, $dV_i/dy = dV_j/dy$ for $i,j = 1,2,...,N$. These outcomes of the theoretical model are the basis for designing the experiments described further.

4 Experimental Design

4.1 Minimum Effort Game

The MECG has been useful to examine groups' ability to coordinate (Myung, 2009) in many economic (Bryant, 1983) and management (Fatas et al., 2006) phenomena. Previous studies on the MECG have focused on different issues such as communication and signals within the group (R. Cooper et al., 1992); entry fees to join the group (Cachon & Camerer, 1996); multiple groups competing with each other (Myung, 2009); group size (R. W. Cooper et al., 1990; Knez & Camerer, 1994; Van Huyck et al., 1990; R. A. Weber, 2006), sequential instead of simultaneous decisions (C. F. Camerer et al., 2004), or pre-game communication (R. Cooper et al., 1992; Riechmann & Weimann, 2008).

The paper proposes a MECG framework to investigate the effect of endogenous/exogenous leadership on team members' behavior. Real problems in companies and industries have been associated with coordination (Fatas et al., 2006). Moreover, there are previous studies in team production with strong complementarities that apply the MECG (Van Huyck et al., 1990). This research proposes teams of three members who privately exert an effort level or contribution. In the first treatment (control), the game is simultaneous, and the second and third treatments (with leadership effect) involve two consecutive decisions: first, the leader chooses its contribution to the team and sends a 'suggestion' on the contribution that each follower should make. The leader's contribution is private information; thus, followers are unaware of the leader's choice, and they simultaneously decide their contribution after receiving the leader's suggestion. Contributions are defined as any natural number between zero and fifty (namely, $C_i \in (0, 50)$, $i \in \{1, 2, 3\}$) that team members wish to devote to the collective task. The output of this task is represented by a Leontief production technology, considering that the inputs are pure complements. Hence, the output is determined by the minimum contribution of the three participants, and any deviation from such a minimum is a loss.

The experiment adopts a 'within' treatment approach, as the same subjects and teams performed the same two consecutive treatments. The payoff function (π_{it}) is the same for three treatments and is computed as the double of the minimum contribution (C_{1t}, C_{2t}, C_{3t}) minus the contribution of subject i in period t (C_{it}).

$$\pi_{it} = 2min\{C_{1t}, C_{2t}, C_{3t}\} - C_{1t} \tag{8}$$

Given that, for the "control treatment", the game is played simultaneously, the dilemma of player i is to predict and choose the minimum effort of the team, taking into account that any positive deviation from this value implies a net utility loss.

For the endogenous and exogenous treatments, the game is sequential; the leader contributes first, and then her two followers simultaneously decide their contribution. Followers made their choice after receiving the leader's suggestion but with no information on the effectiveness of the leader. In this case, leaders are expected to convince followers that only the maximum contribution is optimal. Nevertheless, any situation in which $C_1 = C_2 = C_3$ is a Nash equilibrium in pure strategies for both treatments. Given that C_1 is an integer bounded at 50 as a maximum, it becomes clear that $C_1 = C_2 = C_3 = 50$ is the unique efficient (Pareto-optimal) equilibrium. The key difference between treatments is rooted in the kind of leadership and whether the game is simultaneous or sequential. The rationale of the sequential game with leadership implies that the leader will use her suggestions to the followers to achieve coordination at a more efficient equilibrium. Since communication between the leader and the followers is feasible, the suggestion made by the leader can be an effective way to improve coordination and, thus, efficiency (Brandts & Cooper, 2007; Sahin, Eckel, & Komai, 2015; R. Weber, Camerer, Rottenstreich, & Knez, 2001). If followers trust the leader, they should infer that the (unknown) contribution of the leader equals her suggested contribution. The theoretical predictions of the model in Sect. 3 and the above arguments lead us to formulate the following proposition:

P1: Leadership induces more efficient contributions/outcomes in teamwork.

Conversely, if followers do not trust their leader, they can adopt two behaviors: (a) choosing their contributions as if there were no leader, i.e. their choices will be solely based on the experience from previous decisions; or (b) selecting a lower contribution than that suggested by the leader on the belief that the leader is trying to deceive them. Both behaviors of followers would lead to rejecting P1, but they differ in terms of efficiency levels. When followers behave as if the leader is 'useless' (case a), the efficiency of the outcome will be similar to the treatment with no leadership, but if the followers believe that their leader is a 'deceiver' (case b), efficiency can be even lower than teams with no leadership.

There are also differences between teams depending on the selection process of the leader. A team member should bid higher than their mates when she is more confident in her ability to achieve better coordination of the team and, thus, maximize her profits by leading followers to contribute the maximum. Moreover, the leader, as the auction winner, must incur an upfront cost, an investment only recoverable if the team's output is high. These arguments support the following proposition:

P2: Endogenous leadership implies more efficient equilibria than exogenous leadership.

4.2 Procedures

The experiment was programmed in the Z-tree toolbox (Fischbacher, 2007) and conducted in the computer room of the Faculty of Economics and Management at the University of Salamanca. At the beginning of every session of the experiment, three-player teams were randomly chosen. These teams remained unaltered during the experiment, and their members were also kept anonymous during and after the experiment. The experiment consisted of three treatments: the "control treatment" (Control) that was performed considering that there was no leader, and thus, the decisions of the three subjects were simultaneous; the "exogenous leadership" treatment, in which the leader is selected randomly; and the "endogenous leadership" treatment, in which subjects had an initial endowment of $1000 to bid in an auction for the position of the leader. Thus, the member with the highest bid on every team was selected as the leader. In both exogenous and endogenous treatments, once the leader had been chosen, she or he remained unchanged during all the treatment decisions. There were programmed five sessions (groups), where only two of the three treatments were applied in every session. Thus, it is considered a 'within group' approach. The treatment order changed in the different sessions to control for possible 'order effects'.

Experimental subjects consisted of 138 students enrolled in two undergraduate programs of the aforementioned University ('Economics' and 'Business Administration'). Subjects were considered unexperienced as they had never participated in a similar activity before, and they were incentivized according to their performance during the experiment and in terms of their payoffs.

All sessions were organized according to the availability of the schedules of the participants and limited to a maximum of 33 participants per group. Information exchange between team members was not allowed during the treatment without a leader. In both treatments with leadership, the leader must send a suggested contribution for the next decision in every round to the remaining members of the team. The message was '*I suggest you to make a contribution of x in your next decision*', where x was an integer between 0 and 50. Once all subjects made their decisions, they were privately informed of their own payoffs, but not about the payoffs or decisions of their partners, although from the payoff function (Eq. 8), they might infer some kind of information related to them (i.e., the minimum contribution).

4.3 Hypotheses

The MECG has multiple and symmetrical Nash-equilibria: any profile with identical contributions from members within a team. Nevertheless, there exists a unique Pareto-optimal equilibrium that corresponds to the maximum contribution for any teammate

($C_1=C_2=C_3=50$). Unlike this theoretical prediction, previous experimental studies have found that subjects might converge to the low-effort equilibrium (Devetag & Ortmann, 2007).

Consistent with our proposition P1, leadership (either endogenous or exogenous) can be a solution to overcome such inefficiency in teamwork. This proposition is also supported by studies that find that the presence of a leader in a team improves the overall outcome (Van der Heijden & Moxnes, 2003). Leaders influence and motivate teams; they do not coerce, as they achieve results by developing a shared vision and communicating it to the team (Sohmen, 2013). However, early findings show that behavior can differ depending on whether a role is earned or randomly assigned (Hoffman, McCabe, Shachat, & Smith, 1994; Hoffman & Spitzer, 1985). Randomly selected leaders failed in their aim to improve coordination in teams (R. Weber et al., 2001), mainly when team members felt the leader's suggestion as an upper bound on their own decisions (Levy, Padgitt, Peart, Houser, & Xiao, 2011).

It is well known, that there is no evidence about the role that the selection procedure of the leader plays in the outcome of the team. The proposal is justified as an attempt to approximate the process of leader selection without compromising the anonymity of the team members. The logic of the 'leader by auction' is applicable to democratically elected leaders since they should incur upfront commitments and/or costs to earn this position. In this framework, teams with an elected leader tend to coordinate at higher effort levels (Reuben & Timko, 2017), since the elected leader has more influence or legitimacy over followers because of the way in which the leader is selected (Brandts et al. 2015). Also, effective team performance derives from characteristics like the need to integrate individual actions, perform in complex and dynamic environments, and finally, the need for team leadership (Zaccaro et al., 2001).

Therefore, the main hypothesis of this work, which conjectures that leadership increases cooperation in teamwork, can be subdivided in two, depending on the type of leadership:

H1: *Members of teams with exogenous (H1a) or endogenous (H1b) leadership contribute more that members of teams without a leader.*

5   Results and Discussion

The results are described in terms of three comparisons. The first compares both endogenous and exogenous leadership against the control treatment, and the second studies team performance based on exogenous versus endogenous leadership. In both cases, the main descriptive statistics analyze the effort levels of the different groups and the treatments. Then, the hypotheses H1 and H2 were tested with non-parametric statistics (Wilcoxon test). In the third section, the panel presents data models to analyze the dynamics of the contributions and test the three main hypotheses of our research using a parametric approach.

5.1 Leadership Treatments Versus Control Treatment

5.1.1 Control Treatment Versus Exogenous Treatment

In the first stage, groups 1 and 2 are compared. These groups correspond to control and exogenous treatment, albeit in a different order.

Descriptive Statistics

The main descriptive statistics of the contributions of individuals for Control and Exogenous treatment are displayed in Table 1 with Panels A (Group 1) and B (Group 2). Both panels only differ in the order in which both treatments were run. Additional data like measures of central tendency (mean, median, and mode) and dispersion (standard deviation) are shown, as well as the maximum and minimum values in the first and last rounds of the corresponding experiment.

Table 1. Descriptive Statistics for Control and Exogenous treatments

	DESCRIPTIVE STATISTICS					Initial Contribution	Final Contribution
Treatment	N	Mean	Median	Standard Deviation	Mode	Max/Min	Max/Min
Panel A: Group 1							
Control	27	7.01	1	13.24	0	50/0	50/0
Exogenous	27	4.84	0	12.17	0	50/0	50/0
Panel B: Group 2							
Exogenous	33	7.29	0	13.30	0	50/0	40/0
Control	33	4.65	0	11.53	0	50/0	50/0

The table reports main descriptive statistics for every group session and the maximum and minimum contribution at the beginning and end of the experiment.

As shown in Table 1, the mean and standard deviation of subjects' contributions are higher for the treatment administered in the first place. Actually, subjects of Group 1 contribute more, on average, to the Control than to the Exogenous treatment, whereas in Group 2, these results are reversed, namely, the Exogenous treatment offers a higher average contribution than the Control treatment. Similar results were obtained when comparing standard deviations. There are no differences in the ranges of initial and final contributions except when the exogenous treatment is performed in the first place (Group 2), where the maximum contribution is not achieved. These results support a clear 'order effect' since subjects seem to contribute more on average and with a higher deviation in the first treatment regardless of the existence of the exogenous leader. In addition, there is a decreasing pattern in contributions, particularly in the Exogenous treatment. This fact suggests that learning effects play an important role when the leader is randomly chosen, and thus, exogenous leadership is not effective in increasing contributions over time. In Sect. 5.3. This argument is better explained.

Figure 1 depicts the mean and standard deviation (S.D.) for the Control and Exogenous treatments in both groups by round. In Group 1, Exogenous treatment starts with higher values but tends to have lower contributions than Control treatment in subsequent rounds. Group 2 shows a more smoothly decreasing trend, but contributions from exogenous leadership remain higher than those of the Control with the exception of the first and last rounds. In both groups, standard deviation fluctuates without a clear trend.

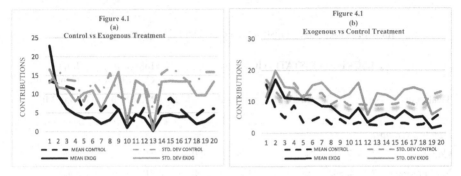

Fig. 1. Mean and standard deviation of the contributions over time

This figure shows the evolution of the mean contribution and its standard deviation (S.D.) for Group 1 and 2 in both the Control and Exogenous treatment.

5.1.2 Nonparametric Analysis

Given the 'within-subjects' nature of our experimental design, the Wilcoxon signed-rank statistic (Table 2) is used to confirm that the difference in average contributions between the exogenous and control treatments is ambiguous and fully determined by the order of the treatment. However, when the game starts with exogenous leadership, teams achieve a better average performance. Hence, non-parametric analysis partially supports our hypothesis H1a, since teams with an exogenous leader contribute more than those without a leader, but it cannot be discarded that these results are influenced by a learning effect.

Table 2. Wilcoxon Test for mean contributions in the different groups

	GROUP 1		GROUP 2	
Mean Contribution	Control	Exogenous	Exogenous	Control
	7,02	4,83	7,28	4,65
Z*	−5,28		5,51	
p-value	,000		,000	

*The test evidenced a clear order effect and then differences are due to learning more than treatment effects

5.2 Control Treatment Versus Endogenous Treatment

5.2.1 Descriptive Statistics

Measures of central tendency (mean, median, and mode) and dispersion (standard deviation) from endogenous and control treatments are shown in Table 3. As in the previous comparison, Panels A (Group 3) and B (Group 4) show the pooled values of the contributions of subjects for both treatments and each group session in the experiment.

Table 3. Descriptive Statistics for Control and Endogenous treatments

		DESCRIPTIVE STATISTICS				Initial Contribution	Final Contribution
Treatment	N	Mean	Median	Standard Deviation	Mode	Max/Min	Max/Min
Panel A: Group 1							
Control	27	7.01	1	13.24	0	50/0	50/0
Exogenous	27	4.84	0	12.17	0	50/0	50/0
Panel B: Group 2							
Exogenous	33	7.29	0	13.30	0	50/0	40/0
Control	33	4.65	0	11.53	0	50/0	50/0

The table reports main descriptive statistics for every group session and the maximum and minimum contribution at the beginning and end of the experiment.

Central tendency measures (mean, median, and mode) in all groups are higher in the Endogenous than in the Control treatment. The standard deviation in both groups also exhibits a higher dispersion in the Endogenous treatment compared to the Control. Maxima, minima, and ranges of initial and final contributions are equal for all treatments/orders, and they exhibit an extreme dispersion of contributions. The most frequent value of contribution when the control treatment was performed first was the minimum (zero) while for the remaining treatments and orders, the mode was the maximum (50).

Figure 3 shows the mean and standard deviation (S.D.) for the Control and Endogenous treatments by round. Mean in both groups is higher in the Endogenous treatment regardless the treatment order. In Group 4 standard deviation is higher and exhibits a positive trend (Fig. 2).

This figure shows the evolution of the mean contribution and its standard deviation (S.D.) for Group 3 and 4 in both the Control and Endogenous treatment.

Nonparametric Analysis The hypothesis H1b was tested (i.e. the existence of significant differences in the median contribution between the two treatments) through the Wilcoxon signed-rank statistic. In this case, the test confirms that, regardless of the treatment order, teams contribute significantly more to the Endogenous than to the Control treatment (Table 4).

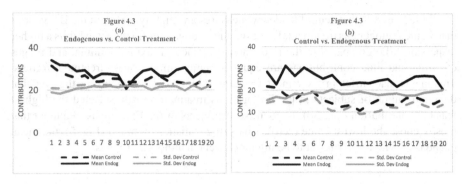

Fig. 2. Mean and standard deviation of the contributions over time

Table 4. Wilcoxon Test for mean contributions in the different groups

	GROUP 3		GROUP 4	
Mean Contribution	Endogenous	Control	Control	Endogenous
	28,26	25,06	15,65	25,23
Z*	−7.42		10.30[b]	
p-value	.000		.000	

[*]Endogenous treatment presents significantly higher contributions regardless the treatment order.
[b]The ranks of the test are based on the difference between the second and first treatment.

5.3 Exogenous Versus Endogenous Leadership

5.3.1 Descriptive Statistic

Table 5 displays the main descriptive statistics of the contributions of individuals to Exogenous and Endogenous treatment in Group 5. Note that in this case, possible order effects were not controlled for in this comparison.

Table 5. Descriptive Statistics for Control and Endogenous treatments

	DESCRIPTIVE STATISTICS					Initial Contribution	Final Contribution
Groups	N	Mean	Median	Standard Deviation	Mode	Max/Min	Max/Min
Panel A: Exogenous treatments							
Group 5	18	21.76	20	18.93	0	50.0	50.0
Panel B: Endogenous treatments							
Group 5	18	21.16	15	20.29	50.0	50.0	50.0

The table reports main descriptive statistics for group session and the maximum and minimum contribution at the beginning and end of the experiment.

Table 5 reveals that central tendency measures are slightly higher in the Exogenous than in the Endogenous treatment. However, the Endogenous treatment exhibits a higher dispersion (SD) compared to the Exogenous treatment. Maxima, minima, and ranges of initial and final contributions are equal or quite similar for all treatments/orders. Treatments also differ in their most frequent value (mode), supporting the fact that the contribution of subjects in the Endogenous treatment mostly selected the highest feasible contribution (i.e., 50), in contrast to subjects in the Exogenous treatment that mostly chose the lowest value (zero). Analyzing statistics by round (Fig. 5), the mean (standard deviation) turns out to be higher (lower) in almost all rounds.

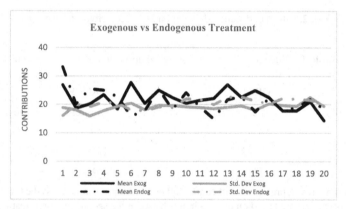

Fig. 3. Mean and deviation of the contributions over time

This figure shows the evolution of the mean contribution and its standard deviation (S.D.) for Group 5 in both the Exogenous and Endogenous treatment.

Figure 6 exhibits the median, maximum (MAX) and minimum (MIN) values of contributions along the sequence of decisions for every group. In general, the Endogenous treatment reveals higher median contributions, albeit the trend is unclear. The minimal and maximum contributions achieve the most feasible values in all cases.

5.3.2 Nonparametric Analysis

The Hypothesis H2 was testes through the Wilcoxon statistic, i.e. our conjecture that Endogenous treatment leads to higher contributions than the Exogenous treatment. However, in Group 5, Wilcoxon test does not find significant differences in contributions in both treatments, as shown in Table 6.

5.4 Econometric Analysis

This section provides dynamic panel data models to test the impact of the different types of leadership on the contribution of any subject of a three-player team i, namely, subject 1 (C_{1it}). The different treatments are tested through a dummy variable (T_{it}), which takes a value of 1 in the main scenario and 0 in the control scenario (further

Table 6. Wilcoxon Test for mean contributions in the different groups

GROUP 5		
Mean Contribution	Exogenous	Endogenous
	21,75	21,16
Z*	−1.67	
p-value	.096	

* No difference between Exogenous and Endogenous treatment is found at 5% level.

details for every model are provided below). To control for possible learning effects (i.e., the effect of the past on future decisions), not only the dynamics of contributions are considered, but also the treatment variable is introduced in a multiplicative way with the lagged values of both the dependent variable and the minimum contribution within a team, i.e.,$\min\{C_{1it-1}, C_{2it-1}, C_{3it-1}\}$. These interaction terms are aimed at capturing the marginal effects of past information on the treatment scenario. Finally, control variables such as nationality and gender are considered and included in the vector X_{it}. Consequently, it is proposed the following basic model for subject 1 contributions to team i in period t:

$$C_{1it} = \beta_0 + \beta_1 C_{1it-1} + \beta_2 T_{it} + \beta_3 T_{it} \times C_{1it-1} + \beta_4 \min\{C_{1it-1}, C_{2it-1}, C_{3it-1}\}$$
$$+ \beta_5 T_{it} \times \min\{C_{1it-1}, C_{2it-1}, C_{3it-1}\} + \alpha' X_{it} + \eta_i + \varepsilon_{it}, \qquad (9)$$
$$for\ i = 1, 2, \ldots, N\ and\ t = 1, 2, \ldots 40.$$

Where C_{1it-1} represents the subject's 1 contribution in period $t - 1$, $\min\{C_{1it-1}, C_{2it-1}, C_{3it-1}\}$ is the minimum contribution of the three members of team i in period $t - 1$, and T_{it} is the dummy variable treatment scoring zero in the control treatment and one in the main treatment. It is noteworthy that the main treatment involves the first (second) 20 observations for groups 2 and 3 (1, 4 and 5). X_{it} is a vector containing the remaining control variables used in the various regressions (such as gender and nationality), η_i s the variable capturing the individual effects, and ε_{it} the error term (both satisfying the standard assumptions in panel data models).

The model, given the dynamic of its nature, was estimated by Generalized Method of Moments (GMM). Lagged endogenous variables were used as valid instruments to control for endogeneity (Arellano & Bond, 1991). The validity of the instruments was checked by the Sargan and Hansen tests.

Table 7 presents the results of four alternative models for the individual contribution that have a similar structure according to Eq. 9. Model 1 compares Exogenous leadership with the Control (no leadership) (Groups 1 and 2), finding an overall significant and positive treatment effect. Furthermore, subjects seem to be willing to increase their contributions the higher their own past contributions and the minimum efforts (output level) of their teams.

C_{1it-1}. Represent the contributions of subjects in period $t - 1$; $\min_{123it-1}$ Represents the minimum contribution of team i in period $t - 1$; T_{it} is the dummy variable scoring one in the main treatment (Exogenous, Endogenous, Endogenous and Leadership in

Table 7. Econometric models for the contribution of subject 1 (C_{1it}).

	MODEL 1 Exogenous vs. Control		MODEL 2 Endogenous vs. Control		MODEL 3 Exogenous vs. Endogenous		MODEL 4 Leadership vs. Control	
	Coef	P- value	Coef	P-value	Coef	P- value	Coef	P- value
C_{1it-1}	.3826796	0.000	.1048034	0.000	−.1075223	0.228	.1875453	0.000
T_{it}	3.605729	0.002	5.695091	0.002	−2.996537	0.831	5.110931	0.000
$min_{123it-1}$	.3507348	0.000	.4345609	0.000	.5114427	0.000	.5591369	0.000
$T_{it} \times min_{123it-1}$	−.4427721	0.000					−.13184	0.000
$T_{it} \times C_{1it-1}$	−.0901307	0.000					−.0773627	0.000
Nationality	−1.189749	0.140	36.09222	0.000			.019297	0.000
Gender	.6207872	0.034	1.324668	0.072			4.180999	0.000
Intercept	1.254226	0.030	9.046641	0.000	16.09283	0.006	3.374966	0.000
AR1	−4.99	0.000	−4.61	0.000	−2.03	0.042	−7.01	0.000
AR2	1.93	0.054	1.28	0.201	0.44	0.662	2.42	0.015
Sgan	2223.84	0.000	2070.17	0.000	595.94	0.000	4893.55	0.000
Hansen	56.82	1.000	51.65	1.000	10.96	1.000	126.80	1.000
N	60		60		18		138	

Models 1, 2, 3 and 4, respectively) and zero in control treatments with 'no leadership' in all models but Model 3 (Exogenous leadership).Nationality is a dummy variable that takes 0 for Spanish subjects and 1 non-Spanish subjects. Finally, gender takes 0 for men and 1 for women. The Arellano-Bond for testing autocorrelation of order 1 and 2 are labelled as AR1 and AR2, respectively; 'Sargan' and 'Hansen' denote the tests for the validity of instruments and N is the number of observations.

6 Conclusions

An experimental approach and compare the contributions of teams without any kind of leadership (simultaneous decision) to those with either endogenous or exogenous leadership (i.e., a sequential framework where the leader decides her contribution first and sends a message about her recommended contribution to the followers). In endogenous leadership, the leader is chosen through an auction in which all members of any team submit a bid, and the one with the higher bid wins the right to be leader during the whole treatment. In exogenous leadership, the leader is randomly chosen for the whole treatment. A production technology is assumed in which the output depends directly on the minimum contribution within the three-player team, and only this information is revealed to the team members once they have made their decision for every period. A repeated game was implemented within subjects during 20 rounds per treatment with the same teams, and thus learning effects might play an important role in the decisions. On the other hand, it was controlled for possible order effects when testing the impact of treatment as well as possible interactions between input dynamics and treatment.

Leadership has a significant and positive impact on team production, but this effect is different when considering either an endogenous or exogenous selection of the leader.

References

Aghion, P., Tirole, J.: Formal and real authority in organizations. J. Polit. Econ.**105**(1), 1–29 (1997)

Alchian, A.A., Demsetz, H.: Production, information costs, and economic organization. Am. Econ. Rev. **62**(5), 777–795 (1972)

Arce, M., D.: Leadership and the aggregation of international collective action. Oxf. Econ. Pap. **53**(1), 114–137 (2001)

Bass, B.M., Stogdill, R.M.: Bass & Stogdill's handbook of leadership: Theory, research, and managerial applications. Simon and Schuster, New York (1990)

Bolton, P., Brunnermeier, M.K., Veldkamp, L.: Economists' perspectives on leadership. Handb. Leadersh. Theory Pract., 239–264 (2010)

Brandts, J., Cooper, D.J., Fatas, E., Qi, S.: Stand by me—experiments on help and commitment in coordination games. Manage. Sci. **62**(10) (2015)

Bryant, J.: A simple rational expectations Keynes-type model. Q. J. Econ. **98**(3), 525–528 (1983)

Camerer, C.: Behavioral Game Theory: Experiments in Strategic Interaction. Russell Sage Foundation, New York (2003)

Camerer, C.F., Ho, T.-H., Chong, J.K.: Behavioural game theory: thinking, learning and teaching. In: Huck, S. (eds.) Advances in Understanding Strategic Behaviour. Palgrave Macmillan, London (2004). https://doi.org/10.1057/9780230523371_8

Cooper, R., DeJong, D.V., Forsythe, R., Ross, T.W.: Communication in coordination games. Q. J. Econ. **107**(2), 739–771 (1992)

Cooper, R., DeJong, D.V., Forsythe, R., Ross, T.W.: Alternative institutions for resolving coordination problems: experimental evidence on forward induction and preplaycommunication. In Friedman, J.W. (eds) Problems of Coordination in Economic Activity. Recent Economic Thought Series, vol. 35, pp. 129–146. Springer, Dordrecht (1994). https://doi.org/10.1007/978-94-011-1398-4_7

Delarue, A., Van Hootegem, G., Procter, S., Burridge, M.: Teamworking and organizational performance: a review of survey-based research. Int. J. Manag. Rev. **10**(2), 127–148 (2008)

Delarue, A., Van Hootegem, G., Procter, S., Burridge, M.: Teamworking and organizational performance: a review of survey-based research. Int. J. Manag. Rev. **10**(2), 127–148 (2008)

Devetag, G., Ortmann, A.: Classic coordination failures revisited: the effects of deviation costs and loss avoidance (2007)

Fatas, E., Neugebauer, T., Perote, J.: Within-team competition in the minimum effort coordination game. Pac. Econ. Rev. **11**(2), 247–266 (2006)

Gardner, J.: On leadership: Simon and Schuster (1993)

Gerth, H.H., Mills, C.W.: From Weber: Essays in Sociology. 50Gerth50Essays (1946)

Hoffman, E., McCabe, K., Shachat, K., Smith, V.: Preferences, property rights, and anonymity in bargaining games. Games Econom. Behav. **7**(3), 346–380 (1994)

Hoffman, E., Spitzer, M.L.: Entitlements, rights, and fairness: an experimental examination of subjects' concepts of distributive justice. J. Leg. Stud. **14**(2), 259–297 (1985)

Holmstrom, B.: Moral hazard in teams. Bell J. Econ. (1982)

Kahneman, D., Tversky, A.: On the interpretation of intuitive probability: a reply to Jonathan Cohen (1979)

Knez, M., Camerer, C.: Creating expectational assets in the laboratory: coordination in 'weakest-link'games. Strateg. Manag. J. **15**(S1) (1994)

Kocher, M.G., Pogrebna, G., Sutter, M.: Other-regarding preferences and management styles. J. Econ. Behav. Organ. **88**, 109–132 (2013)

Kotter, J.P.: Leading Change. Google Scholar, Boston (1996)

Kreps, D.M.: Game Theory and Economic Modelling. Oxford University Press, Oxford (1990)

León, M., Cornejo, G., Calderon, M., Gonzalez, E., Florez, H.: Effect of deforestation on climate change: A Co-integration and causality approach with time series. Sustainability 14(18), 11303 (2022)

Levy, D.M., Padgitt, K., Peart, S.J., Houser, D., Xiao, E.: Leadership, cheap talk and really cheap talk. J. Econ. Behav. Organ. (2011)

Milgrom, P., Roberts, J.: Informational asymmetries, strategic behavior, and industrial organization. Am. Econ. Rev. 77(2), 184–193 (1987)

Ormiston, M.B., Quiggin, J.: Two-parameter decision models and rank-dependent expected utility. J. Risk Uncertain. 7(3), 273–282 (1993)

Reuben, E., Timko, K.: On the effectiveness of elected male and female leaders and team coordination (2017)

Riechmann, T., Weimann, J.: Competition as a coordination device: experimental evidence from a minimum effort coordination game. Eur. J. Polit. Econ. 24(2), 437–454 (2008)

Rosner, B.: Team players expect real choices. Workforce 80(5), 62–65 (2001)

Rotemberg, J.J., Saloner, G.: Leadership style and incentives. Manage. Sci. 39(11), 1299–1318 (1993)

Sahin, S.G., Eckel, C., Komai, M.J.: An experimental study of leadership institutions in collective action games. J. Econ. Sci. Assoc. 1(1), 100–113 (2015)

Sohmen, V.S.: Leadership and teamwork: two sides of the same coin. J. Inf. Technol. Econ. Dev. 4(2) (2013)

Van der Heijden, E., Moxnes, H.: Leading by Example?: Investment Decisions in a Mixed Sequential-simultaneous Public Bad Experiment, Tilburg University (2003)

Van Huyck, J.B., Battalio, R.C., Beil, R.O.: Tacit coordination games, strategic uncertainty, and coordination failure. Am. Econ. Rev. 80(1) (1990)

Von Neumann, J., Morgenstern, O.: Game theory and economic behavior. Princeton University Press, Princeton (1944)

Weber, R., Camerer, C., Rottenstreich, Y., Knez, M.: The illusion of leadership: Misattribution of cause in coordination games. Organ. Sci. 12(5), 582–598 (2001)

Weber, R.A.: Managing growth to achieve efficient coordination in large groups. Am. Econ. Rev. 96(1), 114–126 (2006)

A GIS Referenced Methodological Approach for the Brownfield Redevelopment

Alfonso Ippolito[1], Yasmine Selim[2], Francesco Tajani[3](✉) , Rossana Ranieri[3] ,
and Pierluigi Morano[4]

[1] Department of History, Design and Restoration of Architecture, Sapienza University of Rome,
00186 Rome, Italy
[2] Department of Architecture, Faculty of Engineering, Ain Shams University, 11566 Cairo,
Egypt
[3] Department of Architecture and Design, Sapienza University of Rome, 00196 Rome, Italy
francesco.tajani@uniroma1.it
[4] Department of Civil, Environmental, Land, Building Engineering and
Chemistry(DICATECh), Polytechnic University of Bari, 70126 Bari, Italy

Abstract. In the perspective of a sustainable development of the urban territory,
the aim of this research is to define a methodology for the characterization of a
brownfield inventory, accessible by the government and the private investors to
facilitate decision making, by reaching the needed information upon land capability, development incentives, public goals, interests and preferences, environmental
concerns. This issue is very current, taking into account the numerous researches
on the urban development of the cities and how the urban sprawl caused the industrial areas that initially existed on the city outskirts to become a part of the city
center. This rapid growth motivates the governments and private investors to look
at these abandoned industrial buildings as important assets. The research discusses
a decision support framework and the benefits of access to geospatial databases
in the decision-making process.

Keywords: Brownfield · GIS · Decision support systems · urban redevelopment

1 Introduction

Brownfields are properties that have been contaminated by hazardous substances and are
often derelict or underused. These properties pose potential health and environmental
risks, and their redevelopment can be costly and complex [1]. Industrial heritage, on the
other hand, refers to the historical legacy of industrial activities and the built environment
that results from them. Industrial heritage sites may include old factories, warehouses,
and other industrial structures, and they may be considered for preservation for their
cultural and historical value [2]. While both brownfields and industrial heritage sites
may be found in urban areas, they are distinct concepts and are managed differently.
The International Council on Monuments and Sites (ICOMOS), and the International
Committee for the Conservation of the Industrial Heritage (TICCIH), acknowledge the

particular nature of industrial heritage and the issues and threats around it, stating that "industrial heritage is highly vulnerable and often at risk, often lost for lack of awareness, documentation, recognition or protection but also because of the changing economic trends, negative perceptions, environmental issues or its sheer size and complexity." [2]. At the same time, physical revitalization and functional restructuring, adaptation of industrial heritage to the needs and requirements of post-industrial society, as well as the aspect of economic revitalization through new ways to utilize an industrial building stock is a matter that is repeatedly talked about regarding industrial heritage. In view of that, the importance of the sustainable conservation of industrial heritage is also recognized. "By extending the life cycle of existing structures and their embodied energy, conservation of the built industrial heritage can contribute to achieving the goals of sustainable development at the local, national, and international levels. It touches the social as well as physical and environmental aspects of development and should be acknowledged as such" [2].

In Central and Eastern Europe, but also elsewhere, de-industrialisation has produced veritable "black holes" in the *Forma Urbis*: in Great Britain it is estimated that there are 128.000 hectares of abandoned land, in France 20,000, in the Netherlands 10,000, in Italy 9,000 and in Switzerland 1,700. Those lands are frequently areas without purpose, filled with rubbish and industrial waste, which have lost their *"raison d'être"* and are awaiting some form of regeneration. [3]. Unused and underused buildings and spaces represent enormous potential for cities; they often exist in desirable waterfront lands, city centers and old industrial zones. Alteration of values generated by functional restructuring, is a subject which is often left behind the general discussion about sustainable conservation and adaptive reuse of industrial heritage. This is because the focus is often on the physical preservation and conservation of industrial heritage sites, rather than on the changes in the values associated with these sites.

The post-industrial society is a term coined by the sociologist Daniel Bell [4] to describe the current state of society in developed countries, in which the service sector has come to dominate the economy and manufacturing has become less important. This shift is often accompanied by changes in social and cultural norms, as well as in the political and economic systems. Some of the key theories of the post-industrial society include: the information society theory, which suggests that the rise of information and communication technologies has led to the growth of the service sector and the decline of manufacturing; the knowledge economy theory, which posits that the value of knowledge and expertise has become more important than physical labor in driving economic growth; the flexible specialization theory, which argues that the post-industrial economy is characterized by the rise of small, specialized firms that are able to quickly adapt to changing market conditions; the cultural capitalism theory, which suggests that the post-industrial society is driven by the production and consumption of cultural goods, such as music, art, and fashion. Overall, the theories of post-industrial society highlight the ways in which the economy and society are changing in response to technological, social, and cultural shifts.

Considering the aesthetic of brownfield and the shift of the modern society needs, there is a demand for spaces that are flexible and different. Industrial heritage fits this scheme, establishing itself in the landscape of contemporary art and culture. Old factories can be transformed into cultural spaces in a variety of ways: repurposing the factory as a museum or exhibit space, it could involve showcasing the history of the factory and its role in the local community, or it could involve hosting temporary or permanent exhibits on a variety of topics. A great example of this reuse is *Centrale Montemartini* in Rome (Fig. 1). An old factory can also be transformed into a venue for concerts, theatre performances, or other live events, *Rawabet* Theatre in Downtown Cairo (Fig. 2) is a successful example of this transformation from an old car warehouse to a theatre hosting cultural events. Another reuse example is *SpazioMensa* (Fig. 3), located inside the former paper mill in Rome divided into smaller spaces that are used as artist studios or galleries, allowing local artists to work and exhibit their work in a shared space. Also, the *Mattatoio* that was inaugurated in 1890, decommissioned in 1975 and remained an empty shell for many years. Most of the old pavilions still stand empty and are closed to the public. However, others are now to a contemporary art space and architecture school (Fig. 4).

Fig. 1. Cent. Montemartini, Rome

Fig. 2. Rawabet Theatre, Cairo

Fig. 3. SpazioMensa, Rome

Fig. 4. Mattatoio, Rome

The Industrial Revolution left substantial marks on the appearance of cities, certain stereotypes and a negative image of industrial urban landscape emerged, which was reinforced by many depictions of the rough aesthetic of the heavy industrial architecture in cities and of the pollution that came with it. De-industrialization crisis and the profound structural change enriched the negative image by leaving numerous disused industrial spaces, run-down factories, and industrial complexes behind. Being aware of the socio-cultural formation of post-industrial Western societies, their tendencies, and dynamics, is crucial to understand the evolution of the post-industrial urban landscape and the transformation of its single elements, e.g., post industrial production spaces and the current strategies of their management. Nonetheless, it is important to consider the alteration of values generated by functional restructuring when planning for the sustainable conservation and adaptive reuse of industrial heritage. This is because changes in values can have a significant impact on the long-term sustainability of these sites. For example, if the values associated with an industrial heritage site are altered in a way that makes it less appealing to visitors or less valuable to the local community, it may become difficult to generate the resources needed to preserve and maintain the site over time. This can involve engaging with local stakeholders and communities to understand their priorities and concerns, as well as conducting research to identify the potential consequences of functional restructuring. By taking these factors into account, it is possible to develop conservation and adaptive reuse strategies that both preserve the physical heritage of industrial sites and support the long-term sustainability of these sites.

The work is organized in the following Sections. In Sect. 2, an analysis of the current literature on brownfields and the methods/technique to assess them is reported. In Sect. 3, the methodological approach and its main phases are illustrated. In Sect. 4, the conclusions and possible further insights are drawn.

2   Literature Review

Urbanized spaces are undergoing major changes due to the higher number of people moving to the city. In particular, urban transformation and deindustrialization in advanced economies have left numerous vacant and abandoned lands that can become an opportunity for positive city improvement [5–7]. With the aim to reduce land consumption, Public Administrations have begun to pay more attention to the issue of brownfields redevelopment. There are numerous contributions in current literature that propose tools and methodological approaches for the analysis of brownfield and related transformation projects [8–11]. According to these studies, the assessments of brownfield programs could be complex, especially because there are no available databases for tracing ample information on policy activity. In this sense, Bacot and O'Dell [12] have tried to identify proper environmental criteria for analyzing local government brownfield programs; Hartmann et al. [13] have proposed a multi-objective examination and evaluation method for extensive analysis of the conditions of the brownfields, in order to support investor that aims to utilize the property for energy generation purposes. The energy purpose redevelopment of brownfield sites is frequent: there are in fact many studies related on wind and solar power, biopower, waste, and mixed uses [14–18]. Those studies highlight that is important to take the social aspects into consideration, by revitalizing urban areas and involving local governance and communities in the projects. In particular, Wang et al. [19] have proposed a quantitative methodology to support negotiations on the allocation of costs and benefits in brownfield redevelopment projects applying cooperative game theory.

Another key aspect of brownfield management is related to the ability for city planners to have access to georeferenced quantitative information. In this regard, Geographic Information System (GIS) tools have been very effective in managing urban planning and real estate developments, with particular reference to brownfields [20–22]. Ahamad et al. [23] have developed a consensus-based brownfield definition and an evaluation index system to evaluate brownfield redevelopment in Pakistan using a methodology combining Triangular Fuzzy Numbers and Grey Relational Analysis. Aktas et al. [24] have proposed a method to screen numerous brownfields over large geographic areas by using GIS and to assess and prioritize such sites for green building suitability based on leadership in energy and environmental design criteria. Thomas et al. [25], in order to evaluate land use options with respect to brownfields inventory, characterization, and potential for redevelopment, have defined a GIS based land use modeling application to support decision system that provides access to state, regional, and local geospatial databases, several informational and visualization tools, and assumptions useful in providing a better understanding of issues, options, and alternatives in redeveloping brownfields. Furthermore, Li et al. [26] have integrated the Data Envelopment Analysis method with a GIS based site selection systems that can determine the most suitable site objectively and visually. Zeng et al. [27] have developed a prototype real estate GIS by integrating fuzzy set theory, a rule-based system and GIS.

3 Methodological Approach

Referring to Anne Lacatan's approach "Never demolish. Never subtract, remove, or replace. Always add, transform, and utilize, with and for the inhabitants" [28]. Adaptive reuse refers to the process of repurposing or converting an industrial building for a new use, rather than demolishing it and starting from scratch. This approach can be a sustainable and cost-effective way to reuse existing buildings and infrastructure, and it can also help to preserve the character and history of a place.

The main objective of adaptive reuse is to give new life to existing buildings or sites that are no longer being used for their original purpose. Raising the awareness and appreciation of industrial heritage is another objective of adaptive reuse, preserving historical or cultural landmarks can support to protect important buildings, structures, and sites that may have architectural, historical, or cultural significance. This can maintain the character and sense of place of a community and can also support local tourism and economic development. Heritage recycling has a great impact on environment preservation, reducing waste and thus allowing for the reincorporation of old materials, to reduce the amount of waste generated by demolishing old buildings and constructing new ones. It can also minimize the environmental impact of development by reducing the amount of energy, water, and other resources required to build new structures. This leads to the economic benefits of the brownfields redevelopment creating commercially viable assets for owners and users: adding to the economic and environmental benefits the social well-being by the adaptation of spaces according to the community and stakeholders needs; designing accessible, usable public places can support sustainability and resilience by promoting the use of existing infrastructure and resources, and by helping to create compact, mixed-use developments that can support diverse and vibrant communities; providing opportunities for designers and developers to think outside the box and to come up with creative solutions for repurposing old buildings and sites, to foster a sense of ingenuity and entrepreneurship within a community [29].

Noting that the benefits provided by a framework for brownfields redevelopment are aligning with the adaptive reuse goals and benefits, it leads to following a similar strategy approaching the brownfields redevelopment planning.

The phases of adaptive re-use of brownfields can be divided into the following steps:

i. Mapping. This involves creating an inventory of brownfields in the area, including information about ownership, environmental conditions, and potential uses. This step helps to identify the properties that are suitable for redevelopment.
ii. Visualising. This phase involves collecting ideas and proposals from the community and stakeholders for the re-use of the vacant properties. This can include public input sessions, design competitions, and other methods of engaging the community in the planning process.
iii. Decision making and financing. This phase involves evaluating the economic and social impact of different alternatives for the use of the brownfields. This may include analysing the feasibility of different development proposals, considering the costs and benefits of each option, and identifying potential sources of funding.
iv. Evaluating. This final phase involves creating a mechanism for collecting feedback and modifying the strategy as needed. This may involve ongoing monitoring of the redevelopment process, soliciting feedback from the community, and adjusting the plan as needed to ensure that the redevelopment meets the needs and goals of the community.

3.1 Road Map

Reusing brownfields can be a challenging process due to several barriers, including environmental contamination, as many brownfields are contaminated with hazardous substances, which can be expensive and time-consuming to clean up; liability concerns, as property owners may be liable for any environmental contamination that occurs on their property, which can be a deterrent to reuse. The unknown remediation costs associated with brownfield clean up and redevelopment can make it difficult for developers to secure financing for these projects; complex regulatory environment, as brownfields are often subject to a variety of state regulations, which can be complex and time-consuming to navigate; community opposition, as local communities may resist the reuse of brownfields due to concerns about environmental impacts or other issues; limited availability of technical assistance, as developers may lack the technical expertise or resources needed to navigate the complex process of brownfield reuse.

In order to overcome these barriers, both the government and the private investors need an easily accessible database to assess the criteria of redevelopment and facilitate the brownfields redevelopment not only on the public municipal level, nor on the financial revenue to private entities, but also on the public-private partnership approaches [30]. Public-private partnerships can be a useful tool for brownfields development that can support the challenges associated with brownfields development by bringing together the resources and expertise of both the public and private sectors. One key benefit is that the financial burden and risk associated with cleaning up and developing contaminated properties are spread over both parties. The public sector can finance, regulatory support, and other resources, while the private sector can bring expertise, innovation, and financial resources to the table. Assessing the reduction of i) the cost of brownfields development and making it more feasible for both the public and private sectors, ii) the amount of time and effort required to clean up and regenerate contaminated properties, which in turn stimulate economic growth and revitalize communities [31].

The use of decision support systems in the business world is well established. According to Sauter [32], decision support systems, by definition, should aid in and strengthen the process of choice. The goal of a Decision Support System (DSS) is to provide users with the information and tools they need to make informed decisions. This includes understanding the needs and abilities of the user, as well as the context in which the information will be used. To be effective, a land use decision support system must ensure access to data, the tools or mechanisms to transform data into useful information, and the context from which understanding is derived. With the addition of GIS-based models and other analytical tools, decision-makers can begin to manipulate data in a true planning environment [25].

A decision-support framework for brownfields development can be a useful tool to help alter the narrative of brownfields and make them more competitive with Greenfields. There are several benefits to having such a framework in place. A decision-support framework can guarantee a structured approach for evaluating the potential of a brownfield site, including its environmental, economic, and social impacts. Decision-makers can use this to swiftly find the most promising sites and forward development plans and can also demonstrate the viability of a brownfields development project, making it more attractive to potential funding sources.

Based on the project marketability it will attract different approaches of funding, as generally more marketable brownfield development projects are more likely to attract private funding, while less marketable projects may be more reliant on funding from government sources and medium marketable sites depend more on public-private partnerships. Factors that may influence the marketability of a brownfield development project include the location of the site, the potential for economic development, and the environmental risks and liabilities associated with the site. Projects that are located in high-demand areas, have a clear economic benefit, and pose minimal environmental risks are likely to be more marketable and therefore more attractive to private investors. On the other hand, projects that are located in less desirable areas, have uncertain economic prospects, or pose significant environmental risks may be less marketable and may need to rely on government funding sources.

When creating a decision-support framework, it is crucial to take the marketability of a brownfield development project into account as it can assist identify the most suitable funding sources and guarantee that the project has the resources it needs to be successful.

There are several benefits to using a framework for the stakeholders. Investors, by analyzing data and alternative uses, can make informed decisions about which projects to invest in and can potentially reduce financial risk. The framework assesses the government to easily track and manage brownfield sites, which can be incorporated into city planning and development decisions. From a community perspective, the framework ensures that development projects align with the needs and priorities of the community as identified through surveys and other forms of public input. Non-governmental organizations (NGOs) can use a framework to focus on both community needs and environmental issues, helping to ensure that development projects have a positive impact on both people and the environment. Providing urban planners with access to data and surveys that can support them prioritize development projects and make informed decisions about how to use land and resources in the most effective and efficient way.

The main goal of this project is to develop a *vademecum* that could help local governments and developers make informed decisions about the development of brownfield sites. It would use GIS-based visualization models and decision criteria, as well as access to various geospatial databases and web-based tools that inventory brownfield sites, to help users assess the feasibility of different development options. The system has been designed to be accessible and affordable for local governments and developers, and to involve extensive public input and engagement.

3.2   Description of GIS Approach

To create the inventory of brownfields, the first step is identifying the potential sites in the targeted geographical area. The study was done using QGIS, an open-source geographic information system, also using data from online public sources e.g., Rome Transportation map, *Geoportale cartografico* [33]. Figure 5 shows some of the industrial sites in Europe collected during this study, located with coordinates on QGIS and using the software in registering related data to the site, e.g. current and previous ownership, previous use, current use, structure condition, all collected in one database to show the efficiency of the system in data accessibility and analysis [34, 35].

Field1	Field2	Field5	Field6
0	Project_Name	Country	Former Use
1	Hammer	Germany	Former industrial estate
2	Frederiksvaerk	Denmark	Used as Cannon Foundry untill 1928
3	Merthyr Tydfil	UK	Iron Industrial village
4	Balenavon	UK	Coal mining and iron working industries
5	Elbeuf	France	Wool production center
6	Roubaix-Tourcoing	France	Main French production hub for Cotton
7	Verviers	Belgium	One of the oldest Cité ouvrière
8	Mongiana	Italy	NULL
9	Larderello	Italy	NULL
10	Alvisopoli	Italy	NULL
11	Wielczka	Poland	NULL
12	Solivar	Slovakia	NULL
13	Oberhasen	Germany	NULL
14	Kuchen	Germany	NULL
15	Bochum	Germany	NULL
16	Frankfurt on the main	Germany	NULL
17	Dortmund	Germany	NULL
18	Augsburg	Germany	NULL
19	Halifax	UK	NULL
20	Chateauroux	France	NULL
21	Nord-Pas-De-Calais	France	NULL
22	Tergnier	France	NULL
23	Arnao	Spain	NULL
24	Bustiello	Spain	NULL
25	Lieres	Portugal	NULL
26	Vista Algere	Portugal	NULL
27	Biella	Italy	NULL
28	Collegno	Italy	NULL
29	Piazzola sul Brenta	Italy	NULL

Fig. 5. Demo of mapping industrial heritage sites in Europe and registering variable data on QGIS

Using open-source GIS software (QGIS) to find the data related to the targeted geographic area, not only analyzing the data available from the local government but also collecting data from the urban planners' surveys and benefiting from the modern technology having public community surveys about the brownfield area. Data including the location and characteristics of brownfields in the area can be used and analyzed on the QGIS, as well as data on the surrounding community, such as population demographics, land use, and infrastructure. Collecting and analyzing data is just one step in the process of considering brownfield redevelopment. It is also important to engage with the community and other stakeholders to ensure that any redevelopment plans take into account the needs and concerns of the community.

Open data GIS can be used by community stakeholders and decision makers to help them consider the reuse of brownfields in their community. This could include data and analysis at the neighborhood level, and help stakeholders track brownfields and consider the potential benefits and impacts of different redevelopment options for existing residents. Using GIS technology could help decision makers make informed decisions about brownfields redevelopment, which can have a significant impact on the community. Redevelopment of brownfields can promote economic and social benefits, such as creating jobs, revitalizing the local economy, and improving the overall quality of life in the community. However, it is important to carefully consider the potential impacts on existing residents, including any potential negative effects on the environment or public health. It is important to involve the community in the decision-making process and to ensure that any redevelopment plans take into account the needs and concerns of the community. This can be done through community engagement efforts, such as holding public meetings, using geotagged surveys, seeking input from local organizations, and working with community leaders.

The relevant level of resolution will depend on the specific decision-making context. There are many different types of data that can be useful to consider when making decisions about brownfields redevelopment using a GIS system. Some of the key data include: location and characteristics of brownfields (e.g. location, size, condition of brownfields in the area, as well as information about any contamination or other environmental issues that may need to be addressed); community data including population demographics, land use, and infrastructure. This can help decision makers understand the potential impacts of brownfields redevelopment on the community and ensure that any plans take into account the needs and concerns of the community; economic data on employment, income, and other economic indicators, as well as data on the potential economic benefits of different brownfields redevelopment options; environmental data on air quality, water quality, and other environmental factors that could be impacted by brownfields redevelopment; social data indicators, such as housing, education, and public health, as well as data on the potential social impacts of different brownfields redevelopment options. Table 1 shows some of these criteria and the possible data sources.

By collecting and analyzing this data using a GIS system, decision makers can get a more complete picture of the potential benefits and impacts of different brownfields redevelopment options and make informed decisions about the reuse of these sites.

Table 1. Synoptic framework of the criteria to be considered for an effective brownfield redevelopment

Site Criteria	Stakeholder questions	Possible answers
Land area	Is the site large enough?	Area (sqm)
Existing contamination	Is the site ready for development? Are there remediation costs before development?	Cost (Euros)
Land Use and land cover	Is the site vacant? What is the existing land use?	Location Survey
Land Value	What is the land purchase cost?	Valuation (euro/sqm)
Incentives	How will the site attract development?	Survey for local financial incentives
Targeted users	Will the proposed use be attractive for users?	Demographic and economic data of the area
Appropriate Zoning	Is the proposed development suitable with the city planning?	Municipality planning
Population demographics	Does development provide a variety of social and economic opportunities?	Demographic and economic data of the area
Community Involvement	Development impact on community improvement, safety, and benefits?	Surveys
Proximity to transportation	How well is the site connected to the city?	Physical survey for transportation accessibility
Existing infrastructure condition	Does water, telephone and different services need upgrade?	Municipal sources and Area surveying

3.3 Framework for Brownfield Redevelopment

The framework for brownfield redevelopment involves the following steps.

1. *Target geographic areas.* To import data from land surveys and local information sources for a specific geographic area, identifying the sources of data that are relevant to your research or project. These may include land surveys, municipal urban planning documents, local government websites.
2. *Identify brownfield sites.* Identifying brownfields on the maps, benefiting from the GIS systems for mapping to visualize and analyze the brownfield sites identified. Overlaying additional data, such as environmental data or demographic information, to understand the potential impact of the sites on the surrounding community. Analyzing the potential risks and challenges associated with each site, such as the extent and type of contamination, the feasibility of clean-up and redevelopment, and any

legal or regulatory barriers that may be in place, to prioritize which sites to focus on first and develop strategies for addressing the challenges they pose.

3. *Traditional Source of Funding based on marketability.* It is important to note the marketability of the project, as a factor that can influence the availability and terms of funding from these sources. Funding sources for redevelopment vary based on the site's intended use.

4. *Screen potential community benefits.* Evaluating the potential impacts of the project on the local community and identifying opportunities for the project to provide benefits that go beyond the financial returns to the developer or investors. Some Important points for community development are job creation, community amenities, economic development by attracting new businesses, increasing property values, or generating tax revenues for the community, and environmental benefits by incorporating sustainable design elements and the rehabilitating of the existing property.

5. *Evaluate impacts of cultural redevelopment.* Since contaminated fields cannot be used as residential for health and hazards risks, most municipalities intend them for cultural and commercial uses. Which may involve the development of parks, museums, or other cultural amenities, or the construction of commercial or industrial buildings. These types of uses may be considered less risky from a public health perspective because they typically do not involve long-term exposure to the site by residents. Cultural redevelopment projects can also impact the cultural heritage and identity of the local community. These impacts may be positive, if the project helps to preserve or celebrate the cultural heritage of the area, or negative, if the project involves the demolition or alteration of significant cultural landmarks or ignores the cultural values and traditions of the community.

6. *Develop strategy for redevelopment activities.* Brownfield sites can also pose challenges for cultural and commercial development. These sites may require significant clean-up and remediation efforts to address the contamination, which can be costly and time-consuming. In addition, there may be legal or regulatory barriers to development on brownfield sites, such as liability concerns or restrictions on land use. As a result, it can be important for municipalities to carefully evaluate the feasibility and risks of cultural and commercial development on brownfield sites.

One of the city's most notable abandoned sites is the former "Fiera di Roma", which is located in the VIII Municipality. With resolution no. 66 of July 3, 2014, the Capitoline Council began the process of developing an urban variation, confirming the interest in its redevelopment and upgrading. The Municipal Administration of Rome has in fact decided to involve citizens in selecting which interventions and works they want to see carried out in the area of the Municipio, using the economic resources allocated by private operators within the convention [36].

The Municipal Administration of Rome has a dual purpose in executing this project: on one hand, starting a regeneration process to reshape the area, possibly impacting the entire neighborhood, and, on the other hand, creating a building that is both multifunctional and innovative, able to combine the hopes and needs of a community with the demands and the potential of the institutional partner involved [37].

The former "Fiera di Roma" is an excellent illustration of the advantages of data visualization using QGIS, using the accessible GIS data and with the potential for public surveys with the locals, demonstrating the potential of available data and how it may assist in the creation process and final decision-making. By means of the available online data, an accurate analysis of distances of the neighboring services can be carried out. Figures 6 and 7 respectively describe the distances of several metro lines and the density of bus stops in relation to the site of the former "Fiera di Roma", highlighting the importance of service availability.

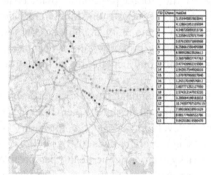

Fig. 6. Metro lines around the former "Fiera di Roma, colour coded according to distances.

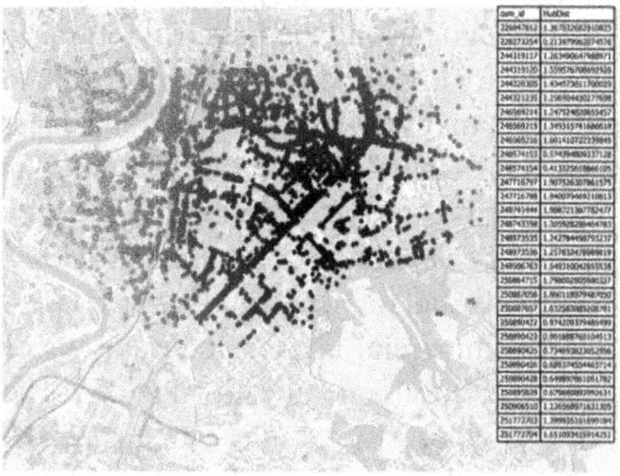

Fig. 7. Density of bus stops around the former "Fiera di Roma", colour coded according to distances.

4 Conclusions

One of the main objectives for using GIS analysis is related to the redevelopment project prioritization. The GIS maps the location and extent of contaminated sites, and allows to identify potential risks and impacts on human health and the environmental context. These information data can be used to prioritize brownfield sites for clean-up and redevelopment, and to elaborate strategies for mitigating any potential risks. Secondly, the GIS analysis gives an integrated tool that includes not only data from municipal sources, but also from community surveys; furthermore, all the geospatial data available are also taken into account, such as demographic, land use, environment and transportation. This allows decision-makers to get a more complete picture of the social, economic, and environmental factors that may impact brownfield regeneration efforts [38–42]. Lastly, it allows to create interactive maps and other visualizations that can be easily shared with stakeholders and the public entities. This can effectively support the brownfield regeneration projects and let the communities know about the potential benefits and impacts of these projects.

References

1. CLARINET. https://haemers-technologies.com/wp-content/uploads/2018/02/Brownfields_and_Redevelopment-Urban_Areas.pdf. Accessed 14 Feb 2023

2. TICCIH. https://ticcih.org/about/about-ticcih/dublin-principles. Accessed 21 Feb 2023
3. Rey, E., Laprise, M., Lufkin, S., Rey, E., Laprise, M., Lufkin, S.: The Multiple Potentials of Urban Brownfields. In: Neighbourhoods in Transition, Brownfield Regeneration in European Metropolitan Areas, pp. 47-63. Springer, Cham (2022). https://doi.org/10.1007/978-3-030-82208-8_3
4. Bell, D.: The Coming of Post-Industrial Society: A Venture in Social Forecasting. Basic Books, New York (1999)
5. Adams, D., De Sousa, C., Tiesdell, S.: Brownfield development: a comparison of North American and British approaches. Urban Stud. **47**(1), 75–104 (2010)
6. Loures, L., Vaz, E.: Exploring expert perception towards brownfield redevelopment benefits according to their typology. Habitat Int. **72**, 66–76 (2018)
7. Loures, L.: Post-industrial landscapes as drivers for urban redevelopment: Public versus expert perspectives towards the benefits and barriers of the reuse of post-industrial sites in urban areas. Habitat Int. **45**, 72–81 (2015)
8. Ahmad, N., Zhu, Y., Ibrahim, M., Waqas, M., Waheed, A.: Development of a standard brownfield definition, guidelines, and evaluation index system for brownfield redevelopment in developing countries: the case of Pakistan. Sustainability **10**(12), 4347 (2018)
9. De Sousa, C.A.: Brownfield redevelopment in Toronto: an examination of past trends and future prospects. Land Use Policy **19**(4), 297–309 (2002)
10. Alker, S., Joy, V., Roberts, P., Smith, N.: The definition of brownfield. J. Environ. Plan. Manage. **43**(1), 49–69 (2000)
11. Hammond, E.B., et al.: A critical review of decision support systems for brownfield redevelopment. Sci. Total Environ. **785**, 147132 (2021)
12. Bacot, H., O'Dell, C.: Establishing indicators to evaluate brownfield redevelopment. Econ. Dev. Q. **20**(2), 142–161 (2006)
13. Hartmann, B., Török, S., Börcsök, E., Groma, V.O.: Multi-objective method for energy purpose redevelopment of brownfield sites. J. Clean. Prod. **82**, 202–212 (2014)
14. Adelaja, S., Shaw, J., Beyea, W., McKeown, J.C.: Renewable energy potential on brownfield sites: a case study of Michigan. Energy Policy **38**(11), 7021–7030 (2010)
15. Venter, T.: Brownfield development is the new green for sustainable mine-dump redevelopment. Town Reg. Plan. **76**, 42–55 (2020)
16. Mosey, G., Heimiller, D., Dahle, D., Vimmerstedt, L., Brady-Sabeff, L.: Converting limbo lands to energy-generating stations: renewable energy technologies on underused, formerly contaminated sites (No. EPA/600/R-08–023; NREL/TP-640–41522). National Renewable Energy Lab, Golden (2007)
17. Uyarra, E., Gee, S.: Transforming urban waste into sustainable material and energy usage: the case of Greater Manchester (UK). J. Clean. Prod. **50**, 101–110 (2013)
18. Matchak, P.: Proposed reuse and redevelopment of the Salem harbor power station, Salem, Massachusetts. University of Massachusetts (2012)
19. Wang, L., Fang, L., Hipel, K.W.: Negotiation over costs and benefits in brownfield redevelopment. Group Decis. Negot. **20**, 509–524 (2011)
20. Morano, P., Tajani, F., Locurcio, M.: GIS application and econometric analysis for the verification of the financial feasibility of roof-top wind turbines in the city of Bari (Italy). Renew. Sustain. Energy Rev. **70**, 999–1010 (2017)
21. Locurcio, M., Morano, P., Tajani, F., Di Liddo, F.: An innovative GIS-based territorial information tool for the evaluation of corporate properties: an application to the Italian context. Sustainability **12**(14), 5836 (2020)
22. Wyatt, P.J.: The development of a GIS-based property information system for real estate valuation. Int. J. Geogr. Inf. Sci. **11**(5), 435–450 (1997)

23. Ahmad, N., Zhu, Y., Lin, H., Geng, L.: Integrating triangular fuzzy numbers & grey relational theory to evaluate brownfield redevelopment projects. In: 2017 IEEE International Conference on Systems, Man, and Cybernetics, pp. 3495–3500 (2017)

24. Aktas, C.B., Bartholomew, P., Church, S.: Application of GIS to prioritize brownfield sites for green building construction based on LEED criteria. J. Urban Plan. Dev. **143**(3), 04017004 (2017)

25. Thomas, M.R.: A GIS-based decision support system for brownfield redevelopment. Landsc. Urban Plan. **58**(1), 7–23 (2002)

26. Li, H., Yu, L., Cheng, E.W.: A GIS-based site selection system for real estate projects. Constr. Innov. **5**(4), 231–241 (2005)

27. Zeng, T.Q., Zhou, Q.: Optimal spatial decision-making using GIS: a prototype of a real estate geographical information system (REGIS). Int. J. Geogr. Inf. Sci. **15**(4), 307–321 (2001)

28. Archdaily. https://www.archdaily.com/475507/frac-of-the-north-region-lacaton-and-vassal?ad_medium=office_landing&ad_name=article. Accessed 21 Feb 2023

29. Bullen, P.A., Love, P.E.: Adaptive reuse of heritage buildings. Struct. Surv. **8** (2011)

30. Anelli, D., Tajani, F.: Spatial decision support systems for effective ex-ante risk evaluation: an innovative model for improving the real estate redevelopment processes. Land Use Policy **128**, 1–16 (2023)

31. Tajani, F., Morano, P., Di Liddo, F.: The optimal combinations of the eligible functions in multiple property assets enhancement. Land Use Policy **99**, 1–11 (2020). 105050

32. Sauter, V.: Decision Support Systems: An Applied Managerial Approach. Wiley, Hoboken (1997)

33. Geoportale Roma. https://geoportale.cittametropolitanaroma.it/attivita-del-gis. Accessed 21 Feb 2023

34. Gritti, A., Fontana, G.L.: Architecture at Work. Towns and Landscape of Industrial Heritage. Forma Edizioni srl, Florence (2020)

35. Torelli, E.: Roma memorie della città industriale: storia e riuso di fabbriche e servizi nei primi quartieri produttivi. Palombi, Roma (2007)

36. Urbanistica Comune di Roma. http://www.urbanistica.comune.roma.it/partec-ex-fiera.html. Accessed 21 Feb 2023

37. Urbanistica Comune di Roma. http://www.urbanistica.comune.roma.it/concorsi/centro-cultur ale-tormarancia.html. Accessed 21 Feb 2023

38. Tajani, F., Guarini, M.R., Sica, F., Ranieri, R., Anelli, D.: Multi-criteria analysis and sustainable accounting. Defining indices of sustainability under Choquet's integral. Sustainability **14**(5), 2782 (2022)

39. Morano, P., Tajani, F., Di Liddo, F., La Spina, I.: The evaluation in the urban projects planning: a logical-deductive model for the definition of "warning areas" in the Esquilino District in the City of Rome (Italy). Smart Cities **6**(1), 469–490 (2023)

40. Spatari, G., Lorè, I., Viglianisi, A., Calabrò, F.: Economic Feasibility of an Integrated Program for the Enhancement of the Byzantine Heritage in the Aspromonte National Park. The Case of Staiti. In: Calabrò F., Della Spina L., Piñeira Mantiñán M.J. (eds.), New Metropolitan Perspectives, NMP 2022. Lecture Notes in Networks and Systems, LNNS, vol. 482, pp. 313–323.Springer, Cham (2022). https://doi.org/10.1007/978-3-031-06825-6_30

41. Calabrò, F., Mafrici, F., Meduri, T.: The valuation of unused public buildings in support of policies for the inner areas. the application of sostec model in a case study in Condofuri (Reggio Calabria, Italy). In: Bevilacqua C., Calabrò F., Della Spina L. (eds.) New Metropolitan Perspectives, NMP 2020. Smart Innovation, Systems and Technologies, SIST, vol. 178, pp. 566–579. Springer, Cham (2021). https://doi.org/10.1007/978-3-030-48279-4_54

42. Massimo, D.E., Del Giudice, V., Malerba, A., Bernardo, C., Musolino, M., De Paola, P.: Valuation of ecological retrofitting technology in existing buildings: a real-world case study. Sustainability **13**(13), 7001 (2021)

A Methodological Approach for the Assessment of Parametric Costs of Sustainable Urban Roads: An Application to the City of Rome (Italy)

Spartaco Paris[1] ⓘ, Francesco Tajani[2](✉) ⓘ, Elisa Pennacchia[2], Rossana Ranieri[2] ⓘ, and Felicia Di Liddo[3]

[1] Department of Structural and Geotechnical Engineering, Sapienza University of Rome, 00196 Rome, Italy
[2] Department of Architecture and Design, Sapienza University of Rome, 00196 Rome, Italy
francesco.tajani@uniroma1.it
[3] Department of Civil, Environmental, Land, Building Engineering and Chemistry, Polytechnic University of Bari, 70125 Bari, Italy

Abstract. In the context of the maintenance of urban and extra-urban road infrastructures, the need to support Public Administrations in the selection of technological solutions able to, on one hand, pursue compliance with i) environmental issue, ii) urban planning and iii) protection of cultural and landscape heritage regulations, and, on the other hand, to be financially sustainable, is relevant. The aim of the present research concerns the definition of a methodological approach for the assessment of the parametric costs of innovative technological solutions, by taking into account their differentials compared to the traditional ones, i.e. the solutions generally applied in the considered contexts. With reference to twenty roads located into the city of Rome (Italy), assumed as case studies, the parametric costs for the traditional solutions and the innovative ones have been built, by evaluating all the working expenses that occur for their realization. Finally, the cost differentials between them have been highlighted.

Keywords: Urban roads infrastructures · parametric costs · working · evaluation

1 Introduction

It is widely agreed that the construction industry contributes significantly to pollution, resource depletion, waste generation, global warming, and climate change [1]. The last years has been characterized by a scarce public economic resources availability that has determined the increasing need to develop adequate evaluation tools for the optimization of their allocation (especially with reference to the current and relevant European funding) [2]. Within the mentioned framework, the main driver of the building sector has concerned the refurbishment and redevelopment investments [3, 4]. With reference to the topic of the present research, the construction and the maintenance of the road infrastructures constitutes an intensive process. The finished structure strongly impacts the aesthetics of the urban context and can affect the noise pollution and, in general terms, the existing ecosystem [5–9].

From a quality point of view, the pavements in urban spaces are one of the largest and significant elements in defining the perception of the urban landscape, both aesthetically and functionally. The surfaces of these areas must respond to multiple needs, by including the perceptive-landscape and historical-iconographic nature and guaranteeing high levels of safety, well-being, usability and liveability. Therefore, the urban infrastructures should have functional requirements according to their type of use that, necessarily, affects the choice of the materials and layings.

The resurfacing of an urban pavement requires, where it is possible, the preservation of the construction traditions of the site, by respecting its material and chromatic characteristics, and by considering climatic and lighting conditions and the needs for comfort, efficiency and sustainability [10].

Effective road design can make a significant contribution not only to mobility, but also to the environment through, for example, the planting of trees, the adoption of specific materials to improve the microclimate, to reduce air and noise pollution, and to increase the resilience of the urban system [11, 12]. In fact, the road pavements construction sector is constantly evolving both to optimise the performance and the durability levels and to pursue goals such as i) the reduction of air pollution, ii) the decrease of noise pollution, iii) the decline of heat island, iv) the increase of the water drainage, v) the improvement of the energy efficiency, vi) the growth of the perceptive quality.

In order to support the Public Administration in the selection of effective technological solutions for the urban road infrastructure, the aim of the present research is to define a methodological approach to compare the costs of traditional technologies and innovative ones. The pursued objective is developed with reference to the case study, i.e. by considering twenty roads in the city of Rome (Italy), and by determining a parametric cost for the construction and maintenance of road infrastructures. The obtained outputs could constitute a valid support for the local Public Administration, within the preliminary assessment phases of the projects, for an effective allocation of the available resources. In fact, the results of the present analysis consists of useful economic references both for the different types of interventions generally carried out and for those related to the innovative solutions.

The paper is organized in the following Sections. In Sect. 2, the methodological approach and its main phases are illustrated. In Sect. 3, the conclusions and possible further insights are drawn.

2 Methodological Approach

The methodological approach proposed in the present research is illustrated with reference to the chosen case study, referred to twenty roads located into the city of Rome (Italy). The assessment of the parametric costs and the determination of the percentage cost differentials between the traditional solutions referred to an ordinary maintenance intervention of the selected roads and the innovative ones, require the following five phases implementation:

1. Systematic analysis of the tendering procedures (active and performed), within the road infrastructures pertaining to the *Dipartimento Sviluppo Infrastrutture e Manutenzione Urbana* (CSIMU) [13], included in the city of Rome. This phase has firstly allowed to identify the categories of workings that mostly contribute to defining the construction costs of the interventions, as well as the main types of project on the road infrastructures.
2. Evaluation of the parametric construction costs per type of performance solution related to the traditional interventions, i.e. defined in the technical and economic documents of the Master Agreement for the *"Ordinary maintenance and emergency maintenance of the roads of the so-called Grande Viabilità, the roads of EUR, the Tramway Headquarters and the relevant works of art (bridges, tunnels, overpasses, subways, etc.) - divided into twelve lots for the three-year period 2021–2023"* (hereinafter the "Master Agreement") [14]. In this phase, the classification of the workings set in the Master Agreement ("superficial", "medium", "deep", "deep-bis") has been borrowed, by considering the macro-categories of workings constituting the roadway (e.g. pavements, and driveway paving). For each of them, an estimated metric calculation has been developed for the assessment of the parametric cost ($€/m^2$), by adopting the Price List of the Lazio Region updated to 2022 for the unit workings costs identification [15].
3. Determination of the parametric cross-sectional costs per longitudinal linear meter related to the twenty roads included in the case study and with reference to the classification of the traditional interventions reported by the Master Agreement. These values have been assessed by parameterizing the construction costs per linear meter of road, taking into account the actual cross-sectional dimension of the different components for each of the identified twenty roads.
4. Estimation of the parametric construction costs for the designed innovative solutions. This phase has allowed to obtain at both a cost per square meter, by remodeling the cost items of the workings related to the traditional interventions through the improved technological solutions, and at a new parametric cost per longitudinal linear meter for the twenty roads identified as case studies.
5. Calculation of the percentage cost differentials between the traditional solutions referred to a possible ordinary maintenance of the chosen roads and the planned innovative ones.

2.1 Phase 1: Systematic Analysis of the Tendering Procedures

The analysis has been carried out by consulting primarily two online portals made available by the Municipality of Rome, one referring to all workings and services tenders [16], and the other one specifically dedicated to road infrastructure maintenance [17].

In order to draw up a representative framework of the reference context, both the documents of tenders with the traditional procedure and those referring to the Master Agreement have been considered. Firstly, from the processing of the collected data, it has been possible to identify the most recurring workings categories, and, for these, the percentage of incidence on the total cost of the intervention has been calculated. This analysis allows to verify the empirical evidence, by highlighting that the categories of workings related to the driveway component of the road infrastructure (as binder and layering) are those that mostly contribute to the definition of the total intervention cost (Fig. 1).

Following this analysis, a further research has been carried out with reference to the presence (or absence) of possible new costs related to special or specific workings that could not be attributed to the items already included in the regional reference Price List. In this sense, a list of the "new prices" adopted in the consulted economic documents has been drawn up, as a further market reference for the interventions involving these specific workings.

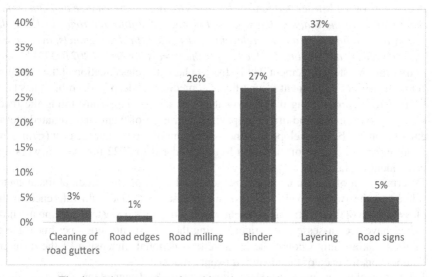

Fig. 1. Main categories of workings in road infrastructure contracts

2.2   Phase 2: Evaluation of the Parametric Construction Costs Per Type of Performance Solution Related to the Traditional Interventions

First of all, it should be highlighted that the analysis of the documentation related to the current Master Agreement has allowed the identification of the different types of performance solution for each type of intervention ("superficial", "medium", "deep" and "deep-bis") and for the macro-category of workings, used as a reference for the parametric costs assessment. In particular, the following macro-categories are identified in the Master Agreement:

- sidewalk;
- paved pavements;
- road paving.

For the workings on the pavements, the following categories are distinguished in relation to the used materials:

- type A - bituminous conglomerate pavement;
- type B - poured asphalt pavement;
- type C - basalt slab pavement;
- type D - concrete pavement;
- type E - paved pavement/porphyry.

As far as the paving is concerned, the main differentiation among the types of intervention regards the specific envisaged workings, which are progressively (from "superficial" to "deep-bis") more substantial and relevant.

In order to determine the parametric cost of each performance solution distinguished by type of intervention ("superficial", "medium", "deep" and "deep-bis") and with respect to the used materials, for the fundamental portions that characterize the road resurfacing interventions (pavements and carriageway), the stratigraphy of the performance solutions defined in the Master Agreement has been analyzed.

The construction unit costs to be associated with the different layers identified in each section relating to the "driveway pavement" and "pavement" components have been borrowed by the Lazio Region 2022 Price List and the unit of measurement has been specified. The aggregation of the different unit prices in the parametric cost of the intervention has been carried out by considering a portion of the road of 1 m^2 (1 m for the length x 1 m for the width).

In this way, to each performance solution a parametric cost has been associated: this differs according to the considered workings, the type of intervention ("superficial", "medium", "deep" and "deep-bis") and the used materials.

As an example, Table 1 reports the analytical calculation for one typological section related to the sidewalk of the Master Agreement. The assessed parametric cost is equal to 47.76 €/m^2.

This type of calculation has been performed for all the traditional materials included in the Master Agreement. The synthesis of this analysis is reported in Tables 2, 3 and 4.

Table 1. Calculation for the sidewalk in bituminous conglomerate - "superficial" type

Working description	Quantity	Unit of measurement	Unit cost [€]	Total cost [€]	Code of the Lazio Region 2022 Price List
Demolition of existent pavement	0.80	m^2	5.61	4.49	A 03 01 015 j
Alignment road edges or substitution (when needed)	0.80	m	25.96	25.96	B 1 06 6 b
Foundation curb	0.01	m^3	185.99	1.86	A 06 01 001 01 a
New paving in bituminous conglomerate	0.80	m^2	19.32	15.46	B 01 05 005

Table 2. Summary of the assessed parametric costs related to sidewalk work [€/m^2]

Type	Bituminous conglomerate	Asphalt	Basalt	Concrete pavements	Paved pavements
Superficial	47.76	49.46	201.32	70.78	159.69
Medium	69.26	70.95	221.60	89.94	186.11
Deep	116.43	118.12	257.92	137.11	
Deep-bis	118.86	120.56	260.36	139.55	

Table 3. Summary of assessed parametric costs related to paving work [€/m^2]

Type	Bituminous conglomerate
A1 – Squared	147.99
A2 – Round	195.61

Table 4. Summary of assessed parametric costs related to road works [€/m²]

Type	Bituminous conglomerate
B1	12.19
B2	16.25
B3	20.31
B4	34.31
B5	33.26
B6	71.34

2.3 Phase 3 and Phase 4: Determination of the Parametric Cross-Sectional Costs for the Traditional Solutions and for the Designed Innovative Ones

For each of the twenty roads identified as case studies in the city of Rome, an assessment of the parametric costs per longitudinal linear meter of section has been carried out. The selected roads have been defined as representative of the heterogeneity of the city's road system, that includes "main" and "local" types streets. In Fig. 2 the types and the specific roads considered are reported.

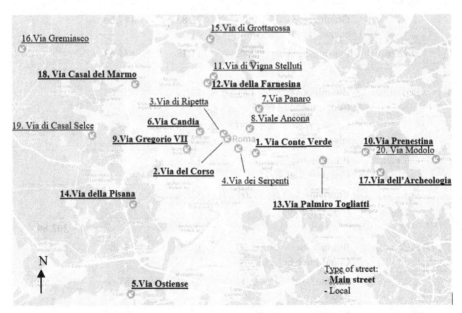

Fig. 2. Identification of the selected twenty roads located in the city of Rome

Table 5. Evaluation of the parametric construction costs for the traditional solutions

n	Type of function	Material	Length [m]	Unit cost [€/m^2]	Total cost [€/m]	Parametric cost [€/m]
1	Pedestrian	Bituminous Conglomerate	3.10	12.19	37.79	
		Granite road edges	2.00	93.83	187.66	
	Car Park	Bituminous Conglomerate	10.00	12.19	121.90	
	Driveway	Bituminous Conglomerate	11.50	12.19	140.19	
						487.53
2	Pedestrian	Basalt slabs	9.60	114.67	1 100.83	
		Granite road edges	2.00	93.83	187.66	
	Driveway	Bituminous Conglomerate	5.30	12.19	64.61	
						1 353.10
3	Pedestrian	Basalt slabs	2.60	114.67	298.14	
		Granite road edges	2.00	93.83	187.66	
	Driveway	Pavement paving	7.48	111.18	831.63	
						1 317.43
4	Pedestrian	Bituminous Conglomerate	4.81	12.19	58.63	
		Granite road edges	1.00	93.83	93.83	
	Car Park	Bituminous Conglomerate	6.70	12.19	81.67	
	Driveway	Bituminous Conglomerate	5.64	12.19	68.75	
						302.89
5	Pedestrian	Bituminous Conglomerate	2.60	12.19	31.69	
		Granite road edges	2.00	93.83	187.66	
	Driveway	Bituminous Conglomerate	23.35	12.19	284.64	

(*continued*)

Table 5. (*continued*)

n	Type of function	Material	Length [m]	Unit cost [€/m^2]	Total cost [€/m]	Parametric cost [€/m]
	Car Park	Bituminous Conglomerate	8.50	12.19	103.62	
						607.61
6	Pedestrian	Bituminous Conglomerate	5.00	12.19	60.95	
		Granite road edges	2.00	93.83	187.66	
	Car Park	Bituminous Conglomerate	5.00	12.19	60.95	
	Driveway	Bituminous Conglomerate	9.00	12.19	109.71	
						419.27
7	Pedestrian	Bituminous Conglomerate	6.32	12.19	77.04	
		Granite road edges	2.00	93.83	187.66	
	Car Park	Bituminous Conglomerate	6.85	12.19	83.50	
	Driveway	Bituminous Conglomerate	5.90	12.19	71.92	
						420.12
8	Pedestrian	Bituminous Conglomerate	5.00	12.19	60.95	
		Granite road edges	2.00	93.83	187.66	
	Car Park	Bituminous Conglomerate	6.55	12.19	79.84	
	Driveway	Bituminous Conglomerate	3.50	12.19	42.67	
						371.12
9	Pedestrian	Bituminous Conglomerate	8.60	12.19	104.83	
		Granite road edges	2.00	93.83	187.66	

(*continued*)

Table 5. (*continued*)

n	Type of function	Material	Length [m]	Unit cost [€/m²]	Total cost [€/m]	Parametric cost [€/m]
	Cycle path	Bituminous Conglomerate	3.00	12.19	36.57	
	Car Park	Bituminous Conglomerate	10.00	12.19	121.90	
	Driveway	Bituminous Conglomerate	9.00	12.19	109.71	
	Driveway pref	Bituminous Conglomerate	6.00	12.19	73.14	
						633.81
10	Pedestrian	Bituminous Conglomerate	8.40	12.19	102.40	
		Granite road edges	4.00	93.83	375.32	
	Cycle path	Bituminous Conglomerate	3.00	12.19	36.57	
	Car Park	Bituminous Conglomerate	5.00	12.19	60.95	
	Driveway	Bituminous Conglomerate	20.49	12.19	249.77	
	Quay	Paving in concrete	1.30	64.79	84.23	
						909.24
11	Pedestrian	Bituminous Conglomerate	5.09	12.19	62.05	
		Granite road edges	2.00	93.83	187.66	
	Car Park	Bituminous Conglomerate	5.00	12.19	60.95	
	Driveway	Bituminous Conglomerate	8.67	12.19	105.69	
						416.34
12	Pedestrian	Bituminous Conglomerate	2.95	12.19	35.96	

(*continued*)

Table 5. (*continued*)

n	Type of function	Material	Length [m]	Unit cost [€/m²]	Total cost [€/m]	Parametric cost [€/m]
		Travertino road edges	2.00	43.87	87.74	
	Driveway	Bituminous Conglomerate	12.40	12.19	151.16	
						274.86
13	Pedestrian	Bituminous Conglomerate	10.74	12.19	130.92	
		Travertino road edges	3.00	43.87	131.61	
	Cycle path	Bituminous Conglomerate	2.00	12.19	24.38	
	Car Park	Bituminous Conglomerate	5.68	12.19	69.24	
	Driveway	Bituminous Conglomerate	19.23	12.19	234.41	
	Driveway	Bituminous Conglomerate	7.57	15.85	119.96	
						710.53
14	Pedestrian	Bituminous Conglomerate	2.60	12.19	31.69	
		Travertino road edges	2.00	43.87	87.74	
	Car Park	Bituminous Conglomerate	7.80	12.19	95.08	
	Driveway	Bituminous Conglomerate	7.20	12.19	87.77	
						302.28
15	Pedestrian	Bituminous Conglomerate	3.20	12.19	39.01	
		Travertino road edges	2.00	43.87	87.74	
	Driveway	Bituminous Conglomerate	6.80	12.19	82.89	

(*continued*)

Table 5. (*continued*)

n	Type of function	Material	Length [m]	Unit cost [€/m^2]	Total cost [€/m]	Parametric cost [€/m]
						209.64
16	Pedestrian	Bituminous Conglomerate	2.58	12.19	31.45	
	Driveway	Bituminous Conglomerate	7.11	12.19	86.67	
						118.12
17	Pedestrian	Bituminous Conglomerate	4.34	12.19	52.90	
		Travertino road edges	2.00	43.87	87.74	
	Driveway	Bituminous Conglomerate	13.23	12.19	161.27	
						301.92
18	Pedestrian	Bituminous Conglomerate	1.35	12.19	16.46	
		Travertino road edges	1.00	43.87	43.87	
	Driveway	Bituminous Conglomerate	8.03	12.19	97.89	
						158.21
19	Pedestrian	Bituminous Conglomerate	2.00	12.19	24.38	
		Travertino road edges	1.00	43.87	43.87	
	Driveway	Bituminous Conglomerate	7.00	12.19	85.33	
						153.58
20	Pedestrian	Bituminous Conglomerate	2.60	12.19	31.69	
		Travertino road edges	2.00	43.87	87.74	
	Driveway	Bituminous Conglomerate	16.36	12.19	199.43	
						318.86

For each road, the existing road section, the main components of the infrastructure (pedestrian, car park, driveway), the characteristics and types of performance solutions adopted for its construction and their main dimensions have been studied. Starting from this analysis, the appropriate costs included in the Lazio Region 2022 Price List have been identified. Then, the costs for one meter of road section have been assessed, taking into account the ordinary maintenance interventions, and the cost of the workings envisaged by the proposed design guidelines has been evaluated. The parametric cost has been obtained in € per meter in the longitudinal direction, since the width of the road and the subdivision of its parts are known both from the survey and from the project. Tables 5 and 6 show, respectively, the parametric costs assessed for the twenty roads, by considering the traditional solutions and the innovative ones.

Table 6. Evaluation of the parametric construction costs for the designed innovative solutions

n	Type of function	Material	Length [m]	Unit cost [€/m²]	Total cost [€/m]	Parametric cost [€/m]
1	Pedestrian	Basalt slabs	3.30	114.67	378.41	
		Granite road edges	1.00	93.83	93.83	
	Car Park	Drainage paving	10.00	138.98	1 389.75	
	Driveway	Draining bituminous conglomerate	11.50	17.07	196.26	
						2 058.25
2	Pedestrian	Basalt slabs	10.00	114.67	1 146.70	
		Granite road edges	2.00	93.83	187.66	
	Driveway	Drainage paving	5.30	138.98	736.57	
						2 070.93
3	Pedestrian	Basalt slabs	3.00	114.67	344.01	
		Granite road edges	1.00	93.83	93.83	
	Driveway	Drainage paving	7.48	138.98	1 039.53	
						1 477.37

(*continued*)

Table 6. (*continued*)

n	Type of function	Material	Length [m]	Unit cost [€/m²]	Total cost [€/m]	Parametric cost [€/m]
4	Pedestrian	Drainage paving	5.01	138.98	696.26	
		Granite road edges	1.00	93.83	93.83	
	Car Park	Drainage paving	6.70	138.98	931.13	
	Driveway	Drainage paving	5.64	138.98	783.82	
						2 505.05
5	Pedestrian	Draining bituminous conglomerate	2.60	17.07	44.37	
		Granite road edges	2.00	93.83	187.66	
	Driveway	Draining bituminous conglomerate	23.35	17.07	398.49	
	Car Park	Draining bituminous conglomerate	8.50	17.07	145.06	
						775.58
6	Pedestrian	Draining bituminous conglomerate	3.40	17.07	58.02	
		Granite road edges	2.00	93.83	187.66	
	Car Park	Drainage paving	5.00	138.98	694.88	
	Driveway	Draining bituminous conglomerate	9.00	17.07	153.59	
						1 094.15
7	Pedestrian	Draining bituminous conglomerate	6.32	17.07	107.86	

(*continued*)

Table 6. (*continued*)

n	Type of function	Material	Length [m]	Unit cost [€/m^2]	Total cost [€/m]	Parametric cost [€/m]
		Granite road edges	2.00	93.83	187.66	
	Car Park	Eco-active screeds	6.85	50.71	347.34	
	Driveway	Draining bituminous conglomerate	5.90	17.07	100.69	
						743.54
8	Pedestrian	Draining bituminous conglomerate	5.00	17.07	85.33	
		Granite road edges	2.00	93.83	187.66	
	Car Park	Draining bituminous conglomerate	6.55	17.07	111.78	
	Driveway	Draining bituminous conglomerate	3.50	17.07	59.73	
						444.50
9	Pedestrian	Basalt slabs	8.60	114.67	986.16	
		Granite road edges	2.00	93.83	187.66	
	Cycle path	Draining colored bituminous conglomerate	3.00	41.04	123.12	
	Car Park	Drainage paving	10.00	138.98	1 389.75	
	Driveway	Draining bituminous conglomerate	9.00	17.07	153.59	

(*continued*)

Table 6. (*continued*)

n	Type of function	Material	Length [m]	Unit cost [€/m²]	Total cost [€/m]	Parametric cost [€/m]
	Driveway pref	Draining bituminous conglomerate	6.00	17.07	102.40	
						2 942.69
10	Pedestrian	Draining bituminous conglomerate	8.40	17.07	143.35	
		Granite road edges	4.00	93.83	375.32	
	Cycle path	Draining bituminous conglomerate	3.00	17.07	51.20	
	Car Park	Draining bituminous conglomerate	5.00	17.07	85.33	
	Driveway	Draining bituminous conglomerate	12.30	17.07	209.91	
	Dock	Draining bituminous conglomerate	1.30	138.98	180.67	
						1 045.78
11	Pedestrian	Basalt slabs	5.09	114.67	583.67	
		Granite road edges	2.00	93.83	187.66	
	Car Park	Draining bituminous conglomerate	5.00	17.07	85.33	
	Driveway	Drainage paving	8.67	138.98	1 204.91	
						2 061.57
12	Pedestrian	Draining bituminous conglomerate	2.95	17.07	50.34	

(*continued*)

Table 6. (*continued*)

n	Type of function	Material	Length [m]	Unit cost [€/m²]	Total cost [€/m]	Parametric cost [€/m]
		Travertino road edges	2.00	43.87	87.74	
	Driveway	Draining bituminous conglomerate	12.40	17.07	211.62	
						349.70
13	Pedestrian	Draining bituminous conglomerate	10.74	17.07	183.29	
		Travertino road edges	3.00	43.87	131.61	
	Cycle path	Draining colored bituminous conglomerate	2.00	41.04	82.08	
	Car Park	Draining bituminous conglomerate	5.68	17.07	96.93	
	Driveway	Draining bituminous conglomerate	19.23	17.07	328.18	
	Driveway interrail	Draining bituminous conglomerate	7.57	22.19	167.95	
						990.04
14	Pedestrian	Draining bituminous conglomerate	2.60	17.07	44.37	
		Travertino road edges	2.00	43.87	87.74	
	Car Park	Draining bituminous conglomerate	7.80	17.07	133.11	
	Driveway	Draining bituminous conglomerate	7.20	17.07	122.88	
						388.10

(*continued*)

Table 6. (*continued*)

n	Type of function	Material	Length [m]	Unit cost [€/m^2]	Total cost [€/m]	Parametric cost [€/m]
15	Pedestrian	Draining bituminous conglomerate	3.20	17.07	54.61	
		Travertino road edges	2.00	43.87	87.74	
	Driveway	Draining bituminous conglomerate	6.80	17.07	116.05	
						258.40
16	Pedestrian	Draining bituminous conglomerate	2.18	17.07	37.20	
		Travertino road edges	2.00	43.87	87.74	
	Driveway	Draining bituminous conglomerate	7.11	17.07	121.34	
						246.28
17	Pedestrian	Draining bituminous conglomerate	9.67	17.07	165.03	
		Travertino road edges	4.00	43.87	175.48	
	Driveway	Draining bituminous conglomerate	10.23	17.07	174.59	
	Cycle path	Colored bituminous conglomerate	2.60	41.04	106.71	
	Car Park	Draining bituminous conglomerate	11.25	17.07	191.99	

(*continued*)

Table 6. (*continued*)

n	Type of function	Material	Length [m]	Unit cost [€/m²]	Total cost [€/m]	Parametric cost [€/m]
						813.79
18	Pedestrian	Draining bituminous conglomerate	1.35	17.07	23.04	
		Travertino road edges	1.00	43.87	43.87	
	Driveway	Draining bituminous conglomerate	8.03	17.07	137.04	
						203.95
19	Pedestrian	Draining bituminous conglomerate	2.00	17.07	34.13	
		Travertino road edges	1.00	43.87	43.87	
	Driveway	Draining bituminous conglomerate	7.00	17.07	119.46	
						197.46
20	Pedestrian	Draining bituminous conglomerate	2.60	17.07	44.37	
		Travertino road edges	2.00	43.87	87.74	
	Driveway	Draining bituminous conglomerate	16.36	17.07	279.20	
						411.31

Phase 5: Calculation of the percentage cost differentials between the traditional solutions and the innovative ones.

Once calculated the costs both for the traditional and the innovative solutions, the percentage cost differentials between the two types of solutions have been calculated (Table 7) The results have allowed to provide the Municipal Administration with a relevant and useful indication on the main categories of workings that affect the total cost of the maintenance of urban road infrastructures interventions and the relative contribution. It is evident that the main differences occur when a significant change in the materials choice are planned, or new elements are considered for the realization and include in the overall project (e.g. a cycle path).

It should be noted that for both the parametric costs evaluation - traditional and innovative one - the road infrastructure subgrades have been assumed unchanged: therefore, the construction cost of the interventions has been estimated referring only to the surface component of the system.

Table 7. Comparison between the assessed parametric costs of traditional and innovative solutions for the considered twenty roads

No	Traditional solution	Innovative solution	Delta
	Parametric cost [€/m]	Parametric cost [€/m]	
1	487.53	2 058.25	322%
2	1 353.10	2 070.93	53%
3	1 317.43	1 477.37	12%
4	302.89	2 505.05	727%
5	607.61	775.58	28%
6	419.27	1 094.15	161%
7	420.12	743.54	77%
8	371.12	444.50	20%
9	633.81	2 942.69	364%
10	909.24	1 045.78	15%
11	416.34	2 061.57	395%
12	274.86	349.70	27%
13	710.53	990.04	39%
14	302.28	388.10	28%
15	209.64	258.40	23%
16	118.12	246.28	109%
17	301.92	813.79	170%
18	158.21	203.95	29%
19	153.58	197.46	29%
20	318.86	411.31	29%

3   Conclusions

In the present research a methodological approach for the assessment of parametric costs of innovative technological solutions related to urban road infrastructures intervention has been proposed. In particular, the developed operational tool represents a valid reference for the Public Administrations: it allows to calculate the parametric construction cost differentials between the traditional solutions (those generally applied in the considered contexts) and the innovative ones. In this sense, the approach can be applied at two different levels, from the urban scale to the construction details and technical architectural design specifications. The proposed five phases implementation intends to pursue a harmonic management of maintenance interventions of the urban road pavements, in order to interrupt the current process of fragmentation that frequently characterises the cities' road systems.

The application of the approach to the case study related to twenty roads located in the city of Rome has pointed out, on the one hand, the heterogeneity and richness of the different urban tissues, and, on the other hand, the opportunity to differentiate the intervention strategies consistently with the considered context [18].

The design experimentation activity has been subsequently checked for suggestions and recommendations in order to update the parametric reference costs for maintenance workings (mainly extraordinary) and for performance specifications. In this direction, a dynamic and continuously updatable system of street mapping, starting from the elaboration and updating of digital mapping in open form, could be carried out. Therefore, future insights of the research may concern the development of a digital mapping of the roads within the competence of the CSIMU in GIS environment [19–22], in order to test the management of maintenance interventions of the entire road network and public spaces of the city of Rome and to export the developed approach to other national and international contexts.

References

1. Cheng, E.W., Chiang, Y.H., Tang, B.S.: Exploring the economic impact of construction pollution by disaggregating the construction sector of the input–output table. Build. Environ. **41**(12), (2006)
2. Tajani, F., Di Liddo, F., Ranieri, R.: The effective use of national recovery and resilience plan funding: a methodological approach for the optimal assessment of the initiative costs. Land **11**(10), 1812 (2022)
3. Morano, P., Tajani, F., Di Liddo, F., Anelli, D.: A feasibility analysis of the refurbishment investments in the Italian residential market. Sustainability **12**(6), 2503 (2020)
4. Tajani, F., Morano, P., Di Liddo, F., Doko, E.: A model for the assessment of the economic benefits associated with energy retrofit interventions: an application to existing buildings in the Italian territory. Appl. Sci. **12**(7), 3385 (2022)
5. Zhang, M., Liu, X., Ding, Y.: Assessing the influence of urban transportation infrastructure construction on haze pollution in China: a case study of Beijing-Tianjin-Hebei region. Environ. Impact Assess. Rev. **87**, 106547 (2021)
6. Giunta, M.: Assessment of the impact of co, nox and pm10 on air quality during road construction and operation phases. Sustainability **12**(24), 10549 (2020)
7. Sun, C., Zhang, W., Luo, Y., Li, J.: Road construction and air quality: empirical study of cities in China. J. Clean. Prod. **319**, 128649 (2021)
8. Morano, P., Tajani, F., Di Liddo, F., Darò, M.: Economic evaluation of the indoor environmental quality of buildings: the noise pollution effects on housing prices in the city of Bari (Italy). Buildings **11**(5), 213 (2021)
9. Tarimo, M., Wondimu, P., Odeck, J., Lohne, J., Lædre, O.: Sustainable roads in Serengeti national park: gravel roads construction and maintenance. Procedia Comput. Sci. **121**, 329–336 (2017)

10. Shackel, B., Ball, J., Mearing, M.: Using permeable eco-paving to achieve improved water quality for urban pavements. In: Proceedings of 7th International Conference on Concrete Block Paving (2003)
11. Akbari, H., Pomerantz, M., Taha, H.: Cool surfaces and shade trees to reduce energy use and improve air quality in urban areas. Sol. Energy **70**(3), 295–310 (2001)
12. Marchioni, M., Becciu, G.: Experimental results on permeable pavements in urban areas: a synthetic review. Int. J. Sustain. Dev. Plan. **10**(6), 806–817 (2015)
13. CSIMU. https://www.comune.roma.it/web/it/dipartimento-sviluppo-infrastrutture-e-manutenzione-urbana-uffici-e-contatti.page. Accessed 14 Feb 2023
14. Tuttogare. https://gare.comune.roma.it/gare/id28128-dettaglio. Accessed 21 Feb 2023
15. Regione Lazio. https://www.regione.lazio.it/cittadini/lavori-pubblici-infrastrutture/tariffa-prezzi-lavori-pubblici. Accessed 18 Feb 2023
16. Tuttogare. https://gare.comune.roma.it/gare/. Accessed 19 Feb 2023
17. StradeNuove. http://www.comune.roma.it/servizi2/stradenuove/index.jsp. Accessed 21 Feb 2023
18. Carneiro, J., Rossetti, R.J., Silva, D.C., Oliveira, E.C.: BIM, GIS, IoT, and AR/VR integration for smart maintenance and management of road networks: a review. In: 2018 IEEE International Smart Cities Conference (ISC2), pp. 1–7 IEEE (2017)
19. Corazza, M.V., D'Alessandro, D., Di Mascio, P., Moretti, L.: Methodology and evidence from a case study in Rome to increase pedestrian safety along home-to-school routes. J. Traffic Transp. Eng. **7**(5), 715–727 (2020)
20. Shrestha, P.P., Pradhananga, N.: GIS-based road maintenance management. In: Computing in Civil Engineering, pp. 472–484 (2009)
21. Pantha, B.R., Yatabe, R., Bhandary, N.P.: GIS-based highway maintenance prioritization model: an integrated approach for highway maintenance in Nepal Mountains. J. Transp. Geogr. **18**(3), 426–433 (2010)
22. Kramberger, T., Žerovnik, J., Štrubelj, G., Prah, K.: GIS technology as an environment for testing an advanced mathematical model for optimization of road maintenance. CEJOR **21**, 59–73 (2013)

The Usufruct Right as an Effective Strategy for the Enhancement of Properties in Disuse

Marco Locurcio[1]([✉]), Pierluigi Morano[1], Francesco Tajani[2], and Rossana Ranieri[2]

[1] Department of Civil, Environmental, Land, Building Engineering and Chemistry (DICATECh), Polytechnic University of Bari, 70126 Bari, Italy
marco.locurcio@poliba.it

[2] Department of Architecture and Design, "Sapienza" University of Rome, 00196 Rome, Italy

Abstract. The aim of the present research is to highlight the central role of the usufruct right in the context of property valuations, in particular with reference to the need of supporting the Public Administration (PA) in the proper definition of effective strategies in order to achieve its real estate objectives while containing financial exposure. Often, public properties are owned by entities that do not have the skills and the spending capacity required for their enhancement, which causes the progressive degradation of the assets with a negative impact on the entire territory in which they are located. Such assets, even when placed in the market for sale, frequently do not attract the interest of market operators due to the constraints and the generally high costs of renovation. PAs, which are interested in the enhancement of their properties, in the positive effects on the surrounding areas and in the benefits to the population, do not have the resources necessary to bear the costs of redevelopment. The case study developed in this research, concerning the valuation of the usufruct right of a building in disuse located in a municipality in Southern Italy, is an opportunity to highlight the potential of this strategy.

Keywords: usufruct · bare ownership · property enhancement · market value · net present value

1 Introduction

Public administrations (PAs) have the need to enhance portions of their real estate assets in order to meet the needs of the community [1]. This need clashes with the scarcity of resources to be allocated to such operations, especially in cases where the PA interested in the valorization of the asset is not the owner because to the considerable costs of valorization and renovation, should also add the amount necessary to acquire ownership of the asset. To contain the acquisition costs associated with the full ownership of an asset, it is possible to take possession of property rights, which still enable the PA to achieve its goals over a medium/long-term horizon and to access the many financing opportunities provided [2]. Specifically, in the Italian legislative framework, it is possible to split ownership into two complementary property rights, namely, usufruct and bare ownership. This allows the usufructuary to enjoy possession of an asset for a specific time horizon, and the bare owner to regain possession of the asset when the usufruct expires; in this sense the usufructuary has to pay the bare owner a monetary amount that restores from the temporary lack of ownership of the asset for the stipulated amount of time. The ownership value, i.e., the market value, is divided into two complementary monetary amounts corresponding to the usufruct and bare ownership rights, which allow the usufructuary to contain the financial exposure in the face of certain limitations, and the bare owner to receive a monetary amount for an asset deemed non-strategic with respect to its purposes.

The objective of this paper is to highlight the central role of the usufruct right in the context of real estate development initiatives, and the importance of supporting the PA in the proper definition of strategies to achieve its goals while containing financial exposure. The case study, concerning the estimation of the usufruct right of a building in disuse located in a municipality in Southern Italy, is an opportunity to highlight the potential of such a strategy.

2   The Usufruct Right

2.1   Legislative Framework

Usufruct is a property right originated in the law of Roman legislative framework of the classical period, found in the legal system of many European (Italy, France, Spain, Germany, etc.), American (USA, Cuba, Guatemala, etc.), Asian (China, Philippines, Thailand, etc.) and African (Ghana, etc.) countries [3, 4]. The analysis of the current literature shows that most of the researches focus on the legal aspects of the partial rights of bare ownership [5–7], and on studies about the methodological and financial issues of the related estimation models [8, 9]. The present research does not focus specifically on the legal or estimation aspects of the usufruct right, but it is aimed in describing the use of this approach as a way to support the enhancement of public properties in contexts characterized by scarcity of resources.

In Italy, usufruct is regulated by Articles 978 et seq. of the Civil Code [10] and consists of the right of a subject (usufructuary) to enjoy a property owned by another subject (bare owner) and to obtain the benefits by applying the diligence of the "good family man" in the management of the property. The usufruct is always temporary and has a duration not exceeding the life of the usufructuary, if the usufructuary is a person, or 30 years, if the usufruct is established in favor of a legal entity. The usufructuary has the right to enjoy the property, but its economic purpose should be respected, and the change of intended use is not allowed. However, the usufructuary could make improvements that do not alter the main use and that should be removed at the end of the right, if this does not damage the property. If this is not possible, the usufructuary is entitled to an indemnity at the time he/she returns the property, equal to the lesser of the amount of the expenditure and the increase in value associated with the improvements. Expenses and, in general, charges related to the custody, administration and ordinary maintenance of the property shall be borne by the usufructuary; extraordinary repairs necessitated by failure to fulfill the obligations of ordinary maintenance shall also be charged by the usufructuary, while extraordinary repairs are up to the owner.

The usufruct is extinguished in the following cases: *i)* by reaching the stipulated term; *ii)* in case of non-use of the property for continuous 20 years; *iii)* by the unification of the usufruct in the same person; *iv)* by the total perishing of the property; *v)* by abuse of the usufructuary.

2.2 Possible Evaluation Approaches

At the time when the right of usufruct occurs, full ownership ceases to exist and usufruct and bare ownership are associated with two different stakeholders, whether natural or legal persons, are created. For estimating the value of usufruct right, i.e., the amount that the usufructuary has to pay to the bare owner to purchase the right of usufruct, it is possible to consider two different approaches: *i)* the one indicated by the "Consolidated Text of Provisions Concerning Registration Tax" [11]; *ii)* the valuation best practices indicates by Appraisal reference. The first approach is designed to determine the tax base to be used for tax purposes, while the second is borrowed from market rationality.

The approach used in this paper refers to valuation practices on usufruct, and the provisions of the Consolidated Act of Provisions Concerning Registration Tax will be only used for comparison purposes. According to estimative best practices, the value of the usufruct right (V_U), is the Net Present Value (NPV) associated with the net cash flows of the usufructuary, in formulas:

$$NPV = \sum_{t=1}^{n} \left[\frac{R}{(1+i)^t} \right] - \left[\frac{C}{(1+i)^t} \right] \tag{1}$$

where R and C are respectively the revenues and costs in the hands of the usufructuary, i the discount rate, t the time point at which the revenues and costs occur, and n the duration of the usufruct right.

Essentially, net income, limited by the duration of the usufruct right, could be equated with a hypothetical rent whose duration is precisely the duration of the usufruct right. Otherwise, it is possible to determine the net income associated with the specific person who will use the property according to the current economic use; this option is scarcely used in valuation practices, because the determination of costs and revenues of the actual user, instead of the rent, makes compliance with the principle of ordinariness more complicated, and it is easy to switch from a generally valid appraisal judgment to a specifically valid one of economic convenience. For these reasons, it is preferred to discern the purely real estate component from that associated with management.

The discount rate, which is necessary to carry forward to the valuation date the amounts that occur over the life of the usufruct, is determined according to market logic and thus by means of the Weighted Average Cost of Capital (WACC). The WACC represents the average cost of capital weighted compared to the two financial coverage components of capital employed, namely debt [12] and equity. The formula for determining the discount rate using WACC is:

$$WACC = k_E \cdot E + k_D \cdot D \tag{2}$$

where k_E and k_D are the cost of equity and debt, respectively, and E and D are the percentage of equity and debt capital. To estimate k_E, the Capital Asset Pricing Model

(CAPM) can be applied by applying the following formula:

$$k_E = R_f + \beta(R_m - R_f) \tag{3}$$

where R_f is a risk-free yield, β is a coefficient that measures the responsiveness of the yield to movements in the reference market, and R_m is the yield associated with the specific reference market. For the determination of k_D, it is possible to consider the cost of financing obtainable by placing the property or, as in the present case, the usufruct right as collateral.

3 Case Study

In order to highlight the limitations and potential of splitting full ownership into usufruct and bare ownership as a strategy for facilitating property enhancement, in accordance with what has been previously illustrated, the assessment of the usufruct right related to a property in disuse has been carried out. This case study takes into account the need of a PA to use a property for a period of 20 years, in order to intercept a public financing provided for the enhancement of this type of asset; this objective collided the PA's inability to obtain full ownership of the property due to both a lack of resources to allocate and the owner's will to maintain the property right, despite the fact that the asset was not strategic with respect to its medium/long-term objectives. The mutual requirements have taken the form of the 20-year usufruct in favor of the PA, the monetary consideration for which has been assumed to be paid in 20 annual down payments in favor of the bare owner, given the inability of the entity interested in managing the property to pay the total amount in one lump sum.

3.1 Description of the Property and the Context

The property is located on the peripheral area of a Southern Italian municipality, in a strategic location, less than one kilometer from the city center, 400 m from the train station, and in close proximity to an outpatient clinic in which there are several services (cardiology, general surgery, endocrinology, geriatrics, internal medicine, nephrology, neurology, and the blood draw center). The property consists of (i) a main building originally used as a kindergarten; (ii) a secondary building used as a garage; (iii) an enclosed area used as a courtyard within which the two buildings are located; (iv) an adjacent pine forest. The extrinsic-positional and intrinsic characteristics of the property seem to be responsive to the needs expressed by the PA in question, seeking a building to be used for the specialized accommodation of the over-65 population.

The main building, accessed by 3 entrances, consists of 1 basement and 3 floors connected by a stairwell and elevator. Also, the main building and the secondary building have been built presumably in 1960–1970 and consist of a reinforced concrete structure and curtain wall cladding with face brick. Over the years there have been interventions aimed at partially replacing part of the flooring, changing the articulation of the interior rooms, and introducing the elevator. The building was used in its original function until the early 2000s, then it was occasionally used by the ownership for recreational and hospitality activities until 2013. Currently, the property is in a state of neglect and has been subject to vandalism and theft. The main building and the secondary building have a total gross internal area of about 2,700 m^2; the total area of the lot is about 4,800 m^2 of which 900 m^2 are covered and the residual occupied by the courtyard and pine forest.

3.2 Identification of the Economic Purpose of the Asset

In order to proceed with the assessment of the value of the usufruct right, it is necessary to identify the economic destination of the property, which must remain unchanged throughout the duration of the usufruct and compatible at the same time with the urban zoning of the area, the stacking of the buildings, the specificities of the building and with the needs of the reference real estate market, as expressed by the PA interested in purchasing the usufruct right. Based on the analysis of these elements, it has been considered that the property lends itself to becoming a *"senior accommodation"* in which: (i) the basement floor of the main building can house the service rooms (kitchen, dining room, kitchenette, laundry, linen storage); (ii) on the *mezzanine* floor, it is possible to develop the common rooms for recreation and leisure activities, gymnasium, a bar room, infirmary, management, administrative employee offices, staff service room with attached toilets, and guardhouse; (iii) related to the *mezzanine*, first and second floors, a total of 37 rooms are planned, including 10 single and 27 double rooms, for a total of 64 guests.

The outline hypothesis of space re-functionalization (see Fig. 1) has been conceived with the view that the facility aims to provide long-term care and maintenance services, including rehabilitation services, delivered to non-self-sufficient patients with low need for health care protection, ensuring the achievement of appropriate scale economies. In addition to being compatible with stacking, urban planning requirements and technically feasible, the hypothesized intended use must be economically viable; therefore, the last step in identifying the economic intended use of the asset consists of the analysis of the target market i.e., the supply/demand ratio and their respective prospective evolution. The potential demand has been identified in the population over 65 residing in the reference province, while the supply consists of the similar facilities currently present.

In Italy, the life expectancy is 83.6 years, which is higher than the OECD average (equal to 81 years) [13] and, based on the analysis of the age pyramid relative to the next 20 years (see Fig. 2), against a decrease in the resident population in Italy of 6%, an increase in the over-65s of 37% is expected, thus a potential increase in the elderly in need of care. Currently in our country, the demand for long term care appears to be largely unmet, the number of beds allocated for long-term care of the over 65s is among the lowest in Europe as is the investment in such facilities. Therefore, the use of *"senior accomodation"* represents a possible new use for the property in line with the concept of economic destination of an asset suitable to usufruct.

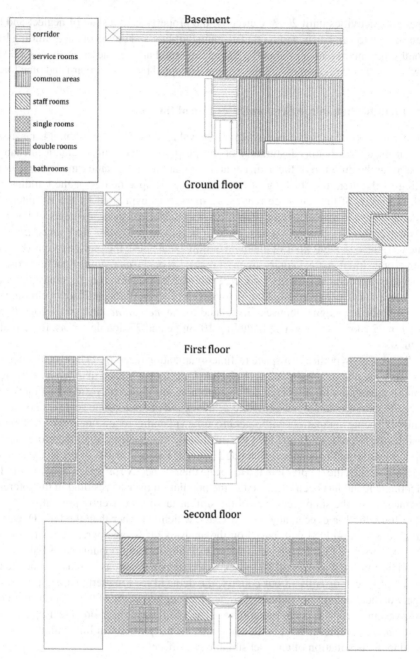

Fig. 1. Outline hypothesis of the re-functionalization of spaces.

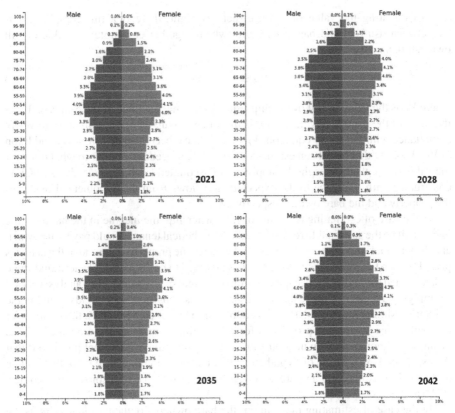

Fig. 2. Age pyramid of the Italian population processed by PopulationPyramid.net on data from United Nations, Department of Economic and Social Affairs, Population Division.

3.3 Determination of the Usufruct Right's Value

To assess the value of the usufruct right, it is necessary to define the stakeholder involved in the transaction:

- the bare owner, who receives from the usufructuary an annual payment for the duration of 20 years equivalent to the corresponding value of usufruct right for 20 years;
- the usufructuary, who pays the above amount to the bare owner and receives from a tenant a rent for the period of time between the end of the renovation work and the end of the term of the usufruct right;
- the hypothetical lessee, who pays the usufructuary the above rent and takes care of the management of the senior accommodation by making a profit.

Given the poor state of maintenance of the property and its original use, it is necessary to provide renovation works to enhance the value of the property; in light of the usufruct law, it is reasonable to assume that the usufructuary will bear the necessary costs for the improvement of the property by receiving a reimbursement at the term of the usufruct from the bare owner, equal to the costs incurred.

In estimating the value of the usufructuary right, there is a full complementarity between usufruct and bare ownership, which together constitute the value of full ownership, namely:

$$V_P = V_U + V_N \tag{4}$$

where V_P is the value of full ownership, equal to the market value of the property, V_U is the value of the usufruct right, and V_N is the value of bare ownership. In order to verify compliance with the above equation, V_P and V_N have been also determined in addition to V_U. V_P e V_N that have been estimated by indirect procedure, similar to what done for the value of the usufruct right, by applying a Discounted Cash Flow Analysis (DCFA) constructed with reference to the expected cash flows from the hypothetical owner of the property and the bare owner, respectively.

In the case of estimating the value of full ownership, the income in the hands of the owner will be the sustainable rent, which the hypothetical tenant should pay to the owner, and the terminal value, which is the residual value of the property at the end of the analysis period (which for consistency of approach is assumed to be 20 years). The terminal value is determined through a direct capitalization of the rent received at the last analysis period by applying a gross cap rate equal to 5.5%, which is consistent with yields found in the market for similar structures. The costs to be borne by the owner will be the same as for the usufructuary, to which provisions for extraordinary maintenance are added. These quantities, although they do not constitute actual cash outlays, represent provisions that the owner makes by virtue of hypothetical extraordinary maintenance work that will be performed over the years and are set equal to 1% of the cost of reconstruction to new (CRN).

In the case of estimating the value of the bare ownership, the terminal value is the only income in the hands of the bare owner, relative to the end of the analysis period, cleared of the costs for extraordinary maintenance that he/she will have to reimburse the usufructuary.

With regard to the technical parameters identified, the valuation is developed under current prices, assuming the evolution over time of the quantities involved (sustainable rent, prices, revenues, maintenance costs, etc.) due to the prospective trend of monthly changes in the consumer price index for blue and white-collar families (FOI) as measured by ISTAT [14]. For this purpose, the variability of the FOI index has been analyzed (see Fig. 3) from which a 2% inflation trend growth can be conservatively assumed. Rent has been indexed to 75% of the FOI index, and prices and costs to 100% of the FOI index.

Regarding the other technical parameters, the following assumptions have been applied to the analysis. The discount rate has been determined through the WACC approach, identifying the European β for the Real Estate - Development sector published by Professor Damodaran [15], the market risk (R_m) equal to the sum of the Return On Equity (ROE) of the Real Estate - Development sector and an increase function of the specificities of the real estate initiative (ΔR_m), while the risk free R_f is equal to the gross yield of the 15-year BTPs [16] placed on July 13–14, 2022; the k_D is given by the sum of the yield of the 20-year EURIRS [17] (17/08/2022) and the adjusted default spread for Italy.

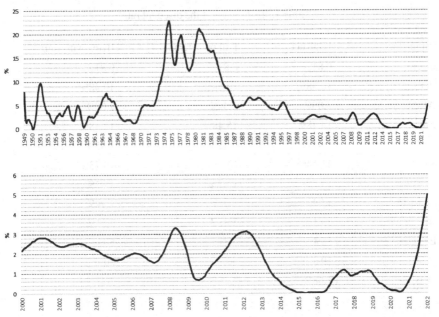

Fig. 3. Annual moving average (on a monthly basis) of changes in the FOI-ISTAT index for the periods 1949–2022 and 2000–2022. Elaborations made by setting negative values equal to zero.

Depending on the appraised value (usufruct, full ownership, and bare ownership) and thus the point of view from which the cash flows are constructed (usufructuary, owner, and bare owner) ΔR_m is going to vary. The owner assumes all the risks of the transaction and therefore is expected to have a higher return on equity, as opposed to the bare owner to whom a lower risk profile, and therefore return, corresponds. The usufructuary is in an intermediate position, although he/she has to burden the costs of extraordinary maintenance, like the owner, that has the expectation of returning these amounts at the end of the usufruct. Another parameter that distinguishes the different profiles is the equity/debt ratio, set equal to 50%/50%, in the case of usufructuary and bare owner, because of the limitations they have compared to the owner, for whom it can be assumed a greater bank exposure and thus in equity/debt ratio equal to 40%/60%. Table 1 shows the parameters used and the rates obtained; the usufructuary's discount rate turns out to be the highest precisely because of the high extraordinary maintenance costs it has to incur in the 2 years following the establishment of the usufruct right, and the uncertainties about future revenues; the owner, although has to incur the same costs, has revenue prospects that do not end after 20 years and could have a higher Loan To Value (LTV), having a slightly lower rate than the usufructuary; finally, the bare owner has an even lower rate resulting from the lower risks incurred.

Table 1. Estimation of the discount rate

Parameters	Usufruct	Full ownership	Bare ownership
β	0.81	0.81	0.81
ROE	10.48%	10.48%	10.48%
ΔRm	3.00%	5.00%	2.00%
Rm	13.48%	15.48%	12.48%
BTP	3.45%	3.45%	3.45%
K_E	11.54%	13.15%	10.73%
spread	1.87%	1.87%	1.87%
EURIRS	1.94%	1.94%	1.94%
K_D	3.81%	3.81%	3.81%
E	50%	40%	50%
D	50%	60%	50%
WACC	**7.68%**	**7.55%**	**7.27%**

The costs charged to the usufructuary, according to the evaluation approach described, are:

- extraordinary maintenance;
- routine maintenance;
- insurance premium;
- property tax [18];
- administrative management;
- registration tax.

The assessment of unit costs associated with the extraordinary maintenance and the CRN has been carried out by means of parametric costs related to recurring building types [19] adjusted according to the differences in workmanship, geography [20] and time [21] existing between the type sheets and the specifics of the case under consideration. Technical (design, construction management, testing, etc.) and general (operation preparation, consulting, secretariat. etc.) expenses have been added to the construction costs.

In summary: the extraordinary maintenance operation has a total estimated cost of about € 3,135,000, corresponding to a unit cost of 1,173 €/m^2 and a cost per room of 77,604 €/room; the CRN is about € 4,670,000, corresponding to a unit cost of 1,746 €/m^2 and a cost per room of 126,177 €/room; the property tax is 10,756 €/year [22]. Administrative management costs are assumed to be 1.5% of the rent, while the registration tax is set at 2% of the rent; these amounts will fluctuate over time depending on the indexation of the rent.

The revenues in the hands of the usufructuary are the sustainable rents, which the hypothetical tenant pays until the end of the usufruct, and the reimbursement for maintenance expenses incurred, which the bare owner will pay to the usufructuary at the end of the usufruct right.

In determining the sustainable rent that the manager of the nursing home pays to the usufructuary, it is necessary to reconstruct the costs and revenues of the initiative. The sustainable rent, in line with valuation best practices, is assumed to be 25 percent of gross management revenue, obtained by considering a room rate of 60 €/day for single rooms and 100 €/day for double rooms, determined based on analyses of the tariffs of similar facilities in the surrounding area. Given the low vacancy associated with these facilities, an average annual occupancy of 95% has been assumed; total revenue, i.e., gross revenue, is given by the sum of room revenue and ancillary revenue (bar management, vending machines, etc.) equal to 5% of room revenue.

In order to verify that the profit of the nursing home operator is consistent with the expectations of the stakeholder, the costs of operation have been parametrically determined [23]. The sustainable rent in fully operational condition is equal to 300,000 €/year, which corresponds to an Estimated Rental Value (ERV) of 110 €/m^2; the profit of the nursing home operator is about 200,000 €/year, i.e. 17% of the total estimated turnover.

It is assumed that after the conclusion of the enhancement workings, there is a lease contract between the usufructuary and the manager of the facility with a duration of 9 + 9 years, indexed to 75% of the previously estimated FOI-ISTAT index; in order to facilitate the manager in starting the business, it is assumed that the usufructuary grants the tenant a step rent of the first 2 periods (1st period 60% of the sustainable rent and 2nd period 80% of the sustainable rent).

Reimbursement of extraordinary maintenance expenses without interest at the end of the usufruct is paid in the 20th year by the bare owner in favor of the usufructuary.

As described in the introduction, the parties have agreed that the value of the usufruct right is not paid in a single tranche at the time of establishment of the right in favor of the usufructuary, but in 20 equal annual down payments compensated by the usufructuary to the bare owner at the beginning of each period. Following the estimation of the value of the usufruct right, it is then necessary to divide this amount into 20 constant annual payments in advance as they are given at the beginning of each period; the value of the usufruct right is equivalent to the initial accumulation A_0 (as of the valuation date) of the 20 annual payments (r) previously defined, in formulas:

$$A_0 = r \cdot q \frac{q^{20}-1}{q^{20} \cdot s} = r \cdot \frac{q^{20}-1}{q^{19} \cdot s} \tag{5}$$

where $q = 1 + s$ is the unit amount and s is the interest rate. In the present case, given the initial accumulation equal to the value of the estimated usufruct right ($A_0 = V_U$), the annual installment is equal to:

$$r = \frac{V_U \cdot q^{19} \cdot s}{q^{20}-1} \tag{6}$$

The interest rate s is equated to a risk free rate set equal to the gross yield on 15-year BTPs as placed on July 13–14, 2022, which is equal to 3.45%.

The value of the usufruct right with a 20-year term, relating to the subject property, determined as of 08/31/2022 is equal to € 302,000 corresponding to an equivalent annual down payment of € 20,448.

The value of the full ownership determined as of 08/31/2022 is equal to € 779,000, corresponding to a unit value with respect to the commercial area of 284 €/m^2; the value of the bare ownership is equal to € 481,000; the sum of the values of usufruct and bare ownership is equal to € 783,000, which is € 4,000 higher than the value of the full ownership (+0.51%); this difference appears negligible and attributable to the different approximations used.

4 Conclusions

The present research, applied to a concrete case, has shown that the usufruct right could take a central role in property development initiatives, especially when there are several stakeholders with different interests; in fact, properties of public value are often owned by entities who do not have the interest and spending capacity necessary to develop them, and this causes the progressive degradation of the assets with a consequent negative impact on the entire territory in which they are located. Such assets, even when offered for sale, often do not attract the interest of market operators, due to the current constraints and the high costs of renovation. PAs, which are interested in the enhancement of the properties and the positive effects on the surrounding areas and the benefits to the population, do not have the resources necessary to purchase full ownership and to bear the costs of redevelopment. The usufruct right makes it possible to overcome this situation since it permits the usufructuary to: *i)* be able to enjoy the asset for a period of time necessary for the enhancement of the asset; *ii)* have the ownership of a real property right necessary to access possible public financing; *iii)* contain the initial costs since the monetary consideration to be paid for the possession of the usufruct right is less than the market value of the asset. The bare owner, on the other hand, obtains: *i)* a monetary amount without depriving himself of ownership of the asset; *ii)* containment of costs associated with maintenance of the asset. The proposed approach could be extended in many different contexts characterized by public properties to be enhanced missing resources [24].

Note

The research has been developed within the project "MISTRAL - a toolkit for dynaMic health Impact analysiS to predicT disability-Related costs in the Aging population based on three case studies of steeL-industry exposed areas in Europe"- HORIZON-HLTH-2022-ENVHLTH04 - Grant Agreement Project n. 101095119 of the Polytechnic University of Bari (Italy).

References

1. Anelli, D., Tajani, F.: Valorization of cultural heritage and land take reduction: an urban compensation model for the replacement of unsuitable buildings in an Italian UNESCO site. J. Cult. Herit. **57**, 165–172 (2022)

2. NextGenerationEU. https://next-generation-eu.europa.eu/index_en. Accessed 09 Feb 2023
3. Pereña Vicente, M.: La constitución voluntaria del usufructo. Ciencias jurídicas y Sociales **32** (2005)
4. Morano, P., Tajani, F.: Estimative analysis of a segment of the bare ownership market of residential property. In: Computational Science and Its Applications – ICCSA 2013. ICCSA 2013. LNCS, vol. 7974. Springer, Berlin (2013). https://doi.org/10.1007/978-3-642-39649-6_31
5. LeVan, G.: The usufructuary's obligation to preserve the property. Lousiana Law Rev. **22**(4), 808–818 (1962)
6. Yiannopoulos, A.N.: Usufruct: general principles Louisiana and comparative law. Louisiana Law Rev. **27**(3), 369–422 (1966)
7. Christensen, H.: International Estate Planning, 2nd edn., LexisNexis, Conklin (2013)
8. Brueggeman, W.B., Fisher, J.D.: Real Estate Finance and Investments, 13th edn. McGraw-Hill International, Boston (2008)
9. Morano, P., Tajani, F.: Bare ownership of residential properties: insights on two segments of the Italian market, Int. J. Hous. Mark. Anal. **9**(3), 376–399 (2016)
10. The Italian Civil Code (Testo del Regio Decreto 16 marzo 1942, n. 262 and D.Lgs. 10 ottobre 2022, n. 149)
11. Consolidated Text of Provisions Concerning Registration Tax (26 april 1986 n. 131)
12. Locurcio, M., Tajani, F., Morano, P., Anelli, D., Manganelli, B.: Credit risk management of property investments through multi-criteria indicators, Risks **9**(6), 106 (2021)
13. OECD: Health at a Glance 2021: OECD Indicators, OECD Publishing, Paris (2021)
14. ISTAT FOI. https://www.istat.it/it/archivio/FOI. Accessed 09 Feb 2023
15. Damodaran, A. https://pages.stern.nyu.edu/~adamodar/New_Home_Page/datacurrent.html. Accessed 9 Feb 2023
16. BTP. https://www.dt.mef.gov.it/it/debito_pubblico/emissioni_titoli_di_stato_interni/risultati_aste. Accessed 9 Feb 2023
17. EURIRS. https://mutuionline.24oreborsaonline.ilsole24ore.com/guide-mutui/irs.asp, Accessed 9 Feb 2023
18. Tajani, F., Morano, P., Torre C.M., di Liddo F.: An analysis of the influence of property tax on housing prices in the Apulia Region (Italy), Buildings **7**(3), 67 (2017)
19. Collegio degli Ingegneri e Architetti di Milano: Prezzi tipologie edilizie, DEI – Tipografia del Genio Civile, Milano (2019)
20. Manganelli B.: Il deprezzamento degli immobili urbani, Franco Angeli, Milano (2011)
21. Bianca M., C.: Diritto Civile – la proprietà, Giuffrè Editore, Milano (2016)
22. Amministrazioni Comunali. https://www.amministrazionicomunali.it/main/. Accessed 9 Feb 2023
23. Unione nazionale istituzioni e iniziative di assistenza sociale. I costi e i ricavi nelle RSA: come renderli più efficienti. 26 ottobre 2010. https://www.uneba.org/i-costi-e-i-ricavi-nelle-rsa-come-renderli-pi-efficienti/. Accessed 9 Feb 2023
24. Morano, P., Tajani, F., Di Liddo, F., La Spina, I.: The evaluation in the urban projects planning: a logical-deductive model for the definition of "warning areas" in the Esquilino District in the City of Rome (Italy). Smart Cities **6**(1), 469–490 (2023)

Specifics of Smart Cities Development in Europe (SPEED 2023)

Engagement and Inclusion Experiences for Energy Communities. An Ongoing Case Study in Cagliari, Italy

Ivan Blečić, Alessandro Sebastiano Carrus, Emanuel Muroni$^{(\boxtimes)}$, Valeria Saiu, and Maria Carla Saliu

University of Cagliari, Via Corte d'Appello 78, Cagliari, Italy
{ivanblecic,emanuel.muroni,vsaiu,mariacarla.saliu}@unica.it,
a.carrus2@studenti.unica.it

Abstract. In recent years, we see further progress in the interest of the concept of energy communities. They have been able to attract much attention and research effort both because of their central role in the development of sustainable energy systems and because they are able to include and engage many people. Research indicates that participation in desirable energy activities is one of the keys to the effective enforcement of energy transition and, consequently, to the successful fight to climate change. Despite the potential for inclusion that energy communities hold, the classical governance tools favour the technical side rather than focusing on encouraging the active involvement of stakeholders and citizens who are potential participants in the energy community. For this reason, the overall aim of this article is to propose a method, projects, and engagement activities to build the conditions in which participation in the energy system can trigger virtuous behaviour by developing a certain dose of self-sufficiency in terms of management. We will argue that such method of engagement influences the extent to which parties can or cannot engage in the whole framework for the collective management of energy communities. To exemplify this approach, we present a still ongoing experience of a Solar Energy Community, the first in the city of Cagliari, to demonstrate how the dynamics of inclusion and exclusion in renewable energy projects can contribute to producing spatial, social, cultural, and economic context that can adapt to changing circumstances, capacity demands, technological innovations, demographic, social, and economic trends.

Keywords: Renewable energy community · REC · Local energy community · Energy transition · Social behaviours · Social acceptance · Community engagement · Cagliari (Italy)

1 Introduction

The European Union (EU) in 2019 introduced the Clean Energy Package for All Europeans (CEP) [1], a broad set of measures to promote high energy efficiency buildings, renewable energy, consumer rights on self-generation, and cross-border cooperation,

O. Gervasi et al. (Eds.): ICCSA 2023 Workshops, LNCS 14109, pp. 513–528, 2023.
https://doi.org/10.1007/978-3-031-37120-2_33

among others. To achieve these goals, the CEP introduced the concept of energy communities in its legislation, notably as Renewable Energy Communities (RECs). The Renewable Energy Directive (2018/2001/EU) [2], also known as RED II, aims to make renewable energy more accessible to citizens by providing them the opportunity to engage in joint renewable energy projects. The directive introduces the need to make citizen-driven RECs capable of consuming and producing renewable energy and, in some cases, also storing and selling renewable energy and providing flexibility services to the grid through demand response and storage as legal entities. In Italy, for instance, energy communities are subject to the technical rules outlined by the GSE ("Gestore Servizi Energetici") the Italian Energy Services Operator [3], and by the regulation 318/2020/R/EEL of the ARERA ("Autorità di Regolazione per Energia Reti e Ambiente") the Italian Regulation Agency for Environment, Network and Energy [4]. In this way, citizens have the opportunity to become increasingly environmentally and socially conscious towards energy issues. RECs therefore need to develop democratic processes that allow citizens to actively participate in energy policies and the energy market.

During recent years, we have had the chance to witness the strong increase in calls for energy transition in terms of assigning a fundamental role to Energy Communities [5–14]. The recent literature on RECs has addressed issues related to normative barriers [15], maximizing self-sufficiency [16], local energy sharing strategies [17], and the interaction of RECs with the electricity system. The analysis of the energy and climate issues, however, as correctly observed by Mignani [18], reveals a topical predominance of engineering and economic sciences. Traditional approaches emphasise the technical and legal side when setting up the energy community, in order to find the optimal configuration of technologies and energy-sharing strategies among members. The social elements of energy systems and their consequences are often neglected or underestimated, especially in processes that involve local governments [19, 20]. According to Mignani [18] this happens because energy is considered only a basic factor whose diverse forms structure the temporal and spatial organization of social life. Actually, there is a tendency to neglect both step and organization of direct personal/collective engagement of citizens. Through the presentation of an ongoing case study, we will highlight how instead humans and social behavior are central as they are able to profoundly influence the future energy scenarios. This article starts from the general aforementioned consideration and has the general objective of highlighting the sociological relevance of the energy question.

The paper is structured as follows: Sect. 2 will highlight the key theoretical perspectives that have been emerging in the literature around the topic of energy communities, with a focus on the weight that dominant approaches give to sociological aspects; Sect. 3 deals the way in which the methodology can be applied; in Sect. 4, the type of results, critical aspects and suggestions it yields are illustrated, and both outcomes and difficulties faced by these community energy initiatives are discussed; finally, Sect. 5 presents concluding remarks, and outlines potential future perspectives.

2 Literature Review

The topic of RECs is attracting attention from researchers, local stakeholders, such as mayors, energy planners, and citizens. Energy, its consumption and its production have been at the center of the public and scientific debate, as well as the subject of national and European policies. In the literature, it is easier to find papers closely connected to highly topical issues, even general, such as climate change, the reduction of emissions, natural disasters, the security of supply, and the sustainability of the current model of economic development, just to name a few. Issues that intertwine with each other in complex and often contradictory ways [18]. The way in which these issues are often dealt with is through focus on technical aspects of design, e.g. designing various local energy systems [21]. Despite the fact that we can handle the topic from various perspectives, a substantial part of the literature does not refer to the evaluation of social impacts and benefits as part of the structure of RECs.

There is however a significant number of papers focusing on the design and operational phase of energy communities [22]. Di Silvestre et al. [23], for instance, provide an analysis of the European regulatory context, focusing on two adopted directives on the promotion of the use of energy from RECs and on the increase of energy efficiency. With these directives emerge the leading role of citizens (called "prosumers") in the energy transition. In this model in which even small domestic surplus productions could be an active part of the energy supply sector, another focus is about RECs as new actors in the electricity market. Instead, Cutore et al. [22] define, in accordance with the Italian regulation, two different energy-sharing configurations, distributed and centralized, to obtain a techno-economic comparison. By the analysis of energy performance assessment and cost-effectiveness of the investment the authors presented an optimization model and demonstrate that the configuration which improve the rates of total self-consumption has higher investment and maintenance costs, which means that greater investment in technologies reduce beneficial social impact on REC's participants.

In these lines of research there is a lack of attention to the involvement of the inhabitants. This method has for too long focused on *hardware* rather than on the human and social *software* that underlies energy systems. Among the lacking aspects related to the social phenomena, there are, for example, ignorance of social processes which, if present, would determine the acceptance and use of the technological solutions promote by researchers to obtain an optimized REC, the social factors and dynamics underlying the demand for energy services and the use of technologies, social perceptions regarding energy risks, communication methods in relation to energy choices [24].

On the other hand, there is a growing social relevance of energy that does not escape contemporary sociological reflection. In recent years, various aspects of energy communities have been studied what rally should it mean [25], with a focus to promote community initiatives [26]. Among these, some did through a quantitative [27] and others through qualitative research [15] on the motivations behind participation. Most of these were focused on both the willingness of citizens to participate, and the factors that influence their motivations to participate. Soeiro and Ferreira Dias [27], inter alios, define the citizens' participation as a crucial point for the development of this type of communities, adding that trust is very important for the development of any REC. Whereas Raven et al. [28] presents an interesting best practice in the field of engagement, with a particular attention to the acceptance of energy community. Indeed, as pointed out by Azarova et al. [29], vast literature is available on the social acceptance of renewable energy sources and technologies [18, 30], also for the acceptance of RECs on the energy markets recommendations for the transposition [31]. Existing researches focus on specific local energy system management activities, especially in Italian urban realities that aim to build a dense network of RECs in their cities. It lacks attention for project and context specific explanations of how acceptance mechanisms are articulated according to the characteristics of the project, site, community, region, and the project development and engagement process. In order to further elucidate and improve this line of research, we present our experience that aims to ease traditional acceptance problems through a specific community engagement programme.

In the next section, we will show our approach based on participatory actions and the steps of community engagement.

3 Methodology

The methodology is illustred through the presentation of a specific case study [32]. The case study on which the empirical work draws is "CER-CA", an acronym of "Comunità Energetica Rinnovabile (English: Renewable Energy Community) and Cagliari"[1]. It is an initiative of the Municipality and the University of Cagliari to promote the first REC in Cagliari, the capital city of Sardinia and the most populous municipality on the island. The ongoing project includes a pilot program involving the installation of photovoltaic (PV) system in a socially difficult residential sector.

In this study we present an experience that is part of a project "Energy Efficiency in 40 Schools Support Communities – EE(40)Sco" from the NESOI (New Energy Solutions Optmised fo Islands) program (see Table 1), led by the Munincipality of Cagliari.

The proposal envisages an articulated plan of interventions involving about half of the city's school buildings around which to establish RECs. The area identified by the municipality to start the project is Piazza Medaglia Miracolosa (PMM) and consists of a square surrounded by buildings, forming a central block at the intersection of the main urban connecting roads in the San Michele neighborhood (see Fig. 1). It is a residential sector in a neighborhood characterised by a high density of urban commons and a socio-economic vulnerability of many residents. The kindergarten, located in the middle of the residential sector, serves as a meeting point for many families in the area, as well as the square. Despite its poor state of maintenance, the square remains a place of great interest to the community due to its strategic location and the presence of the kindergarten.

The pioneering project envisages the establishment of a REC through the installation of 1 PV system, divided into two lots respectively one on the best oriented residential block and one on the kindergarten. The municipality envisages that through the cooperation of 80 households and the electricity consumption of the kindergarten, the electricity produced by the PV will be almost completely self-consumed by the REC members.

---

[1] In the Sect. 3.2, we will explain in detail reasons and meanings behind the choice of this naming.

Table 1. Short history of the project development process and actors involved.

Year	Project milestones and involved actors
2019	NESOI received funding from the European Union's Horizon 2020 research and innovation programme under grant agreement Opening of a window of opportunity for REC through EU support schemes and Italian project development aid
2020	First open call from the European Island Facility NESOI offers grants of up to € 60k per proposal as well as up to € 60k worth of Technical Assistance to help local European islands reach their energy transition ambitions
2021	Cagliari Municipality identified Piazza Medaglia Miracolosa site as a suitable location for the first REC in the city. Dominant characteristics found: shape, size, social condition of residential blocks, distance from existing infrastructure and connectivity, and vitality of the neighbourhood Cagliari Municipality developed the project proposal called "Energy Efficiency in 40 Schools Support Communities - EE(40)Sco" The proposal made for the city of Cagliari, in Sardinia, receives the financial support from the EU Inslands Facility NESOI
2022	The University of Cagliairi is called upon to assist the Municipality of Cagliari in managing the engagement step The research group of University of Cagliari developed the project proposal called "CER-CA" The proposal made for the research group is accepted by the Munincipality Implementing Agreement between Munincipality and University of Cagliari Approval of the executive project for the establishment of a REC in Piazza Medaglia Miracolosa Arrival, erection, and commissioning of the PV system (two lots) Work begins on the first lot (kindergarten)
2023	End of work: first lot (kindergarten) Work begins on the second lot (residential block)
2024	End of work: second lot (residential block) Commissioning of photovoltaic energy

The large presence of not-for-profit cultural, social, and recreational activities managed by the community, the high degree of community-ownership, several years of operation, and the active community organisation pursuing a variety of community development goals, and more in generally the vivacity of the neighbourhood emerged during in-field analysis carried out on previous projects. These are used as selection criteria to find a matured project (despite still in progress) most likely to display a considerable and diverse impact on the community it is part of.

These criteria and these characteristics, including the fact that it is a well-delineated island community increase the visibility of local impacts, make this case study more of a critical case study that is especially helpful to illustrate by testing the methodology that we present here.

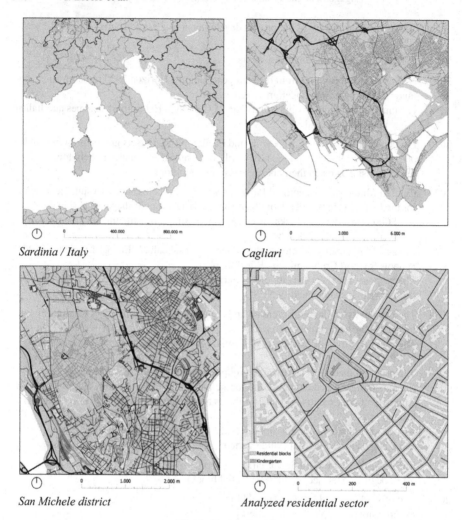

Sardinia / Italy

Cagliari

San Michele district

Analyzed residential sector

Fig. 1. Project location.

3.1 Survey Process

For the empirical study, data were collected during several fieldwork visits to the residential sector of PMM. Data were collected through a first probing activity, including an exploratory survey addressed to community members, in-depth interviews, focus groups with households, school administrators, representatives of local activities, cultural associations, religious leaders, and other group members, and finally the dissemination activity, carried out through a rich program of workshops addressed to different categories of stakeholders.

For operationalising actions, this study draws on a definition from the field of Social Impact Assessment, which studies "the processes of analysing, monitoring and managing the intended and unintended social consequences, both positive and negative, of planned interventions [...] and any social change processes invoked by those interventions" [33, p. 1].

Each step we will present was affected by an initial approach that could be called a step zero of engagement. A first contact operated via letter and email to ensure the willingness of the candidate to be a REC member generated negative impacts. Due to this approach, described by the technicians of the Municipality themselves as "unsuccessful communication attempts", in zero days of fieldwork, we had both a response of 10 out of approximately 240 and an already established condition of hostility between community and administration[2].

Without losing the nuance and in-depth analysis that are necessary for a complex issue such as social acceptance of the REC project, the methodology has been simplified. The survey steps are presented in the following sub-sections.

Step 1. Probing

This phase of initial community engagement is structured by involving key actors. It is a step that aims at the acquisition of contacts through subjects 'already loyal/established', so to speak, in other contexts or previous project experiences such as the exploratory study conducted in San Michele-Is Mirrionis neighbourhoods [34]. The project, called "NeighbourHub" (NHub), developed over two years (2019–2022) has provided a participation process that involved over 30 associations. These group members were contacted in order to assist us in our first phase of presentation and introduction to the households of the PMM area.

The ethnographic fieldwork included two interactions with key actors in preparation for a meeting with each potential participant/REC member:

i) A first contact via phone or email to key actors. In this approach is necessary to inform key actors about the intentions and main issues of the REC project, but above all ask them if they would be available to be 'social pivot point' in this step of the project;

ii) A first contact with the households through key actors. In this interaction phase all known representatives of local activities (ice cream makers, bartenders, tobacconists), cultural associations, and religious leaders of the neighborhood have to be approached by us. Key actors have to explain to the latter who we are, present the general outline of the REC project and ask if they would like to hear from us.

These small groups of subjects will become our gateway to residential blocks. In the next step, the approach of direct engagement of households will be presented.

Step 2. Community Survey

In this step the key actors are identified. Three representatives from cultural associations in the neighbourhood of San Michele, the parish priest of the Church of Medaglia Miracolosa adjacent to the homonymous residential sector, and several representatives of

---

[2] A preliminary survey of potential real estate units and associated households revealed different living situations: owners, renters, and squatters. Any letter approach made by the municipality, if not ignored, scared the community.

local activities assist us during our extensive ethnographic fieldwork. It is a sort of "loyalty operation" aimed at implementing the number of key actors by recruiting them from among households. Initial surveys and meetings with residents, school administrators and local activities/cultural associations within the residential sector took place.

Step 2 is required in order to create a core group of members through the identification of kay actors in the community.

Step 3. Focus Group

Participants were recruited via the first exploratory survey assisted by the key actors. Tha phase of intensive community engagement and consolidation can therefore begin.

In this step, an initial information meeting will be organised with the stakeholders. These meetings will be repeated every 2–3 months. On this occasion, the project is promoted and disseminated to the local community. A mention will also be made of the presentation of the different tools available that will be used in the next steps, information materials, social media and the web, but also educational channels. One example pointing in this direction is the activity we explain in detail in the next section.

Step 4. Other Activities

The support process continues through the acquisition of new contacts and the consolidation of key actors among the households, with an eye on the potential REC members. To ease the problems of acceptability and invasiveness, we organised a series of activities.

A fundamental activity was conducted with young children of the kindergarten located in the middle of residential blocks, in order to create new opportunities to meet the community. The main focus is on the cleaning and redevelopment of the square.

In these terms, the activity with the school becomes more than a didactic activity aimed at imparting knowledge or skills. The activity becomes a tactical urban intervention with an ambivalent character: (i) Trojan Horse designed to increase curiosity, build an additional informative moment, expand the network of contacts, and consequently find the earliest REC members. The school activity in the square will take advantage of the "eyes on the street" [35] favoured by the shape of the residential sector, capturing the attention of all households; (ii) a trasformation of the space aimed at triggering important mechanism, including affection towards public space. Howcan these activities create affection or "attachment to place" [36]?

Here activity is defined as a temporary perturbance related to a planned intervention that affects or concern people and space, directly or indirectly, perceptual or corporeal. The activity ends with the placement of a mark in the square. The children will sign their work with their name or more simply by leaving the imprint of their hand. Finally, they will be given a bright lamp. This lamp, which will have the symbol of the CER-CA project imprinted on it, will be left by the children in the square as a further physical sign of their appropriation of space. The action was planned to be antifragile [37], in that if the lamps remain in the square they will contribute to the aesthetic value of the public space, on the contrary if the lamps are stolen (as we expect) they will spread like a sort of 'information virus' in the houses of the citizens[3]. In fact, each bright lamp will be

---

[3] We could call it the physical concretisation of the the concept of contagion [40] at the basis of transference of emotions that spread through groups of people accompanying the behaviour and choices of individuals.

marked with a logo and a Qr code of the project. This will allow anyone to connect via a simple smartphone to the digital platform of CER-CA. Practice that becomes a tangible urban sign of rootedness, affection and attachment.

The project phases outlined have taken place and effects produced are discussed in Sect. 4. From now on, we will describe the planned future steps of the survey process as they really are, i.e. a plan of upcoming activities, we will explain which reasons are behind our choices and explore the expected outcomes.

Step 5. Recreational and Convivial Moments

Convivial launch events will be organised during this step.

The space transformed by the children through the tactical intervention now has a specific mark that makes it recognisable to the families living in residential blocks. The piece of square will become a REC pivot point in the study area. An information gazebo will be placed within the space circumscribed by the children's intervention, becoming the place where citizens will have the opportunity to engage in a safe environment about problems and concerns related to the project.

These recreational and convivial events can also be the celebration of activities such as the one described in the previous section. Moreover, these types of practices, if combined with informal practices active in residential blocks (e.g. barbecues), can become further auspicious occasions, pivotal moments for approaching future REC members. The pivotal idea is to stimulate the community through tactical or otherwise temporary activities in order to promote the energy community in the city.

Step 6. Focus Group

This step works in the same way as step 3. The actors and topics involved will change, but not the pattern. If before the target group was the key actors among the community now it is the households and potential REC members. If in the first focus group the project was presented together with its benefits, now we will try to give detailed information about the amounts that each household can save each month on its electricity bills, the incentives that can be received through certain targeted behaviours and in general how become REC member. At this stage, due in part to the trust gained, we will ask residents for their electricity bills. We will assess with them, through a simple formula, their current consumption and what it would become if they decide to become REC members.

Step 7. Workshop

In this step we would like to emphasise the learning dimension of the project CER-CA. This phase is preparatory to the consolidation of the methodology aimed at achieving a robust form applicable to other city contexts. A separate information workshop for the community and the REC members will be organise, so both groups could talk in a safe environment about the problems of the project. Participants were recruited via the exploratory survey, focus groups, other activities, and through information materials (e.g. poster announcements, flyers, brochures, gadgets).

The aim of this step is to construct theories of behavioral change. However, there will be no lack of constant follow-up to the process, aimed at triggering and reinforcing virtuous behaviors by developing a certain amount of self-sufficiency in terms of management. Outline and define a clear methodology applicable and extendable to other contexts in the city was the pivotal prerogative.

Each step and activity presented (see Table 2) has been structured and designed in order to ensure constant follow-up, i.e. a continuous, periodic and planned control phases.

In the next section the parallel project of graphic design is presented.

3.2 Graphic Project

In this section, the design processes of the communication programme (logo, graphics, language code effectiveness and attractiveness) are presented.

The communication campaign came from the conception of a logo and naming. The output is a replicable object which can be adaptable to other contexts and social schemes. References to visual identities close to the symbol of the sun and local traditions were important.

The naming "CER-CA" was born from the meeting of the acronyms Renewable Energy Community and Cagliari specifically to represent the modular and replicable aspect of the project. Furthermore, CERCA in Italian means "search". The need to simplify the language codes and make them as effective as possible led us to choose this option to better integrate the information materials in the spaces of residential blocks. Like a sort of treasure hunt, the households are accompanied in their search not only for the object (the poster) but also for what each one represents (savings, community, etc.).

From the early steps of the project, 5 poster announcements (see Fig. 2) have been distributed in the four entrances of the residential sector. Each poster (size 85 × 150 cm) will have a head/slogan (variable depending on access points, info on savings, sense of community, and other REC benefits) and a body (fixed text with purely informational data), which aimed to tell the community who we are by informing them that "we are coming". The result will be posters announcements covering the residential sector with slogans such as "CER-CA il risparmio (Find the Saving)", etc. Through a triptych system of modular and increasing information, with consequential and non-substitutive outputs, the release of poster announcements has been scheduled. Every 2 weeks a new poster will implement information side by side, not replacing the previous one.

Modularity is the pivotal concept [37]. It was important to work in terms of simplification and replicability, producing reversible elements that are able to accept possibilities for remodeling. All this because of the needs related to the future intention of a program that aims to include 40 new energy projects in the city of Cagliari.

This will be followed by the production of information and communication materials, physical (e.g. flyers and brochures) and digital (social media and web) tools. Flyers and brochures have been distributed to the local shop adjacent to the residential blocks, but in the coming months we plan to extend the dissemination of materials.

Table 2. The data gathering process.

Methods	Description
Probing	*Purpose:* Project and community context *Target group:* Actors involved in accomplished and ongoing cultural projects (e.g. local government, intermediaries, school administrators, representatives of Non-Governmental Organizations (NGOs), local activities, cultural associations, religious leaders), and other key actors *Methodological steps:* Community profile and project profile
Community survey	*Purpose:* General impression and perceived impacts *Target group:* Key actors, households and community members *Methodological steps:* Input for the upcoming experiences
Focus Group	*Purpose:* Activity planning *Target group:* Key actors among families living in residential blocks *Methodological steps:* Structuring the field activity (e.g. cultural activities, experimentation of tactical urban planning activities)
Other activities	*Purpose:* Project and specific activity *Target group:* Key actors, households and community members *Methodological steps:* Experience of temporary projects and activities
Recreational and convivial moments	*Purpose:* Information activity *Target group:* All community *Methodological steps:* Station for the collection of REC members
Focus Group	*Purpose:* Deepening understanding of how benefits come through behaviour and lifestyle adjustments *Target group:* All community including REC members *Methodological steps:* Input for theories of behavioural change in the workshops

(*continued*)

Table 2. (*continued*)

Methods	Description
Workshops	*Purpose:* Deepening understanding of how benefits come through behaviour and lifestyle adjustments that is not feasible in a focus group. For example, because of personal nature or other sensitivities, or because the person is exceptionally knowledgeable on a pattern of behaviour related to the energy transition. Another reason may be because some groups may not be able to visit a focus group or comfortable to talk in this setting *Target group:* All community including REC members *Methodological steps:* Constructing theories of behavioural change

Fig. 2. Overview of posters announcements.

4 Results and Discussions

The general theme of this paper concerns the relationship between energy and community, with particular attention on the social acceptance of RECs. In the previous sections we presented some of the outcomes of the qualitative approach in an ongoing progress process, aimed at identifying the main operational models and organisational frameworks put in place for the development of a REC.

In 7 steps we identified possible practices that could overcome the technical and social challenges leading to the formation of a REC in a difficult residential sector in the city of Cagliari. In each step of engagement, the governance of the community was deemed as a fundamental pillar for the success of the project. Concerning the first steps already carried out, we can enunciate some considerations which we think will be fundamental for the work in progress. These considerations applied particularly to 3 steps out of 7: step 1, during which some of the households we came into contact with have not replied and others did not give their availability mainly because did not know anyone from the study area. Several, however, have been available to assist us and contacted the known families living in residential blocks directly; step 2, during which the first meeting with households confirms the profound citizens' distrust towards institutions. In general, there is a problem with the acceptability of top-down administrative proposals. This area has often been faced with coercive policies and actions (see the recent project for the adjacent Piazza San Michele, which was never accepted by the residents). It was found by Warren and McFadyen [38] that the community element can ease opposition and create support. While considering that it is neither or a panacea for local acceptability of REC, or nor a guarantee of solely positive outcomes we believe that the French philosopher René Girard would have agreed with this thought. In this respect, the idea was to turn an apparently negative condition such as the distrust of households towards institutions into an opportunity. The approach we used is close to the Girardian concept of the scapegoat mechanism, in which social cohesion is strengthened by uniting against an arbitrary other [39, 40]. This fundamental approach has been instrumental in easing the classic problem of community division on the matter, which, especially in small communities, can be detrimental [41]. The approach, was also helpful in opening to some interesting confessions, which gave us a more precise framework of the socio-democratic profile and some informal activities within the residential sector. Forms of extension of the private and appropriation to the public areas manifested (e.g. the presence of barbecues and gazebo built by residents on the sides of the square); step 4, during which demands, needs and desires prevail over initial fears and perplexity of the community. In addition the activity proved to be an opportunity on several fronts. One of them aims to discover new contacts among teachers and many school children's families who live within residential blocks.

The two critical aspects that could were identified are teamwork and empowerment. An important point that we need to work on is the engagement of the critical community members. Their attendance at the activities, focus group and, in the best-case scenario, workshop is not necessary but important if we aim to activate empowerment processes. Effective teamwork and coordination are critical to the success of REC like CER-CA.

Empowerment enables households to have the proper tools to participate in engagement activities, which are useful in building the conditions in which participation in the energy system can trigger virtuous behaviour by developing a certain dose of self-sufficiency in terms of REC management, while ensuring that they are accountable for their decision-making and actions.

Aspects identified by others as problematic (e.g. the opportunistic behavior [28] or the individual wishes [42]) were overcome through some specific and targeted engagement practices only because these were designed to be adaptable to the changing dynamics of the context. We also observed how engagement activities through projects of space (interim use) can offer new scenarios for urban regeneration. It is therefore important to ensure a modular design [37], among other things.

In these terms, this study aims to contribute methodologically to facilitate the process of social acceptance of REC in order to both produce motivation [43] for participating in a joint transition project based clean energy production and to trigger mechanism of attachment to place [36] in which it takes place. We believe this is necessary if we aim to achieve a truly effectiveness future-proof REC.

5 Conclusions

This section concludes the paper by discussing the results of the case study, as well as the potential of the methodology used. In this paper, we presented the still ongoing CER-CA project and in particular the role of a CER within a programme that will include 40 new energy projects in the city of Cagliari. Experience is showing us some general challenges that are important to deal with when developing new energy projects.

Recognising the energy transition as a chance not only to expand its community empowerment policy, but also to trigger processes of revaluing space, from an affective point of view, of attachment to place, rather than merely identity, can be considered one of the original contributions of this research. To arrive at the definition of a methodology applicable in other contexts, accompanied by other specific work plans, it is necessary to begin to recognize energy communities as evolving and changing objects. The social impacts of the first completed steps show us an effective method of engagement because it is able to influence the extent to which parties (key actors, social point pivot and REC members, iter alia) can engage in the whole framework for the collective management of energy communities. The still ongoing status of the practice does not allow us to fully discuss our experiences here, so we prefer to present some critical aspects noted and suggestions for the next steps.

In conclusion there is a remaining research question, i.e. if is whether CER-CA is more widely applicable beyond the residential sector of PMM. Applying the CER-CA pattern to other contexts, observing how it changes and adapts to other actors and frameworks, could provide an interesting and fruitful research contribution. We extracted lessons with an overall validity for the transferability of drivers and success factors. Creating evidence of the positive impacts requires dedicated surveys, qualitative, experiential accounts, and preferably also a before and after measurement to track change reliably. This is the track we intend to follow in the next steps.

References

1. Clean energy for all Europeans, European Commission, Directorate-General for Energy (2019). [Online]. https://data.europa.eu/doi/https://doi.org/10.2833/9937. Accessed 29 Apr 2023
2. C. o. t. E. U. European Parliament, «Directive (EU) 2018/2001 of the European Parliament and of the Council of 11 December 2018 on the promotion of the use of energy from renewable sources,» 11.12.2018. [Online]. https://eur-lex.europa.eu/legal-content/EN/TXT/?uri=uriserv%3AOJ.L_.2018.328.01.0082.01.ENG. Accessed 29 Apr 2023
3. Gestore Servizi Energetici GSE S.p.A., «Comunitàdi energia rinnovabile e gruppi di autoconsumatori, aggiornate le regole tecniche per l'accesso al servizio,» 11 April 2022. [Online]. https://www.gse.it/servizi-per-te/news/comunit%C3%A0-di-energia-rinnovabile-e-gruppi-di-autoconsumatori-aggiornate-le-regole-tecniche-per-l%E2%80%99accesso-al-servizio. Accessed 29 April 2023
4. Autorità di Regolazione per Energia Reti e Ambiente ARERA, «Regolazione delle partite economiche relative all'energia elettrica condivisa da un gruppo di autoconsumatori di energia rinnovabile che agiscono collettivamente in edifici e condomini oppure condivisa in una comunità di energia rinnovabile,» 4 August 2020. [Online]. https://www.arera.it/allegati/docs/20/318-20.pdf

5. Kellett, D.J.: «Community-based energy policy: a practical approach to carbon reduction.» J. Environ. Plan. Manag. **50**(3), 381–396 (2007)
6. Koirala, B.P., Koliou, E., Friege, J., Hakvoort, R.A., Herder, P.M.: «Energetic communities for community energy: a review of key issues and trends shaping integrated community energy systems.» Renew. Sustain. Energy Rev. **56**(1), 722–744 (2016)
7. Moroni, S., Alberti, V., Antoniucci, V., Bisello, A.: «Energy communities in the transition to a low-carbon future: a taxonomical approach and some policy dilemmas.» J. Environ. Manag. **236**(1), 45–53, (2019)
8. Hain, J.J., Ault, G.W., Galloway, S.J., Cruden, A., McDonald, J.: «Additional renewable energy growth through small-scale community orientated energy policies.» Energy Policy **33**(9), 1199–1212 (2005)
9. Denis, G.S., Parker, P.: «Community energy planning in Canada: the role of renewable energy.» Renew. Sustain. Energy Rev. **13**(8), 2088–2095 (2009)
10. Bomberg, E., McEwen, N.: «Mobilizing community energy.» Energy Policy **51**(1), 435–444 (2012)
11. Romero-Rubio, C., De Andrés Díaz, J.R.: «Sustainable energy communities: a study contrasting Spain and Germany.» Energy Policy **85**(1), 397–409 (2015)
12. Van der Schoor, T., Scholtens, B.: «Power to the people: local community initiatives and the transition to sustainable energy.» Renew. Sustain. Energy Rev. **43**(1), 666–675 (2015)
13. De Vries, G.W., Boon, W.P., Peine, A.: «User-led innovation in civic energy communities.» Environ. Innov. Soc. Trans. **19** (1), 51–65 (2016)
14. Süsser, D., Döring, M., Ratter, B.M.: «Harvesting energy: place and local entrepreneurship in community-based renewable energy transition.» Energy Policy **101**(1), 332–341 (2017)
15. De Vidovich, L., Tricarico, L., Zulianello, M.: Community Energy Map. Una ricognizione delle prime esperienze di comunità energetiche rinnovabili, Milano: Franco Angeli (2021)
16. Secchi, M., Barchi, G., Macii, D., Moser, D., Petri, D.: «Multi-objective battery sizing optimisation for renewable energy communities with distribution-level constraints: A prosumer-driven perspective.» Appl. Energy **297** (2021)
17. Moncecchi, M., Meneghello, S., Merlo, M.: «Energy Sharing in Renewable Energy Communities: The Italian Case.» In: 55th International Universities Power Engineering Conference (UPEC), Turin, italy, (2020)
18. Magnani, N., Carrosio, G.: Understanding the Energy Transition. Civil society, Territory and Inequality in Italy. Palgrave Macmillan, London (2021)
19. Saiu, V.: «The three pitfalls of sustainable city: a conceptual framework for evaluating the theory-practice gap.» Sustainability **9**(12), 2311 (2017)
20. Saiu, V., Blečić, I., Meloni, I.: «Making sustainability development goals (SDGs) operational at suburban level: potentials and limitations of neighbourhood sustainability assessment tools,» Environ. Impact Assess. Rev. **96** (2022)
21. Gjorgievski, V. Z., Cundeva, S., Georghiou, G.E.: «Social arrangements, technical designs and impacts of energy communities: a review.» Renew. Energy **169**(1), 1138–1156 (2021)
22. Cutore, E., Volpe, R., Sgroi, R., Fichera, A.: «Energy management and sustainability assessment of renewable energy communities: the Italian context.» Energy Conv. Manag. **278**, 116713 (2023)
23. Di Silvestre, M.L., Ippolito, . M.G., Sanseverino, E.R., Sciumè, G., Vasile, A.: «Energy self-consumers and renewable energy communities in Italy: new actors of the electric power systems.» Renew. Sustain. Energy Rev. **151**, 111565 (2021)
24. Sovacool, B.K., et al.: «Integrating social science in energy research.» Energy Res. Soc. Sci. **6**(1), 95–99 (2015)
25. Walker, G., Devine-Wright, P.: «Community renewable energy: what should it mean?» Energy Policy **32**(2), 497–500 (2008)

26. Heras-Saizarbitoria, I., Sáez, L., Allur, E., Morandeira, J.: «The emergence of renewable energy cooperatives in Spain: a review.» Renew. Sustain. Energy Rev. **94**(1), 1036–1043 (2018)

27. Soeiro, S., Ferreira Dias, M.: «Renewable energy community and the European energy market: main motivations.» Heliyon **6**(7) (2020)

28. Raven, R.J., Mourik, R.M., Feenstr, C.J., Heiskanen, E.: «Modulating societal acceptance in new energy projects: towards a toolkit methodology for project managers» Energy **34**(5), 564–574 (2009)

29. Azarova, V., Cohen, J., Friedl, C., Reichl, J.: «Designing local renewable energy communities to increase social acceptance: Evidence from a choice experiment in Austria, Germany, Italy, and Switzerland.» Energy Policy **132**(1), 1176–1183 (2019)

30. Wüstenhagen, R., Wolsink, M., Bürer, M.J.: «Social acceptance of renewable energy innovation: An introduction to the concept.» Energy Policy **35**(5), 2683–2691 (2007)

31. Jeans, L.: «Consumer stock ownership plans (csops) - the prototype business model for renewable energy communities.» Energies**13**(1), 1–24 (2019)

32. Yin, R.K.: Case Study Research: Design and Methods. Sage, California (2013)

33. Vanclay, F.: «International principles for social impact assessment» Impact Assess. Project Appr. **21**(1), 5–12 (2012)

34. Saiu, V., Blečić, I.: «NeighbourHub. Un circuito aperto di spazi per usi temporanei e a rotazione, per un distretto culturale diffuso nei quartieri di Is Mirrionis e San Michele a Cagliari.» In: IV COngresso Internazionale dell'Abitare COllettivo Sostenibile, Alghero (2020)

35. Jacobs, J.: The Death and Life of Great American Cities. Random House, New York (1961)

36. Kolers, A.: Land, Conflict, and Justice A Political Theory of Territory. Cambridge University Press, Cambridge (2008)

37. Blečić, I., Cecchini, A.: «Antifragile planning.» Plan. Theory **19**(2), 172–192 (2020)

38. Warren, C. R., McFadyen, M.: «Does community ownership affect public attitudes to wind energy? A case study from south-west Scotland,» Land Use Policy **27**(2), 204–213 (2008)

39. Girard, R.: The Scapegoat. Johns Hopkins University Press, Baltimore (1986)

40. Girard, R.: Violence and the Sacred. The Johns Hopkins Unniversity Press, Baltimore (1977)

41. Walker, G., Devine-Wright, P., Hunter, S., High, H., Evans, B.: «Trust and community: exploring the meanings, contexts and dynamics of community renewable energy.» Energy Policy **38**(6), 2655–2663 (2010)

42. O'Neill-Carrillo, E., Mercado, E., Luhring, O., Jordan, I., Irizarry-Rivera, A.: «Community energy projects in the caribbean: advancing socio-economic development and energy transitions.» IEEE Technol. Soc. Mag. **38**(3), 44–55 (2019)

43. Dóci, G., Vasileiadou, E.: «Let's do it ourselves" Individual motivations for investing in renewables at community level» Renew. Sustain. Energy Rev. **49**(1), 41–50 (2015)

Citizen Participation in the Transition of Greek Cities to Smart Cities: Does Size Matter?

Pagona-Xanthi Psathopoulou, Andreas Alexopoulos[✉], and Vasileios Panagou[✉]

Department of Accounting, University of West Attica, Athens, Greece
{ppsathopoulou,a.alexopoulos}@uniwa.gr, vas.panagou@gmail.com

Abstract. This paper focuses on the concept of the smart city and the factors that work for its formation. One of them is related to the size of the city. The concept of the "smart city" has been particularly widespread in recent years both within the academic community and more widely in the field of self-government and society itself. In this context, emerging 'smart city' strategies around the world, with an emphasis on 'smart citizens' and their role in shaping smart cities, are at the center of research, business and policy initiatives. Since the size of cities in Greece varies significantly, it is important to investigate whether this particular characteristic affects the process of transforming cities into smart cities.

For this reason, the paper focuses on the investigation of the concept of the smart city and its specific components, in relation to the importance of size, through the conduct of a qualitative research on representatives of different sized municipalities in Greece.

The results of the research highlight the fact that the idea of smart cities in Greek local society is more widespread in urban centers. In addition, in the smaller cities the daily communication and contact of the citizens with the representatives of the local authority is a primary way of citizen participation. Finally, the size of the municipalities under study seems to have a significant impact on issues related to staffing, resources, the operation of economies of scale, etc. and which determine the operational capacity of each municipality.

Keywords: Smart cities · city size · citizens participation

1 Introduction

In recent decades, the concept of smart cities is more widespread than ever, since it is associated with the provision of new, innovative solutions in areas of urban development such as mobility, environment, economy, governance, quality of life, education, etc. etc. Indeed, smart city is a conceptual umbrella that includes smart urbanism, smart economy, smart and sustainable environment, smart technology, smart energy, smart mobility, smart healthcare and a range of related topics (Jasrotia 2018).

Although the interest in smart cities was initially closely linked to new technologies to solve various urban issues (Perera et al. 2014), the interest soon shifted to citizens and how they can contribute to developing smart cities. (Simonofski et.al. 2021).

© The Author(s), under exclusive license to Springer Nature Switzerland AG 2023
O. Gervasi et al. (Eds.): ICCSA 2023 Workshops, LNCS 14109, pp. 529–546, 2023.
https://doi.org/10.1007/978-3-031-37120-2_34

In this context, citizen participation emerged as an alternative solution in order to give citizens an active role. And this is because citizens are often excluded from the decision-making process of the rulers, while they could act as experts and information providers for their cities (Secinaro et al. 2022).

The first scientific research on citizen participation in public decision-making began in the late 1960s, with Arnstein's famous article "The Ladder of Citizen Participation". In his article Arnstein presented a scale for levels of citizen participation. Thus, citizen participation is captured on a scale that includes various levels, from non-participation of the citizen, providing ideas but without impact on decision-making, and active participation where he co-decides and participates in the various processes.

Today the debate about the participation of citizens in decision-making both more broadly and specifically in relation to their participation in the transition of cities to smart ones is perhaps more relevant than ever. Elements such as the value of participation, the ways but also the means, by which this participation can be enhanced, are emerging.

The purpose of this paper is, after delineating the concept and importance of the smart city, to investigate the degree of citizen participation mainly in decision-making for the formation of a smart city and secondarily in the provided smart services that are available. A central parameter in this investigation is the variable of the size of the cities which, as a basic hypothesis, is considered decisive.

The work is structured in 5 sections. In Sect. 2 the process of citizen participation in smart cities is analyzed, in Sect. 3 research data is listed regarding the size of the cities under consideration and how this affects the transition of cities to smart cities, in Sect. 4 the research methodology is described and in Sect. 5 the analysis and discussion of the research results are presented.

2 Citizens Participation in Smart Cities

In the last few years, there are more and more studies regarding the participation of citizens in the smart cities under development. These studies focus each time on different applications, services and dimensions of under development smart cities, as well as on the ways through which citizen participation can be enhanced. Briefly, we list some of these studies around the world.

In particular, in a study by Yeh (2017), the importance of services to citizens in developing smart cities in Taiwan was studied. The research highlighted the fact that citizens were more receptive to smart services when their ideas were taken into account while designing the services. In addition, it was recorded that citizens are more accepting of services based on new technologies, especially when their design stands out for innovation, ensures personal data protection and high quality. On the contrary, in a research by Belanche et al. (2016), in Zaragoza, Spain, it was recorded that the participation of citizens in planning and decision-making regarding the smart city, ultimately contributes to the use of these services.

In addition, in the research of Castelnovo (2016), the participation of citizens in the creation and development of services and policies, emerges so important that no smart city can be formed without smart citizens. In the case where the citizens do not accept the cities becoming smart, the whole project towards the transformation of a city into a smart city is said to have many chances of failure. The cooperation of citizens with the designers and creators of smart cities is a prerequisite.

In the research of Tadili and Fasly (2019), on smart city experts around the world, the need for citizen participation in smart cities is emphasized, both at the initial stage of planning public services (as co-creators), and afterwards by voicing the experiences and their knowledge on a variety of issues. Awareness of the importance of citizen participation in smart cities was prioritized.

Also, in a research by Berntzen and Johannessen (2016), it emerged that the development of smart cities in India requires emphasizing the opinions of both citizens and governments.

Moreover, in the research of Berntzen and Karamagioli (2010), in Norwegian cities, citizens seem to take on different roles in order to contribute to the development of smart city services. On the one hand there are citizens who can influence political decisions, while on the other hand there are those who do not have access to decision-making or general participation. However, all citizens have the opportunity to share their knowledge, experiences and time.

In the research of Simonofski et.al. (2021), in the cities of Namur (Belgium) & Linköping (Sweden), the active participation of citizens in the design of the smart city and the presentation of their ideas are taken into account in order for the smart city to meet their real needs. In addition, each city has its own unique characteristics that should be taken into account when designing a strategy that favors citizen participation.

Also, in Hollands (2008) research, smart city experts attempted to identify ways and means to increase citizen participation in smart cities. The research documented a variety of factors that affect citizens in a smart city, such as the transfer of power, addressing inequalities, redefining the concept of "smart city", using new technologies to benefit peoples' needs.

In research by Myeong et al. (2018), the determinants influencing the development of smart cities were investigated. The results of the study highlighted the participation of citizens as the most important factor, followed by leadership, infrastructure, the reorganization of the legal system, the willingness of governments to cooperate, etc.

Finally, in a research by Georgiadis et al. (2021), the active participation of citizens is emphasized as a vital part for the development of any smart city. In particular, in the same research, the perceptions of Greek and Cypriot citizens regarding the concept of the smart city, their opinions and their beliefs regarding the level of "smartness" of their city were studied. Municipal authorities should adopt methods that inspire and encourage the participation of citizens, provide them with incentives, identify the reasons for which they are reluctant to participate (e.g. lack of trust, dissatisfaction), work closely to solve local problems and implement innovative ideas.

From what was discussed in this section, the question arises "since the participation of citizens is recognized as important, why is this not a priority during the development of smart cities?". Perhaps this can be justified to the fact that the two sides start from different points, focusing on different dimensions of the cities each time. As an example, we mention the results of Gupta and Hall's (2017) research, where citizens focus on issues such as mobility, environment, governance and economy, while city officials prioritize environment, economy, mobility and governance. It is likely that citizen participation varies from country to country, from city to city and is related to a number of factors such as the culture of participation, the existence of strong centralized and paternalistic models in public administration, the degree of integration of technology, the institutional framework, etc. Therefore, citizens' participation in smart cities needs further investigation.

3 The Size of Cities and Smart Cities

In this section we present research data regarding the size of the cities under consideration and how this affects the transition of cities to smart cities.

In particular, according to Kumar and Dahiya (2016), there is strong evidence that the city's population size matters, especially in EU member states, when it comes to developing a smart city.

In research by Gupta and Hall (2017), the size of cities is a critical factor for the development of smart cities. Size seems to influence the priorities of citizens and officials (governors and people in positions of power) of developing smart cities in India. Thus, the concept of a smart city varies, related to the population and infrastructure of each city.

In Berntzen and Johannessen's (2016) research in India, city size can influence the formation of smart cities by determining the priority areas for project development.

Furthermore, Borsekova's et al. research on 158 European smart cities explored the ways in which the size of each city shapes individual smart city characteristics and indicators. The survey found that the size of cities is significantly related to the profile of smart city participants, as well as the ways in which these cities manage their resources. In particular, regarding the profile of the participants, citizens in medium-sized cities are described as more open-minded compared to larger cities, which seems to affect their decisions as well. This is due to the fact that in larger cities there are citizens of different ethnicities, with different interests and pursuits, as well as the fact that life in larger cities is much more impersonal, with a more fragmented sense of community. In addition, citizens in medium-sized cities are shown to be more innovative than citizens in larger cities. This is probably justified, according to the results of the research, by the fact that in medium-sized cities, citizens do not have the same intense rhythms in their daily lives and are not as busy as those in large cities. In the same research on resource management, the research highlighted that large investments in new technologies may not always be the best or most efficient solution for smaller and medium-sized smart cities. Small and especially medium-sized cities are constantly forced to look for new growth opportunities and make more efficient use of internal resources. On the contrary, larger cities (metropolitan cities) have more money to invest in new technologies, are more interesting from a business point of view, in terms of investment sizes and their returns, as well as the market scope which is of considerable interest. Finally, the research concluded that the dimension of city size still remains undervalued when studying smart cities.

In contrast, for Duygan et al. (2022), who studied 22 Swiss cities to determine the factors that make some cities more advanced than others in smart city development, city population size was less important. In particular, population (or city size), which is widely recognized as a favorable factor for the promotion of smart projects and innovation, turned out to be not a critical factor (in Switzerland) in the case of Swiss cities. These data are attributed to the political and institutional conditions, since in Switzerland, even the smallest municipalities have considerable power in institutionalizing and planning the use of infrastructure. The legal and fiscal autonomy of cities can enable local governments to initiate and implement smart city projects. However, the results showed that high participation of the service sector, the presence of research institutions and high urban density are sufficient for the development of smart cities, while population size, new residential development and participation in international networks seem less significant. The case of Switzerland therefore reveals that progress towards the smart city transition is not limited to large, metropolitan areas, but as it turns out, even small suburbs with a population of around 20,000 (e.g. Pully) can also be centers for the implementation of smart city projects, due to their denser population, the large share of the service sector, the proximity to major cities and the universities of the region.

From what was mentioned above in the cities under consideration, we notice that size seems to influence the development of smart cities. However, is population size enough to rank cities as small or large? According to Oliveira et al. (2018), population size alone is not sufficient to classify a city as small, medium or large. It is necessary to take into account other factors, such as the relations established with the nearby cities, the influence of the periphery, the movements and the activities developed in the cities under review.

In the same direction contributes the research of Simonofski et al. (2021), in which it is pointed out that each city has particularities that must be taken into account in order to design a meaningful citizen participation strategy, which must be adapted to factors such as the city's context, values, organization, size, the peculiarities of a country, etc.

Ultimately, nowadays it is difficult to follow a single smart city recipe, due to the geographical heterogeneity and urban diversity of cities. After all, smart thinking pre-supposes an understanding of the complexity of the city and its interrelated components. It is important to understand what kind of city is to be analyzed and in which sector. Thus, small and medium-sized cities cannot aim for the same "performance" but often have the same means and resources to achieve smart projects, just like large regional metropolises (Caruso et al. 2022).

Therefore, research is required in cities of different sizes, in order to establish the degree to which of the above considerations apply, but also to capture how the size of towns ultimately affects or not the participation of citizens in them. In this context, a qualitative research was carried out in selected Greek cities of different sizes, described in the next section.

4 Research Methodology

As mentioned above in the theoretical part of our work, the existing literature receives more extensive research, is intensified, regarding the role of citizens and how it is outlined during the development of smart cities of different sizes. Thus, in the present work, the investigation of the ways and means utilized by different size Municipalities is attempted, in order to transform the cities into smart ones and operate by providing better quality services, being at the same time more competitive in the context of the global economy. In addition, the research focuses on the participation of citizens in the formation of smart cities and in the relevant decision-making.

In particular, the research focuses on the following research fields:

- The ways in which the inhabitants of the cities under examination participate in the transformation of the cities into smart cities,
- In the correlations between citizens' participation in the planning and development/implementation of innovative actions and their demographic characteristics,
- In the inhibiting factors of the development of smart cities,
- In the role of local authorities in encouraging the participation of citizens in the "intelligence" - digitization of each city,
- Usability-friendliness of new technologies to encourage citizen participation in existing or developing smart cities,
- The impact of the pandemic period on enhancing citizen participation in smart cities (at the level of decision-making and service provision).

The paper aims to investigate the transformation of cities into smart cities, while addressing the following research questions: (1) How do Municipalities of different sizes manage their transformation into smart cities? (2) What are the main conversion axes (how they transform cities into smart cities)? (3) What are the main obstacles faced by Municipalities of different sizes in their transformation into smart cities? (4) What is the role of the citizens in the process of co-creating products or services in cities of different sizes? (5) How did the pandemic affect citizen participation in cities of different sizes?

By focusing on the above research questions, we can derive information that depends on how the situation regarding citizen participation is shaped in smart cities of different sizes or under development. This information can then contribute to the study of all cases of Greek smart cities.

This research aims to explore the process and critical factors of transforming cities into smart cities and at the same time to examine the role of citizens in this process. The qualitative method and in-depth interviews were chosen to conduct the research since, as mentioned above, our aim is to study in depth the phenomenon of citizen participation in the development of smart cities of different sizes. Through qualitative research, the formation of a global perception is sought on the basis of contexts and detailed elements, as they appear in their natural social context (Mason 2003).

The present qualitative research was conducted with individual interviews with representatives of municipalities of different sizes in Greece and involved both political figures and executives involved in decision-making regarding the digital strategy of each city.

All the data were collected by 6 representatives of municipalities selected from the total of 332 municipalities in the country. More specifically, each representative came from a different category of municipality as defined in the "Existing model of city typologies n. 3852/2010 "New Architecture of Self-Government and Decentralized Administration - Kallikratis Program"" More specifically, these are the following categories:

(a) Municipalities of Metropolitan Centers,
(b) Large Mainland Municipalities and Capital Prefecture Municipalities,
(c) Mid-Continental Municipalities,
(d) Small Continental and Small Mountain Municipalities,
(e) Large and Medium Island Municipalities,
(f) Small Island Municipalities.

More specifically, respondents from the municipalities of Peristeri, Trikkaia, Domoko, Deskatis, Syros, Astypalaia participated in the survey. The interviews were conducted online and had the form of a semi-structured interview, in the Greek language. The survey was conducted from June 2022 to October 2022.

The interview as a means of collecting research material is considered to offer higher quality information with a lower degree of statistical bias than other methods (Howard and Sharp 2001). In particular, this method was preferred, as the purpose of the research was to study elements, such as perceptions of the phenomenon of citizen participation in cities of different sizes, the beliefs regarding the strengthening of participation, the context in which the factors that act as inhibitors are formed in the development of smart Greek cities. The sample of respondents can be considered suitable, because it has the elements we want to investigate, the knowledge, the characteristics and the will to give more complete and in-depth answers to the question about the degree of citizen participation in the formation of different sized smart cities.

5 Analysis and Discussion of Research Results

The analysis and discussion of the research results is presented based on the above axes.

Regarding the current situation, in terms of the degree of development of smart cities in the Greek area, the respondents consider that the idea of smart cities is not widespread in Greek society. Some of them (a finding from respondents in smaller cities) express the belief that the idea of smart cities is more widespread in larger municipalities, compared to smaller ones. More generally, there is a confusion on the issue of "what is considered a smart city", since also through the data of our research, the incorrect interpretation that is often attributed to the concept of a smart city is captured. Bibliographic data from a survey of municipalities in Greece confirm our findings by documenting that most participants have a vague understanding of the conceptual framework of a smart sustainable urban area (Siokas et al. 2021).

However, some of the interviewees point out that gradually this picture seems to be changing for the better, as citizens are gradually adopting smart city practices, making use of the infrastructure offered to them, without the majority of them, however, currently being able to understand "the big idea" of smart cities. Bibliographic data validates the fact that citizens recognize the concept of smart cities, as well as the benefits they can bring to their quality of life (Kontothanasi 2021).

Summing up, from all the answers given, it can be seen that in Greek local communities the idea of smart cities is not particularly developed. In particular, what seems to emerge is that the practice of smart cities in Greece is more widespread in urban centers compared to smaller, more remote municipalities. The following can be considered as the main reasons: a) the fact that citizens are limited to enjoying the benefits of smart applications and services, without participating in their design and development and essentially without understanding the "idea" of smart cities, b) in the wrong handling of local government agencies regarding the promotion of new technologies and, in particular, in the fact that no emphasis had been placed on the use of new technologies, which could facilitate the daily life of citizens, c) in a lack of knowledge or lack of awareness from the part of citizens about what is considered as a smart city (what is a smart city, what services are provided by a smart city, etc.) and what is the role of decision-makers in them (limited perceptions - mentality), d) the geographical heterogeneity of cities and the possibilities (practices) given for the development of projects in them.

The role of local government is multi-dimensional, decisive and critical for the development of smart cities according to all respondents in the survey. In particular, they consider that it provides infrastructure, information, education, inspires and motivates the citizen to use new technologies to their advantage, while absorbing resources through the European and other programs it secures. However, there is a strong perception that smaller municipalities cannot compete with larger municipalities (for reasons discussed below) and that larger municipalities will serve as role models for the smaller cities surveyed by us.

The value of citizen participation and the need to implement projects and provide services based on the real needs of citizens, is evident from the results of the survey. The internal organization is set as a necessary condition by the research participants, in order for any projects to be successful and last over time. Therefore, the question arises "in what ways/instruments can we strengthen the participation of citizens in smart cities?", which will be attempted to be answered below.

In addition, citizen participation in smart cities is seen as crucial by survey participants. This finding is also confirmed in other research, where the importance of citizens' participation in the design of the smart city is highlighted in order to benefit from their ideas, so that the smart city meets their real needs (Simonofski et.al. 2021).

However, this participation of citizens is often presented as "virtual", in the sense that the elected bodies pick the priorities and choose each time what will happen in practice. In particular, for the smaller cities, according to the answers given "in practice it has been proven that the citizen hardly participates at all". The participation of citizens is limited to the use of any applications or services and concerns use by younger citizens. However, to lead to a real smart city, the active participation of the citizen should be ensured (Zubizarreta et al. 2016). Therefore, the question of real citizen participation should be put at the center of research.

The next axis concerns practices and initiatives to encourage citizen participation in smart cities.

Thus, according to the research data, citizen participation in the cities under study is expressed through a) participation/use of citizen applications and electronic services, b) online councils and consultations, c) communication/contact with the citizen, d) social media, e) conducting surveys and polls at local level (Table 1).

Table 1. Practices and initiatives to encourage citizen participation in smart cities. Source: Editing of Own Research Data.

Municipalities category (as described in the section "*4. Research methodology*")/Inhibiting factors	Face to face communication	Online councils - Consultation	Use of application/Electronic services	Sureys/Polls	Social Media
(a)	-	X	X	X	X
(b)	-	X	X	X	X
(c)	X	-	-	-	-
(d)	X	-	-	-	-
(e)	-	-	X	X	X
(f)	X	-	-	-	-

Conducting surveys and polls is considered important by the people interviewed in the survey, although up to the time of conducting our survey, there has rarely been any relevant research with an emphasis on the needs of the citizens. In particular, for the smaller cities, the understaffed municipal staff, the staff's technological training, but also the staff's willingness to "run" surveys, is recorded and acts as an inhibiting factor. In addition, for these cities, any investigation that has been carried out, it is recording "...zero participation of citizens in surveys with questionnaires".

The emphasis on personal contact and real-life communication with the citizen is considered decisive for all the participants in the research, in order for the citizens to get involved in the "smartening" processes of the city. In particular, in the smaller cities, the daily communication and contact of the citizens with the representatives of the local authority is a primary way of citizen participation. Personal contact appears to be a more popular tactic for smaller municipalities, while leveraging new technologies is a more popular tactic for larger municipalities.

At this point, the following questions rightly arise "How can one measure the impact that each service and/or application has on citizen satisfaction during the development of smart cities? How can it be established whether the existing, implemented and planned services and applications are useful in the development of smart cities, since there is no sufficient and accurate data resulting from the essential participation of citizens? How can we involve the citizens of smaller cities more technologically/electronically?".

In particular, initiatives that have been developed concern the user identification and authentication platform (gov.hub), consultations that take place online per municipality, as well as the utilization of municipalities' social media to record and collect data on citizens' needs. But also the gathering and quantification of the data of each city in practice, through measurements and surveys (e.g. "...we put bicycles and suddenly we saw a terrible reduction in the streets and squares...") are valuable elements for the further planning and development of smart cities.

In the above context, one of the respondents also mentioned the need to create a consultation platform, where collective bodies will be able to put forward citizens' proposals, discuss and make decisions. Also, the size of the city seems to influence the aforementioned consultations. Thus, the participation of citizens in the smaller cities often registers low levels ("participation was too small, the percentage was too small, not even 5%") and mainly by the youngest citizens.

Here the question arises "Couldn't the existing websites that the municipalities already have, technically support this need?" In any case, the need to create a platform, adapted to the needs of each municipality of different size, where all opinions from and in every direction will be taken into account, is deemed necessary. After all, this has been emphasized in other research where the collaborations created by cities become more beneficial when they involve not only municipalities and private companies but also NGOs, research institutions as well as different political organizations (Jablonska 2018).

However, the following question was raised here: "Who will make the final decisions?" Who will choose what will be given importance?' The majority of respondents believe that the final decision should be made by those in power, because citizens think and act individually and not according to the "common good". In particular, on the one hand, the opinion is expressed that participation, the expression of ideas and opinions is required, and on the other hand, the very concept of participation is often negated, from opinions expressed by the respondents who argue that the municipality should give direction to the citizens, because either they themselves do not know what they should do, or in order to speed up any formal procedures. Ultimately, citizens do not seem to be recognized as 'smart citizens' and remain largely outside or peripheral to power structures and decision-making processes, limiting the boundaries of the smart city and its ability to claim and restructure. The citizen still remains marginal to the existing smart city (Shelton and Lodato 2019).

The participation of the citizens is limited to the use of any application/infrastructure, but also to the sending of corrections, etc., and does not concern their substantial participation in the decision-making for the development of smart cities.

Regarding the type of participation recorded during the development of smart cities, it seems to be mostly pretentious. In particular, the views of the citizens recorded in the consultations are often of a "pretend" nature. We would say that once again, although the efforts start with pure intentions, ultimately in the majority of cases any citizen participation in Greek smart cities seems to be treated by the municipal authorities virtually and superficially.

It appears that, despite efforts to reframe the smart city as 'citizen-centred', smart urbanism remains rooted in pragmatic, instrumental and paternalistic discourses and practices rather than those of social rights, political citizenship and the common good (Cardullo and Kitchin 2019). Indeed, to become smart, a city should develop a service approach that will focus mainly on citizens who are also the main beneficiaries of the services offered by a Smart City (Georgiadis et al. 2021).

But what is finally happening in the Greek reality? From what was presented above, it seems that in Greek cities the transformation towards the achievement of intelligence meets several obstacles.

Regarding the factors that affect the motivation of citizens' participation, various factors are recorded that work, either positively and reinforcing, or inhibiting.

Thus, on the one hand, the provision of incentives, the satisfaction of the real needs of citizens, the use of new technologies to simplify and reduce the time of the services offered, act as positive factors, while the established culture in the municipalities is recorded among the inhibiting factors (at all levels, citizens, employees, municipal authorities), along with the insufficient resources, the inability to distribute responsibilities, the multiplicity of legislation, the size of the municipalities, etc.

More specifically, citizens' participation in the formation and operation of smart cities could be enhanced through incentives, that are related to realistic goals that actually concern the improvement of citizens' quality of life.

With regard to the strategies to strengthen citizens' participation in the formation and operation of smart cities, three basic elements are necessary according to the respondents, as follows: time, mood and will.

The following table (Table 2) summarizes the main inhibiting factors in the development of smart Greek cities.

The most important problem that remains, according to the research data, concerns polynomiality and legislation. The need for rewording, correction, completion, etc. of the lawsis emphasized, in order for them to facilitate the procedures and not be obstacles in the development of smart cities. In addition, the difficulty arising from the fact that most cities have a history, a culture, a character that must be preserved, as well as resources that must be protected, redistributed, supported when developing a smart city or region is highlighted. Therefore, any change should be governed by creativity that supports the development of the city or region based on its particular characteristics.

Strengthening the level of citizen participation can be achieved through "internal reorganization". In particular, in the smaller municipalities, the opinion is recorded that several projects are still at the level of contracts and tenders, because the specific municipalities are able to support a limited number of projects based on the staff they own.

In regards to the creation of the aforementioned consultation platform, it is proposed in order to increase participation. The contribution of new technologies is considered crucial for the completion of such a plan. Finally, once again research data is confirmed according to which, the main challenges faced by policy makers when developing applications and services are organizational and not technological (Mondschein et al. 2021). Furthermore, despite the fact that the majority of cities have incorporated various forms of smart projects, a rather partial implementation of related initiatives in their daily operations is observed (Siokas et al. 2021).

The size of municipalities seems to have a decisive effect on citizen participation. More specifically, the staffing of small municipalities, their strategic planning, the low level of education (e.g. the absence of universities or other institutions through which citizens could be educated), the inability to attract investment and the lack of business activity, the lack of connection with Academic institutions and research centers, the lack of civil society organizations, define the culture of a city's citizens and contribute to their participation or non-participation in the transition of cities to smart cities.

In addition, the size of cities plays a decisive role in the quantity and quality of projects and the citizens' use of them.

Table 2. Inhibiting factors in the development of smart Greek cities. Source: Editing of Own Research Data.

Municipalities category (as described in the section "4. Research methodology")/Inhibiting factors	Size of cities	Resources - Manage resources	Legislation/Polynomy	Culture	Unknown fear	Technological involvement	Age	Municipality capabilities	Lack of research	Internal organization
(a)	-	-	X	-	-	X	X	X	-	-
(b)	-	-	-	X	-	X	-	-	-	-
(c)	X	X	-	X	X	X	-	X	-	X
(d)	X	X	-	X	-	-	-	X	-	X
(e)	-	X	-	X	X	X	X	X	-	X
(f)	X	X	X	X	-	X	X	X	-	-

In addition to size, the geographic location of each municipality determines citizen participation in smart cities. People living in island regions are more innovative, on the contrary, people living in small villages (e.g. farmers), often do not have access to knowledge or sometimes are not interested (different priorities and cultures) and therefore, a part of them remains technologically and typically illiterate.

Furthermore, the geographical location or topography of smaller municipalities often renders any planned projects incomplete, as practical (geographical) difficulties are inhibiting factors.

The issue of the unevenness of the municipalities is recorded as another factor affecting the operational capacity of each municipality, in the sense of the impossibility of horizontalizing certain initiatives that could be implemented at the national level, which concern either directly or indirectly the citizen. This finding is confirmed bibliographically, since each city has its own unique characteristics that must be taken into account in order to design a citizen participation strategy, truly adapted to the context at hand (Simonofski et al. 2021).

Moreover, the culture of a city's citizens can play a decisive role in their participation in the development of smart cities. In addition, the prevailing culture and specifically the lack of culture of political leadership on participatory issues, combined with the aforementioned lack of coordination and legislation, is another important inhibiting factor noted.

In addition, the culture of a municipality's employees, their receptivity to structural operational changes and participatory practices, can influence citizen participation in smart cities to a very large extent. In particular, the opinion is recorded that it would be useful to emphasize the training of employees, in order to remove the aforementioned obstacles. The need to invest in training and familiarizing employees with modern digital tools, has also been highlighted in other research (Siokas et al. 2021).

In addition, the culture of the society as a whole and the role played by the companies cooperating with the local government in the overall organization, is an issue for further investigation. Through the answers given, the need for redefining strategies emerges in combination with the culture that exists as a whole in society (a factor mentioned above), elements that act as an inhibitor during the development of smart cities.

Another inhibiting factor recorded concerns the responsibilities, the resources and the ways in which they are distributed. Moreover, another problem that emerged from smaller municipalities was the lack of software and the uneven distribution of resources. The issue of lack of resources is often one of the most important barriers recorded that can be improved by combining resources through an inter-municipal collaboration (Mavroyianni 2019; Karahasan and Hagane 2018). The lack of synergy and convergence between the various interventions, leads to the impossibility of exploiting the added value offered by the coordination of resources and the joint efforts of organizations (Phararaj et al. 2018).

Therefore, the provision of incentives, the formation of a relevant culture (of the municipality, the citizens, the employees), the correct strategic planning, the decentralization of responsibilities and the correct distribution of resources, the redefinition of laws, the size of the cities and their geographical location are listed as decisive factors for the development of smart cities. Indeed, some of the inhibiting factors recorded in the present research are also found in the research of Tadili and Fasly (2019). In particular, obstacles to the active participation of citizens are related to factors, such as bridging the digital divide, the lack of a long-term vision and the lack of a specific allocation of the budget in the developing smart cities.

With reference to the demographic characteristics and the degree to which they affect the participation of citizens in smart cities, the sample under examination varies its answers, focusing on the factors of age, education, technological-digital training, human geography and professional status.

Regarding the education of citizens, more than half of the respondents state that it is a very important factor, while the rest consider that "educational level does not play any role".

Furthermore, while for some of the respondents, age is not considered one of the factors that determine the degree of participation, for some others it is a determining factor. In particular, the opinions are recorded that age plays a role, but not a decisive one. The age of the citizens is a decisive factor for the representatives of smaller cities, regarding the use of technology. Also, emphasis was placed on the training required for these people, in order to facilitate the use of the new technologies.

However, according to literature, the age factor and factors related to the city (city-factors), seem not to be decisive for the development of smart cities in the research of Georgiadis et al. (2021).

With reference to the professional qualification, this seems to determine the mentality and the opportunities to deal with new technologies and, to a further extent, the technological training of the citizens, in the smaller cities. However, as noted, technological means strengthen the interface, but there should be a desire and willingness on both sides for any technological venture to work well.

In particular, on technology training, the respondents seem to be divided into two parts. More specifically, for smaller cities, technological training/competence is considered a decisive factor. Thus, in these cities "younger citizens participate to some extent using online services and applications, while older citizens lack the motivation for such engagement and often exhibit a technophobia." These findings seem to agree with research where, indeed, there is a portion of citizens with low levels of digital access and digital literacy who even tend to be excluded, receiving limited benefits from digital urban services and infrastructure in smart cities (Shin et al., 2021). In particular, as reported by Zdjelar and Keleman (2019), the number of e-service users aged 54+ is extremely low, however bridging the digital gap will be achieved by looking for the best way related to abilities, skills and needs of each person.

In addition, respondents as a whole, place a strong emphasis on providing incentives as a strategy to enhance participation.

Moreover, the activation of civil society in a logic where everyone can contribute and solve problems of the local society, develop their ideas, testify their experiences, co-create, is suggested by an interviewee, as a way of substantial active participation. In the same logic, actions – updates of new applications and services, as well as seminars, workshops, conferences for the citizens are proposed.

Furthermore, open consultations are recorded as an important mean to enhance citizen participation, in the sense that, through them, citizens can determine the development and progress of their city.

Finally, social media are proposed as means of enhancing participation that gives the possibility of immediacy, attracting younger citizens, while at the same time it is an economic tool for municipalities (as long as it does not require any significant financial investment) and which is already used by the whole of the municipalities under study. These data seem to be confirmed in a study by Triantafillidou et al. (2022), where "smart cities in Greece use Facebook mainly to publish information of interest to various audiences in the form of announcements and press releases about activities and services of municipalities". However, it should be noted (as mentioned above) that, for smaller municipalities, information through direct contact is a priority, since citizens are not yet used to being informed through the municipality's website (or modern technological means).

In summary, regarding the strategies to enhance citizen participation in smart cities, this is presented on two levels. On the one hand, the participation in decision-making and in the formation of smart applications and services and on the other hand in their operation.

Finally, regarding the role played by the pandemic in the participation of citizens in the formation of smart cities, it seems to be more strengthened after the period of the pandemic. In particular, it seems to have acted as an accelerator of citizens' technological involvement, since according to all respondents in the survey, the pandemic played a decisive role in introducing citizens to the concept of digital transformation and the use of new technologies - applications. In addition, on a practical level, it helped people who either lived in remote areas, or who feared for their health due to the pandemic and were facilitated by electronic exchange. However, according to some of the interviewees in the research, it seems that at the level of infrastructure development, it often acted as a hindrance since it was not possible due to practical difficulties (prohibition of movement) for the municipality's projects to develop smoothly.

At the level of everyday life, a relative disturbance was created for the citizen after it forced them to take actions unknown (to them) until then.

From what was discussed above, it appears that the compulsion caused by the pandemic, the effort to satisfy needs through smart services and applications, pushed the active participation of citizens to use smart applications and services. However, concerns are raised as to whether and to what extent this participation is active or passive. In particular, the manner of citizen participation is under investigation, since citizens participated in the use of data and services produced by local self-government organizations or the government, without being given the opportunity to choose or co-create it. Possibly conducting studies regarding the way the pandemic affected the active or passive participation of citizens, as well as strategies to strengthen their role could be the subject of future research.

6 Conclusions

The concept of the smart city and the participation of citizens in it is a modern, dynamic and evolving research field, which cannot be studied statically and in isolation.

In our research, an attempt is made through the primary research that was carried out to capture the general picture of the situation regarding the participation of citizens in making decisions for the formation of smart cities, particularly examining the size parameter. However, further investigation, at the level of municipalities - local self-government, is deemed imperative and necessary in order to examine other factors that may be related to the geographical area, the organizational culture of each body and its citizens.

In the Greek area, the development of smart cities cannot be considered to be at the same level as that found in many developed countries. Also, the range of factors associated with the participation process work differently in cities of different sizes, sometimes enhancing and sometimes inhibiting. Among the most important problems for the development of smart cities remains the culture (citizens, employees-executives, political leadership), finding resources, the inability to distribute responsibilities, polynomy - legislation, organization, etc. In particular, in smaller municipalities, the understaffing and training (mainly technological) of the staff, as well as the culture of the citizens, is recorded as acting as a hindrance to the development of the cities.

The role of the citizen in the transformation of cities into smart ones remains limited and passive, while time, will, methodicality, cultural change, etc. are required, in order for the citizen to be at the center, at least according to what emerges from all the cities under study, with any limited generalizations that could be made here, since this is a qualitative research. Citizens in large cities gradually seem to be adopting the practices of the smart city, while at the same time making use of the relevant infrastructure and tools offered to them. In particular, they send requests to citizen service platforms, participate in online councils and consultations, actively participate in social media, express their opinions and positions through surveys and polls at the local level. Of course, even in this case there is still great room for improvement and several steps to be taken. On the other hand, the majority of citizens, mainly in small provincial towns, seem to stick to a daily communication and traditional practices without giving much importance to the advantages that the development of digital services and projects brings to them. In the great majority, in these cases, citizens do not seem to be able to understand "the big idea" of smart cities and thus their participation is often recorded as limited, low and problematic. This does not mean that at the city level there are not some exceptions.

In addition, it appears that larger cities have had more ICT-related projects, which is attributed to their ability to absorb larger funds/resources, the economies of scale that they can develop, as well as geographic factors.

Undoubtedly, the research data cannot be generalized. However, they provide a first insight into the progress of Greek cities towards the process of "smartness".

We believe that an in-depth study of local government officials (elected officials and technocrats), on a larger scale, in municipalities of different sizes, could more adequately reflect the current situation.

References

Arnstein, S.: A ladder of citizen participation. J. Am. Inst. Plann. 3(54), 216–224 (1969)
Belanche, D., Casaló, L.V., Orús, C.: City attachment and use of urban services: Benefits for smart cities. Cities 50, 75–81 (2016)

Berntzen, L.Johannessen, M.R.: The role of citizens in "smart cities. In: Proceedings of the Management International Conference, Pula, Croatia (1–4 June 2016)

Berntzen, L., Karamagioli, E.: Regulatory measures to support eDemocracy. In: Proceedings of the IEEE 2010 Fourth International Conference on Digital Society, Saint Maarten, Netherlands Antilles, pp. 311–316 (10–16 February 2010)

Borsekova, K., Korónya, S., Vaňováb, A., Vitálišová, K.: Functionality between the size and indicators of smart cities: a research challenge with policy implications. Cities **78**, 17–26 (2018)

Cardullo, P., Kitchin, R.: Being a "citizen" in the smart city: up and down the scaffold of smart citizen participation in Dublin Ireland. GeoJournal **84**, 1–13 (2019)

Caruso, G., Pumain, D., Thomas, I.: No "Prêt à Porter" but a multi-scalar perspective of "Smart Cities". In: Laurini, R., Nijkamp, P., Kourtit, K., Bouzouina, L. (eds.) Knowledge Management for Regional Policymaking, pp. 123–148.Springer, Cham (2022). https://doi.org/10.1007/978-3-031-15648-9_7

Castelnovo, W.: Co-production makes cities smarter: citizens' participation in smart city initiatives. In: Co-Production in the Public Sector; pp. 97–117. Springer: Cham (2016)

Duygan, M., Fischer, M., Pärli, R., Ingold, K.: Where do Smart Cities grow? The spatial and socio-economic configurations of smart city development. Sustain. Cities Soc. **77**, 103578 (2022)

Georgiadis, A., Christodoulou, P., Zinonos, Z.: Citizens' perception of smart cities: a case Study. Appl. Sci. **11**(6), 2517 (2021)

Gupta, K., Hall, R.P.: The Indian perspective of smart cities. In; Smart City Symposium Prague (SCSP), Prague, Czech Republic, pp. 1–6 (2017)

Hollands, R.G.: Will the real smart city please stand up? Intelligent, progressive or entrepreneurial? City **12**, 303–320 (2008)

Howard, K., Sharp, J.: The Scientific Study (Trans. Dalakou B.). Gutenberg, Athens (2001)

Jablonska, J.: Smart Cities in practice. a comparative case study between Warsaw, Gdynia, Copenhagen and Malmö. A public actor's perspective with a secondary focus on collaboration and digitization. Master Thesis. Lund University (2018)

Jasrotia, A.: Smart cities & sustainable development: a conceptual framework. Asian J. Res. Bus. Econ. Manag. **8**(2), 42–50 (2018)

Karahasan, A., Hagane, P.: Exploring the smart city mindset in small municipalities: a case study an embedded single case study of small Norwegian municipalities. University of Agder (2018)

Kontothanasi, Th.: Smart cities and their contribution to improving citizens' quality of life. The case of the Municipality of Vari, Voula, Vouliagmeni. Thesis. Aigaleo: PADA (2021)

Kumar, T.M.V., Dahiya, B.: Smart Economy in Smart Cities. Springer, Singapore (2016). https://doi.org/10.1007/978-981-10-1610-3

Mason, J.: Conducting Qualitative Research. Translated from English by N. Kyriazi. Greek Letters, Athens (Originally published 1996) (2003)

Mavrogianni, A.: The transformation of modern cities into intelligent cities: the case of Heraklion, Crete. Diploma thesis. University of Piraeus (2019)

Mavroyianni, A.: The transformation of modern cities into smart cities: the case of Heraklion, Crete. Bachelor's thesis. Piraeus University (2019)

Mondschein, J.S., Clark-Ginsberg, A., Kuehn, A.: Smart cities as large technological systems: overcoming organizational challenges in smart cities through collective action. Sustain. Cities Soc. **67** (2021)

Myeong, S., Jung, Y., Lee, E.: A study on determinant factors in smart city development: an analytic hierarchy process analysis. Sustainability **10**(8), 2606 (2018)

Oliveira, L., Oliveira, R., Bracarense, L., Meira, L., Bertoncini, B.: An overview of problems and solutions for UrbanFreight transport in Brazilian Cities. Sustainability **10**, 1233 (2018)

Perera, C., Zaslavsky, A., Christen, P., Georgakopoulos, D.: Sensing as a service model for smart cities supported by internet of things. Trans. Emerg. Telecommun. Technol. **25**(1), 81–93 (2014)

Praharaj, S., Han, H., Hawken, S.: Urban innovation through policy integration: critical perspectives from 100 smart cities mission in India. City Cult. Soc. **12**, 35–43 (2018). ISSN 1877-9166, Available at: https://doi.org/10.1016/j.ccs.2017.06.004

Secinaro, S., Brescia, V., Iannaci, D., Gideon Mekonnen, J.: Does citizen involvement feed on digital platforms? Int. J. Public Adm. **45**(9), 708–725 (2022)

Shelton, T., Lodato, T.: Actually existing smart citizens: expertise and (non) participation in the making of the smart city. City **23**(1), 35–52 (2019)

Shin, S.Y., Kim, D., Chun, S.: Digital divide in advanced smart city innovations. Sustainability, **13**(7), 4076 (2021)

Simonofski, A., Serral Asensio, E., De Smedt, J., Snoeck, M.: Hearing the voice of citizens in smart city design: the citivoice framework. Bus. Inf. Syst. Eng. **61**(6), 665–678 (2019)

Simonofski, A., Vallé, T., Serral, E,. Wautelet, Y.: Investigating context factors in citizen participation strategies: a comparative analysis of Swedish and Belgian smart cities. Int. J. Inf. Manag. **56** (2021)

Siokas, G., Tsakanikas, A., Siokas, E.: Implementing smart city strategies in Greece: appetite for success. Cities **108** (2021)

Tadili, J., Fasly, H.: Citizen participation in smart cities: a survey. In: Proceedings of the 4th International Conference on Smart City Applications (2019)

Triantafillidou, A., Lappas, G., Yannas, P.: E-Government, dialogic communication principles and social media engagement: an empirical investigation of Greek smart cities. SSRN (2022)

Yeh, H.: The effects of successful ICT-based smart city services: from citizens' perspectives. Gov. Inf. Q. **34**, 556–565 (2017)

Zdjelar, R., Keleman, R.: The smart cities are implemented – are citizens also "smart"? Smart cities and regional development (SCRD). Univ. Acad. Publ. House **3**(1), 47–62 (2019)

Zubizarreta, I., Seravalli, A., Arrizabalaga, S.: Smart city concept: what it is and what it should be. J. UrbanPlan. Dev. **142**(1), (2016)

Impacts of Smart Governance on Urban Development

Katarína Vitálišová[✉], Anna Vaňová, Artur Ivan, Ivana Hačková,
and Kamila Borseková

Faculty of Economics, Matej Bel University, Tajovského 10, 974 01 Banská Bystrica, Slovakia
{katarina.vitalisova,anna.vanova,kamila.borsekova}@umb.sk,
{artur.ivan,ihackova}@student.umb.sk

Abstract. The present paper focuses on the identification of the smart governance impacts on the urban development verified by the empirical research carried out in the cities of the Slovak Republic in 2021. The literature review refers to the various positive and negative effects of smart governance that can be applied at the level of cities. In the paper, the effects mapped in the already published research works were tested by the questionnaire survey, where the respondents were representatives of the cities. The unique contribution of the paper is a verification of these effects in practice, subsequently, by factorial analysis also a specification of the factors (positive effects and barriers) that are key to implementation of smart governance in an integrated and systematic way.

Keywords: Smart Governance · Slovakia · Cities · Factors · Impact

1 Introduction

Over the past decades, urban development has undergone various economic, political, demographic, social, cultural and technological changes that have significantly impacted the current state of cities, both positive and negative. Cities have been the areas in which innovations, new technologies, and efficient and smart solutions are created for a better quality of life for people.

These changes are also reflected in the new approaches in city management. From the new public management, the shift towards public governance and network governance focusing on collaboration can be identified [1–5]. It strongly supports the involvement of stakeholders to carry out a public purpose that could not be achieved due to the boundaries of public administration [6] and digital transformation that focusses on adapting organizational structures and fundamental public service delivery processes [7].

The challenges of urban and local development therefore require appropriate policy responses. In addition to an integrated approach to urban development, the issue of 'multi-level governance' and the participation of relevant actors in city governance is coming to the fore. Both of these approaches require openness, transparency, efficiency, effectiveness, exploration of needs and promotion of active participation of relevant actors in public decision-making while involving them in local community life. For this

O. Gervasi et al. (Eds.): ICCSA 2023 Workshops, LNCS 14109, pp. 547–564, 2023.
https://doi.org/10.1007/978-3-031-37120-2_35

task, it is necessary to introduce new management tools, measures and processes that will create procedures for seeking consensus among representatives of the public, private and non-profit sectors [8, 9]. It is part of smart governance concept.

The aim of the paper is to identify the impacts of smart governance on urban development verified by the empirical research carried out in the cities of Slovak Republic in 2021. It explains, based on the factorial analysis, the pros and cons of smart governance and identify the key factors influencing its implementation.

The paper is divided into three chapters. The first part presents the theoretical review of the research topic, including the main theoretical presumptions used in the primary research. Subsequently, the data and methodology are described and the research results are presented. In the processing of research data, we used descriptive statistics and a software - IBM SPSS Statistics for factorial analysis (KMO and Bartlett's tests).

The added value of the paper lies in the identification of the crucial factors that influence the implementation of the smart governance concept in cities and should be reflected by policy makers and transformed into monitoring and evaluation criteria.

2 From Traditional to Smart Governance in Cities

The concept of governance is generally associated with theories and problems of social coordination and the establishment of its rules. These theories abandon the previous emphasis on the importance of the hierarchical role of the state and highlight the role of the market and networks [10]. Regarding the public sector, the term public governance is used as an alternative approach to public sector management [11–17]. It is a new process of governance in which society, comprising the public, private and not-for-profit sectors, actively participates while accepting the state's authority [13, 18].

Due to rapid technological rapid progress, the governance has to face new challenges and transform to a digital one. This creates new opportunities for improving the participation and interaction of municipalities with relevant stakeholders through conventional and multi-channel communication, including virtual space [19, 20].

Many organizations view digital transformation primarily as the implementation of IT systems [21–23]. It is important to note that an essential prerequisite for the success of digital transformation is, first and foremost, a change in the way of working, organising and managing. At the local level, cities with established technological infrastructure, resources, vision and political leadership see digital technologies as key enablers and infrastructure enablers capable of addressing the growing challenges of urbanisation, population growth, and environmental and fiscal pressures. The use of information and communication technologies (from now on ICTs) enables 'smart' city transformation [24].

Smart governance can be seen as a starting point for the development of smart administration through the use of new ICTs in the management of municipalities [25–30, 56]. Smart governance through ICTs allows improved decision-making through better collaboration between stakeholders. However, even in this approach, innovative technologies should be seen only as a medium or channel that helps cities to streamline management and administrative processes and thus achieve better results for municipalities [25–28, 31].

Moreover, Gil-Garcia, Zhang and Puron-Cid [32]. State that smart local governance is based on integration, innovation, evidence-based decisions, citizen-centricity, sustainability, creativity, efficiency, effectiveness, equity, entrepreneurship, citizen engagement, openness, resilience, technological capabilities.

To the key elements in building a smart governance system in cities belong the efforts of politicians and city leadership to seek new opportunities for the collaboration and empowerment of residents, entrepreneurs and different communities in the city, the efforts to implement these opportunities through relevant tools and methods in decision-making and local policy formulation (Vaňová 2021; Lee, Lee 2014; Lombardi et al. 2011). The next preconditions are an appropriate legislative and organisational framework, financial support and technological infrastructure. A significant challenge for cities is not only to educate and train end-users of smart governance tools but it is also essential to support activities that aim to improve the digital skills of employees [33–37].

Building a smart governance system is a long-term transformation process based on the shared understanding of the concept of smart governance, vision, strategy and shared responsibility. The level of smart governance can then be assessed based on the transparency of urban governance, the involvement of social partners, the level of public services and the implementation of development strategies [38–40, 57].

Based on the scope of the transformation of municipal management, four forms of smart governance can be identified in cities [41]. The least invasive form of smart governance in cities is the preservation of the original government structure in the city with an attempt to adapt it to a smart one. As a rule, the smart attribute is used as a marketing item and becomes part of the city's brand. Externally, this approach is manifested in innovative city websites or the sophisticated use of social networks. The second variant of smart governance is based on decision-making processes that use actual data over time to make decisions that should be the right solution to society's challenges. The third variant of smart governance is smart public administration. Its essence is the reconstruction and integration of the internal processing system through electronic government tools using advanced digital technologies. The fourth form of smart governance is identified as collaborative governance. It is a large-scale transformation of the organisation of city governance, linked to the integration of internal structures and building partnerships with relevant stakeholder, especially within the decision-making processes.

Based on studies by authors working on smart governance [28, 42–47] it is possible to identify three groups of benefits. The first group includes impacts on urban quality of life (improved social and economic conditions, value creation, social equity, urban performance, sustainability, resilience, improved services, economic development based on knowledge and innovation, maximization of socio-economic and environmental development indicators, and the like). The second group relates to local municipalities and the benefits concerning governance processes (e.g. greater administrative efficiency, interoperability, the effectiveness of public policies, strengthening openness and accountability, changes in the structure of municipal organisation, strengthening citizen orientation, and the like). The last group is more stakeholder-oriented and empowering their standing in local politics (e.g. stakeholder participation in public life, equity of their role in local politics, promoting their awareness to build trust in municipalities and social inclusion).

The concept of smart governance in cities also has its critics, who focus on defining the pitfalls [45–47] associated with implementing this concept. The success of implementing the concept depends on the will and capacity of the local municipality to learn. The concept of smart governance requires the continuous development of the skills and capabilities of municipal staff, managers, and stakeholders; otherwise, it cannot be systematically developed.

Several authors [among others, 48–51] often point out that it is not yet possible to realistically assess the long-term benefits of smart governance in practice. At the same time, these authors question the value digital co-production brings concerning the political and social impact in the context of the potential for some marginalisation of parts of the population. Some doubts are associated with the meaning and, in particular, the effect of participatory processes as part of smart governance. The evaluation of the effectiveness and efficiency of participatory processes and identifying their actual contribution to sustainable urban development needs to be addressed [52, 53]. Royo and Yetano [50], for example, point out that the use of new technologies, sensors, and chips can lead to the perception that the citizen as an active public policymaker taking a back seat. According to these authors, the citizen can only be perceived as a unit of information gathering or a particular statistic. Prioritisation of technological innovations can exacerbate the situation without considering the real needs and expectations of users. Thus, unnecessary innovations may represent an unnecessary financial investment.

The benefits and pitfalls of smart governance in the context of smart city governance we researched in the next text in the context of the Slovak Republic.

3 Data and Methodology

To identify the potential positive and negative impacts of smart governance on the local development we used following research studies [28, 42–47, 52–54]. The list of identified impacts was verified in the practice of Slovak cities.

In this paper, we present the partial results of the empirical research realized in a form of questionnaire survey. The research was conducted in the first half of 2021 using a questionnaire survey method, with which we addressed all 141 Slovak cities, with a return rate of 67 responses (47.52%).

The questionnaire was filled out either independently by a city representative or in a guided interview with a city representative. The questionnaire contained 17 questions. For the paper we selected the results that are oriented on the definition of pros and cons of the smart governance in cities.

Four questions were of an identifying nature (city name, position, gender, age). By the size of the cities, 32.84% of respondents were from cities with 5000–9999 inhabitants; 22.39% of the respondents from cities with 10,000–19 999, 20.90% of respondents from cities with 20,000–49 999 inhabitants, 14.93% respondents from cities with inhabitants up to 5000, 7.46% respondents were from cities with 50 000–99 9999 inhabitants, and 1.49% of the respondents were from cities with more than 100 000 inhabitants. Based on the Chi-square test, the research sample is representative of the size categories of the cities.

$$G = \sum_{k=1}^{K} \frac{(n_k - n\prod_k)^2}{n\prod_k}$$

$\chi^2 = 9.49$ $(a = 0,05)$
$G = 0.52682$
Degrees of freedom $= 4$

The respondents of the represented cities were mayors (35.8%), deputy mayors (31.3%), and heads of municipal authorities (32.8%). As many as 64 respondents (95.5%) were university educated, while three had a secondary school education. Regarding age, 3% of the respondents were in the 18–30 age category; 22.4% in the 31–40 age category; 31.3% in the 41–50 and 51–60 age categories; and 11.9% in the 61 + age category.

In the research results processing we use descriptive statistic methods, statistical induction and factorial analysis. To order the benefits and pitfalls by the priority given by respondents, we used Friedman's tests. The research data was tested by KMO and Bertlet test to check if the data are suitable for factorial analysis. In both cases, they passed, so we could use the factorial analysis based on the rotated matrix of factor saturations.

4 Research Results and Discussion

Based on in-depth literature review we identified relatively broad scope of potential positive impacts of digitalization and introduction of innovative methods of governance at the local level. By their summarization, they include:

1. increasing administrative efficiency and operational capability;
2. strengthening openness and accountability;
3. improving services;
4. increasing the effectiveness of public programmes and policies;
5. changes in the structure of the organization of local municipality and its bodies, as well as in its position in relation to stakeholders;
6. strengthening the orientation towards the interests of the citizen (transparency and trust);
7. increasing the involvement of citizens in public life;
8. increasing the participation of other stakeholders in public life;
9. enabling stakeholders to become more informed, qualified and skilled in engaging in public affairs, which increases mutual understanding and trust;
10. sustainability and resilience;
11. economic development based on knowledge and innovation;
12. combined creation of social and economic values;
13. social inclusion;
14. promoting social justice;
15. improving the quality of life in cities;
16. maximizing indicators of socioeconomic and ecological development.

Within the questionnaire survey, we asked the respondents to evaluate each statement as a possible positive impact of smart governance in the city on the scale-fully disagree (1), disagree (2), neither agree, nor disagree (3), agree (4), fully agree (5). Figure 1 presents the share of respondents' answers of the respondents, as well as the average evaluation of each item. The numbers in legends 1–16 identify the evaluated potential benefit below.

As Fig. 1 shows that the most important advantage of a modern municipality is increasing administrative efficiency and operational capability and improving service. Respondents consider the third and fourth advantages to be the strengthening of the orientation towards the interests of the citizen and the strengthening of openness and responsibility. Increasing the efficiency of public programmes and policies is in fifth place, and economic development based on knowledge and innovation is in sixth. Increasing the participation of citizens on the seventh and increasing the participation of other actors on the eighth. The respondents consider changes in public administration organizations and their position in relation to other actors to be the least significant advantage. Changes are followed by social inclusion and social justice.

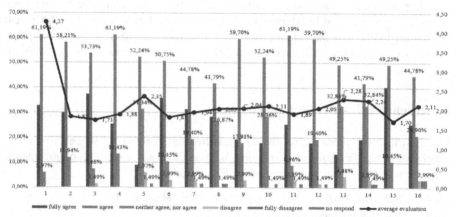

Fig. 1. Potential benefits of smart governance in cities. Legend: 1. Increasing administrative efficiency and operational capability; 2. strengthening openness and accountability; 3. improving services; 4. increasing the effectiveness of public programs and policies; 5. changes in the structure of the organization of local municipality and its bodies, as well as in its position in relation to stakeholders; 6.strengthening the orientation towards the interests of the citizen (transparency and trust); 7. increasing the involvement of citizens in public life; 8. increasing the participation of other stakeholders in public life; 9. enabling stakeholders to become more informed, qualified and skilled in engaging in public affairs, which increases mutual understanding and trust; 10. sustainability and resilience; 11. economic development based on knowledge and innovation; 12 combined creation of social and economic values; 13. social inclusion; 14. promoting social justice; 15. improving the quality of life in cities; 16. maximizing indicators of socioeconomic and ecological development

The research results confirm the priority of cities to improve their quality of life and the services they provide through a smart governance approach. This priority is only possible if, at the same time, the local municipality is transparent and prioritises the citizen, has built an excellent organisational structure and set processes that contribute to administrative efficiency and interoperability. All these aspects also influence the implementation of public policies and programmes.

This assessment was tested with the Friedman test (significance level 0.01), which determined the following order of significance of the individual benefits of smart governance in the cities of the Slovak Republic (Table 1).

Table 1. Order of potential benefits of smart governance by Friedman's test

Improving the quality of life in cities	10.45
Improving services	10.01
Strengthening citizen-orientation (transparency and trust)	9.91
Increasing administrative efficiency and operational capacity	9.68
Strengthening openness and accountability	9.33
Economic development based on knowledge and innovation	9.14
Increasing citizen participation in public life	8.94
Increasing the effectiveness of public programmes and policies	8.93
Increase participation of other stakeholders in public life	8.40
Enabling stakeholders to become more informed, skilled and knowledgeable in engaging in public affairs, increasing mutual understanding and trust	8.20
Combined social and economic value creation	8.12
Maximising socio-economic and environmental development indicators	7.92
Sustainability and resilience	7.54
Promoting social justice	6.82
Social inclusion	6.48
Changes in the structure of the organisation of local municipalities and their bodies, as well as in their position in relation to stakeholders	6.13

Because the results of KMO and the Bertlet test of sphericity showed that the data are suitable for factorial analysis, we try to identify the factors that can be seen as crucial in the perception of benefits of smart governance in cities. We used the principal method analysis and the Varimax method of rotation (Table 2).

Table 2. Eigenvalues and the proportion of explained variability with the original number of variables – positive effects of smart governance

Component	Initial Eigenvalues			Rotation Sums of Squared Loadings		
	Total	% of Variance	Cumulative %	Total	% of Variance	Cumulative %
increasing administrative efficiency and operational capability	6,447	40,294	40,294	3,631	22,692	22,692

(*continued*)

Table 2. (*continued*)

Component	Initial Eigenvalues			Rotation Sums of Squared Loadings		
	Total	% of Variance	Cumulative %	Total	% of Variance	Cumulative %
strengthening openness and accountability	1,878	11,741	52,035	2,926	18,285	40,977
improving services	1,225	7,654	59,689	2,490	15,565	56,542
increasing the effectiveness of public programs and policies	1,095	6,844	66,533	1,599	9,991	66,533
changes in the structure of the organization of local municipality and its bodies, as well as in its position in relation to stakeholders	0,920	5,749	72,282			
strengthening the orientation towards the interests of the citizen (transparency and trust)	0,763	4,768	77,050			
increasing the involvement of citizens in public life	0,755	4,717	81,767			
increasing the participation of other stakeholders in public life	0,576	3,599	85,367			

(*continued*)

Table 2. (*continued*)

Component	Initial Eigenvalues			Rotation Sums of Squared Loadings		
	Total	% of Variance	Cumulative %	Total	% of Variance	Cumulative %
enabling stakeholders to become more informed, qualified and skilled in engaging in public affairs, which increases mutual understanding and trust	0,544	3,398	88,764			
sustainability and resilience	0,426	2,665	91,430			
economic development based on knowledge and innovation	0,366	2,288	93,717			
combined creation of social and economic values	0,359	2,244	95,962			
social inclusion	0,221	1,382	97,344			
promoting social justice	0,168	1,050	98,394			
improving the quality of life in cities	0,138	0,863	99,257			
maximizing indicators of socioeconomic and ecological development	0,119	0,743	100,000			

Based on the Eigenvalues, the software recommended four factors that together explain 66% of the variability from the original sixteen variables. Thus, the data also meet the percentage of explained variability criterion, which is required in the social sciences to be at least 60%. Their influence is illustrated in Table 3 the rotated matrix of factor saturations (Table 3).

Table 3. Rotated matrix of factor saturations – positive effects of smart governance

Rotated Component Matrix

	Component			
	1	2	3	4
increasing administrative efficiency and operational capability	,008	-,057	,603	,573
strengthening openness and accountability	,662	,134	,180	,417
improving services	,272	,128	,712	,053
increasing the effectiveness of public programs and policies	,236	,326	,536	,183
changes in the structure of the organization of local municipality and its bodies, as well as in its position in relation to stakeholders	,491	,210	,416	-,504
strengthening the orientation towards the interests of the citizen (transparency and trust)	,766	,128	,298	-,056
increasing the involvement of citizens in public life	,848	,098	,051	,081
increasing the participation of other stakeholders in public life	,772	,233	,264	,016
enabling stakeholders to become more informed, qualified and skilled in engaging in public affairs, which increases mutual understanding and trust	,745	,186	,077	,021
sustainability and resilience	,129	,382	,096	,689
economic development based on knowledge and innovation	,162	,454	,251	,453
combined creation of social and economic values	,123	,836	,211	-,026
social inclusion	,240	,825	,192	,170
promoting social justice	,235	,838	,181	,184
improving the quality of life in cities	,431	,250	,521	,227
maximizing indicators of socioeconomic and ecological development	,096	,357	,709	-,026

Extraction Method: Principal Component Analysis
Rotation Method: Varimax with Kaiser Normalization

From the rotated matrix in Table 4, we see that for the first factor the significant variables are the strengthening of openness and responsibility; strengthening orientation to the interests of the citizen; increasing the involvement of citizens in public life; increasing the participation of other stakeholders in public life and supporting and developing the skills and abilities of other actors. We could interpret the mentioned variables as factor 1 - participation and interested groups. Combined creation of social and economic values; social security and social care support are significant for the second factor, are important for the second factor - social welfare. Variables - increasing administrative efficiency and operational capability; improvement of services; increasing the efficiency of public programs and policies; changes in public administration organizations and their positions in relation to other actors; improving the quality of life in cities and maximizing socioeconomic and ecological development can be summed up in a factor called more efficient services and public policies. Sustainability and resilience and economic development based on knowledge and innovation can be interpreted as factor 4 - sustainability and resilience.

As the second part of the impact analysis, we asked the respondents evaluate on the same scale the potential pitfalls of smart governance in cities. Again, they were identified by the literature review as follows:

– insufficient capacity of local government to learn;
– exclusion of certain population groups;
– higher rate of non-participation of selected population groups (e.g. pensioners), especially in e-participation;
– residents are perceived only as a unit of information collection;
– prioritization of technological innovations instead of user needs and expectations;
– negative impact of technology on ecology.

The share of respondents´ answers and the average assessment of each pitfall are presented in Fig. 2.

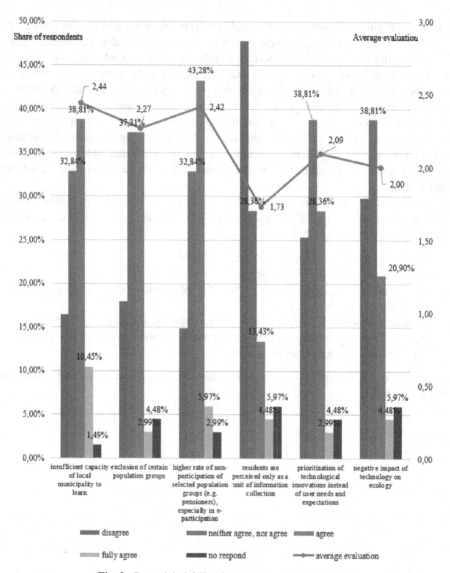

Fig. 2. Potential pitfalls of smart governance in cities

By the Friedman's test (significance level 0.01) of the respondent's answers, the statement with which respondents agree the most is the lack of capacity of local municipalities to learn. Other pitfalls follow this in the following order - a higher level of non-participation of selected population groups (e.g. senior citizens), especially in e-participation; the exclusion of specific population groups; the prioritization of technological innovations instead of users' needs and expectations; the negative impact of technology on ecology; residents are perceived only as a unit of information gathering.

By the results of KMO and Bertlet test of sphericity the research data are suitable for the factorial analysis. We again used the principal method analysis and the Varimax method of rotation (Table 4).

Table 4. Eigenvalues and the proportion of explained variability with the original number of variables – potential pitfalls

Component	Initial Eigenvalues			Loadings			Loadings		
	Total	% of Variance	Cumulative %	Total	% of Variance	Cumulative %	Total	% of Variance	Cumulative %
insufficient capacity of local municipality to learn	2,427	40,443	40,443	2,427	40,443	40,443	1,874	31,228	31,228
exclusion of certain population groups	1,24	20,675	61,118	1,24	20,675	61,118	1,793	29,889	61,118
higher rate of non-participation of selected population groups (e.g. pensioners), especially in e-participation	0,883	14,718	75,836						
residents are perceived only as a unit of information collection	0,626	10,426	86,261						
prioritization of technological innovations instead of user needs and expectations	0,466	7,77	94,031						
negative impact of technology on ecology	0,358	5,969	100,00						

Based on the Eigenvalues, the software recommended 2 factors that can explain 61,118% of variability from all original variables. The relationship of these factors with all variables presents Table 5 Rotated component matrix.

Table 5. Rotated component matrix – potential pitfalls of smart governance in cities

Rotated Component Matrix

	Component	
	1	2
insufficient capacity of local municipality to learn	0,416	0,379
exclusion of certain population groups	0,202	0,788
higher rate of non-participation of selected population groups (e.g. pensioners), especially in e-participation	-0,077	0,877
residents are perceived only as a unit of information collection	0,515	0,503
prioritization of technological innovations instead of user needs and expectations	0,816	0,056
negative impact of technology on ecology	0,851	0,043

Extraction Method: Principal Component Analysis. Rotation converged in 3.

Our research results show that for the first factors are significant that variables 1, 4, 5 and 6, it means insufficient capacity of local government to learn, residents are seen only as a unit of information collection, prioritization of technological innovations instead of the needs and expectations of users, and the negative impact of technology on ecology. Resulting from these obstacles and negative effects, we can name the first factor technology. For the second factor are significant variables 2 and 3, i. e. the exclusion of certain population groups and a higher rate of non-participation of selected population groups (e.g. pensioners), especially in e-participation. Because they are closely associated with stakeholder engagement, the factor can be called barriers of participation.

Our research results verified all identified impacts of smart governance in the cities as relevant. In the field of potential benefits of smart governance, they can be clustered into four main areas. The factorial analysis confirms the importance of the participation and their collaboration. Stakeholder participation can be used at different stages of the public policy cycle and implemented at different levels of involvement in different forms and ways. To achieve the desired effect, it is necessary to develop a participatory process design with a definition of the objective of the participatory process; the target group of stakeholders; the outputs of the participatory process; the forms of stakeholders' participation and engagement; the sequence/logic of the phases of the participation process the timeframe, the staffing and the financial support.

As the second factor, a social welfare was identified. By the in-depth literature review we found out that the smart governance approach should contribute to maximizing the possibilities of economic and social development which is reflected in better quality of life for citizens. This is evident also in the metrics dealing with the smart governance, and verified by our research results. It should be noted here that the assessment of the level of smart governance should not only be based on quantitative assessment but also on qualitative assessment, which often helps to understand better the interrelationships, processes or problems of smart governance.

The third factor in the positive effects of smart governance in cities is more efficient services and public policies. However, it is possible only in case of systematic and integrated implementation of smart governance with the political, organizational and financial support. It creates an opportunity to increase efficiency and strengthen the links between the local municipality and stakeholders to achieve synergies, stimulate coordination on the territory, and thus make governance more effective through the participation of the actors [55]. All previous factors help achieve sustainability and resilience of the city, which were identified as the last factor of positive impacts of smart governance. The sustainability and resilience are supported by the tools of smart governance that are manifested in local municipal functioning, namely transparency, participatory democracy, co-production, and communication that contribute to absorbing economic, environmental, or social changes/shocks, to adapt to them, to mitigate their impacts while at the same time maintaining the ability to perform basic functions of the territory without delegating it to other entities.

In case of potential pitfalls of the smart governance, two factors were identified. The problems in smart governance implementation can be caused by technology. If the priority became technology, the approach to smart governance is only technocratic, without respecting the added value of networks and the development of social capital. The technology is closely associated with the barriers in participation, which is the second identified factor. Due to higher claims (especially computer skills) on forms of stakeholder's engagement it can decrease the rate of participation in the public policy process. The concept of smart governance works with a wide range of tools that can be used in the different phases of participation. To eliminate the possibility of excluding a particular group of the local municipality's population, the solution is a combination of traditional (offline) smart governance tools with new ones in electronic form (online).

We are aware of the limitations in our research, mainly the orientation only on the research sample from one country as well as specifics of questionnaire research results based on the subjective opinion of respondents. On the other hand, the research was original and collected new primary data and the system of local governance in the central European countries is very similar, so the research results can be a starting point for the international comparison or spatial cluster analysis of government behavior of cities in different size.

5   Conclusion

In the present paper, based on our research results and their critical discussion, we identified the impacts of smart governance on urban development. Although, the research was realized in the cities of the Slovak Republic, the principles of municipal self-governance are generally accepted everywhere. Therefore, if cities implement the smart governance approach systematically and in an integrated way, they can expect a relatively wide portfolio of benefits. Moreover, they have to be prepared to face the barriers that can be caused by the progressive technological development. Equally important is the ability of cities to deal with both the opportunities and threats that smart governance brings.

Acknowledgements. This study has been supported by project Vega 1/0311/23 Open Local Municipality and Vega 1/0343/23 Modern approaches to the development of cities and regions.

References

1. Pollitt, C., Bouckaert, G.: Public Management Reform: A Comparative Analysis - into the Age of Austerity. Oxford University Press (2017)
2. Hartley, J.: Innovation in governance and public services: past and present. Public Money Manag. **25**, 27–34 (2005)
3. Hyndman, N., Ligiuri, M.M., Polzer, T., Rota, S., Seiwald, J., Steccolini, I.: Legitimating change in the public sector: the introduction of (rational?) accounting practices in the United Kingdom. Italy Aust. Public Manag. Rev. **20**(9), 1374–13399 (2018). https://doi.org/10.1080/14719037.2017.1383781
4. Torfing, J., Andersen, L.B., Greve, C., Klausen, K.K.: Public Governance Paradigms: Competing and Co-existing. Edward Elgar Publishing (2020)
5. Hammerschmid, G., Palaric, E., Rackwitz, M.A shift in paradigm? Collaborative public administration in the context of national digitalization strategies. In Governance (2023), pp. 1–20. https://doi.org/10.1111/gove.12778
6. Emerson, K., Nabatchi, T., Balogh, S.: An integrative framework for collaborative governance. J. Public Adm. Res. Theory **22**, 1–29 (2011). https://doi.org/10.1093/jopart/mur011
7. Pittaway, J.J., Montazemi, A.R.: Know-how to lead digital transformation: the case of local governments. Govt. Inf. Q. **37**, 15 (2020)
8. Vaňová, A.: Trendy v rozvoji miest, p. 201. Univerzita Mateja Bela v Banskej Bystrici, Belianum (2021)
9. Vitálišová, K., Vaňová, A., Sýkorová, K., Rojíková, D., Borseková, K., Laco, P. Smart Governance v miestnej samospráve. Vládnutie s rozumom (2022) 232pp
10. Bevir, M.: Governance as theory, practice, and dilemma. In: Bevirt, M. (ed.) The SAGE Handbook of Governance, pp. 1–16. Sage, London (2011)
11. Kickert, W.J.M., Klijn, E., Koppenjan, F.M.: Managing Complex Networks. Strategies for the Public Sector. SAGE, London, 224 pp (1997)
12. Pierre, J., Peters, B.G.: Governance, Politics and the State, p. 227. Macmillan, Basingstoke (2000)
13. Rhodes, A.W.: Governance and Public Administration, pp. 54–90. Oxford University Press, Oxford (2000)
14. Bevir, M., Rhodes, R.A.W, WELLer, P.: Traditions of governance: interpreting the changing role of the public sector. Public Adm. **81**(1) 1–17 (2003)
15. Kooiman, J.: Governing as Governance, p. 264. Sage, London (2003)
16. Berry, F. S., et al.: three traditions of network research: what the public management research agenda can learn from other research communities. Publ. Adm. Rev. **64**(5), 539–552 (2004)
17. Klijn, E.H.: Governance and governance neworks in Europe: an assessment of ten years of research on the theme. Public Manag. Rev. **10**, 505–525 (2008)
18. Peters, B.G.: The changing nature of public administration: from easy answers to hard questions. Viešoji Politika IR Administravimas **5**, 1–14 (2003)
19. Huaxiong, J.: Smart urban governance in the 'smart' era: why is it urgently needed? Cities **111**, 6 (2021)
20. Vitálišová, K., et al.: Benefits and obstacles of smart governance in cities. In: EAI International Conference, SmartCity360°. Science and Technologies for Smart Cities: Proceedings, pp. 366-380. Springer, Cham (2022)
21. Greenhalgh, T., Potts, H.W.W., Wong, G., et al. Tensions and paradoxes in electronic patient record research: a systematic literature review using the meta-narrative method. Milbank Q **87,** 729–788 (2009)
22. Wachter, R.M.: Making IT Work: Harnessing the Power of Health Information Technology to Improve care in England, p. 71. National Advisory Group on Health Information Technology in England, London (2016)

23. Benjamin, K., Potts, H.W.W.: Digital transformation in government: lessons of digital health? Digit. Health **4**, 1–5 (2018)
24. Salem, F.A.: Smart City for Public Value: Digital Transformation through Agile Governance – The Case of "Smart Dubai". Dubai: Governance and Innovation Program, Mohammed Bin Rashid School of Government, World Government Summit (2016) 70 pp.
25. Pérez-González, D., Daiz-Daiz, R.: Public services provided with ICT in the smart city environment : the case of Spanish cities. J. Univ. Comput. Sci. **21**(2), 248–267 (2015)
26. Pereira, G.V., Cunha, M.A., Lampoltshammer, T.J., Parycek, P., Testa, M.G.: Increasing collaboration and participation in smart city governance: a cross-case analysis of smart city initiatives. Inf. Technol. Dev. **23**(3), 526–553 (2017)
27. Kleinhans, R., Ham, M., Evans-Cowley, J.: Using social media and mobile technologies to foster engagement and self-organisation in participatory urban planning and neighbourhood governance. Plan. Pract. Res. **30**(3), 237–247 (2015)
28. Castelnovo, A., et al.: Smart Cities governance. the need for a holistic approach to assessing urban participatory policy making. Soc. Sci. Comput. Rev. **34**(6), 724–739 (2015)
29. Khan, Z., Anjum, A., Soomro, K., Tahir, M.A.: Towards cloud based big data analytics for smart future cities. J. Cloud Comput. **4**(1), 1–11 (2015). https://doi.org/10.1186/s13677-015-0026-8
30. Navarro-Galera, A., Alcaraz-Quiles, F.J., Ortiz-Rodriguez, D.: Online dissemination of information on sustainability in regional governments. Effects of technological factors. Govt. Inf. Q. **33**, 53–66 (2016)
31. Castelnovo, W.: Co-production Makes cities smarter: citizens´participation in smart city initiatives, In: Fugini, M., Bracci, E., Sicilia, M. (eds.) Co-production in the Public Sector. Experiences and Challenges, pp. 97–118 (2016)
32. Gil-Garcia, J.R., Zhang, J., Puron-Cid, G.: Conceptualizing smartness in government: an integrative and multi-dimensional view. Gov. Inf. Q. **33**(3), 524–534 (2016)
33. Nam, T., Pardo, T.A.: Smart city as urban innovation: focusing on management, policy, and context. In: Proceedings of the 5th International Conference on Theory and Practice of Electronic Governance, pp. 185–194 (2011)
34. Mellouli, S., Luna-Reyes, L.F., Zhang, J.: Smart government, citizen participation and open data. Inf. Polity **19**, 1–4 (2014)
35. Maheshwari, D., Janssen, M.: Reconceptualizing measuring, benchmarking for improving interoperability in smart ecosystems: the effect of ubiquitous data and crowdsourcing. Govt. Inf. Q. **31**, 84–92 (2014)
36. Nam, T., Pardo, T.A.: The changing face of a city government: a case study of Philly31. Govt. Inf. Q. **31**, 1–9 (2014)
37. GuendueZ, A., Singler, S., Tomaczak, T., Schedler, K., Oberli, M.: Smart governmnet success factors. Swiss Yearbook Adm. Sci. **9**(1), 96–110 (2018)
38. Kumar, V.T.M.: Smart Economy in Smart Cities, 1086 pp. Springer, Singapore (2017). https://doi.org/10.1007/978-981-10-1610-3
39. Zanella, A., Bui, N., Castellani, A., et al.: Internet of things for smart cities. In IEEE Internet of Things J. **1**(1), 22–32 (2014)
40. Caragliu, A., Del Bo, C., Nijkamp, P.: Smart cities in Europe. J. Urban Technol. **18**(2), 65–82 (2011)
41. Praharaj, S., Han, J.H., Hawken, S.: Towards the right model of smart city governance in India. Int. J. Sust. Dev. Plann. **13**(2), 171–186 (2016)
42. Savoldelli, A., Codagnone, C., Misuraca, G.: Undertanding the e-governmnet paradox: learning from literature and practice and barriers to adoption. Gov. Inf. Q. **31**, 63–71 (2014)
43. Osella, M., Ferro, E., Pautasso, M.E.: Toward a methodological approach to assess public value in smart cities. In: Gil-Garcia, J., Pardo, T., Nam, T. (eds.) Smarter as the New Urban Agenda, pp. 129–148. Springer, Schwitzerland (2016)

44. Anand, P.B., Navío-Marco, J.: Governance and economics of smart cities: opportunities and challenges. Telecom. Policy **42**, 795–799 (2018)
45. Pereira, G.V., Parycek, P., Falco, E., Kleinhaus, R.: Smart governance in the context of smart cities: a literature review. Inf. Polity **23**(2), 1–20 (2018)
46. Tomor, Z.: Locally Grown Smart Cities: How the Political-Institutional Context Influences Glasgow, Utrecht and Curitiba. Sussex Innovation Centre, Falmer Brighton, pp. 1–30. East Su (2018)
47. Royo, S., Yetano, A., Acerete, B.: Perceptions about the effectiveness of E-participation: a multistakeholder perspective". In: Bolívar, M.P.R. (ed.) Measuring E-government Efficiency, pp. 257–275. Springer, New York (2014)
48. Washington, V.: Local government, the Internet, and sustainability. Publ. Adm. Rev. **74**(1), 99–100 (2014)
49. Royo, S., Yetano, A.: Crowdsourcing' as a Tool for E-participation: two experiences regarding CO_2 emissions at municipal level. Electr. Com. Res. **15**(3), 323–348 (2015)
50. Cimander, R.: Citizen panels on climate targets: ecological impact at individual level. In: Aichholzer, G., Kubicek, H., Torres, L. (eds.) Evaluating e-Participation. Frameworks, Practice, Evidence, pp. 219–241 Springer International, Basel (2016)
51. Aichholzer, G., Kubicek, H., Torres, L. (eds.) Evaluating e-Participation. Frameworks, Practice, Evidence, 361pp. Springer, Basel (2016). https://doi.org/10.1007/978-3-319-254 03-6
52. Tomor, Z., Meijer, A., Michles, A., Geertman, S.: Smart governance for sustainable cities: findings from a systematic literature review. J. Urban Technol. **26**(4), 3–27 (2019)
53. Dente, B.: Towards a typology of local development policies and programmes. Local Econ. **29**(6–7), 675–686 (2014)
54. Azzari, M., Garau, C., Nesi, P., Paolucci, M., Zamperlin, P.: Smart city governance strategies to better move towards a smart urbanism. In: Gervasi, O., et al. (eds.) ICCSA 2018. LNCS, vol. 10962, pp. 639–653. Springer, Cham (2018). https://doi.org/10.1007/978-3-319-95168-3_43
55. Mills, D., Pudney, S., Pevcin, P., Dvorak, J.: Evidence-based public policy decision-making in smart cities: does extant theory support achievement of city sustainability objectives? Sustainability **14**(1), 3 (2022)

Multi-level Perspective Within the Regulatory Framework of Shared Mobility: A Case Studies Analysis of Italian Demand Responsive Shared Transport Services (DRSTs)

Vincenza Torrisi[1]([✉]) [iD], Roberta Campolo[2]([✉]), Antonio Barbagallo[2],
Pierfrancesco Leonardi[2], Matteo Ignaccolo[2] [iD], and Antonino Longo[2]

[1] Department of Electric, Electronic and Computer Engineering, University of Catania, Viale Andrea Doria, 6, 95125 Catania, Italy
vincenza.torrisi@unict.it
[2] Department of Civil Engineering and Architecture, University of Catania, Viale Andrea Doria, 6, 95125 Catania, Italy
campoloroberta95@gmail.com

Abstract. Shared mobility services belong to the group of Public Transport (PT) services, and they can be divided into two categories: scheduled and on-demand. Line services are characterized by scheduled timetables, fixed routes and stops. Instead, on-demand services are characterized by variable vehicle-routing and timetables considering changes in the mobility demand, in order to satisfy users' requests. In the last decades, innovative shared transport services, i.e., Demand Responsive Shared Transport services (DRSTs) have been implemented in addition to the traditional on-demand services, i.e., taxi and rental car with driver (NCC). The introduction of these new services is part of the legal framework linked to traditional PT, not adapted and detailed for DRSTs, making difficult to fully exploit all potentialities associated with these new transport services. The implementation should require a specific regulation able to define the operational features of the service and to avoid that DRSTs contrast or overlap with PT services. On that basis, this work proposes a Multi-Level Perspective methodology in order to provide a legal framework and analyze the criticalities linked to the introduction and implementation of DRSTs, mainly due to regulatory shortcomings. The paper focuses on the Italian legislation which is characterized by a gap for the implementation of DRSTs. At the regional level, these services have been partially defined and regulated, within the limits imposed by national legislation. Therefore, a comparative analysis is presented by analyzing several case studies (i.e., Piemonte, Valle d'Aosta, Friuli Venezia Giulia and Lombardia). The results of the research will constitute a practical tool to implement DRSTs in a permanent way and within the public transport supply.

Keywords: Demand Responsive Shared Transport services (DRSTs) · Legislation · Local Public Transport (LPT) · Multi-Level Perspective methodology · Sustainable Mobility

O. Gervasi et al. (Eds.): ICCSA 2023 Workshops, LNCS 14109, pp. 565–580, 2023.
https://doi.org/10.1007/978-3-031-37120-2_36

1 Introduction

In the last decade and especially following the pandemic [1], Local public Transport (LPT) is suffering a reduction in the number of passengers [2], increasing the modal imbalance towards the use of private vehicles. This trend contrasts with the cities' environmental and urban planning policies for the promotion of sustainable mobility [3–5]. Indeed, the European Union (EU) has identified the Urban Sustainable Mobility Plans (SUMPs) as a tool for pursuing the improvement of transport mobility [6] of both passengers and goods traffic, in line with environmental, social and economic sustainability policies [7–10]. The main objectives of these tools include interventions to favor the modal integration of different transport modes and to improve the quality and quantity of the services provided. Moreover, considering the new mobility habits, it emerges that users need to have a different transport alternatives respect to the traditional LPT services. Therefore, to satisfy new users' requirements and attract more private transport users, new on-demand shared mobility services have been introduced [11]. These services complement the traditional taxis and NCCs and they are also grouped within the sharing mobility category. They can provide two types of sharing: (i) simultaneous sharing if both the vehicle and the journey are shared or (ii) an exclusive share if only the vehicle is shared. These on-demand services differ from traditional services due to their complete integration with digital platforms which is essential for the use of the service. The platform is useful to provide clear information to users about the service, giving a better perception of the associated quality and, at the same time, the operator can use this tool as a support to optimize the service and try to satisfy a greater number of users' requests. This interaction between transport supply and mobility demand is fundamental for these services in order to offer a greater accessibility and flexibility and attract users of private vehicles [12–15].

Sharing mobility services can be grouped into two categories [16]:

- Vehicle sharing the user shares the vehicle but not the journey, which takes place exclusively.
- Ride sharing: both the vehicle and the journey are shared, and the latter both partially and totally shared with other users.

The first category includes all the services characterized by a fleet of available vehicles (i.e. cars, scooters, bicycles, commercial vehicles). The user books the vehicle, uses it and then relocates it in the reserved areas, thus making the vehicle available to other users [17–20].

Instead, this work intends to deal with ridesharing services. There are different types of ride sharing services, from shared taxi to microtransit/DRST and the difference between these services for users is determined by the degree of flexibility [6, 21–23].

In U.S.A. these services have already been active for several years and there are specific regulations that define the type of service. The U.S. Department of Transportation defines microtransit as *"a privately owned and operated shared transportation system that can offer fixed routes and schedules, as well as flexible routes and on-demand scheduling. The vehicles generally include vans and buses"* [24]. In California they are defined as *"IT-enabled multipassenger transportation services serving passengers based on dynamic vehicle routing and with passengersmaking their way to and from common pick-up or drop-off points. Microtransit vehicles include (but are not limited), large sport utility vehicles, vans, and shuttle buses."* [25].

The European regulatory framework has not explicitly defined these new forms of mobility, however, as the regulation of these services is in line with environmental and social policies, it is becoming a part of the government agenda.

The Italian national regulatory framework does not refer explicitly to demand services, above all to the new service types developed in recent years. Thus, this document aims to clarify the regulatory aspects for the implementation of a DRST service.

In Sect. 2 a legal framework is defined through a Multi-Level Perspective methodology, investigating the regulatory aspects related to the implementation of these innovative services.

Section 3 provides an analysis of Italian case studies and for each service it highlights the regulatory aspects based on which they have been implemented.

In Sect. 4 the results and conclusions are presented. The proposed analysis of legal tools in different contexts can be constitute a guide for administrations, to know and critically examine the key regulatory elements and to equip themselves with these tools.

2 Multi-level Perspective Methodology

The Multi-Level Perspective Methodology has the objective of investigating the possible answers and solutions to main questions related to the adoption and implementation of new on-demand transport services. The first step is the definition of the main issues related to the implementation of the DRST services by identifying four main questions; subsequently an analysis of the Italian legislation is carried out to identify whether and which services can be activated.

2.1 Identification of 4 Questions About On-demand Transport Services

The adopted methodological approach is characterized by the identification of four questions closely related to the implementation of the DRST services. The identification of these questions is linked operational service of these services in Italy, and in some cases as pilot projects. This analysis highlights the critical issues related to the activation of these services. With particular reference to the regulatory framework.

The first question investigates the need to have specific legislative tools for these services. It is necessary to clarify whether these services can be activated only on the basis of national legislation, or if a regional legislation is necessary (in Italy the responsibility for planning LPT services is delegated at the regional level) or even, they can be directly activated through an agreement between local authorities, service providers and operators.

The second question involves the operators. It is not often defined whether these services can be provided by operators, i.e. taxis or NCCs or by LPT companies which already operate urban and suburban services.

The third question concerns the territorial context and the type of service provided to users. On-demand transport services can be provided in areas characterized by weak-demand to replace traditional scheduled services, or in the suburbs areas not yet covered by LPT, to integrate scheduled services.

The fourth question relate to the possibility of obtaining an economic contribution for the service and the methodology for quantifying the provided service in kilometers or equivalent measures. This last aspect turns out to be very important because, unlike traditional scheduled services, demand services can stop due to the lack of mobility demand. During this time intervals, the vehicles are stationary, not generating kilometer production while continuing to offer the service availability to users. This availability implies fixed costs which must be quantified and gave to the transport company. For these reasons it is necessary to provide for a kilometric contribution different from that provided for traditional scheduled services (Fig. 1).

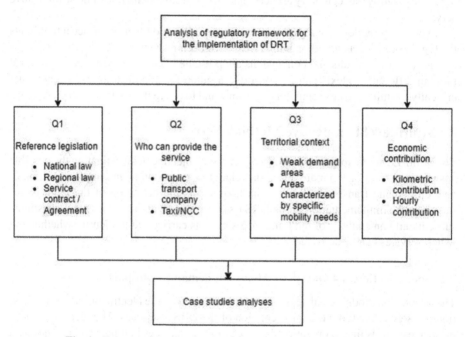

Fig. 1. Four questions within the Multi-Level Perspective Methodology

2.2 Legal Framework at the National Level

At the national level, LPT is regulated by the Legislative Decree 19.11.1997, n. 422 [26] and subsequent amendments. In Art. 6, paragraph 1, it delegates to the Regions the planning of regional and LPT services not included in art. 117 of the Constitution. Similarly, art. 7, paragraph 1, the Regions, confer to the Municipalities and other local entities all the regional functions and tasks in the field of LPT which do not require unitary exercise at the regional level. In particular, the Regions must define guidelines for the planning of LPT and specifically for Basin Plans, must draw up Regional transport plans and must approve the three-year service programs of TPL. The Legislative Decree defines regional and TPL services as transport services for people and goods, not in the national interest. They include road, rail, maritime and air transport systems, operating continuously or periodically or with pre-established itineraries, timetables, frequencies and rates, at regional context. According to art. 14, it is possible to implement particular transport scheduled services in specific weak-demand areas, defined as areas in which the mobility demand is low because the users' trip requests are dispersed due to the territorial structure. Weak-demand areas are identified with the following criteria: a) population density; b) degree of urbanization; c) age of the resident population; d) altitude. The purpose of these services is to guarantee the satisfaction of mobility needs in these particular territories. These services must be assigned through competitive procedures to companies who have the requisites to operate non-scheduled public services or road passenger transport services. The scheduled public service differs from the non-scheduled one, which is regulated at national level by the Law 15.01.1992, n. 21 [27]. Non-scheduled public bus services are collective or individual passenger transport services, with a complementary and supplementary function to scheduled public transport. They are available on users' request, continuously or temporarily with flexible routes and timetables (paragraph 1). They consist of taxi and NCC services (paragraph 2). The taxi service is addressed to a generic user; the vehicles are stationed in a public area and must be distinguishable from other vehicles; the tariffs and the characteristics of the service are determined by the competent authorities; the pick-up points are located within the municipal area (art. 2, paragraph 1); the service provision is mandatory (paragraph 2). According to art. 3, the NCC service is addressed to a specific user, who makes a trip request at the depot for a specific timed also through the use of technological tools (art. 3, paragraph 1). Vehicles cannot wait for requests on public spaces, but only inside the depot (paragraph 2). The operational headquarters and at least one depot must be located in the municipality that provided the authorisation. It is possible to have a depot within other municipalities of the same metropolitan area, with prior communication to those municipalities (paragraph 3). With the Decree Law 07.04.2006, n. 223 [28], the legislator has strengthened the competition for the taxi service, in particular with regard to market access, pricing, increased efficiency of service and quality. After, with the art. 37 of the Decree Law n. 06.12.2011, n. 201 [29], the legislator assigned the Transport Regulatory Authority (ART) specific tasks to improve the taxi service.

In particular:

- increase the number of licenses, if necessary, following comparisons and investigations about costs-benefits analysis, including environmental aspects, in relation to mobility needs and demographic characteristics;
- organize the service with greater flexibility during particular exceptional events or periods with increasing mobility demand, proportionated to user needs. Develop new supplementary services such as taxis for collective use or other forms;
- have greater freedom in tariffs' determination;
- improve the quality of the provided service.

With the "Notification Act to the Government and Parliament about non-scheduled road transport of passengers: taxis, NCCs and technological services for mobility" of 21.05.2015 [30], the Authority highlighted the opportunity to review the rules governing the taxi service. Giving license holders more freedom in organizing the service, for particular extraordinary events or periods of increased demand with flexible timetables and develop new supplementary services such as the collective use of taxis. With a note of 16.07.2020, addressed to the National Association of Italian Municipalities (ANCI, from Italian: "Associazione Nazionale Comuni Italiani) and the Conference of Regions and Autonomous Provinces, the Authority intervened on the use of web connectivity systems and new technologies to facilitate the interaction between the supply and the demand of taxis. On the basis of the decisions of the Council of State, in the sentences of 04.06.2020, n. 3501, n. 3502/2020 and n. 3503/2020, the ART set out these needs:

- remove regional laws and/or municipal regulations that can limit the autonomy of taxis to use the interconnection services between supply and demand;
- promote the development and diffusion of innovative and competitive systems for the interconnection between users and operators of the taxi service, to increase the efficiency and quality of the provided service;
- ensure that the market for intermediation services between supply and demand is open and competitive.

The European Union published the Commission Communication on efficient and sustainable on-demand local transport of passengers (i.e. taxis and NCCs) 2022/C 62/01, which supports the efficiency of services, the access to efficient and sustainability mobility, the environmental sustainability and the use of advantages offered by digitalization. Finally, the Authority on 23.03.2022, with the Resolution n. 46/2022 [31], adopted the Guidelines on adaptation of the taxi service for Regions and Local Authorities regarding the use of web connectivity systems and new technologies to facilitate the interaction between the demand and the supply of taxis. The objective is to provide, also through methodological indications, a decision-support tool for the competent authorities to optimize the service, also considering the technological platforms for the interaction between the supply and the demand, monitor the quality of this tool also through the preparation of customer satisfaction surveys. The use of technological platforms is one of the main problems in terms of sharing mobility. Sharing mobility identifies a set of mobility services, alternatives to one's own vehicle or collective vehicles. These are used temporarily thanks to the use of digital platforms that guarantee the sharing of vehicles and journeys. These platforms also allow to book and pay for the service through IT devices. From a legal point of view, one of the most important issues is the correct qualification of the activities performed by the IT platforms. If they constitute a simple intermediaries between supply and demand or if they are direct suppliers of the transport service. The classification is important because if they are considered direct suppliers of innovative transport services, they must comply with all the legal provisions regarding for example safety, access to the market and responsibility towards users.

3   Case Studies Analysis

In this section four different case studies have been selected, i.e. Regions of Piemonte, Valle d'Aosta, Lombardia and Friuli Venezia Giulia, which have implemented flexible forms of on -demand transport service with different characteristics and within a regional regulatory framework different from each other.

- Case study 1: Piemonte (Torino/Asti) Region

The first case study concerns the regulatory analysis of the flexible mobility systems implemented in the Piemonte Region. In particular, the Regional Law 04.01.2000, n. 1 has been analyzed, which regulates the LPT in the Region, in actuation of the Legislative Decree 19.11.1997, n. 422. Then two Service Contracts have been analyzed, relating to the transport systems in the metropolitan area of Turin and in the Basin of Asti [32].

The Regional Law 04.01.2000, n. 1, art. 2, defines the regional LPT system as the functional integration of regional, provincial and urban scheduled services and supplementary or substitute for scheduled services. These services are carried out in different ways, and they are extended to areas characterized by low population density, with low demand, or able to satisfy complementary mobility or special needs. These services are organized and managed by the mountain communities, or by the interested municipalities together associated, in areas with low demand. Indeed, according to art. 6 of the same Law, within weak-demand areas, local authorities can identify particular procedures for carrying out scheduled services. These services can be self-managed or assigned, through competitive procedure to subjects who have the requisites to operate non-scheduled public bus services or road passenger transport services. If there is no supply of these services, vehicles used for one's own use can be used. In any case, it is required the possession of the professional requisites for the exercise of public transport. In the Service Contract for the management of local suburban road public transport services of passengers by road by bus in the metropolitan area of Turin - valid from 08.01.2012 to 07.31.2018, then followed by provisions for the extension and imposition of Public Service Obligations [33] – it has been envisaged to review the services in relation to the demand trend and revenues. This is possible by (wholly or partially) replacing bus lines with other services, integrating/extending the existing on-demand services and/or setting up new ones. Specifically, the contract has identified these on-demand services as services with flexible or fixed routes and timetables and the service carried out only by reservation. For this type of service, the contract provides for the possibility of using small vehicles (M1 or M2) or vehicles not used for scheduled services (i.e. taxi or NCCs) according to the terms and conditions described in the documents integrating the contract.

The economic compensation for on-demand services have been defined on the basis of an average unit value of €1,407/vehic*km, while the travelled distances (km) have been calculated on the basis of a "distance matrix", pre-defined in agreement with the concessionaire, considering the sum of the travelled route along the entire path of each journey. In addition to the variable compensation, a flat fee has been considered for call center charges of € 18.00/h (with reference to each call-center and each opening day). The compensations would have referred only to the actually made runs, i.e. "commercial runs" with passengers on board. Instead, in the Service Contract for the regulation of the assignment of LPT extra-urban services for the period 2010–2015 in the Basin of Asti, it has been envisaged that a part of the compensation is intended for the implementation of flexible services, on the basis of a unit compensation per kilometer set at €1.11/km within the contract. Specifically, it has been expected that the annual compensation, regardless of the number of travelled kilometers, is to be calculated as the product of the kilometric compensation for flexible services and the kilometers performed by scheduled services changed into flexible services, respecting the limit of kilometers foreseen for flexible services. In the case ok travelled kilometers less than 50% of (changed) kilometers associated to the traditional scheduled service, the compensation would be reduced by 20%. Specifically, it has been agreed in the contract that 891,192.60 km/year for ordinary services could be replaced with alternative services mileage of 712,954.08 km/year.

- Case study 2: Valle D'Aosta Region

The second case study concerns the regulatory analysis of the flexible mobility systems implemented in the Valle D'Aosta Region. In particular, it has been analyzed the Regional Law 09.01.1997, n. 29, "Rules on scheduled public transport services", which regulates LPT in the Region. The Regional Law Valle D'Aosta 09.01.1997, n. 29, in the art. 53, [34] provides that the Region can define, coordinate and authorize transport services supplementary to public transport. Specifically, "supplementary services" are divided into scheduled, non-scheduled and on-demand supplementary services. These last are defined as performed services with fixed or flexible routes upon reservation by users. According to the Law, the purpose of these services is to satisfy specific mobility needs, including tourism, not adequately ensured by scheduled public transport, and meet the mobility needs in weak-demand areas during the day (e.g. afternoon or evening) to supplement scheduled services.

To carry out these services, the Regional Council is authorized to provide specific agreements with the concessionary companies of the scheduled services within the related sub-basins and with NCCs or taxis. The Law defines the cost of the service based on a kilometric or hourly compensation: in the first case it cannot exceed the compensation set out in the sub-basin service contract, which can be increased up to a maximum of 10%; in the second case, the cost is calculated on the basis of the service type offered and the criteria already defined in the contract.

The hourly unit cost is defined by the Regional Council on the basis of the fixed unit compensation following the award to the concessionaire. It is also envisaged that local authorities can set up additional on-demand services to integrate the regional public transport service, if missing or inadequate. This is expected in order to meet mobility needs for students, tourists or for particular periods of the day, i.e. at night in areas with low demand. The Regional Council establishes the criteria for carrying out the services and defines the possible contribution by the Region. The tariffs for these services are determined on the basis of the scheduled service ones, which can be increased in relation to the service characteristics (e.g. frequency) [35].

- Case study 3: Lombardia Region

The third case study concerns the regulatory analysis of the flexible mobility systems implemented in the Lombardia Region. In particular, three legal tools have been analyzed: the Regional Law 04.04.2012, n. 6, which regulates the transport sector in the Region, the Guidelines for the drafting of LPT catchment programs N° X/2486 of 10.10.2014 [36] and the Coordination Guidelines for the assignment of the LPT service and drafting of service contracts approved with D.G.R. no. X/4927 of 14.03. 2016 [37].

The Regional Law 04.04.2012, n. 6, classifies in art. 2, paragraph 2 letter a), regional and LPT services as scheduled services, if they are organized on a continuous or periodic basis with pre-established itineraries, timetables, frequencies, tariffs and conditions, also through innovative services organized with particular modalities, e.g. on-demand services.

The guidelines for the drafting of LPT basin programs N° X/2486 of 10.10.2014 propose two operating models for the creation of on-demand services:

– with fixed routes and journeys made only upon reservation (suitable for extra urban area with low demand);
– with flexible routes and journeys made only by reservation, according to the two commonly used models:

   i. the "many to one" model, with a service that picks-up users at stops within the area and picks-off them to the destination, typically represented by a Point of Interest (POI) or general service, e.g. hospital, shopping center or station;
   ii. the "many to many" model, in which the service does not have route and time constraints, but it is determined only on the basis of user requests, who can book a ride between any two stops in the service network. This model provides for greater operational flexibility, but also greater management complexity, offering a more widespread service and higher user satisfaction rates.

In particular, for on-demand services, the coordination guidelines for the assignment of the LPT service and the drafting of service contracts approved with D.G.R. no. X/4927 of 14.03. 2016, define, in Annex A, how to carry out this conversion of the provided "on-demand" services into equivalent distances.

The document defines two types of trips:

• Equivalent travelled distances for contractual purposes (Peq) are the equivalent distances to which the unit price will be applied;
• Programmed travelled distances (Pprog) are the distances that the service manager actually makes available for the implementation of on-demand services to replace scheduled services.

In the case of services with flexible timetables and (i) a predefined basic route with the possibility of detours; (ii) with flexible routebetween a predefined set of pick-up and drop-off points; (iii) with flexible route with the possibility to explore all the nodes of the network, the equivalent distances are determined considering the working hours of the "driver with vehicle" available during the daily service and the commercial average speed, with the application of a correction factor. This factor concerns the probability of effective service provision and the higher management costs for the flexible service compared to those for the scheduled ones, according to the specific formula defined in the contracts.

- Case study 4: Friuli-Venezia Giulia Region

The fourth case study concernes the regulatory analysis of the flexible mobility systems implemented in the Friuli-Venezia Giulia Region. In particular, it has been analyzed the Regional Law n. 23,20.08.2007, which regulates LPT in the Region and the organization of flexible transport services set out in the General Plan of LPT [38].

The Regional Law n. 23,20.08.2007 (Implementation of Legislative Decree 111/2004 on regional and LPT, freight transport, motorization, road traffic and viability), [39] defines in art. 5 paragraph 1, letter a), the regional and LPT system as the set of transport services of regional interest, including the railway, tramway, automobile and maritime services carried out on a pre-established route or in a flexible way, organized for integrating various transport mobility systems, used for the collective transport of passengers and goods. The art. 5, paragraph 1, lett. h) also defines scheduled bus services, considering them as services with an itinerary between two terminal stops within the first and second level of the transport network; instead, at letter i) flexible car services are differently defined as on-demand services performed in weak-demand areas and low-demand times, with fixed or flexible routes and with the use of technologies, within the third level of the transport network.

The low demand areas are defined by the Regional Plan of Local Public Transport (PRTPL, from Italian "Piano Regionale del Trasporto Pubblico Locale"). The Regional Law (art. 8) also states that the public transport system consists of a) a first-level railway and road network; b) a second-level railway and road distribution network considering arterials (for traffic distribution) and collectors (for traffic penetration); c) a third level network based on flexible services.

Indeed, the Report of the General Plan of LPT defines the structure and organization of public transport. In particular, according to decreasing hierarchical level, transport services become more pervasive across to the local territory and through the third-level network they satisfy mobility needs at local scale, covering routes within restricted territorial areas and with innovative service types, according to flexible mobility needs, time and space-varying. Specifically, during the assignment phase, it is envisaged a concrete definition of flexible services to replace scheduled ones. Then, during the operational phase, according to the results of the monitoring, there is an eventual redefinition of the services, also through the planning of flexible services.

The Report identifies various types of flexible services. (i) The first service type is defined "of improvement" which refers to Municipalities with weak demand, for irregular users and established through the replacement of runs of existing extra-urban line, exercised during pick-off hours. The aim of this type of service is to improve the quality of the service, through the provision of flexible services, because within areas with a high dispersion of settlements the demand for non-systematic mobility is distributed along several directions. These services must be exercised according to the Explanatory Report and the contractualized mileage production, since they derive from the conversion of existing 2nd level services. (ii) The second service type is defined "of extension". It is envisaged for all Municipalities with weak demand, and it has the specific purpose of expanding the LPT network within areas not yet served and improving existing connections.

In addition to these two types of services, there are a third and a fourth type, referring to Municipalities characterized by partial situations of weak demand. (iii) Specifically, the third type refers to services that can be implemented in urban areas during time slots or situations characterized by low demand, e.g. during the night or for public holidays, even replacing existing services. In sub-urban areas these services can be established with the integration of existing extra-urban services with flexible services; in this way it is possible to improve the connection between the provincial capitals and the surrounding municipalities; in the case of Trieste it includes all the municipalities of the city.

(iv) The fourth type of services refers to particular road directories for the connection between the hamlets and the municipal capital, and for particular road directories for which there is the opportunity to transform a part of scheduled services into flexible services or new ones. This consideration derives from the monitoring activities and this services' transformation is possible when the polarities of origin and destination of the connection, even if not overall resulting in weak demand, they are attributable to weak-demand areas for the particular category of users along the connection.

Lastly, the Report specifies that flexible services, as well as replacing existing scheduled services, can be implemented by upgrading them through:

- the use, even partial, of the increases in kilometer production envisaged by the Plan;
- the use of additional available kilometric productions;
- available resources by local authorities for the activation of flexible supplementary services according to the art. 12, paragraph 1, letter d) of the Regional Law 20.08.2007, n.23 (which letter provides that the Municipalities exercise the function of "proposing and establishing flexible supplementary services without charges for the regional budget, in coordination with the territorially competent Province").

4 Discussions and Conclusions

From the analysis of the four case studies, it emerged how the DRT services have been planned and implemented in a partially different way from each other. In all four cases, the Regional Law represents the legal basis for the establishment of the service, because it includes flexible/on-demand services among the LPT services. The Valle d'Aosta Regional Law qualifies this category of services in a clearer and more specific way than the other three Regional Laws. It concretely defines the rules for implementing them. In the case of Piemonte Region, instead, some operational choices have been better identified directly in the Service Contracts (Figs. 2 and 3).

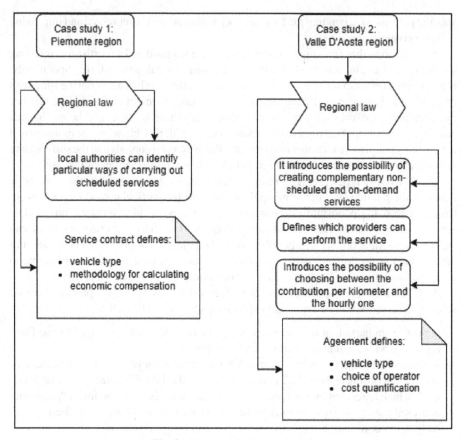

Fig. 2. Framework case study 1–2

The Guidelines drawn up by the Lombardia Region represent a very useful tool to define in advance the operating models for implementing on-demand services. They define how to convert the supply of on-demand services in equivalent travelled kilometers.

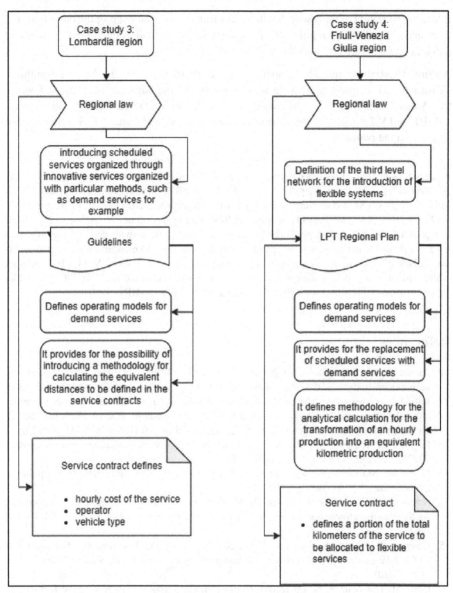

Fig. 3. Framework case study 3–4

From the performed analysis it emerges that flexible services represent a useful tool to better satisfy the mobility demand, where traditional transport are insufficient. However, these flexible services are considered a component within the regulatory framework of the traditional LPT. Consequently, to organize these services it is necessary to respect the existing legislation and its constraints. This makes it more difficult to program totally flexible forms of transport services that fully satisfy the specific users mobility needs. The future development of the research will focus on an in-depth analysis of the other regional laws and the reference regulatory framework in order to introduce new on-demand services characterized by high flexibility.

Author Contributions. This paper is the result of the joint work of the authors. 'Abstract' and 'Introduction' were written jointly by the authors. R.C, P.L, V.T wrote the 'Multi-Level Perspective Methodology'; R.C. and V.T. wrote 'Case studies analysis'; P.L and V.T wrote 'Discussion and conclusions'. V.T, M.I and A.L coordinated and supervised the paper.

Acknowledgements. This work is financed by the MIUR (Ministry of Education, Universities and Research [Italy]) through a project entitled WEAKI TRANSIT: WEAK-demand areas Innovative TRANsport Shared services for Italian Towns (Project code: 20174ARRHT), financed with the PRIN 2017 (Research Projects of National Relevance) programme. We authorise the MIUR to reproduce and distribute reprints for Governmental purposes, notwithstanding any copyright notations thereon. Any opinions, findings and conclusions or recommendations expressed in this material are those of the authors, and do not necessarily reflect the views of the MIUR. This work is also partially supported by the project of V. Torrisi "SAMOTHRACE (ECS00000022) -" under the programme "European Union (NextGeneration EU) - MUR-PNRR).

References

1. Annunziata, A., Desogus, G., Mighela, F., Garau, C.: Health and mobility in the post-pandemic scenario. an analysis of the adaptation of sustainable urban mobility plans in key contexts of Italy. In: Gervasi, O., Murgante, B., Misra, S., Rocha, A.M.A.C., Garau, C. (eds.) Computational Science and Its Applications – ICCSA 2022 Workshops. ICCSA 2022. LNCS, vol. 13382, pp. 439–456. Springer, Cham (2022). https://doi.org/10.1007/978-3-031-10592-0_32
2. ISFORT 19° Rapporto sulla mobilità degli italiani https://www.isfort.it/wp-content/uploads/2023/01/221215_RapportoMobilita2022_Def-1.pdf
3. Gallo, M., Marinelli, M.: Sustainable mobility: a review of possible actions and policies. Sustainability 12(18), 7499 (2020)
4. Schmidt, K., Sieverding, T., Wallis, H., Matthies, E.: COVID-19–A window of opportunity for the transition toward sustainable mobility? Transp. Res. Interdiscipl. Perspect. 10, 100374 (2021)
5. Campisi, T., Basbas, S., Skoufas, A., Akgün, N., Ticali, D., Tesoriere, G.: The impact of COVID-19 pandemic on the resilience of sustainable mobility in Sicily. Sustainability 12(21), 8829 (2020)
6. Campisi, T., Cocuzza, E., Ignaccolo, M., Inturri, G., Torrisi, V.: Exploring the factors that encourage the spread of EV-DRT into the sustainable urban mobility plans. In: Gervasi, O., et al. (eds.) ICCSA 2021. LNCS, vol. 12953, pp. 699–714. Springer, Cham (2021). https://doi.org/10.1007/978-3-030-86976-2_48
7. Pisoni, E., Christidis, P., Thunis, P., Trombetti, M.: Evaluating the impact of "Sustainable Urban Mobility Plans" on urban background air quality. J. Environ. Manage. 231, 249–255 (2019)
8. Torrisi, V., Garau, C., Inturri, G., Ignaccolo, M. (2021, March). Strategies and actions towards sustainability: encouraging good ITS practices in the SUMP vision. In: AIP Conference Proceedings (Vol. 2343, No. 1, p. 090008). AIP Publishing LLC. https://doi.org/10.1063/5.004789a

9. Kiba-Janiak, M., Witkowski, J.: Sustainable urban mobility plans: how do they work? Sustainability **11**(17), 4605 (2019)
10. Torrisi, V., Garau, C., Ignaccolo, M., Inturri, G.: "sustainable urban mobility plans": key concepts and a critical revision on SUMPs guidelines. In: Gervasi, O., et al. (eds.) ICCSA 2020. LNCS, vol. 12255, pp. 613–628. Springer, Cham (2020). https://doi.org/10.1007/978-3-030-58820-5_45
11. Torrisi, V., Campisi, T., Inturri, G., Ignaccolo, M., Tesoriere, G.: Continue to share? An overview on Italian travel behavior before and after the COVID-19 lockdown. In: AIP Conference Proceedings (vol. 2343, No. 1, p. 090010). AIP Publishing LLC (2021, March). https://doi.org/10.1063/5.0048512
12. Garau, C., Desogus, G., Barabino, B., Coni, M.: Accessibility and public transport mobility for a smart (er) Island: evidence from Sardinia (Italy). Sustain. Cities Soc. **87**, 104145 (2022)
13. Engelhardt, R., Dandl, F., Bilali, A., Bogenberger, K.: Quantifying the benefits of autonomous on-demand ride-pooling: a simulation study for Munich, Germany. In: 2019 IEEE Intelligent Transportation Systems Conference (ITSC), pp. 2992–2997. IEEE (2019, October)
14. Tirachini, A., Chaniotakis, E., Abouelela, M., Antoniou, C.: The sustainability of shared mobility: can a platform for shared rides reduce motorized traffic in cities? Transp. Res. Part C: Emerg. Technol. **117**, 102707 (2020)
15. Campisi, T., Tesoriere, G., Ignaccolo, M., Inturri, G., Torrisi, V.: A behavioral and explanatory statistical analysis applied with the advent of sharing mobility in urban contexts: outcomes from an under thirty-age group perspective. In: La Rosa, D., Privitera, R. (eds.) INPUT 2021. LNCE, vol. 146, pp. 633–641. Springer, Cham (2021). https://doi.org/10.1007/978-3-030-68824-0_67
16. IL Monitoraggio Dei Servizi Di Sharing Mobility https://osservatoriosharingmobility.it/wp-content/uploads/2022/03/Linee-guida-su-monitoraggio_sharing-mobility_OSM.pdf
17. Torrisi, V., Ignaccolo, M., Inturri, G., Tesoriere, G., Campisi, T.: Exploring the factors affecting bike-sharing demand: evidence from student perceptions, usage patterns and adoption barriers. Transp. Res. Procedia **52**, 573–580 (2021). https://doi.org/10.1016/j.trpro.2021.01.068
18. Campisi, T, Ignaccolo, M., Tesoriere, G., Inturri, G., Torrisi, V.: The evaluation of car sharing service attributes to raise acceptance of electric vehicles: evidences from an Italian survey among university students (No. 2020-24-0021). SAE Technical Paper. vol. 1, ISSN: 0148-7191, Catania, 4–7 Ottobre 2020. https://doi.org/10.4271/2020-24-0021
19. Campisi, T., Torrisi, V.; Ignaccolo, M., Inturri, G., Tesoriere G.: University propensity assessment to car sharing services using mixed survey data: the Italian case study of Enna city. Transp. Res. Procedia **47**, 433–440, ISSN:2352-1465 (2020). https://doi.org/10.1016/j.trpro.2020.03.155
20. Torrisi, V., Campisi, T., Ignaccolo, M., Inturri, G., Tesoriere, G.: Assessing the propensity to car sharing services in university cities: some insights for developing the co-creation process. Travel Tour. Stud. Transp. Dev. Commun. **24**(3), G1–G14 (2022)
21. Tang, J., Gao, F., Han, C., Cen, X., Li, Z.: Uncovering the spatially heterogeneous effects of shared mobility on public transit and taxi. J. Transp. Geogr. **95**, 103134 (2021)
22. Daganzo, C.F., Ouyang, Y.: A general model of demand-responsive transportation services: from taxi to ridesharing to dial-a-ride. Transp. Res. Part B: Methodol. **126**, 213–224 (2019)
23. Cetin, T., Deakin, E.: Regulation of taxis and the rise of ridesharing. Transp. Policy **76**, 149–158 (2019)
24. U.S. Department of Transportation. Shared Mobility: Current Practices and Guiding Principles APPENDIX B: Glossary (2020). https://ops.fhwa.dot.gov/publications/fhwahop16022/apb.htm
25. California State Assembly Bill No. 149. § 13020 (2021). https://leginfo.legislature.ca.gov/faces/billTextClient.xhtml?bill_id=202120220AB149

26. D.lgs. 19.11.1997, n. 422, Conferimento alle regioni ed agli enti locali di funzioni e compiti in materia di trasporto pubblico locale, a norma dell' 4, comma 4, della l. 15.03.1997, n. 59

27. L. 15.01.1992, n. 21 Legge quadro per il trasporto di persone mediante autoservizi pubblici non di linea

28. D. L. 04.07.2006, n. 223, Disposizioni urgenti per il rilancio economico e sociale, per il contenimento e la razionalizzazione della spesa pubblica, nonchè interventi in materia di entrate e di contrasto all'evasione fiscale, convertito con modificazioni dalla l. 04.08.2006, n. 248

29. D. L. 06.12.2011, n. 201 Disposizioni urgenti per la crescita, l'equità e il consolidamento dei conti pubblici, convertito con modificazioni dalla l. 22.12. 2011, n. 214

30. Atto di segnalazione ART sull'autotrasporto di persone non di linea: taxi, noleggio con conducente e servizi tecnologici per la mobilità, del 21.05.2015. https://www.autorita-trasporti. it/atti-di-segnalazione/anno-2017/

31. Delibera del 23.03.2022, n. 46, Conclusione del procedimento per la definizione delle Linee guida in materia di adeguamento del servizio taxi per Regioni ed Enti locali avviato con delibera n. 146/2021 del 4 novembre 2021. https://www.autorita-trasporti.it/delibere/delibera-n-46-2022/

32. Agenzia della mobilità Piemontese. https://mtm.torino.it/it/servizi-e-contratti/

33. Agenzia della mobilità Piemontese, Servizi a chiamata in Piemonte. https://mtm.torino. it/it/piani-progetti/progetti-a-scala-regionale/servizi-a-chiamata-della-regione-piemonte/#: ~:text=Servizi%20a%20chiamata%20in%20Piemonte%20Sintesi%20dei%20servizi,ser vizio%20Flexibus%20presente%20nelle%20valli%20Sermenza%20e%20Mastallone

34. Legge regionale 01.09.1997, n. 29, Norme in materia di servizi di trasporto pubblico di linea. https://www.regione.vda.it/trasporti/infoutili/leggi/lr_01_09_1997_i.asp

35. Trasporto pubblico locale, Comune di Aosta. https://www.comune.aosta.it/servizi/mobilita-e-trasporti/trasporto-pubblico-locale#:~:text=All%C3%B4%20Nuit%20E%E2%80%99%99% 20un%20servizio%20-%20a%20gestione,prelievo%20presso%20le%20fermate%20del% 20trasporto%20pubblico%20diurno

36. Deliberazione n° X / 2486, seduta del 10.10.2014. Linee guida per la redazione dei programmi di Bacino del trasporto pubblico locale – l. r. N. 6 del 04.04.2012, Art.13, https://www.reg ione.lombardia.it/wps/wcm/connect/fedf80fc-87e7-4c67-bc70-7b349a1a54a6/dgr+linee+ guida+programmi+di+bacino.pdf?MOD=AJPERES&CACHEID=ROOTWORKSPACE-fedf80fc-87e7-4c67-bc70-7b349a1a54a6-mobLPjp

37. Deliberazione n° X, 4927, seduta del 14.03.2016, Linee guida di coordinamento per l'affidamento del servizio di trasporto pubblico locale e la redazione dei contratti di servizio. https://www.regione.lombardia.it/wps/wcm/connect/3419b584-fe6c-4221-9f3a-62f3f6f6c c62/dgr+4927_2016_linee+guida+gare.pdf?MOD=AJPERES&CACHEID=ROOTWORKS PACE-3419b584-fe6c-4221-9f3a-62f3f6f6cc62-lyc4XHU

38. Piano regionale del trasporto pubblico locale. http://arpebur.regione.fvg.it/newbur/vision aBUR?bnum=2013/04/24/17_1

39. Legge regionale 20.08.2007, n. 23, Attuazione del decreto legislativo 111/2004 in materia di trasporto pubblico regionale e locale, trasporto merci, motorizzazione, circolazione su strada e viabilità. https://lexview-int.regione.fvg.it/fontinormative/xml/xmlLex.aspx?anno=2007& legge=23&ART=000&AG1=00&AG2=00&fx=lex

Website as a Tool of Local E-Governance in Czechia: Which CMS is the Most Popular in the Moravian-Silesian Region?

Ingrid Majerova(✉) ⓘ and Radim Dolak ⓘ

School of Business Administration in Karvina, Silesian University in Opava, Univerzitni
Nam1934/3, 73340 Karvina, Czech Republic
{majerova,dolak}@opf.slu.cz

Abstract. If e-governance can be considered as a way for local governments to
provide citizens and other subjects with the fastest and most accurate information
possible, while simultaneously involving them in public affairs, websites appear to
be the best tool for this form of governance. To create and manage these websites,
it is necessary to use an effective content-management system, CMS. The aim of
this paper is to ascertain the most commonly used types of CMS for the creation
of municipal websites in the Moravian-Silesian Region and to determine whether
the use of a particular type of CMS can be related to the size of the municipality
according to its specific needs and financial possibilities. It was discovered that
almost two-thirds of municipalities use commercial systems developed by Czech
companies. Further, it was found that of the size a given type of system depends
upon the size of the municipality, in the sense of a more frequent use of custom
systems as municipalities increase in size.

Keywords: Content Management System · E-Governance · Moravian-Silesian
Region · Municipalities · Websites

1 Introduction

Local governments are mandated to build more powerful and engaged communities.
The Internet is dramatically changing the way that governments serve their citizens and
ensuring the municipal website is accessible to all citizens must be a top priority on the
public digital marketing to-do list [1]. Websites are often the first and primary source
of information that citizens use to make life easier and increase their awareness and
involvement. Municipalities view every interaction with the Web as an opportunity to
learn how to better serve their citizens (and another entities) digitally. Thus, they create
websites that are initially used to publish governmental information for citizens (and
another entities), enabling them to carry out various online transactions directly related
to them and later with third-party organizations from the local community, as well as
facilitating their involvement in decision-making or public service processes [2].

   As the number of citizens (and others) using the internet and mobile technologies
increases, the public sector is constantly innovating to keep pace with these changing

© The Author(s), under exclusive license to Springer Nature Switzerland AG 2023
O. Gervasi et al. (Eds.): ICCSA 2023 Workshops, LNCS 14109, pp. 581–595, 2023.
https://doi.org/10.1007/978-3-031-37120-2_37

technologies and all entities' expectations [3]. So, access to information through systems such as the internet and municipal websites has a very important role to play in ensuring the health of good governance [4].

Good local websites should be constantly updated, as well as properly-organized, content-rich, and easily searchable. Based on using a proper and flexible Content Management System (CMS), when choosing a CMS that best suits local government, there are three possibilities: paid Commercial CMS, a free Open Source CMS and a custom designed CMS that combines both free and paid variants, depending on the objectives of the municipality.

In a majority of municipalities, Open Source CMS prevails, followed by Custom CMS [5]. In the case of Open Source CMS, WordPress is generally the most used system, followed by Drupal and Joomla. According to an analysis of existing studies, is similar in various countries [6–9].

These results are also confirmed in the municipalities of the Moravian-Silesian Region in the Czech Republic. To confirm this fact, a survey was conducted in all three hundred municipalities of this region, in which two research questions were set: 1) Do municipalities in the Moravian-Silesian Region use Open Source CMS on a scale similar to municipalities in other countries? 2) Is the use of a given CMS dependent on the size of the municipality due to their different needs and budgets and can we suppose that the smaller municipalities are using the open source possibilities more than the larger cities?

Thus, the authors of this paper set the aim of their research to determine the most-used CMS for website creation in 300 municipalities across the Moravian-Silesian Region. Both statutory cities, cities, townships and smaller municipalities were analyzed. Thereafter, they determined whether the use of particular types of CMS were related to the size of the municipality, based on a certain type of CSM being more suitable for larger or smaller municipalities.

The motivation for this paper was to clarify whether local Moravian-Silesian governments copy the trend of using open source systems to create their websites like their 'colleagues' abroad or choose other strategies. A second reason was mainly based on the assumption that the financial budgets of municipalities are limited and depend on their size. This can also influence the choice of systems for websites and we find it inspiring (mainly for local governments) to determine whether it is possible to distinguish CMS according to the size of the municipality. These types of studies have not yet been carried out in the Czech Republic and could help optimize the e-services offered to citizens and other economic entities when choosing the most suitable CMS.

This paper is organized as follows. Section Two describes the state of knowledge in the area of the local e-governance in relation to municipal websites. The tool used for creating websites in the form of various CMS systems for public administration is described in Section Three. Section Four is devoted to a brief presentation of the Moravian-Silesian region, its municipalities and problem solving capabilities. Section Five presents the overall results and Section Six contains a conclusion.

2 Literature Review

The internet has only been available to the public for about the last three decades, but has already drastically changed the world. Online services continue to shape the landscape for how people communicate and how information is transferred. Accessing different websites is now a primary way people get their news, check their bank accounts, talk to friends, and much more. Today, there are nearly two billion websites online, with thousands that belong to different government agencies and organizations.

Governments created their own websites as powerful channels for communication and to provide services and miscellaneous other information to public access. As Nicholls [10] claims, since the beginning of the web, there has been a great deal of enthusiasm over the possibilities for digital government, using the internet as a tool for improving public service performance. From the late 1990s onwards, governments have extensively touted the benefits of, and encouraged spending on, web programs at both local and national levels.

As the internet grows, government websites are increasingly used to present public sector information [11]. The emergence of e-government platforms enabled governments to develop and implement environments where diverse interested parties can obtain and request information, conduct operations, and access government services [12]. They comprise a way for governments to use the most innovative information and communication technologies, particularly web-based internet applications, to provide citizens and businesses with more convenient access to government information and services, as well as improve the quality of their services and provide greater opportunities to participate in democratic institutions and processes. These processes are characterized as e-governance [13].

Early researchers described the development of government websites as a series of stages [14, 15]. In the 21st century, globalization is creating offers of interactive initiatives and demands that put governments worldwide under pressure to change and innovate the way in which their bureaucracies relate to citizens [16]. Website progression has been rapid in the public sector, especially in terms of functionality and performance. Public sector websites have sought to go beyond the static dissemination of contact information [17]. Similarly, Huang [18] claims that with the growth of the internet, governmental public service models are gradually changing from traditional manual methods to online e-government websites.

Even so, the purpose of a (local) government website is a bit different from most other sites. It encourages transformation to the 'e-government' paradigm, which emphasizes coordinated network-building, external collaboration and customer services. Websites of municipalities are among the most crucial tools they have for meeting the needs of citizens and connecting with their local community. Thus, it is very important to have an effective government website [19].

According to Piotrowski [20], government websites are quickly becoming the first point of contact for citizens and visitors seeking information. Local government website content is key with regard to transparency. One of the most prominent ways in which governments release information is through their websites. First, governments are increasingly turning to the internet to better their service capabilities. Second, citizens are coming to expect their government to have a presence online.

As e-governance is a tool or application that functions as government information technology [21], official websites are its core instrument: the changes in the quality of municipal websites reflects the changes in its development [22]. The official website is one of the most popular and financially feasible tools for developing e-governance [23], is considered a vital element of any successful e-governance strategy [24] and serves the public as heterogeneous groups of citizens with varied personal attributes, needs, and interests [25]. Through the use of an e-governance system, local authorities are able to provide online services conveniently through the use of modern ICTs, bring services closer to the people, improve communications between local authorities and citizens, reduce local authority operating expenses and be more transparent and accountable for the manner in which they provide services to the public [4].

According to Neves and Silva [26], government websites are an effective tool for increasing information delivery, user interaction, and government services, being the most visible aspects for citizens concerning public management. The implementation of electronic administration aims at simplifying and improving the relationships and transactions between public organizations, their users and citizens [27].

The (local) government is required to take advantage of advances in ICT through the development of e-government to improve the ability to process and distribute, providing quality information and services to the public [28]. Similarly, Yunita [29] claims, the website is one form of effective information technology development in publications and the website is a means for the public to access information.

Through its website, local government can provide services according to the needs of the community and completeness of service information must be considered by the government [30]. Moreover, websites are arguably the most easily accessible, credible and durable form of internet-enabled technology to provide government information in a timely manner [31].

Lastly, websites provide information concerning how public policies shape the lives of local residents, and how local residents can engage with government to shape public policy [32].

3   Content Management Systems Used for Municipal Websites

Quality public websites are not only constantly updated, but also well-organized, content-rich, and easily searchable. This is based on using a proper and flexible Content Management System (CMS). It represents one of the most powerful online content management tools today, by allowing the creation of a web page in a short time, control who has access to information and who creates, alters, and stores content on the platform [6]. Specifically, in public administration, content management promotes a substantial increase in flexibility through remote and updated network access, as well as more selective control of which metadata should be used to steer information correctly, as well as rules that regulate access, search possibilities, and the integration of different information systems [33].

In addition to the above mentioned advantages that CMS offers and to which we can add the low costs and simple updating in the case of self-management or mobile ready access, there are also some disadvantages. We can assign to them: security risk (unless the system is maintained and updated, could be hacked), need for skilled IT specialist (if the system needs to be maintained and updated regularly), users are dependent on plugins and widgets (for most of their functionalities) with the hidden costs and limitations of users´ number and functionalities.

The most-used CMS in the world is WordPress, with a market share of 63.4% [34]. WordPress is used on a third of websites on the internet. Shopify is second (5.5%), followed by Wix (3.7%) and Squarespace (3.1%). The market leader until WordPress came along was Joomla, then occupying second place until 2020 and now in fifth place with a share of about 2.7%. Other positions within the CMS market are Drupal (1.9%), Adobe Systems (1.6%), Google Systems (1.5%) and Bitrix (1.2%).

In public administration, WordPress is used by the official Swedish website as well as by the White House. Joomla is a key CSM tool for the design of municipal websites of several regions in Latin America, e. g. the municipalities of Patzún (Guatemela), David or San Miguelito (Panama) [35]. According to Digital.gov [36], the most used CMS for government agencies in the U.S. are Drupal, Plone and WordPress. In Portugal, Joomla, Drupal and WordPress are the most used systems in public administration [5].

Table 1 shows the ratio of the most popular CMS in selected European countries. The colored areas indicate the most used/popular CMS in particular countries. According to CMScensus [37], in Germany the CMS TYPO3 is most popular, but the difference between this CMS and WordPress is very small, only 3.5 percentage points. WordPress is the most used CMS in Hungary, while Joomla is very close to it – the difference is only 1%.

But as Csontos and Heckl [9] claim, it was very difficult to determine which CMS local governments used, as only 8 were found from the 25 analyzed, leaving 68% unknown. On the contrary, Joomla was used in more than half of municipalities in Italy [8]. The second most popular CMS is OpenCMS, distancing itself by 43 percent from Joomla.

Briggs [7] analyzed 233 local governments in the UK and found that the difference among the first three CMS is not so big. The most popular, JADU, is used by 62 municipalities, Drupal was second, by 60 municipalities and Umbraco was selected by 58 local governments. World Press and Joomla were used by only 14, respectively 7 municipality websites.

Table 1. The Most Used CMS for Municipalities´ Websites in Selected Countries (%).

Country	WordPress	Joomla	Drupal	Umbraco	Others	NF/low
Germany	15.5	7.0	0.5	1.2	19.0 (TYPO3)	41
Hungary	12.0	11.0	8.0	--	--	68
Italy	9.0	57.9	10.1	--	14.6 (OCMS)	*
UK	6.0	2.2	19.0	17.0	20.0 (JADU)	**

Note: NF - not found, * the rest CMS with low ratio 8.3, ** the rest of CMS with low ratio 35.8

4 Problem Solving

To ascertain the tools and technologies that are used for the creation of official websites of municipalities in the Moravian-Silesian Region, the research was carried out during three months from January to March, 2023 and was aimed at examining individual websites of all three hundred municipalities.

4.1 The Study Area

The Moravian-Silesian Region is one of 14 administrative regions of the Czech Republic. The region is defined by the six districts of Bruntál, Frýdek-Místek, Karviná, Nový Jičín, Opava and Ostrava-město, further divided into 22 administrative districts of municipalities with extended remit, which include a total of 300 municipalities. With its area of 5,431 km², it occupies 6.9% of the entire territory of the Czech Republic and is thus ranked 6th among all regions. The location of the Moravian-Silesian region is shown in Fig. 1.

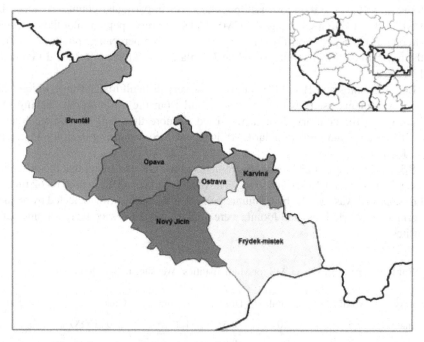

Fig. 1. Location of Moravian-Silesian Region in the Czech Republic

With 1,178 thousand inhabitants, the Moravian-Silesian Region is the third most populous in the Czech Republic (in 2009 it was the first one), but with its 300 municipalities it is one of the regions with the smallest number of settlements. The size of the municipalities in this region is diverse. As shown in Table 1, more than half of them (57.3%) are rural municipalities, 23% are small municipalities and cities form 17.7% of all municipalities. Statutory cities and the regional center (Ostrava) represent only 2% of all municipalities (Table 2).

Table 2. Definition of Municipalities According to their Size and Numbers (2022).

Number of citizens	Definition of municipality	Number of municipalities
1–500	Small municipalities	69
501–3,000	Rural municipalities	172
3,001–30,000	Cities	53
30,001–70,000	Statutory cities	5
279,791	Regional capital (Ostrava)	1

4.2 Content Management System of Municipalities in the Moravian-Silesian Region

Each municipality in the Moravian-Silesian region creates its own website, through which it informs and provides its e-services to all local and external entities. The websites of municipalities have undergone a major transformation over the last decade, with most of the websites currently being created using specialized content management systems focused directly on public administration.

In the past, frequently used tools for creating sites of cities and towns included general content management systems that were freely distributable and free of charge, such as WordPress, Joomla or Drupal. As was mentioned, these CMS were (and still are) the most used in many institutions of public administration or local governments around the world.

In view of the above, it was the intention of the authors of this paper to ascertain whether the above-mentioned CMS are also the most frequently used systems of Moravian-Silesian municipalities (determination of question Q1). In addition, they also tried to ascertain whether the size of the municipality, based on their different needs and financial possibilities, has an effect on the use of different types of CMS (determination of question Q2).

On the basis of the set objectives, research was carried out on all three hundred websites of the municipalities. The first step taken was to enter the name of the municipality in an internet search engine, e.g. karvina.cz. The second step was to find the CMS of the website. Information about the technology used to create the website can often be found in the 'footer' of the website, as shown in Fig. 2. Sometimes, it was necessary to try to find the technology used to create the website directly in the source code. This was mostly the case of Joomla and WordPress.

The data obtained were collected and processed. Results of the survey are presented in the following section of the paper.

Fig. 2. The Case of Websites in Český Těšín (above) and Albrechtice (below).

5   Results of Survey

First of all, it should be noted that the use of CMS for the municipality websites has changed in recent years. While in the past decade it was common that their official websites were using opensource free content management systems such as WordPress, Joomla or Drupal, now these municipalities have moved to use commercial CMS such as GSM (developed by Galileo), Vismo (developed by Webhouse) or IPO (developed by Antee).

Based on research of individual websites of municipalities in the region, we concluded that 214 municipalities out of a total of 300 used one of the three most important editorial systems for their purposes, which is a total market share of 71.33%. The detailed statistic can be seen in the following Table 3.

The best-selling editorial system, GCM (Galileo Content Manager), is provided by GALILEO CORPORATION (https://www.igalileo.cz/). This system is basically very simple and clear for the purposes of managing official websites of municipalities. This system has a dominant position within the creation of websites of towns and municipalities in the Moravian-Silesian Region with almost half market share. According

Table 3. Commercial CMS for Creating Municipalities' Websites.

CMS	Link	Number of municipalities´ websites	Market share
GCM	https://www.igalileo.cz/	140	46.67%
VISMO	https://vismo.cz/	39	13.00%
IPO	https://www.antee.cz/	35	11.67%

to information from the company's official website, the firm already has more than 5,000 customers from municipalities, towns, schools and contributory organizations throughout the Czech and Slovak Republics.

The second strongest player on the market within the region is a content management system called VISMO of company WEBHOUSE (https://vismo.cz/). This CMS is used by substantially fewer municipalities and its share is a quarter compared to GMS in the Moravian-Silesian Region. Editing a website using the vismo Online editing system is very easy because you don't need to know how to program. It applies the principle "WYSIWYG" (what you see is what you get), the website can be edited directly in place, rather than in an administration environment.

The third most used content management system for creating websites of municipalities in the Moravian-Silesian region is the IPO system from company ANTEE (https://www.antee.cz/). This system has only slightly less market share than vismo (by 1 percentage point) in the Moravian-Silesian Region. Content management system IPO is a very practical web management tool. It is possible to easily manage municipal sites through the IPO editorial system, which undergoes regular updates.

Based on research of analysing individual websites of towns and municipalities in the region, we concluded that only 18 municipalities out of a total of 300 use one of the two most used open source content management systems worldwide. Thus, WordPress and Joomla, whose total market share is only 6%. The statistics are shown in Table 4.

Table 4. Table: Open Source CMS for Creating Municipalities' Websites

CMS	Link	Number of municipalities´ websites	Market Share
WordPress	https://wordpress.org/	10	3.33%
Joomla	https://www.joomla.org/	8	2.67%

Based on the above, it can be seen that these free open source systems have already been almost completely replaced in the Moravian-Silesian Region by commercial editorial systems specializing in creating websites for public administration purposes. These commercial systems such as GCM, VISMO or IPO have the undeniable advantage of being run in the cloud in the form of software as a service, so that cities and municipalities need not run them on their own servers. Moreover, these systems fully comply with the requirements for information content of municipalities.

Specialized commercial content management systems, together with general free of charge content management systems, have a market share of 77.34% for creating municipalities' websites in the Moravian-Silesian Region. There is still market share of 22.66% available for other possibilities of creating municipal websites. When we analyzed the websites of municipalities, we found that this segment is made up of more than 40 different smaller companies or individuals involved in creating websites. However, none of these entities has a market share greater than 1.5%.

After dealing with the issue of not/using the given systems, we can focus on the analysis of the results related to question 2 (Q2). That is, whether there is a dependence between the size of the municipality and the CMS used. It can be assumed that the financial conditions of smaller municipalities force them to save in certain ways and therefore use a free open source CMS or the types of CMS that are universal and, in some ways, cheaper. The results of that dependency are shown in Table 5. The biggest city, regional capital Ostrava, is not mentioned because is only one (and uses another CMS).

Table 5. The Relationship between the Size of the Municipality and the Type of CMS.

CMS	SM	RM	C	SC
GMS	34	81	25	-
VISMO	10	17	11	1
IPO	8	26	-	-
WordPress	3	5	1	1
Joomla	4	4	-	-
Others	10	39	16	3

Note: SM – Small Municipalities (1–500 citizens); RM – Rural Municipalities (500–3,000 citizens); C – cities (3,000–30,000 citizens); SC – Statutory Cities (30,000–70,000 citizens)

Unsurprisingly, we see a big difference between the use of open sources and commercial CMS. However, absolute numbers do not have much informative value, it is necessary to convert them into relative numbers – ratios and best to visualize them. Therefore, to answer the second question, pie charts were created (see Fig. 3), according to the size of the given municipalities in the Moravian-Silesian region.

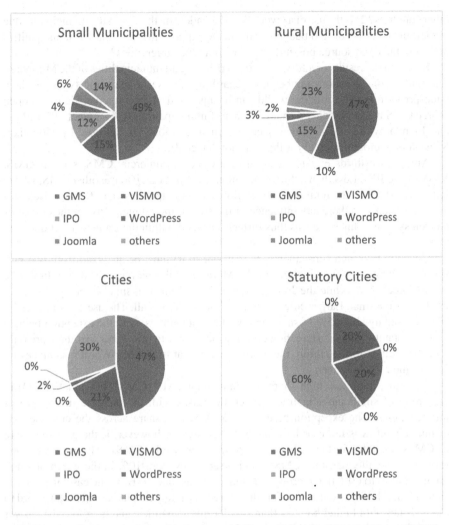

Fig. 3. Visualization of relationship between the Sites of Municipalities and Types of CMS.

6   Conclusions and Discussion

The primary tool for e-governance is the website, whether at the governmental, regional or local level. It can be an official noticeboard, a regional information portal, or an e-administration platform if sufficiently sophisticated [38]. In any case, citizens satisfaction is one of the most important objectives of any e-governance strategy [39]. Clear and transparent websites, providing a large volume of information and e-services, are the basis for choosing a suitable Content Management System. The type of CMS used and its possible dependence on the size of the municipality were the subject of interest of this paper. Thus, two research questions were established: 1) Do municipalities in the Moravian-Silesian Region use Open Source CMS on a scale similar to municipalities in other countries? 2) Is the use of a given CMS dependent on the size of the municipality due to their different needs and budgets and can we suppose that the smaller municipalities are using the open source possibilities more than the larger cities?

Based on the results of a survey conducted among all municipalities of the Moravian-Silesian region, question number one regarding the use of the same types of CMS widespread in the surrounding world can be answered in the negative. Common open source CMS is used by only a small number of municipalities (6%), namely WordPress and Joomla, while other systems such as Drupal or Plone are not used by Moravian-Silesian municipalities at all (or this was not detected).

Almost two-thirds of municipalities use Czech commercial CMS, such as GMS, VISMO and IPO. Less than a third of the municipalities (22.7%) use other CMS, whose individual share in the total use is negligible. If municipalities can afford to use commercial systems, is there any influence of the size of the municipality on the choice of a given system? This issue was thus further analyzed within the framework of question two.

Question two (and subsequently the answer to it) must be analyzed from two perspectives. First, the municipalities of the Moravian-Silesian region use very little free open source CMS, while the Joomla system is used most in small municipalities, but its share is minimal. Larger cities do not use this system at all. The use of WordPress is similar, used by about 5% of small and rural municipalities, with the exception being a group of statutory cities. Here, however, it is necessary to remember that there are only 5 of these cities in the region, therefore one city that uses CMS WordPress makes up 20% of their total number.

Secondly, there is a high share of commercial CMS (GMS, IPO and VISMO) in the group of small municipalities, which decreases with the increase in the size of municipalities. The exception here is VISMO, whose share across the cross-section of municipalities is more or less stable. What is clear, however, is the growing share of CMSs, included in the 'others' group. In other words, CMSs that are tailor-made for cities (so called Custom CMS). Their share rises from 10% in the group of small municipalities to 60% in the group of statutory cities (and 100% in the case of Regional capital, but this city is only one). It is therefore very likely that larger cities can afford to run websites with higher budgets than smaller municipalities, and therefore the answer to question number two is that there is a relationship between the size of the municipality and the CMS system used in terms of its financial demands.

We can add one more interesting remark to the results: according to our findings, not all websites of municipalities in the Moravian-Silesian region have foreign language mutations (and it does not matter the size of the municipality), so they can only serve Czech (at most Slovak) users. This may be a challenge for their operators to change in the future.

Acknowledgement. This study has been financially supported of the Ministry of Education, Youth and Sports of the Czech Republic as part of Institutional Support for the Long-Term Development of Research Organizations in 2023, and created within the grant project CZ.02.1.01/0.0/0.0/17_049/0008452 "Smart Technologies to Improve the Quality of Life in Cities and Regions".

References

1. Valtolina, S., Fratus, D.: Local government websites accessibility: evaluation and finding from Italy. Digit. Govt. Res. Pract. **3**(3), 17 (2022). https://doi.org/10.1145/3528380
2. Zhang, Y., Kimathi, F.A.: Exploring the stages of E-government development from public value perspective. Technol. Soc. **69**, 101942 (2022). https://doi.org/10.1016/j.techsoc.2022.101942
3. Manoharan, A.P., Ingrams, A.: Conceptualizing E-Government from local government perspectives. State Local Govt. Rev. **50**(1), 56–66 (2018). https://doi.org/10.1177/0160323X18763964
4. Matimati, P.T., Rajah, N.: The use of E-governance by Local authorities to improve service delivery: a case of Chitungwiza municipality. J. Glob. Res. Comput. Sci. **6** (2015). http://rroij.com/global-research-in-computer-science.php
5. Louraço, D., Marques, C.G.: CMS in public administration: a comparative analysis. J. Inf. Syst. Eng. Manag. **7**(1), 11688 (2022)
6. Louraço, D., Marques, C.G.: The acceptance of content management systems in portuguese municipalities: a study in the intermunicipal community of Lezíria do Tejo. In: Rocha, Á., Adeli, H., Dzemyda, G., Moreira, F., Ramalho Correia, A.M. (eds.) WorldCIST 2021. AISC, vol. 1366, pp. 503–512. Springer, Cham (2021). https://doi.org/10.1007/978-3-030-72651-5_48
7. Briggs, D.: Content management systems in local government. https://www.linkedin.com/pulse/content-management-systems-local-government-dave-briggs. Accessed 21 Feb 2023
8. Destefanis, G., Tonelli, R., Cocco, L., Concas, G., Marchesi, M.: A case study of the use of open source CMS in public administrations. In: 14th IEEE International Symposium on Web Systems Evolution (WSE), pp. 31–34. Trento, Italy (2012)
9. Csontos, B., Heckl, I.: Accessibility, usability, and security evaluation of Hungarian government websites. Univ. Access Inf. Soc. **20**(1), 139–156 (2020). https://doi.org/10.1007/s10209-020-00716-9
10. Nicholls, T.: Local government performance, cost-effectiveness, and use of the web: an empirical analysis. Policy Internet **11**(4), 480–507 (2019). https://doi.org/10.1002/poi3.209
11. Cunha, M.A., Coelho, T.R., Przeybilovicz, E.: Get into the club: positioning a developing country in the International e-Gov research. Electr. J. Inf. Syst. Dev. Count. **79**(1), 1–21 (2017). https://doi.org/10.1002/j.1681-4835.2017.tb00580
12. OECD: OECD Digital Economy Outlook 2020. OECD Publishing, Paris. https://doi.org/10.1787/bb167041-en (2020)
13. Fang, Z.: E-Government in digital era: concept, practice, and development. Int. J. Comput. Internet Manag. **10**, 1–22 (2002)
14. Layne, K., Lee, J.: Developing fully functional e-government: a four stage model. Gov. Inf. Q. **18**(2), 122–136 (2001)
15. Moon, M.J.: The evolution of E-government among municipalities: rhetoric or reality? Public Adm. Rev. **62**(4), 424–433 (2002)
16. Bonsón, E., Torres, L., Royo, S., Flores, F.: Local e-government 2.0: Social media and corporate transparency in municipalities. Govt. Inf. Q. **29**(2), 123–132 (2012)
17. D'Agostino, M.J., Schwester, R., Carrizales, T., Melitski, J.: A study of E-Government and E-Governance: an empirical examination of municipal websites. Public Adm. Q. **35**(1), 3–25 (2011)
18. Huang, J-Q., Guo, W-I., Fu, L.: Research on E-government website satisfaction evaluation based on public experience. DEStech Trans. Soc. Sci. (2019)
19. Ho, A.T.-K.: Reinventing local governments and the E-government Initiative. Public Adm. Rev. **62**(4), 434–444 (2002). http://www.jstor.org/stable/3110358

20. Piotrowski, S.J., Borry, E.L.: Transparency and local government websites. In: Reddick, C. (ed.) Handbook of Research on Strategies for Local E-Government Adoption and Implementation: Comparative Studies, pp. 390–407 (2009). https://doi.org/10.4018/978-1-60566-282-4.ch020

21. Jalil, M.J., Nurmandi, A., Muallidin, I., Kurniawan, D., Salahudin: quality analysis of local government websites (Study Case DKI Jakarta, Bali, Banten Provinces). In: Stephanidis, C., Antona, M., Ntoa, S. (eds.) HCI International 2021 - Late Breaking Posters. HCII 2021. Communications in Computer and Information Science, vol. 1499 (2021). https://doi.org/10.1007/978-3-030-90179-0_58

22. Gavriluță, N., Stoica, V., Fârte, G.-I.: The official website as an essential e-governance tool: a comparative analysis of the Romanian cities' websites in 2019 and 2022. Sustainability **14**, 6863 (2022). https://doi.org/10.3390/su14116863

23. Potnis, D.D.: Measuring e-Governance as an innovation in the public sector. Gov. Inf. Q. **27**(1), 41–48 (2010). https://doi.org/10.1016/j.giq.2009.08.002

24. Wang, F.: Explaining the low utilization of government websites: using a grounded theory approach. Gov. Inf. Q. **31**(4), 610–621 (2014). https://doi.org/10.1016/j.giq.2014.04.004

25. Lee, T., Lee-Geiller, S., Lee, B.-K.: A validation of the modified democratic e-governance website evaluation model. Gov. Inf. Q. **38**(4), 101616 (2021). https://doi.org/10.1016/j.giq.2021.101616

26. Neves, F., Silva, P.: E-Government in local governments´ websites: from visible to invisible. Revista Catarinense da Ciência Contábil **20**, 1–20. e3160 (2021). https://doi.org/10.16930/2237-7662202131602

27. García-Sánchez, I.-M., Rodríguez-Domínguez, L., Gallego-Alvarez, I.: The relationship between political factors and the development of e–participatory government. Inf. Soc. **27**, 233–251 (2011)

28. Cahyono, T.A., Susanto, T.D.: Acceptance factors and user design of mobile e-government website (Study case e-government website in Indonesia). Procedia Comput. Sci. **161**, 90–98 (2019)

29. Yunita, N.P., Aprianto, R.D.: Current condition of E-government implementation Indonesia: website analysis. In: National Seminar on Information and Communication Technology, pp. 329–336 (2018)

30. Jiang, J.: E-government web portal adoption: the effects of service quality. E-Serv. J. **9**(3), 43–60 (2014). https://doi.org/10.2979/eservicej.9.3.43

31. Tavares, A.F., da Cruz, N.F.: Explaining the transparency of local government websites through a political market framework. Gov. Inf. Q. **37**(3), 101249 (2020). https://doi.org/10.1016/j.giq.2017.08.005

32. Neumann, M., Linder, F., Desmarais, B.: Government websites as data: a methodological pipeline with application to the websites of municipalities in the United States. J. Inform. Tech. Polit. **19**(4), 411–422 (2022). https://doi.org/10.1080/19331681.2021.1999880

33. Svärd, P.: E-Government development and its impact on information management. In: Enterprise Content Management, Records Management and Information Culture Amidst E-Government Development, pp. 1–10, Chandos Publishing, Cambridge (2017)

34. W3Techs: World Wide Web Technology Surveys (2023). https://w3techs.com/. Accessed 16 Mar 2023

35. Lopez-Bachiller, J.: eGovernment - Joomla and Patzun Municipality. In: ICEGOV2012, Electronic Government World Conference (2012). https://magazine.joomla.org/all-issues/december-2012/joomla-patzun-at-icegov2012. Accessed 16 Mar 2022

36. Digital.gov.: Content Management Systems Used by Government Agencies (2023). https://digital.gov/resources/content-management-systems-used-by-government-agencies/. Accessed 21 Feb 2023

37. CMScensus: Municipalities in Germany. Content Management Systems (2022). https://cms census.eu/germany/regions-cities/municipalities. Accessed 21 Feb 2023
38. Król, K., Zdonek, D.: Local government website accessibility - evidence from Poland. Adm. Sci. **10**(2), 22 (2020). https://doi.org/10.3390/admsci10020022
39. Darem, A., Suresha, S., Al-Hashmi, A.: Evaluation of the use of local government websites: Internet users' perspective. IUP J. Inf. Technol. **7**(2), 47–55 (2011)

Author Index

O. Gervasi et al. (Eds.): ICCSA 2023 Workshops, LNCS 14109, pp. 597–598, 2023.
https://doi.org/10.1007/978-3-031-37120-2

Printed in the United States
by Baker & Taylor Publisher Services